An Anthology of
Modern Irish Poetry

An Anthology of
Modern Irish Poetry

EDITED BY

Wes Davis

The Belknap Press of Harvard University Press

Cambridge, Massachusetts, and London, England

First Harvard University Press paperback edition, 2013

Designed by Annamarie McMahon Why

Additional copyright notices appear on pages 955–968,
which constitute an extension of the copyright page.

Library of Congress Cataloging-in-Publication Data

An anthology of modern Irish poetry / edited by Wes Davis.

p.   cm.

Includes bibliographical references and index.

ISBN 978-0-674-04951-2 (cloth : alk. paper)

ISBN 978-0-674-07222-0 (pbk.)

1. English poetry—Irish authors.   2. English poetry—20th century.   I. Davis, Wes.

PR8858.A48 2010

821′.9140809417—dc22   2009037231

CONTENTS

PREFACE

At one point in his wanderings through the fictional Dublin day described in James Joyce's *Ulysses,* Leopold Bloom, the Everyman hero of the novel, imagines that it takes a special set of circumstances to produce poetry—a dreamy disposition, homespun linens, a vegetarian diet, a beard if you're a man or, if you happen to be a woman, stockings that fall loose around the ankles. But the variety and volume of recent Irish poetry argues against his restricted notion of the artist. Irish poets, as a dip into this collection will show, come in all sorts and descriptions. And good ones aren't in short supply. Neither are anthologies devoted to their work.

There have been several recent collections of Irish poetry—Paul Muldoon's *Faber Book of Contemporary Irish Poetry,* Peter Fallon and Derek Mahon's *Penguin Book of Contemporary Irish Poetry,* and Patrick Crotty's *Modern Irish Poetry* are among my favorites—and each has its merits. But the most current of them is already fifteen years old and the poetry keeps on coming. In this new collection I've tried not just to bring the anthologist's snapshot of Irish poetry up to date, but to combine the virtues of depth and breadth by presenting substantial selections from some fifty contemporary Irish poets. They come from North and South. Their styles run the gamut from free verse to formalism. The earliest writers among them were the junior contemporaries of Yeats and Joyce, while the youngest have launched their careers within the last ten years. The collection is *modern,* in the sense of recent, rather than *modernist.*

The volume's introductory material provides two ways into this trove of verse. A general introduction traces the revival of Irish poetry in the years following the Second World War, setting the stage for the rush of literary productivity reflected in the anthology. Readers unfamiliar with Irish poetry or the shape of Irish history may wish to read this narrative account before plunging into the selections that follow. Shorter introductory sketches preface the work of the individual poets. These present a précis of each poet's biography and career, making it convenient for readers to enter the stream of Irish verse at any point in its history.

In choosing the poems I have followed two different principles. The earliest poets in the collection—ancestral figures like Clarke, Kavanagh, and MacNeice —are represented primarily by the kinds of poems that have stuck in the minds of later writers. On the other hand, my goal in selecting work from poets who are still writing—the bulk of the collection—was to show the range of their styles and interests. This meant including greatest hits where appropriate, but favoring less familiar poems when those reveal unexpected sides of well-known poets. With a few exceptions, I have given roughly equal space to each poet, on the assumption that those figures whose long careers or burnished reputations might claim more room are already better represented in readily available individual volumes, while the work of lesser known poets is harder to come by. With so many writers represented by relatively large samples of work, this collection is meant to introduce readers to a wide swath of Irish poetry, while letting them sink down into the stuff they find appealing. It will also serve as a resource for those already familiar with the likes of Heaney, Muldoon, Boland, or Longley, who would like to see where their favorites fit in the broader context of Irish poetry.

What it can't be is complete. There are many worthy poets and still more poems I would like to have included. And no doubt there are writers I don't know about who by rights should be here too. But contemporary literature is uniquely engaging precisely because its landscape is always changing. Think of this anthology as a guidebook to a vibrant terrain you'll want to explore further once you've closed the cover.

ACKNOWLEDGMENTS

I would like to thank John Kulka at Harvard University Press, who proposed this collection and guided the project as it grew to a scale neither of us imagined at the outset. Much of the credit for the book's size and scope goes to Ian Stevenson, who took on the colossal job of acquiring permission to reprint some eight hundred poems. Thanks also to editors Alex Morgan and Matthew Hills.

Earlier versions of some of the introductory essays appeared in the catalog of the Leonard L. Milberg Collection of Irish Poetry. I am grateful to Mr. Milberg and Ben Primer, director of Rare Books and Special Collections at Princeton University Library, for permission to use them here. John Logan deserves particular recognition for editing the essays in that volume. I am also indebted to its compiler, J. Howard Woolmer, and to A. Walton Litz, who recommended me for the job.

Paul Muldoon, Patrick Crotty, and Peter Fallon all offered encouragement despite having anthologies of their own already in print. Donald McNamara advised me on all matters involving the Irish language and he contributed more than his share to the translations on which we collaborated. I was helped in various ways by Neil Olson, James Richardson, Willard Spiegelman, Anne Margaret Daniel, Leslie Brisman, Ben Downing, Barry McCrea, Nathan Suhr-Sytsma, Michael Thurston, and Nigel Alderman, among others—not least the inspiring students who turned up in my Irish literature seminars year after year. For making the writing days pleasurable I thank my virtual colleagues McKay Jenkins, Ben Yagoda, and Bill Deresiewicz,

My deepest gratitude goes to the poets whose work is the whole point of the anthology. And to my wife, Jessica Levenstein Davis. It would be impossible to say whether she helped me more by her unfaltering support, her scholarly advice and skillful editing, or the heroic sacrifices she made to give me time to work. But without her the book would not exist.

An Anthology of
Modern Irish Poetry

Introduction

When the Irish novelist Seán O'Faoláin looked around at the state of his country in 1945 he saw a culture beginning to emerge from a period of dormancy into a new stage of life. The war years had left the Irish "a little dulled, bewildered, deflated," he wrote that July; the country had "a great leeway to make up, many lessons to be learned, problems to be solved which, in those six years of silence, we did not even allow ourselves to state."[1]

O'Faoláin was referring to the stagnant years during which Ireland, still faced with the problems of building an autonomous nation after the revolution that gained it partial independence in 1922, watched its progress falter on the edge of the war in Europe. But 1939—the beginning of what he calls six years of silence—also saw the death of W. B. Yeats. James Joyce died two years later. With those two great losses in the background it was apparent that the emergence O'Faoláin hoped for was as much a cultural rebirth—a revision of the nation's image of itself in poetry and fiction—as it was a matter of history or politics. Together Yeats and Joyce, drawing on the work of Irish, Anglo-Irish, and European forerunners, had called a native Irish literature to life in the English language. Their extraordinary accomplishments established modern Ireland's place in the world's imagination, but it was unclear whether younger writers could continue that work, breaking the recent silence and giving Ireland a proper voice in postwar literature.

As it turned out, O'Faoláin was right to think a culture that could support such a voice was emerging. In the sixty-odd years since 1945 Irish poets have burst out of the shadows of Yeats and Joyce. As a group these writers have produced one of the most vibrant and engaging bodies of poetry written in English in the postwar era. The productivity, political engagement, and thematic and formal range that have marked postwar Irish poetry are exceptional even in an era marked by literary exuberance around the English-speaking world. And given the small size of Ireland—the island has roughly the population of Tennessee in a land area the size of South Carolina—these achievements are still more astonishing.

While Irish poets have become accomplished to an extraordinary degree in the last half century, however, they have done so in large part by emphasizing the richness of ordinary experience as material for poetry. That trend itself shows the challenge faced by poets writing in a tradition pressured with almost equal force by the example of Yeats on the one hand and political turmoil on the other. Although Yeats sometimes wrote in response to political events, in poems like "Easter, 1916" or "September 1913," his poetics depended upon various forms of extravagance that served to distinguish poetry from ordinary experience. That's not to say that he didn't recognize the poetic value of ordinary Irish things— the kettle on the hob or the fisherman in Connemara cloth. He registered their importance directly in poems like "The Fisherman" and obliquely in others like "Adam's Curse"—in which each hard-wrought line must seem "a moment's thought"—and "The Municipal Gallery Revisited," where he recalls the principle that guided his work in the theater with Lady Gregory and John Synge. (The three believed "all that we said or sang / Must come from contact with the soil.") In practice, however, Yeats's writing inclined more toward elaboration than earthiness. When he and his old friend George Moore had a falling out over the shape of a play they had collaborated on, the point of contention was a matter of extravagance versus ordinariness. Yeats complained that Moore wanted *Diarmuid and Grania* to be, like his other plays, "about possible people." Moore "insisted for days upon calling the Fianna 'soldiers'" and he wanted to have "the dying Diarmuid say to Finn, 'I will kick you down the stairway of the stars.'"[2] The colloquialism of "soldiers" and "kick you down the stairway" was completely alien to the idea of poetry Yeats revealed when he argued that the proper effect of verse, in the theater at least, was "to preserve the distance from daily life."[3] But in the years following the Second World War, poetry that distanced itself from daily life was coming to look more and more irrelevant.

The Irish experience of the war in Europe had been shaped by uncertainty about the nation's status and direction. The different roles they played in the war also complicated the already tense relationship between the island's two provinces—the independent Irish Free State and the counties of Northern Ireland that had been partitioned in 1921 and remained under British control after the 1922 Anglo-Irish treaty. On the one hand, Éire, as the Irish Free State was known following the enactment of a new constitution in 1937, remained officially neutral throughout the war. Although forty-three Dubliners were killed in 1941 when two German aircraft mistakenly released their bombs over the city's North Strand, most of Ireland's civilians felt the effects of the Blitz that changed life so radically in London largely in the disappearance of British goods from the market and their replacement by homegrown products. In Northern Ireland, on the other hand, the residents of Belfast suffered two months of heavy bombing in 1941. Since Northern Ireland, as a part of Great Britain, supplied troops and supplies to the war effort, its capital became a target of Luftwaffe raids that damaged more than half the city's houses and left some 100,000 people homeless.[4] In response to the devastation of its neighbors, the government of Éire sent aid north in a move that was at once a humanitarian mission and a political gesture, meant to emphasize that, as the Irish prime minister Éamon De Valera put it, "we are one and the same people."[5] The fields of the North also served as a training and staging ground for the Normandy invasion, an episode in the island's history that would inspire a sequence of poems by Frank Ormsby. Meanwhile, Irish from the South were pouring across the border to join the war effort as well, despite a government policy that censured and ultimately brought about the dismissal of the one parliamentarian who spoke in opposition to neutrality. By recent estimates as many as 70,000 Irish from the South fought in British uniforms, and nearly 10,000 were killed. The altogether confusing situation was summed up by one historian who voiced the period's central question in an appropriately paradoxical phrase: "who are we neutral against?"[6]

As Irish writers began to emerge from this wartime morass, poetry in Ireland underwent a crucial shift. Although few would have acknowledged the fact at the time, the keynote of this new era had been sounded just before the war when Louis MacNeice, in an essay that amounted to a poetic manifesto, declared that "the poet's first business" was not rhetoric or style, but "*mentioning* things." Poetry, in MacNeice's view, was a matter of selection, drawing attention through formal devices to one thing and not another. Its material was ordinary life, not esoteric extremes. Primitivism and occultism were both dead ends. The ideal poet was "a fairly normal person." Neither "half-wits nor out-and-out mystics" were likely to hit the middle key in which the most durable poetry was written.[7] It was a view that many were coming to share. If Irish poetry before the war had flourished under the sway of an out-and-out mystic, the cryptic ideas and elaborate postures Yeats had once made into passionate poetry no longer looked appropriate to writers in this now "dulled, bewildered, deflated" country.

A few of Yeats's younger contemporaries had already begun exploring other poetic terrain. Even before the previous war Padraic Colum, whose early poems had appeared in the *New Songs* anthology edited by Yeats's friend Æ, distinguished himself by writing of rural life. His best poems had shown that cattle could be as authentically poetic in the setting of a country fair as in the epic cattle raid of Cuailgne, and a poor girl's meditations as moving as an aristocrat's. But while Colum saw that the plowman and his peers could be poetry, he tended to romanticize the ordinary world he had learned to draw on. He was capable of following a line on the brute labor of plowing with another that tried to lift that work into the register of "chariots, purples, and splendours." Because later poets had seen the risks of this kind of romanticism made real in the politics of Éamon de Valera—many blamed the country's poverty on his romantic conception of Ireland as an agrarian enclave insulated from the modern world by its Catholic faith and the Irish language—they wanted no part of it in their own work. The two most prominent poets working in the 1950s, Austin Clarke and Patrick Kavanagh, managed by different routes to avoid the trap Colum had slipped into. Both had taken shots at romantic Ireland before the war and their work now staked out the territory over which the first wave of Irish poetry after Yeats would range.

By the 1930s Clarke had already discarded the lumber of Celtic legends he had once borrowed from Yeats and his revivalist circle, shifting his focus first to early Catholic Ireland and then, in the late 1930s, to his own crisis of religious doubt. But that move left his poetic resources depleted and he published nothing during the war. When he finally broke a long poetic silence in 1955, it was with a collection of satirical poems, *Ancient Lights,* that attacked what Clarke saw as the absurdities of contemporary Irish culture. These poems sometimes confronted general problems like poverty, but more often they tackled issues like contraception, on which Clarke felt the Church had misled the nation. Clarke, in other words, was "*mentioning* things" with a vengeance. In a somewhat later poem he would refer to the role he had taken on in the 1950s as that of "local complainer." But *Ancient Lights* was more than simply a Swiftian assault on the shortcomings of Irish culture. Its complaints were registered with an attention to detail that gave the book's depiction of the Irish city a level of realism rarely seen outside *Ulysses* and, some would argue, never seen in Irish poetry until Clarke began writing about Dublin.[8] With the appearance eleven years later of *Mnemosyne Lay in Dust,* a long poem in which dreamlike sequences that might have come from the Nighttown section of *Ulysses* record the nervous breakdown Clarke suffered in 1919, it was clear to anyone who hadn't understood it before that the route forward for many Irish poets was one pioneered by Joyce rather than Yeats.[9] Clarke himself would later return to Irish legend as a subject for poetry, but with a specifically modern emphasis. When an English translation of the episode known as "The Romance of Mis" appeared in the journal *Celtica* in 1954, it captured Clarke's attention because it seemed to him "to anticipate the curative methods of Freud."[10] He later used the story as the basis of a poem, adding material that stressed its psychological aspects. The version of the episode he published in 1970 as "The Healing of

Mis" stands out as the work in which Freudian dream analysis finally replaced the dreaminess of the Celtic twilight.

During the war years Patrick Kavanagh also transformed himself into a species of "local complainer." Kavanagh had published his first book, a volume of mostly conventional lyrics on rural pleasures called *Ploughman and Other Poems*, in 1936. It was a collection that might have appeared in Ireland a good thirty years earlier, combining as it did the stylized verse favored in Palgrave's *Golden Treasury*—Kavanagh's plowman dreams of beauty while he paints a green meadow brown with his plow—with a revivalist interest in the *idea* of rural life. Still, there were passages in the book, like the swerve in "Ploughman" from "star-lovely art" to "dark sod," that hinted at the turn Kavanagh was about to take. Just five years later, under the influence of O'Faoláin, who was forging an anti-revivalist movement through his journal *The Bell*, he was at work on a poem that would obliterate the pastoral spirit of *Ploughman*. Written in one long burst in 1941 and published the next year, "The Great Hunger" uncovers the harsh realities Kavanagh had excluded from the earlier collection's conventional depiction of life in Ireland's rural districts. Field work is nothing like painting in the later poem, and its brutal monotony leaves the plowman with neither time nor imagination for dreaming. Like Clarke in *Ancient Lights*, Kavanagh blames much of his characters' anguish—in particular their devastating sexual dissatisfaction—on the repressive influence of the Catholic Church. But the romantic representation of rural life by the pastoralists of the Celtic Revival is targeted in the poem with equal vehemence. Yeats, to be fair, had resisted the idealized depiction of a wholesome peasantry in much of his poetry and in his leadership of the Irish National Theatre; but at the end of his career he insisted on a view of rural Ireland as a place where peasants and aristocrats held out hope against what he saw as the shabby materialism of the urban Catholic middle class. It is to these two extremes that he directs the attention of Irish writers in "Under Ben Bulben."

> Irish poets, learn your trade,
> Sing whatever is well made,
> Scorn the sort now growing up
> All out of shape from toe to top,
> Their unremembering hearts and heads
> Base-born products of base beds.
> Sing the peasantry, and then
> Hard-riding country gentlemen . . .[11]

But where an idealized peasantry and aristocracy were central to Yeats's vision of Irish poetry's future in "Under Ben Bulben," Kavanagh refused to let either image stand. "The Great Hunger" ridicules the idealized image of the peasant who "has no worries" as he works "his little lyrical fields"; and there is no "hard riding" in his portrait of rural life: "No mad hooves galloping in the sky" but rather "A sick horse nosing around the meadow for a clean place to die."

Writing in journals throughout the 1940s and early 1950s Kavanagh continued the critique of Irish literature and culture he had begun in "The Great Hunger." He found little to praise. To Kavanagh's mind even his fellow complainer Austin Clarke offered no real alternative to the misrepresentations of Ireland that came from the Celtic Twilight school. Although he professed never to have listened to the broadcasts, he argued in one column that the poetry program Clarke presented on Dublin radio in the early 50s was typical of the self-conscious pastoralism and limited range of contemporary poets: "Poems of Fields, Poems of Rocks, Poems of Bogs; Poems of Bigger Fields, Harder Rocks, Deeper Bogs." Calling the poetry produced by Clarke and his school "gilt for the gingerbread of the Philistines," Kavanagh claimed it was "this mentality that drove out O'Casey and Joyce."[12] The problem with Irish poetry was not that it focused on fields and bogs, but that it didn't seem to see them. "There are things that have a local individuality," he wrote in a later column, and "some hint of this local landscape" in the work of literary writers "would help to establish their genuineness. What proof have we that a man's poetical vision is genuine," he asked, "when we know that to the immediate scene he is totally blind?" Because he wanted to see a more recognizable representation of Ireland in its poetry, Kavanagh went back to "Under Ben Bulben" to rewrite Yeats's instructions for Irish poets. The opening lines of his version echo Yeats's "Irish poets learn your trade," but the poem quickly turns its attention toward a very different Ireland than the one peopled by peasants and country gentlemen.

> Irish poets open your eyes,
> Even Cabra can surprise;
> Try the dog-tracks now and then—
> Shelbourne Park and crooked men.

It was not that a poet ought to be the proverbial "blunt man of the people," Kavanagh explained in the column in which the poem appeared. Nor did he want poets to lower their ambitions. In fact much of his complaining in these years was directed at middle-class mediocrity. But it was time poets in Ireland learned, as he put it, "to achieve the illusion of life . . . the most difficult thing of all." The poem's concluding stanzas link the lived experience of the ordinary Irishman to a literary achievement that transcends, for Kavanagh, the momentary popularity of bogs, fields, and rocks.

> Enter in and be a part
> Of the world's frustrated heart,
> Drive the golf ball of despair,
> Supperdance away your care.
>
> Be ordinary.
> Be saving up to marry.
> Kiss her in the alleyway.
> Part—"Same time, same place"—and go.
>
> Learn repose on Boredom's bed,
> Deep anonymous, unread,
> And the god of Literature
> Will touch a moment to endure.[13]

Because his prescription for Irish poetry took the shape of a response to Yeats, Kavanagh may have felt it necessary to exaggerate his preference for ordinary experience as the basis for poetry. But his humorous revision of "Under Ben Bulben" did reflect a sentiment that was on the rise in Ireland.

Even an English poet living in the North at the time came to share Kavanagh's view that Yeats's poetic posturing was due for revision. When Philip Larkin moved to Belfast in 1950 to take up a post in the library of Queen's University, he had already published *The North Ship*, a collection he would later disparage as the necessary consequence of a youth spent "isolated in Shropshire with a complete Yeats."[14] Over the course of the five years he spent in Belfast, Larkin moved away from Yeats's influence and toward the mature style of poems like "Church Going."[15] The change his work underwent is reflected most clearly in "Born Yesterday," a poem he wrote on the birth of Kingsley Amis's daughter Sally. Responding to the occasion from Ireland, Larkin refashioned the sentiments of Yeats's "A Prayer for My Daughter" in a way that Kavanagh, fresh from his reworking of "Under Ben Bulben," would have applauded. True to his cyclical vision of history, Yeats had imagined his daughter's life unfolding in a future that would rise, "Dancing to a frenzied drum, / Out of the murderous innocence of the sea," while Larkin's future was merely the present extended in all its ordinariness. That distinction led them to quite different hopes for the two children. Whereas Yeats had wished his daughter happiness built on the soul's recovery of a "radical innocence" nurtured by the ceremony and custom of an aristocratic household, Larkin took his cue from the earlier poem's suggestion that a less than extraordinary beauty is best. Others, he wrote, will wish the newborn girl "innocence and love." His wish was different: "May you be ordinary." He went on to define this ordinariness in terms that anticipated both the criticism and praise that would be directed at the poetry that was then emerging.

> In fact, may you be dull—
> If that's what a skilled,
> Vigilant, flexible,
> Unemphasised, enthralled
> Catching of happiness is called.

Larkin's poetry was itself developing a voice that might be described as ordinary, even dull, but certainly skilled, vigilant, and flexible. It is no doubt a coincidence that as this new voice began to be heard, he was frequently mistaken for an Irish poet. (One editor explained that "Irish poets, like Mr. Larkin, though writing in standard English, reflect another regional value, that of rootedness.")[16] But it isn't necessary to believe that Ireland was responsible for Larkin's transformation in order to see in his reworking of Yeats's "Prayer" a reflection of a trend already under way there. A poet's barometer is by necessity a sensitive instrument, and consciously or not the English poet had registered a change in Ireland's literary weather.

In England the new climate spawned a spate of overcast skies rather than literary thunderstorms, the new front taking shape in the ironic and detached poetry of the Movement, a group that Larkin slipped more or less comfortably into when he returned from Belfast in 1955. The wry, disengaged style that Movement poets evolved over the next few years would never quite serve the purpose of poetry in Ireland, however. As the Irish critic Edna Longley put it later, the Movement poets had managed to replace the watery versifiers of the Georgian period "as everyone's favorite Aunt Sally."[17] But in Ireland poets were looking for stronger beer. The new generation of Irish poets was indeed staking a claim to the territory that lay between the peasants and country gentlemen of "Under Ben Bulben," but they were by no means ready to lower the ambitions of their poetry, either in fact or as a poetic posture. James Simmons, who began writing in the middle of the 1950s, saw ordinary experience as the background from which the poet's difficult vocation might emerge, but the vocation itself was still the same high-stakes business it had been in Wordsworth and Coleridge's *Lyrical Ballads*, when poetry had first tried to speak the language of ordinary men. In "The Not Yet Ancient Mariner" Simmons imagines the mariner of Coleridge's poem in the years before "he settled to his hard vocation," a working life that the poem makes as much the poet's recounting of his tribulations as the sailor's living through them. As Simmons conceives the still youthful mariner, "he must just taste the youth that others had" and for a moment at least "be ordinary." If poetry was to begin in the bedrock of ordinary experience, it might still end up at a higher pitch. For these poets ordinary meant "actual," as opposed to Yeats's mythologizing, but drawing on ordinary Ireland needn't lead to mundane or limited writing, as Joyce had shown when he built an epic out of the material of an ordinary day in Dublin.

Irish poets working in the 1950s and 1960s were putting Joyce's example into practice in a number of ways, stretching their poetry between the poles of ordinary Irish life and mythologies employed in newly self-conscious ways. Thomas Kinsella, for example, could write about his life on Baggot Street in the Dublin of the 1950s, but the life he describes there is one always hovering on the edge of prophecy, the river Liffey "sonneting origins" while "Dreamers' heads / Lie mesmerized in Dublin's beds / Flashing with images, Adam's morse." At the same time, Kinsella was also busy doing Yeats one better in the realm of Cuchulain and Oisin, the epic heroes of the Red Branch and Fenian cycles. Kinsella was not just borrowing plots and characters from Irish epic, as his predecessor had done, but going back to the original Irish and wrestling works like *An Táin Bó Cuailgne*, the story of Cuchulain's single-handed defense of Ulster, into a contemporary idiom that crackled with the sounds of ordinary speech. Later, to close the loop between these two modes he wrote about his own experience in retracing the trails taken by the heroes of the *Táin*.

Meanwhile in the North, John Montague was writing about the texture of daily life in rural County Tyrone and relishing its mundane details—like the work of carrying water or the "mug of froth" that is the farmhand's reward for his labor—in a way that emphasized poets' growing understanding of the shift that was taking place in Irish poetry. In *Forms of Exile*, the collection he published in 1958, Montague captured the moment at which he stepped back from the kind of mythic transformation that had once seemed the necessary function of poetry, choosing instead to savor the bare fact of experience for its own sake. Describing one of his childhood chores in "The Water Carrier" he suspends the poem just at the point where he might once have felt it necessary to justify with a poetic flourish the attention he has given to the small details of such a quotidian task. In place of a self-consciously poetic gesture Montague makes a poetic gesture out of the self-consciousness itself, pausing to consider his own reaction to the memory the poem has mined, and its relationship to the practice of poetry:

> Recovering the scene, I had hoped to stylize it,
> Like the portrait of an Egyptian water carrier:
> But pause, entranced by slight but memoried life.

It is worth remarking that the stylized Egyptian water carrier he seems to be rejecting is still present in Montague's poem, but now the mythic image signposts a byway the poem might take, but no longer needs to travel to reach its destination. In later poems, such as his touchstone work "Like Dolmens Round My Childhood," Montague would portray the ordinary people of his youth as already mythic figures, caught by the poem at the moment of their passing into "that dark permanence of ancient forms" for the authority of which poets had once ransacked old Irish legends.

Montague's willingness to make use of tradition even as he distanced himself from its limiting conventions shows up just as clearly in Irish-language poetry of the period. Seán Ó'Ríordáin, who had published his first poems in Irish during the war, wondered in a diary entry in 1947 whether poets writing as he was in modern Irish should "plunge ourselves into the old literature." There was much to gain through association with an ancient tradition. "But, there's mold on Macan Bhaird," he went on to say, referring to the family of hereditary poets active in Donegal in the 16th century. "Well, we'll dry ourselves off under the sun of life after the dip."[18] Writing to a friend a few years later Ó'Ríordáin spelled out what he meant. Old Irish offered poets at the middle of the century a way to add "breadth and scope" to their writing, but "it is in the Irish of this present era that the naturalness and life will be found that will enable us to make use of that breadth and scope."[19] Ó'Ríordáin's original poetry in Irish achieved a balance of ambition and colloquialism that would inspire a renaissance in the language over the next fifty years, but his mid-century translations of medieval Irish poetry into modern Irish are perhaps even more characteristic of the period's effort to strike a compromise between naturalness and the artifices of an established tradition.[20] In trying "to marry heritage with the foreign," as he put it, Ó'Ríordáin also struck a chord that resonated with an emerging strain of Anglo-Irish poetry.[21]

Around the time Ó'Ríordáin was wrestling with tradition in his diary, Pearse Hutchinson, a poet whose work over the last half-century deserves more attention than it has yet received, ventured out across a broader Celtic Europe which the example of Hugh MacDiarmid had emboldened him to explore. Writing in English peppered with Irish phrases Hutchinson demonstrated that the kind of attention to local detail that was emerging in the work of Kinsella and Montague was equally applicable to locales other than Ireland itself. The early poetry Hutchinson wrote from places like Scotland, Spain, Portugal, and Italy always kept one eye on the immediate landscape and the other on the landscape of the Irish language. This double vision allowed him to see the Castilian street signs in Barcelona, for example, as a reminder of the suppression of Catalan, which called up in turn the loss of Irish in Belfast.

Working in different directions and often in isolation, the poets who were finding their voices in the 1950s changed the landscape of Irish poetry within the span of the decade. If the tenets of the new poetry needed articulation beyond the example of the work itself, it came when Northerner John Hewitt's "Freehold" raised a flag over the territory his peers, north and south, were pioneering. In the "Townland of Peace" section of that long poem drafted during the war and revised over the next forty years, Hewitt sounded a retrospective manifesto for poets of the local and particular.

> Against the anthill and the beehive state
> I hold the right of man to stay out late,
> to sulk and laugh, to criticise or pray,
> when he is moved, at any hour of day,
> to vote by show of hands or sit at home,
> or stroll on Sunday with a vasculum,
> to sing or act or play or paint or write
> in any mode that offers him delight.
>
> I hold my claim against the mammoth powers
> to crooked roads and accidental flowers.

The political inflection here is Hewitt's own, but the poetics that pit crooked roads and accidental flowers against mammoth powers were coming into fashion across the political spectrum. Hewitt was careful to account for the narrower focus a poetry like this would necessarily adopt and to emphasize the authenticity of its local discoveries.

> But these small rights require a smaller stage
> than the vast forum of the nations' rage,
> for they imply a well-compacted space
> where every voice declares its native place,
> townland, townquarter, county at the most,
> the local word not ignorantly lost
> in the smooth jargon, bland and half alive,
> which wears no clinging burr upon its sleeve
> to tell the ground it grew from, and to prove
> there is for sure a plot of earth we love.

Hewitt's confidence in the force of the local word against the depleting effects of placeless cosmopolitan jargon provided a retrospective sanction for the sort of verse Irish poets were writing throughout the 1950s and that he had himself published in collections like *No Rebel Word* (1948). It also signaled the growing strength of a sentiment that began in the early 1960s to embolden a new generation of poets in Northern Ireland. The burr upon the sleeve that tells the ground it grew from could serve, in particular, as a banner for the group that was then gathering around Philip Hobsbaum, a critic and poet who arrived at Queen's University, Belfast, a few years after Philip Larkin left the library there. In Hobsbaum's view, the Movement that Larkin's poetry had spawned back home in England had given modern poetry "a necessary spring cleaning," but the next important wave of poetry would come from writers who understood as Hewitt did the force of local subjects and diction.[22] And it was on these grounds that Belfast looked due for a literary blossoming.

By the 1960s universities in Northern Ireland were beginning to feel the full effect of the Education Act of 1947, which had extended secondary and higher education to students for whom it had once been economically impractical to remain in school beyond the primary years. The result of this move for poetry was the "rising into articulation," as critic Neil Corcoran puts it, "of social classes which would previously have been tongue-tied by the lack of educational opportunity."[23] As it happened, this injection of new perspectives into Northern poetry coincided with the escalation of sectarian tensions known as the Troubles, which would break into open violence in the late 1960s. That combination of circumstances, fostering the emergence of new voices just as those voices began to seem most necessary, provoked a literary renaissance in the North, and its epicenter was in the group of poets—including Seamus Heaney and Michael Longley—that gathered around Hobsbaum in Belfast.

Writing in the short-lived *Kavanagh's Weekly* in 1952, Patrick Kavanagh had casually proposed a set of terms that now gave these Belfast poets the confidence to step outside the traditions of English poetry and write in voices that declared their native place. Accused of parochial views, Kavanagh had taken up the criticism and made it into a kind of manifesto for marginals. "Parochialism and provincialism," he wrote, "are direct opposites. The provincial has no mind of his own; he does not trust what his eyes see until he has heard what the metropolis—towards which his eyes are turned—has to say on any subject. This runs through all his activities." The parochial writer, on the other hand, keeps his eye on the local horizon and therefore "is never in any doubt about the social and artistic validity of his parish." To Kavanagh's mind the Ireland of the 1950s was still a provincial place, not a parochial one; what made it so, however, was an absence of courage, not of material for poetry. It is fitting that his own version of parochialism encouraged poets of Heaney's generation to write from a sense of place that was untrammeled by the expectations of English tradition.

Michael Longley in his "Letter to Derek Mahon" recalls one upwelling of this parochial spirit in the fall of 1969, when in the midst of the burgeoning civil rights movement the two poets, "minus muse and lexicon," staged what amounted to a poetic occupation of a Belfast that had once seemed entirely unpoetic. "And did we come into our own" at that moment, Longley wonders,

> Two poetic conservatives
> In the city of guns and long knives,
> Our ears receiving then and there
> The stereophonic nightmare
> Of the Shankill and the Falls,
> Our matches struck on crumbling walls
> To light us as we moved at last
> Through the back alleys of Belfast?

The Shankill and Falls Road neighborhoods are, respectively, Protestant and Catholic enclaves bordering each other in west Belfast. One achievement of the Belfast group was in lifting their chorus of disparate voices above the "stereophonic nightmare" of sectarian rhetoric and actual unrest that was then the soundtrack of the city. As a group these poets managed under the most challenging circumstances to introduce poetry into the public discourse of Northern Ireland, even as they staked their claim, as Yeats and Joyce had done before them, on a tradition of English language poetry that had once seemed explicitly British.

The remarkable accomplishment of the Belfast poets would serve as an impetus for writers in Ulster and the Republic alike. What is sometimes called the Belfast renaissance turned out to be the stirring of a poetic revival that has since spread across the island. Over the next decades a striking number of new voices would emerge in Ireland and many previously overlooked aspects of Irish life came to be represented in poetry. Women like Eavan Boland and Eiléan Ní Chuilleanáin added their accents to the poetic tradition once dominated by men, in turn opening the field for a wave of younger women. Poets working in the Irish language—such as Michael Davitt, Nuala Ní Dhomhnaill and Cathal Ó Searcaigh —enriched both languages when the foremost English language poets began to read and translate their work. The conception of poetry in Ireland expanded to include everything from Derek Mahon's cosmopolitan formalism and Paul Muldoon's verbal pyrotechnics to Paul Durcan's surrealist vignettes and Matthew Sweeney's minimalist fantasies. Its province stretched from Ciaran Carson's Belfast to Mary O'Malley's Connemara, from Conor O'Callaghan's East to Cathal

Ó Searcaigh's West. New strains of poetry came from the suburbs and the midlands, from the farmland and the office cubicle. And reports from Irish poets would be heard from as far away as Japan and the Czech Republic.

Following the course prescribed by MacNeice, poets in the coming years embraced the ordinary world around them, reflecting and sometimes advancing the changes taking place in every sphere of Irish life from social mores to politics to popular culture. Poetry in Ireland continued to contemplate literature and the arts, but it also grappled in turn with the Troubles, the economic stagnation of the 1970s, the rise of the Celtic Tiger, and, more recently, the easing of hostilities in the North. In the relatively small space of an island nation this renewed literary vigor has fed on itself, with poets North and South reading and reviewing each other's work, encouraging and disparaging their peers in poetry as well as in prose. That lively interplay of voices has made poetry a prominent feature of contemporary Ireland's cultural identity, adding a resonant element to the nation's dialogue with itself and with the world at large. A portion of this complex and varied conversation may be overheard in the selections that follow.

NOTES

1. "The Price of Peace," *Bell*, vol. X, no. 4 (July 1945), p. 288. Quoted in Terence Brown, *Ireland: A Social and Cultural History, 1922 to the Present* (Ithaca: Cornell University Press, 1985), p. 162.

2. W. B. Yeats, *Autobiographies* (London: Bracken Books, 1995), p. 435. The play was produced by the Irish Literary Theatre in 1901.

3. W. B. Yeats, *Explorations* (London: Macmillan, 1962), pp. 109–110.

4. See Diarmaid Ferriter, *The Transformation of Ireland* (New York: Overlook Press, 2005), p. 387.

5. Quoted in Ferriter, *The Transformation of Ireland*, p. 387.

6. J. P. Duggan, review of Brian Barton, *Northern Ireland in the Second World War*, History Ireland, vol. 4, no. 1, Spring 1996, p. 61. Quoted in Ferriter, *The Transformation of Ireland*, p. 389.

7. Louis MacNeice, *Modern Poetry: A Personal Essay* (Oxford: Clarendon Press, 1968), p. 5.

8. See, for example, Robert F. Garratt, who in reference to *Night and Morning* calls Clarke "the first real poet of the city." *Modern Irish Poetry: Tradition and Continuity from Yeats to Heaney* (Berkeley: University of California Press, 1989), p. 119.

9. Dillon Johnston would codify the image of Joyce as the ancestral figure for younger poets in *Irish Poetry After Joyce* (Mountrath, Ireland: Dolmen Press, 1985).

10. See Clarke's note to "The Healing of Mis" in this anthology.

11. W. B. Yeats, "Under Ben Bulben," in *The Collected Poems of W. B. Yeats*, rev. 2nd ed., ed. Richard J. Finneran (New York: Scribner, 1996), p. 328.

12. "Diary," *Envoy*, vol. 2, no. 7 (June 1950), p. 84.

13. "Diary," *Envoy*, vol. 3, no. 10 (September 1950), pp. 84–85.

14. Philip Larkin, Introduction to *The North Ship* (London: Faber and Faber, 1966), pp. 9–10.

15. Terry Whalen provides a useful overview of Larkin's Irish years in "'Strangeness Made Sense': Philip Larkin in Ireland," *Antigonish Review* 107 (Autumn 1996), pp. 157–169.

16. G. S. Fraser's slip in *Springtime* is quoted in a note to Blake Morrison, *The Movement* (Oxford: Oxford University Press, 1980), p. 287. Morrison also points to the Spring 1955 issue of *Departures,* where Larkin is said to have been born in Northern Ireland. The inclination of editors to describe Larkin as Irish became a topic of discussion on the BBC radio program *First Reading* during a broadcast on 1 July 1953. See Morrison, p. 45.

17. Quoted in Morrison, *Movement*, p. 7, but also see Longley, "Larkin, Edward Thomas and The Tradition," *Phoenix*, nos. 11–12 (1973–74), p. 64.

18. Seán Ó'Ríordáin, diary entry, 7 September 1947; quoted in Kaarina Hollo, "The Shock of the Old: Translating Early Irish Poetry into Modern Irish," *Eire-Ireland: a Journal of Irish Studies,* vol. 38, 2003.

19. Seán Ó'Ríordáin, letter to Donncha O Laoghaire, 17 March 1953, quoted in Hollo, "Shock of the Old."

20. The compromise is perhaps already evident in the act of translating from Old Irish to modern, but Ó'Ríordáin carries his negotiation between the two languages down to the most minute level. For example, he uses in his modern Irish translation whatever words of the Old Irish still have some currency, while translating those that have been lost, or, when he can, reviving an older word preserved in local use in one dialect or another. For a discussion of his practices see Hollo, "Shock of the Old."

21. Letter to Donncha O Laoghaire.

22. Philip Hobsbaum, "The Growth of English Modernism," *Wisconsin Studies in Contemporary Literature*, vol. 6, no. 1 (Winter–Spring 1965), p. 100.

23. Neil Corcoran, *After Yeats and Joyce* (Oxford: Oxford University Press, 1997), p. 131. My description of the Belfast renaissance owes much to Corcoran's excellent chapter on "Ulsters of the Mind: The Writing of Northern Ireland."

Padraic Colum (1881–1972)

Of the world imagined in Padraic Colum's 1907 volume *Wild Earth*, W. B. Yeats wrote admiringly: "It is unbeautiful Ireland, he will contrast finely with our Western dialect-makers."[1] Yeats's praise for Colum came at a time when the two men were moving apart, Colum having broken with Yeats's Abbey Theatre earlier that year to escape the dictatorial rule of its founder.

In 1905, Colum's play *The Land* had given the newly opened Abbey its first major success.[2] Joseph Holloway, a playgoer present that night, describes the event in his journal:

> Friday, June 9: A goodly crowd of patrons put in an appearance at the Abbey Theatre where Padraic Colum's three-act play, *The Land*, was produced for the first time on any stage. . . . I must say at once that the new piece was received with genuine enthusiasm. The actors were recalled after each act, and the author at the end of the play. He came forward and shyly bowed, returning hurriedly as if scared by the sight of the audience. Colum is a strange lad and always looks to me as if a good square meal would do him a world of good. A slight, fragile scrap of humanity with the look of a startled fawn ever hovering about his eyes.[3]

Colum, who was born in 1881 at Longford in the Irish Midlands, was only twenty-four on that night, and had come a long way to reach the stage of the Abbey. His Catholic childhood was nothing like the comfortable life of the Protestant aristocracy from which Yeats and other founders of the Abbey had come. His father, a teacher in the Longford workhouse when Colum was born, struggled against debt and heavy drinking, at one point leaving his wife and children in Ireland to try his fortune in America. Eventually the family moved to Dublin, where they lived on the small wages of the father's railway job, allowing Colum to spend eight years at the Glasthule National School. At seventeen he passed the railway examination and began working long hours as a clerk.[4]

Little time was left for literary pursuits, but in 1902 Colum began publishing poems in the *Irish Independent* and *United Irishman*. The poems drew the attention of Yeats and of Æ, to whom Colum would dedicate *Wild Earth* five years later. This volume, Colum's later editor John Sweeney writes,

> was a delicate distillation of all that Colum had learned from his study of speech rhythms for the stage, and . . . a deep undertone of compassion related to the universal human plight which he had pondered in local terms for his plays. Here, above all, was a brilliant new voice and a fine free music in a very old tradition.[5]

Two of these musical poems were in fact Colum's restorations, from one or two extant lines, of traditional Irish folksongs. Giving musical voice to the often disappointing realities of Irish rural life, they are typical of Colum's early work, and one, "She Moved Through the Fair," has become so fully integrated into the folk tradition that its author has been upgraded, in some anthologies, to "Anonymous" status.

Despite the critical success of *Wild Earth*, Colum found it difficult to make a living as a serious writer in Dublin. Broke and without patronage, he and his new wife Mary, herself an incisive critic and journalist, were glad to accept the gift of a honeymoon trip offered by Colum's aunt in Pittsburgh. They left Ireland on what was meant to be a brief visit to America in the autumn of 1914. In New York the pair found writing more profitable, and, encouraged by friends wary of the war breaking out in Europe, they decided to stay. Except for visits to Ireland and a brief residence in France, Colum would live and write in America until his death in 1972.

Over his long career Colum's poetry sometimes slipped into the shadows as he gained recognition as a folklorist and children's writer, but his belief in the importance of poetry and its ability to aid in the construction of an autonomous Irish future never lagged. In his last collection, with poems like "Roger Casement" and "Odysseus: In Memory of Arthur Griffith," he was still recalling the figures who shaped an independent Ireland. But, with the perspective of old age, he was also able to reconcile himself to those who had imagined a different future. "Ave Atque Vale" makes the poet's peace with his brother who, like many relatives of nationalists, chose to serve as a soldier for the British. Colum's *Collected Poems* closes with "Before the Fair," a poem that recalls the music of *Wild*

Earth, and reaches back beyond the Troubles to find the Ireland both sides sacrificed in the struggle.

Colum, late in life, became a harsh critic of his own achievement. Perhaps regretting the time given over to less serious writing, he felt betrayed by the bright future Yeats had predicted for him. Eavan Boland describes meeting Colum in the 1960s, when the older poet was in his eighties. Boland asked him about the early praise from Yeats. "He paused for a moment," Boland remembers. "His voice had a distinctive treble resonance. When he answered, it was high and emphatic. 'Yeats hurt me,' he said. 'He expected too much of me.'"[6]

NOTES

1. Quoted in Eavan Boland, *Object Lessons: The Life of the Woman and the Poet in Our Time* (Manchester, England: Carcanet Press, 1995), p. 138.

2. Sanford Sternlicht, *Padraic Colum,* Twayne English Authors Series (Boston: Twayne Publishers, 1985), p. 7. The Abbey occupied space vacated by the Mechanics Theatre and an adjacent morgue.

3. *Joseph Holloway's Abbey Theatre: A Selection from His Unpublished Journal,* ed. Robert Hogan and Michael J. O'Neill (Carbondale, Illinois: Southern Illinois University Press, 1967), p. 60. (Quoted in Sternlicht, p. 7.)

4. Sternlicht, *Padraic Colum,* pp. 2–3.

5. John L. Sweeney, "Padraic Colum and His Poetry," preface to *The Collected Poems of Padraic Colum* (Old Greenwich, Connecticut: Devin-Adair, 1953), p. vi.

6. Boland, *Object Lessons,* p. 139.

The Plougher

Sunset and silence! A man; around him earth savage, earth broken;
Beside him two horses, a plough!

Earth savage, earth broken, the brutes, the dawn-man there in the sunset,
And the plough that is twin to the sword, that is founder of cities!

"Brute-tamer, plough-maker, earth-breaker! Canst hear? There are ages
    between us—
Is it praying you are as you stand there alone in the sunset?

Surely our sky-born gods can be nought to you, earth child and earth-
    master—
Surely your thoughts are of Pan, or of Wotan, or Dana?*

Yet why give thought to the gods? Has Pan led your brutes where they
    stumble?
Has Dana numbed pain of the child-bed, or Wotan put hands to your
    plough?

What matter your foolish reply! O man standing lone and bowed earth-
    ward,
Your task is a day near its close. Give thanks to the night-giving god."

Slowly the darkness falls, the broken lands blend with the savage;
The brute-tamer stands by the brutes, a head's breadth only above them.

A head's breadth? Aye, but therein is hell's depth and the height up to
    heaven,
And the thrones of the gods and their halls, their chariots, purples, and
    splendours.

A Connachtman

It's my fear that my wake won't be quiet,
Nor my wake house a silent place:
For who would keep back the hundreds
Who would touch my breast and my face?

For the good men were always my friends,
From Galway back into Clare;
In strength, in sport, and in spending,
I was foremost at the fair;

In music, in song, and in friendship,
In contests by night and by day,
By all who knew it was given to me
That I bore the branch away.

Now let Manus Joyce, my friend
(If he be at all in the place),
Make smooth the boards of the coffin
They will put above my face.

The old men will have their stories
Of all the deeds in my days,
And the young men will stand by the coffin,
And be sure and clear in my praise.

But the girls will stay near the door,
And they'll have but little to say:
They'll bend their heads, the young girls,
And for a while they will pray.

And, going home in the dawning,
They'll be quiet with the boys;
The girls will walk together,
And seldom they'll lift the voice;

And then, between daybreak and dark,
And between the hill and the sea,
Three women, come down from the mountain,
Will raise the keen over me.

But 'tis my grief that I will not hear
When the cuckoo cries in Glenart,
That the wind that lifts when the sails are loosed,
Will never lift my heart.

She Moved Through the Fair*

My young love said to me, "My brothers won't mind,
And my parents won't slight you for your lack of kind."
Then she stepped away from me, and this she did say
"It will not be long, love, till our wedding day."

She stepped away from me and she moved through the fair,
And fondly I watched her go here and go there,
Then she went her way homeward with one star awake,
As the swan in the evening moves over the lake.

The people were saying no two were ere wed
But one had a sorrow that never was said,
And I smiled as she passed with her goods and her gear,
And that was the last that I saw of my dear.

I dreamt it last night that my young love came in,
So softly she entered, her feet made no din;
She came close beside me, and this she did say
"It will not be long, love, till our wedding day."

The Poor Girl's Meditation

I am sitting here
Since the moon rose in the night,
Kindling a fire,
And striving to keep it alight;
The folk of the house are lying
In slumber deep;
The geese will be gabbling soon:
The whole of the land is asleep.

May I never leave this world
Until my ill-luck is gone;
Till I have cows and sheep,
And the lad that I love for my own;

I would not think it long,
The night I would lie at his breast,
And the daughters of spite, after that,
Might say the thing they liked best.

Love takes the place of hate,
If a girl have beauty at all:
On a bed that was narrow and high,
A three-month I lay by the wall:
When I bethought on the lad
That I left on the brow of the hill,
I wept from dark until dark,
And my cheeks have the tear-tracks still.

And, O young lad that I love,
I am no mark for your scorn;
All you can say of me is
Undowered I was born:
And if I've no fortune in hand,
Nor cattle and sheep of my own,
This I can say, O lad,
I am fitted to lie my lone!

Legend

There is an hour, they say,
On which your dream has power:
Then all you wish for comes,
As comes the lost field-bird
Down to the island-lights;
There is an hour, they say,
That's woven with your wish:
In dawn, or dayli' gone,
In mirk-dark, or at noon,
In hush or hum of day,
May be that secret hour.

A herd-boy in the rain
Who looked o'er stony fields;

A young man in a street,
When fife and drum went by,
Making the sunlight shrill;
A girl in a lane,
When the long June twilight
Made friendly far-off things,
Had watch upon the hour:
The dooms they met are in
The song my grand-dam sings.

Men on Islands

Can it be that never more
Men will grow on Islands?
Ithaka and Eriskey,
Iceland and Tahiti!
Must the engines he has forged
Raven so for spaces
That the Islands dwindle down,
Dwindle down!—
Pots that shelve the tap-root's growth?
Must it be that never more
Men will flower on Islands?
Crete and Corsica, Mitylene,
Aran and Iona!

In the Carolina Woods

Here you should lie, ye Kings of eld,
Barbarossa, Boabdil,*
And Czar Lazar and Charlemagne,
Arthur, Gaelic Finn—
Here where the muffling Spanish mosses
Forests with forests fill!

Not in a cavern where the winds
Trample with battle-call,
But in these woods where branch and branch
From tree and tree let fall—
Not moss, but grey and cobweb beards,
Kings' cabalistic beards!

Here should you sleep your cycles out,
Ye Kings with hoary beards!

Jackdaw

Aloof from his tribe
On the elm-tree's top,
A jackdaw perched
A hand-reach up.

Silent he sat
On the branch, nor stirred,
And I saw in him
A changeling bird.

Grass was worn
Round pots and a pan,
A flea-bitten horse,
And a tilted van,

Where tinker's or gypsy's
Brats at play
Made vagrant's game of
Some citizen's way.

I watched the daw
On the branch, beguiled:
I saw a vagrant
From the wild.

The entail broken
What had he?
The humour of one
Out of his degree.

The franchise of one
Without kith or kind,
And only the pauper's
Single mind!

The daws on the elms
Kept tribal speech,
And he perched there,
Within a hand's reach—

He flew; his flight
Neither high nor wide
Was a vagabond's
To a seedman's stride.

A dog on the ground
Was rubbing for fleas;
Rags were there—
He fluttered to these:

Held a bright rag up
Like a banner won,
And went and hid it
Behind a stone!

Ave Atque Vale*

Thorough waters, thorough nations I have come
To lay last offerings at your low abode,
Brother, and to appeal
To ashes that were you.

Since that which none can check has borne you
From my regard, poor brother, these gifts take—
The tokens that are due
To ancient pieties;

But find them washed with tears, the many tears
A brother shed; and now I say Farewell—
Henceforth and for all time,
Hail, brother, and Farewell!

Odysseus: In Memory of Arthur Griffith*

You had the prose of logic and of scorn,
And words to sledge an iron argument,
And yet you could draw down the outland birds
To perch beside the ravens of your thought—
The dreams whereby a people challenges
Its dooms, its bounds. You were the one who knew
What sacred resistance is in men
That are almost broken; how, from resistance used,
A strength is born, a stormy, bright-eyed strength
Like Homer's Iris, messenger of the gods,
Coming before the ships the enemy
Has flung the fire upon. Our own, our native strength
You mustered up. But I will never say this,
Walking beside you, or looking on you,
With your strong brow, and chin was like a targe,*
And eyes that were so kindly of us all.

And sorrow comes as on that August day,
With our ship cleaving through the seas for home,
And that news coming sparkling through the air,
That you were dead, and that we'd never see you
Looking upon the state that you had builded.

The news that came was like that weight of waters
Poured on our hopes! Our navies yet unbuilded,
Our city left inglorious on its site,
Our fields uncleared, and over
Our ancient house the ancient curse of war!
And could we pray, touching the island-homeland,
Other than this: "Odysseus, you who laboured
So long upon the barren outer sea;
Odysseus, Odysseus, you who made
The plan that drove the wasters from the house,
And bent the bow that none could bend but you:
Be with us still:
Your memory be the watcher in our house,
Your memory be the flame upon our hills."

Roger Casement*

They have hanged Roger Casement to the tolling of a bell,
Ochone, och, ochone, ochone! *
And their Smiths, and their Murrays, and their Cecils say it's well,
Ochone, och, ochone, ochone!
But there are outcast peoples to lift that spirit high,
Flayed men and breastless women who laboured fearfully,
And they will lift him, lift him, for the eyes of God to see,
And it's well, after all, Roger Casement!

They've ta'en his strangled body from the gallows to the pit,
Ochone, och, ochone, ochone!
And the flame that eats into it, the quicklime, brought to it,
Ochone, och, ochone, ochone!
To waste that noble stature, the grave and brightening face,
In which courtesy and kindliness had eminence of place,
But they—they'll die to dust which the wind will take a-pace,
While 'twas yours to die to fire, Roger Casement!

Before the Fair

"Lost," "lost," the beeves and the bullocks,
The cattle men sell and buy,
Crowded upon the fair green,
Low to the lightless sky.

"Live," "live," and "Here," "here," the blackbird
From the top of the bare ash-tree,
Over the acres whistles
With beak of yellow blee.*

And climbing, turning, and climbing
His little stair of sound,
"Content," "content," from the low hedge
The redbreast sings in a round.

And I who hear that hedge-song
Will fare with all the rest,
With thoughts of lust and labour,
And bargain in my breast.

The bare hedge bright with rain-drops
That have not fallen down,
The golden-crowded whin-bush—
Nor know these things my own!

Austin Clarke (1896–1974)

Austin Clarke stands in remarkable isolation from the movements and schools of twentieth-century literature. Clarke's career began at a time, near the end of the Great War, when a cosmopolitan worldview was giving shape to literary modernism in London and Paris. Rather than turning to Paris, though, or even Dublin, Clarke found material for poetry in Ireland's past. "The problems of modernism," he wrote later, "can have little practical value in this country, where our literary development is so distinctively different."[1] Already working with this assumption that modernity in Ireland would take forms that hadn't been anticipated by English and American writers, Clarke in his first volume, *The Vengeance of Fionn*, updated the legend of Diamuid and Grainne not by the application of modernist technique, but through a fullness of detail that evoked, in the shadow of the Easter Rising, the continuity of landscape, poetry, and turmoil in the history of Ireland.

Clarke was born in Dublin in 1896, to middle-class parents. Like James Joyce a decade earlier, he was educated by the Jesuits of Belvedere College where, also like Joyce and his character Stephen Dedalus, Clarke experienced a great conflict between adolescent desires and Jesuit repression. He eventually married a woman with whom he shared these experiences, an older writer who was at work on a novel to be called, predictably, *Portrait of the Artist as a Young Woman*. Equally predictable, the apparently unconsummated marriage fell apart within weeks. Clarke's obsession with the issues of desire and repression expressed in Joyce's *Portrait* outlived the marriage, however, and would eventually guide his own poetic confrontation with the dilemmas of Catholic childhood in *Night and Morning*.[2] Poems like "Repentance" in this volume, published in 1938, map the conflicts of his Jesuit experience onto the landscape of medieval monasticism which Clarke had explored in earlier works, like *Pilgrimage and Other Poems* (1929), that had followed *The Cattledrive in Connaught* (1925), the last of his early narratives to focus on pre-Christian Ireland. "The Frenzy of Suibhne"—a poem in which Clarke reworks the medieval Irish legend of a pagan king whose assault on a newly established church results in a curse of madness that transforms him into a monstrous birdlike beast—is drawn from that 1925 collection.

After *Night and Morning,* Clarke did not publish a volume of poetry again until 1955, but despite the gap separating it from the earlier work, his *Ancient Lights, Poems and Satires: First Series* still displays Clarke's interest in the Church's effect on Irish life. His most important later poems were more explicitly personal. In *Mnemosyne Lay in Dust,* published in 1966, Clarke returned to his early narrative mode to document the mental breakdown that had hospitalized him during his twenties. It was with this long poem more than any other that Clarke exerted his influence on coming generations of Irish poets. Clarke himself moved on from this example. His demons in some sense exorcised by the return to youthful struggle and madness in *Mnemosyne,* Clarke wrote, through the final years of his career, poems like "The Healing of Mis" that for the first time embrace physicality in an exuberant and playful language.

In addition to poetry Clarke wrote plays, novels, memoirs, and criticism. He died in Dublin in 1974.

NOTES

1. Quoted in Gregory A. Schirmer, *The Poetry of Austin Clarke* (Notre Dame, Indiana: University of Notre Dame Press, 1983), p. 11.

2. See Robert F. Garratt's discussion of Joyce's influence on Clarke in "'Non Serviam': James Joyce and Modern Irish Poetry," *James Joyce and His Contemporaries,* ed. Diana A. Ben-Merre and Maureen Murphy (New York: Greenwood Press, 1989), pp. 121–129.

The Frenzy of Suibhne*

Run, run to the sailmaker—
While I pluck the torn white hedges
Of sea to crown my head—
And tell him to bind hard the canvas
For the waves are unhorsed to-night;
I cracked a thought between my nails
That they will light a candle
When I swim from the loud grass
To the holy house of Kieran.*

Storm is masted in the oakwood
Now and the fire of the hags
Blown out by the tide; in wet smoke
Mannanaun* splashes by with a bagful
Of music to wager for the food
In a house where the women mull
Ale; workmen dream of their furnace
And the male jewels that are alive:
But I hear the hounds of the black queen race
As I nest in the drenching ivy.

The rain is drowning in Glenveigh*
Where once the vats of brightness poured
Until the wet green branches hid
The black ridge of the boar:
Garlic was good there and the pignut;
Upon the clean tops of the wells
A tender crop was rooted—
But the wild-eyed man of the water
Was feathered like a hawk to the foot.

I hurried at evening
From the glen of birches
When longer shadows
Were cropping
Their way: on a sudden,
Darkness was nearer,
Hazels had ripened,
I heard the rain drop.

Far down a dark hollow
Of sloe-trees, a bird
Cried and black swine
Ran under the fences
Of rain for a tall man
Followed, his one eye
Redder than grey turf
When it is stirred:
Far down the hollow,
Sloe-bushes ran.

A black drove of boulders
Was crossing the ford:
O to what household,
Swineherd, Red Swineherd,
Do you hurry unbidden
That men may carouse?
Breathe on their eye-lids,
And bound to the rafters
May three naked women drip
Blood;* in their hearing
Strange laughter and rapine

Of phantoms that tumble
From nothing, till fear
Empty the bladder,
Swineherd, Red Swineherd,
And shadows madden
The heart like a drum.

I hurried to the paddock
While stablemen were brawling
And under the bellies
Of horses I crawled:
Dark, dark was the harness,
(The wheelwright said I was mad)
But I flung back the lock
And I loosed forty hoofs to
The storm in the grass.

A juggler cried. Light
Rushed from doors and men singing:
"O she has been wedded
To-night, the true wife of Sweeny,
Of Sweeny the King!"
I saw a pale woman
Half clad for the new bed:
I fought them with talons, I ran
On the oak-wood—O Horsemen,
Dark Horsemen, I tell ye
That Sweeny is dead!

Stark in the rushlight
Of the lake-water,
I heard the heads talking
As they dripped on the stake:
Who runs with the grey moon
When ravens are asleep?
It is Sweeny, Little Sweeny
Looking for his mind.
When roots were barking in the wood,
I broke the horns of a goathead
For I heard them on the water
Call: *Sweeny, Little Sweeny*
Is looking for his mind.
But Robbers, dark Robbers, I tell ye
That Sweeny is dead!

If I sleep now, the hag
Of the haggard, will steal
My feathers, though I drowned her
In the dark pool of Achill*
That has no sound.

When tides were baying
The moon, in a glen
Of pools, I fed on
Grey cowdung: a hundred
Men hauling a slab
Upon the great dolmen*
Of Sweeny the King,
From the shovels and barrow,

Fled. Nailing, I dug up
The gold cup and collar
And hid them in rain.
But how can mind hurry
As reeds without feet,
And why is there pain in
A mind that is dead?

I have heard the little music
Of Midna,* I have seen
Tara in flame and a blooded moon
Behind the Ridge of Judgment . . .
But how can they find my name
Though they are crying like gulls
That search for the sea?
Nine years I hurried from mankind
And yet, O Christ, if I could sail
To the Island of the Culdees,*
I would sleep, sleep awhile
By the blessing of the holy Kieran.

from Mnemosyne Lay in Dust*

I

Past the house where he was got
In darkness, terrace, provision shop,
Wing-hidden convent opposite,
Past public-houses at lighting-up
Time, crowds outside them—Maurice Devane
Watched from the taxi window in vain
National stir and gaiety
Beyond himself: St Patrick's Day,
The spike-ends of the Blue Coat school,
Georgian houses, ribald gloom
Rag-shadowed by gaslight, quiet pavements
    Moon-waiting in Blackhall Place.*

For six weeks Maurice had not slept,
Hours pillowed him from right to left side,
Unconsciousness became the pit
Of terror. Void would draw his spirit,
Unself him. Sometimes he fancied that music,
Soft lights in Surrey, Kent, could cure him,
Hypnotic touch, until, one evening,
The death-chill seemed to mount from feet
To shin, to thigh. Life burning in groin
And prostate ached for a distant joy.
But nerves need solitary confinement.
    Terror repeals the mind.

Cabs ranked at Kingsbridge Station, Guinness
Tugs moored at their wooden quay, glinting
Of Liffey mudbank; hidden vats
Brewing intoxication, potstill,
Laddering of distilleries
Ready to sell their jollities,
Delirium tremens. Dublin swayed,
Drenching, drowning the shamrock: unsaintly
Mirth. The high departments were filed,
Yard, store, unlit. Whiskey-all-round,
Beyond the wealth of that square mile,
    Was healthing every round.

The eighteenth century hospital
Established by the tears of Madam
Steevens,* who gave birth, people said, to
A monster with a pig's snout, pot-head.
The Ford turned right, slowed down. Gates opened,
Closed with a clang; acetelyne glow
Of headlights. How could Maurice Devane
Suspect from weeping-stone, porch, vane,
The classical rustle of the harpies,
Hopping in filth among the trees,
The Mansion of Forgetfulness
    Swift gave us for a jest?*

II

Straight-jacketing sprang to every lock
And bolt, shadowy figures shocked,
Wall, ceiling; hat, coat, trousers flung
From him, vest, woollens, Maurice was plunged
Into a steaming bath; half-suffocated,
He sank, his assailants gesticulating,
A Keystone reel gone crazier;
The terror-peeling celluloid,
Whirling the figures into vapour,
    Dissolved them. All was void.

Drugged in the dark, delirious,
In vision Maurice saw, heard, struggle
Of men and women, shouting, groans.
In an accident at Westland Row,
Two locomotives with mangle of wheel-spokes,
Colliding: up-scatter of smoke, steel,
Above: the gong of ambulances.
Below, the quietly boiling hiss
Of steam, the winter-sleet of glances,
    The quiet boiling of pistons.

The crowds were noisy. Sudden cries
Of "Murder! Murder!" from a byway,
The shriek of women with upswollen
Bodies, held down in torment, rolling
And giving birth to foundlings, shriek
After shriek, the blanket lifting unspeakable
Protrusions. The crowds were stumbling backward,
Barefooted cry of "Murder" scurried.
Police batoned eyesight into blackness,
    Bandages were blurred.

Maurice had wakened up. He saw a
Circular peep-hole rimmed with polished
Brass within the door. It gloomed.
A face was glaring into the bed-room
With bulging eyes and fierce moustache.
Quicker than thought, a torchlight flashed
From wall to pillow. Motionless,

It spied until the face had gone.
The sound of sleepers in unrest:
    Still watchful, the peep-hole shone.

What night was it, he heard the creaking
Of boots and tiptoed to the peep-hole?
Four men were carrying a coffin
Upon their shoulders. As they shuffled,
Far in his mind a hollaloo
Echoed: "The Canon of Killaloe . . ."
Death-chill would mount from feet to limbs,
His loins, secretion no longer burn.
Those shoulderers would come for him with
    The shroud, spade, last thud.

Nightly he watched a masquerade
Go by his cell and was afraid
Of one – the stooping, bald-headed madman
Who muttered curse after curse, his hands
Busily knitting, twiddling white reeds:
So huge, he seemed to be the leader.
The others tormented by their folly,
The narrows of the moon, crowded
Together, gibboned his gestures, followed
    That madman knitting reed, brow.

Once, getting out of bed, he peeped
Into the dormitory. Sheet
And slip were laundry-white. Dazes
Of electric light came down. Patients
Stirred fitfully. Their fidgeting marred
With scrawls the whiteness of the ward,
Gift of the moon. He wondered who
He was, but memory had hidden
All. Someone sat beside him, drew
    Chair nearer, murmured: "Think!"

One afternoon, he looked in dread
Into the ward outside. The beds
Were empty. Quiet sunshine glowed
On waxed floor and brass. He hurried
Across to the high window, stood

On the hot pipes to see the view.
Below there was a widespread garden,
With shrubberies, walks, summerhouses,
He stared in wonder from his bars,
    Saddened by the boughs.

VI

One night he heard heart-breaking sound.
It was a sigh unworlding its sorrow.
Another followed. Slowly he counted
Four different sighs, one after another.
"My mother," he anguished, "and my sisters
Have passed away. I am alone, now,
Lost in myself in a mysterious
Darkness, the victim in a story."
Far whistle of a train, the voice of steam.
Evil was peering through the peep-hole.

Suddenly heart began to beat
Too quickly, too loudly. It clamoured
As if it were stopping. He left the heat
And stumbled forward, hammered
The door, called out that he was dying.
Key turned. Body was picked up, carried
Beyond the ward, the bedwhite row
Of faces, into a private darkness.
Lock turned. He cried out. All was still.
He stood, limbs shivering in the chill.

He tumbled into half the truth:
Burial alive. His breath was shouting:
"Let, let me out." But words were puny.
Fists hushed on a wall of inward-outness.
Knees crept along a floor that stirred
As softly. All was the same chill.
He knew the wall was circular
And air was catchcry in the stillness
For reason had returned to tell him
    That he was in a padded cell.

The key had turned again. Blankets
Were flung into blackness as if to mock
The cringer on the floor. He wrapped
The bedclothes around his limbs, shocked back
To sanity. Lo! in memory yet,
Margaret came in a frail night-dress,
Feet bare, her heavy plaits let down
Between her knees, his pale protectress.
Nightly restraint, unwanted semen
Had ended their romantic dream.

Early next morning, he awakened,
Saw only greyness shining down
From a skylight on the grey walls
Of leather, knew, in anguish, his bowels
Had opened. He turned, shivering, all shent.
Wrapping himself in the filthied blankets,
Fearful of dire punishment,
He waited there until a blankness
Enveloped him . . . When he raised his head up,
Noon-light was gentle in the bedroom.

X

In Winter around the fire,
Soldiers at a camp
After the long rout.
Brass helmet tipped with coal
By the fender and fire-guard.
A history-book lying on the floor.

In the dark, secured,
They lie. Every night
The news is going into the past:
The airman lost in Mozambique,
Far shouting at the General Election
And the Great War ending
In drums, processions
And a hooded Preacher
At the Pro-Cathedral.

They lie, in the dark,
Watching the fire, on the edge
Of a storybook jungle: they watch
The high boots of the colonists.

The scales are broken.
Justice cannot reach them:
All the uproar of the senses,
All the torment of conscience,
All that twists and breaks.
Without memory or insight,
The soul is out of sight
And all things out of sight
And being half gone they are happy.

They lie in bed, listening
To the sleet against the bars, train
That whistles from the country. A horse-car
Waits under the oil-lamp at the station
And turns into a drosky.*

On a sun-free day, his senses lied, for
They showed him a man that had been killed.
His severed head lay on the pillow
Beside him, grey-bearded, with lidded eyes.
No axe . . . no blood. How did it happen?
He looked again. Slim palms had placed it
Nearer the window: hallucinatory
Head of an aged John the Baptist.

Soon Mnemosyne made him smaller,
A child of seven, half gone to sleep.
His mother was at her sewing machine,
The shuttle clicking as she followed
A hem. Outside, the praying garden,
Late blossom of the elder-trees:
Twilight was hiding from his elders,
The toolshed, barrel, secret den.

Suddenly over the lower wall,
Madmen were leaping into the yard
With howls of "Murder!" scarcely a yard

From him. He jumped out of the darkfall,
Awake, chill, trembling at the din.
There on his bed, a terrible Twangman*
Was sitting. He muttered "Hang him! Hang him!"
As he nodded, twiddling paper spills.

Maurice would stray through the back streets
By shuttered windows, shadowy Railway
Station, by gas-lamps, iron railings,
Down Constitution Hill. Discreetly
Concealed in every cornerstone
Under the arches, Echo resided,
Ready to answer him. Side by side,
Stepping together, the pair roamed.

Often in priestly robe on a
Night of full moon, out of the waste,
A solitary figure, self-wasted,
Stole from the encampments—Onan,*
Consoler of the young, the timid,
The captive. Administering, he passed down,
The ward. Balsam was in his hand.
The self-sufficer, the anonym.

XII

Nature
Remembering a young believer
And knowing his weakness
Could never stand to reason
Gave him from the lovely hand
Of his despairing mother,
A dish of strawberries
To tempt
And humble the fast
That had laid him nearer than they were
Along her clay.

XVIII

Rememorised, Maurice Devane
Went out, his future in every vein,
The Gate had opened. Down Steeven's Lane
The high wall of the Garden, to right
Of him, the Fountain with a horse-trough,
Illusions had become a story.
There was the departmental storey
Of Guinness's, God-given right
Of goodness in every barrel, tun,
They averaged. Upon that site
Of shares and dividends in sight
Of Watling Street and the Cornmarket,
At Number One in Thomas Street
Shone in the days of the ballad-sheet,
The house in which his mother was born.

The Healing of Mis*

Along that mountain in the south named after her, Mis,
    The only daughter of Dáire Mor, the King
Of Munster, escaped after the battle near Cahirconlish
    Hurled by Fionn and the Fianna from shingle
To rock against the invaders who had sailed out of Greece
    And Spain. Her fingers a-drip with a father's blood, she
Fled up a forest, echoing foreign cries. Streams
    That passed her ran down to faster flood.

Fear put her in caverns, in greenth of fern, on branches that grieved
    About her and for three centuries her mind
Was lost. A raggedness in thorn-set bramble, in greed
    Of gorse, she sprang from gorge to cave-mouth, hind
Of hare in her claws, devoured it raw. A nakedness
    Blue'd by the sea-gales that blew from Dursey, on freezing
Ridges, she lanked her lengthening hair, a mantle that guarded
    The bushiness above her knees.

In winter when turf was raked under the household cauldron,
    Stories were told of a Geilt* that flew over forest top and
Cliff to pray from the sky. Sometimes a shepherd, hatted
    By crack of twig, had a glimpse of hairiness
Crawling from filth and hurried back to safe pasturage.
    Those cloudy cantreds* were dreaded and accursed
For a legend endured from the Paps of Dana to Mount Brandon*
    Of a lonely sorrow time could not cure.

It happened in the third century that word was brought to Felim,
    The King of Munster, as he came from the boar-hunt in a local
Forest. Riding thoughtfully back to Cashel, he felt
    Such pity that when brands flickered in the banquet-hall,
He offered tribute and tax to any man there who could cure
    The Woe of Mis. "Greatness, your wish will be fulfilled,"
A harper called, braving from a corner. "Who's that?" "Duv Ruis.
    She'll listen to strings, but I need a fistful

Of gold coins and silver coins." "Harper, take as much
    As back can carry." "And a farl* from the royal griddle,
Your Grace?" "It's yours. What else?" "Nothing. All can touch
    The bottom of female complaint." "Hard to unriddle.
Faith-healers like to darken their say. But mine is plain. Let
    My steward be summoned to give this man the sum on credit.
If he fails to perform the feat in three months, he has little to gain
    For he will pay the debt with his head."

Laughter unbarred the door: the harper went into the night-rain,
    Journeyed by dysart and dyke, strummed for half-loaf
And the yellowness of ale, sheltered in house or hidy-
    Hole, came to a white battle of waves that broke
Along four promontories. In a sombre glen
    Between the uphills, he stole into the forest of
Slieve Mis. At times a lonely bird-cry vaulted the silence.
    He stopped, listened from a dry course.

When young beaks had been filled and pickaback insects were safe
    As air, Duv Ruis rested awhile in a sun-scented
Vale, then hastened to spread his travelling cloak in the shade
    Of a blossoming quicken-tree, tossed his ring-coins up,

A silver and golden frolic of profit-making pelf,
  Then arranged them carefully in emblems
Along the cloth-edge, lay on his back to greet the Geilt
  Opened his flap, exposed himself.

Holding his harp, the consolation of his bosom,
  He played a suantree* with grace-notes that enspelled
Traditional tunes and, smiling quietly at his ruse,
  Waited. Soon his senses knew that loneliness
Stood by, a bareness modestly draped in tangle-black hair,
  With timesless hands, listening to the special
Melling that drew and soothed her mind as she stared
  In surmise at his rising flesh.

"Are you a man?" she asked. "I am." "What's that you are holding?"
  "A harp." "I remember the triangle." "Pluck it."
"You will not harm me?" "I won't." She tapped the sounding-board,
  Laughed as it answered her. "What's this I'm touching
Below?" "A couple of pouched eggs I like to carry."
  "Can you lay them as the poult-hen?" "Only the glair."
"What's this so high and mighty?" "Marry-come-up, my dear:
  The wand of the feat as scholars declare!"

He spun the gold and silver pieces into a reel
  Around her temples, an oriental garland,
Faster, faster they went. She clapped. "I know that gleam
  For I recall the cargoes of bullion from the harbours
Of Tyre and Gaza." "Eyes cannot gaze at the feat for it closes
  The lids in bliss." "Like this?" She palmed the sun. "Yes."
"Perform the feat," she commanded. Powerfulness held him closely.
  "I cannot. I'm much too hungry."

"Wait here. I'll bring you venison." She leaped over
  The quicken-tree with lifted head. He hurried
To pick up kindling in the forest, gather arm-loads
  Of withered branches, fanned them into up-rushers,
Cracklers, with a flick of his flint, set large stones
  For a nearby cooking-pit the Fianna
Had used, then waited, uneasy as his shoes. At last
  She rose above the rowan branches,

Lightly bearing a buck on her shoulder. "Here's a meal
　　For both our bellies . . . Look, day is aflame on the edge
Of night. Run, run!" "It's only faggots turned into heat."
　　He poked the stones from the ash and the slope sent them,
Red-hot, into the paven pit. He coiled up
　　Each sweeping tress from her filthy body, saw
Her nipples harden into blackberries. "Bogholes have spoiled them.
　　But soon that pair will be redder than haws . . .

I stumbled on a helmet in sand near to washed-in wreckage,
　　Brimmed it from a high cascade, going
And coming patiently to fill your bath." He sloshed
　　Himself as he lathered her down, soaped the skin of her back
With a lump of deer-fat, washed the crack between the slurried
　　Cheeks, like a mother, turned her round, picked crabs from
Her sporran, nit-nurseries hidden in tiny flurries
　　Through tangled tresses, then began

All over again. He soaped her body, washed it down,
　　Drawing the wad of deer-skin to-and-fro
Softly between her glossing thighs, turned her around
　　And frizzled her neglected faddle, noticed
It needed a thorough-going cleansing inside and out, scrubbed
　　And douched it, cursing her ignorance, lack of care,
Then coiled her tresses neatly after he currycombed them
　　As if she was a gainly mare.

"Now canter into dryness, my filly." She galloped, instead, up
　　The smooth slope, became a momentary
Speck on the summit, then flew down again into his arms—
　　The favourite no ostler had led across the Curragh
Or mounted yet. "Lie down with me under the blossoms."
　　He entered so quietly she never felt it
Until a pang shook her. Fearing involuntary loss,
　　He waited, obedient as she helped
His through the hymen. Then at the thrusting of the wand,
　　Her eyelids closed in bliss. The flowers of the quicken-tree
Were poppies. Both drowsed but how could they stop fingers that wan-
　　dered
　　Until their passion was no longer tender?

"Buck, buck me," she cried, "as the stag in rut." Wildly crouping
 Herself while he husbanded roughly, she spent with him in the spasm
That blurs the sight. They lay without words. Soon limbs drooped
 Towards sleep in the deepening grass.

They woke for late supper. He cut and crusted two fillets in dampish
 Clay, left them to bake until the savour
Called to their mouths. He gave her thick slices of bannock.
                                                    When
 The hot meal was over, she said: "Why do you delay
The feat of the wand again?" "We must prepare the bridal
 Bed." Waist-deep in ferns, he gathered sunny swathes.
She ran to pull the fennel bloom, wildering woodbine
 And made a border of braided daisies.

She did not wake until the sun-god had gone by
 Next day. Hidden in foliage, he could hear
Her lamenting: "Ba, be, ba, pleasant the gold and silver on
 Our double bed. Pleasant the grace-notes that appeared
Above his breast. But better than money in a ring
 Coining more bright ones, better than skiddle," she desponded,
As she searched around in vain, hair mantling her from the mist,
 "His pouched eggs and the feat of the wand."

Climbing down from the leaves to comfort her, he thought: "I must trim it
 To-morrow." He held her a minute then led her to the glowing
Branches that waited for her beyond the forest dimness,
 While steaks were broiling, he showed her the honeycomb,
The goat-cheese, the heather-ale, he had bought for the feast at
 A farm near Ventry. After they had eaten, idled
And ale'd, he murmured: "Tell me about those curious dreams."
 "How did you guess?" "From stir and dire cry."
"High tiers of oars from the Mediterranean were dipping whiteness
 In blueness. Ships swept from archipelagoes
Into surds of sound. Hundreds of bucklers lightened
 Through a conflagatory storm: 'Stromboli!' 'Stromboli!'
Look-outs were calling down from a red hail of cinders.
      Main-sails
 Were furling as keels hurtled from fumeroles.
Finger-tips of diluvian fire were piling their rains
 On temple, ziggurat. I zigzagged, stole

In another dream through labyrinthine corridors
    Where serpentries of momentary flashes
Revealed the figurative walls, as iron doors
    Clanged at my heels. Clueless in a subterranean
Maze, I reached a hall where darkness was worshipping
    Itself. The unseen, the unheard-of, moved in self-horror
Around me. Yielding to the force of writhesome limbs,
    Unvirgined by the Minotaur—

I knew my father." "Wrong dreams are dispelled with the help of music
    And the wand." Soon Nature showed them more delightful
Ways as they heaved under the mantle. How could he refuse
    The interplay of limbs that orientalised them?
Daily he scrutinised, scrubbed her, rosied all her skin.
    They stayed in the mountain forest twelve weeks or more
Hugging his harp at night he lulled her to sleep. Then, thinly,
    Tried to serve the longing that woke her.

So Mis was healed. Often she hunted in the forest depths
    While he kept house, moss lodge. When rain-clouds hid
All Ireland, and waters ran down their tumultuous steps,
    Unseen, they warmed themselves in a cave by crowdering
Flame. O she might have come from a Sidhe-mound* for the gods
    Had made her a mortal. "I'll examine her future dreams,
Interpret them, find in chance word much she has forgotten;
    Signs and symbols are underneath."

Early one morning they came down by the turns of a dry course
    And coombe to the highway. Gaily she wore the blue gown,
Shoes and Tyrian cloak he had brought her. A roan horse
    Waited, a servant at the bridle. Her arms were around him
As he rode by ford, rath, to be invested. Goodness
    Blared from the trumpets faring them to the high door
That had laughed him one night from the feast. Blessing,
    Victory, to him who relates this story!

C. Day Lewis (1899–1963)

"You write too little," Cecil Day Lewis once remarked to Philip Larkin; "I've written far too much."[1] Like his contemporaries W. H. Auden and Louis MacNeice, Day Lewis went at poetry with an absolute devotion, turning the most ordinary events of life into occasions for verse. The result is a body of more than four hundred poems that vary as much in quality and energy as in form and content. His best poems, though, now speak as strongly of their time as they once spoke to it.

Day Lewis was born in Ballintubber, in what was then called Queen's County, in 1904, and one of the last poems published in his lifetime, "Kilmainham Jail: Easter Sunday, 1966," recounts a return to Ireland, six years before his death, to commemorate the fiftieth anniversary of the Easter Rising of 1916. His birth and the publication of the volume in which that poem appeared, a nostalgic look back to his childhood entitled *The Whispering Roots,* stand as the essentially Irish bookends of Day Lewis's life. Between them, Ireland arguably figured little. His family moved to England, eventually settling in West London, where his father's career as a clergyman brought the young Day Lewis into contact with both the privileged crowd he would join at Oxford, and the poor working class with whom his socialist politics would later align him. In his last year at Wadham College, Oxford, he became friends with W. H. Auden. In the years following graduation he published four volumes of poetry, ranging from romantic nature lyrics to what he claimed was "unconscious" political allegory, before publishing the book that made his reputation as one of the politically engaged poets of the 1930s. *The Magnetic Mountain* is dedicated to Auden, and its epigraph from R. E. Warner—"Come, then, companions, this is the spring of blood, / Heart's heyday, movement of masses, beginning of good"[2]—sets the program for what today seems an odd mixture of almost Georgian singing and socialist propaganda. The volume's title poem, included here, may well stretch its Audenesque poetics of commitment beyond the point at which formal excellence can contain sheer political rhetoric; combining art and politics in this way undermines both. But it is an appropriate emblem of Day Lewis's personal commitment to social change. Of the famous group—Auden, Spender, Day Lewis—that gave form, and a name, to the spate of political poetry in the 1930s, only Day Lewis in fact joined the Communist Party.

Day Lewis's poetic mode, in the many volumes that followed *The Magnetic Mountain,* drifted between political allegory and romantic lyric, his commitment to socialism being equaled by his commitment to poetry as poetry. Poems of the late 1930s resisted fascism and documented the war in Spain. Through the 1950s and 1960s he was writing long lyric sequences, many of which meditated upon the nature of poetry itself. The graver of these poems express the same regret at the close of his career that gives his quip to Larkin its poignancy. "Unwritten poems loom," Day Lewis writes in "On Not Saying Everything," "as if / They'd cover the whole of earthly life," but the written poem, finally, remains "Purer for this limitation."[3] In "Apollonian Figure" the poet surveys his art with an ironic humor that mocks poetic purity of another sort.

It is with *The Whispering Roots,* the last volume published in his lifetime, that Day Lewis established his claim to be remembered as an Irish poet. Like "Kilmainham Jail," other poems in the volume look back to the history and literary culture of Ireland to find the roots of his personal memories and Anglo-Irish family line, but also the roots of his commitment to social justice. Considering figures like the Irish activist Con Markievicz, on the one hand, and the poor laborers of Ireland's rural West, on the other, these poems restate the social values of Day Lewis's 1930s verse in a new, often colloquial register that has more in common with Ireland's post-war poetic renaissance than is often acknowledged.

Day Lewis was elected Professor of Poetry at Oxford in 1951. He served as Poet Laureate of England from 1968 until his death in 1972. The detective novels he wrote throughout the 1940s under the name Nicholas Blake are still in print and still popular with readers.

NOTES

1. Quoted in Ian Parsons' Introduction to *Poems of C. Day Lewis 1925–1972* (London: Jonathan Cape and Hogarth Press, 1977), p. viii.

2. "The Magnetic Mountain," in *The Complete Poems of C. Day Lewis,* ed. Jill Balcon (London, Sinclair-Stevenson, 1992), p. 135.

3. "On Not Saying Everything," *Complete Poems,* pp. 600–601.

from The Magnetic Mountain

3

Somewhere beyond the railheads
Of reason, south or north,
Lies a magnetic mountain
Riveting sky to earth.

No line is laid so far.
Ties rusting in a stack
And sleepers—dead men's bones—
Mark a defeated track.

Kestrel who yearly changes
His tenement of space
At the last hovering
May signify that place.

Iron in the soul,
Spirit steeled in fire,
Needle trembling on truth—
These shall draw me there.

The planets keep their course,
Blindly the bee comes home,
And I shall need no sextant
To prove I'm getting warm.

Near that miraculous mountain
Compass and clock must fail,
For space stands on its head there
And time chases its tail.

There's iron for the asking
Will keep all winds at bay,
Girders to take the leaden
Strain of a sagging sky.

Oh there's a mine of metal,
Enough to make me rich
And build right over chaos
A cantilever bridge.

16

Look west, Wystan, lone flyer, birdman, my bully boy!
Plague of locusts, creeping barrage, has left earth bare:
Suckling and centenarian are up in air,
No wing-room for Wystan, no joke for kestrel joy.

Sky-scrapers put high questions that quench the wind's breath,
Whose shadow still comes short of truth, but kills the grass:
Power-house chimneys choke sun, ascetic pylons pass
Bringing light to the dark-livers, charged to deal death.

Firework fêtes, love displays, levitation of dead,
Salvation writ in smoke will reassure the town,
While comfy in captive balloons easily brought down
Sit frail philosophers, gravity gone to the head.

Gain altitude, Auden, then let the base beware!
Migrate, chaste my kestrel, you need a change of air!

32

You that love England, who have an ear for her music,
The slow movement of clouds in benediction,
Clear arias of light thrilling over her uplands,
Over the chords of summer sustained peacefully;
Ceaseless the leaves' counterpoint in a west wind lively,
Blossom and river rippling loveliest allegro,
And the storms of wood strings brass at year's finale:
Listen. Can you not hear the entrance of a new theme?

You who go out alone, on tandem or on pillion,
Down arterial roads riding in April,
Or sad beside lakes where hill-slopes are reflected
Making fires of leaves, your high hopes fallen:
Cyclists and hikers in company, day excursionists,
Refugees from cursed towns and devastated areas;
Know you seek a new world, a saviour to establish
Long-lost kinship and restore the blood's fulfilment.

You who like peace, good sorts, happy in a small way
Watching birds or playing cricket with schoolboys,
Who pay for drinks all round, whom disaster chose not;
Yet passing derelict mills and barns roof-rent

Where despair has burnt itself out—hearts at a standstill,
Who suffer loss, aware of lowered vitality;
We can tell you a secret, offer a tonic; only
Submit to the visiting angel, the strange new healer.

You above all who have come to the far end, victims
Of a run-down machine, who can bear it no longer;
Whether in easy chairs chafing at impotence
Or against hunger, bullies and spies preserving
The nerve for action, the spark of indignation—
Need fight in the dark no more, you know your enemies.
You shall be leaders when zero hour is signalled,
Wielders of power and welders of a new world.

34   *for Frances Warner*

What do we ask for, then?
Not for pity's pence nor pursy affluence,
Only to set up house again:
Neither a coward's heaven, cessation of pain,
Nor a new world of sense,
But that we may be given the chance to be men.
For what, then, do we hope?
Not longer sight at once but enlarged scope;
Miraculous no seed or growth of soul, but soil
Cleared of weed, prepared for good:
We shall expect no birth-hour without blood
Nor fire without recoil.

Publish the vision, broadcast and screen it,
Of a world where the will of all shall be raised to highest power,
Village or factory shall form the unit.
Control shall be from the centres, quick brain, warm heart,
And the bearings bathed in a pure
Fluid of sympathy. There possessions no more shall be part
Of the man, where riches and sacrifice
Are of flesh and blood, sex, muscles, limbs and eyes.
Each shall give of his best. It shall seem proper
For all to share what all produced.

Men shall be glad of company, love shall be more than a guest
And the bond no more of paper.

Open your eyes, for vision
Is here of a world that has ceased to be bought and sold
With traitor silver and fairy gold;
But the diamond of endurance, the wrought-iron of passion
Is all their currency.
As the body that knows through action they are splendid,
Feeling head and heart agree;

Young men proud of their output, women no longer stale
With deferred crisis; the old, a full day ended,
Able to stand down and sit still.
Only the exploiter, the public nuisance, the quitter
Receive no quarter.

Here they do not need
To flee the birthplace. There's room for growing and working.
Bright of eye, champions for speed,
They sing their own songs, they are active, they play not watch:
Happy at night talking
Of the demon bowler cracked over the elm-trees,
The reverse pass that won the match.
At festivals knowing themselves normal and well-born
They remember the ancestors that gave them ease,
Harris who fought the bully at Melbourne,
What Wainwright wrote with his blood, Rosa in prison—
All who sucked out the poison.

On Not Saying Everything

This tree outside my window here.
Naked, umbrageous, fresh or sere,
Has neither chance nor will to be
Anything but a linden tree,
Even if its branches grew to span
The continent; for nature's plan

Insists that infinite extension
Shall create no new dimension.
From the first snuggling of the seed
In earth, a branchy form's decreed.

Unwritten poems loom as if
They'd cover the whole of earthly life.
But each one, growing, learns to trim its
Impulse and meaning to the limits
Roughed out by me, then modified
In its own truth's expanding light.
A poem, settling to its form,
Finds there is no jailer, but a norm
Of conduct, and a fitting sphere
Which stops it wandering everywhere.

As for you, my love, it's harder,
Though neither prisoner nor warder,
Not to desire you both: for love
Illudes us we can lightly move
Into a new dimension, where
The bounds of being disappear
And we make one impassioned cell.
So wanting to be all in all
Each for each, a man and woman
Defy the limits of what's human.

Your glancing eye, your animal tongue,
Your hands that flew to mine and clung
Like birds on bough, with innocence
Masking those young experiments
Of flesh, persuaded me that nature
Formed us each other's god and creature.
Play out then, as it should be played,
The sweet illusion that has made
An eldorado of your hair
And our love an everywhere.

But when we cease to play explorers
And become settlers, clear before us
Lied the next need—to re-define
The boundary between yours and mine;
Else, one stays prisoner, one goes free.

Each to his own identity
Grown back, shall prove our love's expression
Purer for this limitation.
Love's essence, like a poem's, shall spring
From the not saying everything.

Apollonian Figure

Careful of his poetic p's and q's,
This self-possessed master of circumspection
Enjoyed a *mariage blanc* with the Muse,
Who never caught his verse in an erection.

Some praise the lapidary figure: but
With due respect to the attendant's spiel,
That fig-leaf there, so elegantly cut—
Just what, if anything, does it conceal?

Ballintubbert House, Co. Laois*

Here is the unremembered gate.
Two asses, a grey and a black,
Have ambled across from the rough lawn
As if they'd been told to greet
The revenant. Trees draw graciously back
As I follow the drive, to unveil
For this drifty wraith, composed and real
The house where he was born.

Nothing is changed from that sixty-year-old
Photograph, except
My father's young face has been brushed away.
On the steps down which he strolled
With me in his arms, the living are grouped,
And it is my son Sean
Who stands upon the dishevelled lawn
To photograph us today.

I walk through the unremembered house,
Note on the walls each stain
Of damp; then up the spacious stair
As if I would now retrace
My self to the room where it began.
Dust on fine furnishings,
A scent of wood ash—the whole house sings
With an elegiac air.

Its owner is not at home—nor I
Who have no title in it
And no drowned memories to chime
Through its hush. Can piety
Or a long-lost innocence explain it?—
By what prodigious spell,
Sad elegant house, you have made me feel
A ghost before my time?

Near Ballyconneely, Co. Galway

i

A stony stretch. Grey boulders
Half-buried in furze and heather,
Purple and gold—Connemara's
Old bones dressed in colours
Out of a royal past.

Inshore the sea is marbled
And veined with foam. The Twelve Pins
Like thunderclouds hewn from rock
Or gods in a cloudy fable
Loom through an overcast.

The roofless dwellings have grown
Back to the earth they were raised from,
And tune with those primordial
Outcrops of grey stone
Among the furze and the heather.

Where man is dispossessed
Silence fills up his place
Fast as a racing tide.
Little survives of our West
But stone and the moody weather.

ii

Taciturn rocks, the whisht of the Atlantic
The sea-thrift mute above a corpse-white strand
Pray silence for those vanished generations
Who toiled on a hard sea, a harsher land.

Not all the bards harping on ancient wrong
Were half as eloquent as the silence here
Which amplifies the ghostly lamentations
And draws a hundred-year-old footfall near.

Preyed on by gombeen men, expropriated
By absentee landlords, driven overseas
Or to mass-burial pits in the great famines,
They left a waste which tourists may call peace.

The living plod to Mass, or gather seaweed
For pigmy fields hacked out from heath and furze—
No eye to spare for the charmed tourist's view,
No ear to heed the plaint of ancestors.

Winds have rubbed salt into the ruinous homes
Where turf-fires glowed once: waves and seagulls keen
Those mortal wounds. The landscape's an heroic
Skeleton time's beaked agents have picked clean.

Land

The boundary stone,
The balk, fence or hedge
Says on one side "I own,"
On the other "I acknowledge."

The small farmer carved
His children rations.
He died. The heart was halved,
Quartered, fragmented, apportioned:

To the sons, a share
Of what he'd clung to
By nature, plod and care—
His land, his antique land-hunger.

Many years he ruled,
Many a year sons
Followed him to oat-field,
Pasture, bog, down shaded boreens.

Turf, milk, harvest—he
Grew from earth also
His own identity
Firmed by the seasons' come-and-go.

Now at last the sons,
Captive though long-fledged,
Own what they envied once—
Right men, the neighbours acknowledge.

Kilmainham Jail: Easter Sunday, 1966

Sunbursts over this execution yard
        Mitigate high, harsh walls. A lowly
Black cross marks the deaths we are here to honour,
        Relieved by an Easter lily.
Wearing the nineteen-sixteen medal, a few
        Veterans and white-haired women recall
The Post Office, Clanwilliam House, the College of Surgeons,
        Jacob's factory—all
Those desperate strongholds caught in a crossfire
        Between the English guns
And Dublin's withering incredulity.
        Against the wall where once

Connolly, strapped to a chair, was shot, a platform
      Holds movie cameras. They sight
On the guard of honour beneath the tricolor,
      An officer with a horseman's light
And quiet hands, and now the old President
      Who, soldierly still in bearing,
Steps out to lay a wreath under the plaque.
      As then, no grandiose words, no cheering—
Only a pause in the splatter of Dublin talk,
      A whisper of phantom volleys.

How could they know, those men in the sunless cells,
What would flower from their blood and England's follies?
Their dreams, coming full circle, had punctured upon
The violence that gave them breath and cut them loose.
They bargained on death: death came to keep the bargain.
Pious postcards of men dying in spruce
Green uniforms, angels beckoning them aloft,
Only cheapen their cause. Today they are hailed
As martyrs; but then they bore the ridiculed shame of
Mountebanks in a tragedy which has failed.
And they were neither the one nor the other—simply
Devoted men who, though the odds were stacked
Against them, believed their country's age-old plight
And the moment gave no option but to act.
Now the leaders, each in his sweating cell,
The future a blind wall and the unwinking
Eyes of firing-squad rifles, pass their time
In letters home, in prayer. Maybe they are thinking
Of Mount Street, the blazing rooftops, the Post Office,
Wrapping that glory round them against the cold
Shadow of death. Who knows the pull and recoil of
A doomed heart?

            They are gone as a tale that is told,
The fourteen men. Let them be more than a legend:
Ghost-voices of Kilmainham, claim your due—
This is not yet the Ireland we fought for.
You living, make our Easter dreams come true.

Remembering Con Markievicz*

Child running wild in woods of Lissadell:
Young lady from the Big House, seen
In a flowered dress, gathering wild flowers: Ascendancy queen
Of hunts, house-parties, practical jokes—who could foretell
(Oh fiery shade, impetuous bone)
Where all was regular, self-sufficient, gay
Their lovely hoyden lost in a nation's heroine?
Laughterless now the sweet demesne,
And the gaunt house looks blank on Sligo Bay
A nest decayed, an eagle flown.

The Paris studio, your playboy Count
Were not enough, nor Castle splendour
And fame of horsemanship. You were the tinder
Waiting a match, a runner tuned for the pistol's sound,
Impatient shade, long-suffering bone.
In a Balally cottage you found a store
Of Sinn Fein papers. You read—maybe the old sheets can while
The time. The flash lights up a whole
Ireland which you have never known before,
A nest betrayed, its eagles gone.

The road to Connolly and Stephen's Green
Showed clear. The great heart which defied
Irish prejudice, English snipers, died
A little not to have shared a grave with the fourteen.
Oh fiery shade, intransigent bone!
And when the Treaty emptied the British jails,
A haggard woman returned and Dublin went wild to greet her.
But still it was not enough: an iota
Of compromise, she cried, and the Cause fails.
Nest disarrayed, eagles undone.

Fanatic, bad actress, figure of fun—
She was called each. Ever she dreamed,
Fought, suffered for a losing side, it seemed
(The side which always at last is seen to have won),
Oh fiery shade and unvexed bone.
Remember a heart impulsive, gay and tender,

Still to an ideal Ireland and its real poor alive.
When she died in a pauper bed, in love
All the poor of Dublin rose to lament her
A nest is made, an eagle flown.

Sailing from Cleggan

Never will I forget it—
Beating out through Cleggan Bay
Towards Inishbofin, how
The shadow lay between us,
An invisible shadow
All but severing us lay
Athwart the Galway hooker.

Sea-room won, turning to port
Round Rossadillisk Point I
Slacken the sheet. Atlantic
Breeze abeam, ahead the sun's eye
Opening, we skirt past reefs
And islands—Friar, Cruagh,
Orney, Eeshal, Inishturk.

Porpoises cartwheeling through
Inshore water, boom creaking,
Spray asperging; and sunlight
Transforming to a lime-green
Laughter the lipcurling of
Each morose wave as they burst
On reefs fanged for a shipwreck.

Miracle sun, dispelling
That worst shadow! Salt and sun,
Our wounds' cautery! And how,
Havened, healed, oh lightened of
The shadow, we stepped ashore
On to our recaptured love—
Never could I forget it.

The Whispering Roots

Roots are for holding on, and holding dear.
Mine, like a child's milk teeth, came gently away
From Ireland at the close of my second year.
Is it second childhood now—that I overhear
Them whisper across a lifetime as if from yesterday?

We have had blood enough and talk of blood,
These sixty years. Exiles are two a penny
And race a rancid word; a meaningless word
For the Anglo-Irish: a flighty cuckoo brood
Foisted on alien nests, they knew much pride and many

Falls. But still my roots go whispering on
Like rain on a soft day. Whatever lies
Beneath their cadence I could not disown:
An Irish stranger's voice, its tang and tone,
Recalls a family language I thrill to recognize.

All the melodious places only seen
On a schoolboy's map—Kinsale, Meath, Connemara:
Writers—Swift, Berkeley, Goldsmith, Sheridan:
Fighters, from Vinegar Hill to Stephen's Green:
The Sidhe,* saints, scholars, rakes of Mallow, kings of Tara:—

Were background music to my ignorant youth.
Now on a rising wind louder it swells
From the lonely hills of Laois. What can a birth-
Place mean, its features comely or uncouth,
To a long-rootless man? Yet still the place compels.

We Anglo-Irish and the memory of us
Are thinning out. Bad landlords some, some good,
But never of a land rightfully ours,
We hunted, fished, swore by our ancestors,
Till we were ripped like parasite growth from native wood.

And still the land compels me; not ancestral
Ghosts, nor regret for childhood's fabled charms,
But a rare peacefulness, consoling, festal,
As if the old religion we oppressed all
Those years folded the stray within a father's arms.

The modern age has passed this island by
And it's the peace of death her revenants find?
Harsh Dublin wit, peasant vivacity
Are here to give your shallow claims the lie.
Perhaps in such soil only the heart's long roots will bind—

Even, transplanted, quiveringly respond
To their first parent earth. Here God is taken
For granted, time like a well-tutored hound
Brought to man's heel, and ghosting underground
Something flows to the exile from what has been forsaken.

In age, body swept on, mind crawls upstream
Toward the source; not thinking to find there
Visions or fairy gold—what old men dream
Is pure restatement of the original theme,
A sense of rootedness, a source held near and dear.

Patrick Kavanagh (1904–1967)

By the time his first collection, *Ploughman and Other Poems,* was published in 1936, Patrick Kavanagh had already submitted nearly a hundred poems for publication. Poetry, against his parents' wish, had become Kavanagh's craft at an early age, and his prolific production may have resulted from an effort to counter the lassitude with which he applied himself to work the family considered more appropriate.

Kavanagh was born in rural County Monaghan in 1904. His family was poor—nine children subsisting on a cobbler's wages. His parents' highest hope for their oldest son was that he would close the "curse o' God books" that enthralled him, and make some money as a cobbler and farmhand.[1] But Kavanagh, more comfortable in the world of words, "was never an enthusiastic worker," his brother Peter remembers, "and it took a skilled slave-driver—of which there were a few around—to get value out him."[2] It isn't surprising, given the conflict between his literary interests and the demands of the farmer's life, that Kavanagh did not immediately adopt an agrarian tone in his poetry. His early poems were shaped by the same tradition that had attracted him before he left school at thirteen: eighteenth- and nineteenth-century English poetry that provided an imaginative alternative to the hardship of country life. Once out of school, Kavanagh began to work as an apprentice to his father, and to write poems that had as little as possible to do with that fact:

> When a country body begins to progress into print he does not write out of his rural innocence—he writes out of Palgrave's *Golden Treasury* . . . The first step out of total rurality is complexity—imitation.[3]

In the 1930s Kavanagh could not yet see the small rural world around him as properly poetic on its own terms. The poems of his first collections are conventionally Romantic lyrics that take their authority on country matters from the literary tradition rather than from a lively authenticity. Still, many of these poems, like "Ploughman," are successful examples of their genre, and they trace the refinement of his craft that is the groundwork of Kavanagh's mature voice. Other early poems point even more clearly toward Kavanagh's later effort to shatter the pieties of pastoral poetry. "Address to an Old Wooden Gate," perhaps the first of his works to appear in print, tempers its romantic apostrophe to the gate as a stock image of rural poetry with a social criticism that asks "How can I love the iron gates which guard / The fields of wealthy farmers?"[4]

By the first years of the next decade, the Edenic view of peasant life that sustains these early lyrics had begun, in another form, to influence Irish politics. Éamon de Valera, the first prime minister, espoused the peasant model as the ideal for the new Irish Republic, and this translation of the pastoral paradigm from literary to social and political matters had a deep effect on Kavanagh. Applied to national life, the pastoral model could only appear inadequate in the light of global economics and the Second World War erupting in Europe. In response, Kavanagh began to send poems like "Stony Grey Soil" to *The Bell*, a journal launched by Sean O'Faoláin in 1940. By publishing realist fiction and poetry in a strongly anti-Romantic mode, O'Faoláin meant to subvert the revivalist spirit in literature and politics. Kavanagh's new poems, in stark contrast to those he had published in 1936, began to express the politics and aesthetics favored in the new journal.

In this period Kavanagh produced his most influential work. "The Great Hunger," a long poem that looks at the influence of a distorted Catholic tradition on the already difficult life of rural Ireland, was written in less than three weeks in 1941. Completely revising the image of country life both of Kavanagh's early poems and of *The Green Fool*, his previously published novel, "The Great Hunger" packs into the character of Patrick Maguire all the potentially repressive and dehumanizing effects of rural society from which Romantic texts turn away. Unlike the blithe inhabitants of pastoral, Maguire is like a man being attacked by two strong assailants—the Church gripping him in a stranglehold while the farm work, year after year, pummels him relentlessly. In this narrow, brutal drama, there's no room for love, and self-esteem is the first human sentiment to be destroyed. In his stark depiction of farm laborers transformed by the work and deprivation into "mechanized scarecrows," Kavanagh challenges the literary tradition of the pastoral alongside the biblical motif of Christ as the word made flesh, asking "is there anything we can prove / Of life as it is broken-backed over the Book / Of Death?" That rhetorical question is repeated throughout the poem in various forms—"Is there some light of imagination in these wet clods? / Or why do we stand here shivering?"—always implying the same negative answer.[5]

In spite of the powerful presence of the Irish working class in "The Great Hunger," Kavanagh did not go on to become a voice of the Irish people. Bitter, perhaps, at his failure to be embraced either by high or low culture, Kavanagh attacked both. Poets and workers alike suffered unrelenting criticism under his attempt to break down the conventions by which Irish poetry maintained its identity as a spiritual entity separate from "poetry." In relentlessly agonistic "Diary" pieces he wrote for the journal *Envoy*, Kavanagh managed, between December 1949 and July 1951, to alienate himself from nearly every figure and school on the Irish literary scene.

But while Kavanagh, during his lifetime, suffered the disappointments of a lone voice clamoring from the metaphorical wilderness between the Dublin literati and the folk of the Irish countryside, his poetry would in subsequent years speak directly to a new generation of Irish poets. For the generation that includes Seamus Heaney and Michael Longley, Kavanagh is one of the ancestral figures who struck a path out of the shadow of Yeats. Kavanagh's efforts to dismantle the conventions of Irish poetry cleared for these younger poets the huge terrain that lies between the extremes of Irishness that Yeats had embraced in "Under Ben Bulben," where he urges Irish poets to "sing the peasantry, and then / / Hard riding country gentlemen, / The holiness of monks, and after / Porter drinkers' randy laughter. . . ."

Much more applicable to the social realities of postwar Ireland, Kavanagh's response to Yeats in one of his "Diary" poems, reproduced here as "Irish Poets Open Your Eyes," not only maps the middle ground Yeats ignored, but does so with a quality of irony that we recognize as an important element in later Irish poetry.

Patrick Kavanagh died of pneumonia in Dublin in 1967.

NOTES

1. Antoinette Quinn, *Patrick Kavanagh: A Critical Study* (Syracuse, New York: Syracuse University Press, 1991), p. 1.

2. *Patrick Kavanagh: Man and Poet*, ed. Peter Kavanagh (Orono, Maine: National Poetry Foundation, 1986), p. 28.

3. Quoted in Quinn, *Patrick Kavanagh*, pp. 4–5.

4. "Address to an Old Wooden Gate," *Collected Poems*, ed. Antoinette Quinn (London: Penguin/Allen Lane, 2004), p. 5.

5. "The Great Hunger," *Collected Poems*, p. 63.

Address to an Old Wooden Gate

Battered by time and weather, scarcely fit
For firewood; there's not a single bit
Of paint to hide those wrinkles, and such scringes
Break hoarsely on the silence—rusty hinges:
A barbed wire clasp around one withered arm
Replaces the old latch, with evil charm.
That poplar tree you hang upon is rotten,
And all its early loveliness forgotten.
This gap ere long must find another sentry
If the cows are not to roam the open country.
They'll laugh at you, Old Wooden Gate, they'll push
Your limbs asunder, soon, into the slush.
Then I will lean upon your top no more
To muse, and dream of pebbles on a shore,
Or watch the fairy-columned turf-smoke rise
From white-washed cottage chimneys heaven-wise.
Here have I kept fair tryst, and kept it true,
When we were lovers all, and you were new;
And many a time I've seen the laughing-eyed
Schoolchildren, on your trusty back astride.
But Time's long silver hand has touched our brows,
And I'm the scorned of women—you of cows.
How can I love the iron gates which guard
The fields of wealthy farmers? They are hard,
Unlovely things, a-swing on concrete piers—
Their finger tips are pointed like old spears.
But you and I are kindred, Ruined Gate,
For both of us have met the self-same fate.

Ploughman

I turn the lea-green down
Gaily now,
And paint the meadow brown
With my plough.

I dream with silvery gull
And brazen crow.
A thing that is beautiful
I may know.

Tranquillity walks with me
And no care.
O, the quiet ecstasy
Like a prayer.

I find a star-lovely art
In a dark sod.
Joy that is timeless! O heart
That knows God!

Spraying the Potatoes

The barrels of blue potato-spray
Stood on a headland of July
Beside an orchard wall where roses
Were young girls hanging from the sky.

The flocks of green potato-stalks
Were blossom spread for sudden flight,
The Kerr's Pinks in a frivelled blue,
The Arran Banners wearing white.

And over that potato-field
A lazy veil of woven sun.
Dandelions growing on headlands, showing
Their unloved hearts to everyone.

And I was there with the knapsack sprayer
On the barrel's edge poised. A wasp was floating
Dead on a sunken briar leaf
Over a copper-poisoned ocean.

The axle-roll of a rut-locked cart
Broke the burnt stick of noon in two.
An old man came through a corn-field
Remembering his youth and some Ruth he knew.

He turned my way. "God further the work."
He echoed an ancient farming prayer.
I thanked him. He eyed the potato-drills.
He said: "You are bound to have good ones there."

We talked and our talk was a theme of kings,
A theme for strings. He hunkered down
In the shade of the orchard wall. O roses,
The old man dies in the young girl's frown.

And poet lost to potato-fields,
Remembering the lime and copper smell
Of the spraying barrels he is not lost
Or till blossomed stalks cannot weave a spell.

Stony Grey Soil

O stony grey soil of Monaghan,
The laugh from my love you thieved;
You took the gay child of my passion
And gave me your clod-conceived.

You clogged the feet of my boyhood,
And I believed that my stumble
Had the poise and stride of Apollo
And his voice my thick-tongued mumble.

You told me the plough was immortal!
O green-life-conquering plough!
Your mandril strained, your coulter blunted
In the smooth lea-field of my brow.

You sang on steaming dunghills
A song of cowards' brood,
You perfumed my clothes with weasel itch,
You fed me on swinish food.

You flung a ditch on my vision
Of beauty, love and truth.
O stony grey soil of Monaghan,
You burgled my bank of youth!

Lost the long hours of pleasure,
All the women that love young men.
O can I still stroke the monster's back
Or write with unpoisoned pen

His name in these lonely verses,
Or mention the dark fields where
The first gay flight of my lyric
Got caught in a peasant's prayer.

Mullahinsha, Drummeril, Black Shanco—
Wherever I turn I see
In the stony grey soil of Monaghan
Dead loves that were born for me.

The Great Hunger

I

Clay is the word and clay is the flesh
Where the potato-gatherers like mechanized scare-crows move
Along the side-fall of the hill—Maguire and his men.
If we watch them an hour is there anything we can prove
Of life as it is broken-backed over the Book
Of Death? Here crows gabble over worms and frogs
And the gulls like old newspapers are blown clear of the hedges, luckily.
Is there some light of imagination in these wet clods?
Or why do we stand here shivering?
   Which of these men
Loved the light and the queen
Too long virgin? Yesterday was summer. Who was it promised marriage
  to himself
Before apples were hung from the ceilings for Hallowe'en?
We will wait and watch the tragedy to the last curtain,
Till the last soul passively like a bag of wet clay
Rolls down the side of the hill, diverted by the angles
Where the plough missed or a spade stands, straitening the way.
A dog lying on a torn jacket under a heeled-up cart,
A horse nosing along the posied headland, trailing

A rusty plough. Three heads hanging between wide-apart
Legs. October playing a symphony on a slack wire paling.
Maguire watches the drills flattened out
And the flints that lit a candle for him on a June altar
Flameless. The drills slipped by and the days slipped by
And he trembled his head away and ran free from the world's halter,
And thought himself wiser than any man in the townland
When he laughed over pints of porter
Of how he came free from every net spread
In the gaps of experience. He shook a knowing head
And pretended to his soul
That children are tedious in hurrying fields of April
Where men are spanging across wide furrows,
Lost in the passion that never needs a wife—
The pricks that pricked were the pointed pins of harrows.
Children scream so loud that the crows could bring
The seed of an acre away with crow-rude jeers.
Patrick Maguire, he called his dog and he flung a stone in the air
And hallooed the birds away that were the birds of the years.
Turn over the weedy clods and tease out the tangled skeins.
What is he looking for there?
He thinks it is a potato, but we know better
Than his mud-gloved fingers probe in this insensitive hair.

"Move forward the basket and balance it steady
In this hollow. Pull down the shafts of that cart, Joe,
And straddle the horse," Maguire calls.
"The wind's over Brannagan's, now that means rain.
Graip up some withered stalks and see that no potato falls
Over the tail-board going down the ruckety pass—
And *that's* a job we'll have to do in December,
Gravel it and build a kerb on the bog-side. Is that Cassidy's ass
Out in my clover? Curse o' God—
Where is that dog?
Never where he's wanted." Maguire grunts and spits
Through a clay-wattled moustache and stares about him from the height.
His dream changes again like the cloud-swung wind
And he is not so sure now if his mother was right
When she praised the man who made a field his bride.

Watch him, watch him, that man on a hill whose spirit
Is a wet sack flapping about the knees of time.
He lives that his little fields may stay fertile when his own body
Is spread in the bottom of a ditch under two coulters crossed in Christ's
    Name.

He was suspicious in his youth as a rat near strange bread
When girls laughed; when they screamed he knew that meant
The cry of fillies in season. He could not walk
The easy road to his destiny. He dreamt
The innocence of young brambles to hooked treachery.
O the grip, O the grip of irregular fields! No man escapes.
It could not be that back of the hills love was free
And ditches straight.
No monster hand lifted up children and put down apes
As here.
        "O God if I had been wiser!"
That was his sigh like the brown breeze in the thistles.
He looks towards his house and haggard. "O God if I had been wiser!"
But now a crumpled leaf from the whitethorn bushes
Darts like a frightened robin, and the fence
Shows the green of after-grass through a little window,
And he knows that his own heart is calling his mother a liar.
God's truth is life—even the grotesque shapes of its foulest fire.

The horse lifts its head and cranes
Through the whins and stones
To lip late passion in the crawling clover.
In the gap there's a bush weighted with boulders like morality,
The fools of life bleed if they climb over.

The wind leans from Brady's, and the coltsfoot leaves are holed with
    rust,
Rain fills the cart-tracks and the sole-plate grooves;
A yellow sun reflects in Donaghmoyne
The poignant light in puddles shaped by hooves.

Come with me, Imagination, into this iron house
And we will watch from the doorway the years run back,
And we will know what a peasant's left hand wrote on the page.
Be easy, October. No cackle hen, horse neigh, tree sough, duck quack.

II

Maguire was faithful to death:
He stayed with his mother till she died
At the age of ninety-one.
She stayed too long,
Wife and mother in one.
When she died
The knuckle-bones were cutting the skin of her son's backside
And he was sixty-five.

O he loved his mother
Above all others.
O he loved his ploughs
And he loved his cows
And his happiest dream
Was to clean his arse
With perennial grass
On the bank of some summer stream;
To smoke his pipe
In a sheltered gripe
In the middle of July—
His face in a mist
And two stones in his fist
And an impotent worm on his thigh.

But his passion became a plague
For he grew feeble bringing the vague
Women of his mind to lust nearness,
Once a week at least flesh must make an appearance.

So Maguire got tired
Of the no-target gun fired
And returned to his headlands of carrots and cabbage,
To the fields once again
Where eunuchs can be men
And life is more lousy than savage.

III

Poor Paddy Maguire, a fourteen-hour day
He worked for years. It was he that lit the fire
And boiled the kettle and gave the cows their hay.

His mother, tall, hard as a Protestant spire,
Came down the stairs bare-foot at the kettle-call
And talked to her son sharply: "Did you let
The hens out, you?" She had a venomous drawl
And a wizened face like moth-eaten leatherette.
Two black cats peeped between the banisters
And gloated over the bacon-fizzling pan.
Outside the window showed tin canisters.
The snipe of Dawn fell like a whirring stone
And Patrick on a headland stood alone.

The pull is on the traces; it is March
And a cold old black wind is blowing from Dundalk.
The twisting sod rolls over on her back—
The virgin screams before the irresistible sock.
No worry on Maguire's mind this day
Except that he forgot to bring his matches.
"Hop back there, Polly, hoy back, woa, wae."
From every second hill a neighbour watches
With all the sharpened interest of rivalry.
Yet sometimes when the sun comes through a gap
These men know God the Father in a tree:
The Holy Spirit is the rising sap,
And Christ will be the green leaves that will come
At Easter from the sealed and guarded tomb.

Primroses and the unearthly start of ferns
Among the blackthorn shadows in the ditch,
A dead sparrow and an old waistcoat. Maguire learns
As the horses turn slowly round the which is which
Of love and fear and things half born to mind.
He stands between the plough-handles and he sees
At the end of a long furrow his name signed
Among the poets, prostitutes. With all miseries
He is one. Here with the unfortunate
Who for half moments of paradise
Pay out good days and wait and wait
For sunlight-woven cloaks. O to be wise
As Respectability that knows the price of all things
And marks God's truth in pounds and pence and farthings.

IV

April, and no one able to calculate
How far is it to harvest. They put down
The seeds blindly with sensuous groping fingers,
And sensual sleep dreams subtly underground.
Tomorrow is Wednesday—who cares?
"Remember Eileen Farrelly? I was thinking
A man might do a damned sight worse . . ." That voice is blown
Through a hole in a garden wall—
And who was Eileen now cannot be known.

The cattle are out on grass,
The corn is coming up evenly.
The farm folk are hurrying to catch Mass:
Christ will meet them at the end of the world, the slow and speedier.
But the fields say: only Time can bless.

Maguire knelt beside a pillar where he could spit
Without being seen. He turned an old prayer round:
"Jesus, Mary and Joseph pray for us
Now and at the Hour." Heaven dazzled death.
"Wonder should I cross-plough that turnip-ground."
The tension broke. The congregation lifted its head
As one man and coughed in unison.
Five hundred hearts were hungry for life—
Who lives in Christ shall never die the death.
And the candle-lit Altar and the flowers
And the pregnant Tabernacle lifted a moment to Prophecy
Out of the clayey hours.
Maguire sprinkled his face with holy water
As the congregation stood up for the Last Gospel.
He rubbed the dust off his knees with his palm, and then
Coughed the prayer phlegm up from his throat and sighed: Amen.

Once one day in June when he was walking
Among his cattle in the Yellow Meadow
He met a girl carrying a basket—
And he was then a young and heated fellow.
Too earnest, too earnest! He rushed beyond the thing
To the unreal. And he saw Sin

Written in letters larger than John Bunyan dreamt of.
For the strangled impulse there is no redemption.
And that girl was gone and he was counting
The dangers in the fields where love ranted.
He was helpless. He saw his cattle
And stroked their flanks in lieu of wife to handle.
He would have changed the circle if he could,
The circle that was the grass track where he ran.
Twenty times a day he ran round the field
And still there was no winning post where the runner is cheered home.
Desperately he broke the tune,
But however he tried always the same melody crept up from the
   background,
The dragging step of a ploughman going home through the guttery
Headlands under an April-watery moon.
Religion, the fields and the fear of the Lord
And Ignorance giving him the coward's blow;
He dare not rise to pluck the fantasies
From the fruited Tree of Life. He bowed his head
And saw a wet weed twined about his toe.

V

Evening at the cross-roads—
Heavy heads nodding out words as wise
As the rumination of cows after milking.
From the ragged road surface a boy picks up
A piece of gravel and stares at it—and then
He flings it across the elm tree on to the railway.
It means nothing,
Not a damn thing.
Somebody is coming over the metal railway bridge
And his hobnailed boots on the arches sound like a gong
Calling men awake. But the bridge is too narrow—
The men lift their heads a moment. That was only John,
So they dream on.

Night in the elms, night in the grass.
O we are too tired to go home yet. Two cyclists pass
Talking loudly of Kitty and Molly—
Horses or women? wisdom or folly?

A door closes on an evicted dog
Where prayers begin in Barney Meegan's kitchen;
Rosie curses the cat between her devotions;
The daughter prays that she may have three wishes—
Health and wealth and love—
From the fairy who is faith or hope or compounds of.

At the cross-roads the crowd had thinned out:
Last words are uttered. There is no tomorrow;
No future but only time stretched for the mowing of the hay
Or putting an axle in the turf-barrow.

Patrick Maguire went home and made cocoa
And broke a chunk off the loaf of wheaten bread;
His mother called down to him to look again
And make sure that the hen-house was locked. His sister grunted in bed,
The sound of a sow taking up a new position.
Pat opened his trousers wide over the ashes
And dreamt himself to lewd sleepiness.
The clock ticked on. Time passes.

VI

Health and wealth and love he too dreamed of in May
As he sat on the railway slope and watched the children of the place
Picking up a primrose here and a daisy there—
They were picking up life's truth singly. But he dreamt of the Absolute
    envased bouquet—
All or nothing. And it was nothing. For God is not all
In one place, complete and labelled like a case in a railway store
Till Hope comes in and takes it on his shoulder—
O Christ, that is what you have done for us:
In a crumb of bread the whole mystery is.

He read the symbol too sharply and turned
From the five simple doors of sense
To the door whose combination lock has puzzled
Philosopher and priest and common dunce.

Men build their heavens as they build their circles
Of friends. God is in the bits and pieces of Everyday—
A kiss here and a laugh again, and sometimes tears,
A pearl necklace round the neck of poverty.

He sat on the railway slope and watched the evening,
Too beautifully perfect to use,
And his three wishes were three stones too sharp to sit on,
Too hard to carve. Three frozen idols of a speechless muse.

VII

"Now go to Mass and pray and confess your sins
And you'll have all the luck," his mother said.
He listened to the lie that is a woman's screen
Around a conscience when soft thighs are spread.
And all the while she was setting up the lie
She trusted in Nature that never deceives.
But her son took it as the literal truth.
Religion's walls expand to the push of nature. Morality yields
To sense—but not in little tillage fields.

Life went on like that. One summer morning
Again through a hay-field on her way to the shop—
The grass was wet and over-leaned the path—
And Agnes held her skirts sensationally up,
And not because the grass was wet either.
A man was watching her, Patrick Maguire.
She was in love with passion and its weakness
And the wet grass could never cool the fire
That radiated from her unwanted womb
In that country, in that metaphysical land,
Where flesh was a thought more spiritual than music,
Among the stars—out of the reach of the peasant's hand.

Ah, but the priest was one of the people too—
A farmer's son—and surely he knew
The needs of a brother and sister.
Religion could not be a counter-irritant like a blister,
But the certain standard measured and known
By which a man might re-make his soul though all walls were down
And all earth's pedestalled gods thrown.

VIII

Sitting on a wooden gate,
Sitting on a wooden gate,
Sitting on a wooden gate,
He didn't care a damn.
Said whatever came into his head,
Said whatever came into his head,
Said whatever came into his head
And inconsequently sang.
Inconsequently sang,
While his world withered away.
He had a cigarette to smoke and a pound to spend
On drink the next Saturday.
His cattle were fat
And his horses all that
Midsummer grass could make them.
The young women ran wild
And dreamed of a child.
Joy dreams though the fathers might forsake them
But no one would take them,
No one would take them;
No man could ever see
That their skirts had loosed buttons,
Deliberately loosed buttons.
O the men were as blind as could be.
And Patrick Maguire
From his purgatory fire
Called the gods of the Christian to prove
That this twisted skein
Was the necessary pain
And not the rope that was strangling true love.

But sitting on a wooden gate
Sometime in July
When he was thirty-four or -five,
He gloried in the lie:
He made it read the way it should,
He made life read the evil good
While he cursed the ascetic brotherhood

Without knowing why.
Sitting on a wooden gate
All, all alone,
He sang and laughed
Like a man quite daft,
Or like a man on a channel raft
He fantasied forth his groan.
Sitting on a wooden gate,
Sitting on a wooden gate,
Sitting on a wooden gate
He rode in day-dream cars.
He locked his body with his knees
When the gate swung too much in the breeze,
But while he caught high ecstasies
Life slipped between the bars.

IX

He gave himself another year,
Something was bound to happen before then—
The circle would break down
And he would curve the new one to his own will.
A new rhythm is a new life
And in it marriage is hung and money.
He would be a new man walking through unbroken meadows
Of dawn in the year of One.

The poor peasant talking to himself in a stable door—
An ignorant peasant deep in dung.
What can the passers-by think otherwise?
Where is his silver bowl of knowledge hung?
Why should men be asked to believe in a soul
That is only the mark of a hoof in guttery gaps?
A man is what is written on the label.
And the passing world stares but no one stops
To look closer. So back to the growing crops
And the ridges he never loved.
Nobody will ever know how much tortured poetry the pulled weeds on the
     ridge wrote
Before they withered in the July sun,

Nobody will ever read the wild, sprawling, scrawling mad woman's signa-
    ture,
The hysteria and the boredom of the enclosed nun of his thought.
Like the afterbirth of a cow stretched on a branch in the wind,
Life dried in the veins of these women and men:
The grey and grief and unlove,
The bones in the backs of their hands,
And the chapel pressing its low ceiling over them.

Sometimes they did laugh and see the sunlight,
A narrow slice of divine instruction.
Going along the river at the bend of Sunday
The trout played in the pools encouragement
To jump in love though death bait the hook.
And there would be girls sitting on the grass banks of lanes
Stretch-legged and lingering staring—
A man might take one of them if he had the courage.
But "No" was in every sentence of their story
Except when the public-house came in and shouted its piece.

The yellow buttercups and the bluebells among the whin bushes
On rocks in the middle of ploughing
Was a bright spoke in the wheel
Of the peasant's mill.
The goldfinches on the railway paling were worth looking at—
A man might imagine then
Himself in Brazil and these birds the Birds of Paradise
And the Amazon and the romance traced on the school map lived again.

Talk in evening corners and under trees
Was like an old book found in a king's tomb.
The children gathered round like students and listened
And some of the saga defied the draught in the open tomb
And was not blown.

X

Their intellectual life consisted in reading
Reynolds' News or the *Sunday Dispatch,*
With sometimes an old almanac brought down from the ceiling
Or a school reader brown with the droppings of thatch.

The sporting results or the headlines of war
Was a humbug profound as the highbrow's Arcana.
Pat tried to be wise to the abstraction of all that
But its secret dribbled down his waistcoat like a drink from a strainer.
He wagered a bob each way on the Derby,
He got a straight tip from a man in a shop—
A double from the Guineas it was and thought himself
A master mathematician when one of them came up
And he could explain how much he'd have drawn
On the double if the second leg had followed the first.
He was betting on form and breeding, he claimed,
And the man that did that could never be burst.
After that they went on to the war, and the generals
On both sides were shown to be stupid as hell.
If he'd taken *that* road, they remarked of a Marshal,
He'd have . . . O they knew their geography well.
This was their university. Maguire was an undergraduate
Who dreamed from his lowly position of rising
To a professorship like Larry McKenna or Duffy
Or the pig-gelder Nallon whose knowledge was amazing.
"A treble, full multiple odds . . . That's flat porter . . .
My turnips are destroyed with the blackguardly crows . . .
Another one . . . No, you're wrong about that thing I was telling you . . .
Did you part with your filly, Jack? I heard that you sold her . . ."
The students were all savants by the time of pub-close.

XI

A year passed and another hurried after it
And Patrick Maguire was still six months behind life—
His mother six months ahead of it;
His sister straddle-legged across it:—
One leg in hell and the other in heaven
And between the purgatory of middle-aged virginity—
She prayed for release to heaven or hell.
His mother's voice grew thinner like a rust-worn knife
But it cut more venomously as it thinned,
It cut him up the middle till he became more woman than man,
And it cut through to his mind before the end.

Another field whitened in the April air
And the harrows rattled over the seed.
He gathered the loose stones off the ridges carefully
And grumbled to his men to hurry. He looked like a man who could give
    advice
To foolish young fellows. He was forty-seven,
And there was depth in his jaw and his voice was the voice of a great
    cattle-dealer,
A man with whom the fair-green gods break even.
"I think I ploughed that lea the proper depth,
She ought to give a crop if any land gives . . .
Drive slower with the foal-mare, Joe."
Joe, a young man of imagined wives,
Smiled to himself and answered like a slave:
"You needn't fear or fret.
I'm taking her as easy, as easy as . . .
Easy there, Fanny, easy, pet."

They loaded the day-scoured implements on the cart
As the shadows of poplars crookened the furrows.
It was the evening, evening. Patrick was forgetting to be lonely
As he used to be in Aprils long ago.
It was the menopause, the misery-pause.

The schoolgirls passed his house laughing every morning
And sometimes they spoke to him familiarly—
He had an idea. Schoolgirls of thirteen
Would see no political intrigue in an old man's friendship.
Love,
The heifer waiting to be nosed by the old bull.
That notion passed too—there was the danger of talk
And jails are narrower than the five-sod ridge
And colder than the black hills facing Armagh in February.
He sinned over the warm ashes again and his crime
The law's long arm could not serve with "time."

His face set like an old judge's pose:
Respectability and righteousness,
Stand for no nonsense.
The priest from the altar called Patrick Maguire's name

To hold the collecting box in the chapel door
During all the Sundays of May.
His neighbours envied him his holy rise,
But he walked down from the church with affected indifference
And took the measure of heaven angle-wise.

He still could laugh and sing,
But not the wild laugh or the abandoned harmony now
That called the world to new silliness from the top of a wooden gate
When thirty-five could take the sparrow's bow.
Let us be kind, let us be kind and sympathetic:
Maybe life is not for joking or for finding happiness in—
This tiny light in Oriental Darkness
Looking out chance windows of poetry or prayer.

And the grief and defeat of men like these peasants
Is God's way—maybe—and we must not want too much
To see.
The twisted thread is stronger than the wind-swept fleece.
And in the end who shall rest in truth's high peace?
Or whose is the world now, even now?
O let us kneel where the blind ploughman kneels
And learn to live without despairing
In a mud-walled space—
Illiterate, unknown and unknowing.
Let us kneel where he kneels
And feel what he feels.

One day he saw a daisy and he thought it
Reminded him of his childhood—
He stopped his cart to look at it.
Was there a fairy hiding behind it?

He helped a poor woman whose cow
Had died on her;
He dragged home a drunken man on a winter's night;
And one rare moment he heard the young people playing on the railway
    stile
And he wished them happiness and whatever they most desired from life.

He saw the sunlight and begrudged no man
His share of what the miserly soil and soul
Gives in a season to a ploughman.

And he cried for his own loss one late night on the pillow
And yet thanked the God who had arranged these things.

Was he then a saint?
A Matt Talbot of Monaghan?

His sister Mary Anne spat poison at the children
Who sometimes came to the door selling raffle tickets
For holy funds.
"Get out you little tramps!" she would scream
As she shook to the hens an apronful of crumbs,
But Patrick often put his hand deep down
In his trouser-pocket and fingered out a penny
Or maybe a tobacco-stained caramel.
"You're soft," said the sister, "with other people's money;
It's not a bit funny."

The cards are shuffled and the deck
Laid flat for cutting—"Tom Malone,
Cut for trump. I think we'll make
This game, the last, a tanner one.
Hearts. Right. I see you're breaking
Your two-year-old. Play quick, Maguire,
The clock there says it's half-past ten—
Kate, throw another sod on that fire."
One of the card-players laughs and spits
Into the flame across a shoulder.
Outside, a noise like a rat
Among the hen-roosts. The cock crows over
The frosted townland of the night.
Eleven o'clock and still the game
Goes on and the players seem to be
Drunk in an Orient opium den.
Midnight, one o'clock, two.
Somebody's leg has fallen asleep.
"What about home? Maguire, are you
Using your double-tree this week?
Why? do you want it? Play the ace.
There's it, and that's the last card for me.
A wonderful night, we had. Duffy's place
Is very convenient. Is that a ghost or a tree?"
And so they go home with dragging feet

And their voices rumble like laden carts.
And they are happy as the dead or sleeping . . .
I should have led that ace of hearts.

XII

The fields were bleached white,
The wooden tubs full of water
Were white in the winds
That blew through Brannagan's Gap on their way from Siberia;
The cows on the grassless heights
Followed the hay that had wings—
The February fodder that hung itself on the black branches
Of the hilltop hedge.
A man stood beside a potato-pit
And clapped his arms
And pranced on the crisp roots
And shouted to warm himself.
Then he buck-leaped about the potatoes
And scooped them into a basket.
He looked like a bucking suck-calf
Whose spine was being tickled.
Sometimes he stared across the bogs
And sometimes he straightened his back and vaguely whistled
A tune that weakened his spirit
And saddened his terrier dog's.
A neighbour passed with a spade on his shoulder
And Patrick Maguire, bent like a bridge,
Whistled good morning under his oxter,
And the man the other side of the hedge
Champed his spade on the road at his toes
And talked an old sentimentality
While the wind blew under his clothes.

The mother sickened and stayed in bed all day,
Her head hardly dented the pillow, so light and thin it had worn,
But she still enquired after the household affairs.
She held the strings of her children's Punch and Judy, and when a mouth
    opened
It was her truth that the dolls would have spoken
If they hadn't been made of wood and tin—

"Did you open the barn door, Pat, to let the young calves in?"
The priest called to see her every Saturday
And she told him her troubles and fears:
"If Mary Anne was settled I'd die in peace—
I'm getting on in years."
"You were a good woman," said the priest,
"And your children will miss you when you're gone.
The likes of you this parish never knew,
I'm sure they'll not forget the work you've done."
She reached five bony crooks under the tick—
"Five pounds for Masses—won't you say them quick."
She died one morning in the beginning of May
And a shower of sparrow-notes was the litany for her dying.
The holy water was sprinkled on the bed-clothes
And her children stood around the bed and cried because it was too late for
    crying.
A mother dead! The tired sentiment:
"Mother, Mother" was a shallow pool
Where sorrow hardly could wash its feet . . .
Mary Anne came away from the deathbed and boiled the calves their gruel.
O what was I doing when the procession passed?
Where was I looking?
Young women and men
And I might have joined them.
Who bent the coin of my destiny
That it stuck in the slot?
I remember a night we walked
Through the moon of Donaghmoyne,
Four of us seeking adventure—
It was midsummer forty years ago.
Now I know
The moment that gave the turn to my life.
O Christ! I am locked in a stable with pigs and cows for ever.

XIII

The world looks on
And talks of the peasant:
The peasant has no worries;
In his little lyrical fields
He ploughs and sows;

He eats fresh food,
He loves fresh women,
He is his own master;
As it was in the Beginning,
The simpleness of peasant life.
The birds that sing for him are eternal choirs,
Everywhere he walks there are flowers.
His heart is pure,
His mind is clear,
He can talk to God as Moses and Isaiah talked—
The peasant who is only one remove from the beasts he drives.
The travellers stop their cars to gape over the green bank into his fields:—

There is the source from which all cultures rise,
And all religions,
There is the pool in which the poet dips
And the musician.
Without the peasant base civilization must die,
Unless the clay is in the mouth the singer's singing is useless.
The travellers touch the roots of the grass and feel renewed
When they grasp the steering wheels again.
The peasant is the unspoiled child of Prophecy,
The peasant is all virtues—let us salute him without irony—
The peasant ploughman who is half a vegetable,
Who can react to sun and rain and sometimes even
Regret that the Maker of Light had not touched him more intensely,
Brought him up from the sub-soil to an existence
Of conscious joy. He was not born blind.
He is not always blind: sometimes the cataract yields
To sudden stone-falling or the desire to breed.

The girls pass along the roads
And he can remember what man is,
But there is nothing he can do.
Is there nothing he can do?
Is there no escape?
No escape, no escape.

The cows and horses breed,
And the potato-seed
Gives a bud and a root and rots
In the good mother's way with her sons;

The fledged bird is thrown
From the nest—on its own.
But the peasant in his little acres is tied
To a mother's womb by the wind-toughened navel-cord
Like a goat tethered to the stump of a tree—
He circles around and around wondering why it should be.
No crash,
No drama.
That was how his life happened.
No mad hooves galloping in the sky,
But the weak, washy way of true tragedy—
A sick horse nosing around the meadow for a clean place to die.

XIV

We may come out into the October reality, Imagination,
The sleety wind no longer slants to the black hill where Maguire
And his men are now collecting the scattered harness and baskets.
The dog sitting on a wisp of dry stalks
Watches them through the shadows.
"Back in, back in." One talks to the horse as to a brother.
Maguire himself is patting a potato-pit against the weather—
An old man fondling a new-piled grave:
"Joe, I hope you didn't forget to hide the spade
For there's rogues in the townland. Hide it flat in a furrow.
I think we ought to be finished by tomorrow."
Their voices through the darkness sound like voices from a cave,
A dull thudding far away, futile, feeble, far away,
First cousins to the ghosts of the townland.

A light stands in a window. Mary Anne
Has the table set and the tea-pot waiting in the ashes.
She goes to the door and listens and then she calls
From the top of the haggard-wall:
"What's keeping you
And the cows to be milked and all the other work there's to do?"
"All right, all right,
We'll not stay here all night."

Applause, applause,
The curtain falls.
Applause, applause

From the homing carts and the trees
And the bawling cows at the gates.
From the screeching water-hens
And the mill-race heavy with the Lammas floods curving over the weir.
A train at the station blowing off steam
And the hysterical laughter of the defeated everywhere.
Night, and the futile cards are shuffled again.
Maguire spreads his legs over the impotent cinders that wake no manhood
    now
And he hardly looks to see which card is trump.
His sister tightens her legs and her lips and frizzles up
Like the wick of an oil-less lamp.
The curtain falls—
Applause, applause.

Maguire is not afraid of death, the Church will light him a candle
To see his way through the vaults and he'll understand the
Quality of the clay that dribbles over his coffin.
He'll know the names of the roots that climb down to tickle his feet.
And he will feel no different than when he walked through Donaghmoyne.
If he stretches out a hand—a wet clod,
If he opens his nostrils—a dungy smell;
If he opens his eyes once in a million years—
Through a crack in the crust of the earth he may see a face nodding in
Or a woman's legs. Shut them again for that sight is sin.

He will hardly remember that life happened to him—
Something was brighter a moment. Somebody sang in the distance.
A procession passed down a mesmerized street.
He remembers names like Easter and Christmas
By the colour his fields were.
Maybe he will be born again, a bird of an angel's conceit
To sing the gospel of life
To a music as flightily tangent
As a tune on an oboe.
And the serious look of the fields will have changed to the leer of a hobo
Swaggering celestially home to his three wishes granted.
Will that be? will that be?
Or is the earth right that laughs, haw haw,
And does not believe
In an unearthly law.
The earth that says:

Patrick Maguire, the old peasant, can neither be damned nor glorified;
The graveyard in which he will lie will be just a deep-drilled potato-field
Where the seed gets no chance to come through
To the fun of the sun.
The tongue in his mouth is the root of a yew.
Silence, silence. The story is done.

He stands in the doorway of his house
A ragged sculpture of the wind,
October creaks the rotted mattress,
The bedposts fall. No hope. No lust.
The hungry fiend
Screams the apocalypse of clay
In every corner of this land.

Irish Poets Open Your Eyes

Irish poets open your eyes,
Even Cabra can surprise;
Try the dog-tracks now and then—
Shelbourne Park and crooked men.

Could you ever pray at all
In the Pro-Cathedral
Till a breath of simpleness
Freed your Freudian distress?

Enter in and be a part
Of the world's frustrated heart,
Drive the golf ball of despair,
Supperdance away your care.

Be ordinary,
Be saving up to marry.
Kiss her in the alleyway,
Part—"Same time, same place"—and go.

Learn repose on Boredom's bed,
Deep anonymous, unread,
And the god of Literature
Will touch a moment to endure.

Epic

I have lived in important places, times
When great events were decided: who owned
That half a rood of rock, a no-man's land
Surrounded by our pitchfork-armed claims.
I heard the Duffys shouting "Damn your soul"
And old McCabe, stripped to the waist, seen
Step the plot defying blue cast-steel—
"Here is the march along these iron stones."
That was the year of the Munich bother. Which
Was more important? I inclined
To lose my faith in Ballyrush and Gortin
Till Homer's ghost came whispering to my mind.
He said: I made the Iliad from such
A local row. Gods make their own importance.

Yeats

Yeats, it was very easy for you to be frank,
With your sixty years and loves (like Robert Graves).
It was thin and, in fact, you have never put the tank
On a race. Ah! cautious man whom no sin depraves.
And it won't add up, at least in my mind,
To what it takes in the living poetry stakes.
I don't care what Chicago thinks; I am blind
To college lecturers and the breed of fakes:
I mean to say I'm not blind really,
I have my eyes wide open, as you may imagine,
And I am aware of our own boys, such as Ben Kiely,
Buying and selling literature on the margin.
Yes, Yeats, it was damn easy for you, protected
By the middle classes and the Big Houses,
To talk about the sixty-year-old public protected
Man sheltered by the dim Victorian Muses.

Louis MacNeice (1907–1963)

In Louis MacNeice's earliest contributions to the thirties magazine *New Verse*, its former editor Geoffrey Grigson wrote in 1949, traditional verse conventions "were stretched to tautness," like "criss-crossing wires of form with this spangled acrobat performing on them." MacNeice's subsequent work is viewed, in Grigson's description, as the sufficient fulfillment of this spectacular early promise:

> The cleverness, as one knows by this time, grew and strengthened itself into a capable and convincing rhetoric, beholden to much, yet chiefly to MacNeice himself. The wires were still silvery and still glittered. The icicles, the ice-cream, the pink and white, the lace and the froth and the fireworks were still there, but underneath the game was the drop, the space, and the knowledge.[1]

Grigson's evaluation seems now wholly appropriate to the displays of technical ability overlain with a modern, though not quite modernist, *sprezzatura* in poems like "The Sunlight on the Garden." But it has taken nearly three decades for the critical mainstream to return to this opinion. The dazzle and light Grigson saw in 1949 were for years hidden under the shadow of MacNeice's friend and sometime collaborator W. H. Auden. At the low point of his critical reputation MacNeice's work was read as little more than a gloss on Auden's 1930s political phase. Fortunately, his reputation survived in the dark long enough to be rehabilitated by the generation of poets who emerged in Belfast in the 1960s. By the early 1970s Seamus Heaney and Derek Mahon were among those endorsing him implicitly and explicitly as an important ancestor of contemporary Northern Irish poetry. Thirty years later his figure is firmly lodged in the Irish poetic psyche. It is because MacNeice's poetry "dramatizes polarities engendered by Ireland, such as that between belonging and alienation," critic Edna Longley has argued, that his work "has become a focus on the literary wing of current debates about 'identity' in Northern Ireland."[2]

Derek Mahon acknowledged MacNeice's influence by placing his elegy to the older poet at the beginning of his own *Selected Poems*. "In Carrowdore Churchyard *(at the grave of Louis MacNeice)*" portrays MacNeice as the prophet and liberator of Northern Ireland's poetic tribe, a figure who "from the ague / Of the blind poet and the bombed-out town" sounds in his poetry the "all-clear to the empty holes of spring."[3] Two generations of Northern poets have been responding to MacNeice's "all clear," by lifting the blackout curtains that obscured Northern writing in the period between MacNeice and Heaney, and by sounding their own paeans to MacNeice, affirming his ancestral place in the genealogy of Irish poetry. In the 1980s Paul Muldoon gave MacNeice the largest allotment of space in his Faber anthology of contemporary Irish poetry, and began in his own work to excavate MacNeice from the strata of the "Auden Generation." Muldoon's long, multi-voiced poem "7 Middagh Street" gives MacNeice the final word in an implicit debate with Auden, whose elegy for W. B. Yeats had argued that "poetry makes nothing happen."

However, toppling Auden still leaves a problem that might, on MacNeice's native ground, cast a darker shadow. He has often been accused of abandoning Ireland. "I thought I was well / Out of it, educated and domiciled in England," he writes in "Autumn Journal." "Though yet her name keeps ringing like a bell / In an under-water belfry."[4] MacNeice's poetry and his life as an adult had far more to do with Auden's England than Kavanagh's Ireland. But while he opposed himself to elements of his Ulster childhood—"guilt, hell fire, Good Friday, the doctor's cough, hurried lamps in the night, melancholia, mongolism, violent sectarian voices," as he catalogs them in one of his memoirs[5]—MacNeice felt an early, romantic attraction to rural Ireland that revealed itself in his response to names. Belfast sounded "hard and unrelenting," while Carrickfergus, where his parents had come from, "was a name to be proud of."[6] Place names and phrases conjured visions of a world at once wilder and more nurturing than his native Ulster.

The first of these dream worlds was "The West of Ireland," a phrase which still stirs me, if not like a trumpet, like a fiddle half heard through a cattle fair. . . . It appeared to be a country of windswept open spaces and mountains blazing with whins and seas that were never quiet, with drowned palaces beneath them, and seals and eagles and turf smoke and cottagers who were always laughing and who gave you milk when you asked for a glass of water.[7]

Seamus Heaney picks up the ambivalence of MacNeice's view of Ireland as the thread that might unravel Ireland's, and particularly Northern Ireland's, ambivalence about itself. In lectures delivered, fittingly, during his tenure as Professor of Poetry at Oxford, Heaney alluded to MacNeice's ability to straddle the divisions that separate Ireland and England, Catholic and Protestant, Britain and Europe:

> MacNeice . . . by his English domicile and his civil learning is an aspect of Spenser, by his ancestral and affectionate links with Connemara an aspect of Yeats and by his mythic and European consciousness an aspect of Joyce. . . . He can be regarded as an Irish Protestant writer with Anglocentric attitudes who managed to be faithful to his Ulster inheritance, his Irish affections and his English predilections.[8]

By his steady, if divided, loyalties MacNeice presents to Heaney's mind a schema of Northern inclusiveness.

> It may be that there is not yet a political structure to reflect this poetic diagram, but the admission of MacNeice in this way within the symbolic ordering of Ireland also admits a hope for the evolution of a political order, one tolerant of difference and capable of metamorphoses within all the multivalent possibilities of Irishness, Britishness, European-ness, planetariness, creatureliness, whatever.[9]

Poems like "Carrick Revisited" give a personal voice to the uncertainties that marked the North's struggle to be born into its own identity. They acknowledge "creatureliness," as Heaney puts it, in an Irish idiom. Nevertheless, much of MacNeice's verse sounds, on first reading, like the English Auden. MacNeice shared with Auden a sense that humor and social critique are not mutually exclusive, and in fact propel each other. His most successful poems of the thirties blend social commentary with a humor and tone at least superficially Audenesque. "Bagpipe Music" is one of the most frequently anthologized examples. Even in that poem, though, the elements he borrowed from Auden are always played against tonal qualities peculiar to MacNeice. A line that begins sounding like Auden, "It's no go the gossip column," is likely to find its end in something totally foreign to Auden's English sensibility: "it's no go the ceilidh."[10]

More important than contesting MacNeice's relationship to Auden, though, is recognizing how this critical subordination may actually have made MacNeice more useful as an ancestral figure for contemporary poets. Unlike Yeats, MacNeice speaks with a voice that is powerful yet relatively unmythologized. As in "Elegy for Minor Poets," it is a voice that, even when modulated by a hint of condescension, recognizes at some level that, although MacNeice is much more than a minor poet himself, it speaks about peers, and to them.

Louis MacNeice died in 1963 of pneumonia that developed after he accompanied sound engineers underground to record cave sounds for an upcoming BBC production of his play *Persons from Porlock*. The selections that follow, though not his best known poems abroad, offer a glimpse of the MacNeice who has exerted the strongest influence on literature in Ireland.

NOTES

1. Quoted in the Preface to Edna Longley, *Louis MacNeice* (London: Faber and Faber, 1988), p. ix.

2. Longley, *Louis MacNeice*, p. xiii.

3. Derek Mahon, "In Carrowdore Churchyard *(at the grave of Louis MacNeice),*" *Selected Poems* (London: Viking / Gallery, 1991), p. 11.

4. "Autumn Journal," *The Collected Poems of Louis MacNeice*, ed. E. R. Dodds (London: Faber & Faber, 1966), p. 132.

5. "Landscapes of Childhood and Youth," in Louis MacNeice, *The Strings Are False* (London: Faber and Faber, 1965), p. 216.

6. Ibid., p. 218.

7. Ibid., pp. 216–217.

8. Seamus Heaney, "Frontiers of Writing," *The Redress of Poetry* (New York: Noonday Press, 1995), p. 200.

9. Ibid.

10. "Bagpipe Music," *Collected Poems 1925–1948*, p. 116.

Belfast

The hard cold fire of the northerner
Frozen into his blood from the fire in his basalt
Glares from behind the mica of his eyes
And the salt carrion water brings him wealth.

Down there at the end of the melancholy lough
Against the lurid sky over the stained water
Where hammers clang murderously on the girders
Like crucifixes the gantries stand.

And in the marble stores rubber gloves like polyps
Cluster; celluloid, painted ware, glaring
Metal patents, parchment lampshades, harsh
Attempts at buyable beauty.

In the porch of the chapel before the garish Virgin
A shawled factory-woman as if shipwrecked there
Lies a bunch of limbs glimpsed in the cave of gloom
By us who walk in the street so buoyantly and glib.

Over which country of cowled and haunted faces
The sun goes down with a banging of Orange drums
While the male kind murders each its woman
To whose prayer for oblivion answers no Madonna.

Turf-Stacks

Among these turf-stacks graze no iron horses
Such as stalk, such as champ in towns and the soul of crowds,
Here is no mass-production of neat thoughts
No canvas shrouds for the mind nor any black hearses:
The peasant shambles on his boots like hooves
Without thinking at all or wanting to run in grooves.

But those who lack the peasant's conspirators,
The tawny mountain, the unregarded buttress,
Will feel the need of a fortress against ideas and against the

Shuddering insidious shock of the theory-vendors,
The little sardine men crammed in a monster toy
Who tilt their aggregate beast against our crumbling Troy.

For we are obsolete who like the lesser things
Who play in corners with looking-glasses and beads;
It is better we should go quickly, go into Asia
Or any other tunnel where the world recedes,
Or turn blind wantons like the gulls who scream
And rip the edge off any ideal or dream.

Train to Dublin

Our half-thought thoughts divide in sifted wisps
Against the basic facts repatterned without pause,
I can no more gather my mind up in my fist
Than the shadow of the smoke of this train upon the grass—
This is the way that animals' lives pass.

The train's rhythm never relents, the telephone posts
Go striding backwards like the legs of time to where
In a Georgian house you turn at the carpet's edge
Turning a sentence while, outside my window here,
The smoke makes broken queries in the air.

The train keeps moving and the rain holds off,
I count the buttons on the seat, I hear a shell
Held hollow to the ear, the mere
Reiteration of integers, the bell
That tolls and tolls, the monotony of fear.

At times we are doctrinaire, at times we are frivolous,
Plastering over the cracks, a gesture making good,
But the strength of us does not come out of us.
It is we, I think, are the idols and it is God
Has set us up as men who are painted wood,

And the trains carry us about. But not consistently so,
For during a tiny portion of our lives we are not in trains,
The idol living for a moment, not muscle-bound
But walking freely through the slanting rain,
Its ankles wet, its grimace relaxed again.

All over the world people are toasting the King,
Red lozenges of light as each one lifts his glass,
But I will not give you any idol or idea, creed or king,
I give you the incidental things which pass
Outward through space exactly as each was.

I give you disproportion between labour spent
And joy at random; the laughter of the Galway sea
Juggling with spars and bones irresponsibly,
I give you the toy Liffey and the vast gulls,
I give you fuchsia hedges and whitewashed walls.

I give you the smell of Norman stone, the squelch
Of bog beneath your boots, the red bog-grass,
The vivid chequer of the Antrim hills, the trough of dark
Golden water for the cart-horses, the brass
Belt of serene sun upon the lough.

And I give you the faces, not the permanent masks,
But the faces balanced in the toppling wave—
His glint of joy in cunning as the farmer asks
Twenty per cent too much, or the girl's, forgetting to be suave,
A tiro choosing stuffs, preferring mauve.

And I give you the sea and yet again the sea's
Tumultuous marble,
With Thor's thunder or taking his ease akimbo,
Lumbering torso, but finger-tips a marvel
Of surgeon's accuracy.

I would like to give you more but I cannot hold
This stuff within my hands and the train goes on;
I know that there are further syntheses to which,
As you have perhaps, people at last attain
And find that they are rich and breathing gold.

Carrickfergus

I was born in Belfast between the mountain and the gantries
   To the hooting of lost sirens and the clang of trams:
Thence to Smoky Carrick in County Antrim
   Where the bottle-neck harbour collects the mud which jams

The little boats beneath the Norman castle,
   The pier shining with lumps of crystal salt;
The Scotch Quarter was a line of residential houses
   But the Irish Quarter was a slum for the blind and halt.

The brook ran yellow from the factory stinking of chlorine,
   The yarn-mill called its funeral cry at noon;
Our lights looked over the lough to the lights of Bangor
   Under the peacock aura of a drowning moon.

The Norman walled this town against the country
   To stop his ears to the yelping of his slave
And built a church in the form of a cross but denoting
   The list of Christ on the cross in the angle of the nave.

I was the rector's son, born to the anglican order,
   Banned for ever from the candles of the Irish poor;
The Chichesters knelt in marble at the end of a transept
   With ruffs about their necks, their portion sure.

The war came and a huge camp of soldiers
   Grew from the ground in sight of our house with long
Dummies hanging from gibbets for bayonet practice
   And the sentry's challenge echoing all day long;

A Yorkshire terrier ran in and out by the gate-lodge
   Barred to civilians, lapping as if taking affront:
Marching at ease and singing "Who Killed Cock Robin?"
   The troops went out by the lodge and off to the Front.

The steamer was camouflaged that took me to England—
   Sweat and khaki in the Carlisle train;
I thought that the war would last for ever and sugar
   Be always rationed and that never again

Would the weekly papers not have photos of sandbags
   And my governess not make bandages from moss

And people not have maps above the fireplace
   With flags on pins moving across and across—

Across the hawthorn hedge the noise of bugles,
   Flares across the night,
Somewhere on the lough was a prison ship for Germans,
   A cage across their sight.

I went to school in Dorset, the world of parents
   Contracted into a puppet world of sons
Far from the mill girls, the smell of porter, the salt-mines
   And the soldiers with their guns.

from Autumn Journal

XVI

Nightmare leaves fatigue:
   We envy men of action
Who sleep and wake, murder and intrigue
   Without being doubtful, without being haunted.
And I envy the intransigence of my own
   Countrymen who shoot to kill and never
See the victim's face become their own
   Or find his motive sabotage their motives.
So reading the memoirs of Maud Gonne,*
   Daughter of an English mother and a soldier father,
I note how a single purpose can be founded on
   A jumble of opposites:
Dublin Castle, the vice-regal ball,
   The embassies of Europe,
Hatred scribbled on a wall,
   Gaols and revolvers.
And I remember, when I was little, the fear
   Bandied among the servants
That Casement would land at the pier
   With a sword and a horde of rebels;
And how we used to expect, at a later date,
   When the wind blew from the west, the noise of shooting

Starting in the evening at eight
    In Belfast in the York Street district;
And the voodoo of the Orange bands*
    Drawing an iron net through darkest Ulster,
Flailing the limbo lands—
    The linen mills, the long wet grass, the ragged hawthorn.
And one read black where the other read white, his hope
    The other man's damnation:
Up the Rebels, To Hell with the Pope,
    And God Save—as you prefer—the King or Ireland.
The land of scholars and saints:
    Scholars and saints my eye, the land of ambush,
Purblind manifestoes, never-ending complaints,
    The born martyr and the gallant ninny;
The grocer drunk with the drum,
    The land-owner shot in his bed, the angry voices
Piercing the broken fanlight in the slum,
    The shawled woman weeping at the garish altar.
Kathaleen ni Houlihan! Why*
    Must a country, like a ship or a car, be always female,
Mother or sweetheart? A woman passing by,
    We did but see her passing.
Passing like a patch of sun on the rainy hill
    And yet we love her for ever and hate our neighbour
And each one in his will
    Binds his heirs to continuance of hatred.
Drums on the haycock, drums on the harvest, black
    Drums in the night shaking the windows:
King William is riding his white horse back
    To the Boyne on a banner.
Thousands of banners, thousands of white
    Horses, thousands of Williams
Waving thousands of swords and ready to fight
    Till the blue sea turns to orange.
Such was my country and I thought I was well
    Out of it, educated and domiciled in England,
Though yet her name keeps ringing like a bell
    In an under-water belfry.
Why do we like being Irish? Partly because
    It gives us a hold on the sentimental English

As members of a world that never was,
    Baptised with fairy water;
And partly because Ireland is small enough
    To be still thought of with a family feeling,
And because the waves are rough
    That split her from a more commercial culture;
And because one feels that here at least one can
    Do local work which is not at the world's mercy
And that on this tiny stage with luck a man
    Might see the end of one particular action.
It is self-deception of course;
    There is no immunity in this island either;
A cart that is drawn by somebody else's horse
    And carrying goods to somebody else's market.
The bombs in the turnip sack, the sniper from the roof,
    Griffith, Connolly, Collins, where have they brought us?
Ourselves alone! Let the round tower stand aloof*
    In a world of bursting mortar!
Let the school-children fumble their sums
    In a half-dead language;
Let the censor be busy on the books; pull down the Georgian slums;
    Let the games be played in Gaelic.
Let them grow beet-sugar; let them build
    A factory in every hamlet;
Let them pigeon-hole the souls of the killed
    Into sheep and goats, patriots and traitors.
And the North, where I was a boy,
    Is still the North, veneered with the grime of Glasgow,
Thousands of men whom nobody will employ
    Standing at the corners, coughing.
And the street-children play on the wet
    Pavement—hopscotch or marbles;
And each rich family boasts a sagging tennis-net
    On a spongy lawn beside a dripping shrubbery.
The smoking chimneys hint
    At prosperity round the corner
But they make their Ulster linen from foreign lint
    And the money that comes in goes out to make more money.
A city built upon mud;
    A culture built upon profit;

Free speech nipped in the bud,
    The minority always guilty.
Why should I want to go back
    To you, Ireland, my Ireland?
The blots on the page are so black
    That they cannot be covered with shamrock.
I hate your grandiose airs,
    Your sob-stuff, your laugh and your swagger,
Your assumption that everyone cares
    Who is the king of your castle.
Castles are out of date,
    The tide flows round the children's sandy fancy;
Put up what flag you like, it is too late
    To save your soul with bunting.
Odi atque amo:
    Shall we cut this name on trees with a rusty dagger?
Her mountains are still blue, her rivers flow
    Bubbling over the boulders.
She is both a bore and a bitch;
    Better close the horizon,
Send her no more fantasy, no more longings which
    Are under a fatal tariff.
For common sense is the vogue
    And she gives her children neither sense nor money
Who slouch around the world with a gesture and a brogue
    And a faggot of useless memories.

XXIV

Sleep, my body, sleep, my ghost,
    Sleep, my parents and grand-parents,
And all those I have loved most:
    One man's coffin is another's cradle.
Sleep, my past and all my sins,
    In distant snow or dried roses
Under the moon for night's cocoon will open
    When day begins.
Sleep, my fathers, in your graves
    On upland bogland under heather;
What the wind scatters the wind saves,
    A sapling springs in a new country.

Time is a country, the present moment
    A spotlight roving round the scene;
We need not chase the spotlight,
    The future is the bride of what has been.
Sleep, my fancies and my wishes,
    Sleep a little and wake strong,
The same but different and take my blessing—
    A cradle-song.
And sleep, my various and conflicting
    Selves I have so long endured,
Sleep in Asclepius' temple
    And wake cured.
And you with whom I shared an idyll
    Five years long,
Sleep beyond the Atlantic
    And wake to a glitter of dew and to bird-song.
And you whose eyes are blue, whose ways are foam,
    Sleep quiet and smiling
And do not hanker
    For a perfection which can never come.
And you whose minutes patter
    To crowd the social hours,
Curl up easy in a placid corner
    And let your thoughts close in like flowers.
And you, who work for Christ, and you, as eager
    For a better life, humanist, atheist,
And you, devoted to a cause, and you, to a family,
    Sleep and may your beliefs and zeal persist.
Sleep quietly, Marx and Freud,
    The figure-heads of our transition.
Cagney, Lombard, Bing and Garbo,
    Sleep in your world of celluloid.
Sleep now also, monk and satyr,
    Cease your wrangling for a night.
Sleep, my brain, and sleep, my senses,
    Sleep, my hunger and my spite.
Sleep, recruits to the evil army,
    Who, for so long misunderstood,
Took to the gun to kill your sorrow;
    Sleep and be damned and wake up good.

While we sleep, what shall we dream?
    Of Tir nan Og or South Sea islands,*
Of a land where all the milk is cream
    And all the girls are willing?
Or shall our dream be earnest of the real
    Future when we wake,
Design a home, a factory, a fortress
    Which, though with effort, we can really make?
What is it we want really?
    For what end and how?
If it is something feasible, obtainable,
    Let us dream it now,
And pray for a possible land
    Not of sleep-walkers, not of angry puppets,
But where both heart and brain can understand
    The movements of our fellows;
Where life is a choice of instruments and none
    Is debarred his natural music,
Where the waters of life are free of the ice-blockade of hunger
    And thought is free as the sun,
Where the altars of sheer power and mere profit
    Have fallen to disuse,
Where nobody sees the use
    Of buying money and blood at the cost of blood and money,
Where the individual, no longer squandered
    In self-assertion, works with the rest, endowed
With the split vision of a juggler and the quick lock of a taxi,
    Where the people are more than a crowd.
So sleep in hope of this—but only for a little;
    Your hope must wake
While the choice is yours to make,
    The mortgage not foreclosed, the offer open.
Sleep serene, avoid the backward
    Glance; go forward, dreams, and do not halt
(Behind you in the desert stands a token
    Of doubt—a pillar of salt).
Sleep, the past, and wake, the future,
    And walk out promptly through the open door;
But you, my coward doubts, may go on sleeping,
    You need not wake again—not any more.

The New Year comes with bombs, it is too late
   To dose the dead with honourable intentions:
If you have honour to spare, employ it on the living;
   The dead are dead as Nineteen-Thirty-Eight.
Sleep to the noise of running water
   To-morrow to be crossed, however deep;
This is no river of the dead or Lethe,
   To-night we sleep
On the banks of Rubicon—the die is cast;
   There will be time to audit
The accounts later, there will be sunlight later
   And the equation will come out at last.

Carrick Revisited

Back to Carrick, the castle as plumb assured
As thirty years ago—Which war was which?
Here are new villas, here is a sizzling grid
But the green banks are as rich and the lough as hazily lazy
And the child's astonishment net yet cured.

Who was—and am—dumbfounded to find myself
In a topographical frame—here, not there—
The channels of my dreams determined largely
By random chemistry of soil and air;
Memories I had shelved peer at me from the shelf.

Fog-horn, mill-horn, corncrake and church bell
Half-heard through boarded time as a child in bed
Glimpses a brangle of talk from the floor below
But cannot catch the words. Our past we know
But not its meaning—whether it meant well.

Time and place—our bridgeheads into reality
But also its concealment! Out of the sea
We land on the Particular and lose
All other possible bird's-eye views, the Truth
That is of Itself for Itself—but not for me.

Torn before birth from where my fathers dwelt,
Schooled from the age of ten to a foreign voice,
Yet neither western Ireland nor southern England
Cancels this interlude; what chance misspelt
May never now be righted by my choice.

Whatever then my inherited or acquired
Affinities, such remains my childhood's frame
Like a belated rock in the red Antrim clay
That cannot at this era change its pitch or name—
And the pre-natal mountain is far away.

Coda

Maybe we knew each other better
When the night was young and unrepeated
And the moon stood still over Jericho.

So much for the past; in the present
There are moments caught between heart-beats
When maybe we know each other better.

But what is that clinking in the darkness?
Maybe we shall know each other better
When the tunnels meet beneath the mountain.

Samuel Beckett (1906–1989)

Although Samuel Beckett is best known as a dramatist and novelist, it was as a poet that he began and ended his writing career. In the summer of 1930, Beckett, already an associate of James Joyce and a figure on the Paris literary scene, heard that Nancy Cunard's Hours Press was offering a prize of £10 for the best new poem on the subject of time. Little time, it happened, remained before the contest deadline, so Beckett wrote in just one night the work that would become his first published poem. "Whoroscope" draws on Adrien Baillet's biography of Descartes, making of the philosopher a sort of clown whose chief engagement with the question of time lies in a fussy particularity about the preparation of his omelet.

The poem won the contest and Cunard put it out in a small edition. This book ultimately brought Beckett a larger prize when, based on its example of his virtuosity, publishers Chatto and Windus gave him a commission to write a book on Proust. There his inquiry into the nature of time continued. In *Proust*, Beckett's analysis of *À la recherche du temps perdu* proved to be a sketch of the view of time that would inform his own writing of poetry, drama, and fiction over the next sixty years.

> Proust's creatures, then, are victims of this predominating condition and circumstance—Time; victims as lower organisms, conscious only of two dimensions and suddenly confronted with the mystery of height, are victims: victims and prisoners. There is no escape from the hours and the days.[1]

With its explicit statement of what would be his central motif, *Proust* launched Beckett on a writing career, but its composition also propelled him into a terrific emotional crisis. He spent the next year nearly paralyzed by depression. The despair was partly a practical response to his inability to find a publisher for his novel, *Dream of Fair to Middling Women*. More of the problem, though, arose from internal strife, and Beckett was convinced to undergo psychoanalysis. Since he was not allowed to write fiction during the course of therapy, Beckett turned from the novel, which he thought of as his primary genre, back to poetry. He published his first collection of poems, *Echo's Bones and Other Precipitates*, in 1935. In this volume, the influence of Joyce, evident in the verbal energy and fragmentation of "Whoroscope," melds with the mendicant restlessness that will characterize Beckett's novels from *Molloy* on. The lyric eye roves through these poems as through a Fellini landscape, registering the most startling evidence that the human condition is utterly impoverished. The diminished Everyman in "Enueg I," glimpsed "scuttling along between a crutch and a stick," is a figure that becomes familiar in Beckett's work, the victim of time as a disfigured kind of clown. In this early poem he appears in a distinctly Irish landscape.

The critic Hugh Kenner was close to this scuttling image when he suggested that "[t]he antecedents of his plays are not in literature but—to take a rare American example—in Emmett Kelly's solemn determination to sweep a circle of light into a dustpan."[2] For Kenner this image of the clown—sedulous, ridiculously bound by fidelity to an arbitrary task—reflects the tragic sense of duty that, in his most famous play, has Beckett's characters waiting endlessly, pointlessly, for Godot. His mime show *Act without Words* plays explicitly on this knowledge that the things we continually reach for won't do even if we can manage to get hold of them. A similar atmosphere of impossible effort permeates Beckett's poetry, though his later poems retreat from any active engagement with the world. "Something there" gives us a moment somehow prior to Kenner's image: the ironic clown-eyes taking in the broom and the light and the dustpan, and seeing that it can't be done, but that one thing, a poem, will be done, nonetheless.

In Beckett's early poems the "something there" had begun as an idea with fuller dimension, and still vulnerable, like the eggs in "Whoroscope," to a capricious kind of poetic violence. By the end of his life, though, even the nebulous *something* is just a question, lingering in the nothingness of words. "Tailpiece," published as an addendum to *Watt* in 1953, brings this question back to the Proustian fascination with the ineffability of time. Beckett placed the poem as an envoi to his *Collected Poems*. It makes a fitting close, like a final echo to the themes of *Proust*, where Beckett had already been thinking of the immeasurable nature of a life's span. The poem resounds with Proust's problem of fitting the expansive weightlessness of all time into literary form:

He accepts regretfully the sacred ruler and compass of literary geometry. But he will refuse to extend his submission to spatial scales, he will refuse to measure the length and weight of man in terms of his body instead of in terms of his years.[3]

In "Tailpiece," Beckett only has to add the formal signals of verse to turn this sentiment into poetry.

Beckett's last original work, written early in 1989, is a short piece of fragmentary poetry that continues to reach for that nothingness on the periphery of perception. "Comment dire" ends with a glimpsed sensation withdrawing from perception, through thought, until finally it disappears into a who's-on-first sort of comic tautology.

Samuel Beckett was born in a well-to-do suburb of Dublin in 1906, perhaps on Good Friday, as he maintained, though the date is disputed. He was educated at Trinity College, Dublin, and at the École Normale Supérieure in Paris. He won the Nobel Prize for Literature in 1969. Until his death in 1989, Beckett lived just outside Paris in a small house he called "the house that *Godot* built."[4]

NOTES

1. *Proust* and *Three Dialogues with Georges Duthuit* (London: John Calder, 1987), pp. 12–13.

2. Hugh Kenner, *Samuel Beckett: A Critical Study* (Berkeley and Los Angeles: University of California Press, 1968), p. 13.

3. *Proust*, p. 12.

4. Quoted in *Dictionary of Literary Biography*, vol. 13, p. 69.

Whoroscope*

What's that?
An egg?
By the brothers Boot it stinks fresh.
Give it to Gillot.

Galileo how are you
and his consecutive thirds!
The vile old Copernican lead-swinging son of a sutler!
We're moving he said we're off—Porca Madonna!
the way a boatswain would be, or a sack-of-potatoey charging Pretender.
That's not moving, that's *moving*.   10

What's that?
A little green fry or a mushroomy one?
Two lashed ovaries with prostisciutto?
How long did she womb it, the feathery one?
Three days and four nights?
Give it to Gillot.

Faulhaber, Beeckman and Peter the Red,
come now in the cloudy avalanche or Gassendi's sun-red crystally cloud
and I'll pebble you all your hen-and-a-half ones
or I'll pebble a lens under the quilt in the midst of day.   20

To think he was my own brother, Peter the Bruiser,
and not a syllogism out of him
no more than if Pa were still in it.
Hey! pass over those coppers,
sweet millèd sweat of my burning liver!
Them were the days I sat in the hot-cupboard throwing Jesuits out of the
    skylight.

Who's that? Hals?
Let him wait.

My squinty doaty!
I hid and you sook.   30
And Francine my precious fruit of a house-and-parlour foetus!
What an exfoliation!
Her little grey flayed epidermis and scarlet tonsils!
My one child

scourged by a fever to stagnant murky blood—
blood!
Oh Harvey belovèd
how shall the red and white, the many in the few,
(dear bloodswirling Harvey)
eddy through that cracked beater? 40
And the fourth Henry came to the crypt of the arrow.

What's that?
How long?
Sit on it.

A wind of evil flung my despair of ease
against the sharp spires of the one
lady:
not once or twice but. . . .
(Kip of Christ hatch it!)
in one sun's drowning 50
(Jesuitasters please copy).
So on with the silk hose over the knitted, and the morbid leather—
what am I saying! the gentle canvas—
and away to Ancona on the bright Adriatic,
and farewell for a space to the yellow key of the Rosicrucians.
They don't know what the master of them that do did,
that the nose is touched by the kiss of all foul and sweet air,
and the drums, and the throne of the faecal inlet,
and the eyes by its zig-zags.
So we drink Him and eat Him 60
and the watery Beaune and the stale cubes of Hovis
because He can jig
as near or as far from His Jigging Self
and as sad or lively as the chalice or the tray asks.
How's that, Antonio?

In the name of Bacon will you chicken me up that egg.
Shall I swallow cave-phantoms?

Anna Maria!
She reads Moses and says her love is crucified.
Leider! Leider! she bloomed and withered, 70
a pale abusive parakeet in a mainstreet window.

No I believe every word of it I assure you.
Fallor, ergo sum!
The coy old frôleur!
He tolle'd and legge'd
and he buttoned on his redemptorist waistcoat.
No matter, let it pass.
I'm a bold boy I know
so I'm not my son
(even if I were a concierge)   80
nor Joachim my father's
but the chip of a perfect block that's neither old nor new,
the lonely petal of a great high bright rose.

Are you ripe at last,
my slim pale double-breasted turd?
How rich she smells,
this abortion of a fledgling!
I will eat it with a fish fork.
White and yolk and feathers.
Then I will rise and move moving   90
toward Rahab of the snows,
the murdering matinal pope-confessed amazon,
Christina the ripper.
Oh Weulles spare the blood of a Frank
who has climbed the bitter steps,
(René du Perron . . . !)
and grant me my second
starless inscrutable hour.

NOTES

René Descartes, Seigneur du Perron, liked his omelette made of eggs hatched from eight to ten
days; shorter or longer under the hen and the result, he says, is disgusting.

He kept his own birthday to himself so that no astrologer could cast his nativity.

The shuttle of a ripening egg combs the warp of his days. [This note and the notes that follow
are Beckett's.]

3   In 1640 the brothers Boot refuted Aristotle in Dublin.

4   Descartes passed on the easier problems in analytical geometry to his valet Gillot.

5–10   Refer to his contempt for Galileo Jr., (whom he confused with the more musical Galileo
       Sr.), and to his expedient sophistry concerning the movement of the earth.

17   He solved problems submitted by these mathematicians.

21–26	The attempt at swindling on the part of his elder brother Pierre de la Bretaillière—The money he received as a soldier.
27	Franz Hals.
29–30	As a child he played with a little cross-eyed girl.
31–35	His daughter died of scarlet fever at the age of six.
37–40	Honoured Harvey for his discovery of the circulation of the blood, but would not admit that he had explained the motion of the heart.
41	The heart of Henri IV was received at the Jesuit college of La Flèche while Descartes was still a student there.
45–53	His visions and pilgrimage to Loretto.
56–65	His Eucharistic sophistry, in reply to the Jansenist Antoine Arnauld, who challenged him to reconcile his doctrine of matter with the doctrine of transubstantiation.
68	Schurmann, the Dutch blue-stocking, a pious pupil of Voët, the adversary of Descartes.
73–76	Saint Augustine has a revelation in the shrubbery and reads Saint Paul.
77–83	He proves God by exhaustion.
91–93	Christina, Queen of Sweden. At Stockholm, in November, she required Descartes, who had remained in bed till midday all his life, to be with her at five o'clock in the morning.
94	Weulles, a Peripatetic Dutch physician at the Swedish court, and an enemy of Descartes.

Enueg I

Exeo in a spasm
tired of my darling's red sputum
from the Portobello Private Nursing Home
its secret things
and toil to the crest of the surge of the steep perilous bridge
and lapse down blankly under the scream of the hoarding
round the bright stiff banner of the hoarding
into a black west
throttled with clouds.

Above the mansions the algum-trees
the mountains
my skull sullenly
clot of anger
skewered aloft strangled in the cang of the wind
bites like a dog against its chastisement.

I trundle along rapidly now on my ruined feet
flush with the livid canal;

at Parnell Bridge a dying barge
carrying a cargo of nails and timber
rocks itself softly in the foaming cloister of the lock;
on the far bank a gang of down and outs would seem to be mending a
    beam.

Then for miles only wind
and the weals creeping alongside on the water
and the world opening up to the south
across a travesty of champaign to the mountains
and the stillborn evening turning a filthy green
manuring the night fungus
and the mind annulled
wrecked in wind.

I splashed past a little wearish old man,
Democritus,
scuttling along between a crutch and a stick,
his stump caught up horribly, like a claw, under his breech, smoking.
Then because a field on the left went up in a sudden blaze
of shouting and urgent whistling and scarlet and blue ganzies
I stopped and climbed the bank to see the game.
A child fidgeting at the gate called up:
"Would we be let in Mister?"
"Certainly" I said "you would."
But, afraid, he set off down the road.
"Well" I called after him "why wouldn't you go on in?"
"Oh" he said, knowingly,
"I was in that field before and I got put out."
So on,
derelict,
as from a bush of gorse on fire in the mountain after dark,
or in Sumatra the jungle hymen,
the still flagrant rafflesia.

Next:
a lamentable family of grey verminous hens,
perishing out in the sunk field,
trembling, half asleep, against the closed door of a shed,
with no means of roosting.
The great mushy toadstool,
green-black,

oozing up after me,
soaking up the tattered sky like an ink of pestilence,
in my skull the wind going fetid,
the water . . .

Next:
on the hill down from the Fox and Geese into Chapelizod*
a small malevolent goat, exiled on the road,
remotely pucking the gate of his field;
the Isolde Stores a great perturbation of sweaty heroes,
in their Sunday best,
come hastening down for a pint of nepenthe or moly or half and half*
from watching the hurlers above in Kilmainham.

Blotches of doomed yellow in the pit of the Liffey;
the fingers of the ladders hooked over the parapet,
soliciting;
a slush of vigilant gulls in the grey spew of the sewer.

Ah the banner
the banner of meat bleeding
on the silk of the seas and the arctic flowers
that do not exist.

Something there

something there
where
out there
out where
outside
what
the head what else
something there somewhere outside
the head

at the faint sound so brief
it is gone and the whole globe
not yet bare
the eye

opens wide
wide
till in the end
nothing more
shutters it again

so the odd time
out there
somewhere out there
like as if
as if
something
not life
necessarily

Tailpiece

who may tell the tale
of the old man?
weigh absence in a scale?
mete want with a span?
the sum assess
of the world's woes?
nothingness
in words enclose?

John Hewitt (1907–1987)

"I know my corner in the universe," John Hewitt writes in "Freehold," "my cor-
ner, this small region limited / in space by sea, in the time by my own dead."[1] The
poem reverberates with the Scots-Irish planter tradition through which Hewitt
claims descent, so that these lines at once attest to the deep roots his heritage has
permitted him to sink in the landscape of Northern Ireland and the deeply con-
flicted sense that his own inheritance leaves him "cornered" in the land of his
birth.

The same tension is evident throughout the poem, in its rhetoric, but more sig-
nificantly and characteristically in Hewitt's shaping of images drawn from rural
life in the region "where the bog-brown Dall / cuts through the seashore with a
lazy scrawl / and leaves a mounded tongue of sand whereon / the patriarchal
heron stands alone."[2] It is typical of Hewitt's poems to account the beauty of the
Northern landscape against the strain of religious difference, here inscribed as a
natural truth in the heron's "patriarchal" isolation on a "tongue" of sand thrown
up by the river's "lazy scrawl."

Hewitt's sense of alienation contends with his fluent rendering of the imagery
of his native place. He was born in Belfast in 1907 and studied there, at Method-
ist College and at Queen's University. He died in the city in 1987. Throughout
Hewitt's life, Belfast and its environs gave shape to his private and poetic experi-
ence. A Hewitt family anecdote that recalls him on a childhood pram ride in the
charge of his mother suggests that even at the earliest moment of his verbal life he
was prepared to speak in the idiom of his native landscape:

From this road you could see Belfast below in its smoke, and the lough with
the gantries and docks, a narrow strip of sea cutting off the wooded little
hills of the County Down from the southward sloping Antrim you were

in. On this road, at a gate or a hedge-gap, I rose, one bright day, battling against my harness, and pointing, spoke my first important words—"Ship-Boat-Water." I heard this recounted so often that although I do not honestly remember the occasion, it stands indisputably at the forefront of my life of talk.[3]

Hewitt expresses his surprise that this event did not prove prophetic of a life at sea, and something of Ulster's sectarian tension emerges when he goes on to confess bewilderment that he has "remained a rooted person."

Hewitt speaks his quarrel with Northern Irish Catholicism more directly in "The Glens," a poem that again plays his attachment to the native land against a religious revulsion that, viewed from outside the contending traditions, is difficult to comprehend. "I fear their creed," he writes, "as we have always feared / the lifted hand against unfettered thought. / I know their savage history of wrong."[4] Hewitt had previously published the poem with the second line reading "the lifted hand between the mind and truth," but moderated his position to the present form for inclusion in *Collected Poems*. Commenting on the change in an interview, he explained the shift in terms that put the desire to lighten the offense to Catholics in balance with his wish for greater poetic accuracy:

> When I wrote that it seemed true to me. I wanted no bar on my thinking. I admitted no censorship of my thought by anyone. But I found that I was giving offence to kindly and gentle Catholics.[5]

The new line, he went on to say, represented his thoughts "more exactly." The poem concludes the issue with Hewitt's affirmation of a tie to place that exceeds in strength the centrifugal effect of religious difference: "And yet no other corner in this land / offers in shape and colour all I need / for sight to torch the mind with living light."[6] John Wilson Foster notes this turn as one characteristic of Hewitt's poetry. He suggests that Hewitt senses "that birth and residence are *not* sufficient" to constitute a valid Irishness and, "unable to fall back on race or religion, turns to landscape . . . in order to join native and settler."[7]

While the poetry would seem to sustain Foster's suggestion that Hewitt's takes recourse to native imagery in place of a native religious tradition, however, the poet's own critical essays complicate the matter. In "Irish Poets, Learn Your Trade" Hewitt develops a framework that makes his attention to landscape look like an aesthetic gesture meant to combat what he registers as a central defect of Irish poets, that they "generally lacked skill in the recall of visual experience." The effort to pinpoint this deficiency critically coincides with a reflexive bend in much of Hewitt's poetry. Continually he returns to the theme of poetic "craft," as he does here in "Ars Poetica."

Hewitt's early notebooks show a young poet working to discover the boundaries of his craft through his exploration of the vast terrain of poetic possibility. Beginning with free verse on the model of Walt Whitman's, Hewitt, like the apprentice carpenter learning by feel the various techniques of joinery, applied himself in turns to a spectrum of poetic forms, from ballads and sonnets to dramatic monologue, *terza rima,* dialogue poems, and translations.[8]

Profiting from this early apprenticeship, Hewitt's later work settles into a lovely organicism of form. Formal rhythmic structures fold unobtrusively around the poet's thematic embrace of directness and simplicity in poems that range from the personal ("The Last Summer, for Roberta (1975)") and political ("Bogside, Derry, 1971") to the professional ("Ars Poetica"). It is this range, perhaps, that lead Seamus Heaney to declare in his obituary for Hewitt that the categories of Ulster poet and Planter poet by which he had been defined were insufficient, and that Hewitt would be remembered instead as a "universal poet."[9]

NOTES

1. "Freehold," *Collected Poems of John Hewitt,* ed. Frank Ormsby (Belfast: Blackstaff Press, 1991), p. 382.

2. Ibid., p. 370.

3. John Hewitt, "Planter's Gothic," in *Ancestral Voices: The Selected Prose of John Hewitt,* ed. Tom Clyde (Belfast: Blackstaff Press, 1987), p. 1.

4. "The Glens," *Collected Poems,* p. 310.

5. Quoted in Frank Ormsby's notes to *Collected Poems,* p. 626.

6. "The Glens," *Collected Poems,* p. 310.

7. John Wilson Foster, "The Dissidence of Dissent," *Across a Roaring Hill: The Poetic Imagination of Northern Ireland,* ed. Gerald Dawe and Edna Longley (Belfast: Blackstaff Press, 1985), p. 142.

8. For a thorough analysis of Hewitt's development, see Frank Ormsby's Introduction to *Collected Poems,* p. xli.

9. Quoted in Frank Ormsby, "Introduction," *Collected Poems,* p. lxxiii.

Once Alien Here

Once alien here my fathers built their house,
claimed, drained, and gave the land the shapes of use,
and for their urgent labour grudged no more
than shuffled pennies from the hoarded store
of well-rubbed words that had left their overtones
in the ripe England of the mounded downs.
The sullen Irish limping to the hills
bore with them the enchantments and the spells
that in the clans' free days hung gay and rich
on every twig of every thorny hedge,
and gave the rain-pocked stone a meaning past
the blurred engraving of the fibrous frost.

So I, because of all the buried men
in Ulster clay, because of rock and glen
and mist and cloud and quality of air
as native in my thought as any here,
who now would seek a native mode to tell
our stubborn wisdom individual,
yet lacking skill in either scale of song,
the graver English, lyric Irish tongue,
must let this rich earth so enhance the blood
with steady pulse where now is plunging mood
till thought and image may, identified,
find easy voice to utter each aright.

Because I Paced My Thought

Because I paced my thought by the natural world,
the earth organic, renewed with the palpable seasons,
rather than the city falling ruinous, slowly
by weather and use, swiftly by bomb and argument,

I found myself alone who had hoped for attention.
If one listened a moment he murmured his dissent:
this is an idle game for a cowardly mind.
The day is urgent. The sun is not on the agenda.

And some who hated the city and man's unreasoning acts
remarked: He is no ally. He does not say that
Power and Hate are the engines of human treason.
There is no answering love in the yellowing leaf.

I should have made it plain that I stake my future
on birds flying in and out of the schoolroom window,
on the council of sunburnt comrades in the sun,
and the picture carried with singing into the temple.

O Country People

O country people, you of the hill farms,
huddled so in darkness I cannot tell
whether the light across the glen is a star,
or the bright lamp spilling over the sill,
I would be neighbourly, would come to terms
with your existence, but you are so far;
there is a wide bog between us, a high wall.
I've tried to learn the smaller parts of speech
in your slow language, but my thoughts need more
flexible shapes to move in, if I am to reach
into the hearth's red heart across the half-door.

You are coarse to my senses, to my washed skin;
I shall maybe learn to wear dung on my heel,
but the slow assurance, the unconscious discipline
informing your vocabulary of skill,
is beyond my mastery, who have followed a trade
three generations now, at counter and desk;
hand me a rake, and I at once, betrayed,
will shed more sweat than is needed for the task.

If I could gear my mind to the year's round,
take season into season without a break,
instead of feeling my heart bound and rebound
because of the full moon or the first snowflake,
I should have gained something. Your secret is pace.
Already in your company I can keep step,
but alone, involved in the headlong race,

I never know the moment when to stop.
I know the level you accept me on,
like a strange bird observed about the house,
or sometimes seen out flying on the moss
that may tomorrow, or next week, be gone,
liable to return without warning
on a May afternoon and away in the morning.

But we are no part of your world, your way,
as a field or a tree is, or a spring well.
We are not held to you by the mesh of kin;
we must always take a step back to begin,
and there are many things you never tell
because we would not know the things you say.

I recognise the limits I can stretch;
even a lifetime among you should leave me strange,
for I could not change enough, and you will not change;
there'd still be levels neither'd ever reach.
And so I cannot ever hope to become,
for all my good will toward you, yours to me,
even a phrase or a story which will come
pat to the tongue, part of the tapestry
of apt response, at the appropriate time,
like a wise saw, a joke, an ancient rime
used when the last stack's topped at the day's end,
or when the last lint's carted round the bend.

Gloss, On the Difficulties of Translation

Across Lock Laig
the yellow-billed blackbird
whistles from the blossomed whin.

Not, as you might expect,
a Japanese poem, although
it has the seventeen
syllables of the haiku.

Ninth-century Irish, in fact,
from a handbook on metrics,
the first written reference
to my native place.

In forty years of verse
I have not inched much further.
I may have matched the images;
but the intricate wordplay
of the original—assonance,
rime, alliteration—
is beyond my grasp.

To begin with, I should
have to substitute
golden for *yellow*
and *gorse* for *whin*,
this last is the word we use
on both sides of Belfast Lough.

Bogside, Derry, 1971

Shielded, vague soldiers, visored, crouch alert;
between tall houses down the blackened street
the hurled stones pour hurt-instinct aims to hurt,
frustration spurts in flame about their feet.

Lads who at ease had tossed a laughing ball,
or, ganged in teams, pursued some shouting game,
beat angry fists against that stubborn wall
of faceless fears which now at last they name.

Night after night this city yields a stage
with peak of drama for the pointless day,
where shadows offer stature, roles to play,
urging the gestures which might purge in rage
the slights, the wrongs, the long indignities
the stubborn core within each heart defies.

Mary Hagan, Islandmagee, 1919

She wore high sea-boots and a wave-dowsed skirt,
a man's cloth cap, a jersey, her forearms freckled,
wind-roughened her strong face; with the men
she hauled the boat up, harsh upon the shingle,
and as they hauled they called out to each other,
she coarse as the rest. A skinny twelve-year-old,
pale from the city, watched this marvellous
creature, large-eyed, from my sun-warmed boulder.

I cannot remember her at any time
tossing the lapped hay, urging home the cattle,
or stepping out on a Sunday: she exists
in that one posture, knuckles on the gunwale,
the great boots crackling on the bladderwrack;
one with Grace Darling, one with Granuaile.*

Ars Poetica

I

Press on the thought till every word is proved
by evidence of sense; let no phrase fly
unballasted, but high as trees are high
that hold the sap still in the utmost leaf:
only of what you've cherished claim you loved,
and know the heart-scald if you'd name the grief.

This was my craft and discipline. I wrought
along the grain as with a steady tool,
its clean edge tempered and allowed to cool;
no surface scored by any wristy trick,
I have, obedient to my sober thought,
disdained the riper curves of rhetoric.

With what I made I have been satisfied
as country joiner with a country cart
made for a like use, fitting part to part,
built to endure all honest wear and tear

so long as needed, till it's laid aside
to flake and splinter back to earth and air.

My symbol's master was the solid man,
that slow and independent carpenter,
lord of an acre, no man's pensioner,
fixed in a place which knew his proper skill,
not waited on like chance of rain or sun,
but like a quarry or a spring-fed well.

But there were instants when that symbol failed,
when what I made stood idle; no one came
to buy or beg its use. Then I would blame
both time and place and thrust my tools aside
to find my hands a calling better scaled
to fill the empty pockets of my pride.

Or I would say: Not yours the time's demands.
Your heart's grown callous. Let the truth be told.
The savaged child, the lonely old and cold,
the hungry mother, beggared refugee,
the prisoner for conscience, in all lands,
utter blunt challenge to all poetry.

What word of yours can ever succour these?
Give life and purpose to workless lad?
The hearthless house? Restore the strength they had
to the smashed fingers? For the prisoners
break down the bars? For mercy pray, and peace,
for that unravished kingdom rightly theirs?

Which one of these, if chance should let him spell
your wisest verse, would surely recognise
the certain comfort in your grave replies
to the harsh questions time has set your heart?
If you can frame the questions, it is well;
if not, you are defeated from the start.

2

Let the mind grasp the symbol which has grown
out of the thresh and welter of my words,
as somehow in spring's gale of singing birds

the grateful ear plucks out a single call,
not richest in its range, or of subtlest tone,
that offers core and melody of all.

That symbol now's the farmer on his ground,
hill-farmer with his yowes upon the moss,*
and his brown horses moving slow across
the steep glen-acres with the jolting plough.
At any hour or season he'll be found
a master of the tasks his years allow.

He does not ask, before he casts his seed,
that it be pencilled in who'll use each grain,
and when the red cart climbs the long white lane
with cargoed lint, his slow thought does not run
beyond the scutch-mill, that it be decreed
the finished web serve such or such a one.

And there are times, too, when his labour's lost,
by misadventure lost, by flood or drought
or heavy snowstorm when the lambs are out,
or by world-accidents of war or trade.
He takes his chances, reckons all the cost,
repairs his reaper or rehafts his spade.

So be the poet. Let him till his years
follow the laws of language, feeling, thought,
that out of his close labour there be wrought
good sustenance for other hearts than his.
If no one begs it, let him shed no tears,
five or five thousand—none will come amiss.

The Last Summer, for Roberta (1975)

Deck-chaired in our back yard among your flowers,
bee-rifled poppies, tall *Impatiens*
in delicate blossom, triggers not yet set—
we brought its seeds first from Glendun,
a rank weed by the stream-side, of no repute
in any gardener's handbook, dear to me—

and rose of Sharon in a golden bush,
thrift with mop-heads on bare stems,
carnations tattered past their noon still sweet,
delphiniums, *Oxalis, Mimulus,*
in all their coloured companies . . .
We draw the sunlight in to warm our bones
against the creaking months, nor vex our wits
for metaphors to flourish round their names
or sprig our myth of being where we are.

These flowers are free of ambiguity
or other function than their single lives.
Our senses are not focused to accept
more than here is offered; we accept
the momentary excellence, content
with mood, with instant, knowing all will pass.

The Glens

Groined by deep glens and walled along the west
by the bare hilltops and the tufted moors,
this rim of arable that ends in foam
has but to drop a leaf or snap a branch
and my hand twitches with the leaping verse
as hazel twig will wrench the straining wrists
for untapped jet that thrusts beneath the sod.

Not these my people, of a vainer faith
and a more violent lineage. My dead
lie in the steepled hillock of Kilmore*
in a fat country rich with bloom and fruit.
My days, the busy days I owe the world,
are bound to paved unerring roads and rooms
heavy with talk of politics and art.
I cannot spare more than a common phrase
of crops and weather when I pace these lanes
and pause at hedge gap spying on their skill,
so many fences stretch between our minds.

I fear their creed as we have always feared
the lifted hand against unfettered thought.
I know their savage history of wrong
and would at moments lend an eager voice,
if voice avail, to set that tally straight.

And yet no other corner in this land
offers in shape and colour all I need
for sight to torch the mind with living light.

from Freehold: III Townland of Peace

Once in a showery summer, sick of war,
I strode the roads that slanted to Kilmore,
that church-topped mound where half the tombstones wear
my people's name; some notion drew me there,
illogical, but not to be ignored,
some need of roots saluted, some sought word
that might give strength and sense to my slack rein,
by this directed, not to lose again
the line and compass so my head and heart
no longer plunge and tug to drag apart.

Thus walking dry or sheltered under trees,
I stepped clean out of Europe into peace,
for every man I met was relevant
to the harsh clamour of my eager want,
gathering fruit, or leading horse uphill,
sawing his timber, measuring his well.
The crooked apple trees beside the gate
that almost touched the roadside with the weight
of their clenched fruit, the dappled calves that browsed
free in the netted sunlight and unhoused
the white hens slouching round the tar-bright sheds,
the neat-leafed damsons with the smoky beads,
the farm unseen but loud with bucket and dog
and voices moving in a leafy fog,

gave neither hint nor prophecy of change,
save the slow seasons in their circled range;
part of a world of natural diligence
that has forgotten its old turbulence,
save when the spade rasps on a rusted sword
or a child in a schoolbook finds a savage word.

Old John, my father's father, ran these roads
a hundred years ago with other lads
up the steep brae to school, or over the stile
to the far house for milk, or dragging the long mile
to see his mother buried. Every stride
with gable, gatepost, hedge on either side,
companioned so brought nearer my desire
to stretch my legs beside a poet's fire
in the next parish. As the road went by
with meadow and orchard, under a close sky,
and stook-lined field, and thatched and slated house,
and apples heavy on the crouching boughs,
I moved beside him. Change was strange and far
where a daft world gone shabby choked with war
among the crumpled streets or in the plains
spiked with black fire-crisped rafters and buckled lines,
from Warsaw to the Yangtze, where the slow-
phrased people learn such thought that scourge and blow
may school them into strength to find the skill
for new societies of earth and steel,
but here's the age they've lost.
                                The boys I met
munching their windfalls, drifting homeward late,
are like that boy a hundred years ago,
the same bare kibes, the heirloom rags they show;
but they must take another road in time.
Across the sea his fortune summoned him
to the brave heyday of the roaring mills
where progress beckoned with a million wheels.

The bearded man who jolted in his cart
on full sack nodding, waking with a start,
giving his friendly answer to my call,

uncertain of the right road after all,
might have been he, if luck had let him stay
where no shrill hooters break across the day,
and time had checked its ticking. Had I passed
a woman by a gate, I should have paused
to crack about the year the Lough was hard
and safe as frozen bucket in the yard,
and fit to bear the revel and the feast
when merry crowds devoured the roasted beast
beneath the bright stars of a colder year
than any living man remembers here,
to ask if she had lost her mother too
from famine-fever, or if it were true
she bore my family name. There's scarce a doubt
she would have, or, at worst, have pointed out
a house whose folk did, for it's common there
as berries on the hedges anywhere.

I found my poet-parson and his fire
expecting me. When unobtrusive care,
that natural acceptance of a friend,
had eased my tired bones, and my weary mind
had stretched its knotted sinews, that still man
and his quick wife, the doctor, once again
confirmed intention, slowly making plain
that by the heart's blind wisdom I had found
my seeming-aimless feet on solid ground;
then, when good talk had brimmed my singing head,
the lamp, the shallow stairs, the friendly bed,
till chortling blackbird in the neighbour trees
woke me to sunshine and the cruising bees.

The next day, in the old cathedral town,
I saw my friend the painter, tall and brown,
his long skilled fingers on the handlebars,
weaving his high way through the close-parked cars.
I signalled, he dismounted leisurely.
The slow laconic words we always say
when we two meet were said again. We crossed
wide streets and narrow streets till we had passed
out of the town and over the old bridge,

above the sunken river thick with sedge.
He urged a detour to the rising lane
from which he'd made that drawing of the scene.
We stopped till I recalled, as best I could,
the bridge, the hedges and the skyline wood,
the squat cathedral tower, the headless mill,
as they'd been noted by his pencil's skill,
comparing his with earth's reality.
Resumed our journey then, our talk came free,
as each reported gay but urgently
what things he'd done worth doing, what he'd thought,
or read or heard, or what the times had brought
that showed once more how strangely parallel
the paths we find to life's rare miracle.
The long five miles of road to Killylea
held only half the things we had to say;
and once again the night was nearly gone
before the logs were ash and we were done.

Somehow that easy journey, every minute,
and every field and face and word within it,
not to be split or shredded line by line
to smooth equations easy to define,
has not the random shape of accident,
but the warm logic of a testament
by which since then my better moments move,
assured of certainties I need not prove.

Now and for ever through the change-rocked years,
I know my corner in the universe;
my corner, this small region limited
in space by sea, in the time by my own dead,
who are its compost, by each roving sense
henceforward mobilised in its defence,
against the sickness that has struck mankind,
mass-measured, mass-infected, mass-resigned.

Against the anthill and the beehive state
I hold the right of man to stay out late,
to sulk and laugh, to criticise or pray,
when he is moved, at any hour of day,

to vote by show of hands or sit at home,
or stroll on Sunday with a vasculum,
to sing or act or play or paint or write
in any mode that offers him delight.

I hold my claim against the mammoth powers
to crooked roads and accidental flowers,
to corn with poppies fabulously red,
to trout in rivers, and to wheat in bread,
to food unpoisoned, unpolluted air,
and easy pensioned age without a care
other than time's mortality must bring
to any shepherd, commissar, or king.

But these small rights require a smaller stage
than the vast forum of the nations' rage,
for they imply a well-compacted space
where every voice declares its native place,
townland, townquarter, county at the most,
the local word not ignorantly lost
in the smooth jargon, bland and half alive,
which wears no clinging burr upon its sleeve
to tell the ground it grew from, and to prove
there is for sure a plot of earth we love.

Máirtin Ó Direáin (1910–1988)

Máirtín Ó Direáin was born in 1910 at Inishmore, a Gaelic community in the Aran Islands off the coast of County Galway. Unlike the majority of Irish-language poets, Ó Direáin spoke only Irish throughout his childhood. He learned English as a second language when he was in his teens. At the age of eighteen he moved to Galway, where he worked in the postal service for ten years, transferring to Dublin in 1938 to take another civil service job. In Dublin, far removed from the rural environment in which he learned the language, Ó Direáin began to write and publish poetry and journalism in Irish.

Ó Direáin's poems are unquestionably motivated by a nostalgia for the life he left behind in the western islands. At his best, he evades the trap of sentimentality by holding the physical privations of island life in sharp focus, balancing Romantic simplicity and actual adversity in a crisply descriptive poetic vocabulary as spare as the landscape it depicts. Poetry, rather than serving as a reservoir of Romantic images, becomes the way imagination reconciles the life of those forced to leave the island with that of the ones who, staying behind, experience its reality without the mediating effects of memories savored and rehearsed in absence. His "Rún na mBan," translated here as "The Women's Secret," expresses this reconciliation in the link between poetic discovery and the more immediate arts of island life.

Although his poetry is rooted in the experiences of a childhood cut off from the mainstream of modern Irish life, Ó Direáin's engagement with Irish literature and intellectual history is evident in poems like "Homage to John Millington Synge" and "Berkeley," which build bridges between the dominant Anglo-Irish culture of the mainland and the Irish Gaelic tradition of the Western Islands that Ó Direáin is himself extending.

Máirtín Ó Direáin died in Dublin in 1988.

I Will Find Solace

I will find solace
For a short time only
Among my people
On a sea-girt island,
Walking the shore
Morning and evening
Monday to Saturday
      In my western homeland.

I will find solace
For a short time only
Among my people,
From what vexes the heart,
From a troubled mind,
From soured solitude,
From wounding talk,
      In my western homeland.

[Translated by Tomás Mac Síomóin and Douglas Sealey]

The Women's Secret

Nearly every Sunday evening
There they were by the fire,
The women with their shawls
Wrapped about their heads.
There was always tea
On such occasions,
And they passed a sup around
From one to another.

The talk started,
The nudge and the whisper,
Elbow on knee emphasizing the words;
I used to be ordered out on the roads,
Not to be inside wolfing each word,

I'd be healthier out in the air
Like the rest of the lads.

I left in the end,
Blushing and hurt
But I wish I had stayed:
When I think of it now
Who knows what secret lore
Unknown to any man alive
I'd have snatched from the women
Ranged round a fire,
Drinking tea
With their shawls on their heads?

[Translated by Tomás Mac Síomóin and Douglas Sealey]

Ó Mórna*

Traveller straying in from the mainland,
You who gaze at a tomb on a cliff-top,
Who gaze at a coat of arms and a slogan,
Who gaze at inscription and flagstone,
Do not leave the graveyard by the bay
Before you know the dead man's story.

The man was Cathal Mór the son of Rónán,
Son of Conn son of Conán Ó Mórna,
But don't rely on common hearsay
Nor crone signing the cross on her forehead
To give you a true report of the man
Who entered the grave in that churchyard.

Don't condemn the dead man because of women's whispers,
Following a hint let fall between elbow
And knee by the old people's hearth,
Before you consider his blood and lineage,
His station, his power, the age he lived in,
And the snares that loneliness sets for his sort.

Consider also the dead man's heredity,
How he sprang from the line of great Ó Mórna,

Think of all he heard, all he saw,
As he went around he listened intently,
Remember also no prize was denied him
But all that he took was taken by right.

He saw the washing and then the thickening,
Saw the women scouring frieze,*
Each naked leg from knee to heel
Like a wash-staff pounding the cloth,
Woman sitting opposite woman
Along the sides of the makeshift trough,

Saw and noted each white wash-staff,
Saw the young women gazing at him,
Sizing him up and tantalizing him.
The blood of the robust male responded,
Traversed his body, suffused his face
And urged him on to swift demand.

"Press in there close to them like a man,
I warrant you'll feel an answering pressure,
Sure they know already
You're no empty spunkless cod
But a man of your rank and direct ancestry."
Pádhraicín the bailiff spoke those words.
A worthless rascal! You should have ignored him.

After the death of the titular lord,
Rónán the son of Conn the son of Conán,
The young Cathal took over his prerogative,
His lands and his jurisdictions,
His stewards and bailiffs as the law appointed,
He took his title and his power.

The knowledge gained in the cabins
Frequented before his accession,
He'd remembered every least bit of it,
Saved it up and treasured each detail;
He used it later for his own advantage
When he laid his law on the people.

He thought of the one who'd been stiffnecked,
Who wouldn't readily comply with his schemes,
He thought of the one who'd been obsequious,

The one who'd truly grovel before him,
He thought long of each virginal prize
For which he hankered with unbridled passion.

Our chief lived prey to melancholy's assaults,
Odd man out on a remote island,
An understanding friend from across the sound
Seldom came to his rescue
And he hunted on across the crags
Yearning for ease and alleviation.

He was advised to take in marriage
A woman who would bear him as heir
A legitimate and noble male-child
To continue the line of mighty Ó Mórna,
Instead of consorting with Alehouse Nuala,
Peg of Ard and Kate of Glen.

The wife, after Ó Mórna found her,
Bore him no son, no proper heir;
Ó Mórna lay with her only a while,
His newfound bride made a frigid mate;
In her drowsy bed his right was denied,
His marriage was nothing but torture.

Ó Mórna departs once more in haste,
Rampaging beyond the legal limits,
Digging the fallow land, digging the furrowed,
Ploughing with headlong violence,
Forcing the gate of virginity,
Crossing the bounds of marriage.

Breaking pledge and word,
Breaking commandment and vow,
Prompted by his greed's excess,
Listening to the whisper of desire
Increasing the clamour of his blood
In its rich and restless springtide.

Sated, they said, of base-born flesh,
Ó Mórna followed the ways of his forebears,
Used to take jaunts from known domains
To lush domains, to vast domains,

Abandoning all for the sake of pleasure,
Abandoning all for the harlot's embrace.

Stewards and bailiffs were at his disposal,
Administering his territories on his behalf,
Cruelly carrying out his instructions,
Causing grievous loss to many;
They had the whole of the apple to themselves,
Each starveling had the peel.

I give you the names of the stewards,
Wiggins, Robinson, Thomson and Ede,
Four crafty men who shunned no evil,
Who collected rents, who evicted tenants,
Who drove the orphan away from his hovel,
Who left hundreds without field or strand.

No sooner had Ó Mórna been back
On his native ground for a while
Than he quickly got up to the same tricks
Which had already gained him disrepute;
He ploughed again the base-born flesh
In open defiance of priest and layman.

One day he came on horseback,
Laden to the gills with drink,
Stopped beside the strand of Kilcolman
To scatter a handful of gold for sport;
The starvelings snatched at each sovereign
The lord tossed at their feet.

Ó Mórna roared and gave a shout,
The dead of his kin in the graveyard above
Must have heard that shout;
He declared as well with a sneer of contempt
That he could easily put up a sovereign
To match each louse in their arm-pits.

The priest named him on Sunday,
Threatened to use the powers against him,
Denounced him for profaning virginity,
Vehemently denounced the scandal to his flock,
But Ó Mórna set off in his coach
At an arrogant trot past the church.

Denounced by all for raiding and rapine,
Denounced by the girl for taking her maidenhead,
Denounced by the mother for her family scattered,
Denounced by the father for field and strand,
Denounced by the youth for raping his sweetheart,
Denounced by the husband for raping his wife.

Each day that passed meant one day less,
Each year that passed meant another gone,
Ó Mórna was falling to flesh and greyness,
More sour and petulant in his drunken bouts,
Venting his spleen on the stewards
But the worm in his flesh he could not defeat.

When the years caught up with Ó Mórna
The aches of desire were replaced by pain,
He lay for a while in the house of Kilcolman,
His ancestral house in the heart of the wood,
A house that grace had never shone on,
A house where laughter seldom sounded.

Threescore he was and a year besides
When he was buried in Cill na Manach*
After Unction, Penance, prayer and Mass:
Among his ancestors in Cill na Manach
Along with the tally of his kin,
On the tomb a coat of arms and a slogan.

The worm that gnawed you in the grave,
Great Ó Mórna, lord of Kilcolman,
Was not the worm of your vigour nor of your hauteur
But a worm that heeds not birth nor blood.
Calm be your slumber in the tomb tonight,
Cathal, son of Rónán son of Conn.

[Translated by Tomás Mac Síomóin and Douglas Sealey]

Homage to John Millington Synge*

The impulse that brought you to my people
From the distant pasture to the harsh rock

Was partnered by the living clay
And the intimations of loss and sorrow.

You didn't listen to the tale of the stones,
Greatness lived in the tale of the hearth,
You paid no heed to tombstone or graveyard,
No whimper escapes the lifeless dust.

Deirdre appeared before you on the road
And Naoise's currach weathered Ceann Gainimh;*
Deirdre and Naoise went to their death
And Pegeen flung abuse at Shawneen.*

The book was always in your hand—
You brought the words in it to life;
Deirdre, Naoise and Pegeen took form
And leaped like heroes from the pages.

The ways of my people decay.
The sea no longer serves as a wall.
But till Coill Chuain comes to Inis Meáin
The words you gathered then
Will live on in an alien tongue.

[Translated by Tomás Mac Síomóin and Douglas Sealey]

Stout Oars

Stand your ground, my soul;
Cleave to every rooted stock;
Don't behave like a callow youth
When your false friends depart.

You've often seen a redshank
Alone on a wet rock;
Though he drew no wealth from the wave
His lapse incurred no censure.

From your dark realm you brought
No lucky caul around your head
But the ritual wands were placed
To protect you in your cradle.

Useless sticks were placed around you;
An iron tongs above,
Beside you a piece of your father's clothing,
A poker placed in the fire.

Lean on your own stout oars
Against neap-tide and ebb,
Keep alight the coal of your vision;
To part with that is death.

[Translated by Tomás Mac Síomóin and Douglas Sealey]

The Smirk

That yellow, dried-up skull in the shrine
In the church beside the Boyne*
Didn't wipe that smirk from your mouth,
But I wanted to ask
What brought you there
Since I judged a skull no cause for laughter,
And I thought to myself you'd been born too late
For if you'd lived when Herod was king,
You would have brought the Saint's head in
With a smile on your lips.

[Translated by Tomás Mac Síomóin and Douglas Sealey]

The Eunuchs

"Let's collaborate" say the eunuchs
So no account will be read
Of what this man fathered,
Not in paper nor journal:
And they collaborated,
Downing their drinks
In the evil alcoves,
For there's no keener envy

Than that of the eunuch
For the man with balls.

[Translated by Tomás Mac Síomóin and Douglas Sealey]

To Ireland in the Coming Times

The man who bared his blade on high
In your defence when Easter blazed—
If he thought he'd freed you from too much shame,
What odds! He was only a simple fellow,
A poet-hero who had nothing saved
And nothing to bequeath but glory;
His glory you'll be forced to sell,
As you were compelled, before he came,
To be the slave of each foreign lout,
And if you're looked on as a whore again
Play the famous whore in earnest
And sell his glory and satiate
Each lout who sidles up to solicit,
Betray his ideal as well and lead
A new mate and his wealth to bed,
For you're no longer the mate of Conn nor Eoghan,
The mate of Pearse nor the beloved of heroes,
But if the attachment must be consummated
Let me beseech you, you darling of the Fianna,
To make no contract without wads of dollars.

[Translated by Tomás Mac Síomóin and Douglas Sealey]

Berkeley

On a rock, Bishop of Cloyne,*
I was reared as a boy;
And the grey stones
And barren crags encompassed me,

But far from such you lived,
Bishop and philosopher.

Swift himself, the great Dean,
Was not mad, if it's true
He left you on his doorstep;
Was not the closed door a dream
In your mind, for thus you taught?
And why would he want to open it for you
Since it was only a ghost of itself?

Dr. Johnson too
Kicked an adjacent stone
As if the assault
On the pure entity smashed
Your vision, and its implication
That in the mind was contained
All living substance and all inanimate matter.

I don't deny I agreed
With those great men for a while,
But since the grey stones began
To turn to dreams in my mind,
I do not know, my dear Bishop,
That you weren't the one who went on the deep
While the great men stayed on the shore.

[Translated by Tomás Mac Síomóin and Douglas Sealey]

The Yoke of Custom

The man who cast an ember from the bonfire
Into the garden outside his door
Didn't know the father of his deed;
But he fulfilled the dictate of custom
That made one clan
Of all the tillers of the soil
From India to Sruthán.*

[Translated by Tomás Mac Síomóin and Douglas Sealey]

The Essence is not in the Living

When fire and drink were a shelter
From the blast of the cold night
You were a compact bundle of sensuousness—
The warmth of the fire before you,
The cheering wine at your side;
But you were still intent on your interests
In spite of fire, drink and warmth,
But you were not the essence of an island
Nor any of the group who were with you.

The old lord on the wall
With his formal paunch,
And his good lady facing him
With her formal bust,
Have been captured in two portraits
Unliving and unchanged
For three hundred years and more—
Those two are the essence of an island,
As are stone rock and strand
In the cold midnight.

Unliving things slip
Away from life and leave it:
Was it thus
The island left my poem,
Or did you notice?

[Translated by Tomás Mac Síomóin and Douglas Sealey]

Seán Ó Ríordáin (1916–1977)

Seán Ó Ríordáin is credited with resuscitating a dying tradition of Irish-language poetry. At a time when the poetic practice descended from the Irish poets of the eighteenth century appeared exhausted and unable to confront modernism and the modernizing demands of a recently independent Irish culture, Ó Ríordáin began to write poetry in Irish that asserted a conscientious rendering of contemporary experience, breaking from the conventions of Irish poetry both in subject and meter, while remaining faithful to its linguistic tradition. His example sent a generation of young Irish writers into the Gaeltacht, to find in the Irish language the modes and sources of expression they might, by contemporary convention, have been expected to seek abroad.

Ó Ríordáin's career, whatever ameliorative effect it would have on an infirm literary tradition, itself began primarily in response to a much more particular malady. In 1940, he started to keep a diary, now celebrated though still unpublished, marking the origin of his life as a serious writer at a point closely, and consciously, linked to the diagnosis of tuberculosis he received in 1938. From the outset, chronic illness provided the recurrent metaphors that shaped Ó Ríordáin's poetry. Poems like "Fiabhras" (The Fever), transform the symptomatic profile of disease into the landscape of his experience: "The mountains of the bed are rather high and sickness a heat in there, the floor a long journey, and miles, miles away, life's sittings and standings go on."[1] But, unlike Proust, for whom the isolating effect of illness is reconciled in a subjectivist aesthetic, Ó Ríordáin found in the rhetoric of invalidism a model of human experience shaped on an armature of helplessness and fear and filled out by the specific threats of suffocation and collapse.

Throughout his poetry, Ó Ríordáin presents these threats as simultaneously physical and spiritual. The sense of mortality always palpable in his physical symptoms exerted a pressure on the sense of eternity that would sustain his religious belief. As a result his poems flutter between the desire to find security, even immunity, in religious life and the sense that such well-being is itself false, a kind of disorder within human reality. "Cnoc Mellerí," translated by Patrick Crotty as "Mount Melleray," provides an exemplary illustration of this tension. In that poem, the mind's questions become a weight that disturbs the balance of belief, and their answers tip Ó Ríordáin's balance in the direction of skepticism, as he comes to believe that "God's church was a spancel on my mind, / The priest a eunuch, the Faith / Mere lip-service." But in "Mount Melleray" Ó Ríordáin presents this breaking of faith as a moment of liberation. It leads momentarily to a philosophy not unlike the Horatian "seize the day": "drink up without anguish," Ó Ríordáin writes. "Let's live till we die!"[2] Living, though, is never an unchallenged act for Ó Ríordáin, and since sin and sickness are related in his mind, living sinfully is a double peril. Ultimately, belief, like a desperate dying grasp on life, has to be maintained, but in order to be maintained it must be transformed into poetry.

> The snoring of the storm in Melleray last night
> And days of soft sin on my memory like sickness,
> The days that will follow them lie hidden in God's fist,
> But a drowning man's grip on Melleray is this twist of poetry.[3]

Seán Ó Ríordáin was born in Ballyvourney in County Cork in 1916. He lived and worked in the city of Cork from 1932 until his death in 1977.

NOTES

1. "The Fever," prose translation by Seán Dunne in his *Poets of Munster: An Anthology* (Dublin: Anvil Press, 1985), p. 53.

2. "Cnoc Mellerí / Mount Melleray," *Modern Irish Poetry: An Anthology*, ed. Patrick Crotty (Belfast: Blackstaff, 1995), p. 123.

3. Ibid.

Death

Death was at hand.
I said I would go
with no grief or delay.
I looked at myself
in wonder
and said:
"So that's
all I was . . .
Goodbye then
my friend."

I look back now
upon that time
when death came up
in his hurry to take me
and yield I must—
and I think I know
the delight of a maid
as she waits for her love,
though I am
no woman.

[Translated by Thomas Kinsella]

Tulyar

O Tulyar, O Stallion,
Bought by De Valera from the Aga Khan,
A most chaste land, my ancestral land,
Land of virgins, land of abbots,
Land of psalters and of gospels
And friars poor but great in learning.
That is history, Tulyar:
But now, Stallion, give ear:
Don't you think it somewhat strange

That a practitioner of your fame
Surpassing every horsey name
To us came
Here to exercise your trade
In land of scholars, land of saints,
Land blest by Patrick when *he* came?
Not that it's sin when horses mate,
But your coming has set seed a-shake;
Not Patrick's gospel do you bring
But quite a different thing
That Eisirt would understand.
Sin is less sinful in our land
Now that you at stud will stand,
A public stallion, with official backing,
On behalf of government acting.
    Was it that we had gone all barren
    And needed the example of a stallion?
    Or were we to be deemed heretical
    Unless you were classified official?

[Translated by Criostoir O'Flynn]

The Moths

Delicate sound of a moth; a page turning;
a tiny wing destroyed.
In my bedroom on a night in autumn
a delicate thing hurt.

Another night, I saw in dream
two moth wings
wide as the wings of angels
and delicate as women.

I was to restrain them,
not to have them escape,
to possess them, as I held them,
and bring them to full bliss.

But I spilled the holy powder
spattered on each wing
—and I knew I was without digits,
without the digits of manhood for ever.

And the digits stalked away from my blunder
with a new and firm authority,
and everyone could be heard, talking about them,
everyone, except myself.

Delicate sound of a moth; a page turning;
a moth membrane ruined;
an autumn night; moths flying.
Such fierce attention to their tiny uproar.

[Translated by Thomas Kinsella]

My Mother's Burial

June sun in an orchard
    And a whispering in the afternoon's silk,
A malicious bee's drone
    Scream-tearing the day's fabric.

An old soiled letter in my hand:
    With every word that I drank
A venomous pain stung my breast,
    Each word bruised out its individual tear.

I recalled the hand that did the writing,
    A hand as recognisable as a face,
A hand that dealt out old Biblical kindness,
    A hand that was like balm when you were ill.

And June collapsed back into winter:
    The orchard was a white cemetery by a river
And from the heart of the silent whiteness all about me
    The black hole roared in the snow.

The whiteness of a girl on her first Communion Day,
    The whiteness of the wafer on a Sunday altar,
The whiteness of milk drawing free from the breasts,
    When they buried my mother, the whiteness of the sod.

My mind was scourging itself in the attempt
    To savour the burial entire
When there gently flew into the bright silence
    A robin, unflustered, unafraid.

It hovered above the grave as if it knew
    The reason for its coming was hidden from all
But the one lying waiting in the coffin:
    I resented their extraordinary exchange.

The air of Heaven landed on that grave,
    A terrible, saintly merriment held the bird:
I was barred from the mystery like a layman
    And the grave, though right before me, was miles away.

The freshness of sorrow washed my lascivious soul,
    Pure snow fell on my heart:
In my white heart now I will bury the memory
    Of she who carried me three seasons in her womb.

The labourers came with a harsh sound of shovels
    And roughly swept earth into the grave.
I looked away, a neighbour was brushing his knees;
    I looked at the priest and there was worldliness in his face.

June sun in an orchard
    And a whispering in the afternoon's silk,
A malicious bee's drone
    Scream-tearing the day's fabric.

Little halting verses I'm writing,
    I'd like to catch the tail of a robin,
I'd like to vanquish the spirit of the knee-brushers,
    I'd like to fare in sorrow to the end of day.

[Translated by Patrick Crotty]

Second Nature

After Seán Ó Ríordáin, Malairt

"Come over here," says Turnbull, "till you see the sorrow in the horse's eyes.
If you had hooves as cumbersome, there would be gloom in your eyes too."

And it was clear to me, that he had understood the sorrow in the horse's eyes
So well, had dwelt so long on it, that he was plunged in the horse's mind.

I looked over at the horse, that I might see the sorrow pouring from its eyes;
I saw the eyes of Turnbull, looming towards me from the horse's head.

I looked at Turnbull; I looked at him again, and saw beneath his brows
The too-big eyes that were dumb with sorrow, the horse's eyes.

[Translated by Ciaran Carson]

Mount Melleray

The snoring of the storm in Melleray last night
And days of soft sin on my memory like sickness,
Days that were life's beds of ease
With fleas of lust hopping in them in their thousands.

A fairy wind of footsteps rose in the night
—Monks going to Mass,
Gaiety, turning about and dancing in the air,
The chanting of sandals.

A brother in the dining-hall dispensing supper,
A silence so soft it was balm for the mind,
The saintly poverty of his speech
And unaffected demeanour of a good Christian.

Deformed sunlight was slowly poured
Through the hive-like window
Until it took the shape of a monk from head to toe,
A shape that began to read.

The white malevolent monk was reading a book
When a bell suddenly coughed—
The sun-monk was obliterated
And the word lost from his cheeks.

Compline was rung and every guest
Hurried, subdued, towards the chapel;
These saints' lives seemed sheet-white
Where ours were beetle-black.

Perspiration on the beads gripped in my hands,
My trousers stuck to my knees,
A hooded procession of monks glided past;
Though it would have been vulgar to stare,

Stare at them I did, without pity or compassion
As the Jews stared long ago
At Lazarus shyly issuing from the tomb,
Their keen eyes all round burning him.

They filed past us one by one,
A cemetery in perpetual prayer,
And a thick cloud of sepulchral mildew
Settled like melancholy on the evening's cheek.

"Death casts a frost over life here,
The monks are his retinue,
He the Abbot they serve,
It's for him they endure fast and abstinence.

"A youth walking like an enfeebled old man
Is an insult to the mercy of God;
Whoever would inflict such wrong on a boy
Would pull a hood over the sun;

"Would spread night across midday,
Would rip the tongue from the river,
Plant lechery in the minds of birds
And fill the world with shame.

"This boy is blind to the wild imagination
That fertilises diversity of thought,
That cares nothing for Abbot or bell or rule
But lies down with its own deepest desire.

"He will never be woman-drunk
With the longing that moves mountains,
The desire that once opened the heavens for Dante
When angels descended in the shape of verses."

So spoke the arrogant, insubordinate ego,
Blind with the world's fury;
But I thought later, as music pealed over us,
That the individual is less than the congregation.

I looked back at the waste of my life,
With the beads still tight in my fist,
Sin, idleness, bent prodigality
—A ghastly nettle-bed of years.

I looked at the life of the monks
And recognised there the form of a poem
—Measure, clarity, profundity and harmony—
My mind buckled under the weight of its questions.

This morning I savoured the release of Confession,
Restoration, a load laid aside,
The anchor was raised, I danced in Latin
And almost set foot in Heaven.

But I savoured too, once more, over-confidence:
My blood coursing with delight,
I imagined the Holy Spirit took up residence in me,
That my words had their origin in Heaven.

That God's church was a spancel on my mind,
The priest a eunuch, the Faith
Mere lip-service; drink up without anguish,
Let's live till we die!

The monks sounding through my head like bees,
My mind buckled from questioning,
Sung notes wheeling hither and thither:
Suddenly Compline was over.

The snoring of the storm in Melleray last night
And days of soft sin on my memory like sickness,
The days that will follow them lie hidden in God's fist,
But a drowning man's grip on Melleray is this twist of poetry.

[Translated by Patrick Crotty]

Claustrophobia

Next to the wine
Stand a candle and terror,
The statue of my Lord
Bereft of its power;
What's left of the night
Is massing in the yard,
Night's empire
Is outside the window;
If my candle fails
Despite my efforts
The night will leap
Right into my lungs,
My mind will collapse
And terror be made for me,
Taken over by night,
I'll be darkness alive:
    But if my candle lasts
    Just this one night
    I'll be a republic of light
    Until dawn.

[Translated by Patrick Crotty]

Fever

The mountains of the bed are high,
The sick-valley sultry with heat,
It's a long way down to the floor,
    And miles and miles further
    To a world of work and leisure.

We're in a land of sheets
Where chairs have no meaning,
But there was a time before this levelled time,
    A walking time long ago,
    When we were high as a window.

The picture on the wall is heaving,
The frame has liquefied,
Without faith I can't hold it at bay,
　　Everything's driving at me
　　And I feel the world falling away.

A whole district's arriving from the sky,
A neighbourhood's set up on my finger,
Easy now to grab a church—
　　There are cows on the northern road
　　And the cows of eternity are not so quiet.

[Translated by Patrick Crotty]

Padraic Fiacc (1924–)

Like many poets in a century that has seen economic concerns overshadow poetic ones, Padraic Fiacc gained critical acclaim a good while before he secured a publisher for his first full-length volume. Padraic Colum, working at Macmillan's at the beginning of the 1940s, responded with interest to the collection of verse submitted by a student at Haaren High School in New York City, but apparently could not convince his firm to publish the work. He did persuade the young poet, Patrick Joseph O'Connor, to make more of his Irish immigrant background. O'Connor assumed the name Padraic Fiacc, and within a few years was publishing poems in the *Irish Times* and *Poetry Ireland*.[1]

Turning the mind of his art toward Ireland soon led Fiacc to make a literal return. In 1946 he went back to Belfast. He had been born there in 1924, but five years later his parents had moved the family to New York. In America, Fiacc later remembered, his father "fulfilled the American Dream and rose from a Belfast bartender to someone who owned his own grocery stores, one in Harlem and one on Amsterdam Avenue."[2] The dream, though, was not without its nightmarish elements. His father's little commercial empire collapsed when his customers proved unable to pay their bills. As a result of the family's diminished economic position, his son grew up in the midst of just the sort of depravity and everyday violence the parents had left Belfast to escape:

> We had a kind of childhood, or in my own case, boyhood or youth, but this was of such a complex, inexplicable nature. Materialism pushed nature itself out the door, so that it came in the window from the fire escape in the guise of a sex fiend.[3]

Childhood is the supposed realm of simplicity and innocence, but in Fiacc's view it turns out to be frighteningly complex, and not simply because economic reality has displaced the natural order. Even when nature successfully insinuates itself it is in a perverted form. In Fiacc's vocabulary, everything, even beauty, is couched in terms that reveal an inherent threat; yet shining through the threat is, nonetheless, a strange beauty, as when he describes the polluted Hudson River "Shining like a ringworm that is a rain / -bow."[4]

Fiacc's early experience in New York shaped his perception of Belfast, and his meditations on childhood help explain how he became one of the earliest of contemporary Irish poets to concentrate his art on the urban landscape. Breaking from the stream of Irish poetry written under the influence of Yeats or Kavanagh, Fiacc's poems often originate in imagistic urban vignettes: "A grey cloud of pollution from Power / Chimneys, mill houses, laundries, cars,"[5] or "Sinking on iron streets, the bin-lid / -shielded, battleship-grey-faced kids."[6] In poems peopled more often with "kids" than adults, Fiacc's view of the city is oddly childish, not naïve or innocent, but filled with amazement and horror at the amazing and horrible things adults learn to take as normal.

NOTES

1. See Aodán Mac Póilin's "Biographical Outline," in *Ruined Pages: Selected Poems of Padraic Fiacc*, ed. Gerald Dawe and Aodán Mac Póilin (Belfast: Blackstaff Press, 1994), pp. 13–16.

2. "Hell's Kitchen: An Autobiographical Fragment," *Ruined Pages*, p. 156. ("[T]he text of a programme written and presented by Padraic Fiacc on BBC Radio Ulster. It was first broadcast on 1 June 1980, and produced by Paul Muldoon" [p. 151].)

3. "Hell's Kitchen," *Ruined Pages*, p. 152.

4. Ibid., p. 153.

5. "Our Fathers," *Ruined Pages*, p. 46.

6. "The Black and the White," *Ruined Pages*, p. 109.

Leaving the Monastery

Goodbye giant pine.
Black branch give way
And each copper nut
Of star in the cloud.

I trek back down
Black blind blood
To the mill-tall town.

What did I learn up there?
What do I now know?

Boots go slip shod;

It is already
Blindly
Snowing.

The Boy and the Geese   *for Brigid*

The swans rise up with their wings in day
And they fly to the sky like the clouds away

Yet with all their beauty and grace and might
I would rather have geese for their less-smooth flight.

I would rather have geese for they're ugly like me
And because they are ugly, as ugly can be

I would rather have geese for their mystery.

The Let Hell Go of It

After I helped you tear up
The gangplank from the Law
As I mounted the bus back

Into town, and my old umbrella
Cracked from an ice-storm wind our
"old acquaintanceship," I

Gaped at and prayed to the driver;
"It would be a good idea," he swore,
"to let friggin go-of-it!"

Yes, day is night out in
This hailstone-skinning sky
As I watch my broken stick

(All spokes)—fly
Down the whimpering street,
Your liner far out into

The bitch Atlantic now:
An elongated neck of the snow
Goose in flight ship-horn

Honk of the cow in heat,
An art-long, ram-rod flicker
Of fingers, then: GONE!

Well then, good, great, I love
You all the more because
You are not here . . .

Tenth-Century Invasion

Doves beat their wings
Against their breasts

Bloodying their wings
Bloodying their breasts . . .

Bells ring throughout the book
At the bottom of the lough

Gold running over the
Ruined page

Drowned
Emerald and lilac ink

From the song written in
The shaft of the sun

In the moment on the
Margin
Never to be sung.

Orange Man

for Norman Dugdale *

The sparrow and the bluetit eating
Greased potato skins are chased

By the blackbird. He's chased by
His own brown mate. She's chased

By a shell-in-beak stone-banging
Puffed-out Norwegian thrush that

A gang of tough-looking starlings
Easily chases until a shrewd-eyed

Navy blue jackdaw, the brute size
Of a graveyard raven, invades

The territory that the tiny orange
-breasted robin only thinks is all

His own garden, just can't get let
To stay that dead lonely in.

More Terrorists

The prayer book is putting on fat
With *in memoriam* cards.

The dead steal back
Like snails on the draining board

Caught after dark
Out of their shells.

Their very
Outnumbering, swarmy cunning
Betters

My "cut head" and
Scares me as
Pascal was

At too many stars.

First Movement

Low clouds, yellow in a mist wind,
Sift on far-off Ards*
Drift hazily . . .

I was born on such a morning
Smelling of the Bone Yards

The smoking chimneys over the slate roof tops
The wayward storm birds

And to the east where morning is, the sea
And to the west where evening is, the sea

Threatening with danger

And it would always darken suddenly.

Vengeance

I am a child of the poor.

For me there will have to be

Tinfoil: the pink light
-ning pale aquamarine
Morning sea-splashed

Soil dream against

The grave night gale.

Haemorrhage

I bleed by the black stream
For my torn bough.   James Joyce

Entries patent leather with sleet
Mirror gas and neon light . . .
A boy with a husky voice picks a fight
And kicks a tin down home in pain

To tram rattle and ship horn
In a fog from where fevers come
In at an East Wind's
Icy burst of black rain . . .

Here I was good and got and born

Cold, lost, not predictable
Poor, bare, crossed in grain
With a shudder no one can still

In the damp down by the half-dried river
Slimy at night on the mud flats in
The moonlight gets an un
-earthly white Belfast man.

The Wearing of the Black

Black velvet short trousers, the shoes
Black patent leather with crystal buttons!

"Awnie, you have them like the Prince of Wales!"

Mother is playing, "See the Conquering Hero Comes"
And "The Bluebells of Scotland" on the piano.

"Where, O where has my Highland Laddie gone?"

O he is gone to America for
He is on the bloody run!

Our hostess, a bony white-haired Highland woman
Brings us a cup of tea in a rice-paper thin
Porcelain, so delicate, I fumble and drop it . . .

Now, near half a century after, why
Can I recall that flash of fire on the tile
Floor as I scalded my bare knees when I pray
To care even that this rotting self-dinner

-jacketed hero's grave, tonight, in black cuff

Links, at least has the wit to dress for death.

Son of a Gun

Woe to the boy for whom the nails, the crown of thorns, the sponge of gall were the
first toy.   François Mauriac*

Between the year of the slump and the sell out, I
The third child, am the first born alive . . .

My father is a Free Stater "Cavan Buck."
My mother is a Belfast factory worker. Both

Carry guns, and the grandmother with a gun
In her apron, making the Military wipe

Their boots before they rape the house. (These
Civil wars are only ever over on paper!)

Armed police are still raping my dreams
Thump-thud. Thump-thud. I go on nightmaring

Dead father running. There is a bull
In the field. Is father, am I, running away

From the bull to it? Is this the reason why
I steal

      time, things, places, people?

Barman father, sleeping with a gun under
Your pillow, does the gun help you that much?
                                        I wonder

For the gun has made you all only the one
In of sex with me the two sexed son (or three

Or none?) you bequeathed the gun to
Still cannot make it so. I can

Never become your he-man: shot
Down born as I was, sure, I thought

And thought and thought but blood ran . . .

Our Father   *for my sister Mary Galliani*

Our father who art a Belfast night
-pub bouncer had to have
A bodyguard, drilled recruits for
The IRA behind the scullery door in
The black back yard,
                        died
In your sleep, in silence like
The peasant you stayed
Never belonging on Wall Street,
Your patience a vice
Catching as a drug!
                        With no hankering
To fly back "home," the way that you never
Left lifting your feet out of the dung
Of the fields of that crossroad town between
Leitrim, Longford and Cavan,* begot
Such a high-strung, tight-knit man, but
For a drinking fit when you vented your spleen
On heaven "took your woman"
Hissing between nicotined teeth
Collapsing over the "Hope Chest"
Demolishing the delph closet . . .
Bull-bellowing out in

That hollowing slum subway
"God damn it Christ, why?
That child belonged to me!"
                              Pray
For us now that you and she
Bed together in your American grave
And at what an unnatural price!
The eaten bread is soon forgotten years
Sweltering in the subway—bought
Under Mike Quill* nightshift days
Hungering and agitating for
Civil Rights, a living wage
And still, still the injustices,
The evil thing being
That which crushes us . . .

Icon

for my brother Peter
serving in the Alps

Unholy mother Ireland banging
on the wall in labour

Each season believed
Ivy and thorn would flower

Fell
          slumped over
The Sewing Machine

"Christ of Almighty" swore
Down through a childhood
                              only
A woman or a child could
                                        bear
Left each one of us with
A grave grace, dark

Not just the same thing as
Wisdom, that what

A *Terribilita**frowning
Nefertiti brow

Vowed never to
Scratch a grey hair
And now, indeed, did not:

We were born in her

Screams to "Get Out!"

Enemies

At the Gas and Electric Offices
Black boats with white sails
Float down the stairs

Frightening the five-year-old
Wee Protestant girls . . .

"Nuns, nuns," one of them yells,
"When are yez go'n to git
                              married?"

The British Connection

In Belfast, Europe your man
Met the Military come to raid
The house:
              "Over my dead body
Sir," he said, brandishing
A real-life sword from some
Old half-forgotten war . . .

And youths with real bows and arrows
And coppers and marbles good as bullets
And oldtime thrupenny bits and stones
Screws, bolts, nuts (Belfast confetti),

And kitchen knives, pokers, Guinness tins
And nail-bombs down by the Shore Road

And guns under the harbour wharf
And bullets in the docker's tea tin
And gelignite in the tool shed
And grenades in the scullery larder
And weedkiller and sugar
And acid in the french letter

And sodium chlorate and nitrates
In the suburban garage
In the boot of the car

And guns in the oven grill
And guns in the spinster's shift

And ammunition and more more
Guns in the broken-down rusted
Merry-Go-Round in the Scrap Yard

Almost as many hard-on
Guns as there are union jacks.

Elegy for a "Fenian Get"

Patrick Rooney *
Aged nine
Shot dead

Clouded with slow moving orange smoke
Swirls over the hill-street, the shop

Where I bought the First Holy Communion
                                        Dress
Is boarded up with wire around the
                            back
Of it the altar boy was shot dead
By some trigger-happy cowboy cop

Whose automatic fire penetrated
The walls of the tower flat the young
                                    father

Hid the child in out of a premonition!

O holy Christ, why?
                    "Well, it's like this:
Fenian* gets out of hell are spawned in
Filthy Fenian beds by Fenian she-devils
                                    will

Bloody not take the pill!"
                                The other
Little children altogether shouted:

"Rats, pigs (nits make lice!)—Burn 'im
Burn 'im, Burn the scum, Burn the vermin!"

A Slight Hitch

March 1972

We wanted to think it was the quarry
but the pigeons roared with the white
smoke, black smoke, and the ghost

-faced boy-broadcaster
fresh from the scene broke down
into quivering lips and wild

tears (can you imagine, and him
"live" on the TV screen!)

had to be quickly replaced
so that the News could be announced
in the usual cold, acid
and dignified way by the

NORTHERN IRELAND BRITISH
BROADCASTING CORPORATION.

Goodbye to Brigid/an *Agnus Dei*

I take you by the hand. Your eyes,
Mirroring the traffic lights,
Are green and orange and red.

The Military lorries by our side
Drown out your child-heart
Thumping tired under the soot

-black thorn trees these
Exhaust-fumed greasy mornings.

My little girl, my Lamb of God,
I'd like to set you free from
Bitch Belfast as we pass the armed

-to-the-back-teeth barracks and
Descend the road into the school
Grounds of broken windows from

A spate of car-bombs, but
Don't forgive me for not.

Intimate Letter 1973

Our Paris part of Belfast has
Decapitated lamp posts now. Our meeting
Place, the Book Shop, is a gaping
Black hole of charred timber.

Remember that night with you, in
-valided in the top room when
They were throwing petrol bombs through
The windows of Catholics, how
My migraine grew to such
A pitch, Brigid said "Mommy,
I think Daddy is going to burst!"

We all run away from each other's
Particular hell. I didn't
Survive you and her thrown
To the floor when they blew up the Co
-Op at the bottom of the street or Brigid
Waking screaming after this
Or that explosion. Really,
I was the first one to go:

It was I who left you . . .

Credo Credo

You soldiers who make for our holy
Pictures, grinding the glass with your
Rifle butts, kicking and jumping on them

With your hob-nailed boots, we
Are a richer dark than the Military
Machine could impose ever.

We have the ancient, hag-ridden, long
-in-the-tooth Mother, with her ugly
Jewish Child

Hangs in the depths of our dark
Secret being, no rifles can reach
Nor bullets, nor boots:

It was our icons not our guns
You spat on. When you found our guns
You got down on your knees to them

As if our guns were the holy thing . . .
And even should you shoot the swarthy
-faced Mother with her ugly Jewish Child

Who bleeds with the people, she'll win
Because she loses all with the people,
Has lost every war for centuries with us.

Pearse Hutchinson (1927–)

Pearse Hutchinson remembers Maurice Lindsay's *Modern Scottish Poetry* as one of the first books he ever bought first-hand. The anthology has given Hutchinson "recurrent pleasure for nearly half a century," but it was through another scrap of writing that Lindsay may have had a greater effect on Hutchinson's life as a poet.[1] In 1948 Lindsay gave the young Hutchinson the Glasgow address of Hugh MacDiarmid. Hutchinson, having worked up his "partly Dutch courage," made a pilgrimage to see the most influential poet in Scotland. What he discovered in MacDiarmid's presence was a form of courage that did not require a bottle:

> I was, like others of my generation, in full flight from the far-from-hidden Ireland of sexual repression, with which I mistakenly, though understandably, identified Irish nationalism. Many of us in the Dublin of those days looked to the London of Horizon and the "posh" papers for enlightenment. Meeting MacDiarmid at that point, listening to his talk of my country and his, was one of the things that helped me come to terms with Ireland, but also to begin to struggle free from the thralldom of London. That MacDiarmid had no difficulty in being both a Socialist and a Nationalist gave me courage.[2]

Socialist, Nationalist, and, in a linguistic rather than an ideological sense, a dialectician, MacDiarmid was largely responsible for the revival of Scottish interest in vernacular poetry. Following the course of that early meeting, Hutchinson's own poetry has continued to engage the causes of labor, Irish nationalism, and the preservation of the Irish language.

Hutchinson was born to Irish Catholic parents in 1927 in Glasgow, Scotland, and was educated at University College, Dublin. With one biographical foot in each of these Gaelic regions, Hutchinson took a natural interest in language. What that interest has produced is surprising in its variety. Hutchinson has written poetry in Irish and English and has translated poetry into English from Catalan and Galaicoportuguese, and from Old Irish into Italian.

His early volumes of poetry ended with pages of notes meant to guide the reader through complex linguistic mazes. Annotations for *Barnsley Main Seam*, published in 1995, are briefer and fewer in number, reflecting the fact that simpler wonders of language are shaping its poems. In "Legend," for example, the title inscribes the poem in the realm of the fabulous, while holding out the possibility that, like the legend on a map, its comparative lexicon presents a key to understanding all the same. "Legend" uses the moment of linguistic discovery as an occasion for intimate lyric, but Hutchinson is equally, if not more, attentive to the way linguistic subtleties can wrap an obscuring cloak around social and political issues. Hutchinson's poems often call attention to issues by undermining the naturalness of the language that surrounds them, as in "British Justice," his brief poetic response to the British government's convicting Paddy Joe Hill, one of the six men accused, wrongly, of bombing a pub in Birmingham, England. "She Fell Asleep in the Sun" performs a similar, and more linguistically intriguing, operation on the practice of calling "illegitimate" any children born outside of a legally recognized relationship.

Hutchinson's best-known poem is also perhaps the one most successful at bringing together issues of language, nationalism, and oppression. "The Frost is All Over" was published by Gallery Press in a volume by the same name in 1975, and was later anthologized in the *Penguin Book of Contemporary Irish Poetry*. Its title was picked up by Robert Welch to describe his sense "that the colonial, or post-colonial, or post-post-colonial repression is over and done with."[3] Hutchinson may be less optimistic. "To kill a language," his poem maintains, "is to kill a people."

NOTES

1. Pearse Hutchinson, "Drinking MacDiarmid Down," *Chapman*, nos. 69–70 (Autumn 1992), p. 65.
2. Ibid.
3. Robert Welch, *Changing States: Transformations in Modern Irish Writing* (London: Routledge, 1993), p. 229.

Eight Frontiers Distant

for John Jordan

Eight frontiers distant
from the company and gesture of his true friends,
each man becomes less perfect in affection.
Divided by a hundred seas and lakes
from the second-rate, the tenth-rate, and the unspeakable,
each man recalls their faces and their names
with gradually less disdain.
Travel is in this matter, so,
more specious than trite death.
Till, having crossed back over two frontiers,
or ten extensive deserts of water,
confronted suddenly at a café-table
with choice between his own alone integrity,
with all its dangerous peepshows,
and the fourth- or fifteenth-rate with an eager face,
and a Nansen passport somewhere in the background,*
each man hears need, putting on the voice of duty,
re-assert itself; and into his mind again
his true friends come,
smiling and loving and mercilessly absent.

Travel Notes

Some men are scarcely conscious of
more than their own parishes yet
could hurt no foreigner nor scorn the strangest;
but they are few not many, let
no prideful island take
them for a sanction of each new mistake.

Some, through visiting many countries,
have grown less cocky on self, birth-place,
and glittering tags, while more sure of the earth;
but they're not many, you couldn't base
much hope, on them, for those
who know what time all bars in Europe close.

Two foreigners in a century,
perhaps, break through to a nation's core:
to them, honour; let grateful others take
some personal boons, and claim no more;
respect and love dispense
at once with blindness and omniscience.

Two foreigners—and how many
nationals, balladeers?

Fleadh Cheoil*

Subtle capering on a simple thought,
the vindicated music soaring out
each other door in a mean twisting main street,
flute-player, fiddler and penny-whistler
concentrating on one sense only
such a wild elegance of energy gay and sad
few clouds of lust or vanity could form;
the mind kept cool, the heart kept warm;
therein the miracle, three days and nights
so many dances played and so much drinking done,
so many voices raised in singing but none
in anger nor any fist in harm—
Saint Patrick's Day in Cambridge Circus might
have been some other nation's trough of shame.

Hotel-back-room, pub-snug, and large open lounges
made the mean street like a Latin fête,
music for once taking all harm out—
from even the bunting's pathetic blunderings,
and the many mean publicans making money fast,
hand over fat fist, pouring the flat
western porter from black-chipped white enamel,
Dervorgilla's penitent chapel
crumbling arch archaic but east,
only music now releasing her people
like Sweeney's cousins on a branch unable

to find his words, but using music
for all articulateness.

But still the shabby county-town was full,
en fête; on fire with peace—for all
the black-and-white contortionists bred
from black and white enamel ever said.
From Easter Snow and Scartaglin
the men with nimble fingers came
in dowdy Sunday suits,
from Kirkintilloch and Ladbroke Grove came back
in flashy ties and frumpish hats,
to play an ancient music, make it new.
A stranger manner of telling than words can do,
a strange manner, both less and more than words or Bach,
but like, that Whitsuntide, a stained-glass in summer,
high noon, rose window, Benedictbeuern pleasure,
and Seán Ó Neachtain's loving singing wood,
an Nollaig sa tSamhradh.*

Owls and eagles, clerks and navvies,
ex-British Tommies in drab civvies,
and glorious-patriots whose wild black brindled hair
stood up for the trench-coats they had no need to wear
that tranquil carnival weekend,
when all the boastful maladies got cured—
the faction-fighting magniloquence,
devoid of charity or amorous sense,
the sun-shunning pubs, the trips to Knock.

One said to me: "There's heart in that,"
pointing at: a thick-set man of middle age,
a thick red drinker's face,
and eyes as bright as good stained-glass,
who played on and on and on
a cheap tin-whistle, as if no race
for petty honours had ever come to pass
on earth, or his race to a stale pass;
tapping one black boot on a white flag,
and us crowding, craning, in at the door,
gaining, and storing up, the heart in that.

With him a boy about eighteen,
tall and thin, but, easy to be seen.
Clare still written all over him
despite his eighteen months among the trim
scaffoldings and grim digs of England;
resting his own tin-whistle for his mentor's riff,
pushing back, with a big red hand, the dank mousy quiff,
turning to me to say, "You know what I think of it,
over there?
                    Over there, you're free."
Repeating the word "free," as gay and sad as his music,
repeating the word, the large bright eyes convinced
of what the red mouth said, convinced beyond
shaming or furtiveness, a thousand preachers,
mothers and leader-writers wasting their breath
on the sweet, foggy, distant-city air.
Then he went on playing as if there never were
either a famed injustice or a parish glare.

    Ennis

Gaeltacht*   *for Liam Brady*

Bartley Costello, eighty years old,
sat in his silver-grey tweeds on a kitchen chair,
at his door in Carraroe, the sea only yards away,
smoking a pipe, with a pint of porter beside his boot:
"For the past twenty years I've eaten nothing only
periwinkles, my own hands got them off those rocks.
You're a quarter my age, if you'd stick to winkles
you'd live as long as me, and keep as spry."

In the Liverpool Bar, at the North Wall,
on his way to join his children over there,
an old man looked at me, then down at his pint
of rich Dublin stout. He pointed at the black glass:
"Is lú í an Ghaeilge ná an t-uisce sa ngloine sin."*

Beartla Confhaola, prime of his manhood,
driving between the redweed and the rock-fields,

driving through the sunny treeless quartz glory of Carna,
answered the foreigners' glib pity, pointing at the
small black cows: "You won't get finer anywhere
than those black porry cattle." In a pub near there,
one of the locals finally spoke to the townie:
"Labhraim le stráinséirí. Creidim gur chóir bheith
ag labhairt le stráinséirí." Proud as a man who'd claim:
"I made an orchard of a rock-field,
bougainvillea clamber my turf-ricks."

A Dublin tourist on a red-quarter strand
hunting firewood found the ruins of a boat,
started breaking the struts out—an old man came,
he shook his head and said:
"Áá, a mhac: ná bí ag briseadh báid."

The low walls of rock-fields in the west
are a beautiful clean whitegrey. There are chinks between
the neat stones to let the wind through safe,
you can see the blue sun through them.
But coming eastward in the same county,
the walls grow higher, darkgrey:
an ugly grey. And the chinks disappear:
through those walls you can see nothing.

Then at last you come to the city,
beautiful with salmon basking becalmed black below
a bridge over the pale-green Corrib; and ugly
with many shopkeepers looking down on men like
Bartley Costello and Beartla Confhaola because they
speak in Irish, eat periwinkles, keep
small black porry cattle, and on us
because we are strangers.

Bright after Dark

for Sebastian Ryan

In the first country,
what you must do when the cow stops giving milk
is climb, after dark, a certain hill,
and play the flute: to kill your scheming neighbour's curse.

If you can find a silver flute to play,
the spell will break all the faster, the surer.
But silver is not essential. But: the job must
be done after dark:
otherwise, it won't work.

In the second country,
when you send a child out of the house at night,
after dark, you must, if you wish it well,
take, from the fire, a burnt-out cinder
and place it on the palm of the child's hand
to guard the child against the dangers of the dark.
The cinder, in this good function, is called aingeal,
meaning angel.

In the third country,
if you take a journey at night, above all
in the blind night of ebony, so good for witches to work in,
you dare not rely on fireflies for light,
for theirs is a brief, inconstant glow. What you must hope
is that someone before you has dropped grains of maize
on the ground to light your way; and you must drop
grains of maize for whoever comes after you:
for only maize can light the way on a dark night.*

Movement

The blind men stumble round
a small, unmoving bird
they feel is brightly coloured
on a grey field.

Achnasheen

for Eoghan Ó Néill

"You'd miss the Gaelic from the placenames,"
you said, turning from the danger-seat to me in the back swigging Talisker,
driving through Wester Ross making for the Kyle of Lochalsh.
And the next signpost we came to was Achnasheen.*

How could there be any Gaelic "for" Achnasheen?
It isn't Gaelic any more. It could never be English.
Despite the murderous maps,
despite the bereft roadsigns,
despite the casual distortions of illiterate scribes,
the name remains beautiful. A maimed beauty.

Hiding behind it somewhere
its real name.

You'd almost think the conquerors thought
Gaelic was God:
its real name unnameable.

And I remembered the first-time crossing the Border,
not the Highland Line but the one from Cavan into "Ulster,"
and missing the Gaelic placenames, the maiming ugliness of that;
guessing the real names, failing to guess, the irk of that,
like a horsehair down the back.

The Gaelic names beating their wings madly
behind the mad cage of English;
the new names half the time transparent, but half the time
silent as the grave
                        English would bury Irish in.

Later we saw Beinn Ailleagan: the jewelled mountain—
but not called that but keeping its true name:
Beinn Ailleagan
                        wearing its name like a jewel
upon its snow-white breast
                                    like the jewel of the Gaelic tongue
that old men and young women keep shining and singing
all over the Catholic islands and the Calvinist
islands for all the invader
and his canting quisling ministers could reek.

And will the black sticks of the devil, Eoghan,
ever pipe us into heaven at last—
as one night down the torchlit street of Áth Dara—
into a heaven of freedom to give
things back
                        their true names?

Like streets in Barcelona,
like Achnasheen,
Belfast*

The Frost is All Over   *for Michael Hartnett*

To kill a language is to kill a people.
The Aztecs knew far better: they took over
their victims' language, kept them carving
obsidian beauties, weeded their religion
of dangerous gentleness, and winged them blood-flowers
(that's a different way to kill a people).
The Normans brought and grew, but Honor Croome
could never make her Kerryman verse English:
Traherne was in the music of his tears.

We have no glint or caution who we are:
our patriots dream wolfhounds in their portraits,
our vendors pose in hunting-garb, the nightmare
forelock tugging madly at some lost leash.
The Vikings never hurt us, xenophilia
means bland servility, we insult
ourselves and Europe with artificial trees,
and coins as gelt of beauty now
as, from the start, of power.

Like Flemish words on horseback, tongue survives
in turns of speech the telly must correct;
our music bows and scrapes on the world's platforms,
each cat-gut wears a rigorous bow-tie.
The frost, we tell them, is all over, and they love
our brogue so much they give us guns to kill
ourselves, our language, and all the other gooks.

Bobrowski would have understood, he found
some old, surviving words of a murdered language,
and told a few friends; but he knew how to mourn,
a rare talent, a need not many grant.

To call a language dead before it dies
means to bury it alive; some tongues do die
from hours or days inside the coffin, and when
the tearful killers dig it up they find
the tongue, like Suarez, bitten to its own bone.
Others explode in the church, and stain the bishop,
whose priest could speak no Gaelic to his "flock"
but knew to sink a splendid tawny goblet
as deep as any master of the hunt.

Is Carleton where the tenderness must hide?
Or would they have the Gaelic words, like insects,
crawl up the legs of horses, and each bite,
or startle, be proclaimed a heritage?
Are those who rule us, like their eager voters,
ghosts yearning for flesh? Ghosts are cruel,
and ghosts of suicides more cruel still.
To kill a language is to kill one's self.

Summer 1973

She Fell Asleep in the Sun

"She fell asleep in the sun."

That's what they used to say
in South Fermanagh
of a girl who gave birth
unwed.

A woman from Kerry told me
what she'd always heard growing up was
leanbh ón ngréin:
a child from the sun.

And a friend of mine from Tiernahilla
admired in North Tipperary
a little lad running round a farmyard
the boy's granda smiled:
"garsúinín beag mishtake."*

A lyrical ancient kindliness
that could with Christ accord.
Can it outlive technolatry?
or churches?

Not to mention that long, leadránach,
latinate, legal, ugly
twelve-letter name not
worthy to be called a name,
that murderous obscenity—to call

any child ever born
that excuse for a name
could quench the sun for ever.*

Barnsley Main Seam   *for Peter Kiddle*

Impeccable snow, eternally fresh, gold-clustering—
limitless icefield sparkled with golden igloos,
an ordered sprinkling, all mathematics
made sumptuous like the sound
of Ceva's theorem—the whole ceiling
so boundless a roof so soaring
as almost babellious in its worship,
                              Vatican-voluptuous,
higher than God's own sky,
higher and whiter than even serenest
clouds over the Brecklands. Look! look up
at us, honey-knobs, pommes mousseline:
perfection of man's making—

Yet for-all-that a feast, true, an even chaste
feast for spirit as for eye—
Stefansdom, Gaudí—
and for-all-that more accessible
to the tiny floored nape craning up
(like Čapek flat on his back in the pocked Alhambra)
than the Five Grey Sisters:
                              grey-stained infinite-oblong glass,

austerest glass, how rich a grey,
an almost velvet grey, bleak brocade,
stuff so harsh hauteur
                              you'd never want to stroke,
noli-me-tangere-vaginistic charm—
and flat on his back forever
the lissome silvery armour-body of young Prince William,
only thirteen, poor mite,
endless gazing sightless up
at buttertub slobs in a muslin-spud expanse,
no Amsterdancing prinsiade now for him,
his long grey slim steel as graced
as the five giant Sisters but him stretched
only one young boy, not five pious bayonets,
just one dead boy who never chose
to be born a prince but perhaps more easily
forgot he didn't
                      than
the miners who made the timber model
of Barnsley Main Seam*

Not of high stone
not of deep coal
not of gold snow
nor grey glass
they built their small model
nestling modest into the minster wall:
"The Tribute of the Yorkshire Miners
to the Minster"—
or so it says and there the little model men are
not in sumptuous colours woven
not in bleak brocade
but well worked in wood
working away at the coal face—

A hunk of white bread, spattered in blood,
and a black rag, aloft on a pike:
the hungry women of Honiton made their protest clear.
But that was in the bad old days, long before
enlightened centuries when the milk-thief drove
Derby and Merthyr Tydfil to hunger-strike.*

Black white and red, those women planting a pike
in high gold-spattered snow
like a dominion flag in a polar icefield:
were *they* in the miners' minds when
they made
and gave
that blunt, matter-of-fact model of a pit-place,
dwarfed by antique splendour,
dwarfing splendour?

Were those riotous women and all the toiling mothers
of miners and masons and all the guilds and all
the muscle called unskilled
back to the tower of Babel and Brú na Bóinne*
deep in the miners' minds? as though to say
to all antique splendour (so buoyant still):
Men like us made you,
without us
you could not be.

Did Primitivo Pérez from
Where the Air is Clear*
signing his name in the big book in the narthex
buying a minster minute
observe the miners' tribute, how
clear the sacred air must be
down pit?
Young miners flaunting shoulder-bags in the cage
grinning all over their glad eyes
ready for a prinsiade but
the old honey walls
of York are a different colour entirely—
and is there honey still for tea
in Honiton?
Or black bread, white faces, bad blood?

British Justice

*for Paddy Joe Hill**

For British
　　read English.
For Justice
　　read Law.

Legend

The Russian word for beautiful
is the Russian word for red.
The Chinese word for silk
is the Chinese word for love.

Beautiful red silk love.

Silk isn't always red—
is love always beautiful?
When you are with me,
yes.

Yet Another Reason for Writing in Irish

"He"
is cold,
hard,
weak.

"She"
is warm,
soft,
strong.

Manifesto

Universal courtesy—
now that would be
revolutionary

Two Young Men

Two young men in Belfast fell in love,
hands reaching out in real peace
across the dangerous peace-line.
They gave each other pleasure—
maybe even happiness, who knows?—
and one day the protestant lad
gave his catholic lover
a plant from his window-sill,
a warm geranium.

Then the catholic street was torched,
and the catholic boy killed.
His lover ran both gauntlets
across the god-fearing city
and rescued back, against the odds,
that plant of trust,
his flower of love.

That flower was all his own now,
his loss replete.

2000

River

for Sujata Bhatt

She plucked a flower and leaving the village
walked as far as the river.
She stood for a minute, watching the water move,
then bending down she placed—not cast—

the flower on the water.
Standing there for a short while, relaxing,
she watched the river carry the flower away,
till it was out of sight beyond the trees.
Then she walked back home.

Richard Murphy (1927–)

When Richard Murphy calls the village of Aughrim "the navel of the country" in an essay entitled "The Use of History in Poetry," he is in part recognizing its geographical place "in the center of Ireland." But the town and the battle that took place there are of central importance in Irish history, as well. "My connection with it was accidental at first," Murphy recalls, when he describes his initial encounter with the town whose history would play a pivotal role in his own career as a poet. Like Henry James sensing the *donnée* of a novel in a seemingly insignificant event of daily life, Murphy "felt an ominous sense" of history and poetical potential at Aughrim during an accustomed car trip between Dublin and his one-time home in Connemara. "That was the germ," he recalled, "of what became a long sequence of poems—not an epic, because nowadays, certainly in this century, the epic has been taken over by the historical novel—but a way of coming at certain events in our past that have shaped the country we live in today."[1]

The sequence that grew from this germ was "The Battle of Aughrim," a long narrative work in several sections, each comprising a number of meditative, lyrical subsections that are closer to dramatic monologue than to epic. The poem integrates Murphy's own experience and family history with legends and historical accounts of the battle, so that personality shapes history. Murphy's later comments on the poem make no pretense to objectivism: "I was harsher, I think, on the Protestant side because I was reared on that side and because I was living at the time in a small fishing village on the west coast of Ireland with Catholic friends." Throughout the poem, Murphy's speaking voice confesses to guilt that wells up from the roots of his family tree, and as a result the historical situation of the battle takes on a palpable presence otherwise lost in documentary evidence: "Sifting clay on a mound, I find / Bones and bullets fingering my mind: / The past is happening today." What's happening, the great loss of life, Murphy goes on to say, "Has a beginning in my blood."[2]

In the widely read early poem "Sailing to an Island," Murphy documents a sailing trip that turns into a similar search for the tangible reality of history on Clare Island off the western coast of Ireland:

> We point all day for our chosen island,
> Clare, with its crags purpled by legend:
> There under castles the hot O'Malleys,
> Daughters of Granuaile, the pirate queen
> Who boarded a Turk with a blunderbuss,
> Comb red hair and assemble cattle.[3]

A storm hits before the boat can make Clare, though, and the questers wind up spending the night at Inishbofin, where history comes alive in words as the local fishermen, a "whispering spontaneous reception committee," relate the story of a previous storm that killed nine of their number. This shift of attention in "Sailing to an Island" from the legends of Gaelic Ireland to the circumscribed reality of contemporary rural life mirrors Murphy's concern with the antagonisms that stretch across Irish history. At an elementary level Murphy sees these worked out in the central duality of his work, the play between his English education and Irish feeling. His approach to the battle of Aughrim caught hold of the literal conflict between English and Irish armies as one metaphor for the struggle he himself experiences as an internal one.

Murphy was born in County Galway in 1927, but spent a portion of his early life in Ceylon, the country now known as Sri Lanka, where his father was an official of the British colonial government. He was sent to school in England at an early age, and eventually won a scholarship to Magdalen College, Oxford. His tenure at Oxford was interrupted, though, when he spent a part of a term in a rented cottage in Connemara. Murphy returned to Magdalen and eventually completed an M.A. degree, but his experience of rural Ireland would continue to stand in a tense relationship with his Oxford education. Perhaps more crucial to his poetry than the obvious distinction between English and Irish influences is the more subtle delineation between his aristocratic Anglo-Irish heritage and the Catholic present in which he has placed himself. Between the two, Seamus Heaney argues, is "the constricted space [Murphy] moves in and writes out of . . . a space at once as neutral and torn as the battlefield at Aughrim . . . sometimes nostalgic for the imperial, patrician past, sometimes hospitable to deprivations and disasters that somehow rebuke that heritage."[4]

Murphy, in recent years, has discovered the poetic version of this ironically

charged neutrality less in the narrative line of history than in the multivalent im-
plications of the words that transmit and make it. This discovery of the history
embedded in language is perhaps a natural development of his portrayal of the
speakers that figure in his early poems as more vital for the way they give voice to
history than for the content of the stories they tell. "Sailing to an Island" finds
that its safe port coincides with the whispering voices of fishermen, while the
monologues of "The Battle of Aughrim" bring to life material that Murphy found
dead in documentary narratives; the life is in the language brought to life by
voices. "I believe that the best, the most important, history in all poetry is in the
words themselves," he writes, "the history that is latent in all the words we use.
To a poet that is the most important history—the etymology of words. And when
history is assumed into the body of the poem and becomes another sense of it, as
when it is assumed in the words themselves, then it is of more value than writing
poems about history."[5]

NOTES

1. Richard Murphy, "The Use of History in Poetry," in Audrey S. Eyler and Robert F. Garratt,
eds., *The Uses of the Past: Essays on Irish Culture* (Newark, Delaware: University of Delaware
Press, 1988), p. 19.

2. "The Battle of Aughrim," in Richard Murphy, *New Selected Poems* (London: Faber and
Faber, 1985), p. 54.

3. "Sailing to an Island," *New Selected Poems*, p. 3.

4. Seamus Heaney, "The Poetry of Richard Murphy," *Irish University Review*, vol. 7, no. 1
(Spring 1977), p. 19.

5. Richard Murphy, "The Use of History in Poetry," p. 23.

Sailing to an Island

The boom above my knees lifts, and the boat
Drops, and the surge departs, departs, my cheek
Kissed and rejected, kissed, as the gaff sways
A tangent, cuts the infinite sky to red
Maps, and the mast draws eight and eight across
Measureless blue, the boatmen sing or sleep.

We point all day for our chosen island,
Clare, with its crags purpled by legend:
There under castles the hot O'Malleys,
Daughters of Granuaile, the pirate queen*
Who boarded a Turk with a blunderbuss,
Comb red hair and assemble cattle.
Across the shelved Atlantic groundswell
Plumbed by the sun's kingfisher rod,
We sail to locate in sea, earth and stone
The myth of a shrewd and brutal swordswoman
Who piously endowed an abbey.
Seven hours we try against wind and tide,
Tack and return, making no headway.
The north wind sticks like a gag in our teeth.

Encased in a mirage, steam on the water,
Loosely we coast where hideous rocks jag,
An acropolis of cormorants, an extinct
Volcano where spiders spin, a purgatory
Guarded by hags and bristled with breakers.

The breeze as we plunge slowly stiffens:
There are hills of sea between us and land,
Between our hopes and the island harbour.
A child vomits. The boat veers and bucks.
There is no refuge on the gannet's cliff.
We are far, far out: the hull is rotten,
The spars are splitting, the rigging is frayed,
And our helmsman laughs uncautiously.

What of those who must earn their living
On the ribald face of a mad mistress?
We in holiday fashion know
This is the boat that belched its crew
Dead on the shingle in the Cleggan disaster.*

Now she dips, and the sail hits the water.
She luffs to a squall; is struck; and shudders.
Someone is shouting. The boom, weak as scissors,
Has snapped. The boatman is praying.
Orders thunder and canvas cannonades.
She smothers in spray. We still have a mast;
The oar makes a boom. I am told to cut
Cords out of fishing-lines, fasten the jib.
Ropes lash my cheeks. Ease! Ease at last:
She swings to leeward, we can safely run.
Washed over rails our Clare Island dreams,
With storm behind us we straddle the wakeful
Waters that draw us headfast to Inishbofin.

The bows rock as she overtakes the surge.
We neither sleep nor sing nor talk,
But look to the land where the men are mowing.
What will the islanders think of our folly?

The whispering spontaneous reception committee
Nods and smokes by the calm jetty.
Am I jealous of these courteous fishermen
Who hand us ashore, for knowing the sea
Intimately, for respecting the storm
That took nine of their men on one bad night
And five from Rossadillisk in this very boat?
Their harbour is sheltered. They are slow to tell
The story again. There is local pride
In their home-built ships.
We are advised to return next day by the mail.

But tonight we stay, drinking with people
Happy in the monotony of boats,
Bringing the catch to the Cleggan market,
Cultivating fields, or retiring from America
With enough to soak till morning or old age.

The bench below my knees lifts, and the floor
Drops, and words depart, depart, with faces
Blurred by the smoke. An old man grips my arm,
His shot eyes twitch, quietly dissatisfied.
He has lost his watch, an American gold
From Boston gas-works. He treats the company
To the secretive surge, the sea of his sadness.
I slip outside, fall among stones and nettles,
Crackling dry twigs on an elder tree,
While an accordion drones above the hill.

Later, I reach a room, where the moon stares
Through a cobwebbed window. The tide has ebbed,
Boats are careened in the harbour. Here is a bed.

The Last Galway Hooker

Where the Corrib river chops through the Claddagh*
To sink in the tide-race its rattling chain
The boatwright's hammer chipped across the water

Ribbing this hooker, while a reckless gun
Shook the limestone quay-wall, after the Treaty
Had brought civil war to this fisherman's town.

That "tasty" carpenter from Connemara, Cloherty,
Helped by his daughter, had half planked the hull
In his eightieth year, when at work he died,

And she did the fastening, and caulked her well,
The last boat completed with old Galway lines.
Several seasons at the drift-nets she paid

In those boom-years, working by night in channels
With trammel and spillet and an island crew,
Tea-stew on turf in the pipe-black forecastle,

Songs of disasters wailed on the quay
When the tilt of the water heaved the whole shore.
"She was lucky always, the *Ave Maria,*"

With her brown sails, and her sleek skin of tar,
Her forest of oak ribs and larchwood planks,
Cut limestone ballast, costly fishing gear,

Fastest in the race to the gull-marked banks,
What harbour she hived in, there she was queen
And her crew could afford to stand strangers drinks,

Till the buyers failed in nineteen twenty-nine,
When the cheapest of fish could find no market,
Were dumped overboard, the price down to nothing;

Until to her leisure a fisher priest walked
By the hungry dockside, full of her name,
Who made a cash offer, and the owners took it.

Then like a girl given money and a home
With no work but pleasure for her man to perform
She changed into white sails, her hold made room

For hammocks and kettles, the touch and perfume
Of priestly hands. So now she's a yacht
With pitch-pine spars and Italian hemp ropes,

Smooth-running ash-blocks expensively bought
From chandlers in Dublin, two men get jobs
Copper-painting her keel and linseeding her throat,

While at weekends, nephews and nieces in mobs
Go sailing on picnics to the hermit islands,
Come home flushed with health having hooked a few dabs.

*

Munich, submarines, and the war's demands
Of workers to feed invaded that party
Like fumes of the diesel the dope of her sails,

When the priest was moved inland to Athenry
From the stone and reed patches of lobstermen
Having sold her to Michael Schofield, PC,

Who was best of the boatsmen from Inishbofin,
She his best buy. He shortened the mast, installed
A new "Ailsa Craig,"* made a hold of her cabin,

Poured over the deck thick tar slightly boiled;
Every fortnight he drained the sump in the bilge
"To preserve the timbers." All she could do, fulfilled.

The sea, good to gamblers, let him indulge
His fear when she rose winding her green shawl
And his pride when she lay calm under his pillage:

And he never married, was this hooker's lover,
Always ill-at-ease in houses or on hills,
Waiting for weather, or mending broken trawls:

Bothered by women no more than by the moon,
Not concerned with money beyond the bare need,
In this boat's bows he sheathed his life's harpoon.

A neap-tide of work, then a spring of liquor
Were the tides that alternately pulled his soul,
Now on a pitching deck with nets to hand-haul,

Then passing Sunday propped against a barrel
Winding among words like a sly helmsman
Till stories gathered around him in a shoal.

She was Latin blessed, holy water shaken
From a small whiskey bottle by a surpliced priest,
Madonnas wafered on every bulkhead,

Oil-grimed by the diesel, and her luck lasted
Those twenty-one years of skill buoyed by prayers,
Strength forged by dread from his drowned ancestors.

She made him money and again he lost it
In the fisherman's fiction of turning farmer:
The cost of timber and engine spares increased,

Till a phantom hurt him, ribs on a shore,
A hulk each tide rattles that will never fish,
Sunk back in the sand, a story finished.

*

We met here last summer, nineteen fifty-nine,
Far from the missiles, the moon-shots, the money,
And we drank looking out on the island quay,

When his crew were in London drilling a motorway.
Pricing the priceless, I made a fair offer
For the *Ave Maria,* and he agreed to sell.

Then he was alone, stunned like a widower—
Relics and rowlocks pronging from the wall,
A pot of boiling garments, winter everywhere,

Especially in his bones, watching things fall,
Hooks of three-mile spillets, trammels at the foot
Of the unused double-bed—his mind threaded with all

The marline of his days twined within that boat,
His muscles' own shackles then staying the storm
Which now snap to bits like frayed thread.

*

So I chose to renew her, to rebuild, to prolong
For a while the spliced yards of yesterday.
Carpenters were enrolled, the ballast and the dung

Of cattle he'd carried lifted from the hold,
The engine removed, and the stale bilge scoured.
De Valera's* daughter hoisted the Irish flag

At her freshly adzed mast this Shrove Tuesday,
Stepped while afloat between the tackle of the *Topaz*
And the *St John,* by Bofin's best boatsmen,

All old as himself. Her ghostly sailmaker,
Her inherited boatwright, her dream-tacking steersman
Picked up the tools of their interrupted work,

And in memory's hands this hooker was restored.
Old men my instructors, and with all new gear
May I handle her well down tomorrow's sea-road.

from The Battle of Aughrim

1. Now

On Battle Hill

Who owns the land where musket-balls are buried
In the blackthorn roots on the esker, the drained bogs
Where sheep browse, and credal war miscarried?
Names in the rival churches are written on plaques.

Behind the dog-rose ditch, defended with pikes,
A tractor sprays a rood of flowering potatoes:
Morning fog is lifting, and summer hikers
Bathe in a stream passed by cavalry traitors.

A Celtic cross by the road commemorates no battle
But someone killed in a car, Minister of Agriculture.
Dairy lorries on the fast trunk-route rattle:
A girl cycles along the lane to meet her lover.

Flies gyrate in their galaxy above my horse's head
As he ambles and shies close to the National School—
Bullets under glass, Patrick Sarsfield's "Would to God . . ."
And jolts me bareback on the road for Battle Hill:

Where a farmer with a tinker woman hired to stoop
Is thinning turnips by hand, while giant earth-movers
Shovel and claw a highway over the rector's glebe:
Starlings worm the aftergrass, a barley crop silvers,

And a rook tied by the leg to scare flocks of birds
Croaks as I dismount at the death-cairn of St Ruth:
Le jour est à nous, mes enfants, his last words:
A cannonball beheaded him, and sowed a myth.

History

One morning of arrested growth
An army list roll-called the sound
Of perished names, but I found no breath
In dog-eared inventories of death.

Touch unearths military history.
Sifting clay on a mound, I find
Bones and bullets fingering my mind:
The past is happening today.

The battle cause, a hand grenade
Lobbed in a playground, the king's viciousness
With slaves succumbing to his rod and kiss,
Has a beginning in my blood.

2. Before

Legend

The story I have to tell
Was told me by a teacher
Who read it in a poem
Written in a dying language.
Two hundred and fifty years ago
The poet recalled
Meeting a soldier who had heard
From veterans of the war
The story I have to tell.

Deep red bogs divided
Aughrim, the horse's ridge
Of garland hedgerows and the summer dance,
Ireland's defence
From the colonists' advance:
Twenty thousand soldiers on each side,
Between them a morass
Of godly bigotry and pride of race,
With a causeway two abreast could cross.

In opposite camps our ancestors
Ten marriages ago,
Caught in a feud of absent kings
Who used war like a basset table
Gambling to settle verbal things,
Decide if bread be God
Or God a parable,
Lit matches, foddered horses, thirsted, marched,
Halted, and marched to battle.

Planter

Seven candles in silver sticks,
Water on an oval table,
The painted warts of Cromwell
Framed in a sullen gold.
There was ice on the axe
When it hacked the king's head.
Moths drown in the dripping wax.

Slow sigh of the garden yews
Forty years planted.
May the God of battle
Give us this day our land
And the papists be trampled.
Softly my daughter plays
Sefauchi's Farewell.

Dark night with no moon to guard
Roads from the rapparees,
Food at a famine price,
Cattle raided, corn trod,
And the servants against us
With our own guns and swords.
Stress a hymn to peace.

Quiet music and claret cups,
Forty acres of green crops
Keep far from battle
My guest, with a thousand troops
Following his clan-call,
Red-mouthed O'Donnell.
I bought him: the traitor sleeps.

To whom will the land belong
This time tomorrow night?
I am loyal to fields I have sown
And the king reason elected:
Not to a wine-blotted birth mark
Of prophecy, but hard work
Deepening the soil for seed.

Rapparees

Out of the earth, out of the air, out of the water
And slinking nearer the fire, in groups they gather:
Once he looked like a bird, but now a beggar.

This fish rainbows out of a pool: "Give me bread!"
He fins along the lake shore with the starved.
Green eyes glow in the night from clumps of weed.

The water is still. A rock or the nose of an otter
Jars the surface. Whistle of rushes or bird?
It steers to the bank, it lands as a pikeman armed.

With flint and bundles of straw a limestone hall
Is gutted, a noble family charred in its sleep,
And they gloat by moonlight on a mound of rubble.

The highway trees are gibbets where seventeen rot
Who were caught last week in a cattle-raid.
The beasts are lowing. "Listen!" "Stifle the guard!"

In a pinewood thickness an earthed-over charcoal fire
Forges them guns. They melt lead stripped from a steeple
For ball. At the drumming of a snipe each can disappear

Terrified as a bird trapped in a gorse fire,
To delve like a mole or mingle like a nightjar
Into the earth, into the air, into the water.

3. During

St Ruth

St Ruth trots on a silver mare
Along the summit of the ridge,
Backed by a red cavalcade
Of the King's Life Guards.
He wears a blue silk tunic,
A white lace cravat,
Grey feathers in his hat.

He has made up his mind to put
The kingdom upon a fair combat:

Knowing he cannot justify
Losing Athlone
Before his Most Christian master,
He means to bury his body
In Ireland, or win.

The army commander only speaks
French and Italian:
His army speaks either
English or Irish.
When he gives an order
His jowls bleach and blush
Like turkeycock's dewlap.

Lieutenant-General Charles Chalmont,
Marquis of St Ruth
The Prince of Condé's disciple
In the music of war,
Jerks with spinal rapture
When a volley of musket fire
Splits his ear.

Picture his peregrine eyes,
A wife-tormentor's thin
Heraldic mouth, a blue
Stiletto beard on his chin,
And a long forked nose
Acclimatized to the sulphurous
Agony of Huguenots.

He keeps his crab-claw tactics
Copied from classical books
An unbetrayable secret
From his army of Irishmen.
He rides downhill to correct
A numerical mistake
In his plan's translation.

He throws up his hat in the air,
The time is near sunset,
He knows victory is sure,
One cavalry charge will win it.

"Le jour est à nous, mes enfants,"
He shouts. The next minute
His head is shot off.

The Winning Shot

Mullen had seen St Ruth riding downhill
And Kelly held a taper. "There's the Frenchman!"
Trench laid the cannon, a breeze curved the ball.

The victory charge was halted. Life Guards stooped down
And wrapped the dripping head in a blue cloak,
Then wheeled and galloped towards the setting sun.

Chance, skill and treachery all hit the mark
Just when the sun's rod tipped the altar hill:
The soldiers panicked, thinking God had struck.

Sarsfield

Sarsfield rides a chestnut horse
At the head of his regiment,
His mountainous green shoulders
Tufted with gold braid,
Over his iron skull-piece
He wears the white cockade.
A bagpipe skirls.

Last summer after the Boyne
When King James had run,
He smashed the Dutch usurper's
Waggon-train of cannon
Benighted at Ballyneety.
Patrick Sarsfield, Earl of Lucan
Commands the reserve today.

The saviour of Limerick knows
Nothing of St Ruth's plan,
Not even that the battle
Of Aughrim has begun.
He has obeyed since dawn
The order to wait for further
Orders behind the hill.

He sees men run on the skyline
Throwing away muskets and pikes,
Then horsemen with sabres drawn
Cutting them down.
He hears cries, groans and shrieks.
Nothing he will do, or has done
Can stop this happening.

Luttrell

Luttrell on a black charger
At the rear of his regiment
Stands idle in a beanfield
Protected by a tower.
He wears a dandy yellow coat,
A white-feathered hat
And a gilded sabre.

When he hears the word spread
Along the line, "St Ruth is dead,"
He retreats at a trot:
Leading his priding cavalry
To betray the humble foot:
Ten miles to a dinner, laid
In a mansion, then to bed.

Prisoner

Night covers the retreat.
Some English troops beating a ditch for loot
Capture a wounded boy. "Don't shoot!"

"What'll we do with him?"
"I'll work in the camp." "Strip him!"
Naked he kneels to them. They light a lamp.

"Pretty boy." "Castrate the fucker!"
"Let the papist kiss my flute."
"Toss a coin for the privilege to bugger . . ."

He cries like a girl. "Finish him off."
"No, keep him alive to be our slave."
"Shove a sword up his hole." They laugh.

A tipsy officer calls out:
"You men be on parade at eight.
I want no prisoners, d'you hear me? Shoot

The crowd we took, when it gets light.
We've no more food. Good night.
God knows you all put up a splendid fight."

4. After

The Wolfhound

A wolfhound sits under a wild ash
Licking the wound in a dead ensign's neck.

When guns cool at night with bugles in fog
She points over the young face.

All her life a boy's pet.
Prisoners are sabred and the dead are stripped.

Her ear pricks like a crimson leaf on snow,
The horse carts creak away.

Vermin by moonlight pick
The tongues and sockets of six thousand skulls.

*

She pines for his horn to blow
To bay in triumph down the track of wolves.

Her forelegs stand like pillars through a siege,
His Toledo sword corrodes.

Nights she lopes to the scrub
And trails back at dawn to guard a skeleton.

Wind shears the berries from the rowan tree,
The wild geese have flown.

She lifts her head to cry
As a woman keens in a famine for her son.

*

A redcoat, stalking, cocks
His flintlock when he hears the wolfhound growl.

Her fur bristles with fear at the new smell,
Snow has betrayed her lair.

"I'll sell you for a packhorse,
You antiquated bigoted papistical bitch!"

She springs: in self-defence he fires his gun.
People remember this.

By turf embers she gives tongue
When the choirs are silenced in wood and stone.

Patrick Sarsfield's Portrait

Sarsfield, great-uncle in the portrait's grime,
Your emigration built your fame at home.
Landlord who never racked, you gave your rent
To travel with your mounted regiment.

Hotly you duelled for our name abroad
In Restoration wig, with German sword,
Wanting a vicious murder thrust to prove
Your Celtic passion and our Lady's love.

Gallant at Sedgemoor, cutting down for James
The scythe-armed yokels Monmouth led like lambs,
You thought it needed God's anointed king
To breathe our Irish winter into spring.

Your ashwood lance covered the Boyne retreat:
When the divine perfidious monarch's rout
From kindred enemy and alien friend
Darkened the land, you kindled Ireland.

At Limerick besieged, you led the dance:
"If this had failed, I would have gone to France."
When youths lit brandy in a pewter dish
You were their hazel nut and speckled fish.

A French duke scoffed: "They need no cannonballs
But roasted apples to assault these walls."
Sarsfield, through plague and shelling you held out;
You saved the city, lost your own estate.

Shunning pitched battle was your strategy:
You choose rapparee mountain routes to try
The enemy's morale, and blew his train
Of cannon skywards in the soft night rain.

Your king, who gave St Ruth supreme command,
Mistrusted you, native of Ireland.
"Await further orders," you were told
At Aughrim, when your plan was overruled.

You stood, while brother officers betrayed
By going, and six thousand Irish died.
Then you assumed command, but veered about:
Chose exile in your courteous conqueror's boat.

"Change kings with us, and we will fight again,"
You said, but sailed off with ten thousand men;
While women clutched the hawsers in your wake,
Drowning—it was too late when you looked back.

Only to come home stronger had you sailed:
Successes held you, and the French prevailed.
Coolly you triumphed where you wanted least,
On Flemish cornfield or at Versailles feast.

We loved you, horseman of the white cockade,
Above all, for your last words, "Would to God
This wound had been for Ireland." Cavalier,
You feathered with the wild geese our despair.

Battle Hill Revisited

Strangers visit the townland:
Called after wild geese, they fly though Shannon.

They know by instinct the sheepwalk
As it was before the great hunger and the exodus:

Also this cool creek of traitors.
They have come here to seek out ancestors.

They have read that the wind
Carried their forebears' gunsmoke, to make blind

The enemy, but nevertheless the Lord
Permitted the wicked to purify the good.

They know little about God
But something of the evil exploded by the word.

They are at the navel of an island
Driving slowly into well-drained battleground,

To follow the glacial esker
By the new signpost the credal slaughter,

Blood on a stone altar:
Seed, there should be seed, buried in a cairn.

If they listen, they may hear
Doubtless the litany of their houseled father.

Soon they located the dun
Where St Ruth spun the thread of his fatal plan:

They try to imagine
Exactly what took place, what it could mean,

Whether by will or by chance:
Then turn in time to catch a plane for France.

Seals at High Island

The calamity of seals begins with jaws.
Born in caverns that reverberate
With endless malice of the sea's tongue
Clacking on shingle, they learn to bark back
In fear and sadness and celebration.
The ocean's mouth opens forty feet wide
And closes on a morsel of their rock.

Swayed by the thrust and backfall of the tide,
A dappled grey bull and a brindled cow
Copulate in the green water of a cove.
I watch from a cliff-top, trying not to move.

Sometimes they sink and merge into black shoals;
Then rise for air, his muzzle on her neck,
Their winged feet intertwined as a fishtail.

She opens her fierce mouth like a scarlet flower
Full of white seeds; she holds it open long
At the sunburst in the music of their loving;
And cries a little. But I must remember
How far their feelings are from mine marooned.
If there are tears at this holy ceremony
Theirs are caused by brine and mine by breeze.

When the great bull withdraws his rod, it glows
Like a carnelian candle set in jade.
The cow ripples ashore to feed her calf;
While an old rival, eyeing the deed with hate,
Swims to attack the tired triumphant god.
They rear their heads above the boiling surf,
Their terrible jaws open, jetting blood.

At nightfall they haul out, and mourn the drowned,
Playing to the sea sadly their last quartet,
An improvised requiem that ravishes
Reason, while ripping scale up like a net:
Brings pity trembling down the rocky spine
Of headlands, till the bitter ocean's tongue
Swells in their cove, and smothers their sweet song.

Coppersmith

A temple tree grew in our garden in Ceylon.
We knew it by no other name.
The flower, if you turned it upside down,
Looked like a dagoba with an onion dome.
A holy perfume
Stronger than the evil tang of betel-nut
Enticed me into its shade on the stuffiest afternoon,

Where I stood and listened to the tiny hammer-stroke
Of the crimson coppersmith perched above my head,
His *took took took*
And his *tonk tonk tonk*
Were spoken in a language I never understood:
And there I began to repeat
Out loud to myself an English word such as *beat beat beat,*

Till hammering too hard I lost the meaning in the sound
Which faded and left nothing behind,
A blank mind,
The compound spinning round,
My brain melting, as if I'd stood in the sun
Too long without a topee and was going blind,
Till I and the bird, the word and the tree, were one.

Trouvaille

This root of bog-oak the sea dug up she found
Poking about, in old age, and put to stand
Between a snarling griffin and a half-nude man
Moulded of lead on my chimney-piece.
It looks like a heron rising from a pond,
Feet dipped in brown trout water,
Head shooting arrow-sharp into blue sky.

"What does it remind you of?" she wanted to know.
I thought of trees in her father's demesne
Levelled by chainsaws;
Bunches of primroses I used to pick
Before breakfast, hunting along a limestone lane,
To put at her bedside before she woke;
And all my childhood's broken promises.

No, no! It precedes alphabets,
Planted woods, or gods.
Twisted and honed as a mind that never forgets
It lay dead in bog acids, undecayable:

Secretively hardening in a womb of moss, until
The peat burnt off, a freak tide raised
The feathered stick she took to lure me home.

Connemara Quay

I should have done this, that and all those things
Goodwill intended when I was designed
To end the poor land's hunger. Failure brings
Catches that slip through nets too close to mind.

Men stood me up here, promising that I'd be
Their godsend: ocean would provide more food.
The green earth should have married the grey sea,
But fell foul of her storms, her moody tide.

Attached by strings of warps to my stone head,
Fine wooden craft came, to be overcome
By torpor. Keels took root in silt of seabed,
Ribbed frames rotted in a frayed hemp dream.

You played in these hulks half a century ago.
What did you think you might do? Now you know.

Friary

Each time you breathe my name—Ross Errilly—
Young leaf-growth rustles in the druid wood,
Felled to convert my land so thoroughly
Stone crosses stand on grass where forest stood.

Here the rain harps on ruins, plucking lost
Tunes from my structure, which the wind pours through
In jackdaw desecration, carping at the dust
And leprous sores my towers like beggars show.

Now my fish-ponds hold no water. Doors and aisles
Are stacked with donors' tombs, badly invested,
A gift for peeping toms: my lecherous gargoyles
Hacked off by thieves, the bones unresurrected.

Here, too, buried in rhyme, lovers lie dead,
Engraved in words that live each time they're read.

Anthony Cronin (1928–)

Anthony Cronin, born in 1928 in Enniscorthy, County Wexford, is widely known as the author of novels that reflect the literary life of modern Dublin and London. Cronin's close acquaintance with many of the literary figures of postwar Dublin enlivens both the novels and the collection of literary criticism he published as *A Question of Modernity*. In the nonfiction work *Dead as Doornails*, Cronin playfully documents the early tribulations of fellow Irish writers, giving sharp pictures of Brendan Behan and Patrick Kavanagh, among others. His portrait of the novelist Flann O'Brien, *No Laughing Matter*, was praised by Denis Donoghue as "an extremely telling document, written with the intelligence and generosity for which, not only in Ireland, he is admired."[1]

The wit and insight characteristic of Cronin's novels and memoirs also give a lively and discerning voice to his poetry. He has published several volumes of poems ranging in form from sonnet series to long narrative verse. Whatever the genre, Cronin's poetry is often preoccupied with criticizing mass society's ready acceptance of lies. His approach to truths that might replace specious ideas, however, is usually indirect. Cronin looks for deeper insight by focusing, paradoxically, on the surface details of daily life, attending to the drain smell in the street, the "gearings," and "descriptions" we wade through "[s]o that we may come to a point where the true images can re-exist."[2] The poet writes, Cronin insists, "to come to a hallstand, a fountain or a change of heart."[3] Each image, true to its particular referent, is at the same time a potential reservoir of human truths.

Cronin's most widely read poem is the long work "R.M.S. Titanic." The poem, published in 1960, has become influential in recent years for its apparent premonition of the Troubles that would erupt in the late 1960s. Cronin himself denies any prophetic impulse in the poem, but Paul Durcan calls attention to its foresight in understanding the coming turmoil in economic rather than sectarian terms; he cites as one of the poem's themes "Samuel Johnson's 'general massacre of gold.' The rich and the poor. The riff-raff of the English rich on the upper deck, and the emigrant Irish poor in the holds of hell below."[4] The poem has its origin in a film on the Titanic that Cronin saw in the early 1950s. Documentary facts, though, are of less importance to the poem's final structure than the legends about the disaster preserved from Cronin's childhood:

> that the ship foundered because anti-Papist slogans were painted on its hull by the Belfast shipyard workers; that the sinking caused a tidal wave; that the *S.S. California* lay in full sight of the doomed throughout; and that the band played "Nearer My God to Thee" to the end.[5]

Under pressure of these memories, the narrative of the disaster fractures into sections that conflate images of the ship with those of Ireland—itself adrift and in danger on the North Atlantic—and of the many Irish emigrants washing ashore to populate the doss-houses of London. It is, in other words, a story of adversity, dispersal and persistence that resonates throughout Cronin's poetry.

NOTES

1. Denis Donoghue, *Times Literary Supplement*, October 27, 1989, p. 1171.
2. "An Apology for Various Forms," *New and Selected Poems* (Dublin: Raven Arts Press, 1982), p. 135.
3. Ibid.
4. Introduction to *R.M.S. Titanic* (Dublin: Raven Arts Press, 1981), p. [5].
5. Afterword to *R.M.S. Titanic*, p. [23].

Writing

Our happiness is easily wronged by speech,
Being complete like silence, globed like summer,
Without extension in regret or wish.
Outside that sky are all our past and future.

So in those moments when we can imagine
The almost perfect, nearly true, we keep
The words away from it, content with knowledge,
Naming it only as we fall asleep.

In suffering we call out for another,
Describing with a desperate precision.
We must be sure that this is how all suffer.

Or be alone forever with the pain,
And all our search for words is one assertion:
You would forgive me if I could explain.

Surprise

Since we are told it we believe it's true,
Or does as it's intended. Birds eat worms,
The water flows downhill and aunts depart.
Sea heaves, sky rains and can be blue.
Always love cherishes and firelight warms.
That knocking sound you hear is just your heart.

Nothing is angry long and all surprises
Are well provided for. That dog that died
Became a legend and then had its day.
Sooner or later someone realises
That a mistake occurred and no one lied.
If it is said to be then that's the way.

But soon when doors are opened hints are found
Of strange disorders that have no because.
In one room on the ceiling is a stain.

Someone is missing who should be around.
Some games are stopped by arbitrary laws
And an odd I does things it can't explain.

Nothing is order now and no forecast
Can be depended on. The thing declared
To be may not be so. The dear face wears
A false expression. Yet the very last
Surprise of all still finds us unprepared:
Although we say I love you no one cares.

The Elephant to the Girl in Bertram Mills' Circus

I, like a slow, morose and shabby fatalist,
Unfitted for presumption, trousers too loose,
Shamble towards you, scented, delicate,
Your eyes glittering myopically back at the front rows,
Shoulder blades bared to me,
Imagining, although I cannot see
Your faintly trembling lips, white teeth, those fixed bright eyes,
Your desperate smile and stare.
I stoop, mournful that this should be
Over your lacquered hair,
My soft tongue touches it,
My loose pink lips enclose
Your closing eyes and nose,
Between the inside of your thighs
And the front rows' avid gaze
I drop my trunk.
Then you lean back, breasts taut
And grip my ears,
Abandoned to decision now you raise
Your legs and close them round my forehead bone
And we proceed on circuit, we alone,
You in my dark, my gravity, my space
Waiting for your release.
You are my victim, yes, but all my care,
Your face invisible and your shining hair

Within my mouth's pink softness,
My foul breath
Your fierce preoccupation.
The rest possess
Only your white long arms and legs,
Your backside's elevation
And whatever consolation
Lies in the fact that they can watch our progress.
Yet when I set
Gently your beautiful buttocks down again
And, lifting lip and trunk, reveal your face,
Your smile, your hair in place,
Only a slight
Worry about mucus mingles with your response
To them and their applause.
And when you twist and show on solid ground
Around the ring to all of them the tight
Behind and breasts which I have carried round,
And doing so invite
With effulgent wave and kiss
Them all to re-possess
The high-heeled girl that lately ran such risk—
I am the loser for my tenderness.

R.M.S. Titanic

I

Trembling with engines, gulping oil, the river
Under the factories glowering in the dark
Is home of the gulls and homeless; cold
Lights on the sucking tideway, scurf and sewage,
Gobbets of smoke and staleness and the smell,
The seaweed sour and morning smell of sea.

Here in the doss the river fog is dawn.
Under the yellow lights it twists like tapeworm,

Wreathes round the bulbs and, with the scent of urine,
Creeps down the bare board corridors, becomes
The sour, sweet breath of old men, sleepless, coughing.

Lights on the glistening metal, numinous fog
Feathering to mist, thin garlands hung
On the wet back of the Mersey. Out to sea
A great dawn heaves and tugs the tide past Crosby.

II

On the bog road the blackthorn flowers, the turf-stacks,
Chocolate brown, are built like bricks but softer,
And softer too the west of Ireland sky.
Turf smoke is chalked upon the darker blue
And leaves a sweet, rich, poor man's smell in cloth.
Great ragged rhododendrons sprawl through gaps
And pink and white the chestnut blossom tops
The tumbled granite wall round the demesne.
The high, brass-bound De Dion coughing past,
O'Conor Don and the solicitor,
Disturbs the dust but not the sleeping dogs.

Disturb the memories in an old man's head.
We only live one life, with one beginning.
The coming degradations of the heart
We who awake with all our landfalls staring
Back at us in the dawn, must hold our breath for.
The west is not awake to where *Titanic*
Smokes in the morning, huge against the stars.

III

No one spoke of this in the parlour bookcase.
R. M. Ballantyne held no hint of chaos.
There was no astonishing ship in the morning sky,
Slanting and falling in appalling ruin.
There was only the deliberate enunciation of an April Sunday
Announcing twelve o'clock:
A bobbined green cloth on the parlour table,

The prolonged anticipatory pleasure of a boy's boredom,
Church bells and baking smells, the buff and throaty hens.
A Protestant hymn vibrates in the musty sunlight,
Nearer my God to Thee, nearer to Thee.

O nothing so huge and wonderful as disaster
(Fenimore Cooper could have foretold that,
Or all of the foolish liars in the bookcase
Prognosticated something of the kind
In terms of a boy's heroics—
The long gashed hull, the officers, the boats)
But led by a cyclopedia to the slaughter,
Expecting a world of fountain pens and clippings;
And led like a romantic to the slaughter,
Imagining voices in the song-washed dusk.
O who in that bookcase foretold the derisive laughter?

IV

Those who lately took the notion
To cross the rolling and roaring Atlantic Ocean
Where the dead of the coffin ships once washed
To and fro on the shingle, shoals of corpses,
Ocean dividing the parishes of Bertraghboy and Boston,
Are battened now beside the pounding engines,
Oil and varnish floating on the darkness,
While it wanders like a headland through the North Atlantic,
Or like a city oscillating across a landscape,
Into whose basements the emigrants are crowded with their worries.
It is impossible not to feel for the poor of this nation
Sentiments of companionship and love,
For although the forgiving of misfortune is among the most dangerous of
      human operations,
In the alleyways of our need we turn for help
Not to those who judge but to those who do not care,
Companions now under the naked bulbs
In the communal forgetting of drunken consociation
Where the lies are allowed for an hour between one day and another.

V

Now Lightoller* sees with pride the order of reasonable magnitude
Bulking and glistening round him, metallic, echoing,
As he stands on his bridge over vibrating darkness,
A capable man and therefore entitled to pride,
And truly also neither a bore nor a prig;
Or at least on this April night of nineteen twelve,
Standing decent and quiet under the towering smokestacks,
While the great ship, lighted like late-night London,
Moves towards a rising and falling horizon over the respiring ocean
Into disaster he cannot foresee, has no reason to enquire
Into the truth he might not be able to endure.
Mr Lightoller, last of the line, now, let us take you, of likeable men,
As you move through the cloud of the night with a cap set square on your
    head
And your responsibilities shouldered,
For it is possible that there were such simplicities,
A schoolboy autumn order with no rot at the core,
Without the knowledge of interior and exterior degradations,
The cracked voice, the face crumbling into that of a fool or a bully
And already that of a bore:
But there will soon in the habited world be only the blind and the ruined,
The active who, claiming to be just, are devoid of compassion and self-
    knowledge,
And those who will never act again, who tremble with disgust,
The half men and the crippled, neither good,
Who demand from omnipotent god excluding dispensations,
Mercy and justice,
Or at best meet together in an obscene embrace
Like the criminal and the boyish police.
The limited man may act and judge, Mr Lightoller,
But prepare to incur some contempt.

VI

Down underneath the Irish poor are singing
Their songs of Philadelphia in the morning,
In comradeship romantically clinging

To those whom they would murder without warning.
A warm frieze crowd where every eye is crying
And all the songs are always of misfortune,
Inured to the snug, cosy slop of dying
They watch the grey rats creeping to the ocean.
Down here no one will judge, and all's forgiven.
Every man loves the thing he kills and slowly,
With many a tear the smiler does the knifing.
Down here the failure to redeem is holy.
Their songs of loss, of exile, desolation,
Hang on the wide still night. They shout of loving.
Each heart is full of black midnight emotion
And will create a sorrow for its proving.

Surely among the rich men's snowy linen
The dignified and decent can be found,
The stainless, crystal, cut-glass attitudes
And mouths shut on the boy's need to impress,
Instead of the hysterical moist palm,
The smiling urgencies of need and love,
The trader's charm, the clever one's reply.
Familiarities of skin and cloth
Clinging in fecundation to the sweat,
What won't wash out, the bit of shit on shirt,
The fungoid socks, the broken shoe, skinned heel,
The hanging round for hours, the aptly named,
Indeed intrusive, hand on the shoulder touch—
Surely the rich, who know the tiny shiver
Caressing the dry, lonely, selfish skin
Contrive to keep some attitudes intact,
Reptiles who change, three times a day, their cloth?

Sick in the bilboes of the world the poor
Cling to each other, but the rich cling more
Closely to the cruelty that prevents
The dissolution of the modelled stance,
The waxwork melting of the features down,
The blubber sympathy when sorrows drown.
Oh if this face concealed great pain we might
Call it necessity and concede its right,
But, multiplied in the racing mirrors here,
The eyes of money, vacantly severe,

The polished surfaces, the silver knives,
The gorgon heads which model the good lives
Presume a reckoning from the weak, the odd,
The young, to proffer to a glutton god.
The face of justice does not mask its grief
But emptiness and greed and disbelief,
A solemn bully's face, pretentious, grave,
Loathing the brother that it fears to save
Lest money and attendance might not get
Their due reward, their prior claims be met.
To all the decent scriveners it lied
Who bit upon that coin before they died
And found it hollow and who took the blame,
Bearing their own, their son's and father's shame.

VII

A tragedy is only one mistake,
Or the last in a series, making all irretrievable.
The tragic accident is the one which leaves
The knowledge that a desired possibility has been finally destroyed
By neglect, foolishness, or bad luck.
When the shock ran back along the narrow alleys
The lights were suddenly darkened,
Bringing the consciousness of error.
But although the voices rose again after the silence
The lights did not fully recover.
Then the engines stopped,
For now they were in the interval between two events,
The irretrievable mistake in the past
And the inevitable consequence in the future.
And as knowledge of the nature of the mistake grew in each mind
So did the penalty loom clearer out of the small hours.

VIII

Who can make plausible what happens?
Only the inexplicable rules
Over the worst of our lives,
The intimate degradations,
The disproportionate punishments

For the trivial mistakes.
Loud in the echoless night
Titanic is not alone,
Also enclosed by the sky
The *Californian's** lights
Deny necessity
And dignity to its fate.
Around her boarded decks
Fear infects the dark,
Slowly its floors slop down
Into the freezing peace
Of the calm and ridiculous sea.
Lightoller clings to the real,
The world that cannot be regained,
And those lustrous lights shine on
Like the ordinary overheard
After the end of the world.
They call out for help, they wait
For the casual world to reply,
But the *Californian's* lights,
Cosy in great, cold dark,
Simply inform the damned
The households are happy and safe.
Over and over again
Their rockets flare through the cold
But no answer at all returns
As from an inanimate phone
Incredibly ringing on
While the seconds expand in the head.
They stare at a shocking thing,
Mankind untouched by their fear,
The *Californian's* lights
Like a pierhead glistening there.
Nothing can ever explain
This further grotesque mischance,
Redeem with cause and effect
Their aloneness inside the vast
Cloud which obscures the real,
Which makes their voice unheard,

Their foghorn shaking the stars,
Their rockets shocking the dark,
Their courage, their casual jokes,
Their anxious, ordinary talk.

Many at home will awake
To find this gigantic ship
Has sailed into the bay
Whose waves lulled them to sleep,
Preternaturally great,
Obscuring most of the sky,
While the darkness spreads overhead
As the great ship comes close,
The appalling shape in the bay
Towering over the house.

IX

Coagulate wtih cold and dark the sea
Sucks down *Titanic* as the hiss of steam
Dies over empty distance. The boats gaze
On what was home, eleven storeys high,
Commotion crowding on its decks, its lights
Tilting above them as the band plays on.

Is Horatio Bottomley* who climbs now by the stairs
To the sliding platforms of the ship
Strength or weakness? Are the deceptions the late king practiced,
Flitting between the cabins, dishonour?

The freezing sea heaves slowly as it sinks
Into a tidal wave as high as it
Which licks the stars. The screaming rich sucked under
And the poor cry in that icy darkness
One last time, and then the cowering boats
Are hoisted up among the stars themselves.
The great ship gone the lucky count their loss
And search and search again to find the gain,
What guttered in the darkness of that wave,
For why else may the living not believe

The lies that served the first-class passengers
As passports to redemption from the dirt?

Under soft showers of April lies the west,
Belled washed-out skies, the angelus, drenched birds.
Before our fathers stretches nineteen twelve,
The cloudy evenings and the river pools.
The freemen's journals soon will tell the story
And life rub in the lesson day by day.
There is no decency except a lie.

X

The hot breath of the brass, the drum's insistence,
Tar-barrels flaming in the market square,
And then the declinations of the heart.
Troubled by drums and scent the blood is trembling,
And caverned under canvas, taunting, white,
The girls twist, sensuously touched by light.

Rain beats on the branches, scattering
Debris of April, blossoms and leaves on the ground.
Petals and twigs afloat on the sky in the roadway,
Deciduous stonework black as the big house crumbles,
The roofs with afterglow of rain still bright,
Auguring autumns to come in a cold light.

We live by living, survive by mere surviving.
Stubborn beyond our stubbornness or strength
Our virtues, like our weaknesses, prevail.
A man may suffer goodness like a growth
Intimate with his life. See, in his face
His gentleness encounter its disgrace.

XI

The dreams born in the mists of autumn evenings,
Cold, blue, tingling leaf-falls after rugby,
With lights in passing buses: promises:
Remembrances of wrongs in mothers' eyes:
Money's smooth hum: migrating newspapers
Flocking across the skies: the cameras purring

On whores' ecstasies of self-possession:
Insane and fearful punctualities
Will keep the bands still playing, the great ship
Towering above the roadsteads of the world.
And they will bless the Pope this time in building
It in a Belfast of exorbitant virtue,
Bound still by decent business's iron tramlines.

As the world drifts with dismal Sunday bells
Into an April half a century on,
Sweating awake, their skin next to the blankets,
Many reflect on how their lives were not
As once imagined. Sepia photographs
Whose background was a swathe of shimmering sea,
Gone, with the cupboards, washstands, bedroom ceilings
Under which decencies perished hour by hour,
The patterns made by sunlight on those ceilings,
The German band tromboning on the corner
Fading laments for Genevieve and June,
Damp smells, diplomas, cobwebs, cindered yards,
Lugubrious moustaches, high-winged collars,
Tied bundles of old newspapers and books
On esperanto, self-help, concentration,
The wastages of effort and of love.

Coughing and spitting by the radiator,
The old men listen to the wireless now
The world has turned into a coalyard where
Life which had died in shame is reborn free.
These years that saw declensions of the heart
Unguessed at on assistants' summer evenings
When ghostly skirts were whispering in the dark,
Saw also freedoms, huge across the sky
Grimy with blood and fire against which foundered
Towering gasometers, crossed girders, gantries.
Disgust itself is freedom, as is fear.
What steers us to destructions has released
Many from corridors, the servant's guile,
The clerk's reliable, deft-fingered grace,
Imperial mirrors cracked across the smile

Of duty on the dowager's creamed face.
A daily drudgery of approximate justice
Is incumbent yet upon the brave who crouch
Still over tasks upon the drumming floor.
But the eyes of survivors will ask both more and less.
And no one now need ever fear a disgrace.
The responses the night is listening to are aware
Of the irrelevant ignobility of distress.

Homage to the Rural Writers, Past and Present, at Home and Abroad

Country origins, country roots
Seduce long after our transplantment,
The mechanic round, the mud-caked boots
Retain or gain a strange enchantment.

The endurance of the rural breed
Seems, like the rugged landscape, stoical.
Rural grasping, rural greed,
Are somehow, unlike ours, heroical.

The rural rancour, dampened down,
The rural passions, smouldering, steaming,
The rural smile, the rural frown,
Compared to ours are realer seeming.

And when two rural lovers meet,
Escaping rural interdiction,
The rural suddenness and heat,
Intemperate, beyond restriction,

Which visits all with complex dooms,
With family feuds and endless fighting
Has still involved the primal grooms
In passionate, envied, early plighting.

While haze on the long barrow's back,
The winter-misted lane's sad squelchings,
Great nature's oozings and her wrack,
Unlike our factory chimney's belchings,

Endorse their ardours as intense,
Not like our own, which are verbal, flagging,
Ensure they show no grain of sense,
Remove the reasonable and nagging;

Till kindly nature takes away
The rougher, rawer edge of feeling,
Shows them the main-spring of the play,
The moral tragedy revealing,

And country habitudes, country ways
Reconcile all to nature's purpose.
The floorboards creak, the house decays
And no surprise will now disturb us.

The realer seeming spade has struck,
The realer seeming sod is turning.
All lie in realer seeming muck,
While autumn leaves are really burning.

Completion

for Robert MacBryde

All things tend to completion,
Towards a resultant end.
The heat of a harvest noonday
With an August night will blend.

The rose burns out in its calyx.
The leaf yields to the ground.
Almost every appearance
Is with disappearance crowned.

1798

Commisioned by Comoradh '99 and read on Vinegar Hill

They wore their Sunday best for early battle,
Coming with ribbons in their hats to join
Their neighbours at the crossroads by the chapel
As on a holy day of obligation.

War is release and sudden holiday,
For some, release now from a nightly horror,
The flaming thatch, the mingled oaths and screams.

The lovely summer weather gave them leave
To sleep beneath the bright and beckoning stars
And wake each day to Liberty's wide dawn.
But nothing happens as a wish would have it;
And war is chance, its currents rip us far
Beyond all headlands and all reach of rescue,
Beyond what heart can hope or soul can stomach.

Too soon the Slaney's waves were stained, the Barrow
Carried its cargo seawards from New Ross
To cold, wide waters where no sail appeared.
Their columns heaving now with frantic households,
Not heroes, merely people, but the pikes
Their hedge and shelter in the broken weather,
Here on this hill they stood, where we assemble,
A civic gathering in a different time.

History, the nightmare from which all mankind
Must struggle to awake, recedes at last;
And our normality accommodates
The dream of Liberty, Equality
For which they had to rend the normal day,
To take the lives of others, give their own;
Which seemed so distant then, to us mundane.
We should recall the price they had to pay.

Thomas Kinsella (1928–)

"I wrote my first poem, when I was eighteen, out of curiosity," Thomas Kinsella once remarked, "my second at twenty, as a joke. The third was written soon after with a faint foreboding."[1] His foreboding came, on the one hand, from entering into a process that once begun could never end, since there is an unlimited terrain of the unpoetic to be mapped by poetry. At the same time, Kinsella must have sensed early on that his own poetry would have its commerce primarily with suffering, with the conversion through art of the harsh realities of human life. Later in his career, he could articulate these matters more clearly:

> It is certain that maturity and peace are to be sought through ordeal after ordeal, and it seems that the search continues until we fall. We reach out after each new beginning, penetrating our context to know ourselves, and our knowledge increases until we recognize again (more profoundly each time) our pain, indignity and triviality. This bitter cup is offered, heaped with curses, and we must drink or die. And even though we drink we must also die, if every drop of bitterness—that rots the flesh—is not transmuted.[2]

For Kinsella, it is poetry, in other words, that offers us our best opportunity to transform bitterness into something of value.

Kinsella was born in Dublin in 1928, and began his poetic career at a low point in the history of Irish literature. During the late 1940s, poetry in Ireland seemed to have nowhere left to go. Poets of the previous generation, most notably Austin Clarke and Patrick Kavanagh, had carried out an attack on the Romantic poetics of the revival—the valorization of a lost Irish pastoralism which, under the influence of Yeats, had produced countless poems filled with noble peasants and rural aristocrats. But having challenged the standing image of Ireland, each poet had retreated into his own concerns, Clarke struggling with personal issues of religion, Kavanagh's focus tightened to the borders of a small farm by his poetics of parochialism.[3]

Unlike the previous generation, Kinsella and his contemporaries—John Montague and Richard Murphy among them—first looked outside Ireland for models that might circumvent the restrictions Irish society placed on them. Kinsella himself did not go abroad, but, still in Dublin, read widely outside the Irish tradition, embracing Goethe, Donne, Keats, and especially the modernists Ezra Pound, T. S. Eliot, and W. H. Auden.

James Joyce's modernism in particular gave Kinsella a route back into the poetic material of Irish life, so that when he turned inward as Clarke and Kavanagh had done, it was to a Joycean inner reality manifest in a modernist human isolation, rather than an isolation particular to the Irish society Clarke and Kavanagh had reacted against. Given the larger framework of international modernism, Irish society itself seemed to Kinsella like one symptom of a larger, universal condition:

> I find in practice that social or political matters, for example, or any motifs characteristic of a group, never arise; little is relevant but the dignity of the isolated person, whose conscious or unconscious bargainings with time insist, like those of a condemned or dying man, that they be respected.[4]

Kinsella's most explicit use of a Joycean poetics of individual consciousness comes in what is likely to be his most influential poem. "Nightwalker," published in 1968, is credited with ratifying the literary revaluation of everyday Irish experience that Joyce had begun in *Ulysses*. Set on Sandymount Strand, Kinsella's poem substitutes Joyce's Martello tower for the Norman one Yeats had placed at the heart of Ireland's artistic sensibility, symbolically opening the way for the distinctively Joycean poetry that has come out of Ireland and the North in recent years.

Following Joyce, Kinsella uses the newspaper as a link between individual experience and national history. Kinsella's poem weaves into its night landscape images of Éamon de Valera's wedding, reported in the morning *Times,* thereby multiplying each image's field of reference in a way that signals the solid installation of Joycean methods in contemporary Irish poetry.[5] Late in "Nightwalker" Kinsella imagines the ultimate reconciliation of this new poetics with the more conservative Irish tradition. Joyce's methods, he had already conceded, "may give offense / But this should pass." Now he watches as a book assembled from the fragments of modernity flows into the light of a "Virgin" moon. Looking on the "Scattered notes, scraps of newspaper, photographs" that are the elements of the poem itself, the moon first "darkens" as she reads, much to the poet's horror,[6] "But she soon brightens a little," as if accepting and affirming Kinsella's new poetics.[7]

While Joyce provided a model for innovation, Irish epic gave Kinsella a ground in which his poetry might sink its roots. The year after *Nightwalker* appeared, he published a translation of the Ulster epic *An Táin Bó Cuailgne*. The influence that project had on his own poetry may be seen in "The Route of *The Táin*."

Contemporary events in Ulster were even more influential, and one crisis in particular led Kinsella to an innovation he calls "draft publication," a way of putting poetry abroad more quickly than is possible through journals.[8] When the Widgery Report on the Bloody Sunday massacre appeared in 1972, exonerating the British soldiers who had killed thirteen civil rights protesters in Derry, Kinsella's poetic response was immediate. A week after the report was published he issued his response in a long poem entitled *Butcher's Dozen*, having in the mean time founded a press for the purpose. He named the enterprise Peppercanister Press, after the peppershaker shape of the steeple of St. Stephen's Church, which he could see from his house in Dublin. Peppercanister has published Kinsella's occasional verse ever since.

NOTES

1. Quoted in Maurice Harmon, *The Poetry of Thomas Kinsella: "with darkness for a nest"* (Atlantic Heights, New Jersey: Humanities Press, 1975), p. 7.

2. *Nightwalker and Other Poems* (Dublin: Dolmen Press, 1968), p. 23.

3. See Harmon, *The Poetry of Thomas Kinsella*, p. 7.

4. *Poetry Book Society Bulletin*, March 1958, quoted in Harmon, *The Poetry of Thomas Kinsella*, p. 14.

5. For a discussion of Kinsella's debt to Joyce, see Thomas H. Jackson, *The Whole Matter: The Poetic Evolution of Thomas Kinsella* (Syracuse, New York: Syracuse University Press, 1995), p. 49ff.

6. This quotation is from the version of Kinsella's poem published in *Nightwalker and Other Poems* (New York: Alfred A. Knopf, 1986), p. 66. This line does not appear in the version reproduced below, which is drawn from Kinsella's *Collected Poems 1956–2001* (Manchester: Carcanet, 2001).

7. "Nightwalker," *Poems 1956–1973* (Montrath, Portloaise, Ireland: Dolmen Press, 1980), p. 112.

8. Thomas Kinsella, "Note on Peppercanister Poems," *Collected Poems 1956–2001* (Manchester: Carcenet, 2001).

Echoes

Alone we make symbols of love
Out of echoes its lack makes in an empty word.
Inaccessible softness of breast or voice in the dove
Or high gull grace are what we are thinking of,
The poise in quality of a bird.
Time must pare such images to the heart.
Love I consider a difficult, scrupulous art.

A drumming of feet on a lake
When a stretched word touches the meaning like a swan
Points in the vanishing whisper of its wake
The course of argument that love must take
Until word and image are gone.
Out of a certain silence it may bring
The softer dove or a skylit glitter of wing.

Across the deepest speech,
When what is said is less than what is heard,
Gift to the shaken giver melts into each,
Receipt on the lips alights and returns to teach
What further words can be spared
Till graven language centres love with quiet
More full than spoken gesture can supply it.

So, much that the instant needs
Being faded token of what the next replaces,
An echo deepens as the past recedes;
Words like swans are swallowed into the reeds
With lapping airs and graces.
Speechless white necks dip in the fugal pause
When streaming images transfigure the dove that was.

What beats in its flaming throat
Or under its plumes, or what transfigures its flight
—A detail of light—what inexplicable mote
Drifts in the slanted shaft where loves are afloat
Flowers in no single sight;
In composite hearts there sings a full repose:
Mute splendour of a breast-soft, sea-graced close.

Baggot Street Deserta

Lulled, at silence, the spent attack.
The will to work is laid aside.
The breaking-cry, the strain of the rack,
Yield, are at peace. The window is wide
On a crawling arch of stars, and the night
Reacts faintly to the mathematic
Passion of a cello suite
Plotting the quiet of my attic.
A mile away the river toils
Its buttressed fathoms out to sea;
Tucked in the mountains, many miles
Away from its roaring outcome, a shy
Gasp of waters in the gorse
Is sonneting origins. Dreamers' heads
Lie mesmerised in Dublin's beds
Flashing with images, Adam's morse.

A cigarette, the moon, a sigh
Of educated boredom, greet
A curlew's lingering threadbare cry
Of common loss. Compassionate,
I add my call of exile, half-
Buried longing, half-serious
Anger and the rueful laugh.
We fly into our risk, the spurious.

Versing, like an exile, makes
A virtuoso of the heart,
Interpreting the old mistakes
And discords in a work of Art
For the One, a private masterpiece
Of doctored recollections. Truth
Concedes, before the dew, its place
In the spray of dried forgettings Youth
Collected when they were a single
Furious undissected bloom.
A voice clarifies when the tingle
Dies out of the nerves of time:

Endure and let the present punish.
Looking backward, all is lost;
The Past becomes a fairy bog
Alive with fancies, double crossed
By pad of owl and hoot of dog,
Where shaven, serious-minded men
Appear with lucid theses, after
Which they don the mists again
With trackless, cotton-silly laughter;
Secretly a swollen Burke
Assists a decomposing Hare
To cart a body of good work
With midnight mutterings off somewhere;
The goddess who had light for thighs
Grows feet of dung and takes to bed,
Affronting horror-stricken eyes,
The marsh bird that children dread.

I nonetheless inflict, endure,
Tedium, intracordal hurt,
The sting of memory's quick, the drear
Uprooting, burying, prising apart
Of loves a strident adolescent
Spent in doubt and vanity.
All feed a single stream, impassioned
Now with obsessed honesty,
A tugging scruple that can keep
Clear eyes staring down the mile,
The thousand fathoms, into sleep.

Fingers cold against the sill
Feel, below the stress of flight,
The slow implosion of my pulse
In a wrist with poet's cramp, a tight
Beat tapping out endless calls
Into the dark, as the alien
Garrison in my own blood
Keeps constant contact with the main
Mystery, not to be understood.
Out where imagination arches
Chilly points of light transact

The business of the border-marches
Of the Real, and I—a fact
That may be countered or may not—
Find their privacy complete.

My quarter-inch of cigarette
Goes flaring down to Baggot Street.

Nightwalker

Mindful of the shambles of the day,
  But mindful, under the blood's drowsy humming,
Of will that gropes for structure; nonetheless
  Not unmindful of the madness without,
The madness within—the book of reason
  Slammed open, slammed shut:

I

I only know things seem and are not good.

A brain in the dark and bones out exercising
Shadowy flesh. Fitness for the soft belly,
Fresh air for lungs that take no pleasure any longer.
The smell of gardens under suburban lamplight;
Clipped privet; a wall blotted with shadows:
Monsters of ivy squat in lunar glare.
There above the roof it hangs,
A mask of grey dismay, like a fat skull.
Or the pearl knob of a pendulum
At the outermost reach of its swing, about to detach
Its hold on the upper night, for the return.
That dark area the mark of Cain.

*

My shadow twists above my feet in the light
Of every passing street lamp. Window after window
Pale entities, motionless in their cells like grubs,
Stare in a blue trance.

A laboratory
Near Necropolis. Underground. Embalmers,
Their arms toil in unearthly light,
Their mouths opening and closing.

                        A shade enters.
Patrolling the hive of his brain.

*

I must lie down with them all soon and sleep,
And rise with them again when the new day
Has roused us. We'll come scratching in our waistcoats
Down to the kitchen for a cup of tea.
Then with our briefcases, by the neighbours' gardens,
To wait at the station, assembled for the day's toil,
Fluttering our papers, palping the cool wind.
Ready to serve our businesses and government
As together we develop our community
On clear principles, with no fixed ideas.
And (twitching our thin umbrellas) agreeable
That during a transitional period
Development should express itself in forms
Without principle, based on fixed ideas.
Robed in spattered iron she stands
At the harbour mouth, Productive Investment,
And beckons the nations through our gold half-door:
Lend me your wealth, your cunning and your drive,
Your arrogant refuse. Let my people serve them
Holy water in our new hotels,
While native businessmen and managers
Drift with them chatting over to the window
To show them our growing city, give them a feeling
Of what is possible; our labour pool,
The tax concessions to foreign capital,
How to get a nice estate though German.
Even collect some our better young artists.

*

Our new constellations are rising into view
At the end of the terrace. You can pick them out,
With their pale influences.

The Wakeful Twins

Bruder und Schwester . . .

Two young Germans I had in this morning
Wanting to transfer investment income.
The sister a business figurehead, her brother
Otterfaced, with exasperated smiles
Assuming—pressing until he achieved—response.
Handclasp; I do not exist; I cannot take
My eyes from their pallor. A red glare
Plays on their faces, livid with little splashes
Of blazing fat. The oven door closes.

There: The Wedding Group . . .
The Groom, the Best Man, the Fox, and their three ladies.
A tragic tale.

Soon, the story tells,
Enmity sprang up between them, and the Fox
Took to the wilds. Then, to the Groom's sorrow,
His dear friend left him also, vowing hatred.
So they began destroying the Groom's substance
And he sent out to hunt the Fox, but trapped
His friend instead; mourning he slaughtered him.
Shortly in his turn the Groom was savaged
No one knows by whom. Though it's known the Fox
Is a friend of Death, and rues nothing.

And there, in the same quarter,
The Two Executioners—Groom and Weasel—
"77" burning onto each brow.

And there the Weasel again,
Dancing crookbacked under the Player King.
A tragicomical tale:
How the Fox discovered
A great complex gold horn left at his door;
Examined it with little curiosity,
Wanting no gold or music; observed the mouthpiece,
Impossible to play with fox's lips;
And gave it with dull humour to his old enemy,
The Weasel. Who bared his needle teeth,
Recognising the horn of the Player King.
He took it, hammered on it with a stick,

And pranced about in blithe pantomime,
His head cocked to enjoy the golden clouts.
While the Fox from time to time nodded his mask.

2

The human taste grows faint, leaving a taste
Of self and laurel leaves and rotted salt.
And gardens smelling of half-stripped rocks in the dark.

A cast-iron lamp standard on the sea wall
Sheds yellow light on a page of the day's paper
Turning in the gutter:
                              Our new young minister
Glares in his hunting suit, white haunch on haunch.

Other lamps are lighting along a terrace
Of high Victorian houses, toward the tower
Rising into the dark at the Forty Foot.
The tide drawing back from the promenade
Far as the lamplight can reach, into a dark
Alive with signals. Little bells clonk in the channel
Beyond the rocks; Howth twinkling across the Bay;
Ships' lights moving along invisible sea lanes;
The Bailey light sweeping the middle distance,
Flickering on something.

     *

                         Watcher in the tower,
Be with me now. Turn your milky spectacles
On the sea, unblinking.

                         A dripping cylinder
Pokes up into sight, picked out by the moon.
Two blazing eyes. Two tough shoulders of muscle
Lit from within by joints and bones of light.
Another head: animal, with nostrils
Straining open, red as embers. Google eyes.
A phantom whinny. Forehooves scrape at the night.
A spectral stink of horse and rider's sweat.
The rider grunts and urges.

Father of Authors!
It is himself! In silk hat, accoutred
In stern jodhpurs. The Sonhusband
Coming in his power, climbing the dark
To his mansion in the sky, to take his place
In the influential circle, mounting to glory
On his big white harse!

A new sign: Foxhunter.
Subjects will find the going hard but rewarding.
You may give offence, but this should pass.
Marry the Boss's daughter.

*

The soiled paper settles back in the gutter.
THE NEW IRELAND . . .

Awkward in the saddle

But able and willing for the foul ditch,
And sitting as well as any at the kill,
Whatever iron Faust opens the gate.

It is begun: curs mill and yelp at your heel,
Backsnapping and grinning. They eye your back.
Beware the smile of the dog.

But you know the breed,
And all it takes to turn them
To a pack of lickspittles running as one.

3

The foot of the tower. An angle where the darkness
Is complete. A backdrop of constellations,
Crudely done and mainly unfamiliar.
They are arranged to suggest a chart of the brain.

In the part of the little harbour that can be seen
The moon is reflected in low water. Beyond,
A line of lamps on the terrace.

From the vest's darkness,
Smell of my body; faint brutality;
Chalk dust and flowers.

Music far off.

The loins of Brother Burke
Flattened in his soutane against my desk:

. . . And Dublin Castle used the National Schools
To try to conquer the Irish national spirit
At the same time exterminating our "jargon"
—The Irish language, in which Saint Patrick, Saint Bridget
And Saint Colmcille taught and prayed!

Edmund Ignatius Rice founded our Order
To provide schools that were national in more than name.
Pupils from our schools have played their part
In the fight for freedom. And you will be called
In your various ways.

To show your love

By working for your language and your country.
Today there are past pupils everywhere
In the Government service. Ministers of State
Have sat where some of you are sitting now.

The Blessed Virgin smiles from her pedestal
Like young Victoria. Celibates, adolescents,
We make our vows to God and Ireland; thankful
That by our studies here they may not lack
Civil Servants in a state of grace.

*

A seamew passes over, whingeing: *Eire,*
Eire. Is there none to hear? Is all lost?
Alas, I think I will dash myself at the stones.

I will become a wind on the sea again.
Or a wave of the sea,
or a sea sound.

At the first light of the sun I stirred on my rock.
I have seen the sun go down at the end of the world.
Now I fly across the face of the moon.

A dying language echoes
across a century's silence.

4

Moon of my dismay, Virgin most pure,
Reflected enormous in her shaggy pool,
Quiet as oil. My brain swims in her light
And gathers into a book beneath her stare.
She reads and her mask darkens.
But she soon brightens a little:

It was a terrible time.
Nothing but horrors of one kind or another.
My tears flowed again and again.
But we came to take the waters, and when I drank
I felt my patience and trust coming back.

From time to time it seems that everything
Is breaking down. But we must never despair.
There are times it is all part of a meaningful drama
Beginning in the grey mists of antiquity
And reaching through the years to unknown goals
In the consciousness of man, which makes it less gloomy.

A wind sighs. The pool shivers. The tide
At the turn. An odour of the sea bed.
She rules on high, queenlike, pale with control.

Hatcher of peoples!
Incline out of your darkness into mine.
I stand at the ocean's edge,
My head fallen back heavy with your control,
And oppressed.

5

        A pulse hisses in my ear.
I am an arrow piercing the void, unevenly
As I correct and correct. But swift as thought.

I arrive enveloped in quiet.
          A true desert,
Sterile and odourless. Naked to every peril.

A bluish light beats down,
To kill every bodily thing.
But the shadows are alive.

They scuttle and flicker across the surface,
Searching for any sick spirits,
To suck at the dry juices.

If I stoop down and touch the dust
It has a human taste:
                              massed human wills.

I believe
                   I have heard of this place. I think
This is the Sea of Disappointment.

＊

It is time I turned for home.

Her dear shadow on the blind.
The breadknife. She was slicing and buttering
A loaf of bread. My heart stopped. I starved for speech.

I believe now that love is half persistence,
A medium in which from change to change
Understanding may be gathered.

Hesitant, cogitating, exit.

Butcher's Dozen (1972)

I went with Anger at my heel
Through Bogside of the bitter zeal
—Jesus pity!—on a day
Of cold and drizzle and decay.
A month had passed. Yet there remained
A murder smell that stung and stained.
On flats and alleys—over all—
It hung; on battered roof and wall,
On wreck and rubbish scattered thick,
On sullen steps and pitted brick.
And when I came where thirteen died
It shrivelled up my heart. I sighed

And looked about that brutal place
Of rage and terror and disgrace.
Then my moistened lips grew dry.
I had heard an answering sigh!
There in a ghostly pool of blood
A crumpled phantom hugged the mud:
"Once there lived a hooligan.
A pig came up, and away he ran.
Here lies one in blood and bones,
Who lost his life for throwing stones."
More voices rose. I turned and saw
Three corpses forming, red and raw,
From dirt and stone. Each upturned face
Stared unseeing from its place:
"Behind this barrier, blighters three,
We scrambled back and made to flee.
The guns cried *Stop*, and here lie we."
Then from left and right they came,
More mangled corpses, bleeding, lame,
Holding their wounds. They chose their ground,
Ghost by ghost, without a sound,
And one stepped forward, soiled and white:
"A bomber I. I travelled light
—Four pounds of nails and gelignite
About my person, hid so well
They seemed to vanish where I fell.
When the bullets stopped my breath
A doctor sought the cause of death.
He upped my shirt, undid my fly,
Twice he moved my limbs awry,
And noticed nothing. By and by
A soldier, with his sharper eye,
Beheld the four elusive rockets
Stuffed in my coat and trouser pockets.
Yes they must be strict with us,
Even in death so treacherous!"
He faded, and another said:
"We three met close when we were dead.
Into an armoured car they piled us

Where our mingled blood defiled us,
Certain, if not dead before,
To suffocate upon the floor.
Careful bullets in the back
Stopped our terrorist attack,
And so three dangerous lives are done
—Judged, condemned and shamed in one."
That spectre faded in his turn.
A harsher stirred, and spoke in scorn:
"The shame is theirs, in word and deed,
Who prate of Justice, practise greed,
And act in ignorant fury—then,
Officers and gentlemen,
Send to their Courts for the Most High
To tell us did we really die.
Does it need recourse to law
To tell ten thousand what they saw?
The news is out. The troops were kind.
Impartial justice has to find
We'd be alive and well today
If we had let them have their way.
But friend and stranger, bride and brother,
Son and sister, father, mother,
All not blinded by your smoke,
Photographers who caught your stroke,
The priests that blessed our bodies, spoke
And wagged our blood in the world's face.
The truth will out, to your disgrace."
He flushed and faded. Pale and grim,
A joking spectre followed him:
"Take a bunch of stunted shoots,
A tangle of transplanted roots,
Ropes and rifles, feathered nests,
Some dried colonial interests,
A hard unnatural union grown
In a bed of blood and bone,
Tongue of serpent, gut of hog
Spiced with spleen of underdog.
Stir in, with oaths of loyalty,

Sectarian supremacy,
And heat, to make a proper botch,
In a bouillon of bitter Scotch.
Last, the choice ingredient: you.
Now, to crown your Irish stew,
Boil it over, make a mess.
A most imperial success!"
He capered weakly, racked with pain,
His dead hair plastered in the rain:
The group was silent once again.
It seemed the moment to explain
That sympathetic politicians
Say our violent traditions,
Backward looks and bitterness
Keep us in this dire distress.
We must forget, and look ahead,
Nurse the living, not the dead.
My words died out. A phantom said:
"Here lies one who breathed his last
Firmly reminded of the past.
A trooper did it, on one knee,
In tones of brute authority."
That harsher spirit, who before
Had flushed with anger, spoke once more:
"Simple lessons cut most deep.
This lesson in our hearts we keep:
You condescend to hear us speak
Only when we slap your cheek.
And yet we lack the last technique:
We rap for order with a gun,
The issues simplify to one
—Then your Democracy insists
You mustn't talk with terrorists.
White and yellow, black and blue,
Have learned their history from you:
Divide and ruin, muddle through.
We speak in wounds. Behold this mess.
My curse upon your politesse."
Another ghost stood forth, and wet

Dead lips that had not spoken yet:
"My curse on the cunning and the bland,
On gentlemen who loot a land
They do not care to understand;
Who keep the natives on their paws
With ready lash and rotten laws;
Then if the beasts erupt in rage
Give them a slightly larger cage
And, in scorn and fear combined,
Turn them against their own kind.
The game runs out of room at last,
A people rises from its past,
The going gets unduly tough
And you have, surely, had enough.
The time has come to yield your place
With condescending show of grace
—An Empire-builder handing on.
We reap the ruin when you've gone,
All your errors heaped behind you:
Promises that do not bind you,
Hopes in conflict, cramped commissions,
Faiths exploited, and traditions."
Bloody sputum filled his throat.
He stopped and coughed to clear it out,
And finished, with his eyes a-glow:
"You came, you saw, you conquered . . . So.
You gorged—and it was time to go.
Good riddance. We'd forget—released—
But for the rubbish of your feast,
The slops and scraps that fell to earth
And sprang to arms in dragon birth.
Sashed and bowler-hatted, glum
Apprentices of fife and drum,
High and dry, abandoned guards
Of dismal streets and empty yards,
Drilled at the codeword 'True Religion'
To strut and mutter like a pigeon
'Not An Inch—Up The Queen';
Who use their walls like a latrine
For scribbled magic—at their call,
Straight from the nearest music-hall,

Pope and Devil intertwine,
Two cardboard kings appear, and join
In one more battle by the Boyne!
Who could love them? God above . . ."
"Yet pity is akin to love,"
The thirteenth corpse beside him said,
Smiling in its bloody head,
"And though there's reason for alarm
In dourness and a lack of charm
Their cursed plight calls out for patience.
They, even they, with other nations
Have a place, if we can find it.
Love our changeling! Guard and mind it.
Doomed from birth, a cursed heir,
Theirs is the hardest lot to bear,
Yet not impossible, I swear,
If England would but clear the air
And brood at home on her disgrace
—Everything to its own place.
Face their walls of dole and fear
And be of reasonable cheer.
Good men every day inherit
Father's foulness with the spirit,
Purge the filth and do not stir it.
Let them out. At least let in
A breath or two of oxygen,
So they may settle down for good
And mix themselves in the common blood.
We all are what we are, and that
Is mongrel pure. What nation's not
Where any stranger hung his hat
And seized a lover where she sat?"
He ceased and faded. Zephyr blew
And all the others faded too.
I stood like a ghost. My fingers strayed
Along the fatal barricade.
The gentle rainfall drifting down
Over Colmcille's town
Could not refresh, only distil
In silent grief from hill to hill.

The Route of *The Táin**

Gene sat on a rock, dangling our map.
The others were gone over the next crest,
further astray. We ourselves, irritated,
were beginning to turn down toward the river
back to the car, the way we should have come.

We should have trusted our book.
After they tried a crossing, and this river too
"rose against them" and bore off
a hundred of their charioteers toward the sea
They had to move along the river Colptha
up to its source.
                    There:
where the main branch sharpens away gloomily
to a gash in the hill opposite.

then to Bélat Ailiúin
                        by that pathway
climbing back and forth out of the valley
over to Ravensdale.

Scattering in irritation. Who had set out
so cheerfully to celebrate our book;
cheerfully as we made and remade it
through a waste of hours, content to "enrich the present
honouring the past," each to his own just function.
Wandering off, ill-sorted,
like any beasts of the field,
one snout honking disconsolate,
another burrowing in its pleasures.

When not far above us a red fox
ran at full stretch out of the bracken
and panted across the hillside toward the next ridge.
Where he vanished—a faint savage sharpness
out of the earth—an inlet of the sea
shone in the distance at the mouth of the valley
beneath Omeath: grey waters crawled with light.

For a heartbeat, in alien certainty,
we exchanged looks. We should have known it by now
—the process, the whole tedious enabling ritual.
Flux brought to fullness; saturated;
the clouding over; dissatisfaction
spreading slowly like an ache;
something reduced shivering suddenly
into meaning along new boundaries;

through a forest,
by a salt-dark shore,
by a standing stone on a dark plain,
by a ford running blood,
and along this gloomy pass, with someone ahead
calling and waving on the crest
against a heaven of dismantling cloud,
transfixed by the same figure (stopped, pointing)
on the rampart at Cruachan, where it began.

The morning sunlight pouring on us all
as we scattered over the mounds
disputing over useless old books,
assembled in cheerful speculation
around a prone block, *Miosgán Medba*
—Queen Medb's *turd* . . . ? And rattled our maps,
joking together in growing illness
or age or fat. Before us
the route of the *Táin,* over men's dust,
toward these hills that seemed to grow
darker as we drove nearer.

Tao and Unfitness at Inistiogue on the River Nore

Noon

The black flies kept nagging in the heat.
Swarms of them, at every step, snarled
off pats of cow dung spattered in the grass.

Move, if you move, like water.

The punts were knocking by the boathouse, at full tide.
Volumes of water turned the river curve
hushed under an insect haze.

                               Slips of white,
trout bellies, flicked in the corner of the eye
and dropped back onto the deep mirror.

Respond. Do not interfere. Echo.

Thick green woods along the opposite bank
climbed up from a root-dark recess
eaved with mud-whitened leaves.

*

In a matter of hours all that water is gone,
except for a channel near the far side.
Muck and shingle and pools where the children
wade, stabbing flatfish.

Afternoon

Inistiogue itself is perfectly lovely,
like a typical English village, but a bit sullen.
Our voices echoed in sunny corners
among the old houses; we admired
the stonework and gateways, the interplay
of roofs and angled streets.

The square, with its "village green," lay empty.
The little shops had hardly anything.
The Protestant church was guarded by a woman
of about forty, a retainer, spastic
and indistinct, who drove us out.

An obelisk to the Brownsfoords and a Victorian
Celto-Gothic drinking fountain, erected
by a Tighe widow for the villagers,
"erected" in the centre. An astronomical-looking
sundial stood sentry on a platform
on the corner where High Street went up out of the square.

We drove up, past a long-handled water pump
placed at the turn, with an eye to the effect,
then out of the town for a quarter of a mile
above the valley, and came to the dead gate
of Woodstock, once home of the Tighes.

*

The great ruin presented its flat front
at us, sunstruck. The children disappeared.
Eleanor picked her way around a big fallen branch
and away along the face toward the outbuildings.
I took the grassy front steps and was gathered up
in a brick-red stillness. A rook clattered out of the dining room.

A sapling, hooked thirty feet up
in a cracked corner, held out a ghost-green
cirrus of leaves. Cavities
of collapsed fireplaces connected silently
about the walls. Deserted spaces, complicated
by door-openings everywhere.

There was a path up among bushes and nettles
over the beaten debris, then a drop, where bricks
and plaster and rafters had fallen into the kitchens.
A line of small choked arches . . . The pantries, possibly.

Be still, as though pure.

A brick, and its dust, fell.

Nightfall

The trees we drove under in the dusk
as we threaded back along the river through the woods
were no mere dark growth, but a flitting-place
for ragged feeling, old angers and rumours.

Black and Tan ghosts up there, at home
on the Woodstock heights: an iron mouth
scanning the Kilkenny road: the house
gutted by the townspeople and burned to ruins.

The little Ford we met, and inched past, full of men
we had noticed along the river bank during the week,
disappeared behind us into a fifty-year-old night.
Even their caps and raincoats . . .

Sons, or grandsons. Poachers.
                              Mud-tasted salmon
slithering in a plastic bag around the boot,
bloodied muscles, disputed since King John.

The ghosts of daughters of the family
waited in the uncut grass as we drove
down to our mock-Austrian lodge and stopped.

                    *

We untied the punt in the half-light, and pushed out
to take a last hour on the river, until night.
We drifted, but stayed almost still.
The current underneath us
and the tide coming back to the full
cancelled in a gleaming calm, punctuated
by the plop of fish.

Down on the water . . . at eye level . . . in the little light
remaining overhead . . . the mayfly passed in a loose drift,
thick and frail, a hatch slow with sex,
separate morsels trailing their slack filaments,
olive, pale evening dun, imagoes, unseen eggs
dropping from the air, subimagoes, the river filled
with their nymphs ascending and excited trout.

Be subtle, as though not there.

We were near the island—no more than a dark mass
on a sheet of silver—when a man appeared in mid-river
quickly and with scarcely a sound, his paddle touching
left and right of the prow, with a sack behind him.
The flat cot's long body slid past effortless
as a fish, sinewing from side to side,
as he passed us and vanished.

At the Western Ocean's Edge

Hero as liberator. There is also
the warrior marked by Fate, who overmasters
every enemy in the known world
until the elements reveal themselves.
And one, finding the foe inside his head,
who turned the struggle outward, against the sea.

Yeats discovered him through Lady Gregory,
and found him helpful as a second shadow
in his own sour duel with the middle classes.
He grew to know him well in his own right
—mental strife; renewal in reverse;
emotional response; the revelation.

Aogan O Rathaille felt their forces meeting
at the Western ocean's edge
—the energy of chaos and a shaping
counter-energy in throes of balance;
the gale wailing inland off the water
arousing a voice responding in his head,

storming back at the waves with their own force
in a posture of refusal, beggar rags
in tatters in a tempest of particulars.
A battered figure. Setting his face
beyond the ninth shadow, into dead calm.
The stranger waiting on the steel horizon.

Shop Shut

I pulled the heavy door over
and leaned my head against it,
        the long key coarse in my face.

Inserted the iron teeth in the box lock
and turned the heart of the handle
      on my den of images. Shop shut.

Summer night, Percy Lane.
The last light full of midges.
      Gnats out of nothing.

John Montague (1929–)

John Montague recalls a certain awkwardness in his first encounter with William Carlos Williams, the poet Montague credits with propelling him, by the gentleness of his personality, beyond the sheer craft of what the New Criticism of the day favored with the label of "the well-made poem."[1] When Williams visited the poetry workshop at the University of Iowa, the instructor asked him to comment on a number of his students' poems. On reading Montague's submission, Williams proclaimed that, though the poem was good, it failed to achieve the form of "the American line." Montague then rose to read his poem, and when Williams heard Montague's Ulster Irish accent "his face fell" as he realized that the poet had not been struggling with the American line, but had quite successfully accomplished what Montague calls "the Irish voice."[2]

It was a voice that Montague found through adversity. His parents were Catholics who had left Northern Ireland for America in the 1920s. Montague was born in Brooklyn in 1929, but because of economic difficulties, his parents soon sent him to live with relatives back in Northern Ireland. His two older brothers, both Irish-born, went off together to one relative, and Montague lived alone with two aunts on the family farm at Garvaghey in County Tyrone. The difficulty of that transition is a theme that surfaces in various versions throughout Montague's poetry. One poem recalls an Irish teacher publicly ridiculing his accent as the sound of "an American slum," and warning the other students, "no one should speak like him." In "A Grafted Tongue" Montague imaginatively inverts his own experience in a dreamlike coincidence of personal and national history.[3] Difficult as his childhood appears in those poems, Montague adapted to the new educational climate and eventually attended University College, Dublin. Leaving with an M.A., he went on to do postgraduate work with Robert Penn Warren at Yale before moving to Iowa to pursue an M.F.A.

Neither the time spent abroad nor the adversity of his first encounter with the country turned Montague's poetic attention away from Northern Ireland. His work has focused, some suggest to a fault, on the culture and strife in his adopted home. His long poem *The Rough Field*, for example, weaves together a series of images collected from family history in County Tyrone, assembling these personal materials as commentary upon the tragedies of Irish history from the seventeenth century to the outbreak of the current Troubles in 1968. That this sort of juxtaposition is so facilely made prompts some critics to charge that the "Catholic imagination," in the North, "is too caught up in the nets of history and is addicted to the creation of racial myths and racial landscapes."[4] But Derek Mahon challenges this convention of Montague criticism with the counterargument that "[Montague's] critics do not . . . accuse Yeats of doing the same thing at an earlier period." The deeper implication of this sort of attack, Mahon concludes, "is that something as frivolous as poetry has no business concerning itself with human suffering."[5]

As if echoing Mahon's earlier defense, Montague's *Time in Armagh* offers a model of the way his poetry confronts human misery. A concatenation of poetry and prose pieces that recall his term in a Vincentian school in Northern Ireland's ecclesiastical capital, the book declaims history most fully just in the broader world's subordination to the localized drama of human hardship. Its setting spans 1941–1946, but the war never intrudes beyond the one clear night when the Luftwaffe's bombers strayed wide of Belfast. Instead, conflict irrupts internally, in "the holy war against the growing body" depicted in "Guide." "In the name of chastity," schoolboys are purged of personality, and left "Cowering at the dark soutane's swirl / Along the study hall."[6] It is this sort of internal tension, as often secular as religious, that has been the central concern of Montague's poetry.

NOTES

1. Stephen Arkin, "An Interview with John Montague: Deaths in the Summer," *New England Review and Bread Loaf Quarterly*, vol. 5, nos. 1–2 (Autumn-Winter 1982), p. 233.

2. Ibid.

3. "A Grafted Tongue," *Collected Poems* (Loughcrew, Ireland: Gallery Press, 1995), p. 37.

4. George Watson, "The Narrow Ground: Northern Poets and the Northern Ireland Crisis," *Irish Writers and Society at Large*, ed. Masaru Sekine (Totowa, New Jersey: Barnes and Noble Books, 1985), p. 207.

5. In *Malahat Review*, July 1973; quoted in *Contemporary Authors*, New Revision Series, vol. 9, p. 372.

6. "Guide," *Time in Armagh* (Loughcrew, Ireland: Gallery Press, 1993), p. 15.

The Water Carrier

Twice daily I carried water from the spring,
Morning before leaving for school, and evening;
Balanced as a fulcrum between two buckets.

A bramble-rough path ran to the river
Where you stepped carefully across slime-topped stones,
With corners abraded as bleakly white as bones.

At the widening pool (for washing and cattle)
Minute fish flickered as you dipped,
Circling to fill, with rust-tinged water.

The second or enamel bucket was for spring water
Which, after racing through a rushy meadow,
Came bubbling in a broken drain-pipe,

Corroded wafer thin with rust.
It ran so pure and cold, it fell
Like manacles of ice on the wrists.

You stood until the bucket brimmed
Inhaling the musty smell of unpicked berries,
That heavy greenness fostered by water.

Recovering the scene, I had hoped to stylize it,
Like the portrait of an Egyptian water carrier:
But pause, entranced by slight but memoried life.

I sometimes come to take the water there,
Not as return or refuge, but some pure thing,
Some living source, half-imagined and half real,

Pulses in the fictive water that I feel.

A Drink of Milk

In the girdered dark
of the byre, cattle move;
warm engines hushed
to a siding groove

before the switch flicks
down for milking.
In concrete partitions
they rattle their chains

while the farmhand eases
rubber tentacles to tug
lightly but rhythmically
on their swollen dugs

and up the pale cylinders
of the milking machine
mounts an untouched
steadily pulsing stream.

Only the tabby steals
to dip its radar whiskers
with old-fashioned relish
in a chipped saucer

and before Séan lurches
to kick his boots off
in the night-silent kitchen
he draws a mug of froth

to settle on the sideboard
under the hoard of delph.
A pounding transistor shakes
the Virgin on her shelf

as he dreams towards bed.
A last glance at a magazine,
he puts the mug to his head,
grunts, and drains it clean.

Old Mythologies

And now, at last, all proud deeds done,
Mouths dust-stopped, dark they embrace,
Suitably disposed, as urns, underground.
Cattle munching soft spring grass—

Epicures of shamrock and the four-leaved clover—
Hear a whimper of ancient weapons,
As a whole dormitory of heroes turn over,
Regretting their butchers' days.
This valley cradles their archaic madness
As once, on an impossibly epic morning,
It upheld their savage stride:
To bagpiped battle marching,
Wolfhounds, lean as models,
At their urgent heels.

Forge

The whole shed smelt of dead iron:
the dented teeth of a harrow,
the feminine pathos of donkeys' shoes.

A labourer backed in a Clydesdale.
Hugely fretful, its nostrils dilated
while the smith viced a hoof

in his apron, wrestling it
to calmness, as he sheared the pith
like wood-chips, to a rough circle.

Then the bellows sang in the tall chimney
waking the sleeping metal, to leap
on the anvil. As I was slowly

beaten to a matching curve
the walls echoed the stress
of the verb *to forge*.

To Cease   *for Samuel Beckett*

To cease
to be human.

To be
a rock down
which rain pours,
a granite jaw
slowly discoloured.

Or a statue
sporting a giant's beard
of verdigris or rust
in some forgotten
village square.

A tree worn
by the prevailing winds
to a diagram of
tangled branches:
gnarled, sapless, alone.

To cease
to be human
and let birds soil
your skull, animals rest
in the crook of your arm.

To become
an object, honoured
or not, as the occasion demands;
while time bends you slowly
back to the ground.

The Country Fiddler

My uncle played the fiddle—more elegantly the violin—
A favourite at barn and crossroads dance,
He knew "The Morning Star" and "O'Neill's Lament."

Bachelor head of a house full of sisters,
Runner of poor racehorses, spendthrift,
He left for the New World in an old disgrace.

He left his fiddle in the rafters
When he sailed, never played afterwards,
A rural art stilled in the discord of Brooklyn.

A heavily-built man, tranquil-eyed as an ox,
He ran a wild speakeasy, and died of it.
During the Depression many dossed in his cellar.

I attended his funeral in the Church of the Redemption,
Then, unexpected successor, reversed time
To return where he had been born.

During my schooldays the fiddle rusted
(The bridge fell away, the catgut snapped)
Reduced to a plaything, stinking of stale rosin.

The country people asked if I also had music
(All the family had had) but the fiddle was in pieces
And the rafters remade, before I discovered my craft.

Twenty years afterwards, I saw the church again,
And promised to remember my burly godfather
And his rural craft after this fashion:

So succession passes, through strangest hands.

Like Dolmens Round My Childhood . . .

Like dolmens round my childhood, the old people.

Jamie MacCrystal sang to himself,
A broken song without tune, without words;
He tipped me a penny every pension day,
Fed kindly crusts to winter birds.
When he died, his cottage was robbed,
Mattress and money-box torn and searched.
Only the corpse they didn't disturb.

Maggie Owens was surrounded by animals,
A mongrel bitch and shivering pups,
Even in her bedroom a she-goat cried.
She was a well of gossip defiled,
Fanged chronicler of a whole countryside;
Reputed a witch, all I could find
Was her lonely need to deride.

The Nialls lived along a mountain lane
Where heather bells bloomed, clumps of foxglove.
All were blind, with Blind Pension and Wireless.
Dead eyes serpent-flickered as one entered
To shelter from a downpour of mountain rain.
Crickets chirped under the rocking hearthstone
Until the muddy sun shone out again.

Mary Moore lived in a crumbling gatehouse,
Famous as Pisa for its leaning gable.
Bag-apron and boots, she tramped the fields
Driving lean cattle from a miry stable.
A by-word for fierceness, she fell asleep
Over love stories, *Red Star* and *Red Circle*,
Dreamed of gypsy love-rites, by firelight sealed.

Wild Billy Eagleson married a Catholic servant girl
When all his Loyal family passed on:
We danced round him shouting "To hell with King Billy,"
And dodged from the arc of his flailing blackthorn.
Forsaken by both creeds, he showed little concern

Until the Orange drums banged past in the summer
And bowler and sash aggressively shown.

Curate and doctor trudged to attend them,
Through knee-deep snow, through summer heat,
From main road to lane to broken path,
Gulping the mountain air with painful breath.
Sometimes they were found by neighbours,
Silent keepers of a smokeless hearth,
Suddenly cast in the mould of death.

Ancient Ireland, indeed! I was reared by her bedside,
The rune and the chant, evil eye and averted head,
Fomorian fierceness of family and local feud.*
Gaunt figures of fear and of friendliness,
For years they trespassed on my dreams,
Until once, in a standing circle of stones,
I felt their shadows pass

Into that dark permanence of ancient forms.

A Lost Tradition

All around, shards of a lost tradition:
From the Rough Field I went to school
In the Glen of the Hazels. Close by
Was the bishopric of the Golden Stone;
The cairn of Carleton's homesick poem.*

Scattered over the hills, tribal-
And placenames, uncultivated pearls.
No rock or ruin, *dún* or dolmen
But showed memory defying cruelty
Through an image-encrusted name.

The heathery gap where the Rapparee,
Shane Barnagh, saw his brother die—
On a summer's day the dying sun
Stained its colours to crimson:
So breaks the heart, Brish-mo-Cree.

The whole landscape a manuscript
We had lost the skill to read,
A part of our past disinherited;
But fumbled, like a blind man,
Along the fingertips of instinct.

The last Gaelic speaker in the parish
When I stammered my school Irish
One Sunday after mass, crinkled
A rusty litany of praise:
Tá an Ghaeilge againn arís. . .*

Tír Eoghain: Land of Owen,
Province of the O'Niall;
The ghostly tread of O'Hagan's
Barefoot gallowglasses marching
To merge forces in Dún Geanainn

Push southward to Kinsale!*
Loudly the war-cry is swallowed
In swirls of black rain and fog
As Ulster's pride, Elizabeth's foemen,
Founder in a Munster bog.

A Grafted Tongue

   (Dumb,
bloodied, the severed
head now chokes to
speak another tongue—

   As in
a long suppressed dream,
some stuttering garb-
led ordeal of my own)

   An Irish
child weeps at school
repeating its English.
After each mistake

The master
gouges another mark
on the tally stick
hung about its neck

Like a bell
on a cow, a hobble
on a straying goat.
To slur and stumble

In shame
the altered syllables
of your own name;
to stray sadly home

And find
the turf-cured width
of your parents' hearth
growing slowly alien:

In cabin
and field, they still
speak the old tongue.
You may greet no one.

To grow
a second tongue, as
harsh a humiliation
as twice to be born.

Decades later
that child's grandchild's
speech stumbles over lost
syllables of an old order.

Sweeney

A wet silence.
Wait under trees,
muscles tense,
ear lifted, eye alert.

Lungs clear.
A nest of senses
stirring awake—
human beast!

A bird lights:
two claw prints.
Two leaves shift:
a small wind.

Beneath, white
rush of current,
stone chattering
between high banks.

Occasional shrill
of a bird, squirrel
trampolining along
a springy branch.

Start a slow
dance, lifting
a foot, planting
a heel to celebrate

greenness, rain
spatter on skin,
the humid pull
of the earth.

The whole world
turning in wet
and silence, a
damp mill wheel.

Killing the Pig

The noise.

He was pulled out, squealing,
an iron cleek sunk in the roof
of his mouth.

(Don't say they are not intelligent:
they know the hour has come
and they want none of it;
they dig in their little trotters,
will not go dumb or singing
to the slaughter.)

That high pitched final effort,
no single sound could match it—

a big plane roaring off,
a *diva* soaring towards her last note,
the brain-chilling persistence of an electric saw,
scrap being crushed.

Piercing & absolute,
only high heaven ignores it.

Then a full stop.
Mickey Boyle plants
a solid thump of the mallet
flat between the ears.

Swiftly the knife seeks the throat;
swiftly the other cleavers work
till the carcass is hung up
shining and eviscerated as
a surgeon's coat.

A child is given
the bladder to play with.
But the walls of the farmyard
still hold that scream,
are built around it.

Herbert Street Revisited   *for Madeleine*

I

A Light is burning late
in this Georgian Dublin street:
someone is leading our old lives!

And our black cat scampers again
through the wet grass of the convent garden
upon his masculine errands.

The pubs shut: a released bull,
Behan shoulders up the street,
topples into our basement, roaring "John!"*

A pony and donkey cropped flank
by flank under the trees opposite;
short neck up, long neck down,

as Nurse Mullen knelt by her bedside
to pray for her lost Mayo hills,
the bruised bodies of Easter Volunteers.

Animals, neighbours, treading the pattern
of one time and place into history,
like our early marriage, while

tall windows looked down upon us
from walls flushed light pink or salmon
watching and enduring succession.

II

As I leave, you whisper,
"Don't betray our truth,"
and like a ghost dancer,
invoking a lost tribal strength,
I halt in tree-fed darkness

to summon back our past,
and celebrate a love that eased
so kindly, the dying bone,
enabling the spirit to sing
of old happiness, when alone.

III

So put the leaves back on the tree,
put the tree back in the ground,
let Brendan trundle his corpse down
the street signing, like Molly Malone.*

Let the black cat, tiny emissary
of our happiness, streak again
through the darkness, to fall soft
clawed into a landlord's dustbin.

Let Nurse Mullen take the last
train to Westport, and die upright
in her chair, facing a window
warm with the blue slopes of Nephin.

And let the pony and donkey come—
look, someone has left the gate open—
like hobbyhorses linked in
the slow motion of a dream

parading side by side, down
the length of Herbert Street,
rising and falling, lifting
their hooves through the moonlight.

Guide

Heavy bells that rang above my head,
Sounds loneliness distilled
When Frank Lenny led me, gentle guide,
Under the Cathedral shade
And the gross carillon stirred.

Sick again, I had arrived months late
To hear the shoal's
Seashell roaring along the corridors
While my old neighbours
Fell silent in the parlour.

Garvaghey and Glencull were fleeing,
Leaving me to float,
A stray leaf, down the furious whirlpool
Of a junior seminary
From dawn Mass to Gaelic football.

Cowering at the dark soutane's swirl
Along the study hall;
Harder still, in the long dormitory's chill,
The midnight patrol
With probing torch, and cane's swish!

The holy war against the growing body
In the name of chastity,
As the Dean peers over my writing shoulder
Into my first diary:
"Any little girls' names there, have we?"

Would there have been a warm-breasted army!
Dear Frank Lenny,
For you, the flesh never raised a difficulty,
As you led us all
In solemn procession towards the Cathedral,

Satin-surpliced, with white gloves to uphold
The train of the cardinal.
Pageboy, Head Prefect, ordained priest,
Your path was straight:
One of their own, a natural for the episcopate.

Who would not envy such early certainty?
Across your celibate's bed
You fell last year, gone early upwards
Towards the heavens
Which, steadfast, you still believed in.

If, late again, I arrive flaunting my rival beliefs,
My secular life,
Will you be there, to greet and guide me,
White-gloved, gentle,
Proud of our Tyrone accent, my boyhood Virgil?

The Family Piano

My cousin is smashing the piano.
He is standing over its entrails
swinging a hatchet in one hand

and a hammer handle in the other
like a plundering Viking warrior.

My cousin is smashing the piano
and a jumble, jangle of eighty-eight keys
and chords, of sharps and flats
clambers to clutch at the hatchet,
recoils, to strike at his knees

(*My cousin is smashing the piano!*)
like the imploring hands of refugees
or doomed passengers on the *Titanic*
singing "Nearer My God to Thee"
as they vanish into lit, voiceless seas.

My cousin is smashing the piano
Grandfather installed in the parlour
to hoop his children together.
It came in a brake from Omagh,
but now lists, splintered and riven.

My cousin is smashing the piano
where they gathered to sing in chorus
"My Bonny Lies Over The Ocean"
beneath the fading family portraits
of Melbourne Tom, Brooklyn John.

My cousin is smashing the piano
where buxom Aunt Winifred played
old tunes from scrolled songbooks,
serenely pressing pedals, and singing
"Little Brown Jug," "One Man Went to Mow,"

Or (*My cousin is smashing the piano*)
hammered out a jig, "The Irish Washerwoman,"
while our collie dog lifted its long nose
and howled to high heaven:
John Cage serenading Stockhausen!

White Water

for Line McKie

The light, tarred skin
of the currach rides
and receives the current,
rolls and responds to
the harsh sea swell.

Inside the wooden ribs
a slithering frenzy; a sheen
of black-barred silver-
green and flailing mackerel:
the iridescent hoop
of a gasping sea trout.

As a fish gleams most
fiercely before it dies,
so the scales of the sea-hag
shine with a hectic
putrescent glitter:

luminous, bleached—
white water—
that light in the narrows
before a storm breaks.

James Simmons (1933–2001)

Born into a Protestant family in Derry in 1933, James Simmons as a young man took the path well beaten by previous Northern writers. Like Louis MacNeice—and under the influence of English writers such as W. H. Auden and Philip Larkin—Simmons turned toward England in search of a literary home. He left Ireland to study at the University of Leeds, where he earned a B.A. in 1958. He then taught for some years in Africa. Returning to Ulster in the late 1960s, he found a vibrant and intriguing poetic community that changed his mind about Northern Ireland as material and grounds for poetry: "for whatever it's worth," he said in 1979, "for the last ten years I have been dabbling in the matter of Ireland."[1] Simmons's dabbling took significant form in his foundation and editorship of *The Honest Ulsterman*, the journal that gave a public voice to the poets emerging in Northern Ireland in the 1960s. "It was my belief, more strongly then than now," he later remarked, "that literature might have a dynamic role to play in society. It wasn't that I just wanted popular poetry as one wants popular songs to hum. The way society changes is through its people's minds changing. Possibly the most effective way of changing people's minds is through good writing."[2] As an editor Simmons fostered good writing, and as a poet he has used his own wit and candor to challenge entrenched opinions in the troubled world of Northern Ireland. At the same time, he does want to hum popular songs. Simmons is also a singer, and the title of one of his albums, *City and Western*, typifies the interweaving of popular and high-cultural elements in his music and poetry.

I have always enjoyed singing and listening to singers. I also hanker for times when people relished poems as they do songs, recited them to each other as part of a night's entertainment (poetry readings aren't often the same thing). The poetry world in many of its manifestations is dull and seedy, though some of my best friends are poets. I suppose I try to write for better times, the sort of poems that might be on the lips of those who recite Burns, Shakespeare, or Auden.[3]

Simmons's characterization of his own work here follows a pattern evident in the reflexive turns of the poems themselves. On the one hand he emphasizes his ties to the accessible poetics of popular songs and light verse. Nonetheless, his aspirations are of the highest order, as seen in the company he'd like to keep: Burns, Shakespeare, Auden. He offers a similar view of his work in the poem "Exploration in the Arts," in which Simmons writes that "Shakespeare and I and Byron and Brecht and Burns / offer ourselves as entertainment, turns."[4] Simmons also shares with his targets in "Exploration" an overall concern for poetic quality; like Ezra Pound and T. S. Eliot (the modernists he sets himself against in the poem) Simmons aims at the elevation of literary standards throughout the community of contemporary poets. In his poetry, as in his leadership of *The Honest Ulsterman*, he cultivated a fertile environment for the growth of poetry. It's not surprising that his contention with the modernists takes shape against the way their technical innovations—pushed, in Simmons's terms, to the edge of sense—tend to close off the possibility of future development in the same direction. In the place of Eliot and Pound, he praises writers whose more conservative innovations provide a serviceable foundation for future poets, writers "like Edward Thomas, Hardy, Frost," who "didn't leave industries behind them. No, / they left a land conserved where things still grow."[5] Like the poetry of those figures he admired, his own work is unlikely to spawn an industry. But through his poetry's rich local imagery, as well as its colloquial rhythms and diction, and its passionate insistence on the proximity of life and art, Simmons, who died in 2001, left the ground of poetry in Northern Ireland richer than he found it.

NOTES

1. "The *Honest Ulsterman* and the Ulster Renaissance: Interview with James Simmons," *The Literary Review*, vol. 22, no. 2 (Winter 1979), p. 186.

2. Ibid., p. 184.

3. "James Simmons: Poetry, Bards & Broadway: A Conversation with Kevin T. McEneany," *An Gael*, vol. 3, no. 1 (Summer 1985), p. 14.

4. "Exploration in the Arts," *Poems 1956–1986* (Dublin: Gallery Press, 1986), p. 201.

5. Ibid.

The Not Yet Ancient Mariner

Before he settled to his hard vocation
he must just taste the youth that others had,
be ordinary. He put dark glasses on
and sauntered smiling down the promenade.

There it was usual to chat with strangers.
At first he was quite affable and pliant
until some point involved him, his eyes glittered,
"There was this ship," he said, blushing, defiant.

Words were too precious to be easy with him—
the painful urgency to get things right.
Most girls he cornered, bored by protestations
so qualified, chalked up a wasted night.

He managed to make nicer girls unhappy,
some guilty, some uncertain, some just small,
made little hands applying lipstick tremble
before they left for church or dancing hall.

His solitude, he saw, was part of greatness:
what cut him off was all the things they'd missed;
but when he said goodnight to casual strangers
why did his face still bend down to be kissed?

Puzzled or shocked, some turned their cheeks away.
What was the kiss about? He didn't know.
Some, casual or curious, kissed him back;
but any time was time for him to go.

Here was no solace and no recreation.
There was, as he'd suspected from the start,
no place within his chosen life that chose him
for trivialities so near his heart.

Macushla, Machree*

She is scarred like a soldier,
she droops like a jelly,
there are three distinct ridges
of fat on her belly.
There are varicose veins
on her legs, at the back.
Her vagina is more
a crevasse than a crack.

But I love the old ruin;
each defect and flaw
commemorates something
that both of us saw.
Be it car-crash or childbirth,
each line tells a story,
has a moral, my love,
my *memento mori.*

Lot's Wife

Uneasiness confirmed his words were right:
there was a rottenness in all she knew.
She could not see where she was going to
but love for him felt stronger than her fright.

Yet as she travelled on she was bereft
of every landmark but her husband's eyes:
her whole life echoed in her friends' goodbyes.
How could he take the place of all she left?

For him or them, but not for heaven's sake,
she made decisions: these two were opposed.
He led her on his way, her eyes were closed.
At every step she felt her heart would break.

At last Lot drew his wagon to a halt;
dog-tired but glad, he groped his way inside,
looking for pleasure in his sleeping bride,
kissed her, and on her cold cheek tasted salt.

A Muse

The one I use
is not a moral Muse.
When I'm inadequate
or spite twists me or hate,
or I'm fresh from half-baked sin,
she still comes smiling in
before I'm sorry (and I never ask)
with a full hip-flask
and cigarettes. What's more,
she reclines on the floor,
naked, without a word.

I seldom fail to be stirred
to our mutual satisfaction
and charmed by her kind action.

She walks out into the street;
but our child is my receipt,
a dutiful offspring, glad
to earn cash for his old dad.
It is quite true his mother hates
men who would make dates,
and leaves them hanging about.
There is even some doubt
if fidelity excites her,
however fervent and bright. Her
charm is in being chancy.
She comes at her own fancy
to delight her host

at the weirdest and most
memorable hours.
                    The features
of this delightful creature
are sometimes seen
on others' children. She has been,
to annoy me, elsewhere with her passion,
behaving, doubtless, in the above fashion.

In the Wilderness

I sit alone on the rocks trying to prepare
a man to teach what the laws of life are.
Sunlight and silence, nurses against disease,
are busy fighting my infirmities.
The life is simple, you could not say rough,
a stream, some cans and firewood are enough
to live on; but a hostile shift of weather
would bring me sharply up on the short tether
of endurance. We haven't survived by strength alone.
We have neither fur nor fangs. I will go home,
just as I rise from sleep, eat and get dressed.
This is one more resort, not last or best.

A teacher in the wilderness alone
learns to make bread and sermons out of stone.

Outward Bound   *for Tony Harrison*

Two campers (King Lear and his clown?)
smile to see the skies come down.
The shaken mind finds metaphors
in winds that shake the great outdoors.
As roofs and fences fall in storms

the tranquil mind's protective forms
collapse when passion, grief and fear
stir. We will spend a fortnight here.

To this small wilderness we bring
ourselves to play at suffering,
to swim in lonely bays, immerse
in the destructive elements, nurse
our bare forked bodies by wood fires
where ox-tail soup in mugs inspires
the tender flesh. By rocks we cough
and shiver in the wind, throw off
what history has lent, and lie
naked, alone, under the sky.

Of course, not one of us prefers
the cold; we are sun-worshippers,
wilderness- and storm-defiers,
neither masochists nor liars.

Cheeks whipped by freezing rain go numb.
The baffled blood is stirred, will come
again, glowing like my mind when Lear
speaks in the words of Shakespeare.
Under duress trying to sing
in tune, foretasting suffering
that we will swallow whole, the storm
endured, we hope to come to harm
at home, with better dignity
or style or courage. Anyway
I like to camp and read *King Lear*.
We had a lovely fortnight here.

Stephano Remembers

We broke out of our dream into a clearing
and there were all our masters still sneering.
My head bowed, I made jokes and turned away,
living over and over that strange day.

The ship struck before morning. Half past four,
on a huge hogshead of claret I swept ashore
like an evangelist aboard his god:
his will was mine, I laughed and kissed the rod,
and would have walked that foreign countryside
blind drunk, contentedly till my god died;
but finding Trinculo made it a holiday:
two Neapolitans had got away,
and that shipload of scheming toffs we hated
was drowned. Never to be humiliated
again, "I will no more to sea," I sang.
Down white empty beaches my voice rang,
and that dear monster, half fish and half man,
went on his knees to me. Oh, Caliban,
you thought I'd take your twisted master's life;
but a drunk butler's slower with a knife
than your fine courtiers, your dukes, your kings.
We were distracted by too many things . . .
the wine, the jokes, the music, fancy gowns.
We were no good as murderers, we were clowns.

The Publican   *for Michael Allen*

If God treats the human race like my father
treats customers we needn't worry.
His hand holds up the shutter of the bar
at the same time as he's telling you to hurry.

Drunk eyes always arrest him. He has to come
quietly out from behind, complaining it's late
but hearing accurately the list of quick ones,
the last round for the swing of the gate.

He's always saying Time and always hearing
excuses. He'll even rob his own shelf
on a good night and join the company—
but then wasn't our Saviour a drinker himself?

Still, Power is dangerous. If some wee shit
tells the police, my father has to pay for it.

Drowning Puppies

for Joan Newman

Their small pink mouths were opened
unnaturally wide
and little tongues stuck out too far
because of how they died.

I brought the bucket with its load
into the kitchen. There
the mother with her living pups
enjoyed the warmer air.

I paused before the Raeburn,
but the bitch saw nothing strange—
her master tipping rubbish
into the blazing range.

Epigrams

1.

Happiness can't marry, she only flirts.
Whatever you live with is boring or it hurts.

2.

Declining appetite
made him polite.

3.

When I had curls
I knew more girls.
I do more reading
now my hair is receding.

4.

Now that my faculties give in
I see the need for discipline.

On Circe's Island

for Nell Dunn

1.

One day I found her summer house
most of the glass intact
but the wood riddled by worms,
the white paint flaked.
Age gives such character,
and an odour, strange and good,
of musty red geraniums
from my childhood,
some place where I'd been happy,
at peace to read
books my parents hadn't heard of
but I seemed to need.

2.

Apart from this I was relieved to be
abroad no more on the disastrous sea
that killed companions and servants and cast me

on wrong islands where curving white
sands and bays for shelter and other familiar sights
hid monsters too big for any man to fight.

What with the summer house
and Circe's friendly thighs
this seemed a paradise.

Then one day, lying out, lay next to mine
a familiar face, Joe's face, and yet a swine,
so I knew we were threatened. By magic this time.

3.

Everywhere's unreliable that isn't home.
In guilt I remembered my own wife and my son.
This stunning stranger kept me from my own.

There was always going to be danger being away,
enjoying idleness and novelty.
Destined for hard work and little pay,

I saw my great bow in the arms' store.
I thought, "If Penelope stops watching the shore,
sweet lodgings are all I can hope for."

4.

Circe's charm and humanity
and even her need were not for me.
One is not the same as another.
Responsibility must be particular,
not to every creature under the sun,
not universal love, but cleaving to one.

5.

But that is a moral truth.
My neglected self grows here. The crude
joys of fresh sex and high-class booze
are less than that ruined hot-house, the solitude.

6.

But, degrading my men could never be right.
I walked the perfumed sandhills at night
hearing my brothers grunt and scrape in the sty
while I, if the flesh moved me, was free to lie
on my lovely friend in her goddess's soft bed.

"Love me, love my men," I said.
She grinned and changed the subject, but I stuck
to my point, refusing to chat with her or fuck.
I was stubborn, glum and moody and unfair.
This was a manly quirkiness to her.

7.

She didn't budge an inch till I raised my sword.
Then she promised, and was as good as her word.
Virtue paid out its bonuses all round:
as the boys lifted their forelegs off the ground
their human standing as they stood erect
was more than I'd remembered to expect,
and she had grace to see it was good too,
thereafter helping us with all she knew.

With her beside us hope seemed true at last.
"Wave your wand and waft us homeward, fast,"
I whispered, confident of my charm.
Aside, a little malicious, she took my arm,
"I see your future, being with vision blessed,
and there are more adventures to digest,
crimes to be expiated, chores to do.
No one is going to make it home but you."

Nothing I could discuss with the lads. Again
it was father remote from son, master from men.
We stayed and sort of enjoyed ourselves a year.
And every day new virtues became clear
in Circe that my wife won't have. I will hunger
for her in time, so much sharper and younger.
Instead of thrusting home to love, I will grieve;
but the revelation is tied to the need to leave.

8.

That summer house, the walk there through the wood,
dusty geraniums, sun-warmed solitude.

Her little breasts, thin waist and crooked smile.
The sea of shifting hillocks, cold and vile.

My faithful and unlucky shipmates, friends.
My wife and son, my old age, journey's end.

9.

Joking and kissing, making plans in vain,
we ventured on the wine-dark sea again.

Claudy*   *for Harry Barton, a song*

The Sperrins surround it, the Faughan flows by,
at each end of Main Street the hills and the sky,
the small town of Claudy at ease in the sun
last July in the morning, a new day begun.

How peaceful and pretty if the moment could stop,
McIlhenny is straightening things in his shop,
and his wife is outside serving petrol, and then
a girl takes a cloth to a big window pane.

And McClosky is taking the weight off his feet,
and McClelland and Miller are sweeping the street,
and, delivering milk at the Beaufort Hotel,
young Temple's enjoying his first job quite well.

And Mrs McLaughlin is scrubbing her floor,
and Artie Hone's crossing the street to a door,
and Mrs Brown, looking around for her cat,
goes off up an entry—what's strange about that?

Not much—but before she comes back to the road
that strange car parked outside her house will explode,
and all of the people I've mentioned outside
will be waiting to die or already have died.

An explosion too loud for your eardrums to bear,
and young children squealing like pigs in the square,
and all faces chalk-white and streaked with bright red,
and the glass and the dust and the terrible dead.

For an old lady's legs are ripped off, and the head
of a man's hanging open, and still he's not dead.
He is screaming for mercy, and his son stands and stares
and stares, and the suddenly, quick, disappears.

And Christ, little Katherine Aiken is dead,
and Mrs McLaughlin is pierced through the head.
Meanwhile to Dungiven the killers have gone,
and they're finding it hard to get through on the phone.

Exploration in the Arts

An interviewer made the thrilling case
for Modernists: "They were exploratory!
They made it new!" He brought a blush to my face,

for my own work's all song and story.
"To enter the jungle you really have to invent
techniques! To discover you have to experiment!"

Entering the jungle of what is and is not said
needs guts and talent and experience
to go as deep as Eliot and Pound did;
but let us stay this side of common sense.
Shakespeare and I and Byron and Brecht and Burns
offer ourselves as entertainment, turns.

Old Tom and Ezra battened on the old.
Making it new, my arse. Rapists! Damnation!
Where's the originality, the gold,
when every memorable line's quotation?
"Hast 'ou seen but white lilly grow . . ." The cheek, the gall!
Compare Pound's bits with the original.

ELIOT & POUND, industrial complexes, tower
in academe. Entrepreneurs, they bossed
and forced fashions that gave them power.
Writers like Edward Thomas, Hardy, Frost
didn't leave industries behind them. No,
they left a land conserved where things still grow.

Imperial explorers (at the best
brave and ingenious) only opened doors
into the happy gardens of the West
for bloody Jesuits and Conquistadors.
Greed was their basic right to interfere,
exploit, contaminate a hemisphere.

Undressing (transitive, intransitive)
is the only method. Savour the cooking meat.
Listen and watch precisely as you live.
Look up old recipes. Sit down to eat.
Use ancient forms, the journey, the family curse.
Use farce and tragedy. In the trade immerse.

That frigid crazy pair confessed too late
that what they'd conquered Grub Street with was lies.
Their final years were barren and desolate,
though Eliot warmed to what he'd satirised,

someone to dance with. Well, they weren't pathetic.
God knows they were both bright and energetic.

Tonight I'm hearing Beethoven discovering
depths in himself, trying to outplay
Bach, in his Hammerklavier. The ring
of challenge sorts down to humility.
The best are awed by what they've taken on . . .
imitator, pupil, companion.

Intruder on Station Island

(supposed to be spoken by Seamus Heaney)

I expected the next ghost to shake hands
would equal in fame my previous advisers.
Yeats? Swift? No, they were Protestants.

Imagine my chagrin to feel leather on bone,
a boot up my arse from a former rugby player,
shade of a Catholic policeman I had known.

"Seamus, oul' son, how are ye? I was reading your book in
Mullan's. Where's all the imitations and jokes
you regaled us with? They don't get a look in.

And weemin? Ye must have had many a wee frolic
with hot things in Harvard and the West Coast,
but never a mention, or if there is it's symbolic!"

I expounded my aunt's old leather trowel,
its handle an egret's head, a furled sail,
the rounded hanging lip an Irish vowel;

but he interrupted and had the impudence
to advise me: "Relax, oul' hand. Enjoy your luck,
but give us a rest from the weather and farm implements."

From a cattle-dealing line that would stretch from the Boyne
to Lough Neagh, crookedly, a prefect of *St Columb's*,
I knew how to knee a nuisance in the groin;

but signed pamphlets are more effective than dunts.
I keep them about me. This one argued fiercely
that Faber should pay its Irish poets in punts.

How to escape without giving offense was my pain!
To aid me the air stirred my blow-dried hair
as a helicopter whose pilot was Craig Raine

descended. The nonentity melted in whipped air.

Night Song from a Previous Life

These are my golden times, at night
at the kitchen desk with the table light,

with Bush at my elbow and a bottle of stout
and the family in bed and the cat put out,

a contented island of concentration
that the muse might visit with inspiration.

And what if I turn aside to read?
Fiction is food that you always need.

And what if I pick at my old guitar?
Maybe a singer is what you are.

The piano seldom inveigles me.
That noise would waken the family.

So light up another fag and brood
on the peace and sweetness of solitude.

Don't get nervous. Relax, you bum!
You know the poems have always come.

Even your doubts, when they're from the heart,
presage new terrifying works of art.

Desmond O'Grady (1935–)

In an age of multiculturalism Desmond O'Grady stands out as somehow simultaneously reactionary and avant-garde, an inhabitant of the Old World in the most tremendously inclusive sense. Solidly located within the broad historical swath of Celticism, O'Grady identifies himself, and Ireland, with an old Europe. "From the southern Russian steppe to the boglands of the west of Ireland is the territory and sovereignty of the Celt, and that includes the Arab world. I have no interest in anywhere else."[1]

O'Grady was born in Limerick, and spent his childhood in the Gaeltacht region of western Ireland. After his education in a Cistercian college in Tipperary, he began his exploration of Europe as a Berlitz teacher in Paris, where he received encouragement from Samuel Beckett. Later, while teaching in Rome, O'Grady became a close associate of Ezra Pound who, along with James Joyce, exerted the deepest influence on his work. He continued to travel and teach over the next decades, eventually earning a Ph.D. at Harvard before returning to Ireland.

This biographical Odyssey is recounted, in tones that echo, at a lower volume, the epic voice of Ezra Pound, in the "Exordium" that opens O'Grady's 1991 collection entitled *Tipperary*. Touching England, Paris, Rome Greece, Egypt, the Russian steppe, Persia, even North America, the poem unfolds like a survey map of the vast terrain O'Grady thinks of as Celtic. Its itinerary ends where O'Grady's began, back in Ireland, where the poet, he says, "found reclusive haven" and "evolved my Ithakian / imagination alone."[2]

O'Grady's Ithakian imagination also recognizes what he calls a "different presence" of the same muse that guides his poetry, one that inspires translation rather than composition.[3] Alongside his own poems, and in a voice that he hears as continuous with them, O'Grady has produced hundreds of translations. In 1994, the University of Salzburg Press brought out a collection of translations that display

O'Grady as perhaps the most prolific and eclectic poet-translator after Pound. Translated over a period of forty years, these poems include versions from ancient Greek and Chinese; medieval Welsh, Irish, and Latin; modern Arabic and Baltic languages; as well as contemporary Irish, Italian, Spanish, Russian, and Turkish. Like Pound, O'Grady approaches the originals without the fastidiousness of the philologist, but intent on bringing their tone into a lively, oddly colloquial Irish-English. His goal in this work has been to "bring [his] Ireland into the greater Europe and bring that greater Europe into Ireland."[4]

O'Grady's resourceful translations perform this function effectively, but so do his original poems, a striking number of which work to illuminate the connections between Irish traditions and other world cultures. "On Board Ship," a poem from his *Alexandrian Notebook* that puts Yeats's "Lapis Lazuli" into an alien setting, shows how O'Grady's approach to the foreign, whether in the realm of poetry or experience, allows him to trace the Celtic identity beyond the boundaries of insular Ireland. This broad but precisely focused vision, his unique contribution to Irish poetry, creates in "On Board Ship" an image that might serve as a self-portrait—"an ethnic Celtic type" reading *The Poems of Abu Nuwas* while traveling alone to Alexandria, the ancient capital of world culture.[5]

In his recent work, O'Grady has continued to pull at the Celtic thread in the pattern of human culture. "Kinsale" and "Hugh O'Neill in Rome" both rehearse O'Grady's fixation on the battle of Kinsale, where the British defeat of O'Neill in 1601 sounded the first death knell of Celtic culture in Ireland. Poems like "Celts in Europe," of which there are many in his 2001 collection *The Wandering Celt,* give his lifelong obsession with Celticism an anthropological inflection, while "Ovid from Exile" links the Roman poet to figures like the Celtic chieftain O'Neill by their shared—and O'Grady would say inherently Celtic—experience of exile.

NOTES

1. Quoted in William S. Waddell, Jr., "Desmond O'Grady," *Dictionary of Literary Biography,* vol. 40.

2. "Exordium," *Tipperary* (Galway: Salmon Publishing, 1991), p. 11.

3. Desmond O'Grady, *Trawling Tradition: Translations, 1954-1994* (Salzburg, Austria: University of Salzburg Press, 1994), p. xii.

4. Ibid.

5. "On Board Ship," *Alexandrian Notebook* (Dublin: Raven Arts Press, 1989), p. 11.

Self Portrait of Reilly as a Young Man

Through all the beads and missal mass of days
That bible-bound me down the litany
Of years, from matins child to compline man,
I fidget feared your power of cowl and collar.
And in my mea culpa student fear—
Obedient in the poor sight of chaste eyes—
I'd kneel from habit down in organ night
A monk-made man, toy of a tonsured mind.

Came day when I—strolling the tall toll
Of the convent morning, slow as the swing of the bell,
A choir of woods on either side and centre
Aisle of river in between—walked into
Break bread and bless wine sun in altar sky
And knew, for one quick consecrated catch
Of hallowed hour, the priest-made price and power
Of Mother Church and Mother Land and Mother.
Knew that if I was ever to ordain
My word in adult days, and have a Church;
Create salvation in creating freedom;
I must be priest-poet-layman to myself.

The Poet in Old Age Fishing at Evening

for Ezra Pound

Comes a time
When even the old and familiar ideas
Float out of reach of the mind's hooks,
And the soul's prime
Has slipped like a fish through the once high weirs
Of an ailing confidence. O where are the books
On this kind of death?

Upright as love
Out on the tip of a tail of rock,
The sea ravelling off from the eye,

The line like the nerve
Straining the evening back from the clock,
He merges awhile into the lie
Of his own silhouette.

Professor Kelleher and the Charles River

The Charles river reaps here like a sickle. April
Light sweeps flat as ice on the inner curve
Of the living water. Overhead, far from the wave, a dove
White gull heads inland. The spring air, still
Lean from winter, thaws. Walking, John
Kelleher and I talk on the civic lawn.

West, to our left, past some trees, over the ivy walls,
The clock towers, pinnacles, the pillared university yard,
The Protestant past of Cambridge New England selfconsciously dead
In the thawing clay of the Old Burying Ground. Miles
East, over the godless Atlantic, our common brother,
Ploughing his myth-muddy fields, embodies our order.

But here, while the students row by eights and fours on the river—
As my father used to row on the Shannon when, still a child,
I'd cross Thomond Bridge every Sunday, my back to the walled
And turreted castle, listening to that uncle Mykie deliver
His version of history—I listen now to John Kelleher
Unravel the past a short generation later.

Down at the green bank's nerve ends, its roots half in the river,
A leafing tree gathers refuse. The secret force
Of the water worries away the live earth's under-surface.
But his words, for the moment, hold back time's being's destroyer.
While the falling wave on both thighs of the ocean
Erodes the coasts, at its dying conceptual motion.

Two men, one young, one old, stand stopped acrobats in the blue
Day, their bitch river to heel. Beyond,
Some scraper, tower or ancestral house's gable end.

Then, helplessly, as in some ancient dance, the two
Begin their ageless struggle, while the tree's shadow
With all its arms, crawls on the offal-strewn meadow.

Locked in their mute struggle there by the blood-loosed tide
The two abjure all innocence, tear down past order—
The one calm, dispassionate, clearsighted, the other
Wild with ecstasy, intoxicated, world mad.
Surely some new order is at hand;
Some new form emerging where they stand.

Dusk. The great dim tide of shadows from the past
Gathers for the end—the living and the dead.
All force is fruitful. All opposing powers combine.
Aristocratic privilege, divine sanction, anarchy at last
Yield the new order. The saffron sun sets.
All shadows procession in an acropolis of lights.

Reading the Unpublished Manuscripts of Louis MacNeice at Kinsale Harbour

One surely tires eventually of the frequent references—the gossip,
praise, the blame, the intimate anecdote—to those
who, for one unpredictable reason or other (living
abroad, difference of age, chance, the friends one chose,
being detained too long at the most opportune moment) one
never, face to tactile face, has met; but who
had the way things fall fallen favourably, once met, for some
right physic force, would have been polar, kindred you—
though time, space, human nature, sometimes contract
to force the action done that makes abstraction fact.

Here in this mock of a room which might have been yours,
        might have been
the place of our eventual meeting, I find a berth temporarily
(so long too late) among your possessions. Alone,
except for your face in the framed photos,
I sit with your manuscripts spread over my knees,

reliving the unpublished truths of your autobiography.
On the shelves and table, desk, floor, your books
and papers, your bundles of letters—as if you were just moving in
or out, or had been already for years—
like a poem in the making you'll never now finish.
Through the windows I see down to the hook
      of Old Kinsale Harbour.
Mid-summer. Under the sun the sea as smooth as a dish.
Below on the quays the fishermen wind up the morning's business:
stacking the fishboxes, scraping the scales from
      their tackle and hands.
Behind this house the hills shovel down on the town's slate roofs
the mysterious green mounds of their history.
Flaming fir, clouted holly.
Not an Irish harbour at all, but some other—
the kind you might find along the Iberian coast, only greener.

Down to here, down to this clay of contact between us, Hugh O'Neill
      once marched
from way up your part of the country, the North,
      the winter of sixteen
hundred and one, to connect with the long needed
      Spaniards three months
under siege in the Harbour. Having played the English their own
      game and watched
all his life for his moment, he lost our right lot in one bungled night
and with it the thousands of years of our past and our future.
      He began
what divides the North they brought your ash back to, from the
      South I have left
for Rome—where O'Neill's buried exiled. And here, then, this
      moment, late
as the day is (what matter your physical absence) I grow towards
      your knowing,
towards the reassurance of life in mortality, the importance, the value
      of dying.

Purpose

I looked at my days and saw that
with the first affirmation of summer
I must leave all I knew: the house,
the familiarity of family,
companions and memories of childhood,
a future cut out like a tailored suit,
a settled life among school friends.

I looked face to face at my future:
I saw voyages to distant places,
saw the daily scuffle for survival
in foreign towns with foreign tongues
and small rented rooms on companionless
nights with sometimes the solace
of a gentle anonymous arm on the pillow.

I looked at the faces about me
and saw my days' end as a returned ship,
its witness singing in the rigging.

I saw my life and I walked out to it,
as a seaman walks out alone at night from
his house down to the port with his bundled
belongings, and sails into the dark.

from The Celtic Sura

iii The Poet and his Dog

We pair work alone out here together
day after day in every kind of weather.
His job's to guard the kitchen from wild cats,
mine's to daily make my manuscripts.
More than town, or talk in public places,

I prefer the silence of my house's
study. He, wrapped round my feet, keeps both
us warm. And, because well fed, he's worth
his keep because he keeps those thieving cats
out of the larder of our common eats.
He sometimes growls in sleep about his dreams
while I am plotting literary schemes.
We both get on with what we must each day
which kills the joke of this life's unfair play.
He's master of his trade, devoted worker.
I'm pledged for life to mine and want no other.

from Paraphernalia

Origins

We walked out of ceaseless rain, out of
grey featureless towns into the long
light of the northern summer and found
the fields in the fullness of their season.
We were never the same again.

We surveyed panoramas of low stone walls
numerous and varied as old men's wrinkles;
watched pigeons in piebald flocks
flap about farmyards as children
round church doors on Sundays;
trees looked familiar as locals
and country lanes held a nostalgic
urgency like desire.
When shall we see the same way again?

At one point I realised the sea
lay somewhere beyond all this——a mythology
of stones shored on its beaches;
realised we would some day each
have to pick up the sea shaped
stones one by one for personal

scrutiny: like an archeologist reading
fragments on an ancient site
or like a stranded sailor
hoping for a washed up bottle
with some sort of message in it.

Kinsale

Cúin tSaile or *Ceann tSaile:*
Quiet of the Sea or Head of the Ocean.
Either way, home-haven. Here we all
live "blow-ins": exiles, or exiles from
exile. And we "love our ease, our idleness."
You would too if you lived here among us.

The Bandon river finds sea exit here,
Atlantic spawning salmon entrance.
Kinsale origins flowered beyond the Ice sphere
which makes of Time and History a nonsense.
Here Celtic alternative order fought, died,
sixteen one; left us Ireland's modern divide.

We sleep side by side, together,
enjoying harmony's just measure
without weapons on display for war.

Celts in Europe

Hallstatt of Austria
centre and point of departure
high in the Alps on the lakeside.
One valley flanked by high mountains.
Warlord the caste, material the culture;
economy based on iron and saltmines.
Burial in four-wheeler wagons

bartered out of Etruscan Italy
from which developed
the two-wheeler chariot.

The centre of government moved west
and the trade routes east through Trieste.

And some of us pushed out one spring
after the thaw,
(flow under ice face
like flushed blood under white flesh)
pushed out westward to Pyrene
northeastern Spain.
First by Danube then later traverse of mountain range.
Made contact with Greeks there
for business and barter.

Some others went further down south
through the Ligurians
to deal with Massalians.
That gave access through the Pillars of Hercules
to the land of the Cynesians,
most westerly people in Europe
and family to Minas, Rhadomandhin, Sarpeda.
The isles of the west
mine silver and gold, lime and tin,
have lumber forests for building.
Dealing was easy since we all speak one language
from Styria in Austria down
to those southern and western seaboards.

So Pytheas, navigator, shipped out of Massalia
circa three-twenty-five B.C. to the Pretanic Islands.
Though he probably got only to Cornwall,
presumed the similarity of Ireland.
He may have sailed round Orkney, Shetland,
to Iceland, Norway and entered the Arctic Circle.

Bolgios and Brennus crossed Macedonia
with families, belongings and weaponry,
midwinter and made it to Delphi two-seventy-nine
intending to sack it.

Apollo opposes them
stops them with storm floods
so Brennus for shame suicides.
The Greeks hung our Celtic shield trophies
beside the shields of the Persians
in Apollo's Temple.
Whoever was left crossed into Asia Minor
where we "butchered the males, likewise
old women and babes at their mothers' breasts"
and ruled Anatolia.

Alexandros Megalos in Babylon
drinking for bets
in the thirty-third year of his age.
And we held Anatolia
until Attalos the First of Pergamum
finally knocked us circa two-thirty B.C.
The Dying Gaul statue a Roman copy
of the original bronze erected there by Attalus.

And the crowd who went west into Belgium and Brittany
pushed on into Britain's south chalklands . . .
and so into Ireland
bringing La Tène from the Rhine and the Danube,
result of the wine trade with Greeks and Etruscans.

Ovid from Exile

I vomited the six months' sail all the way
from Rome's Ostia. And I retched when I saw
this barren rock in the Black Sea.

I've been sick in heart since I set
foot on the place. No trees, no growth,
a mist no sun can penetrate.

The sea around lies stiff with ice all winter,
the air so constantly cold that some years
snow remains all summer.

A frozen Danube offers no bar
to barbarian raids from landward.
No sight of a star by which to steer.

Here originally lived Miletian settlements.
The present people are Geto-Celts, half-bred Greeks.
To communicate I've learned the rudiments

of both their languages, Getic and Sarmatian.
I've even tried my hand to verse in one.
But nobody here can language me Latin.

I get on well with these horse-taming people.
My life's the simplest and hospitably tax-free.
I don't drink anymore and don't bother to couple.

Abstemious, fit—if not strong—
my day's kept busy with verses and letters.
I wonder what in God's name went wrong.

I crave Rome's craven life,
my home's vineyards, olive groves, meadows,
old friends of the flesh, family, loyal wife.

At my age, however, I'd happily live
the last of my life in a cosier climate
at home in sweet Sulmo where I'd know my grave.

Here, wrapped in rough furskins, I write sad letters
begging my Roman betters' pardon. No replies.
My plight is neither remarked nor matters.

Now rising sixty, entering my tenth solitary year,
I've no hope at all in a silent Tiberius.
Nothing will change my condition to the contrary.

On my walks by the sea I study the fish
so different here to up around Italy.
I've begun a long poem I doubt I'll finish.

Hugh O'Neill in Rome*

29 April 1608–20 July 1616

Exile chosen, they got here. That pursetight
Paul V housed them without beds, furniture
on a common soldier's miserly monthly pay.
They survive on this Papal-Spanish pension.
We praise their frugal daily life, his fortitude
in his Irish cause nine years here amongst us.

He's the man who invented Ireland's guerilla
war on England with the success of a Castro.
He won but lost. Now he must face the facts:
He'll die in exile, with plans to invade Ireland
with troops from Spain to create his own Irish
Catholic nation protected by the Spanish navy.

His first restless years in Baroque boomtown
Rome he saw his forced stay as brief, before
return and conquest. Back home his Ulster family
and friends have been executed by England;
in Rome they die of fever. That makes him one
of us emigrés who live around the eternal city.

He does not live our Rome's indulgent lifestyle.
His spirit's not broken. He's focused, courageous.
After daily Mass he sits to enormous
correspondence with Spain, Flanders, Ireland,
his stingy Pope to plead his cause and needs.
For exercise he climbs that gardened hill to

the Spaniards' church in Montorio. Raphael's
Transfiguration hangs over, Beatrice Cenci's
corpse lies under the high altar. Outside,
his view of Rome's ruins and winehills necklace.
A spectacle that's the heart of the Catholic world.
His heir lies buried here age twenty-three.

Spanish-English peace pacts thwart his high hopes
for Ireland. Some say this daughter by his fourth wife

Catherine wastes their money on young girls' follies.
At night some wine conjures his past great years
while darkness lengthens, indifferent to his estate.
Tomorrow won't change human nature, or his.

He sees now what then failed: his peasants' frailty
and the strength of those forces he couldn't control.
Ambition galvanized him yet he recoiled
from that. His type of tragic hero is driven
by reason's inflexible demands which nature
denies. He epitomizes his country's defeat.

For him the Counter Reformation gave the world
independence and self-development.
That is modern. Eurovision. That way
the Gaelic world could last. He hopes the Irish
see this and will unite in warwork for it.
If they all fail, it's merely human failure.

The future Ireland he would build would take
its independent place in our new Europe.
As the first Renaissance Irishman he's no
insular patriot self-exiled in dour defeat.
He still lives on as an Irish Euro with vision
and begs to be sent home with troops to conquer.

Self-insight in such men crowns or crucifies.
The comedy or tragedy of human acuity masks each
monarch or martyr. Ireland's atavism martyred him.
Does solace in his European ideals comfort him?
No, his pride affirms. At night his tiger's
eyes stare at those flambeaux in his wineglass.

Most call the Irish drunkards. It's said he takes
his rouse and drains his draughts . . . which takes from his
achievements the pith and marrow of his attribute . . .
One saw him tide and ebb his glass and taunt
his beard till his huge frame shook with sour sobs
and slumped across the table. Wine spilled like blood.

Thirty years he workwarred hard to mature
his world. He failed. O'Donnell died six years past
in Spain; their victor Queen Elizabeth I
(God is my oath) thirteen years gone, at seventy.
They say he takes his naked sword to bed.
Rumoured sick he may not last this summer.

Finis

When Spain advised against, would not finance
his wife's return to Flanders for health reasons
O'Neill withdrew after New Year's to private life.
Unwell, they bled his legs an ounce a day two weeks.
Shakespeare died, sudden, April. O'Neill in July.
Would that the former wrote a tragedy on the latter.

With church pomp and solemnity O'Neill
was buried in San Pietro in Montorio
beside his son. Spain paid the funeral costs.
His sword hangs in St Isidoro's. His wife
got his pension, moved to Naples, died there.
If here 1600 would O'Neill burn Bruno at the stake?

The Poet's Request

I ask
for a house,
not a hovel
for pigs and cattle,
wide open, with dignity in welcome
and a chair
well cushioned with horsehair
at my table.

Sedelius Scottus, 9th c.

The Old Head of Kinsale Says

I'm here in the Atlantic a long time:
two hundred and fifty million years.

My first and only tenants were migrant Celts
from the Mediterranean. They brought a light that
gave safe passage to passerby sailors forever.
They all left us in peace. Thus we have lived more than
two thousand years. No change in my bent grass hair.
It dies, regrows annually. No change in chough,
guillemot, gannet and fulmar, in kittiwake, razor-bill
and skylark that play about my head. No change
in bracken, bell heather and sea thrift in blossom
nor in beef or beastie from beef bullock to pygmy shrew.
No change in the migrating mammals that swim my myth
and no change in me, other than ages' natural weathering.

I have my natural heritage here. I shall keep it for mine.
A land that does not preserve its heritage is not a nation.

Brendan Kennelly (1936–)

Brendan Kennelly was born in 1936 in Ballylongford, a country town in County Kerry where he stayed for some twenty years, observing the rhythms and processes of rural life. He left to attend Trinity College, Dublin, where he eventually became Professor of Modern Literature. The division of his time among country, urban, and academic settings helps to elucidate, Kennelly believes, the fact that his poems "fall naturally into three divisions: poems about the countryside; poems about the city; and poems which, broadly speaking, make an attempt to express some kind of personal philosophy."[1]

But against the apparent distinctness of these categories, Kennelly argues that "there is one poem in every poet which he or she is always trying to write and very rarely succeeds in writing." This, he says,

> helps to account for the repetitiveness, doggedness, obstinate experimentation and moments of self-parody that seem to laugh mockingly at most poets. I sometimes think that poetry takes the mickey out of poets just to show that it refuses to be pinned down or finally defined for the benefit of lazy minds.[2]

Kennelly's own poems span such a breadth of subject matter that the image of a poet continually rewriting the same poem seems inappropriate to his work. But, as he suggests, the surface breadth conceals a consistency of attention; "the way I see a pig-killer at work or the way in which I try to understand history is not separable, essentially, from the way I see scraps of paper in a city street late at night or how I try to understand ideas of, say, goodness and treachery."[3]

Whatever the subject matter, poetry is always, for Kennelly, "basically a celebration of human inadequacy and failure."[4] His early poems look at aspects of this human frailty—moral or physical weakness, defects of character—from a lyric perspective. In a voice isolated from the distortions of personality they sort through the evidence for the inescapable isolation of selves from selves. "Her world approached," he writes of a woman who has just revealed that "she was dying of some incurable disease." "Her world approached, touched, recoiled from mine."⁵ In "Good Souls, to Survive" Kennelly begins to grasp the function of isolation both when it is maintained and when it is transcended. "We see," the poems says, "because we are blind / And should not be surprised to find / We survive because we're enclosed."⁶

The rhyme of "blind" with "find" rings the truth at the core of Kennelly's personal vision. Weakness confronted is a source of power, and mere surviving is not all we can hope to do. It is the willingness to step outside the protective shell and to discover human inadequacy that turns imperfection into strength: "If merit is measured at all, / Vulnerability is the measure." And merit, then, is not revealed in a careful avoidance of defilement. "But from corruption comes the deep / Desire to plunge to the true."⁷ Following this logic, Kennelly has turned his later poetry toward an exploration of treachery and corruption. He published two controversial but critically acclaimed books, *Cromwell* and *The Book of Judas,* that not only look at deceit and betrayal, but try to "enter into" the personalities of "two of the most extreme examples of those forces that cry out (though they're damned to silence, among other things) to be looked at, questioned, listened to, responded to, expressed."⁸ Neither book is squeamish about uncovering depravities, blindness to them being the only debility Kennelly will recognize.

"I believe that each of us is blind in a great number of ways; and that saves us. I believe that occasionally we see things in our blindness; and that elevates us."⁹ By placing human deficiencies in the foreground, Kennelly's poems inherit the strength of human dignity in the face of adversity. "We are cripplingly limited," he writes. "To recognize this is a strength."¹⁰ In the recent volume *Glimpses,* from which are drawn the lapidary miniatures "Home," "Old Irish," and "Still To Be Done," Kennelly overcomes this inherent human blindness by means of the sidewise glance, its vision captured in poems of just a few words.

NOTES

1. Preface to *Selected Poems* (New York: E. P. Dutton & Co. Inc., 1972), p. vii.

2. Preface to *Breathing Spaces: Early Poems* (Newcastle upon Tyne: Bloodaxe Books, 1992), p. 10.

3. Preface to *Selected Poems,* p. vii.

4. Ibid., p. viii.

5. "At the Party," *Selected Poems*, p. 59.

6. "Good Souls, to Survive," *Selected Poems*, p. 37.

7. Ibid.

8. Preface to *Breathing Spaces*, pp. 10–11.

9. Preface to *Selected Poems*, pp. viii–ix.

10. Ibid., p. ix.

James Joyce's Death-mask

He, in this death-mask, warms the vision like a joy,
For whom the cold of exile was the only place
Where home was art's acropolis; now, passions stem
From fretted skin, the hollow landscape of his face.

Eyeing this mask, I see him bending to life's work,
Some prodigal son who scorned, from love, to claim
A fatted calf, but irrevocably estranged,
Strode lonely down the bright meridians of fame.

Inert, the poem-troubled skin squats round the eyes,
Limp hair, white spike of light that strikes the fervent lips
Which opened once to utter sung whisperings; now,
Harsh yearnings hurt wilfully and cold wind rips.

Away, outside, he sees from his total prison,
The bone-bright life of things that grows remote and dim,
A ring of Being, glinting like sunlit water,
Spurting through stoney clouds, outside, away from him.

And yet those eyes knew life's repeated thunder once,
Tumult of images, city roaring and blind,
Leaped wild through his head with a hard, choking wonder,
Stumbling to expression in dark streets of his mind.

His life-work finished and Ireland still blown by the
Wet winds of fear, his death-face has its own life yet;
Some simple no music, birdsong, nor branches
Breaking with full flowers can equal, or we forget.

The Hill of Fire

I saw five counties of Munster
From the top of Scrolm hill,
And later the grey blankets of rain
Swaddling the far fields until

They seemed to disappear in greyness.
Minutes later, the rain was gone,
And the salmon-heavy Cashen
Like a river of silver shone.

The hob-nailed hours trudge slowly
Through that country; the brown
Mountain, bald-headed, lords it
Over the peaceful pastures down

Along the hillside. A name for every field—
Boland's meadow, marvellously green,
And the humped, crooked shoulder
Of grassy Garnagoyteen.

A touch of cold coming in the air,
I threw one last look around
At my mysterious province, and turned my back
On the cold purity of high ground.

From low ground, I saw the sun
Change the entire
World; that towering bulk became
A hill of fire.

The Celtic Twilight

Now in the Celtic twilight, decrepit whores
Prowl warily along the Grand Canal*
In whose rank waters bloated corpses float,
A dog and cat that came to a bad end.
The whores don't notice; perfumed bargainers
Prepare to prey on men prepared to prey
On them and others. Hot scavengers
Are victims, though they confidently strut
And wait for Dublin's Casanovas to appear—
Poor furtive bastards with the goods in hand.

And in the twilight now, a shrill whore shrieks
At one stiff client who's cheated her,
"Misther! If you come back again,
You'll get a shaggin' steel comb through the chest."
Then gathering what's left of dignity,
Preparing once again to cast an eye
On passing prospects, she strolls beside
The dark infested waters where
Inflated carcases
Go floating by into the night
Of lurid women and predatory men
Who must inflict but cannot share
Each other's pain.

Good Souls, to Survive

Things inside things endure
Longer than things exposed;
We see because we are blind
And should not be surprised to find
We survive because we're enclosed.

If merit is measured at all,
Vulnerability is the measure;
The little desire protection
With something approaching passion,
Will not be injured, cannot face error.

So the bird in astonishing flight
Chokes on the stricken blood,
The bull in the dust is one
With surrendered flesh and bone,
Naked on chill wood.

The real is rightly intolerable,
Its countenance stark and abrupt,
Good souls, to survive, select
Their symbols from among the elect—
Articulate, suave, corrupt.

But from corruption comes the deep
Desire to plunge to the true;
To dare is to redeem the blood,
Discover the buried good,
Be vulnerably new.

The Limerick Train

Hurtling between hedges now, I see
green desolation stretch on either hand
while sunlight blesses all magnanimously.

The gods and heroes are gone for good and
men evacuate each Munster valley
and midland plain, gravelly Connaught land

and Leinster town. Who, I wonder, fully
understands the imminent predicament,
sprung from rooted suffering and folly?

Broken castles tower, lost order's monument,
splendour crumbling in sun and rain,
witnesses to all we've squandered and spent,

but no phoenix rises from that ruin
although the wild furze in yellow pride
explodes in bloom above each weed and stone,

promise ablaze on every mountainside
after the centuries' game of pitch-and-toss
separates what must live from what has died.

A church whips past, proclaiming heavy loss
amounting to some forty thousand pounds;
a marble Christ unpaid for on His Cross

accepts the Limerick train's irreverent sound,
relinquishes great power to little men—
a river flowing still, but underground.

Wheels clip the quiet counties. Now and then
I see a field where like an effigy
in rushy earth, there stands a man alone

lifting his hand in salutation. He
disappears almost as soon as he is seen,
drowned in distant anonymity.

We have travelled far, the journey has been
costly, tormented odyssey through night;
and now, noting the unmistakable green,

the pools and trees that spring into the sight,
the sheep that scatter madly, wheel and run,
quickly transformed to terrified leaping white,

I think of what the land has undergone
and find the luminous events of history
intolerable as staring at the sun.

Only twenty miles to go and I'll be
home. Seeing two crows low over the land,
I recognise the land's uncertainty,

the unsensational surrender and
genuflection to the busy stranger
whose power in pocket brings him power in hand.

Realising now how dead is anger
such as sustained us at the very start
with possibility in time of danger,

I know why we have turned away, apart
(I'm moving still but so much time has sped)
from the dark realities of the heart.

From my window now, I try to look ahead
and know, remembering what's been done and said,
that we must always cherish, and reject, the dead.

At the Party

When the woman at the party said
That she was dying of some incurable disease,
I stared into my glass and saw the red
Wine's glittering infinities
Dancing alive between my fingers,
Making me again confront her eyes—
No traces there of any special hunger,
No painful guess, hysterical surmise.
She said, "Christmas in this land is cold,
Maguire's idea to go abroad is good;
As for myself, I like to take a stroll
On winter afternoons. Always heats the blood."
Barely hearing, I agreed. She smiled again.
Her world approached, touched, recoiled from mine.
The room was loud with noise of dying men.
Her parted lips accepted the good wine.

Union

When salmon swarmed in the brown tides
And cocks raised their lusty din
And her heart beat like a wild bird's heart,
She left her kin.

A black ass brayed in the village,
Men ploughed and mowed,
There was talk of rising water
When he struck the road.

Words stranger than were scattered
Over the shuttered dead
Were faint as child-songs in their ears
When they stretched in bed.

The Singing Girl Is Easy in Her Skill

The singing girl is easy in her skill.
We are more human than we were before.
We cannot see just now why men should kill

Although it seems we are condemned to spill
The blood responding to the ocean's roar.
The singing girl is easy in her skill.

That light transfiguring the window-sill
Is peace that shyly knocks on every door.
We cannot see just now why men should kill.

This room, this house, this world all seem to fill
With faith in which no human heart is poor.
The singing girl is easy in her skill.

Though days are maimed by many a murderous will
And lovers shudder at what lies in store
We cannot see just now why men should kill.

It's possible we may be happy still,
No living heart can ever ask for more.
We cannot see just now why men should kill.
The singing girl is easy in her skill.

Clean*

"You know what these Irish bitches are like.
When they're not holy, they're cannibals
Out to munch a man's prick and balls
As an afternoon snack.
There was this mountainous cow of a creature
Who liked to kill and devour others
In a manner not uncommon among Irish mothers.
I decided to hang her.
She was so graceless that not once
Did she cry or call upon God to forgive her

But dangled in silence, gross and obscene.
Afterwards, I went to her house
And found the bones of three of my troopers
Picked clean."

A Holy War

"We suffered the little children to be cut out of women
'Their bellys were rippitt upp'
This was a holy war, a just rebellion
And little lords in the womb must not escape
Their due. Certain women not great with child
Were stripped and made to dig a hole
Big enough to contain them all.
We buried these women alive
And covered them with rubbish, earth and stones.
Some who were not properly smothered
Yet could not rise
(They tried hard) got for their pains
Our pykes in their breasts. People heard
(Or said they heard) the ground make women's cries."

There Will Be Dreams

"Oh yes, there will be dreams," Oliver said
"Be assured, there will always be dreams.
And there will be men, willing makers
And willing destroyers of governments and homes.
I walked the bank of the Cashen this morning
And I stood watching at the edge of the tide
I saw the Ballyduff men turn to their fishing
And every man of them was humble and proud
In his dreaming, touching what he knew to be
True in himself. I saw the boats heading out

And I knew why my life is a long war.
Any man will kill who has known the land's beauty
And though his heart suffer stabs of doubt
This land is a dream to be damned and saved for."

The Big Words

The first time I heard
Transubstantiation
My head fell off.

"Explain it," the teacher said.
I looked around the classroom
Searching for my severed head
And found it near a mouse-hole
Where we used to drop
Crumbs of bread
Turning to turds
Twice as transcendental
As holy words.

"Explain it to me," I said to my father.
From behind the great spread pages of *The Irish Independent*
"It's a miracle," he said,
"I'm reading John D. Hickey on the semi-final
But come back later and we'll see
What's happening to Gussie Goose and Curly Wee."*

I found out what *Transubstantiation* meant.
I trotted out my answer
But the trot turned into a gallop
And I found myself witnessing a race
Between all the big words
Used by all the small men.
I use them myself, of course,
Especially when I have nothing to say,
When I cannot raise dust or hackles, go to town, or make hay
With the little bit of life in my head
Suggesting I should drink the best wine,

Eat the best bread
And thus, with a deft flick of my mind,
Transfigure the blackest hours
On this most holy ground
Where some would make their god
Hide behind big words,
Shields to stop him showing the colour of his blood
And be safe as the bland masters of jargon
Whose blindness is an appetite
For whacking great vocabularies
That cough resoundingly
In some bottomless pit
Of self-importance.

Some night soon, I'm going to have a party
For all the big words.
By the light of a semantic moon
I'll turn the race into a dance,
And with my little words
Both hosts and servants
Catering beyond their best
For even the teeniest need
Of every resonant guest,
Big and small will all be thrilled to see
Exactly what has happened
To Gussie Goose and Curly Wee.

Service*

The best way to serve the age is to betray it.
If it's a randy slut slooping for hump
Hide in a dark ditch, wait, waylay it
And land where no one can extradite you.

If it's a moneyman with a philosophy like
"There's only cash and as many fucks as you can get"
Inspire him to talk of Daddy's tenderness
Till his eyes are wet.

Be a knife, bullet, poison, flood, earthquake;
Cut, gut, shrivel, swallow, bury, burn, drown
Till someone senses things ain't as they should be.

If betrayal is a service, learn to betray
With the kind of style that impresses men
Until they dream of being me.

Halcyon Days

I find the four gospels a darned good read
Though I don't come well out of the scene.
I saw what I saw, did what I did
And shed no tears over what might have been.

These were halcyon days, sane, insane,
Small farmers and fishermen leaving home
On impulse, just up and out, quick adventurous men.

I liked Peter, first Pope and Bishop of Rome.

Far from all that the same Peter was born and bred.
Leaving the wife and kids must have been hard
But Peter always did what Peter had to do.

In this, we were not unalike. I'm glad
These gospels show him in a kindly light.
I once wrote in my scrapbook that what I approve of I tend to regard as
    true.

A Second's Eternity

Even when he was acting the tough around Jerusalem
He had a good word for the bad women
Who liked him for how he saw them
And talked to them in their poxy dens.

Late at night when the screwing has to start
In the moaning towns, villages and cities
Where a longing prick is a pain in the heart
And no one is near to give you the kiss of life

And you, like him, might be out walking by
A river, staring at lights, thinking of simple misery
And the ubiquitous insult to simple dignity

Then he, like you, sees a dead dog in the street,
Bends down, touches, you believe he sighs
As he looks for a second's eternity through the dead eyes.

Lough Derg

Lest anyone should think I am incapable
Of sorrow for sin, I cycled with all
Speed to a boat at a lakeside, a small
Fisherman oared me over to Lough Derg in Donegal*

Where sorrow-for-sin goes to town
And remorseful sinners gather
In the parched weather
Calling on God and his colleagues to come down

And forgive them for doing whatever they've done
Or failed to do. I joined in
And whispered to God to forgive my sin
"Judas" said God, "You're a gas man.

First, you betray me. Then you plead to be forgiven.
D'you think we're gone-in-the-head up here in heaven?
I'm not a God to bear grudges and yet
I think you should hang yourself, you treacherous get!"

This divine advice seemed to me a bit extreme.
I looked around at men and women on their knees.
What in the name of Jesus are they up to at all?
What are they afraid of? Who are they trying to please?

Am I the sole witness of some bad penitential dream?
Are these breastbeating people victims of some immeasurable fall?
Are they stooped in silence because they haven't the heart to scream?
Are the slapping waves the broken hopes of little souls?
Do the blind pretend to see? The deaf let on to hear a call?
Is a man half-happy only when creating his own pain?

What makes a man crave to be a God-licking slave?
What makes him mutter despair to the wind and rain?
Why can't he live with his own voice in this freezing cave?
Are these antics a parody of his preparation for the grave?
O piss into the wind, then piss into the wind again.

I've had some atrocious cups of tea in my time
But Lough Derg tea makes tinkers' piss taste like wine.
I've tasted bread that would scutter a cat
But Lough Derg bread would frighten a starving rat.

Now and then I've found it hard to sleep at night
But after Lough Derg I'll snooze an innocent snooze
While sorrow-for-sin befouls the world like shite
The morning after a monumental, gut-bursting booze.

One encouraging sight I saw, one sight alone:
At the back of the church, triumphant, gasping in joy,
Mr Daniel O'Connell was screwing Miss Molly Malone.*
God bless you, Daniel, may she bear you a happy boy,
I prayed at O'Connell's every emancipated moan.

Then into the boat I got and rhythmed back to land.
Up on my bike I mounted and hit for Sligo town
Where I guzzled Ben Bulbens of fish and chips in grand
Style while hungry gods gaped enviously down.

The True Thing

I don't know anyone who knows what became of the true thing.
If poets think they sing, it is a parody they sing.
In the beginning men of common sense

Knew that for the damned dream to grow
Wholesale massacre of innocence
Was necessary, prophets' blood must flow,
Thieves of little apples be crucified, rebels be put down,
Conspiracies of messianic troglodytes be strangled
And saviours be given the bum's rush out of every pub in town.

Out of the smashed cities
Works of art adorn the Vatican walls
A comfortable living is right for the Archbishop and his wife
Lads and lassies study till their eyeballs burn and their souls know
One must never heed the bitter cries, forsaken calls
Of the man in the beginning burning fear
Like old papers, kissing his death, having given his life.
Yes, and we have double-glazed hearts and committees and promotions
    and pensions
And time off to enjoy and bless
The kids shining out to discos and parties
In the holy light of progress.
And we have learning, we could put Hell in a couplet, Eden in an epigram,
Dish out slices of epics like gifts of land in the Golden Vale
And sweat blood or what feels like blood
To get the right rhythm and thereby hangs a tale
Of an abortive experiment in love
That began in bestial company and ended up in public shame
And started all over again in a sad parody
Of what cannot be understood

Only followed as a blind man follows his expensive dog
Through visionary streets of fluent slavish traffic
Calmly-crazily living the rhythms of my mechanical blood
Yearning occasionally, nevertheless, for dialogue with God.
I would ask, to begin with, what became of the true thing
And after that, well, anything might happen.
I can even imagine a poet starting to sing
In a way I haven't heard for a long time.
If the song comes right, the true thing may find a name
Singing to me of who, and why, I am.

Home

"No place like home," she said,
    eighty in her rocking chair
"where you can spit in the fire
    saucer your tea
      and call the cat a bastard."

Old Irish

The old Irish word for kiss
is drink.
When a man drinks a woman
he knows how stupid it is to think.

Still to be done

Tiredness hits him, failure snuggles in close,
years of work stalk him, bleating
and slipping. One thing he knows, one thing.
Everything is still to be done. Everything.

Seamus Heaney (1939–)

The image Seamus Heaney offers at the opening of his first commercially pub-
lished book, *Death of a Naturalist*, is of himself at work, though the word that
attaches itself to the poet's vocation isn't *work*, but *rest:* "Between my finger and
my thumb / The squat pen rests; snug as a gun."[1] Against that still image of the
poet, pen resting, comes a view of his father, working, first in a flowerbed in the
present, then a potato field remembered from twenty years before. First volumes
are often seen after the fact as prophetic of a writer's career, but it is rare that a
poet's opening lines contain, already, so much of what will come, and rarer that a
poet seems already to know what has to be done to get raw poetic energies under
artistic control. Heaney's anxious preoccupations are here in the tension between
the inactive poet and his occupied father. The anxiety, however, is present in a
form that somehow suggests its own solution, so that Heaney—facing the fear
that writing might not be a proper job of work as farming is, or cutting turf—is
setting up in its practical, manageable form the question that his poetry will con-
tinually ask itself, or invent itself by asking: How is a poem to be of use? And in
particular, how is a poem to be of use in a troubled country where the spade and
the gun appear to have far more immediate utility?

Heaney was born in County Derry in 1939, on a farm called Mossbawn. In
many ways, that place is still the center of his poetic world, its omphalos. Heaney
has used the word to describe the farm, turning the word itself into a kind of
sonic vehicle, like the rasping of his father's spade, for reaching those early mem-
ories.

> I would begin with the Greek word, *omphalos*, meaning the navel, and hence
> the stone that marked the centre of the world, and repeat it, *omphalos,*
> *omphalos, omphalos,* until its blunt and falling music becomes the music of
> somebody pumping water at the pump outside our back door.[2]

The material center of the classical world, given a new form, becomes the music of work done in the workaday world of rural Northern Ireland. That kind of metamorphosis is one Heaney learned to see in his first volume, where poem after poem reworks the Romantic poetic tradition, turning fascination with nature into a poetry of natural practicality.

This turning is useful for Heaney's subsequent poetry because it works in both directions. Reversed, it's like the trick he pulls off in a later essay that takes up Zbigniew Herbert's poem "The Knocker." The poem was published in English translation in 1968, the year the Troubles in Northern Ireland rose to full flare. Appropriately timed, it serves as an indictment of lyric poetry. The charge is disengagement, and, as Heaney puts it, "the poem makes us feel that we should prefer moral utterance to palliative imagery,"

> but it does exactly that, makes us *feel*, and by means of feeling carries truth alive into the heart—exactly as the Romantics said it should. We end up persuaded we are against lyric poetry's culpable absorption in its own process by an entirely successful instance of that very process in action. . . .[3]

Heaney's defense of lyric here tells us something about the strange appearance of a gun, snug in the second line of that first poem. Alongside his sense that poetry might bear some comparison with work, he puts the possibility that the work it does might have some moral bearing on the political situation in Northern Ireland. The gun is another thing that poetry, explicitly, is not, but in the North the two can be imagined in a functional relationship that justifies the simile.

Early in his career, Heaney found in the community of poets coming together in Belfast an endorsement for choosing the work of poetry over the more evident work done with a spade or a gun. In 1963 he began to participate in poetry sessions sponsored by Philip Hobsbaum, a poet and newly-appointed lecturer at Queen's University. Before starting the Belfast group, Hobsbaum had fostered a literary community in London, where he set himself in opposition to the smooth, polished poetics of the Movement poets like Philip Larkin and John Wain.[4] Heaney rejects as a media construction the idea that the poetry coming out of the Hobsbaum group constituted a Belfast "renaissance,"[5] but it is clear that the poets who gathered around Hobsbaum shared a common sense of purpose and enthusiasm, and that for some this sense brought them near to Patrick Kavanagh's conception of the "parochial" as a powerful, informed regionalism ripe for rebirth in Irish, or in this case Northern Irish, poetry. "What happened Monday night after Monday night in the Hobsbaums' house in Fitzwilliam Street somehow ratified the activity of writing for all of us who shared it," Heaney wrote in the *Honest Ulsterman* in 1978.

What Hobsbaum achieved . . . was to give a generation a sense of them-
selves, in two ways: it allowed us to get to grips with one another within the
group, to move from critical comment to creative friendship at our own
pace, and it allowed a small public to think of us as The Group, a single,
even singular phenomenon. . . . It's easy to be blasé about all that now, for
now, of course, we're genuine parochials. Then we were craven provin-
cials. Hobsbaum contributed much to that crucial transformation.[6]

Heaney's first two collections, *Death of a Naturalist* and *Door into the Dark,* have
been read as testimony to the influence of Hobsbaum's anti-Movement sentiment.
Critics wanted to see these volumes as deliberately roughened, and it's true that
Heaney draws his language from the rough, rural world of his childhood, setting
it in stanzas that halt and leap, clanging words against the rhythms of traditional
metrical forms. But the impulse toward polish may be more present in these po-
ems than early readers wanted to acknowledge. Heaney's essay on Robert Frost
owns an admiration for Frost that has to be placed alongside Heaney's early rural
voice. Whatever the source of influence, Heaney's subsequent volumes moved
generally in the direction of formal refinement, and at least one critic has sug-
gested that the early "roughening went against the natural grain in Heaney."[7] In
the deep mirrors of his recent poetry's polished surfaces, though, Heaney contin-
ues to represent the perceptions of an unsettled mind in which the "urgency of
delight," as Helen Vendler puts it, is always in contention with the "urgency of
witness."[8]

During the 1970s Heaney published a series of poems that found a meeting
point for these two imperatives in European prehistory as revealed by the discov-
eries of contemporary archaeology. The convergence of ancient life and current
reality at the tip of the archaeologist's spade offered Heaney both a concrete im-
age for the atrocities committed in the context of the Troubles and a way of en-
gaging the affective content of Northern Ireland's history. "My emotions, my
feelings," he recalls, "whatever those instinctive energies are that have to be en-
gaged for a poem, those energies quickened more when contemplating a victim,
strangely, from 2,000 years ago than they did from contemplating a man at the
end of a road being swept up into a plastic bag—I mean the barman at the end of
our road tried to carry out a bomb and it blew up."[9]

In poems like "The Grauballe Man" and "Punishment," Heaney's identifica-
tion with the suffering victims of prehistoric sacrifice and retribution lets him ac-
knowledge the guilt of complicity shared by all disengaged observers of history:
"I almost love you / but would have cast, I know, / the stones of silence."[10] In the
earlier poem "The Tollund Man," that identification links the bogland of Den-
mark with the landscape of Heaney's native Northern Ireland, creating a north-

ern terrain of atrocity on which various national and sectarian allegiances fade into the single image of brutality. The poem's closing stanza, with its contrary moods, embodies something of the temper of Heaney's mature poetry. "Hung in the scales / with beauty and atrocity," (to use a phrase from "The Grauballe Man") his poems of this period find a kind of stillpoint of lived experience, where truth and beauty are not yet separated.[11]

In "Station Island," this confirmation of the value of lyric takes voice in Heaney's imagination as the ghost of James Joyce. The poem imagines a series of ghosts addressing the poet as he moves through the stations of the traditional Catholic pilgrimage on Lough Derg. Encountering the ghost of Joyce at the end of the poem, Heaney finds himself upbraided for the sort of political worrying he has performed as an expiation for the sins of lyric: "You are raking at dead fires, / a waste of time for somebody your age. // That subject people stuff is a cod's game."[12] Joyce's departing remonstrance not only directs Heaney toward lyrical subjectivity but assumes its language, urging him to put old grievances aside and "fill the element / with signatures on your own frequency, / echo soundings, searches, probes, allurements, / elver-gleams in the dark of the whole sea."[13]

"That subject people stuff is a cod's game," Heaney's Joyce says, because the English language now belongs to the Irish as much as to the British. What the poem recognizes in those elver-gleams and allurements is, again, the broad value of lyric poetry, and the ultimately political effect of Heaney's success in finding an individual poetic signature on an Irish frequency, an Irish claim on the English lyric. Heaney's poems, consistently finding over the last forty years this deep point at which the poet's work becomes the people's, recall the contract, as well as the aesthetic promise, of that first poem: "Between my finger and my thumb / The squat pen rests. / I'll dig with it."[14] Seamus Heaney's lifetime of poetic excavations earned him the Nobel Prize for Literature in 1995.

NOTES

1. "Digging," *Death of a Naturalist* (London: Faber and Faber, 1966), p. 13.

2. "Mossbawn," *Preoccupations: Selected Prose 1968–1978* (London: Faber and Faber, 1980), p. 17.

3. *The Government of the Tongue: The 1986 T. S. Eliot Memorial Lectures and Other Critical Writings* (London: Faber and Faber, 1988), p. 100.

4. The "Movement" denotes a group of poets who emerged in England in the 1950s. Their poems are distinguished by polished form and by clear, clever, and forceful—even, at times, vulgar—language.

5. See Neil Corcoran, *Seamus Heaney* (London: Faber and Faber, 1986), p. 22.

6. "The Group," *Preoccupations*, p. 29.

7. Bernard O'Donoghue, *Seamus Heaney and the Language of Poetry* (London and New York: Harvester/Wheatsheaf, 1994), p. 153.

8. Helen Vendler, "A Nobel for the North," *The New Yorker*, October 23, 1995, p. 84.

9. *Seamus Heaney* ([Copenhagen]: Skoleradioen, 1977), p. 60. This part of the interview is cited in Michael Parker, *Seamus Heaney: The Making of the Poet* (London: Macmillan, 1993), p. 105.

10. "Punishment," *Poems 1965–1975* (New York: Farrar, Straus and Giroux, 1980), p. 193.

11. "The Grauballe Man," *Poems 1965–1975*, p. 191.

12. "Station Island," *Station Island* (London: Faber and Faber, 1984), p. 93.

13. Ibid., pp. 93–94.

14. "Digging," *Death of a Naturalist*, p. 14.

Digging

Between my finger and my thumb
The squat pen rests; snug as a gun.

Under my window, a clean rasping sound
When the spade sinks into gravelly ground:
My father, digging. I look down

Till his straining rump among the flowerbeds
Bends low, comes up twenty years away
Stooping in rhythm through potato drills
Where he was digging.

The coarse boot nestled on the lug, the shaft
Against the inside knee was levered firmly.
He rooted out tall tops, buried the bright edge deep
To scatter new potatoes that we picked,
Loving their cool hardness in our hands.

By God, the old man could handle a spade.
Just like his old man.

My grandfather cut more turf in a day
Than any other man on Toner's bog.
Once I carried him milk in a bottle
Corked sloppily with paper. He straightened up
To drink it, then fell to right away
Nicking and slicing neatly, heaving sods
Over his shoulder, going down and down
For the good turf. Digging.

The cold smell of potato mould, the squelch and slap
Of soggy peat, the curt cuts of an edge
Through living roots awaken in my head.
But I've no spade to follow men like them.

Between my finger and my thumb
The squat pen rests.
I'll dig with it.

Death of a Naturalist

All year the flax-dam festered in the heart
Of the townland; green and heavy-headed
Flax had rotted there, weighted down by huge sods.
Daily it sweltered in the punishing sun.
Bubbles gargled delicately, bluebottles
Wove a strong gauze of sound around the smell.
There were dragonflies, spotted butterflies,
But best of all was the warm thick slobber
Of frogspawn that grew like clotted water
In the shade of the banks. Here, every spring
I would fill jampotfuls of the jellied
Specks to range on window-sills at home,
On shelves at school, and wait and watch until
The fattening dots burst into nimble-
Swimming tadpoles. Miss Walls would tell us how
The daddy frog was called a bullfrog
And how he croaked and how the mammy frog
Laid hundreds of little eggs and this was
Frogspawn. You could tell the weather by frogs too
For they were yellow in the sun and brown
In rain.
      Then one hot day when fields were rank
With cowdung in the grass the angry frogs
Invaded the flax-dam; I ducked through hedges
To a coarse croaking that I had not heard
Before. The air was thick with a bass chorus.
Right down the dam gross-bellied frogs were cocked
On sods; their loose necks pulsed like sails. Some hopped:
The slap and plop were obscene threats. Some sat
Poised like mud grenades, their blunt heads farting.
I sickened, turned, and ran. The great slime kings
Were gathered there for vengeance and I knew
That if I dipped my hand the spawn would clutch it.

The Early Purges

I was six when I first saw kittens drown.
Dan Taggart pitched them, "the scraggy wee shits,"
Into a bucket; a frail metal sound,

Soft paws scraping like mad. But their tiny din
Was soon soused. They were slung on the snout
Of the pump and the water pumped in.

"Sure isn't it better for them now?" Dan said.
Like wet gloves they bobbed and shone till he sluiced
Them out on the dunghill, glossy and dead.

Suddenly frightened, for days I sadly hung
Round the yard, watching the three sogged remains
Turn mealy and crisp as old summer dung

Until I forgot them. But the fear came back
When Dan trapped big rats, snared rabbits, shot crows
Or, with a sickening tug, pulled old hens' necks.

Still, living displaces false sentiments
And now, when shrill pups are prodded to drown,
I just shrug, "Bloody pups." It makes sense:

"Prevention of cruelty" talk cuts ice in town
Where they consider death unnatural,
But on well-run farms pests have to be kept down.

Follower

My father worked with a horse-plough,
His shoulders globed like a full sail strung
Between the shafts and the furrow.
The horses strained at his clicking tongue.

An expert. He would set the wing
And fit the bright steel-pointed sock.
The sod rolled over without breaking.
At the headrig, with a single pluck

Of reins, the sweating team turned round
And back into the land. His eye
Narrowed and angled at the ground,
Mapping the furrow exactly.

I stumbled in his hobnailed wake,
Fell sometimes on the polished sod;
Sometimes he rode me on his back
Dipping and rising to his plod.

I wanted to grow up and plough,
To close one eye, stiffen my arm.
All I ever did was follow
In his broad shadow round the farm.

I was a nuisance, tripping, falling,
Yapping always. But today
It is my father who keeps stumbling
Behind me, and will not go away.

Personal Helicon

for Michael Longley

As a child, they could not keep me from wells
And old pumps with buckets and windlasses.
I loved the dark drop, the trapped sky, the smells
Of waterweed, fungus and dank moss.

One, in a brickyard, with a rotted board top.
I savoured the rich crash when a bucket
Plummeted down at the end of a rope.
So deep you saw no reflection in it.

A shallow one under a dry stone ditch
Fructified like any aquarium.
When you dragged out long roots from the soft mulch
A white face hovered over the bottom.

Others had echoes, gave back your own call
With a clean new music in it. And one
Was scaresome, for there, out of ferns and tall
Foxgloves, a rat slapped across my reflection.

Now, to pry into roots, to finger slime,
To stare, big-eyed Narcissus, into some spring
Is beneath all adult dignity. I rhyme
To see myself, to set the darkness echoing.

Requiem for the Croppies*

The pockets of our greatcoats full of barley—
No kitchens on the run, no striking camp—
We moved quick and sudden in our own country.
The priest lay behind ditches with the tramp.
A people, hardly marching—on the hike—
We found new tactics happening each day:
We'd cut through reins and rider with the pike
And stampede cattle into infantry,
Then retreat through hedges where cavalry must be thrown.
Until, on Vinegar Hill, the fatal conclave.*
Terraced thousands died, shaking scythes at cannon.
The hillside blushed, soaked in our broken wave.
They buried us without shroud or coffin
And in August the barley grew up out of the grave.

Bogland   *for T. P. Flanagan**

We have no prairies
To slice a big sun at evening—
Everywhere the eye concedes to
Encroaching horizon,

Is wooed into the cyclops' eye
Of a tarn. Our unfenced country
Is bog that keeps crusting
Between the sights of the sun.

They've taken the skeleton
Of the Great Irish Elk
Out of the peat, set it up,
An astounding crate full of air.

Butter sunk under
More than a hundred years
Was recovered salty and white.
The ground itself is kind, black butter

Melting and opening underfoot,
Missing its last definition
By millions of years.
They'll never dig coal here,

Only the waterlogged trunks
Of great firs, soft as pulp.
Our pioneers keep striking
Inwards and downwards,

Every layer they strip
Seems camped on before.
The bogholes might be Atlantic seepage.
The wet centre is bottomless.

Anahorish

My "place of clear water,"
the first hill in the world
where springs washed into
the shiny grass

and darkened cobbles
in the bed of the lane.
Anahorish, soft gradient
of consonant, vowel-meadow,

after-image of lamps
swung through the yards
on winter evenings.
With pails and barrows

those mound-dwellers
go waist-deep in mist
to break the light ice
at wells and dunghills.

The Grauballe Man

As if he had been poured
in tar, he lies
on a pillow of turf
and seems to weep

the black river of himself.
The grain of his wrists
is like bog oak,
the ball of his heel

like a basalt egg.
His instep has shrunk
cold as a swan's foot
or a wet swamp root.

His hips are the ridge
and purse of a mussel,
his spine an eel arrested
under a glisten of mud.

The head lifts,
the chin is a visor
raised above the vent
of his slashed throat

that has tanned and toughened.
The cured wound
opens inwards to a dark
elderberry place.

Who will say "corpse"
to his vivid cast?
Who will say "body"
to his opaque repose?

And his rusted hair,
a mat unlikely
as a foetus's.
I first saw his twisted face

in a photograph,
a head and shoulder
out of the peat,
bruised like a forceps baby,

but now he lies
perfected in my memory,
down to the red horn
of his nails,

hung in the scales
with beauty and atrocity:
with the Dying Gaul
too strictly compassed

on his shield,
with the actual weight
of each hooked victim,
slashed and dumped.

Punishment

I can feel the tug
of the halter at the nape
of her neck, the wind
on her naked front.

It blows her nipples
to amber beads,
it shakes the frail rigging
of her ribs.

I can see her drowned
body in the bog,
the weighing stone,
the floating rods and boughs.

Under which at first
she was a barked sapling
that is dug up
oak-bone, brain-firkin:

her shaved head
like a stubble of black corn,
her blindfold a soiled bandage,
her noose a ring

to store
the memories of love.
Little adulteress,
before they punished you

you were flaxen-haired,
undernourished, and your
tar-black face was beautiful.
My poor scapegoat,

I almost love you
but would have cast, I know,
the stones of silence.
I am the artful voyeur

of your brain's exposed
and darkened combs,
your muscles' webbing
and all your numbered bones:

I who have stood dumb
when your betraying sisters,
cauled in tar,
wept by the railings,

who would connive
in civilized outrage
yet understand the exact
and tribal, intimate revenge.

Hercules and Antaeus

Sky-born and royal,
snake-choker, dung-heaver,
his mind big with golden apples,
his future hung with trophies,

Hercules has the measure
of resistance and black powers
feeding off the territory.
Antaeus, the mould-hugger,

is weaned at last:
a fall was a renewal
but now he is raised up—
the challenger's intelligence

is a spur of light,
a blue prong graiping him
out of his element
into a dream of loss

and origins—the cradling dark,
the river-veins, the secret gullies
of his strength,
the hatching grounds

of cave and souterrain,
he has bequeathed it all
to elegists. Balor will die
and Byrthnoth and Sitting Bull.

Hercules lifts his arms
in a remorseless V,
his triumph unassailed
by the powers he has shaken,

and lifts and banks Antaeus
high as a profiled ridge,
a sleeping giant,
pap for the dispossessed.

from Glanmore Sonnets

II

Sensings, mountings from the hiding places,
Words entering almost the sense of touch,
Ferreting themselves out of their dark hutch—
"These things are not secrets but mysteries,"
Oisin Kelly told me years ago
In Belfast, hankering after stone
That connived with the chisel, as if the grain
Remembered what the mallet tapped to know.
Then I landed in the hedge-school of Glanmore
And from the backs of ditches hoped to raise
A voice caught back off slug-horn and slow chanter
That might continue, hold, dispel, appease:
Vowels ploughed into other, opened ground,
Each verse returning like the plough turned round.

The Otter

When you plunged
The light of Tuscany wavered
And swung through the pool
From top to bottom.

I loved your wet head and smashing crawl,
Your fine swimmer's back and shoulders
Surfacing and surfacing again
This year and every year since.

I sat dry-throated on the warm stones.
You were beyond me.
The mellowed clarities, the grape-deep air
Thinned and disappointed.

Thank God for the slow loadening:
When I hold you now
We are close and deep
As the atmosphere on water.

My two hands are plumbed water.
You are my palpable, lithe
Otter of memory
In the pool of the moment,

Turning to swim on your back,
Each silent, thigh-shaking kick
Retilting the light,
Heaving the cool at your neck.

And suddenly you're out,
Back again, intent as ever,
Heavy and frisky in your freshened pelt,
Printing the stones.

Sloe Gin

The clear weather of juniper
darkened into winter.
She fed gin to sloes
and sealed the glass container.

When I unscrewed it
I smelled the disturbed
tart stillness of a bush
rising through the pantry.

When I poured it
it had a cutting edge
and flamed
like Betelgeuse.

I drink to you
in smoke-mirled, blue-
black sloes, bitter
and dependable.

Widgeon   *for Paul Muldoon*

It had been badly shot.
While he was plucking it
he found, he says, the voice box—

like a flute stop
in the broken windpipe—

and blew upon it
unexpectedly
his own small widgeon cries.

from Station Island

VII

I had come to the edge of the water,
soothed by just looking, idling over it
as if it were a clear barometer

or a mirror, when his reflection
did not appear but I sensed a presence
entering into my concentration

on not being concentrated as he spoke
my name. And though I was reluctant
I turned to meet his face and the shock

is still in me at what I saw. His brow
was blown open above the eye and blood
had dried on his neck and cheek. "Easy now,"

he said, "it's only me. You've seen men as raw
after a football match . . . What time it was
when I was wakened up I still don't know

but I heard this knocking, knocking, and it
scared me, like the phone in the small hours,
so I had the sense not to put on the light

but looked out from behind the curtain.
I saw two customers on the doorstep
and an old Land-Rover with the doors open

parked on the street, so I let the curtain drop;
but they must have been waiting for it to move
for they shouted to come down into the shop.

She started to cry then and roll round the bed,
lamenting and lamenting to herself,
not even asking who it was. 'Is your head

astray, or what's come over you?' I roared, more
to bring myself to my senses
than out of any real anger at her

for the knocking shook me, the way they kept it up,
and her whingeing and half-screeching made it worse.
All the time they were shouting, 'Shop!

Shop!' so I pulled on my shoes and a sportscoat
and went back to the window and called out,
'What do you want? Could you quieten the racket

or I'll not come down at all.' 'There's a child not well.
Open up and see what you have got—pills
or a powder or something in a bottle,'

one of them said. He stepped back off the footpath
so I could see his face in the streetlamp
and when the other moved I knew them both.

But bad and all as the knocking was, the quiet
hit me worse. She was quiet herself now,
lying dead still, whispering to watch out.

At the bedroom door I switched on the light.
'It's odd they didn't look for a chemist.
Who are they anyway at this hour of the night?'

she asked me, with the eyes standing in her head.
'I know them to see,' I said, but something
made me reach and squeeze her hand across the bed

before I went downstairs into the aisle
of the shop. I stood there, going weak
in the legs. I remember the stale smell

of cooked meat or something coming through
as I went to open up. From then on
you know as much about it as I do."

"Did they say nothing?" "Nothing. What would they say?"
"Were they in uniform? Not masked in any way?"
"They were barefaced as they would be in the day,

shites thinking they were the be-all and the end-all."
"Not that it is any consolation
but they were caught," I told him, "and got jail."

Big-limbed, decent, open-faced, he stood
forgetful of everything now except
whatever was welling up in his spoiled head,

beginning to smile. "You've put on a bit of weight
since you did your courting in that big Austin
you got the loan of on a Sunday night."

Through life and death he had hardly aged.
There always was an athlete's cleanliness
shining off him, and except for the ravaged

forehead and the blood, he was still that same
rangy midfielder in a blue jersey
and starched pants, the one stylist on the team,

the perfect, clean, unthinkable victim.
"Forgive the way I have lived indifferent—
forgive my timid circumspect involvement,"

I surprised myself by saying. "Forgive
my eye," he said, "all that's above my head."
And then a stun of pain seemed to go through him

and he trembled like a heatwave and faded.

XII

Like a convalescent, I took the hand
stretched down from the jetty, sensed again
an alien comfort as I stepped on ground

to find the helping hand still gripping mine,
fish-cold and bony, but whether to guide
or to be guided I could not be certain

for the tall man in step at my side
seemed blind, though he walked straight as a rush
upon his ashplant, his eyes fixed straight ahead.

Then I knew him in the flesh
out there on the tarmac among the cars,
wintered hard and sharp as a blackthorn bush.

His voice eddying with the vowels of all rivers
came back to me, though he did not speak yet,
a voice like a prosecutor's or a singer's,

cunning, narcotic, mimic, definite
as a steel nib's downstroke, quick and clean,
and suddenly he hit a litter basket

with his stick, saying, "Your obligation
is not discharged by any common rite.
What you do you must do on your own.

The main thing is to write
for the joy of it. Cultivate a work-lust
that imagines its haven like your hands at night

dreaming the sun in the sunspot of a breast.
You are fasted now, light-headed, dangerous.
Take off from here. And don't be so earnest,

so ready for the sackcloth and the ashes.
Let go, let fly, forget.
You've listened long enough. Now strike your note."

It was as if I had stepped free into space
alone with nothing that I had not known
already. Raindrops blew in my face

as I came to and heard the harangue and jeers
going on and on. "The English language
belongs to us. You are raking at dead fires,

rehearsing the old whinges at your age.
That subject people stuff is a cod's game,
infantile, like this peasant pilgrimage.

You lose more of yourself than you redeem
doing the decent thing. Keep at a tangent.
When they make the circle wide, it's time to swim

out on your own and fill the element
with signatures on your own frequency,
echo-soundings, searches, probes, allurements,

elver-gleams in the dark of the whole sea."
The shower broke in a cloudburst, the tarmac
fumed and sizzled. As he moved off quickly

the downpour loosed its screens round his straight walk.

Wolfe Tone

Light as a skiff, manoeuvrable
yet out outmanoeuvred,

I affected epaulettes and a cockade,
wrote a style well-bred and impervious

to the solidarity I angled for,
and played the ancient Roman with a razor.

I was the shouldered oar that ended up
far from the brine and whiff of venture,

like a scratching-post or a crossroads flagpole,
out of my element among small farmers—

I who once wakened to the shouts of men
rising from the bottom of the sea,

men in their shirts mounting through deep water
when the Atlantic stove our cabin's dead lights in

and the big fleet split and Ireland dwindled
as we ran before the gale under bare poles.

from Squarings

Lightenings

iii

Squarings? In the game of marbles, squarings
Were all those anglings, aimings, feints and squints
You were allowed before you'd shoot, all those

Hunkerings, tensings, pressures of the thumb,
Test-outs and pull-backs, re-envisagings,
All the ways your arms kept hoping towards

Blind certainties that were going to prevail
Beyond the one-off moment of the pitch.
A million million accuracies passed

Between your muscles' outreach and that space
Marked with three round holes and a drawn line.
You squinted out from a skylight of the world.

viii

The annals say: when the monks of Clonmacnoise
Were all at prayers inside the oratory
A ship appeared above them in the air.

The anchor dragged along behind so deep
It hooked itself into the altar rails
And then, as the big hull rocked to a standstill,

A crewman shinned and grappled down the rope
And struggled to release it. But in vain.
"This man can't bear our life here and will drown,"

The abbot said, "unless we help him." So
They did, the freed ship sailed, and the man climbed back
Out of the marvellous as he had known it.

xii

And lightening? One meaning of that
Beyond the usual sense of alleviation,
Illumination, and so on, is this:

A phenomenal instant when the spirit flares
With pure exhilaration before death—
The good thief in us harking to the promise!

So paint him on Christ's right hand, on a promontory
Scanning empty space, so body-racked he seems
Untranslatable into the bliss

Ached for at the moon-rim of his forehead,
By nail-craters on the dark side of his brain:
This day thou shalt be with Me in Paradise.

Settings

xxii

Where does the spirit live? Inside or outside
Things remembered, made things, things unmade?
What came first, the seabird's cry or the soul

Imagined in the dawn cold when it cried?
Where does it roost at last? On dungy sticks
In a jackdaw's nest up in the old stone tower

Or a marble bust commanding the parterre?
How habitable is perfected form?
And how inhabited the windy light?

What's the use of a held note or held line
That cannot be assailed for reassurance?
(Set questions for the ghost of W. B.)

Squarings

xlviii

Strange how things in the offing, once they're sensed,
Convert to things foreknown;
And how what's come upon is manifest

Only in light of what has been gone through.
Seventh heaven may be
The whole truth of a sixth sense come to pass.

At any rate, when light breaks over me
The way it did on the road beyond Coleraine
Where wind got saltier, the sky more hurried

And silver lamé shivered on the Bann
Out in mid-channel between the painted poles,
That day I'll be in step with what escaped me.

Weighing In

The 56 lb. weight. A solid iron
Unit of negation. Stamped and cast
With an inset, rung-thick, moulded, short crossbar

For a handle. Squared-off and harmless-looking
Until you tried to lift it, then a socket-ripping,
Life-belittling force—

Gravity's black box, the immovable
Stamp and squat and square-root of dead weight.
Yet balance it

Against another one placed on a weighbridge—
On a well-adjusted, freshly greased weighbridge—
And everything trembled, flowed with give and take.

*

And this is all the good tidings amount to:
This principle of bearing, bearing up
And bearing out, just having to

Balance the intolerable in others
Against our own, having to abide
Whatever we settled for and settled into

Against our better judgement. Passive
Suffering makes the world go round.
Peace on earth, men of good will, all that

Holds good only as long as the balance holds,
The scales ride steady and the angels' strain
Prolongs itself at an unearthly pitch.

*

To refuse the other cheek. To cast the stone.
Not to do so some time, not to break with
The obedient one you hurt yourself into

Is to fail the hurt, the self, the ingrown rule.
Prophesy who struck thee! When soldiers mocked
Blindfolded Jesus and he didn't strike back

They were neither shamed nor edified, although
Something was made manifest—the power
Of power not exercised, or hope inferred

By the powerless forever. Still for Jesus' sake,
Do me a favour, would you, just this once?
Prophesy, give scandal, cast the stone.

*

Two sides to every question, yes, yes, yes . . .
But every now and then, just weighing in
Is what it must come down to, and without

Any self-exculpation or self-pity.
Alas, one night when follow-through was called for
And a quick hit would have fairly rankled,

You countered that it was my narrowness
That kept me keen, so got a first submission.
I held back when I should have drawn blood

And that way (*mea culpa*) lost an edge.
A deep mistaken chivalry, old friend.
At this stage only foul play cleans the slate.

The Gravel Walks

River gravel. In the beginning, that.
High summer, and the angler's motorbike
Deep in roadside flowers, like a fallen knight
Whose ghost we'd lately questioned: "Any luck?"

As the engines of the world prepared, green nuts
Dangled and clustered closer to the whirlpool.
The trees dipped down. The flints and sandstone-bits
Worked themselves smooth and smaller in a sparkle

Of shallow, hurrying barley-sugar water
Where minnows schooled that we scared when we played—
An eternity that ended once a tractor
Dropped its link-box in the gravel bed

And cement mixers began to come to life
And men in dungarees, like captive shades,
Mixed concrete, loaded, wheeled, turned, wheeled, as if
The Pharaoh's brickyards burned inside their heads.

*

Hoard and praise the verity of gravel.
Gems for the undeluded. Milt of earth.
Its plain, champing song against the shovel
Soundtests and sandblasts words like "honest worth."

Beautiful in or out of the river,
The kingdom of gravel was inside you too—
Deep down, far back, clear water running over
Pebbles of caramel, hailstone, mackerel-blue.

But the actual washed stuff kept you slow and steady
As you went stooping with your barrow full
Into an absolution of the body,
The shriven life tired bones and marrow feel.

So walk on air against your better judgement
Establishing yourself somewhere in between
Those solid batches mixed with grey cement
And a tune called "The Gravel Walks" that conjures green.

The Loose Box

Back at the dark end, slats angled tautly down
From a breast-high beam to the foot of the stable wall—
Silked and seasoned timber of the hayrack.

Marsupial brackets . . . And a deep-littered silence
Off odourless, untainting, fibrous horsedung.

*

On an old recording Patrick Kavanagh states
That there's health and worth in any talk about
The properties of land. Sandy, glarry,
Mossy, heavy, cold, the actual soil
Almost doesn't matter; the main thing is
An inner restitution, a purchase come by
By pacing it in words that make you feel
You've found your feet in what "surefooted" means
And in the ground of your own understanding—
Like Heracles stepping in and standing under
Atlas's sky-lintel, as earthed and heady
As I am when I talk about the loose box.

*

And they found the infant wrapped in swaddling clothes
And laid in a manger.
                              But the plaster child in nappies,
Bare baby-breasted little *rigor vitae*,
Crook-armed, seed-nailed, nothing but gloss and chill—
He wasn't right at all.
                              And no hayrack
To be seen.
                              The solid stooping shepherds,
The stiff-lugged donkey, Joseph, Mary, each
Figure in the winter crib was well
And truly placed. There was even real straw
On the side-altar. And an out-of-scale,
Too crockery, kneeling cow. And fairy lights.
But no, no fodder-billowed armfuls spilling over . . .

At the altar rail I knelt and learnt almost
Not to admit the let-down to myself.

*

Stable child, grown stabler when I read
In adolescence Thomas *dolens* Hardy—
Not, oddly enough, his Christmas Eve night-piece
About the oxen in their bedded stall,
But the threshing scene in *Tess of the D'Urbervilles*—
That magnified my soul. Raving machinery,
The thresher bucking sky, rut-shuddery,
A headless Trojan horse expelling straw
From where the head should be, the underjaws
Like staircases set champing—it hummed and slugged
While the big sag and slew of the canvas belt
That would cut your head off if you didn't watch
Flowed from the flywheel. And comes flowing back,
The whole mote-sweaty havoc and mania
Of threshing day, the feeders up on top
Like pyre-high Aztec priests gutting forked sheaves
And paying them ungirded to the drum.

Slack of gulped straw, the belly-taut of seedbags.
And in the stilly night, chaff piled in ridges,
Earth raw where the four wheels rocked and battled.

*

Michael Collins, ambushed at Beal na Blath,
At the Pass of Flowers, the Blossom Gap, his own
Bloom-drifted, soft Avernus-mouth,
Has nothing to hold on to and falls again
Willingly, lastly, foreknowledgeably deep
Into the hay-floor that gave once in his childhood
Down through the bedded mouth of the loft trapdoor,
The loosening fodder-chute, the aftermath . . .

This has been told of Collins and retold
By his biographer:
                                    One of his boy-deeds
Was to enter the hidden jaws of that hay crevasse

And get to his feet again and come unscathed
Through a dazzle of pollen scarves to breathe the air.
True or not true, the fall within his fall,
That drop through the flower-floor lets him find his feet
In an underworld of understanding
Better than any newsreel lying-in-state
Or footage of the laden gun-carriage
And grim cortege could ever manage to.

        Or so it can be stated
                In the must and drift of talk about the loose box.

The Turnip-Snedder
for Hughie O'Donoghue*

In an age of bare hands
and cast iron,

the clamp-on meat-mincer,
the double flywheeled water-pump,

it dug its heels in among wooden tubs
and troughs of slops,

hotter than body heat
in summertime, cold in winter

as winter's body armour,
a barrel-chested breast-plate

standing guard
on four braced greaves.

"This is the way that God sees life,"
it said, "from seedling-braird to snedder,"

as the handle turned
and turnip-heads were let fall and fed

to the juiced-up inner blades,
"This is the turnip-cycle,"

as it dropped its raw sliced mess,
bucketful by glistering bucketful.

The Blackbird of Glanmore

On the grass when I arrive,
Filling the stillness with life,
But ready to scare off
At the very first wrong move.
In the ivy when I leave.

It's you, blackbird, I love.

I park, pause, take heed.
Breathe. Just breathe and sit
And lines I once translated
Come back: "I want away
To the house of death, to my father

Under the low clay roof."

And I think of one gone to him,
A little stillness dancer—
Haunter-son, lost brother—
Cavorting through the yard,
So glad to see me home,

My homesick first term over.

And think of a neighbour's words
Long after the accident:
"Yon bird on the shed roof,
Up on the ridge for weeks—
I said nothing at the time

But I never liked yon bird."

The automatic lock
Clunks shut, the blackbird's panic
Is shortlived, for a second
I've a bird's eye view of myself,
A shadow on raked gravel

In front of my house of life.

Hedge-hop, I am absolute
For you, your ready talkback,
Your each stand-offish comeback,
Your picky, nervy goldbeak—
On the grass when I arrive,

In the ivy when I leave.

Michael Longley (1939–)

Over the course of a career spanning more than forty years, Michael Longley has built a reputation for himself as the master craftsman of Ulster poetry. A self-proclaimed poetic conservative, Longley has injected a strong dose of classicism into Irish poetry, while at the same time rooting his own work firmly in the land-scape of the island's rural west. Both these threads run through the warp of his work. They have remained visible in his poetry since his first collection, *Ten Poems*, appeared in 1965, and they may reflect something of the different worlds he's known in his own life.

Longley has spent a good deal of his time in rural County Mayo, "in the shadow," as he puts it, "of Mweelrea," the highest point in the region. But he was born in Belfast in 1939 and as a boy lived in the suburbs of the city.[1] As Longley has explained, however, growing up in "1930s ribbon development" did not pre-vent him from experiencing a rural childhood. There were, he recalls, "plenty of fields around the houses—playing fields, a field where a riding school trotted horses, a golf course, the remnants of ancient hedges, crab-apple trees like huge cradles, enough space in which to create your own wilderness. And a couple of miles away there was Barnett's Park, which sloped down to the Lagan and the towpath—and, a bit further west, the Minnowburn with its lanky, elegant beech trees; and then up a hilly road to the Giant's Ring, a dolmen set perfectly in a vast, circular grassy arena. I learned to love the countryside in south Belfast."[2]

Longley's poems of the West are sharpened by the contrast with his Belfast background, and he isn't afraid to adopt the posture of an outsider, as he does in "For Ciaran Carson *(On Hearing Irish Spoken)*," a poem in which he listens to the Irish conversation of two fishermen, catching its "echo of technical terms, the one I know / Repeating itself at desperate intervals / Like the stepping stones across a river in spate."[3]

A number of Longley's interests converge in this poem, as the western Ireland he loves is overlain by a West that remains mysterious, the latter coalescing into an image of the former. The poem's last line, recalling Louis MacNeice's "River in Spate," imagines language as a bridge between worlds. That idea of language may derive from the fact that Longley's poetic roots descend, like those of MacNeice, into the literature of ancient languages. Longley read classics at Trinity and says that the experience left him "with some images and themes," but, more important, gave him "a sense of syntactical possibilities—playing a long sentence off against the metrical units."[4] That fluid metrical sensibility emerges in this poem, where the image of "stepping stones" inscribes the stricter rhythms of poetic composition, counting time while the recognizable Irish term is busy "repeating itself at desperate intervals," like a familiar bit of melody recurring in the current of a jazz improvisation. Longley's appreciation for these interactions between the known and the new may account as much for his regard for the West of Ireland as for his love of jazz. Each has given form and subject matter to his poetry. And while the West of Ireland has provided him with a temporal home, Longley remarks that it is the tempo of jazz that holds out the hope of an ultimate poetic leap: "Heaven will be full of saxophones for those who can play," he says, "and kazoos for the rest of us. The joint will be jumping."[5]

But Longley's expeditions into the culture of the West, or into the traditions of jazz, haven't been journeys of escape—either from the Troubles of Belfast or from the goings-on in the larger world. His "Letter to Derek Mahon" sees poetry as a heroic if ill-fated music rising above the noise of the Shankill and Falls Road neighborhoods, Belfast's Protestant and Catholic enclaves.

Though he has been known for the shaped formalism of much of his verse, Longley has begun to write lines that stretch toward the right-hand margin, and strain the boundary between poetry and prose, as in "Baucis and Philemon":

> In the Phrygian hills an oak tree grows beside a lime tree
> And a low wall encloses them. Not very far away lies bogland.[6]

It is not that Longley has abandoned formal structure. These longer lines feel easy and colloquial, but run, at the same time, with a measured confidence that again recalls his classical training and the long lines of Roman poetry. The combination gives Longley the perfect, paradoxical form in which to couch his winking literary envoy in "The White Garden," a poem that bests William Carlos Williams at making poetry out of the most ordinary of messages: "My memorandum to posterity? Listen. 'The saw / Is under the garden bench and the gate is unlatched.'"[7]

Notes

1. Dermot Healy, "An Interview with Michael Longley," *The Southern Review,* vol. 31, no. 3 (Summer 1995), p. 557.

2. Ibid.

3. "For Ciarán Carson (*On Hearing Irish Spoken*)," *Selected Poems, 1963–1980* (Winston-Salem, North Carolina: Wake Forest University Press, 1981), p. 5.

4. Healy, "An Interview with Michael Longley," p. 559.

5. Ibid., p. 561.

6. "Baucis and Philemon," *The Ghost Orchid* (London: Jonathan Cape, 1995), p. 22.

7. "The White Garden," *The Ghost Orchid,* p. 52.

Epithalamion

These are the small hours when
Moths by their fatal appetite
That brings them tapping to get in,
    Are steered along the night
To where our window catches light.

    Who hazard all to be
Where we, the only two it seems,
Inhabit so delightfully
    A room it bursts its seams
And spills on to the lawn in beams,

    Such visitors as these
Reflect with eyes like frantic stars
This garden's brightest properties,
    Cruising its corridors
Of light above the folded flowers,

    Till our vicinity
Is rendered royal by their flight
Towards us, till more silently
    The silent stars ignite,
Their aeons dwindling by a night,

    And everything seems bent
On robing in this evening you
And me, all dark the element
    Our light is earnest to,
All quiet gathered round us who,

    When over the embankments
A train that's loudly reprobate
Shoots from silence into silence,
    With ease accommodate
Its pandemonium, its freight.

    I hold you close because
We have decided dark will be
For ever like this and because,
    My love, already
The dark is growing elderly.

With dawn upon its way,
Punctually and as a rule,
The small hours widening into day,
　　Our room its vestibule
Before it fills all houses full,

　　We too must hazard all,
Switch off the lamp without a word
For the last of night assembled
　　Over it and unperturbed
By the moth that lies there littered,

　　And notice how the trees
Which took on anonymity
Are again in their huge histories
　　Displayed, that wherever we
Attempt, and as far as we can see,

　　The flowers everywhere
Are withering, the stars dissolved,
Amalgamated in a glare,
　　Which last night were revolved
Discreetly round us—and, involved,

　　The two of us, in these
Which early morning has deformed,
Must hope that in new properties
　　We'll find a uniform
To know each other truly by, or,

　　At the least, that these will,
When we rise, be seen with dawn
As remnant yet part raiment still,
　　Like flags that linger on
The sky when king and queen are gone.

Persephone

I

I see as through a skylight in my brain
The mole strew its buildings in the rain,

The swallows turn above their broken home
And all my acres in delirium.

II

Straitjacketed by cold and numskulled
Now sleep the welladjusted and the skilled—

The bat folds its wing like a winter leaf,
The squirrel in its hollow holds aloof.

III

The weasel and ferret, the stoat and fox
Move hand in glove across the equinox.

I can tell how softly their footsteps go—
Their footsteps borrow silence from the snow.

Badger   *for Raymond Piper*

I

Pushing the wedge of his body
Between cromlech and stone circle,*
He excavates down mine shafts
And back into the depths of the hill.

His path straight and narrow
And not like the fox's zig-zags,
The arc of the hare who leaves
A silhouette on the sky line.

Night's silence around his shoulders,
His face lit by the moon, he
Manages the earth with his paws,
Returns underground to die.

II

An intestine taking in
patches of dog's-mercury,
brambles, the bluebell wood;
a heel revolving acorns;
a head with a price on it
brushing cuckoo-spit, goose-grass;
a name that parishes borrow.

III

For the digger, the earth-dog
It is a difficult delivery
Once the tongs take hold,

Vulnerable his pig's snout
That lifted cow-pats for beetles,
Hedgehogs for the soft meat,

His limbs dragging after them
So many stones turned over,
The trees they tilted.

Letter to Derek Mahon

And did we come into our own
When, minus muse and lexicon,
We traced in August sixty-nine
Our imaginary Peace Line
Around the burnt-out houses of
The Catholics we'd scarcely loved,
Two Sisyphuses come to budge
The sticks and stones of an old grudge,

Two poetic conservatives
In the city of guns and long knives,
Our ears receiving then and there
The stereophonic nightmare
Of the Shankill and the Falls,*
Our matches struck on crumbling walls
To light us as we moved at last
Through the back alleys of Belfast?

Why it mattered to have you here
You who journeyed to Inisheer
With me, years back, one Easter when
With MacIntyre and the lone Dane
Our footsteps lifted up the larks,
Echoing off those western rocks
And down that darkening arcade
Hung with the failures of our trade,

Will understand. We were tongue-tied
Companions of the island's dead
In the graveyard among the dunes,
Eavesdroppers on conversations
With a Jesus who spoke Irish—
We were strangers in that parish,
Black tea with bacon and cabbage
For our sacraments and pottage,

Dank blankets making up our Lent
Till, islanders ourselves, we bent
Our knees and cut the watery sod
From the lazy-bed where slept a God
We couldn't count among our friends,
Although we'd taken in our hands
Splinters of driftwood nailed and stuck
On the rim of the Atlantic.

That was Good Friday years ago—
How persistent the undertow
Slapped by currachs ferrying stones,*
Moonlight glossing the confusions
Of its each bilingual wave—yes,

We would have lingered there for less . . .
Six islanders for a ten-bob note
Rowed us out to the anchored boat.

Wounds

Here are two pictures from my father's head—
I have kept them like secrets until now:
First, the Ulster Division at the Somme
Going over the top with "Fuck the Pope!"
"No Surrender!": a boy about to die,
Screaming "Give 'em one for the Shankill!"
"Wilder than Ghurkhas" were my father's words
Of admiration and bewilderment.
Next comes the London-Scottish padre
Resettling kilts with his swagger-stick,
With a stylish backhand and a prayer.
Over a landscape of dead buttocks
My father followed him for fifty years.
At last, a belated casualty,
He said—lead traces flaring till they hurt—
"I am dying for King and Country, slowly."
I touched his hand, his thin head I touched.

Now, with military honours of a kind,
With his badges, his medals like rainbows,
His spinning compass, I bury beside him
Three teenage soldiers, bellies full of
Bullets and Irish beer, their flies undone.
A packet of Woodbines I throw in,
A lucifer, the Sacred Heart of Jesus
Paralysed as heavy guns put out
The night-light in a nursery for ever;
Also a bus-conductor's uniform—
He collapsed beside his carpet-slippers
Without a murmur, shot through the head
By a shivering boy who wandered in

Before they could turn the television down
Or tidy away the supper dishes.
To the children, to a bewildered wife,
I think "Sorry Missus" was what he said.

Wreaths

The Civil Servant

He was preparing an Ulster fry for breakfast
When someone walked into the kitchen and shot him:
A bullet entered his mouth and pierced his skull,
The books he had read, the music he could play.

He lay in his dressing gown and pyjamas
While they dusted the dresser for fingerprints
And then shuffled backwards across the garden
With notebooks, cameras and measuring tapes.

They rolled him up like a red carpet and left
Only a bullet hole in the cutlery drawer:
Later his widow took a hammer and chisel
And removed the black keys from his piano.

The Greengrocer

He ran a good shop, and he died
Serving even the death-dealers
Who found him busy as usual
Behind the counter, organised
With holly wreaths for Christmas,
Fir trees on the pavement outside.

Astrologers or three wise men
Who may shortly be setting out
For a small house up the Shankill
Or the Falls, should pause on their way
To buy gifts at Jim Gibson's shop,
Dates and chestnuts and tangerines.

The Linen Workers

Christ's teeth ascended with him into heaven:
Through a cavity in one of his molars
The wind whistles: he is fastened for ever
By his exposed canines to a wintry sky.

I am blinded by the blaze of that smile
And by the memory of my father's false teeth
Brimming in their tumbler: they wore bubbles
And, outside of his body, a deadly grin.

When they massacred the ten linen workers
There fell on the road beside them spectacles,
Wallets, small change, and a set of dentures:
Blood, food particles, the bread, the wine.

Before I can bury my father once again
I must polish the spectacles, balance them
Upon his nose, fill his pockets with money
And into his dead mouth slip the set of teeth.

Second Sight

My father's mother had the second sight.
Flanders began at the kitchen window—
The mangle rusting in No Man's Land, gas
Turning the antimacassars yellow
When it blew the wrong way from the salient.

In bandages, on crutches, reaching home
Before his letters, my father used to find
The front door on the latch, his bed airing.
"I watched my son going over the top.
He was carrying flowers out of the smoke."

I have brought the *Pocket Guide to London*,
My *Map of the Underground*, an address—
A lover looking for somewhere to live,

A ghost among ghosts of aunts and uncles
Who crowd around me to give directions.

Where is my father's house, where my father?
If I could walk in on my grandmother
She'd see right through me and the hallway
And the miles of cloud and sky to Ireland.
"You have crossed the water to visit me."

Remembering Carrigskeewaun

A wintry night, the hearth inhales
And the chimney becomes a windpipe
Fluffy with soot and thistledown,
A voice-box recalling animals:
The leveret come of age, snipe
At an angle, then the porpoises'
Demonstration of meaningless smiles.
Home is a hollow between the waves,
A clump of nettles, feathery winds,
And memory no longer than a day
When the animals come back to me
From the townland of Carrigskeewaun,
From a page lit by the Milky Way.

An Amish Rug

As if a one-room schoolhouse were all we knew
And our clothes were black, our underclothes black,
Marriage a horse and buggy going to church
And the children silhouettes in a snowy field,

I bring you this patchwork like a smallholding
Where I served as the hired boy behind the harrow,
Its threads the colour of cantaloupe and cherry
Securing hay bales, corn cobs, tobacco leaves.

You may hang it on the wall, a cathedral window,
Or lay it out on the floor beside our bed
So that whenever we undress for sleep or love
We shall step over it as over a flowerbed.

Laertes

When he found Laertes alone on the tidy terrace, hoeing
Around a vine, disreputable in his gardening duds,
Patched and grubby, leather gaiters protecting his shins
Against brambles, gloves as well, and, to cap it all,
Sure sign of his deep depression, a goatskin duncher,*
Odysseus sobbed in the shade of a pear-tree for his father
So old and pathetic that all he wanted then and there
Was to kiss him and hug him and blurt out the whole story,
But the whole story is one catalogue and then another,
So he waited for images from that formal garden,
Evidence of a childhood spent traipsing after his father
And asking for everything he saw, the thirteen pear-trees,
Ten apple-trees, forty fig-trees, the fifty rows of vines
Ripening at different times for a continuous supply,
Until Laertes recognised his son and, weak at the knees,
Dizzy, flung his arms around the neck of great Odysseus
Who drew the old man fainting to his breast and held him there
And cradled like driftwood the bones of his dwindling father.

Ceasefire

I

Put in mind of his own father and moved to tears
Achilles took him by the hand and pushed the old king
Gently away, but Priam curled up at his feet and
Wept with him until their sadness filled the building.

II

Taking Hector's corpse into his own hands Achilles
Made sure it was washed and, for the old king's sake,
Laid out in uniform, ready for Priam to carry
Wrapped like a present home to Troy at daybreak.

III

When they had eaten together, it pleased them both
To stare at each other's beauty as lovers might,
Achilles built like a god, Priam good-looking still
And full of conversation, who earlier had sighed:

IV

"I get down on my knees and do what must be done
And kiss Achilles' hand, the killer of my son."

The White Garden

So white are the white flowers in the white garden that I
Disappear in no time at all among lace and veils.
For whom do I scribble the few words that come to me
From beyond the arch of white roses as from nowhere,
My memorandum to posterity? Listen. "The saw
Is under the garden bench and the gate is unlatched."

The Horses

For all of the horses butchered on the battlefield,
Shell-shocked, tripping up over their own intestines,
Drowning in the mud, the best war memorial
Is in Homer: two horses that refuse to budge
Despite threats and sweet-talk and the whistling whip,

Immovable as a tombstone, their heads drooping
In front of the streamlined motionless chariot,
Hot tears spilling from their eyelids onto the ground
Because they are still in mourning for Patroclus
Their charioteer, their shiny manes bedraggled
Under the yoke pads on either side of the yoke.

An Elegy

in memory of George Mackay Brown

After thirty years I remember the rusty scythe
That summarised in the thatch the deserted village,

And the anchor painted silver so that between showers
Between Hoy and Stromness it reflected the sunshine.*

Now the anchor catches the light on the ocean floor.
The scythe too is gleaming in some underwater room.

The Rabbit

for Ciaran Carson

I closed my eyes on a white horse pulling a plough
In Poland, on a haystack built around a pole,
And opened them when the young girl and her lover
Took out of a perforated cardboard shoe-box
A grey rabbit, an agreeable shitty smell,
Turds like a broken rosary, the slow train
Rocking this dainty manger scene, so that I
With a priestly forefinger tried to tickle
The narrow brain-space behind dewdrop eyes
And it bounced from her lap and from her shoulder
Kept mouthing "prunes and prisms" as if to warn
That even with so little to say for itself
A silly rabbit could pick up like a scent trail
My gynaecological concept of the warren
With its entrances and innermost chamber,

Or the heroic survival in Warsaw's sewers
Of just one bunny saved as a pet or meal,
Or its afterlife as *Hasenpfeffer* with cloves
And bay leaves, onions—enough!—and so
It would make its getaway when next I dozed
Crossing the Oder, somewhere in Silesia
(Silesian lettuce, h'm), never to meet again,
Or so I thought, until in Lodz in the small hours
A fat hilarious prostitute let that rabbit bop
Across her shoulders without tousling her hair-do
And burrow under her chin and nuzzle her ear
As though it were crooning "The Groves of Blarney"
Or "She Walked Unaware," then in her cleavage
It crouched as in a ploughed furrow, ears laid flat,
Pretending to be a stone, safe from stoat and fox.

The Branch

The artist in my father transformed the diagonal
Crack across the mirror on our bathroom cabinet
Into a branch: that was his way of mending things,
A streak of brown paint, dabs of green, an accident
That sprouted leaves,
                          awakening the child in me
To the funny faces he pulls when he is shaving.
He wears a vest, white buttons at his collarbone.
The two halves of my father's face are joining up.
His soapy nostrils disappear among the leaves.

Pipistrelle

They kept him alive for years in warm water,
The soldier who had lost his skin.
                                    At night
He was visited by the wounded bat
He had unfrozen after Passchendaele,

Locking its heels under his forefinger
And whispering into the mousy fur.

Before letting the pipistrelle flicker
Above his summery pool and tipple there,

He spread the wing-hand, elbow to thumb.
The membrane felt like a poppy petal.

Edward Thomas's Poem

I

I couldn't make out the minuscule handwriting
In the notebook the size of his palm and crinkled
Like an origami quim by shell-blast that stopped
His pocket watch at death. I couldn't read the poem.

II

From where he lay he could hear the skylark's
Skyward exultation, a chaffinch to his left
Fidgeting among the fallen branches,
Then all the birds of the Western Front.

III

The nature poet turned into a war poet as if
He could cure death with the rub of a dock leaf.

The Painters

John Lavery rescued self-heal from waste ground
At Sailly-Saillisel in nineteen-seventeen, and framed
One oblong flower-head packed with purple flowers
Shaped like hooks, a survivor from the battlefield.

When I shouldered my father's coffin his body
Shifted slyly and farted and joined up again
With rotting corpses, old pals from the trenches.
William Orpen said you couldn't paint the smell.*

Leaves

Is this my final phase? Some of the poems depend
Peaceably like the brown leaves on a sheltered branch.
Others are hanging on through the equinoctial gales
To catch the westering sun's red declension.
I'm thinking of the huge beech tree in our garden.
I can imagine foliage on fire like that.

Seamus Deane (1940–)

"Any dogsbody can sit up all night / And work in a cube of electric light," Seamus Deane writes in the poem "Power Cut." But, "This is a slight / On creativity."[1] Deane finds in the candle-lit darkness of a power outage a closer connection to past experience. And there is a greater challenge in creativity when the previously lost experience of night, "petrified" and palpable in the waxy light, sits like a devil on his shoulder.

The devil perched on the shoulder of many of Deane's poems is the past itself, especially Irish literary history. Deane was born in Derry in 1940 and studied at Queen's University, Belfast. He is widely known as a critic and literary historian. But Deane has not had a purely congenial relationship with the central characters of the Irish literary tradition his work has documented. His *Short History of Irish Literature*, published in 1986, carries forward his ongoing contention with what he sees as the "myth" of Yeats.

In his role as scholar, Deane attacks the Yeatsian tradition directly. As a poet, however, he is more willing to let confrontation yield to circumvention. Deane acknowledges influence by such decidedly un-Irish poets as W. S. Merwin and Rainer Maria Rilke. And, although many of his poems deal with particularly Irish issues, his poetry most often comes at Ireland by way of a broader narrative of world history. The specific emerges from or comes to rest in the general, and the poems are continually essaying the borderland between public events and private lives.

Deane's poems tend to look for answers to questions that lie, more or less subtly, in the vicinity of those that take explicit shape in "Homer Nods": "Were the seas the surge beneath / The marriage-bed?" the poem asks, "And could it be / We have here an autobiography / Pretending to epic for authority?"[2] Is literature, in other words, the bridge between the subjective experience of individual lives and the larger movement of history? The title poem of his 1983 volume *History Lessons* answers by imagining that the border between epic and autobiography is like the one that separates world history from individual experience. The poem remembers an episode from the epic of modern history in the experiential moment of its discovery by a student in Ireland, as the story of Napoleon's campaign in Russia dissolves to reveal football pitches on the campus of the school where the young Deane encountered it. The result is a kind of archetype of a Deane poem. Ultimately the circumstantial detail of personal experience becomes the vehicle for historical memory, putting the defeat of Moscow on a continuum with the later morning on which a student makes his way, late, to class: "The city is no more. The lesson's learned. / I will remember it always as a burning / In the heart of winter and a boy running."[3]

NOTES

1. "Power Cut," *Selected Poems* (Loughcrew, Ireland: Gallery Press, 1988), p. 11.
2. "Homer Nods," *Selected Poems*, pp. 63–64.
3. "History Lessons," *Selected Poems*, p. 40.

Power Cut

Any dogsbody can sit up all night
And work in a cube of electric light
With only a little spilt ink of shadow
Under the hands and feet. This is a slight
On creativity, the whiter-than-white
Hope to be in there with the black
Shadow-boxers of the past. It's too neat,
Too easy, and it can't be right.

But in candlelight, a high devil looms
On my shoulder and my hand locks on the white
Fire circle. He is so real I can smell
His bad breath of the old rooms
Where the exorcist abandoned him,
The cinemas, jukeboxes and bars
Of a dark city kicked in by winter.
Medusa-light, with yellow wing of flame,

And waxy, serpent head, you are the bright
Petrifier of this darkness, the white lady
Of these locked shadows, the diamond
In the coal-black night, and in you,
As in a lover, I recapture the slight
Moonbeams in the linens of long ago,
The afternoons moiling in the keyhole;
In you, petrified, I recapture night.

Derry

The unemployment in our bones
Erupting on our hands in stones;

The thought of violence a relief,
The act of violence a grief;

Our bitterness and love
Hand in glove.

Roots

Younger,
I felt the dead
Drag at my feet
Like roots
And at every step
I heard them
Crying
Stop.

Older,
I heard the roots
Snap. The crying
Stopped. Ever since
I have been
Dying
Slowly
From the top.

Gradual Wars

The frost is stirring, it
Whitens slow and sudden
On the grass. Darkness
Is pierced by it, it
Has the blind focus
Of a nail shuddering
In the quiet wood
Which is going to
Split as pipes
Choked in ice do;
And whatever shatters
In this cold
Shatters slow and sudden,
Like a writhe of frost,

In stars.
This is the language
That bespeaks
Gradual wars.

The Broken Border

"The only road we can take now
To get us home crosses and recrosses
The border, making a loop
Of quiet fields where there are
Strange, scattered boulders
That look as if a meaning
Might have existed once for their exploded
Circlings. I don't know. But we
Could talk about that on the way back."

"It should be simple, really,
To say why a great stroke of blood
Passed through me when I first
Heard you were sick. Whispers
From our colloquy among the stones
On those border fields with the dark
Approaching, reach me now as
At last the tearing of some silken
Courtesy which it took so many

Patient, later years to weave.
I would unravel all of this,
Take and retake it all apart,
Listening for the first tremor,
The disturbance at your heart;
The deep alto rumour of evening
Surrounding the sharp tenor
Of your son's questioning,
Father. I wanted to penetrate

More than the broken border
And the half-submerged circle
Of stones. I wanted to order
You to tell me what it was like
To lose both parents when you were
Twelve. So that I may be prepared
Father, before we get home,
For losing too. Must the stroke of blood
Fall through us all so cleanly

That even reliving it all with you,
I must be still reliving it alone?
What we both understood easily
In that loop of fields, where the stones
Cropped up and the border
Suffered extinction among the night's
First singular noises, was our own
Compatibility with the scene. Never alone
Then, since it relives us now, in these our two voices."

Shelter

Two years after one war,
And some time before another,
In nineteen forty-seven,
Came a heavy fall of snow
That drifted over the slab
Of the air-raid shelter roof.

Before, there had been an infinite
Summer, full of the pock
And applause of the false spirit
Of cricket. As our reproof,

Came the savage winter
When the boiler burst
And the water in the lavatory bowl
Shook. To tell the truth,

I could see nothing wrong.
Winter was like Russia
At last and the war-games,
Ice-pointed, less uncouth.

Perhaps I heard my mother
Dreading the thaw and frost.
When I turned to look, though,
She was at the fire, face aloof

In concentration. Doing the sums
For food and clothes, the future
In endless hock. I went out
To the air-raid shelter roof

To throw snowballs. The whole summer's
Bowling went into my swing
And I flung them splat on the wall.
Damned winter. Her spirit, unsheltered,
Made me numerate at last
And, since forty-seven, weather-proof.

Osip Mandelstam

"The people need poetry." That voice,
That was last heard asking for warm
Clothes and money, also knew the hunger
We all have for the gold light
The goldfinch carries into the air
Like a tang of crushed almonds.

Nine months before heart-failure
Silenced his silk-sharp whistle
That haunted the steppes as though
A small shrapnel of birds scattered,
Bukharin, his protector, was shot
Along with Yagoda, Rykov, others.

The kerosene flash of his music
Leaps from the black earth,
From the whitening dead of the War
Who burn in its flammable spirit.
The fire-crop smokes in the Kremlin's
Eyes and the scorched marl

Cinders. Son of Petropolis, tell us,
Tell us how to turn into the flash,
To lie in the lice-red shirt
On the bank of the Styx and wait
For the gossamer of Paradise
To spider in our dirt-filled eyes.

History Lessons   *for Roman Sheehan and Richard Kearney*

"The proud and beautiful city of Moscow
Is no more." So wrote Napoleon to the Czar.
It was a November morning when we came
On this. I remember the football pitches
Beyond, stretched into wrinkles by the frost.
Someone was running across them, late for school,
His clothes scattered open by the wind.

Outside Moscow we had seen
A Napoleonic, then a Hitlerian dream
Aborted. The firegold city was burning
In the Kremlin domes, a sabred Wehrmacht
Lay opened to the bone, churches were ashen
Until heretics restored their colour
And their stone. Still that boy was running.

Fragrance of Christ, as in the whitethorn
Brightening through Lent, the stricken aroma
Of Czars in ambered silence near Pavlovsk,
The smoking gold of icons at Zagorsk,
And this coal-smoke in the sunlight
Stealing over frost, houses huddled up in
Droves, deep drifts of lost

People. This was history, although the State
Exam confined Ireland to Grattan and allowed
Us roam from London to Moscow. I brought
Black gladioli bulbs from Samarkand
To flourish like omens in our cooler air;
Coals ripening in a light white as vodka.
Elections, hunger-strikes and shots

Greeted our return. Houses broke open
In the season's heat and the bulbs
Burned in the ground. Men on ladders
Climbed into roselight, a roof was a swarm of fireflies
At dusk. The city is no more. The lesson's learned.
I will remember it always as a burning
In the heart of winter and a boy running.

Guerillas

When the Portuguese came in
From manoeuvres in the North
Atlantic, they brought a scent
Of oranges and dark tobacco
To our Arctic streets. Norwegians,
However, were tall and cold,
Drinkers of cheap wine
That blued their eyes more
Than was good for anyone
Who bothered them. Some women
Became sailors' dolls and others
Disapproved. We smelt corruption
In the hot grease of liquor
And foreign language that spat
Around us in *The Moonlight Club.*
Some pleasure writhed there
And some fear. A fight occurred
And then there came the Military
Police who hammered silence out
With night sticks, wall to wall.

And then we'd steal the drinks
Left on the tables they had pushed
Aside to clear the floor.
The whiskey was watered, we could tell.
A medical treacle had been served
As rum. But that was business.
Pollution entered everything and made it
Fierce. Real life was so impure
We savoured its poisons as forbidden
Fruit and, desolate with knowledge,
Grew beyond redemption. Teachers
Washed their hands of us.
Innocent of any specific crime,
We were beaten for a general guilt,
Regular as clockwork. We watched
And questioned nothing. There would be a time
When the foreign sailors would be gone.
Business would still be business.
Whiskey would still be watered,
Some girls would still be dolls;
The Arctic would have inched nearer,
Pollution have gone deeper
And life, entirely domestic, would carry on.

Exile's Return

We came off the Ozarks at night,
Dreaming the motels we stayed in,
Skirted the snow and parked
On the edge of the Grand Canyon.

Now it is the tinder of border towns,
Greened ruins, locked headlands,
Cow-quilted fields and scattered squalls
Scouting for winter. Honey thins

Out of the blood. At four o'clock
The rivers are dark. Yet, desert-bright,
Sensation is not removed here
From what it loves. The last oasis

Before civilisation, condensed
Out of ocean, malingering far
West of Eden, its truest colour
Nettle-green. Here the heart begins.

Breaking Wood

I was breaking wood in the shed
As dark fell. The wind gusted
And slammed the door, pitching
Me into such blackness that I
Missed my stroke and struck
A spark from the floor.

It brought back my father
Chopping wood in autumn,
And with it came the smell
Of leaf-mould, the hinted
Flights of late swallows,
The shrivelled gold

Of wasps in the notches
Of wide-spoked webs. Memories
Stilled me so long it was dark
Before I rose to gather the sticks.
A sigh of resin and I felt
The stirring of seeds of regret

As I tumbled the white wood
Into the rumbling box
And heard the wind whip
On the trees and bend into
A straight stream of lament
At the razored edge of the wall.

White fall of wood and blue-red
Leaping spark, pitch black
Blow of wind, dark inks
Of still and moving waters,
The seasonable deaths of summers,
The unseasonable deaths of fathers. . . .

Should I have struck with the axe
Near darkness, called the spark
From his deep energies of enrichment
And decay? Still, in this tangled weather
I must break sticks for warmth
And split the flinty wind

For its interior noises.
Soon the red honeycomb of fire
Will sting the poker bright
Up half its length. Soon
The fume of wood upon the air
Will take my feeling to the night.

Tongues

Now and again I have a notion
Of what it will all come to.
Men will be playing noiseless football
In the field far below,
Not working in the factory where
Stones have made black stars
Out of the windows. It will be
The Seventh Sunday after Easter
And at nightfall
We will line up with our torches
In the graveyard to help
Some boy or other lead
His blinded mother
To his father's grave.

For some believe in Pentecost
Though they live in Babel,
Tongues of fire and fiery tongues,
Well-lit but not well-able.

Homer Nods

Were the seas the surge beneath
The marriage-bed? Was this unbelonging
Man escaping over the wine
Of water the fate of having
To belong. Temporary widow,
Forever wife, suitors slaughtered
Nightly in the tapestry

Of their unwound longings;
Ineffectual son. Against this,
Circe and the trek into
The underworld, the sack of Troy,
Gods' angers, favours,
Sex and war and death—
Mature issues that would have made

A better man of that poor
Pawnshipped boy, Telemachus.
Tell us, Ulysses, what we cannot see.
The blind teller lends your story
Wisdom it may not have. The blind leading
The blind on a voyage taken
By a man of infinite clear sight?

Subjects for writers; wife and ocean,
Wandering and stillness; fidelity
Lashed to the mast, destiny?
Or nonsense? Some prefer Circe,
But then is not Penelope
A pearl among swinemen? And could it be
We have here an autobiography

Pretending to epic for authority?
Protean creature, who has come to be
The proof that greatness lives vicariously
In the lies swapped round from men to God.
And when we hear the truth,
Not subject, naturally, to proof,
We allow for Homer and we let him nod.

The Churchyard at Creggan

a translation of Úr-Chill a' Chreagáin *by Art Mac Cumhaigh**

At Creggan churchyard last night
I slept in grief.
And out of the dawnlight
That crimsoned her cheek
A maiden, gold fibre in her hair,
Came to kiss me. Just to stare
On that princess lifted the blight
From the world and gave it relief.

"Good-hearted man, don't be depressed,
Lighten that sorrowful glance;
Rise and come with me to the west
Where the land's not under the trance
Of the stranger; it's honey-sweet there,
And in the high halls the fair
Strains of the music will bless
Your ear and enchant."

"I would not refuse you, not for the gold
Hoarded by all the kings
That lived since the days of old.
But the thought that stings
Is deserting my friends, for I care
For all that remain and more for my fair
Wife to whom in her youth I told
Promises to which her heart clings."

"You have none left alive,
No family nor friends,
Not a jot or a jive
Do you own. You can't fend
For yourself, you are bare,
Hopeless, with nothing to share.
Instead of my filigree love, you'd abide
By your verses that all here deride?"

"O princess, of royal line,
Are you the Helen that brought
Armies to ruin? Or one of the nine
From Parnassus, so sweetly wrought
In their beauty? Star in clear air,
In what land, by what or where
Did you find nurture? And why is mine
The voice you want, as we go west, in your thought?"

"Don't question me; I do not sleep
On this side of the Boyne.
I'm a changeling; on the steep
Side of Gráinneóg, from the loin
Of a fairy race I'm sprung; all aver
It is I who stir music where
There are true poets—in Tara by deep
Night, by morning on the plains of Tyrone."

"It stabs me to know
The Gaels of Tyrone are gone,
The heirs of the Fews are low
Under the slabbed stone;
Niall Frasach's noble heirs
Who would not forsake verse
And at Christmas would bestow
Robes on those whose tribute was their song."

"Since the tribes were torn apart
At Aughrim and, alas, the Boyne,
The Irish, who always gave support
To the learned, cannot again conjoin.
Wouldn't it be better then, to be there

With us in the magic mounds where,
Instead of Orange arrows in your heart,
Each midday you'll have me, closely joined?"

"If it is foretold,
Princess, you are to be my love.
I would have to hold
You to an oath before we move
West on the road. Swear
That when I die, no matter where,
By the Shannon, the Isle of Man, in Egypt old,
I will be laid under in Creggan, its sweet soil above."

Reading *Paradise Lost* in Protestant Ulster 1984

Should I give in to sleep? This fire's warm,
I know the story off by heart,
Was up so late last night and all the harm
That can be done is done. Far apart
From Milton's devils is the present crew
Of zombie soldiers and their spies,
Supergrasses in whose hiss
We hear the snake and sense the mist
Rise in dreams that crowd the new
Awakening with their demobbed cries.

In the old ground of apocalypse
I saw a broken church near where
Two lines of trees came to eclipse
The summer light. Beside the stair
A grey crow from an old estate
Gripped on the book of Common Prayer,
A rope of mice hung on a strip
Of altar-cloth and a blurring date
Smeared the stone beneath the choir.

Awake again, I see the window take
An arc of rainbow and a fusing rain.
None should break the union of this State

Which God and Man conspired to ordain.
But the woe the long evening brings
To the mazy ambushes of streets
Marks us more deeply now than that bower
Of deepest Eden in our first parents' hour
Of sexual bliss and frail enamourings
Could ever do. Our "sovran Planter" beats

Upon his breast, dyadic evil rules;
A syncope that stammers in our guns,
That forms and then reforms itself in schools
And in our daughters' couplings and our sons'.
We feel the fire's heat, Belial's doze;
A maiden city's burning on the plain;
Rebels surround us, Lord. Ah, whence arose
This dark damnation, this hot unrainbowed rain?

Eamon Grennan (1941–)

In his introduction to a collection of essays on contemporary Irish literature published in 1989, Eamon Grennan, who was born in Dublin in 1941 and taught for many years at Vassar College, explained the collection's critical attention to political issues by refuting Conor Cruise O'Brien's warning that "the area where literature and politics overlap has to be regarded with much suspicion."[1] In Grennan's view this may be true as far as it goes, but in reference to Irish literature this sort of generalization never goes very far. Responding in the same essay to Denis Donoghue's argument that politics is of literary interest "only when it invades literature and prescribes the gross conditions under which poems, plays, stories, and novels are written," Grennan pointed out that in Ireland "such a prescriptive invasion seems always in full swing."[2]

That being so, Grennan's own poetry fulfills its political commitments in ways the most aesthetically minded reader would likely find congenial. Its aims are twofold. Grennan once asked a South African poet what were the poet's political responsibilities. "He picked his words with concentrated care," Grennan remembers. "The poet," he replied, "must be . . . an agitator. He must agitate." That is one function of art. But Grennan's poetry falls closer in practice to the ideal Joseph Brodsky described when Grennan asked him the same question. "Brodsky's answer," Grennan says, "was quick, marvelously simple." The poet's political responsibility is: "To the language."[3]

Grennan's sympathy toward both views grows from his perception that, as he puts it in "A Closer Look," "our wars and / the way we live"—the human proclivity for "wasting everything we touch / with our hands" and "crowding the earth with early graves"—result from a general blindness "to the bright little nipples of rain / that simmer on willow twigs, amber shoots / of the stumped willow itself a burning bush / on the scalloped hem of the ice-pond."[4]

This model of political and aesthetic interdependence lends shape to Grennan's work as a poet. His poems are likely to slip from the task of wrapping language skillfully around immediate reality to locating that reality in a broader, more troubled world. They resist the blurring of reality he describes in "A Closer Look" by examining the material world with the care one might bring to looking at works of art. (His poetry often does this in a literal way: among the few poems collected here there are four that focus in one way or another on paintings—"The Cave Painters," "Raeburn's Skater," "Kitchen Vision," and "In the National Gallery, London"—and a fifth, "Women Going," that looks at sculpture with the same ekphrastic gaze.) Whatever political disturbance may lurk in the background, Grennan keeps his discerning eye on such matters as the rain and the twigs and the small dramas unfolding at the edge of the pond, as if intent on confronting history precisely through his poetry's attention to these kinds of overlooked details.

Now retired from teaching, Grennan spends his time in the United States and the West of Ireland.

NOTES

1. *New Irish Writing*, ed. James D. Brophy and Eamon Grennan (Boston: Twayne Publishers, 1989), p. i.

2. Ibid., p. ii.

3. Ibid.

4. "A Closer Look," *What Light There Is & Other Poems* (San Francisco: North Point Press, 1989), p. 97.

A Gentle Art

for my mother

I've been learning how to light a fire
Again, after thirty years. Begin (she'd say)
With a bed of yesterday's newspapers—
Disasters, weddings, births and deaths,
All that everyday black and white of
History is first to go up in smoke. The sticks
Crosswise, holding in their dry heads
Memories of detonating blossom, leaf. Saved
From the ashes of last night's fire,
Arrange the cinders among the sticks:
Crown them with coal nuggets, handling
Such antiquity as behooves it,
For out of this darkness, light. Look,
It's a cold but comely thing
I've put together as my mother showed me,
Down to sweeping the fireplace clean. Lit,
You must cover from view, let it concentrate—
Some things being better done in secret.
Pretend another interest, but never
Let it slip your mind: know its breathing,
Its gulps and little gasps, its silence
And satisfied whispers, its lapping air.
At a certain moment you may be sure (she'd say)
It's caught. Then you simply leave it be:
It's on its own now, leading its mysterious
Hungry life, becoming more itself by the minute,
Like a child grown up, growing strange.

In the National Gallery, London

for Derek Mahon

These Dutchmen are in certain touch
With the world we walk on. Velvet
And solid as summer, their chestnut cows
Repeat cloud contours, lie of the land.

Everything gathers the light in its fashion:
That boat's ribbed bulging, the ripple
Of red tweed at the oarsman's shoulder,
the way wood displaces water, how water
Sheens still, the colour of pale irises.

See how your eye enters this avenue
Of tall, green-tufted, spinal trees:
You tense to the knuckled ruts, nod
To the blunted huntsman and his dog,
A farmer tying vines, that discreet couple
Caught in conversation at a barn's brown angle.
You enter the fellowship of laundered light.

From the ritual conducted around this table
These men in black stare coolly back at you,
Their business, a wine contract, done with.
And on brightly polished ice, these villagers

Are bound to one another by the bleak
Intimacies of winter light—a surface
Laid open like a book, where they flock
Festive and desperate as birds of passage
Between seasons, knowing that enclosing sky
Like the back of their hands, at home
In the cold, making no bones of it.

End of Winter

I spent the morning my father died
Catching flies. They'd buzz and hum
Against the warm illuminated pane
Of the living-room window. Breathless,
My hand would butterfly behind them
And cup their fear in my fist,
Their filament wings tickling
The soft centre of my palm. With my
Left hand I unlatched the window

And opened my right wide in the sunshine.
They'd spin for a second like stunned
Ballerinas, then off with them, tiny
Hearts rattling like dice, recovered
From the fright of their lives. I watch
Each one spiral the astonishing
Green world of grass, and drift
Between the grey branches of the ash.
I see each quick dark shadow
Smudge the rinsed and springing earth
That shone beyond belief all morning.
There must have been at least a dozen
I saved like that with my own hands
Through the morning, when they shook off sleep
In every corner of the living room.

Raeburn's Skater

I want his delicate balance, his
Sturdy, sane, domesticated grace.

Arms crossed, he holds himself together,
Equilibrist of spirit, solid nerve.

Crowblack and solemn, he lives at a tilt
Between limegreen ice and coral air.

Beyond his ken, out of the picture,
The fixed stars hold him fast.

Wing Road

Amazing—
how the young man who empties our dustbin
ascends the truck as it moves
away from him, rises up like an angel
in a china-blue check shirt and lilac

woolen cap, dirty work-gloves, rowanberry
red bandanna flapping at his throat. He plants
one foot above the mudguard, locks
his left hand to a steel bar
stemming from the dumper's loud mouth,
and is borne away, light as a cat, right leg
dangling, the dazzled air snatching at that black-
bearded face. He breaks to a smile, leans wide
and takes the morning to his puffed chest—
right arm stretched far out,
a checkered china-blue wing
gliding between blurred earth
and heaven, a messenger under the locust trees
that stand in silent panic at his passage. But
his mission is not among the trees:
he has flanked both sunlit rims of Wing Road
with empty dustbins, each lying on its side,
its battered lid fallen beside it, each
letting noonlight scour its emptiness
to shining. Carried off in a sudden cloud
of diesel smoke, in a woeful crying out
of brakes and gears, a roaring of monstrous
mechanical appetite, he has left this unlikely
radiance straggled behind him, where the crows—
covening in branches—will flash and haggle.

Men Roofing

for Seamus Heaney

Bright burnished day, they are laying fresh roof down
on Chicago Hall. Tight cylinders of tarred felt-paper
lean against one another on the cracked black shingles
that shroud those undulant ridges. Two squat drums
of tar-mix catch the light: a fat canister of gas
gleams between a heap of old tyres and a paunchy
plastic sack, beer-bottle green. A TV dish-antenna
stands propped to one side, a harvest moon, cocked
to passing satellites and steadfast stars. Gutters
overflow with starlings, lit wings and whistling throats

going like crazy. A plume of blue smoke feathers up
out of a pitch-black cauldron, making the air fragrant
and medicinal, as my childhood's was, with tar. Overhead
against the gentian sky a sudden first flock whirls
of amber leaves and saffron, quick as breath, fine
as origami birds. Watching from a window opposite,
I see a man in a string vest glance up at these exalted
leaves, kneel to roll a roll of tar-felt flat; another
tilts a drum of tar-mix till a slow bolt of black silk
oozes, spreads. One points a silver hose and conjures
from its nozzle a fretted trembling orange lick
of fire. The fourth one dips to the wrist in the green sack
and scatters two brimming fistfuls of granite grit:
broadcast, the bright grain dazzles on black. They pause,
straighten, study one another—a segment done. I can see
the way the red-bearded one in the string vest grins and
slowly whets his two stained palms along his jeans; I see
the one who cast the grit walk to the roof-edge, look over,
then, with a little lilt of the head, spit contemplatively
down. What a sight between earth and air they are, drenched
in sweat and sunlight, relaxed masters for a moment
of all our elements. Here is my image, given, of the world
at peace: men roofing, taking pains to keep the weather
out, simmering in ripe Indian-summer light, winter
on their deadline minds. Briefly they stand balanced
between our common ground and nobody's sky, then move
again to their appointed tasks and stations—as if they were
amazing strangers, come to visit for a brief spell
our familiar shifty climate of blown leaves, birdspin. Odorous,
their column of lazuli smoke loops up from the dark
heart of their mystery; and they ply, they intercede.

Breaking Points   *for Joe Butwin*

They'll all break at some point,
if you can only find it, he says, hoisting
the wedgeheaded heavy axe and coming down with it
in one swift glittering arc: a single *chunnk,*

then the gleam of two half moons of maple
rolling over in the driveway. He finds
his proper rhythm, my strong friend from the west,
standing each half straight up,
then levelling swinging striking
dead centre: two quarters fall
apart from one another
and lie, off-white flesh shining,
on the cracked tarmac. I stand back
and watch him bend and bring to the chopping-place
a solid sawn-off wheel of the maple bough
the unexpected early snow brought down
in a clamorous rush of stricken leafage, a great weight
he walks gingerly under
and gently settles. When he tests it with his eye

I remember a builder of drystone walls
saying the same thing about rocks and big stones,
turning one over and over, hunting its line
of least resistance, then offering it a little
dull tap with his mallet: the stone, as if he'd
slipped the knot holding it together, opened
—cloned—and showed its bright unpolished
inner life to the world. Joe goes on logging
for a furious hour, laying around him
the split quarters, littering the tar-black driveway
with their matte vanilla glitter. Seeing him
lean on the axe-shaft
for a minute's head-bent silence
in the thick of his handiwork,

I remember standing silent at the centre
of the living-room I was leaving for the last time
after ten years of marriage, the polished pine floor
scattered with the bits and pieces
I was in the aftermath taking with me,
the last battle still singing
in my head, the crossed limbs of the children
sofa-sprawled in sleep. And as soon
as he finishes and comes in, steam
sprouting from his red wet neck
and matted hair, dark maps of sweat

staining his navy blue T-shirt, I want to say
as he drains his second glass of lemonade

that this is the way it is
in the world we make and break
for ourselves: first the long green growing, then
the storm, the heavy axe, those shining remnants
that'll season for a year
before the fire gets them; that this is the way
we flail to freedom of a sort,
and—after the heat and blistering deed of it—
how the heart beats in its birdcage of bone
and you're alone
with your own staggered body, its toll
taken, on the nervous verge
of exaltation. But I say nothing, just pour
more lemonade, open a beer, listen
to the tale he tells
of breakage back home—the rending-place
we reach when the labouring heart
fails us and we say
What now? What else? What?
                              And now
in the dusk assembling outside the window
I can see the big gouged maple
radiant where the bough stormed off,
and the split logs
scattered and bright over the driveway—in what
from this Babylonian distance looks like
a pattern of solid purposes or the end of joy.

Kitchen Vision

Here in the kitchen
where we're making breakfast
I find my own view of things
come to light at last: I loom, huge

freckled hands, in the electric kettle's
aluminum belly. In there

the lime-green fridge, military files
of spice jars, and that transfigured window
where the sun breaks flagrant in,
must all recede, draw off, and join
the tiny mourning face
of Botticelli's Venus
hung above a Lilliputian door. In there

all our household effects
are strictly diminished, pared down
to brilliant miniatures
of themselves—the daily
ineluctable clutter of our lives
contained, clarified, fixed in place
and luminous in ordinary light
as if seen once and for all
by Jan Steen or Vermeer. And off

in the silver distance the baby
stares at me from her high chair
of a minute's silence,
and you—a mile away at the stove
turning the eggs—turn round
to see me
gazing at my own
sharply seen misshapen self
in the kettle
that's just starting to sing,
its hot breath steaming.

The Cave Painters

Holding only a handful of rushlight
they pressed deeper into the dark, at a crouch
until the great rock chamber

flowered around them and they stood
in an enormous womb
of flickering light and darklight, a place
to make a start. Raised hands cast flapping shadows
over the sleeker shapes of radiance.

They've left the world of weather and panic
behind them and gone on in, drawing the dark
in their wake, pushing as one pulse
to the core of stone. The pigments mixed in big shells
are crushed ore, petals and pollens, berries
and the binding juices oozed
out of chosen barks. The beasts

begin to take shape from hands and feather-tufts
(soaked in ochre, manganese, madder, mallow white)
stroking the live rock, letting slopes and contours
mould those forms from chance, coaxing
rigid dips and folds and bulges
to lend themselves to necks, bellies, swelling haunches,
a forehead or a twist of horn, tails and manes
curling to a crazy gallop.

Intent and human, they attach
the mineral, vegetable, animal
realms to themselves, inscribing
the one unbroken line
everything depends on, from that
impenetrable centre
to the outer intangibles of light and air, even
the speed of the horse, the bison's fear, the arc
of gentleness this big-bellied cow
arches over its spindling calf,
or the lancing dance of death
that bristles out of the buck's
struck flank. On this one line they leave
a beak-headed human figure of sticks
and one small, chalky, human hand.

We'll never know if they worked in silence
like people praying—the way our monks

illuminated their own dark ages
in cross-hatched rocky cloisters,
where they contrived a binding
labyrinth of lit affinities
to spell out in nature's lace and fable
their mindful, blinding sixth sense
of a god of shadows—or whether (like birds
tracing their great bloodlines over the globe)
they kept a constant gossip up
of praise, encouragement, complaint.

It doesn't matter: we know
they went with guttering rushlight
into the dark; came to terms
with the given world; must have had
—as their hands moved steadily
by spiderlight—one desire
we'd recognise: they would—before going on
beyond this border zone, this nowhere
that is now here—leave something
upright and bright behind them in the dark.

Sea Dog

The sea has scrubbed him clean
as a deal table.
Picked over, plucked hairless,
drawn tight as a drum—
an envelope of tallow
jutting with rib cage, hips, assorted bones.
The once precise pads of his feet
are buttons of bleached wood
in a ring of stubble. The skull—
bonnetted, gap-toothed, tapering
trimly to a caul of wrinkles—
wears an air
faintly human, almost ancestral.

Now the tide falls back
in whispers, leaving the two of us
alone a moment together. Trying
to take in what I see, I see
the lye-bright parchment skin
scabbed black by a rack of flies
that rise up, a humming chorus,
at my approach, settle again
when I stop to stare. These
must be the finishing touch, I think,
till I see round the naked neckbone
a tightly knotted
twist of rope, a frayed noose
that hung him up or held him under
till the snapping and jerking stopped.
Such a neat knot: someone
knelt safely down to do it,
pushing those soft ears back
with familiar fingers. The drag end
now a seaweed tangle around legs
stretched against their last leash.

And nothing more
to this sad sack
of bones, these poor enduring remains
in their own body bag. Nothing more.
Death's head here
holds its own peace
beyond the racket-world of feel and fragrance
where the live dog bent, throbbing
with habit, and the quick children
now shriek by on sand—staring,
averting. I go in over my head

in stillness, and see
behind the body and the barefoot children
how on the bent horizon to the west
a sudden flowering shaft of sunlight
picks out four pale haycocks
saddled in sackcloth

and makes of them a flared quartet
of gospel horses—rearing up,
heading for us.

Women Going

You know the ordinary ways they go
from you and from stark daylight
staring through an open door. This girl
leans her lips to the beak of a dove
she holds against her heart as if
insinuating the best way out and back—
whispering, *Now I have to go.*

On a stone doorpost this young wife
arches her stopped body, one hand
flat across her belly, the other
raised to straighten the seamless veil
through which the full moons of her earrings
just appear, signalling a change of state
and no way back to the here and now
of things, the honeysuckle open air
she's been breathing. And this lady of the house

holds up one necklace after another
chosen from the jewelbox a servant offers
and eyes the way it might belong
between the jut of her neckbone
and where her breasts begin, fitting her
for the road that opens ahead now
and night falling: *This one,* she says
at last, picking the pearls, their clasp
curved like a wishbone. And now

across this busy street you see a man
lean into the back of a taxi
where a woman's face is barely visible
looking back into his face and not flinching

as they dispossess each other into absence,
and the door in that black cloud closes over
whatever it is they say above the roar
of rush-hour traffic. He bends away,

and you know when he looks again
she'll be gone, and in her place will be
this absence beating its stone wings
over every ordinary corner of the day
she's left, and left him in.

These Northern Fields at Dusk

(*Near Newbliss, County Monaghan*)

You'd learn to listen to the big gate
slowly swing in the wind, afloat
on its own all day in a dream of green
and orange light. In the crook
of the hill pasture a scum of flies
has settled on the water
brimming a white cattle trough,
where a congregation of moony eyes
can catch every morning
big-lipped broken glimpses of themselves
gathered together. From the road
you see the whole place
shaped by steel-barred gates
that seem to perch discreetly
on the land—like decorous exchanges
between careful neighbours—
the wildness long ago tamed, trimmed
to use, and garnished with the first
lacy inklings of wild carrot. At this hour
this time of year in this latitude
all the colour that raves by day
gradually leaches out of things, not

towards invisibility but some solid thing—
plain presence—and across the lumpy
quilt of hills you can hear a drumming
ring of metal on metal: someone
hammering a broken pipe or wheel-rim
into better shape. And if you listen
you'll hear whispering: *Nothing
is really lost,* it says, *there is only
this rising up, a shaking out,
a giving back—as these swallows
back from Africa have been given
the swelling heads of grass they shear
their supper from.* This is not the end,
but simply waiting out the waiting itself
until that's the natural state you're in
without fret, a readiness entered: just
walking outdoors—where nothing's changed
for better or worse, but is laid out now
in another light, and being seen by it.

Shed

You wouldn't know it had been there at all, ever,
the small woodshed by the side of the garage
that a falling storm-struck bough demolished
some seasons back, the space and remains now
overcome by weeds, chokecherry, wild rose brambles.
But at the verge of where it stood, a peach tree
I'd never seen a sign of before has pushed
its skinny trunk and sparse-leaved branches up
above that clutter into the thoroughfare of light
and given us, this Fall, a small basketful of
sweet fruit the raccoons love too and sit at midnight
savouring, spitting the stones down where the shed
used to stand, those bony seeds ringing along
the metal ghost of the roof, springing into the dark.

To Grasp the Nettle

Empty your hands. Shake off even the sweat
of memory, the way they burned

to find the cool indented shell of flesh
at the base of her spine, how they cupped themselves

to hold her head, feeling its weight and bones,
every angle of her face and the arc of each earlobe

finding its place in your palm or at your fingertips,
flesh whispering to flesh in its own dialect; or the way

one of them would creep through the breathlessness
of sleep—the sheer unlikely fact of being there, and there

when the light came back—to come to rest on a breast
or claim a hand or settle a warm spot on her belly

or between stilled thighs. Shake it all off:
for as long as they bear the faintest trace

of such hard evidence against you, your hands
will not be steady and the thing will sting you.

Killing the Bees

They'd been there for years, secreted in the ceiling
of the back bedroom—between sealed rafters, plaster
and roof boards—making their own music, leading
a life blind to all but their native needs
and cycles. It couldn't last: armed, masked
under a cloud of sacking-smoke, we knocked a hole
into their cells, sowing anger and panic, a sound
we had, amazed, to shout over, masses of bodies
blackening the light-bulb, a live stalactite of honey
spiralling gold to the floor, the fumes we sprayed
killing them in their thousands. What survived
we dragged outside, drenched in petrol, put a match to,
dug a pit for. Bedroom a battlefield, bodies thick in it.

Detail*

I was watching a robin fly after a finch—the smaller bird
chirping with excitement, the bigger, its breast blazing, silent
in light-winged earnest chase—when, out of nowhere
over the chimneys and the shivering front gardens,
flashes a sparrowhawk headlong, a light brown burn
scorching the air from which it simply plucks
like a ripe fruit the stopped robin, whose two or three
cheeps of terminal surprise twinkle in the silence
closing over the empty street when the birds have gone
about their own business, and I began to understand
how a poem can happen: you have your eye on a small
elusive detail, pursuing its music, when a terrible truth
strikes and your heart cries out, being carried off.

Michael Hartnett (1941–1999)

Michael Hartnett's 1968 volume, *Anatomy of a Cliché*, gives its opening poems titles from various languages—Irish, Italian, French, German, Greek, Russian, Chinese—but soon the titles run out and are replaced in the remaining poems by Roman numerals. None of these poems have titles in English, and seven years later English would disappear from Hartnett's poems themselves.

Hartnett, who was born in 1941 at Croom, in the area of County Limerick that Hartnett refers to as the "seat of the last 'courts' of Gaelic poetry,"[1] remains an influential poet in Ireland, and is among the southern poets most respected in the North.[2] Outside the community of his admirers, though, Hartnett is best known not for what he did but for what he once refused to do. After a decade of publishing poems in English, and translations into English from both Irish and Spanish, Hartnett in 1975 proclaimed what he called "A Farewell to English." "I have made my choice," the poem says, "and leave with little weeping: / I have come with meagre voice / to court the language of my people."[3] In retrospect this public projection of Hartnett's decision to write only in Irish looks like a gesture of insurrection that "A Farewell" itself proposes as the definitive poetic act: "Poets with progress / make no peace or pact. / The act of poetry / is a rebel act."[4] But the poem is less than fully seditious in its relationship to the language. Its tone vacillates—as Hartnett says goodbye to English verse as well as the poetry from other languages that he "found in English nets"—between tenderness toward the English literary tradition and bitterness over the way it has silenced the indigenous Irish voice. William Butler Yeats is a prime target throughout the poem. The third section caricatures the older poet as "Chef Yeats" raiding the cupboard of genuine Irish tradition for the savory and spicy bits that, added to "a glass of University hic-haec-hoc," turn Anglo-Saxon stock into "the celebrated Anglo-Irish stew."

This sort of linguistic cross-breeding in Yeats struck Hartnett, at the time, as detrimental to both of the literary traditions involved. It is interesting to note, though, that in praising Gerard Manley Hopkins, Hartnett is ratifying a similar project that wedded English to the metrical traditions of Welsh poetry. Years later, after publishing several volumes of poems in Irish, Hartnett would himself find a creative energy in the interplay of English and Irish. In 1987 he published *A Necklace of Wrens*, which combined new and selected poems in Irish with English translations by Hartnett himself. *The Killing of Dreams*, published in 1992, was a collection of new poems in English, one of which responds figuratively to the implicit question of language. Pausing to consider that a poem can go out of the poet's control, Hartnett argues that "It is just the case / that in this particular place / an accidental language has / me snarled in its hold." But the poet has survived this "tribal scar" and takes control of the poem, whatever its language:

> What I say is what I am
> and is not open to tirades from you:
> trying not not to be is what I do.[5]

Even in the elevated rhetorical attack of "A Farewell to English," Hartnett recognized that this "trying not not to be" is an effort that unites poets, whatever their relationship to an imperial language. "Struts," another poem in *A Farewell to English*, expresses this sense of connection. The poem figures the community of poets as far-scattered members of a mountaineering expedition, "climbing upwards into time / and climbing backwards into tradition."[6] The surprising number of poems dedicated to Hartnett—several of which appear throughout the anthology—suggests that for many of his contemporaries he was the poet scouting an unexplored Irish Parnassus.

Michael Hartnett died in 1999.

NOTES

1. Author's note to "A Farewell to English," *Collected Poems* (Dublin: Raven Arts Press, 1985), vol. 1, p. 158.

2. Eamon Grennan, "Wrestling with Hartnett," *Southern Review*, vol. 31, no. 1 (Summer 1995), p. 655.

3. "A Farewell to English," *Collected Poems*, vol. 1, p. 163.

4. Ibid., p. 161.

5. "Talking Verses," *The Killing of Dreams* (Loughcrew, Ireland: Gallery Press, 1992), pp. 31–32.

6. "Struts," *A Farewell to English, and Other Poems* (Loughcrew, Ireland: Gallery Books, 1975), p. 11. "Visibility" in line 3 becomes "Visibly" in the version printed in *Collected Poems* (vol. 1, p. 134), which also has "*(for Paul Durcan)*" below the title.

A Small Farm

All the perversions of the soul
I learnt on a small farm,
how to do the neighbours harm
by magic, how to hate.
I was abandoned to their tragedies,
minor but unhealing:
bitterness over boggy land,
casual stealing of crops,
venomous card games
across swearing tables,
a little music on the road,
a little peace in decrepit stables.
Here were rosary beads,
a bleeding face,
the glinting doors
that did encase
their cutler needs,
their plates, their knives,
the cracked calendars
of their lives.

I was abandoned to their tragedies
and began to count the birds,
to deduce secrets in the kitchen cold,
and to avoid among my nameless weeds
the civil war of that household.

Sickroom

Regularly I visited,
since your sickness,
you in the black bedroom
with the gauze of death
around you like your sheets.

Now I must be frank:
these are not roses beside you,
   nor are these grapes,
      and this is no portrait
         of your father's friend.

I know you cannot rise.
You are unable to move.
But I can see your fear,
for two wet mice
    dart
cornered in the hollows
of your head.

Poor Actaeon

Four hounds gone south,
one has your liver in his mouth.
Poor Actaeon.

You understood
her secret action in the nude.
Poor Actaeon.

The female hate
of things too female to relate.
Poor Actaeon.

A mouse, a womb
unfriendly as are life and doom.
Poor Actaeon.

Four hounds went south,
one had your liver in his mouth.
Poor Actaeon.

For My Grandmother, Bridget Halpin

Maybe morning lightens over
the coldest time all the day,
but not for you. A bird's hover,
seabird, blackbird, or bird of prey,
was rain, or death, or lost cattle.
The day's warning, like red plovers
so etched and small the clouded sky,
was book to you, and true bible.
You died in utter loneliness,
your acres left to the childless.
You never saw the animals
of God, and the flower under
your feet; and the trees change a leaf;
and the red fur of a fox on
a quiet evening; and the long
birches falling down the hillside.

Bread

Her iron beats
the smell of bread
from damp linen,
silver, crystal,
and warm white things.
Whatever bird
I used to be,
hawk or lapwing,
tern, or something
wild, fierce or shy,
these birds are dead,
and I come here
on tiring wings.
Odours of bread . . .

from Anatomy of a Cliché

1 *Mo ghrá thú**

> With me, so you call me man.
> Stay: winter is harsh to us,
> my self is worth no money.
> But with your self spread over
> me, eggs under woodcock-wings,
> the grass will not be meagre:
> where we walk will be white flowers.
>
> So rare will my flesh cry out
> I will not call at strange times.
> We will couple when you wish:
> for your womb estranges death.
> Jail me in this gentle land,
> let your hands hold me: I am
> not man until less than man.

2 *Te quiero*

> Your sister, small sister,
> sits: your mother's watchdog.
> *The dance, the dance!*
> Can you hear the soul sing
> of much love
> and little bread,
> an instrument
> thunderous as the soul
> sing pain, sing love?
> *The dance, the dance!*
> Women flash like red flowers!
> Can I not lure your sister down
> so I can kiss behind your ears
> the very fragrance
> of strong sweet wine?

9 "I want you to stand with me . . ."

I want you to stand with me
as a birch tree beside a thorn tree,
I want you as a gold-green moss
close to the bark
when the winds toss
my limbs to tragedy and dark.
You are to be the loveliness
in my cold days,
the live colour in my barrenness,
the fingers that demonstrate
my ways.
I can anticipate no days
unless your graceful sway of hands
arrange my awkward life.
I want you for wife:
keep confronting me as a woman
and make this complex loneliness
more human,
more alive,
and girdered by your graceful sway of hands
we shall ascend from the frigid lands.

from Thirteen Sonnets

9

I saw magic on a green country road—
that old woman, a bag of sticks her load,

blackly down to her thin feet a fringed shawl,
a rosary of bone on her horned hand,
a flight of curlews scribing by her head,
and ashtrees combing with their frills her hair.

Her eyes, wet sunken holes pierced by an awl,
must have deciphered her adoring land:

and curlews, no longer lean birds, instead
become ten scarlet comets in the air.

Some incantation from her canyoned mouth,
Irish, English, blew frost along the ground,
and even though the wind was from the south
the ash-leaves froze without an ash-leaf sound.

from Notes on My Contemporaries

1 The Poet Down   *for Patrick Kavanagh*

He sits between the doctor and the law.
Neither can help. Barbiturate in paw
one, whiskey in paw two, a dying man:
the poet down, and his fell caravan.
They laugh and they mistake the lash that lurks
in his tongue for the honey of his works.
The poet is at bay, the hounds baying,
dig his grave with careful kindness, saying:
"Another whiskey, and make it a large one!"
Priests within, acolytes at the margin
the red impaled bull's roar must fascinate—
they love the dead, the living man they hate.
They were designing monuments—in case—
and making furtive sketches of his face,
and he could hear, above their straining laughs,
the rustling foolscap of their epitaphs.

2 The Poet as Mastercraftsman   *for Thomas Kinsella*

Eras do not end when great poets die,
for poetry is not whole, it is where man
chose mountains to conform, to carve his own
face among the Gothic richness and the sky,
and the gargoyles, and the lesser tradesmen.
Praise from the apprentice is always shown
in miniatures of a similar stone.
I saw the master in his human guise
open doors to let me in, and rhythm out.

He smiled and entertained into the night.
I was aware of work undone. His eyes,
like owls', warned images from the room.
Under the stairs the muse was crying; shields
clashed in the kitchen and the war drum's boom,
men in celtic war dress entered from the right.
I left, my conversation put to rout.

To poets peace poetry never yields.

3 The Poet as Black Sheep   *for Paul Durcan*

I have seen him dine
in middle-class surroundings,
his manners refined,
as his family around him
talk about nothing,
one of their favourite theses.

I have seen him lying
between the street and pavement,
atoning, dying
for their sins, the fittest payment
he can make for them,
to get drunk and go to pieces.

On his father's face
in sparse lines etched out by ice,
the puritan race
has come to its zenith of grey spite,
its climax of hate,
its essence of frigidity.

Let the bourgeoisie beware,
who could not control his head
and kept it in their care
until the brain bled:
this head is a poet's head,
this head holds a galaxy.

5 The Poet as Woman of Ireland

This woman whose dowry was doom
went to a loveless land;
her fragile face enslaved the race
to whom she stretched her hand.
They played fine music at her house
and danced until dawn,
unquivered the dart to find the heart
of that harmless white fawn.
This woman whose dowry was death
sang their requiem,
and hollow bones made the organ's tones
sweet as birdsong to them.
I brought the white flower in spring,
soon the autumn fruit;
with her white ire and her red fire
she killed it at the root.
This woman whose dowry is love,
she sang her ancient songs;
the ardent throngs beat brazen gongs
which she is mistress of.
This woman whose dowry is song
came home to her own place,
her Irish tongue to sing among
her own ungrateful race.

8 The Poet Dreams and Resolves   *for Macdara Woods*

To be alone, and not to be lonely,
to have time to myself, and not be bored;
to live in some suburban house, beside
the mountains, with an adequate supply
of stout and spirits (or of stout only),
and some cigarettes, and writing paper,
and a little cheap food, and a small hoard

of necessary books, where I could write
in dark as monks did, with only blue sky
as interference, wind as soul-reaper.

But what would I do if on certain nights
I was mad in heat for the public lights?
I would chain myself to a living tree
to foil the Sirens of the distant city.

Pigkilling

Like a knife cutting a knife
his last plea for life
echoes joyfully in Camas.
An egg floats
like a navel
in the pickling-barrel;
before he sinks,
his smiling head
sees a delicate girl
up to her elbows
in a tub of blood
while the avalanche
of his offal steams
among the snapping dogs
and mud
and porksteaks
coil in basins
like bright snakes
and buckets of boiling water hiss
to soften his bristles
for the blade.
I kick his golden bladder
in the air.
It lands like a moon
among the damsons.
Life like a knife cutting a knife
his last plea for life
echoes joyfully in Camas.

Death of an Irishwoman

Ignorant, in the sense
she ate monotonous food
and thought the world was flat,
and pagan, in the sense
she knew the things that moved
at night were neither dogs nor cats
but *púcas* and darkfaced men,
she nevertheless had fierce pride.
But sentenced in the end
to eat thin diminishing porridge
in a stone-cold kitchen
she clenched her brittle hands
around a world
she could not understand.
I loved her from the day she died.
She was a summer dance at the crossroads.
She was a card game where a nose was broken.
She was a song that nobody sings.
She was a house ransacked by soldiers.
She was a language seldom spoken.
She was a child's purse, full of useless things.

from A Farewell to English   *for Brendan Kennelly*

I

Her eyes were coins of porter and her West
Limerick voice talked velvet in the house:
her hair was black as the glossy fireplace
wearing with grace her Sunday-night-dance best.
She cut the froth from glasses with a knife
and hammered golden whiskies on the bar

and her mountainy body tripped the gentle
mechanism of verse: the minute interlock
of word and word began, the rhythm formed.
I sunk my hands into tradition
sifting the centuries for words. This quiet
excitement was not new: emotion challenged me
to make it sayable. The clichés came
at first, like matchsticks snapping from the world
of work: *mánla, séimh, dubhfholtach, álainn, caoin.**
they came like grey slabs of slate breaking from
an ancient quarry, *mánla, séimh, dubhfholtach,*
álainn, caoin, slowly vaulting down the dark
unused escarpments, *mánla, séimh, dubhfholtach,*
álainn, caoin, crashing on the cogs, splinters
like axeheads damaging the wheels, clogging
the intricate machine, *mánla, séimh,*
dubhfholtach, álainn, caoin. Then Pegasus
pulled up, the girth broke and I was flung back
on the gravel of Anglo-Saxon.
What was I doing with these foreign words?
I, the polisher of the complex clause,
wizard of grasses and warlock of birds,
midnight-oiled in the metric laws?

5

I say farewell to English verse,
to those I found in English nets:
my Lorca holding out his arms
to love the beauty of his bullets,
Pasternak who outlived Stalin
and died because of lesser beasts;
to all the poets I have loved
from Wyatt to Robert Browning;
to Father Hopkins in his crowded grave

and to our bugbear Mr Yeats
who forced us into exile
on islands of bad verse.

Among my living friends
there is no poet I do not love,
although some write
with bitterness in their hearts;
they are one art, our many arts.

Poets with progress
make no peace or pact.
The act of poetry
is a rebel act.

7

This road is not new.
I am not a maker of new things.
I cannot hew
out of the vacuumcleaner minds
the sense of serving dead kings.

I am nothing new.
I am not a lonely mouth
trying to chew
a niche for culture
in the clergy-cluttered south.

But I will not see
great men go down
who walked in rags
from town to town
finding English a necessary sin
the perfect language to sell pigs in.

I have made my choice
and leave with little weeping:
I have come with meagre voice
to court the language of my people.

from Inchicore Haiku

I

Now, in Inchicore,
my cigarette-smoke rises—
like lonesome pub-talk.

8

My English dam bursts
and out stroll all my bastards.
Irish shakes its head.

30

The cats at civil war
in the partitioned garden.
I stroke my whiskers.

50

My beloved hills,
my family and my friends—
my empty pockets.

64

Blackbird, robin, thrush?
I cannot place the singer.
Exile blunts the ear.

86

All divided up,
all taught to hate each other.
Are these my people?

87

My dead father shouts
from his eternal Labour:
"These are your people!"

Mother Earth

I can't recall an artist's name
who'd paint a woman such as you;
but I've a picture in my purse
(brittle as a caul
kept by a superstitious nurse)
of skin like butter made in country places
with that smell of milking-time,
while sea-urchins like small purple maces
edge along your table
and straw glows in tobacco dung
like slender ingots in the murk
of shed and stable
and your children walk the western rocks
like stooks of oats, gold and full of grain.

But none of this came without pain,
without the social and parental shocks,
the moral alleys where the bigots lurk
who make a lie of what should be a fable,
the pious gang that raves and mocks.
You've felt the rack. Lie back, relax
and let the venom gargle in their throats—
watch your children walk the western rocks
gold and full of grain, like stooks of oats.

The Killing of Dreams

They are encoded and are the past,
cannot be implanted in souls or brains,
not by the learning of lists
nor by learning definitions of names:
this is injecting the dream vaccine
which does not make better but makes die
the entities of the mist
that wait in the hollows of our heads.
We graft the cobbled dream

onto the inbuilt dream:
acid on alkali.
Some of us, afraid we lack
the findings of the analyst,
inject the vaccine in
the sanctum of the heart
only to find that it rejects
the artificial part
and leaves us dreamless in the dark.
This, the learning of lists,
this taking water to the well,
this planting of waterweed in streams,
this addiction to the fix
developed by the alchemists of print—
this is the killing of dreams.

Last Aisling

Helpful and inquisitive, the lads
hauled up his chair
through the side-road, where the briars
(whose ancestors had pulled his hair
and kept some tangled in their thorns)
were still indignant and on guard,
and sat him facing west.
He saw every haybarn, every yard
flow quietly with the hills towards Abbeyfeale,
taking all his life and all the noise of it
beyond there to an island,
long declared unreal and a myth,
but which still rides on a green sea
like a headscarf on the grass.
Among applause and faces,
he heard his praises sung
and saw his old begrudgers trapped
like wasps behind the glass:

but that was now of little consequence
and never was a part of his more real dream—
that his children would stay young
and he'd forever teach them how to say
the names of all the creatures in a stream.
The hills flowed on towards Abbeyfeale,
the lads took down his chair from Tom White's hill
but he was on a walk with Eamon Keane
and they saw a last remaining plover pass
and watched the never-dying children pick
wild strawberries in Glendarragh,
wild raspberries in Glenmageen.

10 June 1991, for John B.

Derek Mahon (1941–)

The Belfast suburb in which Derek Mahon grew up was a mixed neighborhood in which Catholics and Protestants found themselves in close proximity. In the decades after Mahon's birth in 1941, it was the kind of place that provided a thorough elementary education in cultural differences, especially for the only child, as he was, of a Protestant family. At the same time, Belfast's version of suburban culture gave Mahon a peculiar sense of the modern world's distance from the materials of traditional poetry. In the suburbs, he would later write, echoing *Antigone*, "Wonders are many and none is more wonderful than man / Who has tamed the terrier, trimmed the hedge / And grasped the principle of the watering can."[1] Suburban Northern Ireland was certainly not the world of Sophocles or the Anglo-Saxon poets, but Mahon's sense of irony could accommodate that problem, as these lines show. It was, however, much harder to adapt to the stark sectarian division that marked his native place.

In the Belfast of the 1950s and '60s Mahon's complicated sensibility could never resolve itself to a comfortable singularity. Perceiving himself an outsider in the North, Mahon identified early on with the model émigré of Northern Irish letters, Louis MacNeice. But it is not the personal or even the national resonance that Mahon highlights when he considers MacNeice's role in his own development. As he often does in his poems, Mahon translated the sense of isolation he shared with MacNeice into a universal idiom:

> "A tourist in his own country," it has been said, with the implication that this is somehow discreditable. But of what sensitive person is the same not true? The phrase might stand, indeed, as an epitaph for Modern Man, beside Camus's "He made love and read the newspapers."[2]

"In Carrowdore Churchyard," his elegy for MacNeice, is placed as the program piece of Mahon's *Selected Poems*. It imagines the politically pressured, tense future of Irish poetry springing from MacNeice, and figures the relationship between MacNeice and this future in grammatical terms that provide just the sort of pun needed to articulate the connection between these two poets: "This plot is consecrated, for your sake, / To what lies in the future tense. You lie / Past tension now, and spring is coming round / Igniting flowers on the peninsula."[3] The poem's punning hides an almost sentimental core that may be the common center shared by the cosmopolitan, educated personae that Mahon and MacNeice display to the world in their poetry. Mahon's "Preface to a Love Poem" offers a paradoxical disclosure of this kind of hidden core, trying still to hide itself in the conceit of a "preface," even while being exposed. The image Mahon provides there of the poem as a circle sketched around an individual half-truth "[b]eyond which the shapes of truth materialize," reflects his belief that poetry has its most profound effects through reflection and second guessing rather than by expounding ideas or ideologies. His dismissal of the work MacNeice and Auden did in the 1930s makes the same point:

> In fact, most of the verse published by the Auden group at this time was prentice work: the real stuff didn't start to emerge until later, by which time they had rid themselves of their naïve middle-class "socialism" and begun to pursue their individual preoccupations. I would gladly exchange all of Auden's pre-war verse for *New Year Letter,* written in New York when the decade was at an end.[4]

This version of his lineage accounts for Mahon's splendid "letter" poems, but his poetry echoes at the same time a broader tradition, both Irish and English. Mahon has referred to the poet's role as one of "Semiotician, couch potato"[5] and it's true that his poems, juxtaposed one with another, call to mind a sort of channel surfing through literary voices. With transitions as effortless as a click of the remote control, Mahon moves among modes recalling Joyce, Yeats, Beckett. But with each click Mahon accomplishes more than either pastiche or parody.

In a number of poems too long to include here, nearly familiar voices, playing against competing voices, achieve a total effect that is uniquely Mahon's own, as you can hear, for example, in the echoes of Ford Madox Ford, Ezra Pound, and Wyndham Lewis in "A Kensington Notebook." A particularly haunting example of Mahon's mimic muse is "Tithonus," which translates the myth out of the Tennysonian idiom that is its most familiar residence. Mahon heads his "Tithonus" with two tags, one from I Kings—"and after the fire a still small voice"—the other from Beckett; and the poem goes on to give a Beckettian inflection to the still, small voice "at the eastern limit of the world." The result is an unsettling, yet utterly inevitable, revision.[6] As the poem's tonal transposition of Tennyson makes clear, Mahon has a kind of perfect pitch, and the ear that hears tradition is linked to a mind that readily imagines its sound in a contemporary key. His poems also achieve a similar balance in the personal and universal themes they develop. Mahon manages to propel his particular references in the direction of the universal without sacrificing their particularity, as in the lighthouse he writes of, that "might be anywhere—/ Hokkaido, Mayo, Maine; / But it is in Maine."[7]

"The Globe in Carolina," a poem that is included here, has as its central problem the loneliness of lovers, or loved ones—Mahon tends to write these yearning love letters to his children, though the epigraph here suggests a lover—separated by travel. Or, most personally, the problem is the particular one posed by the distance separating North Carolina from London. The universal expansion of this problem starts in the epigraph, Voznesensky's proposition that "There are no religions, no revelations; there are women," which sends the matter whirling into space at once universal and bounded by the geography of the Carolina piedmont. "Globe" binds the competing images of expansiveness and locality together, finally unifying them at the poem's close. Mahon ends the poem singing, but not in the metaphysical falsetto that is the Romantic singing voice of so many post-Romantic poets. Instead, Mahon lowers his voice to achieve a higher level of intensity. From the careful, controlled diction of "The earth spins to my finger tips," he modulates the poem into a stable, enclosing register derived, if derived from anything, from the Blues: "The halved globe, slowly turning, hugs / Its silence, while the lightning bugs / Are quiet beneath the open window, / Listening to that lonesome whistle blow."[8]

This is Mahon's characteristic passage, from elevated description, protected by its own controlled language from what it describes, to a humanized emotional response that comes at the close of the poem because it can't be looked at for long. "Death and the Sun" makes this problem explicit, and is as good a figure as any for the way Mahon's poems are fashioned to collapse into a transcendence, each poem winding up like the sun he describes there, "Listening in silence to his rich despair."[9]

NOTES

1. "Glengormley," *Selected Poems* (London: Viking; Oldcastle: Gallery, in association with Oxford University Press, 1991), p. 12.

2. Derek Mahon, "MacNeice in England and Ireland," *Time Was Away: The World of Louis MacNeice*, ed. Terence Brown and Alec Reid (Dublin: Dolmen Press, 1974), p. 117.

3. "In Carrowdore Churchyard *(at the grave of Louis MacNeice)*," *Selected Poems*, p. 11.

4. "All You Need Is Love," *New Statesman*, vol. 93 (4 February 1977), p. 158.

5. "Beauty and the Beast," *The Hudson Letter* (Loughcrew, Ireland: Gallery Press, 1995), p. 66.

6. "Tithonus," *Selected Poems*, p. 168.

7. "A Lighthouse in Maine," *Selected Poems*, p. 143.

8. "The Globe in Carolina," *Selected Poems*, p. 163.

9. "Death and the Sun (Albert Camus 1913–1960)," *Selected Poems*, p. 194.

Glengormley

Wonders are many and none is more wonderful than man
Who has tamed the terrier, trimmed the hedge
And grasped the principle of the watering can.
Clothes-pegs litter the window-ledge
And the long ships lie in clover; washing lines
Shake out white linen over the chalk thanes.

Now we are safe from monsters, and the giants
Who tore up sods twelve miles by six
And hurled them out to sea to become islands
Can worry us no more. The sticks
And stones that once broke bones will not now harm
A generation of such sense and charm.

Only words hurt us now. No saint or hero,
Landing at night from the conspiring seas,
Brings dangerous tokens to the new era—
Their sad names linger in the histories.
The unreconciled, in their metaphysical pain,
Dangle from lamp-posts in the dawn rain;

And much dies with them. I should rather praise
A worldly time under this worldly sky—
The terrier-taming, garden-watering days
Those heroes pictured as they struggled through
The quick noose of their finite being. By
Necessity, if not choice, I live here too.

In Carrowdore Churchyard

(at the grave of Louis MacNeice)

Your ashes will not stir, even on this high ground,
However the wind tugs, the headstones shake.
This plot is consecrated, for your sake,
To what lies in the future tense. You lie
Past tension now, and spring is coming round
Igniting flowers on the peninsula.

Your ashes will not fly, however the rough winds burst
Through the wild brambles and the reticent trees.
All we may ask of you we have; the rest
Is not for publication, will not be heard.
Maguire, I believe, suggested a blackbird
And over your grave a phrase from Euripides.

Which suits you down to the ground, like this churchyard
With its play of shadow, its humane perspective.
Locked in the winter's fist, these hills are hard
As nails, yet soft and feminine in their turn
When fingers open and the hedges burn.
This, you implied, is how we ought to live—

The ironical, loving crush of roses against snow,
Each fragile, solving ambiguity. So
From the pneumonia of the ditch, from the ague
Of the blind poet and the bombed-out town you bring
The all-clear to the empty holes of spring,
Rinsing the choked mud, keeping the colours new.

A Disused Shed in Co. Wexford

Let them not forget us, the weak souls among the asphodels.

—Seferis, *Mythistorema*

for J. G. Farrell

Even now there are places where a thought might grow—
Peruvian mines, worked out and abandoned
To a slow clock of condensation,
An echo trapped for ever, and a flutter
Of wild flowers in the lift-shaft,
Indian compounds where the wind dances
And a door bangs with diminished confidence,
Lime crevices behind rippling rain-barrels,
Dog corners for bone burials;
And in a disused shed in Co. Wexford,

Deep in the grounds of a burnt-out hotel,
Among the bathtubs and the washbasins
A thousand mushrooms crowd to a keyhole.
This is the one star in their firmament
Or frames a star within a star.
What should they do there but desire?
So many days beyond the rhododendrons
With the world waltzing in its bowl of cloud,
They have learnt patience and silence
Listening to the rooks querulous in the high wood.

They have been waiting for us in a foetor
Of vegetable sweat since civil war days,
Since the gravel-crunching, interminable departure
Of the expropriated mycologist.
He never came back, and light since then
Is a keyhole rusting gently after rain.
Spiders have spun, flies dusted to mildew
And once a day, perhaps, they have heard something—
A trickle of masonry, a shout from the blue
Or a lorry changing gear at the end of the lane.

There have been deaths, the pale flesh flaking
Into the earth that nourished it;
And nightmares, born of these and the grim
Dominion of stale air and rank moisture.
Those nearest the door grow strong—
"Elbow room! Elbow room!"
The rest, dim in a twilight of crumbling
Utensils and broken pitchers, groaning
For their deliverance, have been so long
Expectant that there is left only the posture.

A half century, without visitors, in the dark—
Poor preparation for the cracking lock
And creak of hinges; magi, moonmen,
Powdery prisoners of the old regime,
Web-throated, stalked like triffids, racked by drought
And insomnia, only the ghost of a scream
At the flash-bulb firing-squad we wake them with
Shows there is life yet in their feverish forms.

Grown beyond nature now, soft food for worms,
They lift frail heads in gravity and good faith.

They are begging us, you see, in their wordless way,
To do something, to speak on their behalf
Or at least not to close the door again.
Lost people of Treblinka and Pompeii!
"Save us, save us," they seem to say,
"Let the god not abandon us
Who have come so far in darkness and in pain.
We too had our lives to live.
You with your light meter and relaxed itinerary,
Let not our naive labours have been in vain!"

Courtyards in Delft

—Pieter de Hooch, 1659

for Gordon Woods

Oblique light on the trite, on brick and tile—
Immaculate masonry, and everywhere that
Water tap, that broom and wooden pail
To keep it so. House-proud, the wives
Of artisans pursue their thrifty lives
Among scrubbed yards, modest but adequate.
Foliage is sparse, and clings; no breeze
Ruffles the trim composure of those trees.

No spinet-playing emblematic of
The harmonies and disharmonies of love,
No lewd fish, no fruit, no wide-eyed bird
About to fly its cage while a virgin
Listens to her seducer, mars the chaste
Perfection of the thing and the thing made.
Nothing is random, nothing goes to waste.
We miss the dirty dog, the fiery gin.

That girl with her back to us who waits
For her man to come home for his tea
Will wait till the paint disintegrates
And ruined dikes admit the esurient sea;
Yet this is life too, and the cracked
Outhouse door a verifiable fact
As vividly mnemonic as the sunlit
Railings that front the house opposite.

I lived there as a boy and know the coal
Glittering in its shed, late-afternoon
Lambency informing the deal table,
The ceiling cradled in a radiant spoon.
I must be lying low in a room there,
A strange child with a taste for verse,
While my hard-nosed companions dream of fire
And sword upon parched veldt and fields of rain-swept gorse.

A Garage in Co. Cork

Surely you paused at this roadside oasis
In your nomadic youth, and saw the mound
Of never-used cement, the curious faces,
The soft-drink ads and the uneven ground
Rainbowed with oily puddles, where a snail
Had scrawled its slimy, phosphorescent trail.

Like a frontier store-front in an old western
It might have nothing behind it but thin air,
Building materials, fruit boxes, scrap iron,
Dust-laden shrubs and coils of rusty wire,
A cabbage-white fluttering in the sodden
Silence of an untended kitchen garden—

Nirvana! But the cracked panes reveal a dark
Interior echoing with the cries of children.
Here in this quiet corner of Co. Cork

A family ate, slept, and watched the rain
Dance clean and cobalt the exhausted grit
So that the mind shrank from the glare of it.

Where did they go? South Boston? Cricklewood?
Somebody somewhere thinks of this as home,
Remembering the old pumps where they stood,
Antique now, squirting juice into a cream
Lagonda or a dung-caked tractor while
A cloud swam on a cloud-reflecting tile.

Surely a whitewashed sun-trap at the back
Gave way to hens, wild thyme, and the first few
Shadowy yards of an overgrown cart track,
Tyres in the branches such as Noah knew—
Beyond, a swoop of mountain where you heard,
Disconsolate in the haze, a single blackbird.

Left to itself, the functional will cast
A death-bed glow of picturesque abandon.
The intact antiquities of the recent past,
Dropped from the retail catalogues, return
To the materials that gave rise to them
And shine with a late sacramental gleam.

A god who spent the night here once rewarded
Natural courtesy with eternal life—
Changing to petrol pumps, that they be spared
For ever there, an old man and his wife.
The virgin who escaped his dark design
Sanctions the townland from her prickly shrine.

We might be anywhere but are in one place only,
One of the milestones of earth-residence
Unique in each particular, the thinly
Peopled hinterland serenely tense—
Not in the hope of a resplendent future
But with a sure sense of its intrinsic nature.

The Globe in Carolina

There are no religions, no revelations;
there are women.

—Voznesensky, *Antiworlds*

The earth spins to my fingertips and
Pauses beneath my outstretched hand;
White water seethes against the green
Capes where the continents begin.
Warm breezes move the pines and stir
The hot dust of the piedmont where
Night glides inland from town to town.
I love to see that sun go down.

It sets in a coniferous haze
Beyond Georgia while the anglepoise
Rears like a moon to shed its savage
Radiance on the desolate page,
On Dvořák sleeves and Audubon
Bird-prints; an electronic brain
Records the concrete music of
Our hardware in the heavens above.

From Hatteras to the Blue Ridge
Night spreads like ink on the unhedged
Tobacco fields and clucking lakes,
Bringing the lights on in the rocks
And swamps, the farms and motor courts,
Substantial cities, kitsch resorts—
Until, to the mild theoptic eye,
America is its own night-sky.

Out in the void and staring hard
At the dim stone where we were reared,
Great mother, now the gods have gone
We place our faith in you alone,
Inverting the procedures which
Knelt us to things beyond our reach.
Drop of the ocean, may your salt
Astringency redeem our fault!

Veined marble, if we only knew,
In practice as in theory, true
Redemption lies not in the thrust
Of action only, but the trust
We place in our peripheral
Night garden in the glory-hole
Of space, a home from home, and what
Devotion we can bring to it!

. . . You lie, an ocean to the east,
Your limbs composed, your mind at rest,
Asleep in a sunrise which will be
Your midday when it reaches me;
And what misgivings I might have
About the true importance of
The "merely human" pale before
The mere fact of your being there.

Five miles away a southbound freight
Sings its euphoria to the state
And passes on; unfinished work
Awaits me in the scented dark.
The halved globe, slowly turning, hugs
Its silence, while the lightning bugs
Are quiet beneath the open window,
Listening to that lonesome whistle blow . . .

Ovid in Tomis

What coarse god
Was the gearbox in the rain
Beside the road?

What nereid the unsinkable
Coca-Cola
Knocking the icy rocks?

They stare me out
With the chaste gravity
And feral pride

Of noble savages
Set down
On an alien shore.

It is so long
Since my own transformation
Into a stone,

I often forget
That there was a time
Before my name

Was mud in the mouths
Of the Danube,
A dirty word in Rome.

Imagine Byron banished
To Botany Bay
Or Wilde to Dawson City

And you have some idea
How it is for me
On the shores of the Black Sea.

I who once strode
Head-high in the forum,
A living legend,

Fasten my sheepskin
By greasy waters
In a Scythian wind.

My wife and friends
Do what they can
On my behalf;

Though from Tiberius,
Whom God preserve,
I expect nothing.

But I don't want
To die here
In the back of beyond

Among these morose
Dice-throwing Getes
And the dust of Thrace.

No doubt, in time
To come, this huddle of
Mud huts will be

A handsome city,
An important port,
A popular resort

With an oil pipeline,
Martini terraces
And even a dignified

Statue of Ovid
Gazing out to sea
From the promenade;

But for the moment
It is merely a place
Where I have to be.

Six years now
Since my relegation
To this town

By the late Augustus.
The *Halieutica*,
However desultory,

Gives me a sense
Of purpose,
However factitious;

But I think it's the birds
That please me most,
The cranes and pelicans.

I often sit in the dunes
Listening hard
To the uninhibited

Virtuosity of a lark
Serenading the sun
And meditate upon

The transience
Of earthly dominion,
The perfidy of princes.

Mediocrity, they say,
Consoles itself
With the reflection

That genius so often
Comes to a bad end.
The things adversity

Teaches us
About human nature
As the aphorisms strike home!

I know the simple life
Would be right for me
If I were a simple man.

I have a real sense
Of the dumb spirit
In boulder and tree;

Skimming stones, I wince
With vicarious pain
As a slim quoit goes in.

And the six-foot reeds
Of the delta,
The pathos there!

Whenever they bend
And sigh in the wind
It is not merely Syrinx

Remembering Syrinx
But Syrinx keening
Her naked terror

Of the certain future,
She and her kind
Being bulk-destined

For pulping machines
And the cording
Of motor-car tyres.

Pan is dead, and already
I feel an ancient
Unity leave the earth,

The bowl avoid my eye
As if ashamed
Of my failure to keep faith.

(It knows that I
Have exchanged belief
For documentation.)

The Muse is somewhere
Else, not here
By this frozen lake—

Or, if here, then I am
Not poet enough
To make the connection.

Are we truly alone
With our physics and myths,
The stars no more

Than glittering dust,
With no one there
To hear our choral odes?

If so, we can start
To ignore the silence
Of the infinite spaces

And concentrate instead
On the infinity
Under our very noses—

The cry at the heart
Of the artichoke,
The gaiety of atoms.

Better to contemplate
The blank page
And leave it blank

Than modify
Its substance by
So much as a pen-stroke.

Woven of wood-nymphs,
It speaks volumes
No one will ever write.

I incline my head
To its candour
And weep for our exile.

Antarctica   *for Richard Ryan*

"I am just going outside and may be some time."
The others nod, pretending not to know.
At the heart of the ridiculous, the sublime.

He leaves them reading and begins to climb,
Goading his ghost into the howling snow;
He is just going outside and may be some time.

The tent recedes beneath its crust of rime
And frostbite is replaced by vertigo:
At the heart of the ridiculous, the sublime.

Need we consider it some sort of crime,
This numb self-sacrifice of the weakest? No,
He is just going outside and may be some time—

In fact, for ever. Solitary enzyme,
Though the night yield no glimmer there will glow,
At the heart of the ridiculous, the sublime.

He takes leave of the earthly pantomime
Quietly, knowing it is time to go.
"I am just going outside and may be some time."
At the heart of the ridiculous, the sublime.

from The Hudson Letter   *for Patricia King*

    I

Sometimes, from beyond the skyscrapers, the cry of a tugboat finds you in your
insomnia, and you remember this desert of iron and cement is an island.

                         —Albert Camus, *American Journals*

Winter; a short walk from the 10th St. Pier—
and what of the kick-start that should be here?
The fishy ice lies thick on Gansevoort
around the corner, and the snow shines bright
about your country house this morning: short
the time left to find the serenity
which for a lifetime has eluded me . . .
A rented "studio" apartment in New York
five blocks from the river, time to think and work,
long-suffering friends and visitors, the bars
where Dylan Thomas spent his final hours,
God rest him; but there's something missing here
in this autistic slammer, some restorative
laid like a magic wand on everything—
on bed, chair, desk and air-conditioner.
I often visualize in the neon slush
that great heart-breaking moment in *The Gold Rush*
where Chaplin, left alone on New Year's Eve,
listens to life's feast from his little shack
and the strains of "Auld Lang's Syne" across the snow.
Oh, show me how to recover my lost nerve!
The radiators knock, whistle and sing.
I toss and turn and listen, when I wake,
to the first bird and the first garbage truck,
hearing the "lordly" Hudson "hardly" flow

to New York Harbour and the sea below.
The lights go out along the Jersey shore
and, as Manhattan faces east once more,
dawn's early light on bridge and water-tower,
Respighi's temperate nightingale on WQXR
pipes up though stronger stations throng the ether—
a radio serendipity to illustrate
the resilience of our lyric appetite,
carnivalesque or studiously apart,
on tap in offices, lofts and desperate 'hoods
to Lorca's "urinating multitudes"
while I make coffee and listen for the news
at eight; but first the nightingale. Sing, Muse.

VIII *Ovid on West 4th*

Women are necessarily capable of almost anything in their struggle for survival
and can scarcely be convicted of such man-made crimes as "cruelty."

—F. Scott Fitzgerald, *Tender Is the Night*

When his wronged wife Procne sat him down to eat
King Tereus little knew what was on his plate.
(Afternoon now, some silence in the street
till released children dash to bus and swing.)
Pretending this dinner was a traditional thing,
an Athenian feast fit only for a king,
she excused the servants. Throned in his royal seat,
poor Tereus sipped his wine in solitary state
and, forking his own son hot from a covered dish,
called out: "Hey, send young Itys here to me!"
Procne could barely conceal her wicked glee
and, keen to tell him the ghastly news, replied,
pointing at Tereus' stomach: "There he is inside!"
"What do you mean?" says Tereus, looking foolish,
"I don't see him." Then, as he called once more,
fair Philomela appeared, dripping with blood, and flung
Itys' severed head, itself streaming with gore,
right in Tereus' face, as he picked at his own young.
Oh, how she longed then for the use of her tongue!
Nothing would have given her greater pleasure

than to whisper a few harsh words to her ravisher;
as for the king, he nearly had a seizure
to think that he should eat his . . . own son Itys.
Howling, he swept aside the candlesticks
and called the furies from the depths of Styx—
no, howling he overturned the dinner table
and called the furies from the hobs of Hell.
Unhinged to think this flesh of his own flesh
consumed by the viscera where the genes first grew
and he his own son's charnel-house, he drew
his sword to open his own digestive tract
and pluck the chewed-up gobbets from the mush
but turned instead on the two sisters, who fled
as if on wings; and they *were* winged, in fact,
both of them changed in a twinkling into birds
whirring and twittering inches above his head,
swallow and nightingale hovering in mid-air.
One flew to the roof-top, one flew to the woods
where, even today, the nightingale can be heard
descanting in convent garden and Georgian square—
while Tereus, with hair on end and furious sword-bill,
turned into a hoopoe and is furious still . . .
. . . Never mind the hidden agenda, the sub-text;
it's not really about male arrogance, "rough sex"
or vengeful sisterhood, but about art
and the encoded mysteries of the human heart.

X *St. Mark's Place*

Auden, floppy-slippered bear of St. Mark's Place,
I seem to glimpse your cheesy limestone face
as you stand at your dirty window, gin in paw,
on a hot evening during the great Cold War
where the young Trotsky published *Novy Mir.*
Joseph the druggist, Abe in the liquor store,
Maurice the mailman and Marianne Moore
are the happier for your grumpy love; for, funny
in Hobbit T-shirt and dubious Levi's, you
were a victim of nothing but irony, Gramsci's new
"disease of the interregnum"; and to castration-
and-death phone-threats replied without hesitation:

"I think you've the wrong number." Lord of martini
and clerihew, so insistent on your privacy,
who so valued personal responsibility,
what would you make now of the cosmic *pax
Americana,* our world of internet and fax,
an ever more complex military-industrial complex,
situational ethics, exonerative 12-step programs,
health fascism, critical theory and "smart" bombs?
While we hole up in our bath-houses and catacombs,
votaries of Eros if not always of Aphrodite,
I see you ride at rush-hour with your rich pity
and self-contempt an uptown train packed to the doors
with "aristocratic Negro faces," not like ours,
or reciting "The Unknown Citizen" at the "Y."
When will she—Gaia, Clio—send downpours
to silence the "gnostic chirrup" of her calumniators?
When will we hear once more the pure voice of elation
raised in the nightwood of known symbol and allusion?
Oh, far from Mother, in the unmarried city,
you contemplate a new ode to Euphrosyne,
goddess of banquets; and in the darkest hours
of holocaust and apocalypse, cheap music and singles bars,
you remind us of what the examined life involves—
for what you teach is the courage to be ourselves,
however ridiculous; and if you were often silly
or too "prone to hold forth," you prescribe a cure
for our civilization and its discontents
based upon *agapè,* baroque opera, common sense
and the abstract energy that brought us here,
sustaining us now as we face a more boring future.

from The Yellow Book

XIX *On the Automation of the Irish Lights*

We go to the lighthouse over a golf-course now,
not whins and heather as we used to do,
though we loved golf a generation ago
when it was old sticks and rain-sodden sand—

the sea breeze and first-morning-springy turf,
the dewy, liminal silence of the rough,
the little club-house with its tin roof,
steamers and lightships half a mile from land,
an old sea civilization; but now, unmanned,
the wave-washed granite and limestone towers stand
on the edge of space untouched by human hand,
a routine enlightenment, bright but abandoned.
So long from Alexandria to Fastnet and Hawaii,
to Rathlin, Baily, Kinsale, Mizen, Cape Clear.
These are the stars in the mud, the moth's desire,
the cosmic golf that guides us *ab aeterno*
to "a little cottage with a light in the window";
like Ptolemy and Ussher the mind creates
its own universe with these co-ordinates
marked out by beacons of perpetual fire
from the centuries of monastic candle-power
to the new technologies and the solar glow—
we are star water; as above, below.
Think (i) of evening light and tower shadow,
the families living in the toy buildings there
beneath that generalized, impartial stare,
the children "abstract, neutral and austere,"
star-clustering summer dusk, a single bird;
and (ii) rock keepers. Imagine them off-shore
in their world of siren-song, kelpie and mermaid,
listening to the wind and short-wave radio
and exercising as best they can in tiny
gardens above the sea. Think finally (iii)
of tower lights rising sheer out of the sea
where after gales a grumbling boulder knocks,
shaking the whole place, at igneous rocks.
Wind high among stars, solstice and equinox
will come and go unnoticed by human eye—
no more solitude, dark nights of the soul;
the new noisy knowledge replaces the midnight oil.
Now the ivory towers will be "visitor centres"
visited mostly during the long winters
by sea-birds—gannet, puffin, kittiwake—
and their quartz lenses' own impersonal stroke.

The Cloud Ceiling

An ocean-drop, dash in the dark, flash in the brain,
suspension in the red mist, in the light-grain,
a twitching silence in the hiding place,
fine pearly night-glow of the forming face,
the pushing brow, the twirling ears and knees . . .
Space-girl, soap on a rope, you like cloud-swing,
bath-water and world music; a kidney bean,
you lie there dreaming on your knotted string
listening hard with shut, determined eyes—
a soul of barely determinate shape and size.

Are thoughts a tap trickle, a cloud formation?
Given to light readings and rich inactivity,
alternative galaxies, a-tonal composition
and tentative revisions of quantum gravity,
you drift in a universe of unspoken words
far from the bright lights and story-boards.
A shy girl in your own private microcosm,
you travel from cloud-chasm to cloud-chasm
awaiting the moment when the burbles start,
the camera action, the first signs of art;

and enter like one of Aristophanes' cloud chorus
heard "singing in the distance" though not for us,
daughters of ocean for whom alone we write,
grave sisters of the rainbow, rose and iris
who dip their pitchers in the sea at night
and soak the risen leaf before first light—
capricious dirigibles of the swirling ether,
great wringing sacks above the luminous earth
from whose precipitations images gather
as in the opacity of a developing-bath.

After a night of iron-dark, unmoving skies
you open your eyes; we too open our eyes
on a clear day where hedgerow and high-rise
swivel deliriously round your baby-bed
in the attic studio where you lie safe
like yin and yang in your own secret life.

Sunlight streams like April at the window;
sky-flocks graze above your dreaming head.
Life is a dream, of course, as we all know,
but one to be dreamt in earnest even so.

We've painted a cloud ceiling, a splash of stars
and a thin convective stream, not a bad job:
"Who can number the clouds in wisdom?" (Job).
The indeterminate firmament is all yours.
Rain glitters along a branch, the earth revolves;
soft toys stare, wide-eyed, from the bookshelves.
Will you be Echo, Gráinne, Rosalind? No,
you won't be any of these; you will be you
as, "kitten-soft," you float from the mother-ship,
thirst pockets open for the infinite trip.

I who, though soft-hearted, always admired
granite and blackthorn and the verse hard-wired,
tingle and flow like January thaw-water
in contemplation of this rosy daughter.
Be patient with an old bloke; remember later
one who, in his own strange, distracted youth
awake to the cold stars for the harsh truth,
now tilts a bottle to your open mouth.
So drench the nappies; fluff, bubble and burp:
I probably won't be here when you've grown up.

New Wave

On the first day of principal photography
they sit outside at a St. Germain café
with coffee cups between them on a round
table of chequered oilcloth red and grey.
The hand-held camera looks for natural light,
mikes pick up traffic and incidental sound.
A mid-week noon and the hot bridges sweat;
from ice buckets, from windows, watches, knives,
life flashes back at them their glittering lives.

Silence, the first thing they have in common,
creates a little precise hole in the uproar
and the vague sorrow between man and woman
changes summer to autumn as they conspire
like scientists working from the same data.
When they reach Cabourg beyond a darkening road
and a white hotel room shaken by white waves
in a cloud of powder and brine, they run baths
and stare at the moon through open windows.

While the lamps go off along the promenade
they wake to a dawn silence, curtained light,
mist and the roar of the sea, vast dazzling cloud;
but the stripped mind, still moist and nocturnal,
flinches from confrontation with the infinite.
The sky, its racing stripes and ice-cream colours,
thin cries of children from the beach below,
and the hurtling gulls, are too heartbreaking;
they shut the shutters and return to the dark.

They live the hours as others live the years.
A plane sky-writes, sails flock on the horizon,
their sheets stretch to the white lines of surf
and they doze as if on their own patch of sand
with wind and sun combing their backs and thighs
in a dream of dune-light and rustling quartz
worn smooth by night winds since the dawn of time.
Air reigns, mother-of-pearl; flies come and go;
they open and close their fists like the newly born.

He has given up even on the death of language
and a shower of dots relieves his final page . . .
A singer, tonight she sings in the casino
to a shiny ring of bourgeois, but her heart
has already taken flight from the car-park.
Tide-click; starry wavelengths; aquarium light
from the old world picks out in a double row
their sandy prints where, orphans going home,
they climb back into the waves in a snow of foam.

Eiléan Ní Chuilleanáin (1942–)

Eiléan Ní Chuilleanáin was born in Cork in 1942, and her early life could stand as a model for creating poets without the inconvenience of an unhappy childhood. Free from the ordinary constraints of life within the unconventional intellectual sphere shaped by her parents—her mother was a novelist, her father a professor of Irish—Ní Chuilleanáin spent her adolescence in an enviable exploration of languages and literature. After a primary education at the Ursuline convent in Cork, she went on to study English and history at University College, Cork, and, later, literature at Oxford.

When she returned to Ireland in 1966, Ní Chuilleanáin began to conduct weekly poetry readings in Dublin. While these readings were bringing new poets to a local audience, she sought an international reception for Irish poetry through the journal *Cyphers*, which she founded with Pearse Hutchinson and others in 1975.

Despite these efforts to give poetry a more public voice, however, Ní Chuilleanáin's own work maintains a very private atmosphere. Her longtime interest in history, and in particular the history and literature of the Renaissance, leads her to topics and models that can begin on a large scale but contract under the pressure of analysis into tight, private images. A guided tour through a medieval cloister, for example, becomes the appropriate frame for an image that uncovers a new angle on a childhood attributed to the abbey's founder, but that might just as well be the poet's own:

> What she never saw from any angle but this. . . .
> Herself at fourteen stumbling downhill
> And landing, and crouching to watch
> The sly limbering of the bantam hen
> Foraging between gravestones.[1]

Given the freedom of opportunity she enjoyed in her own life, it is surprising how characteristic this motif of feminine silence and witness has become for Ní Chuilleanáin. Many of her poems evoke what the title of one poem calls "The Absent Girl," a figure who is always "Conspicuous by her silence."[2]

Still more typical, though, is the way this poem moves from the present to a past represented—or in nearly justifiable contemporary critical jargon re-presented—in the traces left after death. "Séamus Murphy, Died October 2nd 1975," a poem Ní Chuilleanáin has cited as her most successful work, models her poetic art along a similar line, turning a graveyard walk into the pathway by which the past inscribes itself in the language of the present, its future.

NOTES

1. "The Architectural Metaphor," *The Brazen Serpent* (Loughcrew, Ireland: Gallery Books, 1994), pp. 14–15.

2. "The Absent Girl," *The Second Voyage* (Newcastle upon Tyne: Bloodaxe Books, 1986), p. 13.

The Absent Girl

The absent girl is
Conspicuous by her silence
Sitting at the courtroom window
Her cheek against the glass.

They pass her without a sound
And when they look for her face
Can only see the clock behind her skull;

Grey hair blinds her eyes
And night presses on the window-panes,

She can feel the glass cold
But with no time for pain
Searches for a memory lost with muscle and blood—
She misses her ligaments and the marrow of her bones.

The clock chatters; with no beating heart
Lung or breast how can she tell the time?
Her skin is shadowed
Where once the early sunlight blazed.

from Site of Ambush

1. *Reflection*

You are not the sun or the moon
But the wolf that will swallow down both sun and moon.

They dance around but they must go down
You will devour them all.

The houses, flowers, the salt and ships
Streams that flow down mountains, flames that burn up trees.

You are the twining gulf Charybdis
Whose currents yield return to none.

6. *Voyagers*

Turn west now, turn away to sleep
And you are simultaneous with
Maelduin setting sail again
From the island of the white cat
To the high penitential rock
Of a spiked Donegal hermit—
With Odysseus crouching again
Inside a fish-smelling sealskin
Or Anticlus suffocating
Back in the wooden horse's womb
As he hears his wife's voice calling.

Turn westward, your face grows darker
You look sad entering your dream
Whose long currents yield return to none.

7. *Now*

I am walking beside Sandymount strand,
Not on it; the tide is nearly at the new wall.
Four children are pushing back and forth
A huge reel that has held electric cable
They are knee deep in the water
I come closer and see they have rubber boots on.
The sand looks level but the water lies here and there
Searching out valleys an inch deep. They interlock
Reflecting a bright morning sky.
A man with a hat says to me "Is it coming in or going out?"
He is not trying to start something, the weather is too fine
The hour early. "Coming in I think" I say
I have been watching one patch getting smaller.

Other people are taking large dogs for walks.
Have they no work to go to? The old baths
Loom square like a mirage.
Light glances off water, wet sand and houses;
Just now I am passing Maurice Craig's
And there he is reading a book at his window.
It is a quarter past ten—
He looks as if he's been at it for hours.

The Second Voyage

Odysseus rested on his oar and saw
The ruffled foreheads of the waves
Crocodiling and mincing past: he rammed
The oar between their jaws and looked down
In the simmering sea where scribbles of weed defined
Uncertain depth, and the slim fishes progressed
In fatal formation, and thought

                              If there was a single
Streak of decency in these waves now, they'd be ridged
Pocked and dented with the battering they've had,
And we could name them as Adam named the beasts,
Saluting a new one with dismay, or a notorious one
With admiration; they'd notice us passing
And rejoice at our shipwreck, but these
Have less character than sheep and need more patience.

I know what I'll do he said;
I'll park my ship in the crook of a long pier
(And I'll take you with me he said to the oar)
I'll face the rising ground and walk away
From tidal waters, up riverbeds
Where herons parcel out the miles of stream,
Over gaps in the hills, through warm
Silent valleys, and when I meet a farmer
Bold enough to look me in the eye
With "where are you off to with that long
Winnowing fan over your shoulder?"
There I will stand still
And I'll plant you for a gatepost or a hitching-post
And leave you as a tidemark. I can go back
And organise my house then.

                           But the profound
Unfenced valleys of the ocean still held him;
He had only the oar to make them keep their distance;
The sea was still frying under the ship's side.
He considered the water-lilies, and thought about fountains
Spraying as wide as willows in empty squares,
The sugarstick of water clattering into the kettle,
The flat lakes bisecting the rushes. He remembered spiders and frogs

Housekeeping at the roadside in brown trickles floored with mud,
Horsetroughs, the black canal, pale swans at dark:
His face grew damp with tears that tasted
Like his own sweat or the insults of the sea.

Ferryboat

Once at sea, everything is changed:
Even on the ferry, where
There's hardly time to check all the passports
Between the dark shore and the light,
You can buy tax-free whiskey and cigars
(Being officially nowhere)
And in theory get married
Without a priest, three miles from the land.

In theory you may also drown
Though any other kind of death is more likely.
Taking part in a national disaster
You'd earn extra sympathy for your relations.

To recall this possibility the tables and chairs
Are chained down for fear of levitation
And a deaths-head in a lifejacket grins beside the bar
Teaching the adjustment of the slender tapes
That bind the buoyant soul to the sinking body,
In case you should find yourself gasping
In a flooded corridor or lost between cold waves.

Alive on sufferance, mortal before all,
Shipbuilders all believe in fate;
The moral of the ship is death.

Old Roads

Missing from the map, the abandoned roads
Reach across the mountain, threading into
Clefts and valleys, shuffle between thick
Hedges of flowery thorn.
The grass flows into tracks of wheels,
Mowed evenly by the careful sheep;
Drenched, it guards the gaps of silence
Only trampled on the pattern day.

And if, an odd time, late
At night, a cart passes
Splashing in a burst stream, crunching bones,
The wavering candle hung by the shaft
Slaps light against a single gable
Catches a flat tombstone
Shaking a nervous beam as the hare passes.

Their arthritic fingers
Their stiffening grasp cannot
Hold long on the hillside—
Slowly the old roads lose their grip.

Letter to Pearse Hutchinson

I saw the islands in a ring all round me
And the twilight sea travelling past
Uneasy still. Lightning over Mount Gabriel:
At such a distance no sound of thunder.
The mackerel just taken
Battered the floor, and at my elbow
The waves disputed with the engine.
Equally grey, the headlands
Crept round the rim of the sea.

Going anywhere fast is a trap:
This water music ransacked my mind
And started it growing again in a new perspective

And like the sea that burrows and soaks
In the swamps and crevices beneath
Made a circle out of food and ill.

So I accepted all the sufferings of the poor,
The old maid and the old whore
And the bull trying to remember
What it was made him courageous
As life goes to ground in one of its caves,
And I accepted the way love
Poured down a cul-de-sac
Is never seen again.

There was plenty of time while the sea water
Nosed across the ruinous ocean floor
Inquiring for the ruinous door of the womb
And found the soul of Vercingetorix
Cramped in a jamjar
Who was starved to death in a dry cistern
In Rome in 46 B.C.

Do not expect to feel so free on land.

Séamus Murphy, Died October 2nd 1975

Walking in the graveyard, a maze
Of angels and families
The path coils like a shaving of wood
We stop to read the names.

In time they all come around
Again, the spearbearer, the spongebearer
Ladder and pillar
Scooped from shallow beds.

Carrying black clothes
Whiskey and ham for the wake
The city revolves
White peaks of churches clockwise lifting and falling.

The hill below the barracks
The sprouting sandstone walls go past
And as always you are facing the past
Finding below the old clockface

The long rambles of the spider
In the narrow bed of a saint
The names inscribed travelling
Into a winter of stone.

Wash

Wash man out of the earth; shear off
The human shell.
Twenty feet down there's close cold earth
So clean.

Wash the man out of the woman:
The strange sweat from her skin, the ashes from her hair.
Stretch her to dry in the sun
The blue marks on her breast will fade.

Woman and world not yet
Clean as the cat
Leaping to the windowsill with a fish in her teeth;
Her flat curious eyes reflect the squalid room,
She begins to wash the water from the fish.

Pygmalion's Image

Not only her stone face, laid back staring in the ferns,
But everything the scoop of the valley contains begins to move
(And beyond the horizon the trucks beat the highway.)

A tree inflates gently on the curve of the hill;
An insect crashes on the carved eyelid;

Grass blows westward from the roots,
As the wind knifes under her skin and ruffles it like a book.

The crisp hair is real, wriggling like snakes;
A rustle of veins, tick of blood in the throat;
The lines of the face tangle and catch, and
A green leaf of language comes twisting out of her mouth.

The Liturgy

He has been invited to perform
The very ancient ceremony, the Farewell to Fire,
And with misgivings has agreed.

The day comes and doubt comes back.
He never thought his initiation
Would lead to this, he planned a quiet life
Studying the epigrams incised
On millennial plaques. And that
Is the reason he was asked to officiate;
The devotees in their casual search
Had spotted the sacred metal in his luggage.

He stands in the September afternoon glow, balancing
The copper shells and their ritual pouch in two hands,
Then clatters off down the stairs of the hostel.

They are waiting outside, the muffled band,
Their boat moored and loaded
With piled blankets, crocheted shawls,
Nets of mellowed fruit. Behind them,
The glitter of the estuary, the honeycomb
Of cliffs riddled with sunlight.

Meanwhile the house is empty
Except for the two women on the ground floor.
The latch of their room will never shut completely.
They hear the hinges of the big door closing,
They know the length of the ceremony, they know
They have just forty minutes.

The Pig-boy

It was his bag of tricks she wanted, surely not him:
The pipkin that sat on the flame, its emissions
Transporting her so she skipped from kitchen to kitchen
Sampling licks of food; she knew who had bacon
And who had porridge and tea. And she needed
The swoop of light from his torch
That wavered as she walked,
Booted, through the evening fair,
Catching the green flash of sheeps' eyes,
The glow of false teeth in the skull:

Its grotto light stroked oxters of arches,
Bridges, lintels, probed cobbles of tunnels
Where the world shook itself inside out like a knitted sleeve:
Light on the frozen mesh, the fishbone curve, the threads
And weights.
    And as day
Glittered on the skin, she stood
In the hood of a nostril and saw
The ocean gleam of his eye.

St Mary Magdalene Preaching at Marseilles

Now at the end of her life she is all hair—
A cataract flowing and freezing—and a voice
Breaking loose from the loose red hair,
The secret shroud of her skin:
A voice glittering in the wilderness.
She preaches in the city, she wanders
Late in the evening through shaded squares.

The hairs on the back of her wrists begin to lie down
And she breathes evenly, her elbows leaning
On a smooth wall. Down there in the piazza,
The boys are skimming on toy carts, warped
On their stomachs, like breathless fish.

She tucks her hair around her,
Looking beyond the game
To the suburban marshes.

Out there a shining traps the sun,
The waters are still clear,
Not a hook or a comma of ice
Holding them, the water-weeds
Lying collapsed like hair
At the turn of the tide;

They wait for the right time, then
Flip all together their thousands of sepia feet.

Chrissie

Escaped beyond hope, she climbs now
Back over the ribs of the wrecked ship,
Kneels on the crushed afterdeck, between gross
Maternal coils: the scaffolding
Surviving after pillage.
                    On the strand
The voices buzz and sink; heads can be seen
Ducking into hutches, bent over boiling pans.
The trees above the sand, like guests,
Range themselves, flounced, attentive.
Four notches down the sky, the sun gores the planks;
Light fills the growing cavity
That swells her, that ripens to her ending.

The tide returning shocks the keel;
The timbers gape again, meeting the salty breeze;
She lies where the wind rips at her left ear,
Her skirt flapping, the anchor-fluke
Biting her spine; she hears
The dull sounds from the island change
To a shrill evening cry. In her head she can see them
Pushing out boats, Mother Superior's shoulder to the stern

(Her tanned forehead more dreadful now
Than when helmeted and veiled)
                                    And she goes on fingering
In the shallow split in the wood
The grandmother's charm, a stone once shaped like a walnut,
They had never found. Salt water soaked its force:
The beat of the oars cancelled its landward grace.

She clings, as once to the horned altar beside the well.

The Architectural Metaphor

The guide in the flashing cap explains
The lie of the land.
The buildings of the convent, founded

Here, a good mile on the safe side of the border
Before the border was changed,
Are still partly a cloister.

This was the laundry. A mountain shadow steals
Through the room, shifts by piles of folded linen.
A radio whispers behind the wall:

Since there is nothing that speaks as clearly
As music, no other voice that says
Hold me I'm going . . . so faintly,

Now light scatters, a door opens, laughter breaks in,
A young girl barefoot, a man pushing her
Backwards against the hatch—

It flies up suddenly—
There lies the foundress, pale
In her funeral sheets, her face turned west

Searching for the rose-window. It shows her
What she never saw from any angle but this:
Weeds nested in the churchyard, catching the late sun,

Herself at fourteen stumbling downhill
And landing, and crouching to watch
The sly limbering of the bantam hen

Foraging between gravestones—
                              Help is at hand
Though out of reach:
                    The world not dead after all.

1989

Woman Shoeing a Horse

This is the path to the stile
And this is where I would stand—
The place is all thick with weeds.

I could see the line of her back and the flash of her hair
As she came from the fields at a call,
And then ten minutes wasted, all quiet

But the horse in the open air clanking his feet
Until the fire was roaring and the work began,
And the clattering and dancing.

I could see by her shoulders how her breath shifted
In the burst of heat, and the wide gesture of her free arm
As she lifted the weight and clung

Around the hoof. The hammer notes were flying
All urgent with fire and speed, and precise
With a finicky catch at the end—

But the noise I could not hear was the shock of air
Crashing into her lungs, the depth
Of the gasp as she turned with a ready hand

As the heat from the fire drew up the chimney,
The flame pressing, brushing out the last thread,
Constantly revising itself upwards to a pure line.

I closed my eyes, not to see the rider as he left.
When I opened them again the sheep were inching forward,
A flock of starlings had darkened the sky.

Studying the Language

On Sundays I watch the hermits coming out of their holes
Into the light. Their cliff is as full as a hive.
They crowd together on warm shoulders of rock
Where the sun has been shining, their joints crackle.
They begin to talk after a while.
I listen to their accents, they are not all
From this island, not all old,
Not even, I think, all masculine.

They are so wise, they do not pretend to see me.
They drink from the scattered pools of melted snow:
I walk right by them and drink when they have done.
I can see the marks of chains around their feet.

I call this my work, these decades and stations—
Because, without these, I would be a stranger here.

Anchoress

In the last season, she changed her ways.
The pilgrim would find only
The mossgrown window beside the church porch
And through it at times a loaf and water were passed.

A few words, a command. Yes she knew who was there,
She still prayed for them all by name. I remember
When she would give me an hour of her visions,
When she would levitate—she was always deaf—
When thin pipe music resounded beyond the grilles.

Agnes Bernelle, 1923–1999

There is no beast I love better than the spider
That makes her own new centre every day
Catching brilliantly the light of autumn,

That judges the depth of the rosemary bush
And the slant of the sun on the brick wall
When she slings her veils and pinnacles.

She crouches on her knife edge, an ideogram combining
The word for *tools* with the word for *discipline*,
Ready for a lifetime of cold rehearsals;

Her presence is the syllable on the white wall,
The hooked shadow. Her children are everywhere,
Her strands as long as the railway-line in the desert

That shines one instant and the next is doused in dust.
If she could only sing she would be perfect, but
In everything else she reminds me of you.

Borders   *for John McCarter*

I am driving north to your wake, without a free hand.
I must start at the start, at the white page in my mind.
I no longer own a ribbed corset of rhymes;
I am the witch who stands one-legged, masking one eye.

Passed under the soldier's lens at Aughnacloy,
I remember how often you crossed the map in a toil
Of love (like Lir's daughter driven to the Sea of Moyle
By spells) from Dublin to Portadown or Armagh to Donegal.

So I leap over lines that are set here to hold and plan
The great global waistline in sober monoglot bands,
I follow the road that follows the lie of the land,
Crossing a stream called *Fairy Water,* to come to the bridge at Strabane.

Gloss/Clós/Glas

Look at the scholar, he has still not gone to bed,
Raking the dictionaries, darting at locked presses,
Hunting for keys. He stacks the books to his oxter,
Walks across the room as stiff as a shelf.

His nightwork, to make the price of his release:
Two words, as opposite as *his* and *hers*
Which yet must be as close
As the word *clós* to its meaning in a Scots courtyard
Close to the spailpín ships, or as close as the note
On the uilleann pipe to the same note on the fiddle—
As close as the grain in the polished wood, as the finger
Bitten by the string, as the hairs of the bow
Bent by the repeated note—
                    Two words
Closer to the bone than the words I was so proud of,
Embrace and *strict* to describe the twining of bone and flesh.

The rags of language are streaming like weathervanes,
Like weeds in water they turn with the tide, as he turns
Back and forth the looking-glass pages, the words
Pouring and slippery like the silk thighs of the tomcat
Pouring through the slit in the fence, lightly,
Until he reaches the language that has no word for *his*,
No word for *hers*, and is brought up sudden
Like a boy in a story faced with a small locked door.
Who is that he can hear panting on the other side?
The steam of her breath is turning the locked lock green.

Eavan Boland (1944–)

"I began to write in an enclosed, self-confident literary culture," Eavan Boland remarks in *Object Lessons*. "The poet's life stood in a burnished light in the Ireland of that time." No one, of course, was handing a life of luxury to Irish poets in the 1960s when Boland's career began; as ever, there was little financial recompense to balance the poet's labors. "But," Boland insists, "the idea of the poet was honored." Boland, born in Dublin in 1944 and educated at Trinity College, was drawn by the luminous image of the poetic life partly because of the antithesis it made to the role she had been prepared by tradition to accept. "A woman's life was not honored," she writes in the same essay. "At least no one I knew suggested that it was exemplary in the way a poet's was."[1]

Not only were the two roles differently valued, but the activities of the one often worked to the detriment of the other, such that "Irish poems simplified women most at the point of intersection between womanhood and Irishness."[2] The challenge for Boland, who had lived in England for much of her childhood, was to find a way of being simultaneously Irish, a woman, and a poet.

Many of her early poems search, self-consciously, for ways of understanding the role of poet in terms as yet uncomplicated by gender. In various contexts they imagine poets as the excavators and explorers of the human condition. In "The Poets" she writes that:

> They like all creatures, being made
> For the shovel and the worm,
> Ransacked their perishable minds and found
> Pattern and form
> And with their own hands quarried from hard words
> A figure in which secret things confide.[3]

As if in recognition of the value of these secrets, Boland's poems reflect the honorific light she had seen her society cast on poets. Poets are the heroes of these poems. "They are abroad. Their spirits like a pride / Of lions circulate / . . . // And they prevail."[4] In "New Territory," a dramatic lyric on the Spanish discovery of the New World, she associates poets with both exploration and prophecy. The poet is able, like the prophet Isaiah, to envision the new territory of the future by "peering down the unlit centuries."[5]

Having become conversant with this traditional and essentially masculine image of the poet, Boland in her later work began to revise it. Peering back through the centuries of Irish poetic tradition she saw the missing women. The poets as conquistadores and prophets faded in the glare of bare suburban kitchen bulbs that shed a new light on the experience of women, especially those who, like the figure in "Suburban Woman," work at turning the "small surrenders" of modern life into poetry.[6] In poems like this the conventional image of the woman as muse, "beautiful, / Young no doubt, protected in your care / From stiffening and wrinkling, not mortal,"[7] is set alongside the reality that muffles women's voices. A series of poems with titles that recall some of the particular challenges of women's lives—"Anorexic," "Mastectomy," "Menses"—culminates in "Making Up," which plays on the way both poets and women make themselves up. This last poem draws the material of a new, feminist poetics out of the dressing-table scene that has provided material for male poets from Pope to Eliot. Boland's version transforms the work of "making up" from a concession to fashion into an act of the imagination that would set the stage for her later poems. Like the speaker here, her poems "Take nothing, nothing / at its face value" and master the "trick" of turning lives into myths or poetry.

As important as Boland has been as a pioneer for women writers, however, her poetic imagination ultimately transcends gender. Her ability to restore lost voices through the imaginative concentration of her poetry has allowed her to reimagine Irish history in general, whether by dipping into the inner life of a figure like W. B. Yeats or looking beneath the surface terrain of the island to discover, as she does in "That the Science of Cartography is Limited," that the traces of the past are always present. Her poetry has created a vision of Irish history that makes it possible to be Irish, a woman, and a poet. And the formal skill and psychological insight that characterize her work have made her one of the most influential poets writing on either side of the Atlantic. Boland now teaches at Stanford University.

NOTES

1. *Object Lessons* (Manchester: Carcanet Press, 1995), pp. ix–x.
2. Ibid., p. 136.
3. "The Poets," *Collected Poems* (Manchester: Carcanet Press, 1995), p. 9.
4. Ibid.

5. "New Territory," *Collected Poems*, p. 5.

6. "Suburban Woman," *Introducing Eavan Boland* (Princeton, New Jersey: Ontario Review Press, 1980), p. 39.

7. "The Other Woman," *Introducing Eavan Boland*, p. v.

Athene's Song

for my father

From my father's head I sprung
Goddess of the war, created
Partisan and soldiers' physic—
My symbols boast and brazen gong—
Until I made in Athens wood
Upon my knees a new music.

When I played my pipe of bone,
Robbed and whittled from a stag,
Every bird became a lover
Every lover to its tone
Found the truth of song and brag;
Fish sprung in the full river.

Peace became the toy of power
When other noises broke my sleep:
Like dreams I saw the hot ranks
And heroes in another flower
Than any there; I dropped my pipe
Remembering their shouts, their thanks.

Beside the water, lost and mute,
Lies my pipe and like my mind
Remains unknown, remains unknown
And in some hollow taking part
With my heart against my hand
Holds its peace and holds its own.

The Poets

They, like all creatures, being made
For the shovel and worm,
Ransacked their perishable minds and found
Pattern and form
And with their own hands quarried from hard words
A figure in which secret things confide.

They are abroad: their spirits like a pride
Of lions circulate,
Are desperate, just as the jewelled beast,
That lion constellate,
Whose scenery is Betelgeuse and Mars,
Hunts without respite among fixed stars.

And they prevail: to his undoing every day
The essential sun
Proceeds, but only to accommodate
A tenant moon,
And he remains until the very break
Of morning, absentee landlord of the dark.

New Territory

Several things announced the fact to us:
The captain's Spanish tears
Falling like doubloons in the headstrong light,
And then of course the fuss—
The crew jostling and interspersing cheers
With wagers. Overnight
As we went down to our cabins, nursing the last
Of the grog, talking as usual of conquest,
Land hove into sight.

Frail compasses and trenchant constellations
Brought us as far as this,
And now air and water, fire and earth
Stand at their given stations
Out there, and are ready to replace
This single desperate width
Of ocean. Why do we hesitate? Water and air
And fire and earth and therefore life are here,
And therefore death.

Out of the dark man comes to life and into it
He goes and loves and dies,
(His element being the dark and not the light of day).
So the ambitious wit

Of poets and exploring ships have been his eyes—
Riding the dark for joy—
And so Isaiah of the sacred text is eagle-eyed because
By peering down the unlit centuries
He glimpsed the holy boy.

Yeats in Civil War

Presently a strange thing happened:
I began to smell honey in places
where honey could not be.

In middle age you exchanged the sandals
Of a pilgrim for a Norman keep
In Galway. Civil war started, vandals
Sacked your country, made off with your sleep;

Somehow you arranged your escape
Aboard a spirit-ship which every day
Hoisted sail out of fire and rape,
And on that ship your mind was stowaway.

The sun mounted on a wasted place,
But the wind at every door and turn
Blew the smell of honey in your face
Where there was none. Whatever we may learn

You are its sum, struggling to survive—
A fantasy of honey your reprieve.

The War Horse

This dry night, nothing unusual
About the clip, clop, casual

Iron of his shoes as he stamps death
Like a mint on the innocent coinage of earth.

I lift the window, watch the ambling feather
Of hock and fetlock, loosed from its daily tether

In the tinker camp on the Enniskerry Road,
Pass, his breath hissing, his snuffling head

Down. He is gone. No great harm is done.
Only a leaf of our laurel hedge is torn—

Of distant interest like a maimed limb,
Only a rose which now will never climb

The stone of our house, expendable, a mere
Line of defence against him, a volunteer

You might say, only a crocus its bulbous head
Blown from growth, one of the screamless dead.

But we, we are safe, our unformed fear
Of fierce commitment gone; why should we care

If a rose, a hedge, a crocus are uprooted
Like corpses, remote, crushed, mutilated?

He stumbles on like a rumour of war, huge,
Threatening; neighbours use the subterfuge

Of curtains; he stumbles down our short street
Thankfully passing us. I pause, wait,

Then to breathe relief lean on the sill
And for a second only my blood is still

With atavism. That rose he smashed frays
Ribboned across our hedge, recalling days

Of burned countryside, illicit braid:
A cause ruined before, a world betrayed.

The Famine Road

"Idle as trout in light Colonel Jones,
these Irish, give them no coins at all; their bones
need toil, their characters no less." Trevelyan's
seal blooded the deal table. The Relief

Committee deliberated: "Might it be safe,
Colonel, to give them roads, roads to force
from nowhere, going nowhere of course?"

"one out of every ten and then
another third of those again
women—in a case like yours."

Sick, directionless they worked; fork, stick
were iron years away; after all could
they not blood their knuckles on rock, suck
April hailstones for water and for food?
Why for that, cunning as housewives, each eyed—
as if at a corner butcher—the other's buttock.

"anything may have caused it, spores,
a childhood accident; one sees
day after day these mysteries."

Dusk: they will work tomorrow without him.
They know it and walk clear; he has become
a typhoid pariah, his blood tainted, although
he shares it with some there. No more than snow
attends its own flakes where they settle
and melt, will they pray by his death rattle.

"You never will, never you know
but take it well woman, grow
your garden, keep house, good-bye."

"It has gone better than we expected, Lord
Trevelyan, sedition, idleness, cured
in one; from parish to parish, field to field,
the wretches work till they are quite worn,
then fester by their work; we march the corn
to the ships in peace; this Tuesday I saw bones
out of my carriage window, your servant Jones."

"Barren, never to know the load
of his child in you, what is your body
now if not a famine road?"

Suburban Woman

I

Town and country at each other's throat—
between a space of truce until one night

walls began to multiply, to spawn
like lewd whispers of the goings-on,

the romperings, the rape on either side,
the smiling killing, that you were better dead

than let them get you. But they came, armed
with blades and ladders, with slimed

knives, day after day, week by week—
a proxy violation. She woke

one morning to the usual story: withdrawing,
neither side had gained, but there, dying,

caught in cross-fire, her past lay, bleeding
from wounds each meant for each, which needing

each other for other wars they could not inflict
one on another. Haemorrhaging to hacked

roads, in back gardens, like a pride
of lions toiled for booty, tribal acres died

and her world with them. She saw their power to sever
with a scar. She is the sole survivor.

II

Morning: mistress of talcums, spun
and second cottons, run tights
she is, courtesan to the lethal
rapine of routine. The room invites.
She reaches to fluoresce the dawn.
The kitchen lights like a brothel.

III

The chairs dusted and the morning
coffee break behind, she starts pawning

her day again to the curtains, the red
carpets, the stair rods, at last to the bed,

the unmade bed where once in an underworld
of limbs, her eyes freckling the night like jewelled

lights on a cave wall, she, crying, stilled,
bargained out of nothingness her child,

bartered from the dark her only daughter.
Waking, her cheeks dried, to a brighter

dawn she sensed in her as in April earth
a seed, a life ransoming her death.

IV

Late, quiet across her garden
sunlight shifts like a cat
burglar, thieving perspectives,
leaving her in the last light
alone, where, as shadows harden,
lengthen, silent she perceives
veteran dead-nettles, knapweed
crutched on walls, a summer's seed
of roses trenched in ramsons, and stares
at her life falling with her flowers,
like military tribute or the tears
of shell-shocked men, into arrears.

V

Her kitchen blind down—a white flag—
the day's assault over, now she will shrug

a hundred small surrenders off as images
still born, unwritten metaphors, blank pages

and on this territory, blindfold, we meet
at last, veterans of a defeat

no truce will heal, no formula prevent
breaking out fresh again; again the print

of twigs stalking her pillow will begin
a new day and all her victims then—

hopes unreprieved, hours taken hostage—
will newly wake, while I, on a new page

will watch, like town and country, word, thought
look for ascendancy, poise, retreat

leaving each line maimed, my forces used.
Defeated we survive, we two, housed

together in my compromise, my craft
who are of one another the first draft.

Making Up

My naked face;
I wake to it.
How it's dulsed and shrouded!
It's a cloud,

a dull pre-dawn.
But I'll soon
see to that.
I push the blusher up,

I raddle
and I prink,
pinking bone
till my eyes

are
a rouge-washed
flush on water.
Now the base

pales and wastes.
Light thins
from ear to chin,
whitening in

the ocean shine
mirror set
of my eyes
that I fledge

in old darks.
I grease and full
my mouth.
It won't stay shut:

I look
in the glass.
My face is made,
it says:

Take nothing, nothing
at its face value:
Legendary seas,
nakedness,

that up and stuck
lassitude
of thigh and buttock
that they prayed to—

it's a trick.
Myths
are made by men.
The truth of this

wave-raiding
sea-heaving
made-up
tale

of a face
from the source
of the morning
is my own:

Mine are the rouge pots,
the hot pinks,
the fledged
and edgy mix
of light and water
out of which
I dawn.

Mise Eire*

I won't go back to it—

my nation displaced
into old dactyls,
oaths made
by the animal tallows
of the candle—

land of the Gulf Stream,
the small farm,
the scalded memory,
the songs
that bandage up the history,
the words
that make a rhythm of the crime

where time is time past.
A palsy of regrets.
No. I won't go back.
My roots are brutal:

I am the woman—
a sloven's mix
of silk at the wrists,
a sort of dove-strut
in the precincts of the garrison—

who practices
the quick frictions,
the rictus of delight

and gets cambric for it,
rice-coloured silks.

I am the woman
in the gansy-coat
on board the *Mary Belle*,
in the huddling cold,

holding her half-dead baby to her
as the wind shifts east
and north over the dirty
water of the wharf

mingling the immigrant
guttural with the vowels
of homesickness who neither
knows nor cares that

a new language
is a kind of scar
and heals after a while
into a passable imitation
of what went before.

The Achill Woman

She came up the hill carrying water.
She wore a half-buttoned, wool cardigan,
a tea-towel round her waist.

She pushed the hair out of her eyes with
her free hand and put the bucket down.

The zinc-music of the handle on the rim
tuned the evening. An Easter moon rose.
In the next-door field a stream was
a fluid sunset; and then, stars.

I remember the cold rosiness of her hands.
She bent down and blew on them like broth.
And round her waist, on a white background,
in coarse, woven letters, the words "glass cloth."

And she was nearly finished for the day.
And I was all talk, raw from college—
week-ending at a friend's cottage
with one suitcase and the set text
of the Court poets of the Silver Age.

We stayed putting down time until
the evening turned cold without warning.
She said goodnight and started down the hill.

The grass changed from lavender to black.
The trees turned back to cold outlines.
You could taste frost

but nothing now can change the way I went
indoors, chilled by the wind
and made a fire
and took down my book
and opened it and failed to comprehend

the harmonies of servitude,
the grace music gives to flattery
and language borrows from ambition—

and how I fell asleep
oblivious to

the planets clouding over in the skies,
the slow decline of the spring moon,
the songs crying out their ironies.

Outside History

There are outsiders, always. These stars—
these iron inklings of an Irish January,
whose light happened

thousands of years before
our pain did: they are, they have always been
outside history.

They keep their distance. Under them remains
a place where you found
you were human, and

a landscape in which you know you are mortal.
And a time to choose between them.
I have chosen:

out of myth into history I move to be
part of that ordeal
whose darkness is

only now reaching me from those fields,
those rivers, those roads clotted as
firmaments with the dead.

How slowly they die
as we kneel beside them, whisper in their ear.
And we are too late. We are always too late.

That the Science of Cartography is Limited

—and not simply by the fact that this shading of
forest cannot show the fragrance of balsam,
the gloom of cypresses
is what I wish to prove.

When you and I were first in love we drove
to the borders of Connacht
and entered a wood there.

Look down you said: this was once a famine road.

I looked down at ivy and the scutch grass
rough-cast stone had
disappeared into as you told me
in the second winter of their ordeal, in

1847, when the crop had failed twice,
Relief Committees gave
the starving Irish such roads to build.

Where they died, there the road ended

and ends still and when I take down
the map of this island, it is never so
I can say here is
the masterful, the apt rendering of

the spherical as flat, nor
an ingenious design which persuades a curve
into a plane,
but to tell myself again that

the line which says woodland and cries hunger
and gives out among sweet pine and cypress,
and finds no horizon

will not be there.

The Pomegranate

The only legend I have ever loved is
the story of a daughter lost in hell.
And found and rescued there.
Love and blackmail are the gist of it.
Ceres and Persephone the names.
And the best thing about the legend is
I can enter it anywhere. And have.
As a child in exile in
a city of fogs and strange consonants,
I read it first and at first I was
an exiled child in the crackling dusk of
the underworld, the stars blighted. Later
I walked out in a summer twilight
searching for my daughter at bed-time.
When she came running I was ready
to make any bargain to keep her.
I carried her back past whitebeams
and wasps and honey-scented buddleias.

But I was Ceres then and I knew
winter was in store for every leaf
on every tree on that road.
Was inescapable for each one we passed.
And for me.
                    It is winter
and the stars are hidden.
I climb the stairs and stand where I can see
my child asleep beside her teen magazines,
her can of Coke, her plate of uncut fruit.
The pomegranate! How did I forget it?
She could have come home and been safe
and ended the story and all
our heart-broken searching but she reached
out a hand and plucked a pomegranate.
She put out her hand and pulled down
the French sound for apple and
the noise of stone and the proof
that even in the place of death,
at the heart of legend, in the midst
of rocks full of unshed tears
ready to be diamonds by the time
the story was told, a child can be
hungry. I could warn her. There is still a chance.
The rain is cold. The road is flint-coloured.
The suburb has cars and cable television.
The veiled stars are above ground.
It is another world. But what else
can a mother give her daughter but such
beautiful rifts in time?
If I defer the grief I will diminish the gift.
The legend will be hers as well as mine.
She will enter it. As I have.
She will wake up. She will hold
the papery flushed skin in her hand.
And to her lips. I will say nothing.

Story

Two lovers in an Irish wood at dusk
are hiding from an old and vengeful king.

The wood is full of sycamore and elder.
And set in that nowhere which is anywhere.

And let the woman be slender. As I was at twenty.
And red-haired. As I was until recently.

They cling together listening to his hounds
get nearer in the twilight and the spring

thickets fill with the sound of danger.
Blossoms are the colour of blood and capture.

We can be safe, they say. We can start
a rumour in the wood to reach the king—

that she has lost her youth. That her mouth is
cold. That this woman is growing older.

They do not know. They have no idea
how much of this: the ocean-coloured peace

of the dusk, and the way legend stresses it,
depend on her to be young and beautiful.

They start the rumour in the last light.
But the light changes. The distance shudders.

And suddenly what is happening is not
what happens to the lovers in the wood

or an angry king and his frantic hounds
and the tricks and kisses he has planned.

But what is whispering out of sycamores.
And over river-noise. And by-passes harebells

and blue air. And is overheard by the birds
which are the elements of logic in an early

spring. And is travelling to enter a suburb
at the foothills of the mountains in Dublin.

And a garden with jasmine and poplars. And
a table at which I am writing. I am writing

a woman out of legend. I am thinking
how new it is—this story. How hard it will be to tell.

The Mother Tongue

The old pale ditch can still be seen
less than half a mile from my house—

its ancient barrier of mud and brambles
which mireth next unto Irishmen
is now a mere rise of coarse grass,
a rowan tree and some thinned-out spruce,
where a child is playing at twilight.

I stand in the shadows. I find it
hard to believe now that once
this was a source of our division:

Dug. Drained. Shored up and left
to keep out and keep in. That here
the essence of a colony's defence
was the substance of the quarrel with its purpose:

Land. Ground. A line drawn in rain
and clay and the roots of wild broom—
behind it the makings of a city,
beyond it rumours of a nation—
by Dalkey and Kilternan and Balally
through two ways of saying their names.

A window is suddenly yellow.
A woman is calling a child.
She turns from her play and runs to her name.

Who came here under cover of darkness
from Glenmalure and the Wicklow hills
to the limits of this boundary? Who whispered
the old names for love to this earth

and anger and ownership as it opened
the abyss of their future at their feet?

I was born on this side of the Pale.
I speak with the forked tongue of colony.
But I stand in the first dark and frost
of a winter night in Dublin and imagine

my pure sound, my undivided speech
travelling to the edge of this silence.
As if to find me. And I listen: I hear
what I am safe from. What I have lost.

Quarantine

In the worst hour of the worst season
    of the worst year of a whole people
a man set out from the workhouse with his wife.
He was walking—they were both walking—north.

She was sick with famine fever and could not keep up.
    He lifted her and put her on his back.
He walked like that west and west and north.
Until at nightfall under freezing stars they arrived.

In the morning they were both found dead.
    Of cold. Of hunger. Of the toxins of a whole history.
But her feet were held against his breastbone.
The last heat of his flesh was his last gift to her.

Let no love poem ever come to this threshold.
    There is no place here for the inexact
praise of the easy graces and sensuality of the body.
There is only time for this merciless inventory:

Their death together in the winter of 1847.
    Also what they suffered. How they lived.
And what there is between a man and woman.
And in which darkness it can best be proved.

Irish Poetry   *for Michael Hartnett*

We always knew there was no Orpheus in Ireland.
No music stored at the doors of hell.
No god to make it.
No wild beasts to weep and lie down to it.

But I remember an evening when the sky
was underworld-dark at four,
when ice had seized every part of the city
and we sat talking—
the air making a wreath for our cups of tea.

And you began to speak of our own gods.
Our heartbroken pantheon.

No Attic light for them and no Herodotus.
But thin rain and dogfish and the stopgap
of the sharp cliffs
they spent their winters on.

And the pitch-black Atlantic night.
How the sound
of a bird's wing in a lost language sounded.

You made the noise for me.
Made it again.
Until I could see the flight of it: suddenly

the silvery lithe rivers of the south-west
lay down in silence
and the savage acres no one could predict
were all at ease, soothed and quiet and

listening to you, as I was. As if to music, as if to peace.

An Elegy for my Mother In Which She Scarcely Appears

I knew we had to grieve for the animals
a long time ago: weep for them, pity them.
I knew it was our strange human duty

to write their elegies after we arranged their demise.
I was young then and able for the paradox.
I am older now and ready with the question:
what happened to them all? I mean to those
old dumb implements which have
no eyes to plead with us like theirs,
no claim to make on us like theirs? I mean—

there was a singing kettle. I want to know
why no one tagged its neck or ringed the tin
base of its extinct design or crouched to hear
its rising shriek in winter or wrote it down with
the birds in their blue sleeves of air
torn away with the trees that sheltered them.

And there were brass firedogs which lay out
all evening on the grate and in the heat
thrown at them by the last of the peat fire
but no one noted down their history or put them
in the old packs under slate-blue moonlight.
There was a wooden clothes horse, absolutely steady
without sinews, with no mane and no meadows
to canter in; carrying, instead of
landlords or Irish monks, rinsed tea cloths
but still, I would have thought, worth adding to
the catalogue of what we need, what we always need

as is my mother, on this Dublin evening of
fog crystals and frost as she reaches out to test
one corner of a cloth for dryness as the prewar
Irish twilight closes in and down on the room
and the curtains are drawn and here am I,
not even born and already a conservationist,
with nothing to assist me but the last
and most fabulous of beasts—language, language—
which knows, as I do, that it's too late
to record the loss of these things but does so anyway,
and anxiously, in case it shares their fate.

In Coming Days

Soon
I will be as old as the Shan Van Vocht—

(although no one knows how old she is.)

Soon
I will ask to meet her at the borders of Kildare.

It will be cold.
The hazel willow will be frozen by the wayside.

The rag-taggle of our history
will march by us.

They will hardly notice two women by the roadside.

I will speak to her. Even though I know
she can only speak with words made by others.

I will say to her: You were betrayed.
Do you know that?

She will look past me at the torn banners,
makeshift pikes, bruised feet. Her lips will move.

To the Currach of Kildare
The boys they will repair.

There is still time, I will tell her. We can still
grow older together.

And will Ireland then be free?
And will Ireland then be free?

We loved the same things, I will say—
or at least some of them. Once in fact, long ago,

Yes! Ireland shall be free,
From the centre to the sea.

I almost loved you.

Paul Durcan (1944–)

To many aficionados, Paul Durcan's distinctive voice is the manifest sound of contemporary Irish poetry. Durcan, who was born in Dublin in 1944, is renowned both in Ireland and abroad for the energy and dramatic style he brings to poetry readings. His poetic incantations can even be heard in a spoken segment of "In the Days Before Rock-n-Roll," a recording by the poet laureate of Irish Rhythm and Blues, Van Morrison.

The characteristic sound, though, is secondary to visual concerns in Durcan's own poetic hierarchy. In his introduction to *Crazy about Women*, a volume of poems commissioned by the Irish National Gallery to accompany reproductions of several works in their collection, Durcan says that "pictures," whether paintings or the flickering images in Dublin's Light House Cinema, have been the breath of his writing life since 1980. Their influence began much earlier:

> In 1967 I was working as a clerk in the North Thames Gas Board adjacent to the Tate Gallery. Every lunchtime I walked out the back gate under the billboard proclaiming "Look Ahead with Gas" to sit in front of the pictures of Francis Bacon. These pictures . . . lit up the gloom of life and turned my eyesight inside out.[1]

Durcan's desire to dissolve the barriers that separate poetry from the other arts is integral to this perceptual conversion experience; he aspires to discover a poetry, as he puts it, "so inclusive as to make the intercourse between what is painted and what is written as reciprocal as it is inevitable."[2]

Cultivating this intercourse is not all a matter of writing about paintings and films. In poems like "They Say the Butterfly is the Hardest Stroke," Durcan locates himself within a specifically literary tradition with a lightness that projects its figures through a literary faith as airy and lambent as cinematic images.

Despite an early reputation for frontal assault on Irish society, Durcan has often taken a subtler track, setting his criticism against the backdrop of a more complex and larger world, whether by imagining "A Vision of Africa on the Coast of Kerry," or simply by expanding the boundaries of his poetry to include the troubled North of Ireland. Edna Longley writes that "Durcan's critique of the South is sharpened by his sense of the North. No other Southern Irish poet has so painfully and continuously responded to the Ulster Troubles."[3]

In his later work Durcan has viewed the social world through a more intimate lens. His poems from the 1990s onward seem determined to dissolve strife into peace not by direct political action, but by an appropriately cinematic technique that views political reality through the filters of those relationships, ideas, and images nearest him. Whatever he writes about, however, Durcan is most distinguished by the boundlessness of his imagination. His is a poetry willing to contemplate, and say, anything.

NOTES

1. Paul Durcan, Introduction to *Crazy about Women* (Dublin: Irish National Gallery, 1990), p. x.

2. Ibid., p. xi.

3. Edna Longley, Introduction to *The Selected Paul Durcan* (Belfast: Blackstaff Press, 1982), p. xiii.

They Say the Butterfly is the Hardest Stroke   *to Richard Riordan*

From coves below the cliff of the years
I have dipped into *Ulysses*,
A Vagrant, Tarry Flynn—
But for no more than ten minutes or a page;
For no more than to keep in touch
With minds kindred in their romance with silence.
I have not "met" God, I have not "read"
David Gascoyne, James Joyce, or Patrick Kavanagh:
I believe in them.
Of the song of him with the world in his care
I am content to know the air.

The Kilfenora Teaboy

I'm the Kilfenora teaboy
And I'm not so very young,
But though the land is going to pieces
I will not take up the gun;
I am happy making tea,
I make lots of it when I can,
And when I can't—I just make do;
And I do a small bit of sheepfarming on the side.

Oh but it's the small bit of furze between two towns
Is what makes the Kilfenora teaboy really run.

I have nine healthy daughters
And please God I will have more,
Sometimes my dear wife beats me
But on the whole she's a gentle soul;
When I'm not making her some tea
I sit out and watch them all
Ring-a-rosying in the street;
And I do a small bit of sheepfarming on the side.

Oh but it's the small bit of furze between two towns
Is what makes the Kilfenora teaboy really run.

Oh indeed my wife is handsome,
She has a fire lighting each eye,
You can pluck laughter from her elbows
And from her knees pour money's tears;
I make all my tea for her,
I'm her teaboy on the hill,
And I also thatch her roof;
And I do a small bit of sheepfarming on the side.

Oh but it's the small bit of furʒe between two towns
Is what makes the Kilfenora teaboy really run.

And I'm not only a famous teaboy,
I'm a famous caveman too;
I paint pictures by the hundred
But you can't sell walls;
Although the people praise my pictures
As well as my turf-perfumèd blend
They rarely fling a fiver in my face;
Oh don't we do an awful lot of dying on the side?

But oh it's the small bit of furʒe between two towns
Is what makes the Kilfenora teaboy really run.

In Memory: The Miami Showband—Massacred 31 July 1975

Beautiful are the feet of them that preach the gospel of peace,
Of them that bring glad tidings of good things

In a public house, darkly lit, a patriotic (sic)
Versifier whines into my face: "You must take one side
Or the other, or you're but a fucking romantic."
His eyes glitter hate and vanity, porter and whiskey,
And I realise that he is blind to the braille connection
Between a music and a music-maker.
"You must take one side or the other
Or you're but a fucking romantic":
The whine is icy
And his eyes hang loose like sheets from poles
On a bare wet hillside in winter

And his mouth gapes like a cave in ice;
It is a whine in the crotch of whose fear
Is fondled a dream gun blood-smeared;
It is in war—not poetry or music—
That men find their niche, their glory hole;
Like most of his fellows
He will abide no contradiction in the mind.
He whines: "If there is birth, there cannot be death"
And—jabbing a hysterical forefinger into my nose and eyes—
"If there is death, there cannot be birth."
Peace to the souls of those who unlike my fellow poet
Were true to their trade
Despite death-dealing blackmail by racists:
You made music, and that was all: You were realists
And beautiful were your feet.

The Haulier's Wife Meets Jesus on the Road Near Moone

I live in the town of Cahir,
In the Glen of Aherlow,
Not far from Peekaun
In the townland of Toureen,
At the foot of Galtee Mór
In the County of Tipperary.
I am thirty-three years old,
In the prime of my womanhood:
The mountain stream of my sex
In spate and darkly foaming;
The white hills of my breasts
Brimful and breathing;
The tall trees of my eyes
Screening blue skies;
Yet in each palm of my hand
A sheaf of fallen headstones.
When I stand in profile
Before my bedroom mirror
With my hands on my hips in my slip,
Proud of my body,

Unashamed of my pride,
I appear to myself a naked stranger,
A woman whom I do not know
Except fictionally in the looking-glass,
Quite dramatically beautiful.
Yet in my soul I yearn for affection,
My soul is empty for the want of affection.
I am married to a haulier,
A popular and a wealthy man,
An alcoholic and a county councillor,
Father with me of four sons,
By repute a sensitive man and he is
Except when he makes love to me:
He takes leave of his senses,
Handling me as if I were a sack of gravel
Or a carnival dummy,
A fruit machine or a dodgem.
He makes love to me about twice a year;
Thereafter he does not speak to me for weeks,
Sometimes not for months.
One night in Cruise's Hotel in Limerick
I whispered to him: Please *take* me.
(We had been married five years
And we had two children.)
Christ, do you know what he said?
Where? Where do you want me to take you?
And he rolled over and fell asleep,
Tanked up with seventeen pints of beer.
We live in a Georgian, Tudor, Classical Greek,
Moorish, Spanish Hacienda, Regency Period,
Ranch House, Three-Storey Bungalow
On the edge of the edge of town:
"Poor Joe's Row"
The townspeople call it,
But our real address is "Ronald Reagan Hill"—
That vulturous-looking man in the States.
We're about twelve miles from Ballyporeen
Or, as the vulture flies, about eight miles.
After a month or two of silence
He says to me: Wife, I'm sorry;
I know that we should be separated,

Annulled or whatever,
But on account of the clients and the neighbours,
Not to mention the children, it is plain
As a pikestaff we are glued to one another
Until death do us part.
Why don't you treat yourself
To a weekend up in Dublin,
A night out at the theatre:
I'll pay for the whole shagging lot.

There was a play on at the time
In the Abbey Theatre in Dublin
Called *The Gigli Concert*,
And, because I liked the name—
But also because it starred
My favourite actor, Tom Hickey—
I telephoned on the Abbey from Cahir.
They had but one vacant seat left!
I was so thrilled with myself,
And at the prospect of Tom Hickey
In a play called *The Gigli Concert*
(Such a euphonious name for a play, I thought),
That one wet day I drove over to Clonmel
And I went wild, and I bought a whole new outfit.
I am not one bit afraid to say
That I spent all of £200 on it
(Not, of course, that Tom Hickey would see me
But I'd be seeing myself seeing Tom Hickey
Which would be almost, if not quite,
The very next best thing):
A long, tight-fitting, black skirt
Of Chinese silk,
With matching black jacket
And lace-frilled, pearl-white blouse;
Black fishnet stockings with sequins;
Black stiletto high-heeled shoes
Of pure ostrich leather.
I thought to myself—subconsciously, of course—
If I don't transpose to be somebody's *femme fatale*
It won't anyhow be for the want of trying.

Driving up to Dublin I began to daydream
And either at Horse & Jockey or Abbeyleix
I took a wrong turn and within a quarter of an hour
I knew I was lost. I stopped the car
And I asked the first man I saw on the road
For directions:
"Follow me"—he said—"my name is Jesus:
Have no fear of me—I am a travelling actor.
We'll have a drink together in the nearby inn."
It turned out we were on the road near Moone.
(Have you ever been to the Cross at Moone?
Once my children and I had a picnic at Moone
When they were little and we were on one
Of our Flight into Egypt jaunts to Dublin.
They ran round the High Cross round and round
As if it were a maypole, which maybe it is:
Figure carvings of loaves and fishes, lions and dolphins.
I drank black coffee from a thermos flask
And the children drank red lemonade
And they were wearing blue duffle coats with red scarves
And their small, round, laughing, freckled faces
Looked pointedly like the faces of the twelve apostles
Gazing out at us from the plinth of the Cross
Across a thousand years.
Only, of course, their father was not with us:
He was busy—busy being our family euphemism.
(Every family in Ireland has its own family euphemism
Like a heraldic device or a coat of arms.)
Jesus turned out to be a lovely man,
All that a woman could ever possibly dream of:
Gentle, wild, soft-spoken, courteous, sad;
Angular, awkward, candid, methodical;
Humorous, passionate, angry, kind;
Entirely sensitive to a woman's world.
Discreetly I invited Jesus to spend the night with me—
Stay with me, the day is almost over and it is getting dark—
But he waved me aside with one wave of his hand,
Not contemptuously, but compassionately.
"Our night will come," he smiled,
And he resumed chatting about my children,

All curiosity for their welfare and well-being.
It was like a fire burning in me when he talked to me.
There was only one matter I felt guilty about
And that was my empty vacant seat in the Abbey.
At closing time he kissed me on both cheeks
And we bade one another goodbye and then—
Just as I had all but given up hope—
He kissed me full on the mouth,
My mouth wet with alizarin lipstick
(A tube of Guerlain 4 which I've had for twelve years).
As I drove on into Dublin to the Shelbourne Hotel
I kept hearing his Midlands voice
Saying to me over and over, across the Garden of Gethsemane—
Our night will come.

Back the town of Cahir,
In the Glen of Aherlow,
Not far from Peekaun
In the townland of Toureen,
At the foot of Galtee Mór
In the County of Tipperary,
For the sake of something to say
In front of our four sons
My husband said to me:
Well, what was Benjamino Gigli like?
Oh, 'twas a phenomenal concert!
And what was Tom Hickey like?
Miraculous—I whispered—miraculous.
Our night will come—he had smiled—our night will come.

Flower Girl, Dublin

AFTER JACK B. YEATS

Afternoons in winter
I sit in Robert Roberts Café
Watching men and women,
Especially women.
I am crazy about women.

Just because I am a man without a woman
Does not mean that I have no interest in women.
In fact, I am preoccupied with fundamentally nothing else.
I read all of Nietzsche when I was seventeen.
Then it was time to grow up.

Would you please hose some of your hot liquid into me?
Mother of five to boy at coffee dispenser.
She must be forty at least but as she sips her grounds—
Her Costa Rican grounds—
As she smacks her lips
Trickling her tongue up along her lip rim
She is a girl not yet nineteen
Haughty as an Englishwoman in Shanghai.
Red cloche hat, grey wool overcoat,
Black low high-heel shoes.

I see in today's newspaper a black-and-white photograph
Of a woman in a black miniskirt at the opening
Of the Seán McSweeney Retrospective last night
(There is a man who can paint—not many can
Since the Great Yeat died in 1957).
But much as that photo causes a stir in me—
An abstract stir in me—
It is as nothing compared to this glimpse of ankle—
Ankle—
Of the mother of five in red cloche hat—
Would you please hose some of your hot liquid into me?

Time to go—home. I dally to loiter
In the doorway of the café eyeing myself
In the shop window opposite, my bowler hat,
My frock coat, my gleaming galoshes.
A flower girl with a single red rose in her hands
Is passing the time of day with the mother of five
Not making any particular pitch to sell.

Timorousness entices me to my right—
But I know, Jack, I know
I should step briskly to my left,
Proffer the single red rose to the mother of five,

Nail my colours to the mast.
Will I or won't I?
And give all my loose change to the flower girl—
All my loose change?

My Belovèd Compares Herself to a Pint of Stout

When in the heat of the first night of summer
I observe with a whistle of envy
That Jackson has driven out the road for a pint of stout,
She puts her arm around my waist and scolds me:
Am I not your pint of stout? Drink me.
There is nothing except, of course, self-pity
To stop you also having your pint of stout.

Putting self-pity on a leash in the back of the car,
I drive out the road, do a U-turn,
Drive in the hall door, up the spiral staircase,
Into her bedroom. I park at the foot of her bed,
Nonchalantly step out leaving the car unlocked,
Stroll over to the chest of drawers, lean on it,
Circumspectly inspect the backs of my hands,
Modestly request from her a pint of stout.
She turns her back, undresses, pours herself into bed,
Adjusts the pillows, slaps her hand on the coverlet:
Here I am—at the very least
Look at my new cotton nightdress before you shred it
And do not complain that I have not got a head on me.

I look around to see her foaming out of the bedclothes
Not laughing but gazing at me out of four-leggèd eyes.
She says: Close your eyes, put your hands around me.
I am the blackest, coldest pint you will ever drink
So sip me slowly, let me linger on your lips,
Ooze through your teeth, dawdle down your throat,
Before swooping down into your guts.
While you drink me I will deposit my scum
On your rim and when you get to the bottom of me,
No matter how hard you try to drink my dregs—

And being a man, you will, no harm in that—
I will keep bubbling up back at you.
For there is no escaping my aftermath.
Tonight—being the first night of summer—
You may drink as many pints of me as you like.
There are barrels of me in the tap room.
In thin daylight at nightfall,
You will fall asleep drunk on love.
When you wake early in the early morning
You will have a hangover,
All chaste, astringent, aflame with affirmation,
Straining at the bit to get to first mass
And holy communion and work—the good life.

A Snail in My Prime

Slug Love:
Older than the Pyramids
Christ Jesus
I am a snail in my prime.

On the banks of the Boyne on a June night,
I lie under the great snail cairn of Newgrange
Watching men go to the moon
While their women give birth to more women.
My snail soul is light-sensitive.
I lie in the central chamber of the passage grave
Inhaling the stillness of the earth
While my daughter daubs slime on my face,
Inserts slime in every crevice of my body,
Between my toes, behind my ears.
Small, plump, sleek thrush on wall-top with snail in beak
Banging it, cracking me open.
Between each embalming, she goes down to the river;
Returns with her hands glistening with snails.
(Oh to hold in my hands my father's walking stick
And to press to my lips its brass ferrule and to lean

On it with his chamois gloves on the handle and to test
The floor with its point—that is the point!)
I have never seen my daughter so congenial
As this evening at the signal of my burial.
I have never heard such laughter on her lips,
Such actual, gratuitous, carefree laughter.
She cries: "Thank you for bringing me to the water."
Under the corbelled roof of her own shell;
In the central chamber of her soul;
In the passage of her root;
At the entrance stone of her eyes;
Behind the kerb stones of her knees;
In the quartz stones of her ears;
In the basin stones of her elbows;
Inside the great stone circle of her hair
I listen to her voice echoing in mud millennia:
"Thank you for bringing me to the water."

I like to spend Christmas in Newgrange
Alone with my extended family
In shells all of different stripes and hues
But unisoned in a bequeathal of slime.
At dawn, at the midwinter solstice,
We creep into the corbelled vault
Of the family tomb.
Down in dark
Death is a revealing of light
When a snail inherits the sky,
Inherits his own wavy lines;
When a snail comes full circle
Into the completion of his partial self.
At my life's end, I writhe
For the sun to fatten in the east
And make love to me;
To enter me
At 8.58 a.m.
And to stay inside me
For seventeen minutes,
My eyes out on stalks.

You feel like a spiral
Inside me; you feel
Like three spirals inside me.
After such early morning lovemaking—
I always preferred making love at daybreak—
I spin out my fate
Under my lady's capstone.
The snails of her breasts
Peep out from behind
Their pink petals.
At my life's end in Newgrange
There is light at the end of the tunnel.

Round and round I trundle my bundle of ego,
My nostril tumbril,
My ham pram, my heart cart,
My dreaming shell, my conscious horns,
My spiral of tongue
Unspiralling over the years,
My crops of teeth.
I am a smudge of froth. All I can hear
Is the tiny squeaking in prehistoric forests
Of my antennae being bent until they snap;
The Great Irish Snail in his prime
Coating the cones of Scots pines with his slime,
The orange aura of desire.
I am not womanizer,
I am a snail.
When it is all over
And my daughters have eaten me,
Cremated me
In earthenware pots
With my stone beads
And there will be from me no more poems,
No more antler, no more horn,
And the last tourist coaches have departed,
Morsels of my antennae will be plucked up
By departing house martins, digested,
Deposited off the shores of Africa

In plankton of the South Seas
To enter into the bloodstream of sea lions . . .
Last night, when we made love up behind our pillows,
A pair of sea lions mated on a sud-strewn rock,
Who moments ago were snails in separate beds,
The River Boyne curled up at our feet,
My tail in your tail, my slime in your slime.

Slug love:
Older than the pyramids
Christ Jesus
I am a snail in my prime.

Self-Portrait as an Irish Jew

I

This is the letter, Mam, I dare not write;
Ear-marked to die in the desert at Alamein;
Affrighted by my fright;
His Majesty's sober soldiery burnt alive
In tanks from which there is no escape.
Tell Rabbi Robinson I kiss his beard
Despite soupstains.
The names of his books help keep me sane.
I swear by Jove if I get home alive
To the sheep farm on the mountain behind Tallaght
I will stop on our hill top, watch the city glow-grow;
"Just those kinds of intimate things."

II

That I do swear—my fantasy, my prayer;
Save nights with my wife at the Stella Cinema
To see Spencer Tracy and his Katharine Hepburn.
I will construct my own bookshelves,
Lectern, table, chair, abacus;
Relearn to read, decipher, even pray

By the light of the bog-oak menorah.
I will read Hone's *Life of George Moore* in bed,
Relearn also how to fall asleep reading—
That phenomenal spectacle of the butterfly page
Trembling off the bevelled edge of the world;
"Just those kinds of intimate things."

III

Stop shelling stop! I hop
Out. Watch myself skip a hornpipe
That I am still alive, still alive!
Ecstatic to be a Joyce, a Ryan's man!
I salute my mate, jitterbug, swear again
And waddle off into our next affray;
Drakes into débâcle.
I can feel the desert dirt lace sand round me,
Its moisture adhering to my cheeks, my chin,
Each grain establishing a hide in my stubble;
If you could see me, Mam, you'd see my eyes;
"Just those kinds of intimate things."

Lady with Portable Electric Fence

Forty-odd years old, but yet a blooming girl
On the verges of new lives leafing,
As you pace the front field
With your portable electric fence and I trumpet
Cheekily: "I am a bullock
Who worships his mistress with dung"
And I fumble in my dewlap as it wags
And unearth my antique Okinawa automatic camera
With which I have photographed you so many thousands—
No, millions—of times
In every inconceivable position in the front field.
Unique albums, but what price
The fidelity-embossed frontispiece?
A cow photographing his mistress as she bends low to
     switch on her portable electric fence.

The Second Coming

All that the infant child can know—
That Infant Child is seeming to say—
Is that the cow is innately good;
Homo sapiens may—may not be—good
But not innately—no way innately.

The infant child is more at home with the cow,
More instinctively, intuitively at home with the cow;
My hooves, my tongue, my ears, my tail.
The infant child comprehends what it is
That keeps me going on head down:

Precisely what it is that motivates me
To adorn and endure the values of Tipperary.
The cow is the palpitating embodiment
Of day-to-day faith in the Second Coming:
I am the personification of innocence.

How could a cow not believe in the Second Coming?
The Second Coming is what gets me up out of it off my knees.
It is what holds me together,
All my parts, my rivets, my cross-struts;
All my floppy berets, all my trailing scarves.

At every Bethlehem you will always find me
In the second row manuring the straw,
Extraterrestrial eyebrows in exuberant excelsis;
The black-and-white cow of the Parousia
Licking the ears of the Mother of God.

John Ennis (1944–)

John Ennis won the Patrick Kavanagh award in 1975. Although the award is intended simply to honor poetic achievement, in Ennis's case its name serves as well to recognize a deep poetic affinity. Ennis's best-known poems are firmly rooted in the narrative tradition exemplified in Ireland by Kavanagh. "Narrative," Ennis writes, "informs my work, poems often being mini-stories, jibing at the constraints of 'verse,' sometimes calling on the archetype."[1] Although his connections to the tradition reach behind Kavanagh—he remembers receiving the collected works of Milton at fifteen—it is Kavanagh's "The Great Hunger" and Robert Lowell's "The Quaker Graveyard in Nantucket" to which he continually returned in his youth.

Ennis's own approach to narrative verse tends toward the use of personae, which, he says, "makes possible a dialectic (the later Yeats found it useful) in a land where the real dialectic of communities, the 'jaw-jaw' has not even begun."

> The poems make comment on collective experience by attempting to focus on particular details of that experience. The "interior" landscape is of less importance than that of the larger community, or communities. The narrator is witness as well as participant. The locale is identifiable to the insular psyche. The *res publica* is never too far away.[2]

Ennis wraps long lines around the consciousness he evokes through such dialectic, making room in this formal gesture, it seems, for both the personal and the public. "Letter to Connla," a long poem from the viewpoint of an anonymous Irish lay-monk living around the ninth century, exemplifies the intertwining of issues that result. Its speaker is in danger from the Church both for the content of actual or imagined letters to his twin brother and for stealing the vellum on which the texts are, or might be, written. Issues having to do with Church tyranny, personal identity, and the questionable value of more public forms of poetic discourse converge in the longing and fear expressed as a dangerous medieval perversion of T. S. Eliot's paradigmatic struggle between tradition and the individual talent.

In later poems Ennis has worked the narrative lumber down to a size more recognizable as lyric. At the same time the speaking persona becomes still more anonymous than that of his ninth-century monk, giving the poems a corresponding lyric quality at the level of voice. Still, the driving force is the story and its implications. And debts to narrative antecedents are still being paid; in these smaller narratives Ennis is adept at acknowledging influence with a rapid gesture across the face of a poem that could otherwise move in quite other directions. His debt to Robert Lowell, for example, shapes a poem, not included here, on the national and sectarian violence in seventeenth-century Ireland, which, oddly echoing the title of Lowell's meditation on the slippery presence of the past in "For the Union Dead," takes the title "To the Considerate Dead." In the still more recent poem "Old Style Country Funeral" Ennis finds himself "suddenly with MacNeice / upon his ferry in the aisle watching all the dead dying."

John Ennis was born in County Westmeath in 1944. He was educated at University College, Cork, and University College, Dublin.

NOTES

1. *Dedalus Irish Poets* (Dublin: Dedalus Press, 1992), p. 206.
2. Ibid.

Bright Days

Often I go in terror of bright days;
The telegraphic arteries of trees sizzling the air,
The sun scalding the eye, the brittle tinsel of cloud
Suddenly limp, vagrant: like the cotton doves of Picasso
Mad paracletes, incongruously puffed, come to warn,
Grotesque decibels of sound muted on their widening beaks.

The leaves agitated, flustered, toss on the chamois
Breeze unable to comprehend the D.T.'s of existence
     or
        Language wobbles on our lips,
And we are shunted onto sidetracks where the weeds
Flourish in couplings, the wren patrols its territory,
Comprehension drivels onto our chins.

Antimony falls from the air, and there's no wild
Flight of gull to steady, arrest the brain
That prays the cooling tide to cross its shingle,
Wipe out the nerve-tracks on its lurid beach
So confined to the gloss of its four walls.

Outside the trees are full of memories
That are unbearable.

I seem here, and not here, on the uncertain verge
Imminent of an abyss of lightness
Carnivorous in intensity
That deepens under the midday's jagged glare
(Where the bright edges allure, the Timothy grass sways).

Terror without, terror within
The small smash of wind on the warm casement
The stony cry of a child, the torn tin of adolescence
The searing tedium of adulthood
The white petrified cloud under the sun.

I crave again the wadable streams of boyhood
Wait for the clatter of drops on the galvanised brain,
The shuffle of the thorny green, the dark squall
Come across to you, ask your forbearance
Read my lot in the cool pale salver of your palm.

Circa July 27

Let rust eat dividers, all cutterbars—
I would (the dark shudder of your care falling as if
Forever) choke the raw world's harvestors
Blunt the oscillating knives
Halt all augers, concaves.
I'd lock in anticlock each hungry combine's
Works, each cry-smoothed hexagon
Cast for the shredding citizens
  of Arles.

A revolving reel
Curves you back.
A pigeon thuds
  first stubble:

Torture of warm absolutes
  and the warm wheat hills
Endearment of heads
Pocked by the crow
  the black deluge
  the black pulling down—
Surrender to dewed blades
  like shoulders' unique give
Guttural in the nard
Triggering this
Anniversary.

  Let us be,
Children of Arles.
See your yield
Windrows on twilit fields.
We're bought elsewhere.

  Grain, we were
Born but for the sieves, air
Blast, intake of the fan
Adjustment of baffles
Magnitude of loss.

*

It is hopeless. This will never end.
In a thousand sacks, grain lorries
          granaries
Lies the dead accumulate
We lead in word, ineffectual
          as palette.

Legion once in a gentle emblematic flame
Mnemonic of deity.
Before your dust like lime whites one mill floor
Who will count the husked, sift, be coherent
Accompany down each unground fear, tot
          what was meant
By these affectionate seas of silica?

The Croppy Boy

It's no use, your wild nightly haggle, horse-pissed over me
At Passage by the Suir or maudlin down in Duncannon stoned.
The piked suns shine on ever more cruelly watery.
Winy streets we littered are innocently crimsoned.

On wet cobbles to the sweaty rope, you'll halo me. Naïve,
O yes, my blond teenage hair is styled like the French.
I'm not crying. To ladies, prance of Hessians, I clench
My bony dream, walk on. My ignorant head's a bee-hive.

From their suite rooms the yogurt mouths of hypocrites
Spit me out like bile. No lusty Patrick sucks their tits.

Rousing Christ, ladies do with me what they please.
While I die, blackbirds sing up the fat-arsed trees.

Mother. It's cruel. Yeoman bar us any last good-bye.
Yesterday I danced, tapped a jig. Noon, see me die.

Villanelle

Red autumn falls around your Samhaintide sycamore.
My knees rat-trap the old bald fat, wheedling king.
The Moyle falls gentler on the grey foreshore.

The green forests all sides are bleeding once more.
Tomorrow, perhaps, my fiery boy, I'll chance my fling.
Red autumn falls around your Samhaintide sycamore.

Soft gossamer dawn whispers, I'm Owen's new whore.
Good-bye to pride. Conor strips me of everything.
The Moyle falls gentler on the grey foreshore.

Twelve bigots smashed into faggots our Derry oak door.
Tied me. I'm not venereal yet. My blue wrists sting.
Red autumn falls around your Samhaintide sycamore.

Every grunt he offers entering me, this ageing rut-hot boar
I'm in Alba with you. I've stopped crying. Robins sing.
The Moyle falls gentler on the grey foreshore.

O, this red lily is as cruel raw as any wound you bore.
I'll see what cliffs the dashing heights to Owen may bring.
Red autumn falls around your Samhaintide sycamore.
The Moyle falls gentler on the grey foreshore.

A Drink of Spring

After the sweat of swathes and the sinking madder sun
The clean-raked fields of a polychrome twilight
With cloudlets of indigo nomadic on the sky,
"A drink of spring" was my father's preface to the night.

As the youngest, I made fast the dairy-window reins,
Sent the galvanized bucket plummeting to sink first
Time, weighted with steel washers at one frost-patterned side.
His request was as habitual as a creaking kitchen joist.

The rope tautened for the upward pull under the damson
Tree and back-biting thorns of a never-pruned rose.
The water, laced with lime, was glacial to the dusty throat.
Mirage of the dying, it brings relief to the lips of the comatose.

Cups furred with cold I handed round the open-door fireless
Kitchen. The taste on my lips was lingering like a first kiss.

from The Burren Days

Ray Daly's Super Yamaha ate up the miles and gleamed
Towards the white portals of the Bord Bainne complex.
The road blurred past the young lab. technician.
April was glowing in the sticky chestnut buds
As Ray remembered Gráinne, their first swim
The Easter Monday previous at Ballybunion.
Love dared the cavern mouth, shock and shudder
Of spume-drunk cliffs. Love kicked into the Atlantic,
Later nestled on the mid-day rocks
Where couples in a trickle of cars hugged the slope
    to the ocean.

Ray and Gráinne dressed, left, passed through Killarney
With its tomb-cold cafés opening for business.
The sun dipped below the rhododendron beyond Tipperary.
And Solomon sang his canticle amid the tangle
    of purple-tipped buds.

Ray's machine fretted across the cement-slabbed enclosure.
The youth gave the Yamaha a long swinging pull,
Set the brilliant machine expertly in position.
Ray Daly parked the Yamaha among executive cars.
His 850 Special stood next to Mr. Joyce's white Renault 30.
Bord Bainne was deep into the Irish export drive.

Young faces flowed up and down the lab. corridors
That smelt mildly of milk and chlorides.
Young hopefuls from the Regional Colleges

Scattered, like Ray, against the Monday clock.
A pigeon flapped against the laboratory window-pane.
Young cherry saplings were pinking into bloom
On the newly landscaped grounds of Bord Bainne Land.

Ray Daly did a good day's work for a wage,
High up in a lab., in a field once riddled with famine
Like a dream of progress from René Magritte.

Ray Daly walked into the Chemistry Lab.
Mr. Joyce told him his morning assignment:
Ray was to test Vitamin A in milk powder.
The powder was bound for the Third World
Reaping the illwind of drought and hunger.
Good money lay in it too for Ireland's Balance of Trade.

As he settled the mixture in a hot waterbath
At 70°C, gently mixing the bottle,
The lab. hand's thoughts swung back to himself and Gráinne.
Exams, with great forbidding clouds, lay on Gráinne's horizon.
Now another week would sludge by. A week gone to pot
    with no Gráinne.
Durex Daly Ray was nicknamed.
At breaktime the other lab. technicians rifled his pockets.
His brother, Malachy, gazed on him coldly at breakfast.
Malachy, a disenchanted cleric, settled for Accountancy;
Accruals, consistency and blue Italian suede.
He once saw Ray and Gráinne making love on Slievenamon
Down a shaft of sunlight between two pines.

Ray hoarded the Burren days,
Their dry, abrasive love in the blue filament of June
As they lay soaking up the sunlight in their bones,
The warm goodness of mid-summer noons on Doomore.
Then the solitudes of Maam before the winter closed
And it was risky riding too far north at week-ends
Shadowed in Antrim glens brimming with leaves.

Now exams were more sacred to her than sex.
After a week the Elba sun was in his eyes.
The wind was soporific in the ripe summer meadow,
As seven days ago among the rhododendron beyond Tipperary,

And above the smoky tumult of Torc waterfall
The forest had breathed with them, on them.
On Gráinne's transistor they heard the new Taoiseach
Bequeath the beaches, lakes and mountains to the nation.
Old joys of Maam and the Burren beckoned and blurred.

Mr. Joyce, Lab. Supervisor, degreed and scrupulous,
Banged the door. His teeth clenched. Ray's eyes
With their salmon blear focused on Seán Joyce.
Ray transferred the aqueous phase
To one set of flasks, the ether to another.
Discarding the spent watery layer,
He remembered the post-alleluia faces
Of church crowds the Yamaha ploughed through on Easter Sunday,
The whey-faced congregations to whom Eros was nausea.
Church and State offices were the shrines
Of a people to whom their love-poetry was anathema.
Love of a god had stuffed them full as ticks.

Ray washed the ether through two 50 *ml*
Portions of distilled water, then a sodium solution.
Gráinne'd lift his wrists to press the Timex digital
(The ritual was the same in Maam, Kerry or Tipperary).
His pulse was as delicate as the heart-beat of a hare.
"Sleep a little," she'd say. The sun was hot on Easter Monday
As she watched over Ray. He might have been
     her twin brother sleeping.
Gráinne sighed. For her Ray'd prepared the birch tops
And the old weather-eaten motor-bike jacket.

Lab. technicians rose like Christs from their test benches.
Refreshment. Ray drained the boggy dregs
Of canteen coffee, went back to work early.
After the shower among the rhododendrons in Tipperary
He and Gráinne boiled water on their gas primus.
An old man with a cataract in one eye,
His other aquamarine, piercing and kind,
Brought them to where a spring well flowed.

Ray recorded the delta OD.
On the long bank-holiday ride back from Ballybunion
Ray and Gráinne came early to the spreading rhododendron,

To the bare sunlit trees and cuckoo already singing.
After, she longed for the berries of the rowan,
But the tree hadn't yet come into blossom,
The red rowan they'd made love under in Autumn
On the Papal Day when the Yamaha was bothersome.

Gráinne'd shaken the pliant sapling.
Crimson berries showered on the lovers.
Ray readied his chart for the data.
The tangent was drawn to the curve.
Ray marked the maximum point of concentration,
Converted the absorbance to international units
From the standard curve. Ray was important.
O Ray Daly was a somebody, a technician.
Now even Gráinne Flynn slipped from his lips.

Gráinne asked the impossible with her eyes.
Her birch bed was springy.
Gráinne's heart slipped into her mouth.
But now Ray was testing a message of milk,
Earning a wage with scores of youths in bright laboratories
Light years away from the Cattle Boat days,
His uncles London-bound down an April road
At their backs the fetid smell of exile.
Ray's Yamaha zoomed back to Gráinne's semi.
The evening in the country wore the sharp blue cold of early April;
They rode back into the outpourings of sulphurous monoxide
        from a thousand estate chimneys.
In the windless evening they found it torture to breathe.
The quartz bulb threw its brilliant white into the indigo
        of the twilight.
"Take me to Maam, or Aran, Friday week after the exams,"
Gráinne begged at the gate. Ray promised faithfully.
And they'd head off to Ben Bulben, maybe, for Whitsuntide
Tasting, here and there, Old-Music festivals.
Ray, all resolve, laid siege to his Tests.

The results were satisfactory,
Conforming to the Food Laws of the Third World
And the exigencies of the Carr-Price Method.

So Monday wore on. Mr. Joyce, Lab. Supremo,
Requested from Ray some routine testing:
Moisture à la Toluene, Acidity of Milk Powder.
Clostridium Welchii Perfringens.
Mr. Joyce was once impressed with Ray Daly.
The RTCs belt out fine boys, he said:
But this youth has a problem.
The present harridan is the most disturbing yet:
Last Hallowe'en he saw her thumb to the gates of Bord Bainne.
Wait for Daly. The whole afternoon she combed her brazen hair.
(And he wouldn't mind sampling her himself.)
The other lads whistling her she treated like vermin.

Daly and Joyce exchanged smiles like sister moons.
Each swung out of the other's solitariness.

And various other tests Ray performed too.
What if the green dye stained his fingers,
In a moment of spillage, hurried sampling?
Ray Daly cheered up, tested in good spirits.
His day had gone like a house on fire.
So he mopped up the brilliant green dye,
Went for a work-out in the Bord Bainne gym.
Gráinne beckoned to him in the naked shower.
He sank into the trailing barley of her hair
Finecombed in the prickly gold river.
"One day I'd like four sons and one daughter," she'd whispered
As the operator called testily for more 1ops.
She vowed to settled nowhere but under a Hone sky.

Far away from Maam the laiety jockeyed,
At Maam there was no papal cheering
But above the stillness of the two lovers
The sun moved through the clouds.

Now green was dyeing the hills and trees.

As his loveless Yamaha 850 fretted out the Bainne concrete,
Ray felt once more a great quietude of combers
The summer moon festooned with galaxies.
Brightness stirred again the waters of Black Head,
The slow rise and fall of the Atlantic they went to sleep over.

Questions for W. C. Williams

on the wheelbarrow and the chickens

In all my years walking round hardware stores
I've yet to embrace it, your red wheelbarrow.
Black, galvanized, they wait on grey co-op floors
To be wheeled across gardens, dour cow-pat yards.

Will, was it all red? What of the wheel? Handles?
And what mix of paint then—a mere cheap oxide?
A glossy finish? Matt coat? An unlikely satin?
Was it out for show like an old bygone pump in a haggard?

If red, what hue of red? Blood bright? Burgundy?
Was it a left-over half-gallon came in handy?
Maybe you mused of a dawn, "I'm going out to paint
        that damned barrow red"?
Pondering this one I woke once in a dark sweat.

The chickens, Will. Were they yellow-beaked leghorns?
White plymouth sisters? Imported minorca? Wyandottes?
Of mixed origins like us? Did an excited wattle-hot
Poulterer crow, "Poet, get an eyeful of these orpingtons"?

Your chickens. Were they downy dayolds, chipped from the egg?
Or sleek white leggy specimens with red fledgling combs?
Or moulting, loved and motley? Broody? Or loud and crawky?
Maybe one or two stood sickly? Hung droopy with blue comb?

Did a white cock among them cluck his luck, dandy fortune?
And it can't have been too dusty a yard, or a mucky one
Either, or you'd have lit on the wings. Were they poised
On cobbles, or concrete, or grass for that still life stumbled on?

Our world depends, you write us, upon this homely scene.
And was the barrow on its side? Or just plain upright?
Was it a great blast of sun resurrected the chickens?
Did one chicken light on a handle for nothing to do?

Your blessed yard scene has dogged me many a year.
I'd love to squeeze your old bony hand for details.
What point? Too late? Rest easy. Let all interrogations cease
In the sun, in this great after-light, after the rain.

Deep Ploughing

We plough familiar ground again and it is good,
The clay pliant, rising with us, free from stone.
All the stubborn and sock-rending rocks are gone.
Here's one love of many to be seen to, to warm the blood

On a winter's day when the storm rises over the wood.
The south-east gale still has the dry cold sting
Of continental Europe where snows are settling.
I am a man reborn and feel all that is good

In your arms up and down the ash bole,
The beech trunk, and the naked sycamore,
That stand by us as we wait on, as if for evermore,
Erect and leafless for the explosive green growth of the soul.

Then let the sleet and the mist and the darkness descend.
We'll wing our cries above them till the end.

Sinking Wells

You open up in me the deeper springs.
These come now welling cold and pristine to the surface.
Deeper loams come first, pale soft sands, way-out imaginings.
The rounded pebbles, then, where subterranean dreams meet,
        interface.

Once I sunk a well and the well sunk me.
I went into debt over it for years, could not
Pipe its iron, lucid, goodness within for my family.
The fruit of my expenditure was set at naught.

But, today, your goodness is on tap all round.
I bring a new comfort to all my kind,
Embrace each for his, or her own worth, find,
And lay down for them the old greatcoat of affection
        on the ground.

Diviner of diviner kind,
You've made to gush the purer fountains of my mind.

Devotees Gathering Round Jim Morrison's Grave

That we would adore You, You took the hammer blows
You found the wood, then were Yourself flung down.
You held the reckless nails. We took off your clothes,
Hoisted You, dear friend, made You a forgotten crown

Of our own sharp devising. And yet You did not cry
Out, banish us with the cold sentence as You might.
And when we plunged the spear beyond your thigh
Only a Merton-like encore filled your inviolate

Eyes. We buried You, unannounced, in a tomb
With inscriptions scrawled like lovers' graffiti.
Till your wild resurrection in us leaves us dumb.
That is why with such awkward affections we

Try to make good to You. Whom we failed. Don't fear
This your darkest hour. Know our embrace is near.

from Letter to Connla

Connla, I'm back in Ochtairbile, Aoife's fields.

In her rath
art is imported
from the steppes,
bronze masks, and dyes, from Persia,
skills of the lotus from North Illyria;
on all sides finesse,
olive oil for cooking,
no stranger to us,
she took me in,
I wonder will she tonight
take in this poor sod on the run, hardly.

Of houses now, do you mind,
her father has a circular

her uncle, a trapezoidal
of evened timbers
with tapestries.
Old gods
guard them within bank and palisade.
She claims kinship with Lagore:
I saw the language of silk rustle on her thighs.
Her people worship in a grove of oak.

Once, our heads amid the beaten foliage,
part of the design, we nestled.
Bronzes hung to feast the eye.
We warmed to red enamel
      (Connla, eat your heart out).
Yes, with your Aoife I have lain
on rushes deep in the souterrain
outscenting the perishable apples of March.
Her father and brothers were dosing the herds.
Robed, and pretending the preacher,
I passed safely through their midst
like Joseph's boy over at Nazareth.
Her gold-brooched mother was off at Fobhar
gave praise where holy springs strain uphill.

Connla, she need not have trekked to Fobhar.
Her sisters were busy in a cabin cheese-making.
In her house I drank wine not common beer.

So intertwined, in one another's arms
like plant and tendrilled animal,
one more species, one with all
we lay, our small cries escaping;

was hers, the melody of harps.
I recall how they caught us naked
how she was laughed to scorn,
how their wolfhound howled.

from Telling the Bees

5 Nirvana
    You fly no more into the cobalt void,
    Your thoughts fly no more into the void
    So numberless your conceptions, deceptions,
    The budburst of theory, the flower that acclaims,
        and is acclaimed,
    Then the wilt, the withering, the seed once more to bloom,
        the ever mutant.
    In the empty house, you said, we can only embody truth,
        not know it:
    You go before me into the blue, blue void.
    You carry nectar home in working sacs,
    Prime pollen in brimming baskets.
    Every day now, honey is pouring in
    Topping up the expectant hexagons.

    Nirvana,
    You fly off into the pollen wind that brings hayfever,
    Makes the eyes weep for days and swell red,
    Southeast wind, yes, that has dimension, is freckled
        with protein,
    Palpable on the cheeks, on the hair, warm breath
        beneath the veil,
    The wind that exists, that can be seen. Why then are we
        so blind?
    So blind to this state beyond states
    Favoured of limes? Touch it, and it can be proved,
        this thousand-winged ether.

    It is laden with honeyed tracts.

    It is packed with gut-filled nectars waiting for the enzyme.

    It is the wiped and brimming jar I've labelled
        to fortify you with affection.

    It is the sacred duty spoken from the mouths of hives.

It is the garden of no release, the prison of sowing,
      prison of weeds, prison of the reaper with the sower
     at his heels and the ash which follows,
      freedom after flames to the dance and the laughter
      of encircling children ordering pizzas of a party size
      when your own funeral is over.

It is the blend of nectars from the hedgerows and the
      phalanxes of whitethorn and the acer of iron and
      insight the world over.

It is the keeper rooted among bees made angry
      by pylons and thundery air, who is harnessing
      swarms and laughing at stings and the drippage
      of venom and set to take on the next thirty thousand.

It is
Waiting, waiting for the sun, milking indifference,
      patience like bees from the dandelions
      of a cool mid-March.

It is
Yourself crawling over every page looking for the mirror.

It is
The roof of the hive which will not blow in the storm
      but remains constant within keeping the heat.

It is
The gentle rap you give daily on the visceral chamber
      letting me know
      letting me know
      I am alive.

It is
The full jar of honey few consumers obtain
      with traces of propolis, pollen and the pale
      queen substance which, if spread across
      the bread of sorrow and the bread of joy,
         will bring equal flavour.

**

Across how many intimate fields and flowers
    have we not journeyed with you
    ambushing the inarticulate petal
    come back to evaporate the vaporous
    till all was sealed in formula
    extracted from the soul.
And then begin, again, the next field,
       the blessed business.

Old Style Country Funeral

He's chiselled out a neat mortise from the black
earth, covered up the once dainty bones
of grandmothers, great grandmothers, aunts who are widespread.
This gravedigger's conscientious as hell, fingers white stones.

I, too, walker from the Graves shoulders down, pass by.
I feel his own snatch at my breath, am suddenly with MacNeice
upon his ferry in the aisle watching all the dead dying.
Envelopes muffle the silver's weeping.

Out in the graveyard, the crow-spired and glare-filled wet sunlight
blooms.
    One man
can't wait, hurries home to grub mangolds. Worked to the bone.
The old maids, Mary and Nan, theirs the headscarved, warm,
rosaried indifference of stone. In the accidental heavens

(deep down in the clanging midland clay one more christian),
two shovels lock in mid-air, ring out with resurrection.

Bernard O'Donoghue (1945–)

Bernard O'Donoghue was born in County Cork in 1945, but his dominant strain of thought has its roots in a much earlier period. O'Donoghue teaches medieval literature at Wadham College, Oxford, and the linguistic issues that center his criticism and poetry are strongly inflected by the tones of his vocation, by the dialogue he hears enacted between widely separated historical periods. He accounts for the breadth of his interests and the unifying concern with language by pointing to his background in rural Ireland:

> I still live in County Cork for part of the year—Ireland is very important to me, socially, linguistically, and historically. The odd mixture of medieval and modern literary worlds interests me, as does the extent to which literary language can be analyzed formally to demonstrate literature's moral and public place or utility.[1]

Followers of Irish poetry recognize O'Donoghue's interest in language and poetic utility from his influential book *Seamus Heaney and the Language of Poetry*. In his reading of Heaney, O'Donoghue applies a method he calls "political formalism" as a way of offsetting the biographical and historical thrust of most criticism of Heaney without cutting Heaney's work off from its historical context.[2] O'Donoghue senses that in the current critical environment, "it may need restating that language is, at least in part, not just material but a means to a definable end which can be aimed at. Heaney's poetry is always to be seen within the context 'of present use.'"[3] At the same time, he argues that the best way of getting at that "present use" is through formal analysis of the poet's language.

O'Donoghue's own quiet poems move in little leaps driven by fortuities of language. In one, a peregrine's call becomes an "anxious *kai*," the onomatopoetic

particle—*kai* is the Greek for *and*—italicized to indicate that we might consider
its status as a sign as well as a sound.[4] Language as a metaphor for artistic process
sneaks into even those poems in which O'Donoghue foregrounds what seems to
be a purely visual aesthetics. The poem "Madonnas" shapes itself around an os-
tensible critique of iconic statuary, but the necessary comparison of art to life
finds its vehicle in a version of life peculiarly attendant to language. When sculp-
tural forms are replaced by animate characters, language even more fully super-
sedes vision as the mode by which readers of O'Donoghue's poems *see* his sub-
jects. It is almost entirely by the way they use language that we know the moral or
ontological status of the characters who people the rural landscape of his poems.
A prophecy of sickness delivered on "A Noted Judge of Horses" works itself out
in a dream in which the failure of health is synonymous with the failure of lan-
guage—"That before September's fair he'll be mumbling / From a hospital bed,
pleading with nurses."[5] *"Lastworda Betst"* remembers a dead father as a bodily
response to his last use of language: "I've never heard / My christian name with-
out a start again / Since he stopped and shouted it, his last word."[6]

O'Donoghue's poems frequently start from a sound or find sounds, whether
heard in sensuous memory or present sensation, that echo their language, themes
and narratives—a falcon crying the debate between faith and doubt in "The Iron
Age Boat at Caumatruish," or the jet's whine that links the harried lives of hares
and people at the end of *"Lepus Timidus Hibernicus."* Despite his attraction to
Heaney's concept of poetry as something of present utility, O'Donoghue may be
suggesting, as in the musical analogy he presents in "Con Cornie," that the poet
at the moment of production is responsible for nothing more than the sound. For
all their interest in the sound of language itself, though, his poems display a strik-
ing fidelity to the world as it is, paying particular attention to the material culture
of everyday life. In "Staples," for example, O'Donoghue measures a working life
against its least significant supplies, while in "Nel Mezzo Del Cammin," he imag-
ines the second half of life as a downhill slide in which the growing list of things
we'll never need to buy again emphasizes the unlikelihood of achieving anything
monumental in the time we have left on earth.

NOTES

1. Quoted in *Contemporary Authors*, vol. 137, p. 334.

2. *Seamus Heaney and the Language of Poetry* (London: Harvester/Wheatsheaf, 1994), p. ix.

3. Ibid., p. 1.

4. "The Humours of Shrone," *The Weakness* (London: Chatto & Windus, 1991), p. 61.

5. "A Noted Judge of Horses," *The Weakness*, p. 79.

6. "Lastworda Betst," *The Weakness*, p. 78.

Poaching Rights

His ochre glowworm waxed and dimmed with the wind
As you looked east from the windows, remember,
To his hide beneath the sally-tree that leaned,
Fish-divining, over the river like
An old man lighting his pipe into the wind.
You know the spot: trawl there tomorrow
And, amid the clean, greasy stones, you'd come
Upon a coal-sack chameleoned against
The depths. Inside, recoiling, you'd find me.

Can you imagine what strong righteousness
Made them, on a sweet summer's evening
That could hardly raise the pigment to grow dusk,
Park on the grey County Council chippings
By the roadside and pad over the fields for me?
Whose bailiffs were they? Who gave them the chain
They killed me with in the doorway?

Hold back your gaff from my polluting flesh.
Wait for the next storm that, quenching lights
And covering three fields, will wash me down
The flood till only the sea's the wiser.
Then once more the salmon lashed to your crossbar,
Blind-eyed, all wrapped-up, can steal into the night.

Lepus Timidus Hibernicus*

Familiar of ditches, coming and going
Over the headland in the boggy acre
Where his form is. A bird of ill omen,
The old woman said, blessing herself.
There he goes (if you have the misfortune
To see him), pulsing away, tan brown
As the wary wren on the polish tin.

"I bless myself because, if he is shot
In the leg, they say I, here in my kitchen

Coven, will find my shoe filling with blood
While I comb out increasingly white tresses."

Which is maybe why it's with our blessing that
Greyhounds slaver in their slipstream to savage
These initiates that spring vibrant from the last
Golden sheaf: such awesome cabbage-stags
Or furze-cats as preside in their hundreds
At Aldergrove, while the jet's whine rises
To hysteria, before taking soldiers
Or civilians towards death or joy or injury.

Enterprise Culture

1159, when John of Salisbury
Writes in his *Metalogicon* about
The followers of Cornificius
(A name derived from Virgil's discommender)
Who "pay no heed to what philosophy
Teaches, and what it shows that we should seek
Or shun. Their sole ambition," in the words
Of John, "is making money: by fair means
If possible, but otherwise by any
Means at all. There's nothing they deem sordid
Or inane except the straits of poverty.
Wisdom's only fruit for them is wealth."

So much for John of Salisbury—a classic case
Of a moralising, moaning so-called thinker.
But now a more hopeful fable for our time:
The case of the loganberry. After great
Creating nature did its bit, along came
Logan to supply the obvious defect:
A red blackberry with an elongated nose.
Everyone's happy: he makes a killing,
And Kate Potosi gets her cut by selling
Them to people to make jam. My point is this:

If John of Salisbury'd taken out a leaf
From Cornificius's book and used his brains

To come up with something practical like that,
He might have saved the whole of western Europe
Centuries of fruitless disputation.

Con Cornie

in memoriam

A farmer's fingers on a flageolet,
Bunched, too crowded, but weaving
A seamless tapestry of sound. A glide
Through a drift of touch, a slur conceded
By a wise, sideways moving of the head.

What complaint was stitched on to the air—
What child bereaved or wife sorrowing—
Was not his part now, intent on making
A fling of notes you could broadcast anywhere.

The Humours of Shrone

The peregrine's anxious *kai* hangs
In the air-bowl of the mountains
Over the limestone lake, water so black
That even in heatwave summer it dims
The sun. There, eighty years ago

On Christmas Eve our young neighbour pulled
His horse's jawing head
Into the blizzard for the eight miles
Of nodding, doddering at the reins
With his swirling load of quicklime.

The red candle in the window was burnt through,
Its warm hole in the frost veil closed
Before his sister heard in the haggard
The frenzied horse clashing his traces
Down the stone yard and the jagged

Shafts leaping behind, trying to keep up.
They found the boy next morning in our quarry
In the snow, with blind holes lime-burned in his face.
So the sister said: ninety, doting and inclined
To roam the quarry-field to search again.

Madonnas

Like a girl at a summer language-school
Making her arms an unnatural platform
For ring-bound folders, the best carry
Their child inexpertly, looking away,
Being ignorant that the garish goldfinch
In his fist denotes his fate on Calvary
Or city-street or battlefield. Some hold on
With desperate, fated protectiveness,
Refusing to respect his father's business.

One, of brown ivory, lowers her eyes
To her empty lap, to the rupture where
One leg of mannered draping and small,
Chiselled toes flow from her right side.
Her own arm is missing on the left,
Perhaps because she clung more tightly to
The innocent than his own human limbs.
But you wouldn't know, so far away
Her eyes which don't yet grasp her tragedy.

Lastworda Betst

So many ways (formal, political,
Witty) of writing poems not on the theme
Of dead parents, it's surprising how many

Have fallen into the trap. Odd too
To find on waking this anniversary
Morning my eyelids—tearless and well-slept—
Were hot to the touch. A *midrash*, maybe,
Whose prophecy is found twenty-four years
Back, at the March-wind final whistle
Of a football-match when, dull and emptied
Like a flask, I watched the crush-barriers
Reappear among celebrating Cork fans.
Their voice rose up, leaving the cold body
With our small company. I've never heard
My christian name without a start again
Since he stopped and shouted it, his last word.

A Noted Judge of Horses

The ache in his right arm worsening
Morning by morning asks for caution.
He knows its boding, cannot be wrong
About this. Yet he is more concerned
For the planks in the float that need
Woodworm treatment before drawing in
The hay, and whether the coarse meadow
Must be limed before it will crop again.

Still in the pallid dawn he dresses
In the clothes she laid out last night,
Washes in cold water and sets off,
Standing in the trailer with his eyes set
On the Shrove Fair. As long as his arm
Can lift a stick to lay in judgement
Down the shuddering line of a horse's back,
He'll take his chance, ignoring his dream
That before September's fair he'll be mumbling
From a hospital bed, pleading with nurses
To loose the pony tied by the western gate.

The Iron Age Boat at Caumatruish

If you doubt, you can put your fingers
In the holes where the oar-pegs went.
If you doubt still, look past its deep mooring
To the mountains that enfold the corrie's
Waterfall of lace through which, they say,
You can see out but not in.
If you doubt that, hear the falcon
Crying down from Gneeves Bog
Cut from the mountain-top. And if you doubt
After all these witnesses, no boat
Dredged back from the dead
Could make you believe.

Nel Mezzo del Cammin

No more overcoats; maybe another suit,
A comb or two, and that's my lot.
So the odd poem (two in a good year)
Won't do to make the kind of edifice
I'd hoped to leave. Flush out the fantasy:
The mid-point being passed, the pattern's clear.
This road I had taken for a good byway
Is the main thoroughfare; and even that
Now seems too costly to maintain.
Too many holes to fill; not enough time
To start again. "I wasn't ready. The sun
Was in my eyes. I thought we weren't counting."

Soon we'll be counting razorblades and pencils.

Staples

When first appointed, along with other
Lesser office necessaries, I bought
A strong stapler and an economy pack
Of five thousand staples. I felt sure
They'd see me out, and for years that seemed
A sound calculation; the red box
Stayed full or nearly full: so packed that,
If one block fell out, it took some skill
To slide it back again. But it's now
A few years since I first noticed them
Loosening and the box rattling
When I held it. I started on the quiet
To use the company's stapler
Whenever possible, to eke them out.
And then last week, with the few mini-blocks
Fast approaching countability,
With no warning, the stapler's hinge snapped.
Who would have thought, however numerous
Those spindly sigla were, they would outlast
The metal arm that banged them into place?

Pied Piper

"Musheroons! Musheroons!," he shouted out,
Flipping the reins so that the foxy horse
Broke into a gallop for us, and the float
Lurched smoothly on its rubber wheels
Down the coarse meadow. Was it the same man
Who picked fights with the most peaceable
Family in the locality?—who
Hired a hackney car to drive to Mallow,
Twenty miles, to lodge a daft complaint
Against the postman?—who seized by the throat
The sole remaining helper on his farm,

A blind, willing old man of eighty,
Until he staggered for breath?

Maybe: because, although he had that first
Modern float, and brooded for years over designs
For a new house, he once left the threshing
So late in the year we could hear the grumble
Of the machine on Christmas Eve
As the damp sleet swept across his grain.
They had no children: him and his dapper wife
Who had the silkest stockings in the parish
And the highest heels, and who'd amassed
Twenty designer hats before she died.

The last time I saw him he was living
In an unfurnished mobile home. He spent
An hour and more patiently rolling
A polish-tin that limped on its opening-catch
Across the concrete floor, over and over,
To keep our anxious one-year-old from crying.
And I suddenly remembered his most foolish
Unexecuted enterprise of all:
That underneath his bed for twenty years
He stored the timber crates that held a *Simplex*
Milking machine for the stall he never built.

Ter Conatus*

Sister and brother, nearly sixty years
They'd farmed together, never touching once.
Of late she had been coping with a pain
In her back, realization dawning slowly
That it grew differently from the warm ache
That resulted periodically
From heaving churns on to the milking-stand.

She wondered about the doctor. When,
Finally, she went, it was too late,
Even for chemotherapy. And still

She wouldn't have got round to telling him,
Except that one night, watching television,
It got so bad she gasped, and struggled up,
Holding her waist. "D'you want a hand?" he asked,

Taking a step towards her. "I can manage,"
She answered, feeling for the stairs.
Three times, like that, he tried to reach her.
But, being so little practised in such gestures,
Three times the hand fell back, and took its place,
Unmoving at his side. After the burial,
He let things take their course. The neighbours watched

In pity the rolled-up bales, standing
Silent in the fields, with the aftergrass
Growing into them, and wondered what he could
Be thinking of: which was that evening when,
Almost breaking with a lifetime of
Taking real things for shadows,
He might have embraced her with a brother's arms.

The Day I Outlived My Father

Yet no one sent me flowers, or even
asked me out for a drink. If anything
it makes it worse, your early death, that
having now at last outlived you, I too
have broken ranks, lacking maybe
the imagination to follow you
in investigating that other, other world.

So I am in new territory from here on:
must blaze my own trail, read alone
the hooftracks in the summer-powdered dust
and set a good face to the future:
at liberty at last like mad Arnaut
to cultivate the wind, to hunt the bull
on hare-back, to swim against the tide.

A Candle for Dolly Duggan

Venice, Easter 2001

Improbabilities of course, we all
know that: that this graceful taper
I force into the tallowed cast iron
beneath the *Assumption* in the Frari
could change the heavens, so that she
can pick up her cigarettes and lighter
to move on to a higher circle, as before
she moved, talking, through the lanes of Cork.

Sir Thomas Browne said there aren't impossibilities
enough in religion for an active faith.
So I'll go on spending liras and francs
and pesetas across the smoky hush
of Catholic Europe until she says
"That's enough," and then I'm free to toast
her in red wine outside in the sunlit squares.

Artistic Block

The great Russian bass Shalyapin
woke up every morning, cleared his throat
and knew his voice was gone: this time for ever.
All through the day his wife cajoled
and comforted, feeding him balsams
and reminding him of past successes
until by 7 p.m. he's ready
once again to take the plaudits
while she fights off sleep in the dress circle.

Usefulness

It was Jim McMahon who first pointed out
that you never come across a bald tinker,
nor do you ever see one in old age.
So the polite man in the hat who knocked
at the door and asked if he could have a look
at the contents of the shed, being fifty-odd,
was as old as they get. As we were going through
the junk, he picked up a bicycle pump,
remarked, "This is no use, is it?" and,
when I agreed, he dropped it in his bag.
Next he picked up an old kitchen pan,
scrutinized it and said "This is no use, is it?"
and, when I said it wasn't, threw it away.

Now I wish I'd asked him while I had him
what things are for, or how he assessed their value,
since these are matters of much greater urgency
for the short-lived who have to make snap-judgements
and can't afford that often to be wrong.

The Potato-Gatherers

(on the painting by George Russell, AE)

They know what they're doing at the worst of times,
these three unpraying desperadoes
on home ground. No time to notice
the sun's orange angelus at their backs,
any more than we, halfway back to them,
used to pause for the grey shine in October skies
as the digger clattered past, anointing us
with wormly wet earth and withered-white
potato-plant pipes as we clutched for the seed,
for cold gold in the seam of gutter.
In that impressionist twilight, you can't make out
their fingers; even their bent backs you'd see better
with our millennial 20-20 sight
from a west-bound jet over Belmullet.

Frank Ormsby (1947–)

In addition to his accomplishments as a poet in his own right, Frank Ormsby is one of the most distinguished editors of Northern Irish poetry. He was the director of *Honest Ulsterman* from 1969 to 1989, a period when the *Ulsterman* provided a venue for work by Seamus Heaney and other poets of his generation as they confronted the escalation of sectarian violence following the events of 1968. Ormsby's insight into the literature and politics of the North has also given shape to a number of important anthologies, including *Northern Windows: An Anthology of Ulster Autobiography*, and two editions of *Poets from the North of Ireland*. His *Collected Poems of John Hewitt* is the standard edition of that fundamental poet of cultural alienation in the North.

When Ormsby applied his editorial skills to the selection of his own poetry for the 1992 anthology, *A Rage for Order: Poetry of the Northern Ireland Troubles,* he chose works that summarized the interests and orientations that have guided his composition over the years. As different as they are from each other, Ormsby's poems in *Rage for Order* are remarkable for their consistent effort to imagine Northern Irish difference in contexts that unsettle the naturalness of its divisions. "Sheepman," for example, maps the Catholic/Protestant divide onto the range wars of the American west, where a sheep farmer in cattle country, like his fellow outcasts the Mexicans and half-breeds, "must wear that special hangdog look, / Say nothing."[1]

In "The War Photographers" Ormsby explores the function of poetic imagery in the face of atrocity through an analogy between poetry and the work of photojournalists in World War II. In the midst of atrocity Ormsby's photographers manage to capture both humor and beauty, affirming "the loved salience of what is always there: / flower of Auschwitz, bird of the Western Front."[2] The aestheticized imagery in this closing line, far from marking the poem's political disengagement, uncovers the mechanism of its social amelioration. The "flower of Auschwitz" and "bird of the Western Front" escape the kind of taxonomic classification—the specificity of Catholic, say, or Protestant—that tends to elevate difference over similarity and diminish the reality of immediate experience.

While Ormsby's poems have often looked at Northern Ireland's political divisions from oblique angles, they have also ranged far beyond the particular problem of the Troubles. His work has touched on subjects that extend from the personal griefs and anxieties of family life, in poems like "The Gap on my Shelf" and "You: The Movie," to the personal experience of history in "Northern Spring," a sequence that imagines the lives and afterlives of the soldiers who trained for the Normandy invasion in the fields of Northern Ireland. Between these two extremes lie such delightful curiosities as "from *The Memoirs*," Ormsby's take on an episode from the youthful exploits of the legendary French detective François Vidocq.

Born in Enniskillen, Northern Ireland, in 1947, Ormsby was educated at Queen's University, Belfast. He serves as Headmaster of the Department of English at the Royal Belfast Academical Institution, a boys' grammar school.

NOTES

1. "Sheepman," *A Rage for Order: Poetry of the Northern Ireland Troubles*, ed. Frank Ormsby (Belfast: Blackstaff Press, 1992), p. 62.

2. "The War Photographers," *A Rage for Order*, p. 207.

On Devenish Island

I am no Norseman, come to plunder.
The stone I sit on is half-under
Your skin. The grey wind that brought
Me here, honing the lough, is your familiar.
I am your next-of-kin.

In drowned valleys you have kept your head
Above water. Church, round tower still spread
On the waves' top. Down fourteen centuries
The rapt soul homes to the embryo it never fled.
I am no Norseman, come to plunder.
I keep what you gave.

Sheepman

Even the barflies move to corner tables,
Mouthing "Sheepman." The barman serves,
But grudgingly. Like Mexicans and half-
Breeds I must wear that special hangdog look,
Say nothing.

There is too much cattle country. The range
Is free in theory, cowmen find
Excuses to resent the different.
They claim that cows won't feed where sheep have fed.
Pathetic.

Don't say the outcast has his dignity.
Perhaps it's something not to thrive
On brawn, or trample those whose small stampedes
Hurt no one; such victories are thin, cold
Consolation.

Unbowed I claim my rights—to herd alone,
And be accepted. When I skirt
The rim of cattle drives, salute me,

And when I come to share your bunkhouse fire,
Make room.

My Friend Havelock Ellis

My first formal lesson on sex I owe
To my mother. Those faded books she bought
At the auction—sixpence the dozen, tied
With a rough string—hid one volume more
Than she bargained for.
For months I harboured him, forbidden one,
Under the green song sheets from *Ireland's Own*.

He never made the bookshelf, even wrapped
In a brown jacket. Consulted daily
Under clumps of trees beyond the hedge
That foiled the window's eye, his lectures turned
Often on mysteries.
I questioned him again until content
He'd yielded all, tutor and confidant.

Even in those days I knew at heart
How much he bored me. The tadpole-diagrams
He labelled Sperm, and cross-sections of organs
Like the cuts in butchers' windows, were less
Than living.
Still I intoned with a determined bliss
Words like fallopian, ovum, uterus.

The real joy was having such a friend,
Sure to be frowned on were his presence known.
He fed my independence, served a need
The set texts neglected. Nothing left then
But to discard him;
Time for fresh schooling, lessons to begin
In the arms of my new friend, Rosita Quinn.

A Small Town in Ireland

The road runs into it and out
　　About the bridge the people go.
Someone was executed there,
　　(Was it two hundred years ago?)

Is sung of still. But I would sing
　　A roof, a door, a set of bricks,
Because you entered Ireland there
　　One night in nineteen forty-six.

These are the rails your fingers touched
　　Passing to school, the waves below
You dipped your toes in. That is all
　　The history I would want to know,

Were not the waters those that eyes
　　Had flung their final glance upon,
Coursing, untouched and blameless, past the loss
　　Of someone's lover, someone's son.

Travelling

I

My grandmother's French journal was full of trains,
the market stalls and stately *grandes horloges* of 1890.
She sketched the beans drying under the eaves,
the sprigging of tulle in doorways, the great cheeses
of Pont L'Evêque,
and an old woman groaning paternosters
in the Rue de la Paix.

Oriels and fine vistas—her France a work
of the selective imagination, fit to grace
that Boston drawing-room,
its polished wood, cheval-glass reflecting

her passion for Europe:
porcelain from Sèvres, a quart of Bushmills
and the novels of Henry James.

II

All my grandmother's travelling was in her head.
She'd never been to Boston or to France.

She died in her Russian phase,
in the hard winter of 1913,
sunk between pillows as though she struggled through
some pass in the Caucasus—
insisting on local colour to the last stroke,
ink-stains amok on the next snowy pages.

from A Northern Spring

1 *The Clearing*

Remote as home and Europe, the broken sounds
drift to me through the laurels, miles from the compound.
Sporadic practice battles. Behind the lodge,
McConnell's axe is attacking another tree.
The manor car glides by on the avenue.

Bluebells and crocuses and saplings' wings.
We came with the Spring. They say our time will come
in the third month, before the Spring is over.
My hammock sways to the swing of a faint march
on distant gravel.

Here is a place I will miss with a sweet pain,
as I miss you always, perhaps because I was spared
the colourless drag of its winter. This is an hour
to dream again the hotel room where we changed
from the once-worn, uncreased garments,

assured and beside ourselves and lonely-strange.

3 *Cleo, Oklahoma*

"I knew he'd be a big shot." My mother's words,
in the third person, as though I'd already gone.
She stepped back through shadows, relinquished me
to sun and bunting, a street of cheers and smiles
from there to the depot. The Mayor struck a pose
for a possible statue,

but the bandsmen stayed in tune until I waved
from the steps of the Greyhound. Already I belonged
to somewhere else, or nowhere, or the next
photograph. The Mayor spread his arms
and had trouble with History.

There was dust everywhere. It was too late to cry
or too early. I heard the Mayor say:
"We've had History before now, folks, in this town.
There'll be more History soon."

4 *Lesson of the War*

I wish this war was over. The other day,
walking from school, I climbed the big oak tree
on the lough shore to watch for aeroplanes.
That was when I saw her, Eileen McConnell
lying with some airman at the foot of a field.
They rolled in their bare skins and gave a cry
and then stopped fighting.

My da was in bad humour when I told.
"Just like her mother," he said and gave me a skite
and warned me to stay away from girls and soldiers.

I wish this war, this *fuckin'* war, was over.

6 *I Died in a Country Lane*

I died in a country lane near Argentan,
my back to a splintered poplar,
my eyes on fields
where peace had not been broken
since the Hundred Years War.
And a family returned to the farm

at the end of the lane.
And Patton sent his telegram: "Dear Ike,
today I spat in the Seine."
And before nightfall Normandy was ours.

8 *I Stepped on a Small Landmine*

I stepped on a small landmine in the *bocage*
and was spread, with three others, over a field
of burnt lucerne.
The bits they shipped to Georgia at the request
of my two sisters were not entirely me.
If dead men laughed, I would have laughed the day
the committee for white heroes honoured me,
and honoured too the mangled testicles
of Leroy Earl Johnson.

13 *Apples, Normandy, 1944*

Was it D + 10 or D + 12 we caught
the war artist sketching apples?

"I'm sick of tanks," he said. "I'm sick of ruins.
I'm sick of dead soldiers and soldiers on the move
and soldiers resting.
And to tell you the truth, I'm sick drawing refugees.
I want to draw apples."

For all we know he's still sitting under a tree
somewhere between the Seine and Omaha,
or, russet with pleasure, striding past old dugouts
towards the next windfall—
sketch-books accumulating as he becomes
the Audubon of French apples,

or works on the single apple
—perfect, planetary—of his imagination.

14 *They Buried Me in an Orchard*

They buried me in an orchard at St Lô
on a pillaged farm. For twelve months I lay
under leaves and ripe windfalls, the thin roots

pressing me, fingering me, till I let them through.
They dug me up and buried me again
one June morning to a roll of drums
in a plain box on the ninety-seventh row
of an immaculate war cemetery.
If anything is left of me, it lives
in Ruth, Nevada, where my people farm
in spite of dust and drought, in spite of my death,
or a small town in Ireland where a child
carries my name, though he may never know
that I was his father.

15 *The Night I Lost World War II*

How do you lose a war? I'll tell you how.

Parachuting after dark, I almost drowned
in the Vire estuary,
stumbled half the night
through woods, cornfields, clover, country lanes,
so far off course the maps were useless.
I looked down one grey road after another
but the war was not to be found.

At dawn the war found me, asleep in a barn.
The first man in the regiment to see the Rhine,
I starved in Bavaria another year
as guest of the Wehrmacht.

Then home to Nebraska without firing a round.

18 *On Devenish Island*

We rowed from Trory on a lough so clear
that even the loughside cows, as Milburn said,
had waded out to stand in their reflections.
Weiss from Milwaukee manned the second oar,
and Pedersen the Slav had trained his lens
on the round tower.

That was a lazy Sunday among the ruins.
When we flicked ash into the saint's stone bed,
or pitched our baseball through the perfect arch

of a church window's crumbling Romanesque,
we meant no harm, the past completed there
was not affected.

It was twilight when we returned. Drifting to sleep
in the hut's darkness I thought of how we had strayed
through empty fields next to the cemetery,
our wake settling before we had reached the shore.

35 *Some of Us Stayed Forever*

Some of us stayed forever, under the lough
in the guts of a Flying Fortress,
sealed in the buckled capsule, or dispersed
with odds and ends—propellers, dogtags, wings,
a packet of Lucky Strike, the instructor's gloves—
through an old world of shells and arrowheads,
dumped furniture, a blind Viking prow.
In ten years or a hundred we will rise
to foul your nets with crushed fuselage.
Our painted stork, nosing among the reeds
with a bomb in its beak, will startle you for a day.

The War Photographers

Working with one eye closed or heads buried
under their drapes, they focus to preserve
the drowned shell-hole, the salient's rubble of dead,
the bleached bones of sepoys torn from the earth.

Their stills haunt us: a stretcher piled with skulls
at Cold Harbour, graves in a barren wood
that in one hour's carnage lost its name
to history and the world's memory of death.

The worst has happened, they confirm the worst:
but show us too the makeshift hospital,
the sad errand of the hospital van
among the ruins. Also enough of sky
to suggest the infinity of angles,

that behind sandbags, under the hostile towers
someone is finding time for a wry note
on bowel movements, an entry that affirms
the loved salience of what is always there:
flower of Auschwitz, bird of the Western Front.

The Gatecrasher

On the lookout for my father in his prime,
I catch him, head down, affecting a bowler,
in John Lavery's *The Weighing Room, Hurst Park*.

He can hardly believe his luck. An hour ago
he dropped his scythe discreetly in the long grass
of a Fermanagh farm, now he is half a length

from that frail figure, poised, posed on the scales.
In a minute he will step forward, paunch drawn in,
to shake the hand of the boul' Steve Donoghue.*

More likely, he'll lose his nerve. More likely still,
those two stewards who have begun to enquire
will show him—there's no justice—the weighing room door.

Before he is turfed out, I hope he takes time
to commend the artist ("You're doing rightly, sur.")
or, as though it might tip the balance, touch him once,

speculatively, on the shoulder, as the jockeys do.

The Gap on my Shelf

Smaller than life, episcopal in death,
he lies, brows frowning
the length of his body,
the *Poems* of Mrs Hemans under his chin.*

The lips sink in his face, his paunch settles
as the hump of a grave levels at last with the earth.
Empty of self, he fills us with the tug
and ebb of his absence.

Where has he gone? When I try to imagine his soul
in flight before dawn or fluttering down at last
on the clouds of a catechism heaven,

what floods my head is dislocated light
and rain at the window,
some no-place, like the space where yesterdays go:

all I can see, the book-size gap on my shelf,
wordless with loss, where poems used to be.

The Graveyard School

Life is no laughing matter. We entered crying
and Melancholy marked us for her own.
Our birth-day was the day we started dying.

Urn-shaped our souls, our fate to wander sighing
where names grow weathered, angels droop in stone.
Life is no laughing matter. We entered crying.

Sepulchral shades, the population lying
under our feet are kindred to the bone.
Our birth-day was the day we started dying.

What are our bodies? Houses putrefying,
clay tenements we moulder in alone.
Life is no laughing matter. We entered crying.

What is our song? A night-piece amplifying
owls in the yews, the universal groan.
Our birth-day was the day we started dying.

Your smile's a death-mask rictus. No denying
what we among the tombs have ever known:

Life is no laughing matter. We entered crying.
Our birth-day was the day we started dying.

from *The Memoirs*

after François Vidocq

Dunkirk, Calais, Ostend. Three times I tried
to embark for the New World. The fares were too high,
the captains unsympathetic. Instead I joined
the Paillasse of the famous Cotte-Comus,*

where first I was master of lamps and chandeliers
and cleaned the cages (the tallow disgusted me,
the monkeys went for my eyes),
then failed trainee-tumbler. For three weeks

(the monkey's leap, the drunkard's leap, the coward's leap,
the chair-leap, the grand fling) I collected bruises,
aches, thrashings, a broken nose. Till Garnier said:
"I like you. You are dirty. Your flesh smells.

You are skeletal. Here is a tiger-skin and club.
From today you are a savage of the South Seas,
who eats raw flesh and cracks flints in his mouth
when he is thirsty. I want you to roll your eyes

and model your walk on the orang-utan
in cage number one." A jar full of round stones
was set at my feet, also a live cock
with its legs tied. "Gnaw this," says Garnier.

"Like fuck I will." I went for him with a stake
and the whole troupe fell on me with kicks and blows.
That night—homeless, broke—I headed for Arras
and my forgiving mother. I was now seventeen.

You: The Movie

We peer through drizzle
on a twelve-inch screen.
Your one-inch shadow
stirs behind the grain.
You are the new star
swum into our ken.
You are, you will be,
may be, might have been.

The bounds of possibility
in one
unfocussed image. The cave
of the unborn—
a silent classic,
a chiaroscuro pan
through ghostly footage
primitive as dawn.

Outside, the window
gathers Arctic showers.
Your photogenic heart
within its layers
is, meanwhile, stealing
the show. No carking cares.
It throbs and throbs
at twice the speed of ours.

Ciaran Carson (1948–)

When Ciaran Carson broke his ten-year poetic silence with *The Irish for No* in 1987, the book's title was a joke that wouldn't have been lost on "Young Flynn," a character in the opening poem of the volume. When Flynn is caught by the Royal Ulster Constabulary while engaged in a smuggling job for the Nationalist cause, his time in prison proves, ironically, to have its own patriotic recompense: "Flynn was in for seven years and learned to speak / The best of Irish. He had thirteen words for a cow in heat; / A word for the third thwart in a boat, the wake of a boat on the ebb tide."[1]

What he wouldn't have had is a word for *no*. The Irish language has no specific words either for *yes* or *no*. Carson's linguistic playfulness would immediately be drawn to the selective specificity of "a word for the third thwart in a boat" and none for "no," a perfect figure for the tendency he saw in Belfast to produce an abundance of language in the vicinity of a problem, without ever confronting it directly. Carson's talent for finding the ideal linguistic emblem for the convergence of artistic and social aims appears again in the title of his next volume, *Belfast Confetti*. The titular phrase has a festive surface that stands well for the scraps of conversation and story that fly when Carson's parade of language starts marching. But in Ulster parlance the idiom refers to the bits of scrap metal— "oldtime thrupenny bits and stones / Screws, bolts, nuts," as Padraic Fiacc catalogues them in "The British Connection"—that became weapons and shrapnel in the hands of sectarian terrorists.[2]

Carson was born in Belfast in 1948, and it is the rhythm of the city that drives his poetry. Poems like those in *The Irish for No* and *Belfast Confetti*, suffused as they are with the language and material particulars of the city, would be useful resources for the mnemonic project undertaken by the regulars at the "Exiles' Club" in Carson's poem of that name, who work to keep their scale reconstruction of Belfast up to date against a tide of bombing constantly changing the face of the city.

That distant émigrés should try to represent not just what they remember of their native city, but the fact and process of loss—the bomb blasts and the blitz alongside the treasured objects pawned between distant paydays—is itself a model of Carson's own poetics of memory and loss. Memory, for Carson as for the exiles, revives a lost time by way of an almost compulsive return to rifts in the temporal landscape. His poems trouble these gaps the way the tongue will trouble the wound left where a tooth was pulled.

> A wound, a suture, an excision will remind us of the physical, of what *was* there. . . . For Belfast is changing daily: one day the massive Victorian fa-çade of the Grand Central Hotel, latterly an army barracks, is *there*, dominating the whole of Royal Avenue; the next day it is gone, and a fresh breeze sweeps through the gap, from Black Mountain, across derelict terraces, hole-in-the-wall one-horse taxi operations, Portakabins, waste ground, to take the eye back up towards the mountain and the piled-up clouds.[3]

In many of Carson's poems the gaps are the only link available between a confusing present and a lost past. "Patchwork" finds in "the perfectly triangular / Barbed wire rip" in the sleeve of the speaker's shirt a sort of textile madeleine that propels the poem on a Proustian swing through spontaneously arising bits of memory.[4] Through the flaw, Carson is able to find a connection between his own art form and his mother's craft. The missing bit—the gap in a shirt, or the invisible bead his father makes the gesture of fingering at his mother's graveside—is the peculiar, characteristic fetish of Carson's later poetry. In this poem, as in the recent book-length sequence *For All We Know*, his own fingering of missing beads manages to recapture a past the poems themselves nearly give up for lost.

NOTES

1. "Dresden," *The Irish for No* (London: Bloodaxe Books, 1987), pp. 12–13.
2. Padraic Fiacc, "The British Connection," *Ruined Pages: Selected Poems of Padraic Fiacc*, ed. Gerald Dawe and Aodán Mac Póilin (Belfast: Blackstaff Press, 1994), p. 110.
3. "Question Time," *Belfast Confetti* (Newcastle upon Tyne: Bloodaxe Books, 1990), p. 57.
4. "Patchwork," *The Irish for No*, p. 59.

Soot

It was autumn. First, she shrouded
The furniture, then rolled back the carpet
As if for dancing; then moved
The ornaments from the mantelpiece,
Afraid his roughness might disturb
Their staid fragility.

He came; shyly, she let him in,
Feeling ill-at-ease in the newly-spacious
Room, her footsteps sounding hollow
On the boards. She watched him kneel
Before the hearth, and said something
About the weather. He did not answer,

Too busy with his work for speech.
The stem of yellow cane creaked upwards
Tentatively. After a while, he asked
Her to go outside and look, and there,
Above the roof, she saw the frayed sunflower
Bloom triumphantly. She came back

And asked how much she owed him, grimacing
As she put the money in his soiled hand.
When he had gone, a weightless hush
Lingered in the house for days. Slowly,
It settled; the fire burned cleanly;
Everything was spotless.

Hearing that soot was good for the soil,
She threw it on the flowerbeds. She would watch
It crumble, dissolving in the rain,
Finding its way to lightless crevices,
Sleeping, till in spring it would emerge softly
As the ink-bruise in the pansy's heart.

The New Estate

Forget the corncrake's elegy. Rusty
Iambics that escaped your discipline
Of shorn lawns, it is sustained by nature.
It does not grieve for you, nor for itself.
You remember the rolled gold of cornfields,
Their rustling of tinsel in the wind,
A whole field quivering like blown silk?

A shiver now runs through the laurel hedge,
And washing flutters like the swaying lines
Of a new verse. The high fidelity
Music of the newly-wed obscures your
Dedication to a life of loving
Money. What could they be for, those marble
Toilet fixtures, the silence of water-beds,
That book of poems you bought yesterday?

Dresden

Horse Boyle was called Horse Boyle because of his brother Mule;
Though why Mule was called Mule is anybody's guess. I stayed there once,
Or rather, I nearly stayed there once. But that's another story.
At any rate they lived in this decrepit caravan, not two miles out of Carrick,
Encroached upon by baroque pyramids of empty baked bean tins, rusts
And ochres, hints of autumn merging into twilight. Horse believed
They were as good as a watchdog, and to tell you the truth
You couldn't go near the place without something falling over:
A minor avalanche would ensue—more like a shop bell, really,

The old-fashioned ones on string, connected to the latch, I think,
And as you entered in, the bell would tinkle in the empty shop, a musk
Of soap and turf and sweets would hit you from the gloom. Tobacco.
Baling wire. Twine. And, of course, shelves and pyramids of tins.

An old woman would appear from the back—there was a sizzling pan in
    there,
Somewhere, a whiff of eggs and bacon—and ask you what you wanted;
Or rather, she wouldn't ask; she would talk about the weather. It had
    rained
That day, but it was looking better. They had just put in the spuds.
I had only come to pass the time of day, so I bought a token packet of
    Gold Leaf.

All this time the fry was frying away. Maybe she'd a daughter in there
Somewhere, though I hadn't heard the neighbours talk of it; if anybody
    knew,
It would be Horse. Horse kept his ears to the ground.
And he was a great man for current affairs; he owned the only TV in the
    place.
Come dusk he'd set off on his rounds, to tell the whole townland the latest
Situation in the Middle East, a mortar bomb attack in Mullaghbawn—
The damn things never worked, of course—and so he'd tell the story
How in his young day it was very different. Take young Flynn,
        for instance,
Who was ordered to take this bus and smuggle some sticks of gelignite

Across the border, into Derry, when the RUC—or was it the RIC?—*
Got wind of it. The bus was stopped, the peeler stepped on. Young Flynn
Took it like a man, of course: he owned up right away. He opened the bag
And produced the bomb, his rank and serial number. For all the world
Like a pound of sausages. Of course, the thing was, the peeler's bike
Had got a puncture, and he didn't know young Flynn from Adam. All he
    wanted
Was to get home for his tea. Flynn was in for seven years and learned to
    speak
The best of Irish. He had thirteen words for a cow in heat;
A word for the third thwart in a boat, the wake of a boat on the ebb tide.

He knew the extinct names of insects, flowers, why this place was called
Whatever: *Carrick*, for example, was *a rock*. He was damn right there—
As the man said, *When you buy meat you buy bones, when you buy land you
    buy stones.*
You'd be hard put to find a square foot in the whole bloody parish
That wasn't thick with flints and pebbles. To this day he could hear the
    grate

And scrape as the spade struck home, for it reminded him of broken bones:
Digging a graveyard, maybe—or better still, trying to dig a reclaimed tip*
Of broken delph and crockery ware—you know that sound that sets your
    teeth on edge
When the chalk squeaks on the blackboard, or you shovel ashes from the
    stove?

Master McGinty—he'd be on about McGinty then, and discipline, the
    capitals
Of South America, Moore's *Melodies,* the Battle of Clontarf,* and
Tell me this, an educated man like you: What goes on four legs when it's young,
Two legs when it's grown up, and three legs when it's old?* I'd pretend
I didn't know. McGinty's leather strap would come up then, stuffed
With threepenny bits to give it weight and sting. Of course, it never did
    him
Any harm: *You could take a horse to water but you couldn't make him drink.*
He himself was nearly going on to be a priest.
And many's the young cub left the school, as wise as when he came.

Carrowkeel was where McGinty came from—*Narrow Quarter,* Flynn
    explained—
Back before the Troubles, a place that was so mean and crabbed,
Horse would have it, men were known to eat their dinner from a drawer.
Which they'd slide shut the minute you'd walk in.
He'd demonstrate this at the kitchen table, hunched and furtive, squinting
Out the window—past the teetering minarets of rust, down the hedge-
    dark aisle—
To where a stranger might appear, a passer-by, or what was maybe worse,
Someone he knew. Someone who wanted something. Someone who was
    hungry.
Of course who should come tottering up the lane that instant but his
    brother

Mule. I forgot to mention they were twins. They were as like two—
No, not peas in a pod, for this is not the time nor the place to go into
Comparisons, and this is really Horse's story, Horse who—now I'm
    getting
Round to it—flew over Dresden in the war. He'd emigrated first, to
Manchester. Something to do with scrap—redundant mill machinery,
Giant flywheels, broken looms that would, eventually, be ships, or
    aeroplanes.

He said he wore his fingers to the bone.
And so, on impulse, he had joined the RAF. He became a rear gunner.
Of all the missions, Dresden broke his heart. It reminded him of china.

As he remembered it, long afterwards, he could hear, or almost hear
Between the rapid desultory thunderclaps, a thousand tinkling echoes—
All across the map of Dresden, store-rooms full of china shivered,
    teetered
And collapsed, an avalanche of porcelain, slushing and cascading: cherubs,
Shepherdesses, figurines of Hope and Peace and Victory, delicate bone
    fragments.
He recalled in particular a figure from his childhood, a milkmaid
Standing on the mantelpiece. Each night as they knelt down for the rosary,
His eyes would wander up to where she seemed to beckon to him, smiling,
Offering him, eternally, her pitcher of milk, her mouth of rose and cream.

One day, reaching up to hold her yet again, his fingers stumbled, and she
    fell.
He lifted down a biscuit tin, and opened it.
It breathed an antique incense: things like pencils, snuff, tobacco.
His war medals. A broken rosary. And there, the milkmaid's creamy hand,
    the outstretched
Pitcher of milk, all that survived. Outside, there was a scraping
And a tittering; I knew Mule's step by now, his careful drunken weaving
Through the tin-stacks. I might have stayed the night, but there's no time
To go back to that now; I could hardly, at any rate, pick up the thread.
I wandered out through the steeples of rust, the gate that was a broken
    bed.

Belfast Confetti

Suddenly as the riot squad moved in, it was raining exclamation marks,
Nuts, bolts, nails, car-keys. A fount of broken type. And the explosion
Itself—an asterisk on the map. This hyphenated line, a burst of rapid
    fire . . .
I was trying to complete a sentence in my head, but it kept stuttering,
All the alleyways and side-streets blocked with stops and colons.

I know this labyrinth so well—Balaclava, Raglan, Inkerman, Odessa
    Street—*
Why can't I escape? Every move is punctuated. Crimea Street. Dead end
    again.
A Saracen, Kremlin-2 mesh. Makrolon face-shields. Walkie-talkies. What
    is
My name? Where am I coming from? Where am I going? A fusillade of
    question marks.

Campaign

They had questioned him for hours. Who exactly was he? And when
He told them, they questioned him again. When they accepted who he
    was, as
Someone not involved, they pulled out his fingernails. Then
They took him to a waste-ground somewhere near the Horseshoe Bend,
    and told him
What he was. They shot him nine times.

A dark umbilicus of smoke was rising from a heap of burning tyres.
The bad smell he smelt was the smell of himself. Broken glass and knotted
    Durex.*
The knuckles of a face in a nylon stocking. I used to see him in the
    Gladstone Bar,
Drawing pints for strangers, his almost perfect fingers flecked with scum.

The Exiles' Club

Every Thursday in the upstairs lounge of The Wollongong Bar they make
Themselves at home with Red Heart Stout, Park Drive cigarettes and
    Dunville's whiskey,
A slightly-mouldy batch of soda farls. Eventually they get down to
    business.
After years they have reconstructed the whole of the Falls Road, and now
Are working on the backstreets: Lemon, Peel and Omar, Balaclava, Alma.

They just about keep up with the news of bombings and demolition, and
    are
Struggling with the finer details: the names and dates carved out
On the back bench of the Leavers' Class in Slate Street School; the Nemo
    Café menu;
The effects of the 1941 Blitz, the entire contents of Paddy Lavery's
    pawnshop.

Patchwork

It was only just this minute that I noticed the perfectly triangular
Barbed wire rip in the sleeve of my shirt, and wondered where I'd got it.
I'd crossed no fences that I knew about. Then it struck me: an almost
    identical
Tear in my new white Sunday shirt, when I was six. My mother, after her
    initial
Nagging, stitched it up. But you can never make a perfect job on tears like
    that.
Eventually she cut it up for handkerchiefs: six neatly-hemmed squares.
Snags of greyish wool remind me of the mountain that we climbed that
    day—
Nearly at the summit, we could see the map of Belfast. My father stopped
For a cigarette and pointed out the landmarks: Gallaher's tobacco factory,
Clonard Monastery, the invisible speck of our house, lost in all the rows
And terraces and furrows, like this one sheep that's strayed into the rags
And bandages that flock the holy well. A little stack of ballpoint pens,
Some broken spectacles, a walking-stick, two hearing aids: prayers
Repeated and repeated until granted.
                                            So when I saw, last week, the crucifix
Earring dangling from the right ear of this young Charismatic
Christian fiddle-player, I could not help but think of beads, beads
Told over and over—like my father's rosary of olive stones from
Mount Olive, I think, that he had thumbed and fingered so much the
    decades
Missed a pip or two. The cross itself was ebony and silver, just like
This young girl's, that swung and tinkled like a thurible. She was playing
"The Teetotaller." Someone had to buy a drink just then, of course: a pint
    of Harp,

Four pints of stout, two Paddy whiskies, and a bottle of Lucozade—the
    baby
Version, not the ones you get in hospital, wrapped in crackling see-through
Cellophane. You remember how you held it to the light, and light shone
    through?
The opposite of Polaroids, really, the world filmed in dazzling sunshine:
A quite unremarkable day of mist and drizzle. The rainy hush of traffic,
Muted car-horns, a dog making a dog-leg walk across a zebra crossing . . .
As the lights changed from red to green and back to red again
I fingered the eighteen stitches in the puckered mouth of my
    appendicectomy.

The doctor's waiting room, now that I remember it, had a print of
    The Angelus *
Above the fireplace; sometimes, waiting for the buzzer, I'd hear the
    Angelus
Itself boom out from St Peter's. With only two or three deliberate steps
I could escape into the frame, unnoticed by the peasant and his wife. I'd
    vanish
Into sepia. The last shivering bell would die on the wind.
I was in the surgery. Stainless steel and hypodermics glinted on the shelves.
Now I saw my mother: the needle shone between her thumb and finger,
    stitching,
Darning, mending: the woolly callous on a sock, the unravelled jumper
That became a scarf. I held my arms at arms' length as she wound and
    wound:
The tick-tack of the knitting needles made a cable-knit pullover.
Come Christmas morning I would wear it, with a new white shirt
    unpinned
From its cardboard stiffener.
                          I shivered at the touch of cold white linen—
A mild shock, as if, when almost sleeping, you'd dreamt you'd fallen
Suddenly, and realised now you were awake: the curtains fluttered
In the breeze across the open window, exactly as they had before.
    Everything
Was back to normal. Outside, the noise of children playing: a tin can
    kicked
Across a tarred road, the whip-whop of a skipping rope, singing—
Poor Toby is dead and he lies in his grave, lies in his grave, lies in his grave . . .
So, the nicotine-stained bone buttons on my father's melodeon clicked
And ticked as he wheezed his way through *Oft in the Stilly Night*—or,

For that matter, *Nearer My God to Thee,* which he'd play on Sundays, just
 before
He went to see my granny, after Mass. Sometimes she'd be sick—*Another*
Clean shirt'll do me—and we'd climb the narrow stair to where she lay,
 buried
Beneath the patchwork quilt.
         It took me twenty years to make that quilt—
I'm speaking for her now—and, *your father's stitched into that quilt,*
Your uncles and aunts. She'd take a sip from the baby Power's
On the bedside table. *Anything that came to hand, a bit of cotton print,*
A poplin tie: I snipped them all up. I could see her working in the gloom,
The shadow of the quilt draped round her knees. A needle shone between
Her thumb and finger. Minutes, hours of stitches threaded patiently; my
 father
Tugged at her, a stitch went wrong; she started up again. *You drink your tea*
Just like your father: two sips and a gulp: and so I'd see a mirror image
Raise the cup and take two sips, and swallow, or place my cup exactly on
The brown ring stain on the white damask tablecloth.
            Davy's gone to England,
Rosie to America; who'll be next, I don't know. Yet they all came back.
I'd hardly know them now. The last time I saw them all together was
The funeral. As the rosary was said I noticed how my father handled the
 invisible
Bead on the last decade: a gesture he'd repeat again at the graveside.
A shower of hail: far away, up on the mountain, a cloud of sheep had
 scattered
In the Hatchet Field.* *The stitches show in everything I've made,* she'd say—
The quilt was meant for someone's wedding, but it never got that far.
And some one of us has it now, though who exactly I don't know.

Bloody Hand

Your man, says the Man, *will walk into the bar like this*—here his fingers
Mimic a pair of legs, one stiff at the knee—*so you'll know exactly*
What to do. He sticks a finger to his head. Pretend it's child's play—
The hand might be a horse's mouth, a rabbit or a dog. Five handclaps.

Walls have ears: the shadows you throw are the shadows you try to throw off.

I snuffed out the candle between finger and thumb. Was it the left hand
Hacked off at the wrist and thrown to the shores of Ulster? Did Ulster
Exist? Or the Right Hand of God, saying *Stop* to this and *No* to that?
My thumb is the hammer of a gun. The thumb goes up. The thumb goes down.

The Ballad of HMS *Belfast*

On the first of April, *Belfast* disengaged her moorings, and sailed away
From old Belfast. Sealed orders held our destination, somewhere in the
    Briny Say.

Our crew of Jacks was aromatic with tobacco-twist and alcoholic
Reekings from the night before. Both Catestants and Protholics,

We were tarry-breeked and pig-tailed, and sailed beneath the White
    Ensign;*
We loved each other nautically, though most landlubbers thought we were
    insane.

We were full-rigged like the *Beagle,* piston-driven, like the *Enterprise*
Express; each system was a back-up for the other, auxiliarizing verse with
    prose.

Our engines ticked and tacked us up the Lough, cranks and link-pins,
    cross-rods
Working ninety to the dozen; our shrouds and ratlines rattled like a
    cross-roads

Dance, while swivels, hook blocks, cleats, and fiddles jigged their
    semi-colons
On the staves. We staggered up the rigging like a bunch of demi-golems,

Tipsy still, and dreamed of underdecks—state-rooms, crystal chandeliers,
And saloon bars—until we got to gulp the ozone; then we swayed like
    gondoliers

Above the aqua. We gazed at imperceptible horizons, where amethyst
Dims into blue, and pondered them again that night, before the mast.

Some sang of Zanzibar and Montalban, and others of the lands
    unascertained
On maps; we entertained the Phoenix and the Unicorn, till we were
    grogged and concertina'ed.

We've been immersed, since then, in cruises to the Podes and Antipodes;
The dolphin and the flying fish would chaperone us like aquatic aunties

In their second, mermaid childhood, till we ourselves felt neither fish nor
    flesh, but
Breathed through gills of rum and brandy. We'd flounder on the randy
    decks like halibut.

Then our Captain would emerge to scold us from his three-days'
    incommunicado
And promenaded on the poop-deck, sashed and epauletted like a grand
    Mikado

To bribe us with the Future: new Empires, Realms of Gold, and precious
    ore
Unheard-of since the days of Homer: we'd boldly go where none had
    gone before.

Ice to Archangel, tea to China, coals to Tyne: such would be our cargo.
We'd confound the speculators' markets and their exchequered, logical
    embargo.

Then were we like the *Nautilus*, that trawls the vast and purple catacomb
For cloudy shipwrecks, settled in their off-the-beam, intractable aplomb.

Electric denizens glide through the Pisan masts, flickering their Pisces'
    lumière;
We regard them with a Cyclops eye, from our bathyscope beneath *la mer.*

Scattered cutlery and dinner-services lie, hugger-mugger, on the murky
    floor.
An empty deck-chair yawns and undulates its awning like a semaphore.

Our rising bubble then went *bloop, bloop* till it burst the swaying
    window-pane;

Unfathomed from the cobalt deep, we breathed the broad Pacific once
  again.

Kon-Tiki-like, we'd drift for days, abandoning ourselves to all the
  elements,
Guided only by the aromatic coconut, till the wind brought us the scent of
  lemons—

Then we'd disembark at Vallambroso or Gibraltar to explore the bars;
Adorned in sequin-scales, we glimmered phosphorescently like stars

That crowd innumerably in midnight harbours. O olive-dark interior,
All splashed with salt and wine! Havana gloom within the humidor!

The atmosphere dripped heavy with the oil of anchovies, tobacco-smoke,
  and chaw;
We grew languorous with grass and opium and *kif,* the very best of draw,

And sprawled in urinous piazzas; slept until the fog-horn trump of
  Gabriel.
We woke, and rubbed our eyes, half-gargled still with braggadocio and
  garble.

And then the smell of docks and ropeworks. Horse-dung. The tolling of
  the Albert clock.
Its Pisan slant. The whirring of its ratchets. Then everything began to
  click:

I lay bound in iron chains, alone, my *aisling* gone, my sentence passed.*
Grey Belfast dawn illuminated me, on board the prison ship *Belfast.*

The Rising of the Moon

As down by the glenside I met an old colleen,
She stung me with the gaze of her nettle-green eyes.
She urged me to go out and revolutionize
Hibernia, and not to fear the guillotine.

She spread the madder red skirts of her liberty
About my head so I was disembodied.

I fell among the people of No Property,
Who gave me bread and salt, and pipes of fragrant weed.

The pale moon was rising above the green mountain,
The red sun declining beneath the blue sea,
When I saw her again by yon clear crystal fountain,

Where poppies, not potatoes, grew in contraband.
She said, *You might have loved me for eternity.*
I kissed her grass-green lips, and shook her bloodless hand.

Catmint Tea

The cat and I are quite alike, these winter nights:
I consult thesauruses; he forages for mice.
He prowls the darkest corners, while I throw the dice
Of rhyme, and rummage through the OED's delights.

He's all ears and eyes and whiskery antennae
Bristling with the whispered broadcast of the stars,
And I have cruised the ocean of a thousand bars,
And trawled a thousand entries at the dawn of day.

I plucked another goose-quill from the living wing
And opened up my knife, while Cat unsheathed his claws.
Our wild imaginations started to take wing.

We rolled in serendipity on the mat.
I forged a chapter of the Universal Laws.
Then he became the man, and I became the cat.

Spraying the Potatoes

Knapsack-sprayer on my back, I marched the drills
Of blossoming potatoes—Kerr's Pinks in a frivelled blue,
The Arran Banners wearing white. July was due,
A haze of copper sulphate on the far-off hills.

The bronze noon air was drowsy, unguent as glue.
As I bent over the big oil-drum for a refill,
I heard the axle-roll of a rut-locked tumbril.
It might have come from God-knows-where, or out of the blue.

A verdant man was cuffed and shackled to its bed.
Fourteen troopers rode beside, all dressed in red.
It took them a minute to string him up from the oak tree.

I watched him swing in his Derry green for hours and hours,
His popping eyes of apoplectic liberty
That blindly scanned the blue and white potato flowers.

Home

hurtling from
the airport down
the mountain road

past barbed wire
snagged with
plastic bags

fields of scrap
and thistle
farmyards

from the edge
of the plateau
my eye zooms

into the clarity
of Belfast
streets

shipyards
domes
theatres

British Army
helicopter
poised

motionless
at last

I see everything

The Forgotten City

after William Carlos Williams, "The Forgotten City"

When on a day of the last disturbances
I was returning from the country, trees
were across the road, thoroughfares and side streets
barricaded: burning trucks and buses, walls
of ripped-up paving-stones, sheets of corrugated
iron fencing, storm-gratings, brown torrents
gushing from a broken water main.
I had to take what road I could to find
my way back to the city. My bike hissed
over crisp wet tarmac as I cycled through
extraordinary places: long deserted avenues
and driveways leading to apartment blocks,
car-ports, neo-Tudor churches, cenotaphs,
and in one place an acre or more of
rusting Nissen huts left over from the War. Parks.
It was so quiet that at one gatekeeper's lodge
I could hear coffee perking. I passed
a crematorium called Roselawn, pleasant
cul-de-sacs and roundabouts with names
I never knew existed. Knots of men and women
gathered here and there at intersections
wearing hats and overcoats, talking
to themselves, gesticulating quietly.
I had no idea where I was and promised myself
I would go back some day and study this
grave people. How did they achieve
such equilibrium? How did they get
cut off in this way from the stream of

bulletins, so under-represented
in our parliaments and media when so near
the troubled zone, so closely surrounded
and almost touched by the famous and familiar?

Zugzwang

As you might hear every possible babble of language
in bells that tumble and peal to celebrate victory;

as the quilters make a pattern of their remnants and rags,
and the jersey, unravelled, becomes a new skein of wool;

as the fugue must reiterate its melodic fragments
in continuously unfinished tapestries of sound;

as the police might have trawled the wreck of your Déesse
in search of the twist in the plot, the point of no return;

as the words of the song when remembered each time around
remind us of other occasions at different times;

as the geographer traces the long fetch of the waves
from where they are born at sea to where they founder to shore—

so I return to the question of those staggered repeats
as my memories of you recede into the future.

Tom Paulin (1949–)

The ultimate concerns of Tom Paulin's poems never lie far from the world of Northern Ireland; but, as if rehearsing the circuitous path of the poet's life, the poetry tends to start somewhere else. Born in Leeds in 1949, Paulin has nonetheless come to be associated more closely than almost any other poet of his generation with the political life of Ulster. His residence in Belfast began in 1953, and he completed elementary and grammar schools there before departing for the University of Hull and an eventual B.Litt. from Lincoln College, Oxford. In 1972 Paulin began teaching at the University of Nottingham. He has since been appointed to the G. M. Young lectureship in English Literature at Hertford College, Oxford, a position from which he continues to observe the Northern Irish scene with the eye of an informed and invested outsider.

Although critics have attacked Paulin for writing poems that are too overtly political, his work has always been more multivalent than that of the stereotypical political poet. His first volume, *A State of Justice,* published in 1977, makes its interest in national politics clear in the title, but the poetry itself displays a complexity of viewpoint that preserves it from collapse into propaganda. "Thinking of Iceland," which is among the more fully realized of these early poems, introduces what now seems Paulin's characteristic technique of layering historical events and personalities within a single lyric structure. It is telling that he returned to this poem in 1993, when he revised it for inclusion in his *Selected Poems.* The revised version printed here projects an even sharper image of Northern Ireland's "sour outback" through the cosmopolitan lens of the W. H. Auden / Louis MacNeice collaboration *Letters from Iceland.*[1] The poem's parenthetical aside in which Paulin "sadly" recalls the letters the two poets sent to Richard Crossman, who had espoused Irish unification during his tenure as editor of *The New Statesman,* betrays the irrepressible presence of Ulster politics in the gaps of Paulin's work. At the same time, its function in motivating the connection between disparate historical and literary moments shows the difficulty of assigning priority either to political or to poetic concerns in Paulin's poetry.

The ideas—or more pejoratively, the ideology—embedded in poetic imagery are for Paulin not separable from the poetry; the melding of idea and image gives evidence of the poet's work, and becomes the medium of poetic social function. In *Seize the Fire*, a version of Aeschylus' *Prometheus Bound*, Paulin's Prometheus is punished by a totalitarian Zeus because he searched out "that one, primal / Idea of all ideas," and, like the poet smuggling ideas in images, "hid it in a cusp of fennel, / a single spark / inside that aromatic / greeny-white bulb."[2] It is typical of Paulin to turn a primal force like fire into a primal idea, but the images in Paulin's poetry are seldom this romantic. Gritty is more usual than "greeny," with the bitter facts of Belfast's political life standing as the point of eternal return. When Prometheus warns Oceanos that opposing Zeus will not result in his freedom, it is in a voice more readily recognizable as Paulin's: "Oceanos: We're comrades still. / I'll see you're freed. // Prometheus: More likely you'll get kneecapped."[3]

In the last few years Paulin has made news more for his inflammatory public statements than for his poetry. In 2002, for example, he told an Egyptian newspaper interviewer that American-born settlers in Israel "should be shot dead."[4] Paulin later distanced himself from the call for violence, while still denying Israel's right to exist. Given his penchant for political complexity, it is perhaps not surprising that the book he published the same year, *The Invasion Handbook*, marked a return to overtly political poetry (after two volumes focused on the artists Paul Klee and Marc Chagall) by recounting the origins of the Second World War, including the persecution of Jews by the Nazis.

NOTES

1. "Thinking of Iceland," *Selected Poems, 1972–1990* (London: Faber and Faber, 1993), p. 5. The earlier version is to be found in *A State of Justice* (London: Faber and Faber, 1977), p. 11. The 1977 text has "unfortunately" rather than "sadly." For a discussion of this parenthetical remark, see Bernard O'Donoghue, "Involved Imaginings," *The Chosen Ground: Essays on the Contemporary Poetry of Northern Ireland*, ed. Neil Corcoran (Bridgend, Wales: Seren, 1992), pp. 175–176.

2. *Seize the Fire: A Version of Aeschylus's "Prometheus Bound"* (London: Faber and Faber, 1990), p. 9.

3. Ibid., pp. 25–27.

4. See Neil Tweedie, "Oxford Poet Wants U.S. Jews Shot," *Daily Telegraph* (London), April 13, 2002.

States

That stretch of water, it's always
There for you to cross over
To the other shore, observing
The lights of cities on blackness.

Your army jacket at the rail
Leaks its kapok into a wind
That slices gulls over a dark zero
Waste a cormorant skims through.

Any state, built on such a nature,
Is a metal convenience, its paint
Cheapened by the price of lives
Spent in a public service.

The men who peer out for dawning
Gantries below a basalt beak,
Think their vigils will make something
Clearer, as the cities close

With each other, their security
Threatened but bodied in steel
Polities that clock us safely
Over this dark; freighting us.

Thinking of Iceland

Forgetting the second cod war
to go North to that island
—just four days' sailing from Hull—
would be what? An escape?
Or an attempt at finding
what's behind everything?
(bit big the last question for a holiday trip.)

Still, reading the letters
they fired back to England

(one, sadly, to Crossman)*
brings back a winter monochrome
of coast and small townships
that are much nearer home:
Doochary, the Rosses, Bloody Foreland.*

An empty road over hills
dips under some wind-bent,
scrub trees: there's a bar
painted pink, some houses,
a petrol pump by a shop;
it's permanently out-of-season
here where some people live for some reason.

A cluster too small for a village,
fields waste with grey rocks
that lichens coat—hard skin
spread like frozen cultures,
green, corroded tufts that make dyes
for tweed—shuttles clack
in draughty cottages based in this sour outback.

On the signposts every place
has two names; people live
in a cold climate, a landscape
whose silence denies efforts
no one feels much like making:
when someone is building
it looks like a joke, as though they're having us on.

They poke laughing faces
through fresh wooden struts and throw
a greeting from new rafters;
on the box in the bar
a sponsored programme begins;
the crime rate is low—wee sins
like poaching or drink. It's far to the border.

Now that a small factory
which cans and dries vegetables
has opened, some girls stay
and scour the country for dances.

In these bleak parishes that seem
dissolved in a grey dream
some men are busy mixing concrete, digging septics.

In winter there is work
with the council on the roads,
or with local contractors.
Each year Packy Harkin
builds a new boat, choosing
for a keel a long curving
branch from a sheltered wood where oaks grow straight.

In the dark panelled bar
through the shop, there's a faded
print of an eviction:
one constable crouches
on the thatch, the family stands
at the door, pale, while bands
of constabulary guard the whiskered bailiff.

In the top corner, clumsily,
the face of a young woman
glimmers: *The Irish Patriot,*
*Miss Maud Gonne.** Sour smell of porter,
clutter of hens in the yard:
no docking in sagaland—
the wish got as far as this coast, then worked inland.

And yet, at Holar, striking matches
in church, trying to snap
a carved altarpiece: strange figures
absent-mindedly slaughtering
prisoners; or "exchanging politenesses"
with Goering's brother at breakfast,
was this coming-full-circle not the question they asked?

In the Lost Province

As it comes back, brick by smoky brick,
I say to myself—strange I lived there
And walked those streets. It is the Ormeau Road
On a summer's evening, a haze of absence
Over the caked city, that slumped smell
From the blackened gasworks. Ah, those brick canyons
Where Brookeborough* unsheathes a sabre,
Shouting "No Surrender" from the back of a lorry.

And the sky is a dry purple, and men
Are talking politics in a back room.
Is it too early or too late for change?
Certainly the province is most peaceful.
Who would dream of necessity, the angers
Of Leviathan, or the years of judgement?

Desertmartin*

At noon, in the dead centre of a faith,
Between Draperstown and Magherafelt,
This bitter village shows the flag
In a baked absolute September light.
Here the Word has withered to a few
Parched certainties, and the charred stubble
Tightens like a black belt, a crop of Bibles.

Because this is the territory of the Law
I drive across it with a powerless knowledge—
The owl of Minerva in a hired car.
A Jock squaddy* glances down the street
And grins, happy and expendable,
Like a brass cartridge. He is a useful thing,
Almost at home, and yet not quite, not quite.

It's a limed nest, this place. I see a plain
Presbyterian grace sour, then harden,

As a free strenuous spirit changes
To a servile defiance that whines and shrieks
For the bondage of the letter: it shouts
For the Big Man to lead his wee people
To a clean white prison, their scorched tomorrow.

Masculine Islam, the rule of the Just,
Egyptian sand dunes and geometry,
A theology of rifle-butts and executions:
These are the places where the spirit dies.
And now, in Desertmartin's sandy light,
I see a culture of twigs and bird-shit
Waving a gaudy flag it loves and curses.

Presbyterian Study

A lantern-ceiling and quiet.
I climb here often and stare
At the scoured desk by the window,
The journal open
At a date and conscience.

It is a room without song
That believes in flint, salt,
And new bread rising
Like a people who share
A dream of grace and reason.

A bit starchy perhaps.
A shade chill, like a draper's shop.
But choosing the free way,
Not the formal,
And warming the walls with its knowing.

Memory is a moist seed
And a praise here, for they live,
Those linen saints, lithe radicals,
In the bottle light
Of this limewashed shrine.

Hardly a schoolroom remembers
Their obstinate rebellion;
Provincial historians
Scratch circles on the sand,
And still, with dingy smiles,

We wait on nature,
Our jackets a dungy pattern
Of mud and snapped leaves,
Our state a jacked corpse
Committed to the deep.

Painting with Sawdust

This may sound insane
but if you take the way a saw
goes ripping and tearing
through a plank of pine or larch
—pine's a softwood while larch
is hard like bone
—if you listen to a saw giving out
those barking yelpy groans
those driven shouts and moans
that're wild as a drowning pup
or raw
like a wet shammy rubbing its knuckles
on a windowpane
—if you listen to the crazy chuckles
thrown out by a saw
in the heat of its only function in life
though to be strictly accurate that jagged blade
can't ever belong to what we call life
—if you reflect on the noises this knife
—this big thrawn toothy rather tinny knife
must make
then they might be a version those chuckles
of the way couples it's said
are always going in and out

of intimacy
which means that when the saw's
dogged panting
suddenly whoops screams and stops
—*chup!*
there's a change of tune
because now that its constant whuffing
has let up
one lover or the other must take a brush
not to paint a picture but lick up
what it seems such a pity not to leave behind
or leave new and untouched
—that tiny dune
of resiny sweet crumbs

Chagall in Ireland   *for Roy and Aisling Foster*

My childhood *shtetl*
—a mourner slumps down the main street
of this tiny settle-
ment as a halfbrick bursts through my window
while the undented kettle
grows warm on the kosangas* stove
like a cat in a basket
—a creaky cricky basket
with a scrap of hairy blanket
that smells of peat
and peat too is hairy
—undaunted the great drayhorse at the forge
turns her luminous eyes
on the nasty fellow
—he's a bad baste—
running down the boreen*
where bats will taste flies in the twilight
—asked what'll happen
the march in the next townland
a woman shakes out her apron

oh the night she says
the night will tell the tale
for a moment it's dark and *lumpen*
sort of *Yellow Pages*
but *bather bather* the smith fettles
four metal shoes
for the horse that's glossy and spruce and brown
as ale
and the hill above
—hill with a rath*
seems somehow engorged
with what?—I
don't want to say blood
but there is for definite metal
—metal and rust—in the image
and we all know how rust tastes
—tastes like sick
or dried shite
and how it's the colour of the culprit's jacket
—see he's got a stick
in his hand now
—the kettle's plumping
I must turn the gas off
he's skulking in the shadows
waiting for me to come down the path
so he can trip this curlyhaired visitor in the mud
but I'll make him and his stick and his brick
shtick
and like someone signing a letter *with love*
I'll paint him into the far corner

Not Musical

Something in the fiddle's tone
that I can't know I know
—which is only to say
that its sound its slow

strutty glumness's too thrawn*
as I hear in its belly an offcolour
sound like furred echoes in a cellar

and does her bow fray
under not over its yelping stresses?
all I know's the clash
of consonants—their broken jaggy tune
like a chough's call
the way they scrape or scringe or smash
—I have no right way to say this
no right to speak at all

August 39

In a house called Invergowrie
—Scotch baronial South Belfast
prosperous and Calvinist
she dreams an open boat
packed with a series
of starved figures
their ribcages bare as laths
—a hint somewhere in the story
(all dreams must tell a story)
that this has to do
with statistics or maths
—the sun is visible and hot
as an almost breeze makes ziggers
on the bluesmooth
surface of the ocean
that's as tight and sinister
as the phrase she'll bring back
from this involuntary journey
—*a dream and a fear*
for now she knows
that many miles from dry land
these ancient mariners

are entering their last sleep
they differ
from the corpse she saw last month
on the dissecting table
the corpse two students dressed
in an old overcoat
and played games with
as if it were a guy
ready for the bonfire
or as if it was a man full
of drink—but as the sea
is also known as the drink
there may be more to this than we think

not an oar but a gaff
—useless thing—leans in one rowlock
and that large hook
it spells out
all that she can see before her
and around and inside her
—a type of horror she hasn't met
with ever that's lodged in her now
like a message from father stamped
on her young mind
that six seven years later
she'll learn to understand
until years beyond
those newsreels of the camps
she hands her dream on
to her eldest son
who wonders if mere dreams
can weigh in the record
or for that matter can poems?

Michael Davitt (1950–2005)

While still a student at University College, Cork, Michael Davitt founded the journal *Innti*, which has played an important role in the renaissance of Irish language poetry in the last three decades. Davitt was a native of Cork, born in 1950, and his own poetry is written in a resonant West Munster dialect, out of which he shaped a lively and contemporary idiom.

Davitt's poetry is remarkable for the ease with which it wraps the Irish language around topics that range from considered nationalism to pop-culture iconography. In his *Selected Poems*, Davitt's recreation of the moment when all Ireland held its breath in anticipation of the death of the Nationalist hunger-striker Bobby Sands stands in powerful symbiosis with the immediately preceding selection on the murder of John Lennon. In translation the poems speak to each other in the same tone of helpless hope, and the uncontrolled velocity of Lennon's rise and the suddenness of his death in "Clay Memories" finds a counterpoint in the drawn-out tension of one night of waiting in "For Bobby Sands on the Eve of his Death." Either poem could end with the lines that close "For Bobby Sands on the Eve of his Death": "Thit suan roimh bhás inniu ort. / Cloisimid ar an raidió" ("You fell today, / into the sleep of death. / We hear on the radio").[1] Like much of Davitt's work, the two poems recognize the interconnectedness of Irish identity and global popular culture, as when the speaker's mother in "Clay Memories" confesses that "no death" but Lennon's "had so grieved her / since Kennedy was shot / in November of that other year,"[2] 1963, the year of the Beatles' first LP.

Paul Muldoon's translation of Davitt's "Do Phound, ó Dhia / To Pound, from God" captures the energy and irreverence by which Davitt has guided a generation of Irish-language poets out of the potentially treacherous bog of antiquarianism, and into a lively engagement with contemporary reality. Addressed to a dog with the poetically multivalent name Pound, the poem swings between the contemporary particularity of a man dealing with the early morning demands of a frenetic dog and the literary humor of a god's-eye view of the equally frenetic persona of Ezra Pound.

Although Davitt has had his greatest influence *as* a writer in Irish *on* writers in Irish, the dual-language edition of his selected poems, which presents his Irish verse alongside versions by some of the most innovative translators on the Irish scene, shows his unusual voice to be one equally fascinating in English. Davitt died in Sligo in 2005.

NOTES

1. "Do Bhobby Sands an Lá sular Éag / For Bobby Sands on the Eve of his Death," *Selected Poems* (Dublin: Raven Arts Press, 1987), pp. 112–113.

2. "Cuimhní Cré / Clay Memories," *Selected Poems*, pp. 110–111.

In Howth

I couldn't give a damn
about rightandwrong
but I love colours

whichever conditional yellow
or past tense blue
might blow through me
let them blend

but after last night
I *do* give a damn
who sees my pink behind
on a dark beach
in Howth

[Translated by Philip Casey]

Joe

A Sunday visit
and you, Joe, in the month
of your first flirtation
with the perpendicular;

terrifyingly beautiful
your toddler's eye,
sweetly scanning
from floor to ceiling

for every porcelain vase,
art-object, ash tray,
typewriter, TV,
every full cup, half-full cup.

Never be a tamed pony
in the tea-taking civilization of the parlour,
on bandy legs
make your bold getaway.

[Translated by Jason Sommer]

Clay Memories

In our teenage world
in the arms of the river Lee
down on the concrete playgrounds
in the hills above the purr
of the city

the beetles descended
their hair combed down
their electric music
full speed in a spiral

we witnessed a miracle
in nineteen sixty three
and no one believed us.

Seventeen years of you
John Lennon
from seed to flower
from sapling to bloody death
outside an apartment block
in the capital of your kind of music
rock 'n roll

you were our sage brother
somehow
and stayed true to your vision
even when love had gone
out of fashion.

And isn't it strange
my own mother saying
that she didn't know why
her heart was broken
nor why no death
had so grieved her
since Kennedy was shot
in November of that other year.

Today is a day of candles
clay memories

in the ten-second silence
a wandering snowflake descends
to deaf ground.

[Translated by Philip Casey]

For Bobby Sands on the Eve of his Death

We wait,
like people
staring up at a man
who stands, tensed
on a fourth-floor window ledge
staring down at us.

But is your sacrifice suicide?
neither surrender, nor escape;
today you don't even have the choice
of jumping or not jumping.

Uncertain of our role
in this madness
we dispute the rights and wrongs
over the background boozer-roar.
We wait for the latest news,
the latest videoed opinions.

We wait,
ducks in our cushy down
staring at hens in the mud
and the strutting cock
threatening his own brood
and his neighbour's
with a pompous crow:
"a crime is a crime is a crime."

You fell today,
into the sleep of death.
We hear on the radio
the grieving voice of your people

sorrow surmounting hatred:
our prayer for you
is that it prevail.

[Translated by Michael O'Loughlin]

The Terrorist

The footsteps have returned again.
The feet for so long still
and silent.

Here they go across my breast
and I cannot
resist;

they stop for a while, glance
over the shoulder, light
a cigarette.

We are in an unlit backstreet
and I can hear who
they belong to

and when I focus to make him out
I see there is
no one

but his footsteps
keeping step with my
heart.

[Translated by Philip Casey]

August

a broad-beamed stately mannish woman
and a silkie man
took a spin of an august evening
along the empty strands

stippled light and shade
turning inside out
between silhouette and sand

a shot of Vladivar a cigarette

her rollicking down to the tide
in her moonstruck hide
his soft shoe shuffle at her hooves
till he bested her on the crest of a wave
and they set themselves up as pillars of salt
and swam through a swell of pubic hair
pleasure-gland to pleasure-gland

until at least one wound
among so many wounds
was salved

a pair of amphibians
in the oomph of quicksilver

[Translated by Paul Muldoon]

The Mirror   *in memory of my father*

I

He was no longer my father
but I was still his son;
I would get to grips with that cold paradox,
the remote figure in his Sunday best
who was buried the next day.

A great day for tears, snifters of sherry,
whiskey, beef sandwiches, tea.
An old mate of his was recounting
their day excursion
to Youghal in the Thirties,
how he was his first partner
on the Cork/Skibbereen route*
in the late Forties.

There was a splay of Mass cards
on the sitting-room mantelpiece
which formed a crescent round a glass vase,
his retirement present from CIE.*

II

I didn't realise till two days later
it was the mirror took his breath away.

The monstrous old Victorian mirror
with the ornate gilt frame
we had found in the three-storey house
when we moved in from the country.
I was afraid that it would sneak
down from the wall and swallow me up
in one gulp in the middle of the night.
While he was decorating the bedroom
he had taken down the mirror
without asking for help;
soon he turned the colour of terracotta
and his heart broke that night.

III

There was nothing for it
but to set about finishing the job,
papering over the cracks,
painting the high window,
stripping the door of the crypt.
When I took hold of the mirror
I had a fright. I imagined him breathing though it.
I heard him say in a reassuring whisper:
I'll give you a hand, here.

And we lifted the mirror back in position
above the fireplace,
my father holding it steady
while I drove home
the two nails.

[Translated by Paul Muldoon]

O My Two Palestinians

18/9/82, having watched a news report on the massacre of
Palestinians in Beirut

I pushed open the door
enough to let light from the landing
on them:

blankets kicked off
they lay askew
as they had fallen:

her nightgown tossed above her buttocks
blood on her lace knickers,
from a gap in the back of her head

her chicken brain retched on the pillow,
intestines slithered from his belly
like seaweed off a rock,

liver-soiled sheets,
one raised bloodsmeared hand.
O my two Palestinians rotting in the central heat.

[Translated by Philip Casey]

Third Draft of a Dream

in Tyrone Guthrie's house, Annaghmakerrig, Co. Monaghan

The door, that shadowy door
Closes. And the mind is closed.
A disembodied eye
Roves through the big house . . .

    the great hall's flagstones
    that sent showers of sparks
    from riding
    boots

a poster announcing
The Merchant of Venice
at Covent Garden
in 1827

the relics
of butter-making
in a bright back-kitchen

the family portraits
of the once-quick
now dead
a dream of fair women
in the first flush of youth
the lady of the house
telling her tale
of a life
lived behind a veil
while out
in the ploughing
a million other versions
of life—no fit subjects
for oil
on canvas—
are conspiring

the lake
the wood
stealing up
through the darkness
their chorus of voices
murmuring the secrets
of fishermen
and lovers
then making their way back
discreetly
to their proper place

In the morning, a hunter of words
Is snatched from his bed
By a squadron of swallows.

He sits at the table
To begin
The second draft
Of the dream.

[Translated by Paul Muldoon]

To Pound, from God

Like the smell of burning fat from the pan,
your whimpering smarms
its way upstairs and sets off my alarm.

7.08 . . . Fuck this for a party.
I suppose you'll want me to wipe your bum
or open a can of Pedigree Chum.

Whether it's your usual morning dog-desolation
or you've finally managed to strangle yourself
I don't know, but I'll get up before I go deaf.

You bow and scrape
with a kind of hangdog genuflection
through the gentle light of the back-kitchen.

Now you take a swing at me,
then tenderly nurse my jaw
between your boxer's bandaged paws

until it's a toss-up
which is greater—
your love for me or mine for you, you cratur.

A love that, in my case, ebbs and flows
from desolation to full bloom,
barometer of my self-hatred or self-esteem.

Aren't you the one who gives the lie
to my grand ideas of the complex, the pre-ordained,
and isn't it you who bears the brunt

of my impatience with the humdrum?
Then my concept of *regulum mundi**
goes right out the window

and I go chasing my own shadow-tail
or truffling about for some bone of contention
in the back of the head's midden.

For when it would be my dearest wish
that you dance a quadrille
you go and trample awkwardly

Miss H.'s pekinese.
Sometimes you can't distinguish the Archangel Gabriel
from a common burglar.

It gives me a kind of sadistic satisfaction
to scare the shit
out of you in the back garden. Then you smugly sit

and watch me scoop it up again
with my poop-bag and poop-shovel . . .
Pound, you old devil,

you have found the hound in me—
we are dreamers both, both at the end of our tether,
and whimpering at God together.

[Translated by Paul Muldoon]

Ceasefire

I'm not holed out in Ballymurphy now
in a backroom on edge
or on a hillside in South Armagh
waiting for a chopper
to come within range
or by the sea in Downings
as peace comes dropping slow.

I'm in MacDonald's, Lisburn,
eating a Fillet o' Fish.
Your enormous lascivious mouth
has polished off a Big Mac
and my eyes here in no man's land
hunger for you:
the explicit way your breasts
fill the space above the Fries.
And though every inch of you
has my trigger cocked
I despise you, tart,
and all the Christmas frenzy
that will destroy me
if I relent.

Later I'll scrape myself off
into the wastebin of your body
and I recoil when I think
of the small door swinging its
Thank You behind me.

Christmas 1994*

[Translated by Louis de Paor and Michael Davitt]

The Call

Whether you're in Clare or Donegal by now,
or somewhere along the ancient way through Galway, Sligo and Mayo,

I'm still here in Dublin waiting for your call.

Here in the Tenters section, the fifties are alive and well.
I have a second-floor room in a Victorian redbrick.
In the hall below, a velvet curtain pulled back
at the foot of the stairs. Under the stairs a cubby-hole
complete with cobwebs. The phone's in there.
I leave my heavy door slightly ajar.
I can't imagine anything worse than missing your call.

I imagine you driving. The exhaust-pipe of your old white Mazda
sending up clouds of smoke along the roads walked by Raftery
at a time when poetry was prized. About your neck a necklace
of wooden beads, the beads of the hundred and eight sorrows
from the Poyhon Temple in North Korea. Your long, graceful
fingers on the wheel. Your eyes taking in the blue
of the Twelve Pins. I imagine you declaiming
"Cast a cold eye . . ." and passing by Yeats's grave
like the horseman in the poem. I imagine you stopping
for a while by the side of Lough Eske in Donegal
where we lay once as one body, naked in the sun,
myself tense as an eel within you, your dolphin-tongue in my mouth.

But no . . . the wind whistling through the window.

A child screeching down in Hamilton Street.

This, then, is Dublin of the rare old time. The kids dancing
and skipping in the street. A horse dragging
a cartful of scrap metal. In the middle of the night,
the squeal of tires of stolen cars like
animals being slaughtered. Women smoking up a storm,
the Bingo halls bursting at the seams,
the smell of disinfectant in shops, trash blowing all
around the Flats, young men finding God
in a needle. I'm safe and sound, though, recovering
from the middle-class flu that's filled my head
and chest for such a long time.

Once you said to me that you had the legs of a mare.
I see them now treading
the clutch and brake as you thread through the Blue Stacks,
Michelle Shocked on tape singing
"Anchorage" at full tilt, your hair streaming
between two windows.

And I imagine you as a chestnut mare under a new moon
racing at low tide along Magheraroarty Strand,
drawing deep on the ocean
for the sense of freedom you yearned for since childhood.

Here in the city, the sky is melting down on the houses.
The rain needles the window pane.
The last days of summer giving way to autumn too.

The phone . . .

No, it's not you. Not you.

[Translated by Paul Muldoon]

So Long

where an age-old icy notion
touches a bright idea newly coined
along the line where touch ends
          and shade begins

you are walking that line
          boarding a train

and I ask if parting
is closer than touch

and at what point are we most apart
          as I stand above you
on the footbridge to nothing?

[Translated by Louis de Paor and Michael Davitt]

Medbh McGuckian (1950–)

"What they ask of women is less their bed," Medbh McGuckian writes in "Ode to a Poetess," "Or an hour or two between trains, than to be almost gone."[1] Always resisting this elision of the feminine, McGuckian has been a powerful literary presence in Northern Ireland since her victory in the British National Poetry Competition in 1979.

McGuckian was born into a Catholic family in Belfast in 1950, and received her secondary education in a Dominican convent, where she decided early on "not to be a nun but a poet."[2] Between 1968 and 1974 she studied English at Queen's University, Belfast, before returning to her former convent school, not, in fact, as a nun, but as a teacher and already a published poet, having placed several of her works in small magazines and newspapers. Critically acclaimed pamphlets followed in 1980. Her first book-length volume, *The Flower Master,* was published by Oxford University Press two years later.

From the beginning McGuckian's poetry has drawn critical praise, with early readers casting her as "a contemporary Irish Emily Dickinson."[3] Her own poetic goals, however, have more to do with survival and personal development than with the achievement of bardic fame. In a conversation with Nuala Ní Dhomhnaill, published in *The Southern Review,* McGuckian recalled a moment when the feeling of rejection following her father's death led her to grasp the role of poetry in her life:

> When that kind of thing happens to me, I think, "Thanks be to God, I can deal with it, because of my poetry." I can deal with the Troubles and I can deal with that and I can deal with my father's death. I imagine I can deal with everything. I feel I can deal with everything, but the poetry is the dealing, and without the poetry it would be a bullet in the head or the mental home.[4]

Her emphasis here on imagination and feeling is played out more fully in the poetry itself. McGuckian has characterized her work as an attempt to find, by feeling or intuition, a "querencia" of the imagination, a poetic vicinity that corresponds to the zone of the bullring that lends the bull its greatest strength.[5] And her poems—as in "The 'Singer,'" which makes the brand name of a sewing machine sound like another name for a poet, or "Red Armchair," in which a shed may be a fishing lodge or an artist's studio—are most likely to find their power at the point where the landscapes of ordinary lives meet the imaginative worlds of artists.

NOTES

1. "Ode to a Poetess," *Venus and the Rain* (Oxford: Oxford University Press, 1984), p. 12.

2. Quoted in Neil Corcoran, "Medbh McGuckian," *Dictionary of Literary Biography*, vol. 40.

3. *Times Literary Supplement* review by Anne Stevenson, quoted in Neil Corcoran's article in the *Dictionary of Literary Biography*.

4. Medbh McGuckian and Nuala Ní Dhomhnaill, "Comhrá, with a Foreword and Afterword by Laura O'Connor," *The Southern Review*, vol. 31, no. 3 (Summer 1995), p. 585.

5. See the poem "Querencia" below.

Smoke

They set the whins on fire along the road.
I wonder what controls it, can the wind hold
that snake of orange motion to the hills,
away from the houses?

They seem so sure what they can do.
I am unable even
to contain myself, I run
till the fawn smoke settles on the earth.

The "Singer"

In the evenings I used to study
at my mother's old sewing-machine,
pressing my feet occasionally
up and down on the treadle
as though I were going somewhere
I had never been.

Every year at exams, the pressure mounted—
the summer light bent across my pages
like a squinting eye. The children's shouts
echoed the weather of the street,
a car was thunder,
the ticking of a clock was heavy rain. . . .

In the dark I drew the curtains
on young couples stopping in the entry,
heading home. There were nights
I sent the disconnected wheel
spinning madly round and round
till the empty bobbin rattled in its case.

The Heiress

You say I should stay out of the low
fields; though my hands love dark,
I should creep till they are heart-shaped,
like Italian rooms no longer hurt by sun.

When I look at the striped marble of the glen,
I see the husbandry of a good spadesman,
lifting without injury, or making sure
where the furrow is this year the ridge
will be the next; and my pinched grain,
hanging like a window on the smooth spot
of a mountain, or a place for fawns, watches
your way with horses, your delicate Adam work.

But I am lighter of a son, through my slashed
sleeves the inner sleeves of purple keep remembering
the moment exactly, remembering the birth
of an heiress means the gobbling of land.

Dead leaves do not necessarily
fall; it is not coldness, but the tree itself
that bids them go, preventing their destruction.
So I walk along the beach, unruly, I drop
among my shrubbery of seaweed my black acorn buttons.

Querencia

Her hands come awake from the apple-green shutters
of sleep. She clasps the end of her leather belt tightly,
as if she can no longer speak for herself or only
with telephone distortions, the meaning of a row
of black spinal buttons between sender and receiver.

Now here is her favourite cup with its matching plate
and a letter so young, something inside her feels
just like the lines and better than sleep.

As she walks to the window, she smooths out her girlhood
into a shadow of body-colour.

It is strange, how his eyelids close from below,
how love blows her hair to the right, his first beard
to the left. A face in a photograph destroyed
since childhood catches her by the gate-legged
oak table—the chance-seen face like a cold moonstone
in the window's sixteen panes.

She remembers his having to throw stones in the water
to break his dream—and how the river returned them—
or seated at the stone table under the yew, explaining
his need for streets.

At which the birds and vine bed-hangings complain, we have
been taken in too many times by leaves against the window:
a window should be a wide-eaved colour beyond anything.

The Blue She Brings with Her

for Teresa

November—like a man taking all
his shirts, and all his ties, little by little—
enters a million leaves, and that
lion-coloured house-number, the sun,
into his diary; with a rounded symbol—
Nothing—to remind himself of callow apples,
dropping with a sense of rehearsal in June
as if their thought were being done by others.

The mirror bites into me as cloud into
the river-lip of a three-cornered lake
that when the moon is new is shaped
like the moon. With a sudden crash
my log falls to ashes, a wood of winter
colours I have never seen—blood-kissed,
the gold-patterned dishes
show themselves for a moment like wild creatures.

While any smoke that might be going loose
the hot room gathers like a mountain
putting out a mist, and not the kind that clears.
Something you add about mountains makes
my mouth water like a half-lifted cloud
I would choose, if I could, to restrain
as a stone keeps its memories.

Your eyes change colour as you move
and will not go into words. Their swanless
sky-curve holds like a conscious star
a promise from the wind about the blue
she brings with her. If beauty lives
by escaping and leaves a mark, your wrist
will have the mark of my fingers in the morning.

The Dream-Language of Fergus

I

Your tongue has spent the night
in its dim sack as the shape of your foot
in its cave. Not the rudiment
of half a vanquished sound,
the excommunicated shadow of a name,
has rumpled the sheets of your mouth.

2

So Latin sleeps, they say, in Russian speech,
so one river inserted into another
becomes a leaping, glistening, splashed
and scattered alphabet
jutting out from the voice,
till what began as a dog's bark
ends with bronze, what began
with honey ends with ice;
as if an aeroplane in full flight

launched a second plane,
the sky is stabbed by their exits
and the mistaken meaning of each.

3

Conversation is as necessary
among these familiar campus trees
as the apartness of torches;
and if I am a threader
of double-stranded words, whose
Quando has grown into now,
no text can return the honey
in its path of light from a jar,
only a seed-fund, a pendulum,
pressing out the diasporic snow.

No Streets, No Numbers   *for Janice Fitzpatrick*

The wind bruises the curtains' jay-blue stripes
like an unsold fruit or a child who writes
its first word. The rain tonight in my hair
runs a firm, unmuscular hand over something
sand-ribbed and troubled, a desolation
that could erase all memory of warmth
from the patch of vegetation where torchlight
has fallen. The thought that I might miss
even a second of real rain is like the simple
double knock of the stains of birth and death,
two men back to back carrying furniture
from a room on one side of the street
to a room on the other. And the weather
is a girl with woman's eyes like a knife-wound
in her head. Such is a woman's very deep
violation as a woman; not like talk,
not like footsteps; already a life crystallises
round it; and time, that is so often only a word,

"Later, later," spills year into year like three days'
post, or the drawing-room with the wall
pulled down.

I look into the endless settees
of the talk-dried drawing-room where all
the colours are wrong. Is that because
I unshaded all the lamps so their sunny,
unhurt movements would be the colour
of emotions which have no adventures?
But I'm afraid of the morning most,
which stands like a chance of life
on a shelf, or a ruby velvet dress,
cut to the middle of the back,
that can be held on the shoulder by a diamond lizard.

A stone is nearly a perfect secret, always
by itself, though it touches so much, shielding
its heart beyond its strong curtain of ribs
with its arm. Not that I want you
to tell me what you have not told anyone:
how your narrow house propped up window
after window, while the light sank and sank;
why your edges, though they shine,
no longer grip precisely like other people;
how sometimes the house won, and sometimes
the sea-coloured, sea-clear dress,
made new from one over a hundred years old,
that foamed away the true break
in the year, leaving the house
masterless and flagless. That dream
of a too early body undamaged
and beautiful, head smashed to pulp,
still grows in my breakfast cup;
it used up the sore red of the applebox,
it nibbled at the fortnight of our violent
Christmas like a centenarian fir tree.

I talk as if the evenings had been fine,
the roof of my shelves not broken

like an oath on crossed rods,
or I had not glimpsed myself
as the Ides of September, white
at the telephone. Two sounds
spin together and fight for sleep
between the bed and the floor,
an uneasy clicking-to of unsorted
dawn-blue plates, the friction
of a skirt of hands refusing to let go.
And how am I to break into
this other life, this small eyebrow,
six inches off mine, which has been
blown from my life like the most aerial
of birds? If the summer that never burnt,
and began two days ago, is ashes now,
autumn's backbone will have the pallor
of the snowdrop, the shape of the stone
showing in the wall. Our first summer-time
night, we will sit out drinking
on the pavement of Bird Street,
where we kissed in the snow, as the day
after a dream in which one really was
in love teases out the voice reserved for children.

Red Armchair

November will dance his night-journey towards me,
Playing his headlamps in a round robin
From leaf to target-leaf.

September will close the eyes of October's fever;
If my father dies in the wasted arms of summer,
The sudden warm flood of his melted life
Will make new constellations.

Like black and white flowers, family photographs
Sparkle to distract death's attention back to love.

May refuses and June extorts
His purple kiss, fog-bound in a restaurant,
Wet with towels in a frosted bathroom.

Through the cornfield above the hawthorn path,
There is a planter's or a trout-fisherman's lodge
Which could also be the studio of two artists:
One stitches a red arboreal background
To the other's marine imagery,
With the perfection of the unseen body,
Into his voice.

Marconi's Cottage

Small and watchful as a lighthouse,
a pure clear place of no particular childhood,
it is as if the sea had spoken in you
and then the words had dried.

Bitten and fostered by the sea
and by the British spring,
there seems only this one way of happening,
and a poem to prove it has happened.

Now I am close enough, I open my arms
to your castle-thick walls, I must learn
to use your wildness when I lock and unlock
your door weaker than kisses.

Maybe you are a god of sorts,
or a human star, lasting in spite of us
like a note propped against a bowl of flowers,
or a red shirt to wear against light blue.

The bed of your mind has weathered
books of love, you are all I have gathered
to me of otherness; the worn glisten
of your flesh is relearned and reloved.

Another unstructured, unmarried, unfinished
summer, slips its unclenched weather
into my winter poems, cheating time
and blood of their timelessness.

Let me have you for what we call
forever, the deeper opposite of a picture,
your leaves, the part of you
that the sea first talked to.

Captain Lavender

Night-hours. The edge of a fuller moon
waits among the interlocking patterns
of a flier's sky.

Sperm names, ovum names, push inside
each other. We are half-taught
our real names, from other lives.

Emphasise your eyes. Be my flare-
path, my uncold begetter,
my air-minded bird-sense.

Shoulder-Length, Caged-Parrot Earrings

Female eyes—male hand—head full of closed sky—
your throat is still open, though your blood is being dried;
the clock you started up in me, leaves the plainest roses
barely aged.
              You play a secret set of muscles
to bring up a rifle to your cheek, your nights
billow no more than truces, swimming towards daylight.

How lightly then your rich body weighed—tonight
it weighs even less—lowflying as meadow-coloured lead

overflying the white ruin of waves, their feeble climaxes
sucking spring from the ground, a nude beach whose skin
rings out like an Angelus in foliage.
                                        Instead of my Communion watch,
I read the hour in the stubble of your beard.

And *now* begin to live, like a too faithful people, whose last
conquered hamlet has ceased signalling.
                                        Bastille Day
weather covers me like waltzing one-horse towns,
caught in ice, or seeds in mad acceleration, Europe-bound.

Your arms are a living robe of earth you halve
with me so death is a quarantine—only half a death.

You hold me like an unlit cigarette, while you burn
match after match, offer yourself in vain.
                                        You run
star-splashed over the rust which would have gushed
through your hands, six-months' obscure sap-thrust
halts the coastline of your so-called "sea-girt isle,"
so-habitable province, serving up its ultimate smile.

The small green plant in the wound on your wrist
became the lens through which I saw how air could pierce
the ground: how black clouds fattening were slave-joys
you rejected.
            Flight-cramped child, hollowed into airworthy place,
your lingering future is less meditated-necessary
than to sail this eve-of-battle, national holiday, sky.

Self-Portrait in the Act of Painting a Self-Portrait

Unreadable day, you must have sat
too often by the dying. Cracked window,
of no property, you must have heard
the busy tinkle of blood.
Never youthful light,

with the minimum of heat,
you collar whole walls
in the feel of trampled flower-ness,
you traverse the city from end to end
in the sky's safety,
to an outer position of a double
circle of positions,
where her Musehood has withdrawn
into a single drop.

The striped gown she lifts
without the painting looking
is the edgeless gunboat surface
on which we all exist.
Each dusting scrapes an internal winter
from her summer missal, like self-caressing,
long-folded clothes, of a sailor
home from sea.
And no answering of siege
but her ears are closed and her lifetime's gaze,
the forced glint of a real pupil
through the inferior blue,
on her own reflection, undigested,
in the fruit with their dismembered trunks
of faces.

The Worship of the Plough

Only old women like the colour
of deep water, when the body is thrown
into a running stream and becomes
the ghost of a childless person.

A coil of twigs brushing out
the sowing basket, like fluid opium
into a catch-basin, as soon as possible
before noon, before the rice flower forms,

drives the water full into
that absolutely level field,
a field left vacant in me,
well-white and smooth.

I go to the field by night,
to the place where the earth begins
to become moist, to a piece
of moist earth stamped and injured

by rain, like an animal black
on the shoulders. The helpless seed
is as much as can be carried
under the arm, the grain as much

as two hands can hold.
And if it is the bright half
of the month, time is a word
formed from action, measured

in Credos, or Pater Nosters,
an Ave Maria said aloud,
a Miserere. A plough is slightly
passed over the field, in a circle,

from corner to corner, and first light
waters the field's pulse
to its supposed extremities,
a hedge of brambles not fixed

in the ground. When the first
leaf shows, the overburnt blisters
give out little shoots which
weaken it a thread-breadth,

then a finger-breadth, till it is
two-thirds grown. In the marriage
of a grove to a well,
or a well to an image,

trees look their best,
half-wearing the produce
of one field less desired
if you weed your fields in me.

The Good Wife Taught her Daughter

Lordship is the same activity
whether performed by lord or lady—
or a lord who happens to be a lady,
all the source and all the faults.

A woman steadfast in looking is a *callot*
and any woman in the wrong place
or outside her proper location
is, by virtue of that, a foolish woman.

The harlot is talkative and wandering
by the way, not bearing to be quiet,
not able to abide still at home,
now abroad, now in the streets,

now lying in wait near the corners,
her hair straying out of its wimple.
The collar of her shift and robe
pressed, one upon the other.

She goes to the green to see to her geese,
trips to wrestling matches and taverns.
The said Margery left her home
in the parish of Bishopshill,

and went to a house, the which
the witness "does not remember,"
and stayed there from noon
of that day until the darkness of night.

Anon the creature was stabled
in her wits as well as ever she was biforn,
and prayed her husband that she might have
the keys to her buttery to take her meat and drink.

He should never have *my* good will
for to make my sister for to sell
candle and mustard in Framlyngham,
or fill her shopping list with crossbows,

almonds, sugar and cloth.
The captainess, the vowess,

must use herself to work readily
as other gentilwomen doon,

in the innermost part of her house,
in a great chamber far from the road.
So love your windows as little as you can,
for we be, either of us, weary of other.

The Currach Requires No Harbours

Infinite racy stir of water.
The rushes became too dense
in the narrow band of soft earth.

A strange hill rose out of the waves,
the island alive and breathing
with delicacy and a sense of space.

There was no current strong enough
to carry me away. There was no street.
The low-slung horizon, never perhaps before so easy,

sabotaged the once-upon-a-time
in a mood of misgiving or the melancholy
of all fragments. I saw her lover

dressing up as a bird, his bride, his vigour,
her old detached griefs and new overlappings,
before she was betrayed by the bare branches.

Peter Fallon (1951–)

Peter Fallon has had a hand in the publishing history of nearly every poet in this collection. As the founder of the Gallery Press, Fallon has given a public outlet to rising Irish writers who benefit from the authority the press earned early on and has maintained by publishing many of Ireland's best-established voices. Gallery has published works by Seamus Heaney, Derek Mahon, Michael Longley, Nuala Ní Dhomhnaill, and Paul Muldoon—to name only a prominent few. Irish fiction has also felt Fallon's guiding influence; he edited the Classic Irish Fiction series and Brendan Behan's novel *After the Wake*.

Fallon was born in Germany in 1951. His father was an officer in the British Army, and his overseas postings separated the family, leaving Fallon, his mother, and his sister to live for most of Fallon's early life on a farm in County Meath. He left the farm to attend Trinity College, Dublin, where as an undergraduate he founded the Gallery Press in 1970. Two years later Gallery would publish *Co-Incidence of the Flesh*, a volume of Fallon's own poetry. Since then Fallon has produced several volumes of poems that circle close around images of life and death in the farmland of County Meath, to which he returned after graduating from Trinity. His poetry, like Patrick Kavanagh's, derives its significance not by subsuming the sweep of large-scale events, but by slowly teasing quiet universal truths out of the quotidian. In Seamus Heaney's words,

> Peter Fallon's poetry confirms Keats's notion that an intelligence becomes a soul through being schooled in a world of pains and troubles. His poems are soul music of this sort, yet they also belong to a particular place and a particular speech: this way of saying has become a way of seeing, eye to eye with griefs and crises he is emotionally well able for. I admire his singular combination of gravity, obliquity, and tenderness.[1]

In a volume that includes Fallon's elegy to a lost infant, the small particular griefs that Heaney registers seem to make survival possible after great personal loss. One of these poems—"Caesarean," in which efforts to deliver the lambs of a dying ewe end in a mournful silence that nonetheless activates the grave and tender voice of the poet—reveals the essence of Fallon's art by lingering on the sacrifices that "clear the way" for hope, but also for a reconciliation with its loss. Whether he is writing about something as familiar as his own farm or—as in his translation of Virgil's *Georgics*—as distant as classical antiquity, it is this kind of tenderness toward sacrifice and careful attention to the minutiae of experience—both physical and emotional—that distinguish Fallon's poetry.

NOTE

1. Seamus Heaney, quoted on the dust jacket of Fallon's *News of the World: Selected Poems* (Winston-Salem, North Carolina: Wake Forest University Press, 1993).

The Lost Field

for Tanya and Wendell Berry

Somewhere near Kells in County Meath
a field is lost, neglected, let by common law.

When the Horse Tobin went to the bad
and sold a farm and drank the money
there was outlying land we couldn't find.

The maps weren't marked.
My people farmed the farm.
They looked and asked about.
They kept an ear to the ground.

They asked the Horse himself.
He handed out handfuls of fivers,
cups of whiskey, and sang dumb.

His sister said, he's fearless but no fool.
He has a fame for fighting
and carried far from himself
caused cases for the County Nurse.
I can't help you. I pray to God
he'll come back to his senses.

Then I came home from Dublin
I found my place.
My part in this is reverence.

Think of all that lasts. Think of land.
The things you could do with a field.
Plough, pasture or re-claim. The stones
you'd pick, the house you'd build.

Don't mind the kind of land,
a mess of nettles even,
for only good land will grow nettles.
I knew a man shy from a farm
who couldn't find a weed
to tie the pony to.

Imagine the world
the place your own windfalls could fall.

I'm out to find this field, to make it mine.

Fostering

He was lost in the blizzard of himself
and lay, a cold white thing, in a drift
of afterbirth. Another stood to drink dry spins.
I put him with the foster ewe who sniffed

and butted him from his birthright, her milk.
I took the stillborn lamb and cleft
with axe on chopping-block its head,
four legs, and worked the skin apart with deft

skill and rough strength. I dressed the living lamb
in it. It stumbled with the weight, all pluck,
towards the ewe who sniffed and smelled and licked
raiment she recognised. Then she gave suck—

and he was Esau's brother and I Isaac's wife
working kind betrayals in a field blessed for life.

My Care

Sometimes we sit in Phil's
and watch a film, *Hill Street Blues,*
or something. But this is new—
we make a point of turning to the news.

A kidnap, check-points, searches,
killers on the run.
The peace-keeping force can't keep
the peace. The new law is the outlaw gun.

The government debates. Here and there
it seems the talk goes on forever.
Talk, talk, talk . . . After a while
it could be a chimney fire, or bad weather.

Should I do more? Is it enough
to keep a weather eye and talk to friends?

I honestly don't know. All I ever wanted was
to make a safe house in the midlands.

"How's all your care?" I'm asked.
"Grand. And yours?" I don't repeat
my worry for my care, my country. When I go home
the animals are healthy, safe. There's that.

I go inside and stir the fire.
Soon I'm sitting by a riot
of kindling, the soft explosions of seasoned logs.
They have shaken the roots of that familiar quiet.

Caesarean

They were clouds come down to ground to yean,
clouds from which clouds of breathing broke.
We went out, night and day, again and again,
to check or correct. One was clearheaded.
She hadn't the fire to make that kind of smoke.

She stood humpbacked, worn out.
We knew she could no longer carry.
One slim chance. No time to doubt
that we would learn what to do by doing.
We did not hesitate or hurry.

This would take its own time. We lay
her down and gently pulled wool from her sides.
We were clearing the way.
We went for towels, soap, beestings, and the gun.
Her lambs could swim in the rough tides

of her death. We shot her to save some drib
from loss, save her pain. She opened like a bloom
beneath the red script of the scalpel's nib
and we found twins, abandoned, perfectly
formed in the warm nest of her womb.

Premature. Too young to live. We had thought
of everything but this, what could not be guessed.
That she was ready and they were not.
They lay like kindlings dazed by daylight,
the tips of their tongues, their front feet pressed

to dive as one into the waters
of the world. We knelt close to hear a heart,
heard our own and thought it one of theirs. Daughters
of death, they'd never know their gifts,
the everyday miracles of which they were part.

They were part instead of that sacrifice
of the whole. James shrugged a smile.
The lambs pulsed once or twice,
and died. We had done what we could. Now there
were other things to do. We said nothing for a while.

Country Music

He is stuck in the mud of four weeks' rain
backing a tractor through a gap
to fodder beasts. They worship at an altar
of a trailer with the tailboard off,

up to their knees in a muck moraine.
They swish the thuribles of their tails, slap
incense breath on the silage psalter,
grain, torn cud; a smothered cough.

He is stuck in the mud of that profane
ritual, his hundred fathers' handicap
of squids and squalls, and asks for a hand. We falter
and spring free. Now I'm dragging water to a frozen trough,

one with them, their muttered Bollocks, Shits and Fuck its,
a cursèd yoke bent beneath a pair of splashing buckets.

The Old Masters

First there was the wonder of their work.
We read their lines and outlines, took asunder
tops of walls, roof remains. Roofing.
A nailbar underneath a granite hundredweight—
how they got up what we could not get down we wonder

yet. We put our plans away. We rode and tied
the horse of their instruction, used all we could
again. We unclenched fists of ivy, hammered home
spiked stays. Wallplates, rafters, runners—
timber felled and treated from a Loughcrew wood.

We nailed sheet iron, shelter for the hay,
the settled flock. That shed's founded on rock
and finished for our time like the work
of woodsmen who, when they have finished
chopping, chop the chopping block.

Windfalls

He is foddering cattle at a gap,
the windiest part of the field.
They were giving out a gale last night,
strong westerlies and warnings.
"That's the wind that peeled

potatoes in New York!"
It skimmed the top of the Atlantic
and tipped it over Ireland.
The blue twine of a bale
is slicing perished fingers. Some antic

power flipped a roof into an outfield;
an undressed outhouse shivers by its edge.
The dervish dance of sleet and hail
has crusted backs of sheep,
cruel comfort by a whitethorn hedge.

Wild days and wicked weather
cut to the bone—not a lot to set store
by. They're troubled times.
"True. They're troubled times.
There's men dying now never died before."

He has seen it all and lived to tell.
A cloudbreak lightens his eyes' frown.
"Don't fear or fret. They made the back
to bear the burden." He'll saw and split
the windfalls when the wind dies down.

Gravities: West

She is stationed between
a briary
bush and a mountainy ash in the hedge
by the edge of bare grazing,
her eyes to high

heaven, her lamb
nibbling nothing, till they bend
in the breeze and she crops
from wild, western commonage
windfalls that depend

on whatever way the wind blows.

Birches

Shadows cross
the road;
a row of birches:
barcode.

Storm at Sea

Winds ruffle the grey hairs of the waves.
They go against the grain
of fields shut off for silage.
Gulls plant themselves inland
in the grazing. They flourish

when a tractor passes
or an edgy collie grumbles.
They say kissing's out of season
when the flower's gone from the gorse.
Though this'd shear the leaves off ivy

the headland's sanctified by petals.
Can this be happening to happy people?
I think of all I should have told you
as I dream into a summer fire.
And my eyes are hands: they hold you.

from *The Georgics of Virgil*

from Book One

I could, if I'd not seen you back away from such concerns,
regale you with a store of ancient learning.
To begin: grade the threshing floor with the heavy roller,
taking pains to tamp it tight with chalk
so that no growth breaks through and it holds firm and doesn't crumble.
Let no blights of pests or parasites squat there
for often, underground, the mouse sets up his house and home
and the groping mole excavates a bolt-hole
and you come upon a shrew or fieldmouse in a hollow
and other creatures earth turns out—the beetle scurries
to spoil heaps of wheat, the emmet hurries to safeguard against a want
some rainy day.
And so pay close attention when stands of walnut trees

disport themselves with blossoms and their fragrant boughs bend down—
if they produce abundant fruit, your corn crop will be bountiful,
great heat will follow and guarantee your harvest.
But if, instead, a luxury of leaves abounds and throws a shadow over
       everything,
you'll waste a world of time at grinding, end up all chaff and little grain.
I've seen with my own eyes plantsmen steeping seeds
before they set them down, drenching them in saltpetre and the dregs of
       olive oil,
so that their deceiving pods would grow a greater yield,
one that might amount to something over a low flame.
    And I have seen long tried and tested crops begin to fail
where no one took the time each year to sort and save
the finest grain, seed by seed. For that's the way it is—
world forces all things to the bad, to founder and to fall,
just as a paddler in his cot struggling to make headway up a river,
if he lets up a minute, will find himself
rushed headlong back between the banks.

from Book Two

       The farmer's chores come round
in seasons and cycles, as the earth each year retraces its own tracks.
And even while the yard relinquishes the last, lingering leaves
and a northerly divests woods of their panache
the keen countryman is turning thoughts to the year ahead
and all to be done in it: with his curved blade he'll prune each branch
and shape it to his own design. Then, as soon as possible,
he'll rake the bed, set fire to his cuttings,
bring under cover vine supports and then, as late as late can be,
he'll draw the harvest home. Time and again, every year,
vines bow beneath a cloud and sink into the grip of undergrowth—ever
       more to do!
So cast a hungry eye on a big estate if you're inclined,
but tend a small one.

from Book Four

Indeed, if I were not already near the limit of my undertaking,
furling my sails and hurrying prow to shore,
it may be that my song would turn to fruitful gardens and the loving labours

that embellish them, to those rose beds that flower twice a year at Paestum,
to how endive delights in drinking from the brook
whose banks are rife with celery, and how cucumber winds its way
through grass and swells into big bladders; nor would I not speak of
the narcissus, late to leaf, nor of the bendy stem of bear's breech, that is
        acanthus,
or pale ivy, or myrtle that's so fond of shores.
    I mind it well, beneath the arched turrets of Tarentum,
where deep Galaesus irrigates the goldening fields,
I set my eyes on an old man, a Cilician who
had a few forsaken roods that wouldn't feed a calf,
not to mention fatten cattle, and no way fit for vines.
Still, he scattered in the thickset his vegetables and a lily border,
vervain and poppies that you'd eat—in his mind the match of anything
a king might have, and when he came home late at night
he'd pile the table high with feasts no one had paid money for.
    In spring, with roses first for picking, and autumn, apples—
and yet, while winter's hardest frosts were splitting
stones in two and putting stops to water's gallop,
he'd be already clipping hyacinth's frail foliage
and muttering about summer's late arrival and the dallying west winds.
Likewise, his bees were first to breed, first to swarm,
and first to gather honey and have it spilling from the comb.
He had lime trees and a wealth of shrubs in flower,
and as many as the blossoms with which each tree
bedecked itself early in the year was the number ripening later on.
He'd been known in his day to set in rows elms that were well-grown,
a hardy pear, and thorns already bearing sloes,
a plane tree that provided shade for drinking under.
The like of this, however, I must forgo—time and space conspiring
to defeat me—and leave for later men to make more of.

The Company of Horses

They are flesh on the bones
of the wind, going full gallop,
the loan of freedom.
But the company of broken

horses is a quiet blessing.
Just to walk in the paddock;
to stand by their stall.
Left to their own devices

they graze or doze, hock to fetlock
crooked at ease, or—head to tail—
nibble withers, hips and flanks.
They fit themselves flat

to the ground. They roll.
But the mere sound or smell
of us—and they're all neighs
and nickerings, their snorts

the splinters of the waves.
And growing out of morning
mists the ghosts of night
form silhouettes along the ridge,

a dun, two chestnuts,
and a bay. A shy colt stares
and shivers—a trembling like
fine feathers in a sudden breeze

around the hooves of heavy
horses. And the dam,
with foal to foot, steadies herself
to find her bearings,

her ears antennae of attention.
Put your hand towards her head-
collar, whispering your *Ohs* and *Whoa,*
Oh the boy and *Oh the girl,*

close your eyes and lean
your head towards
her quiet head, the way
the old grey mare,

hearing that her hero
joined the sleep
of death, spread her mane
across his breast and began to wail and weep.

Fair Game

As if he'd hit
a wall in air,
or slipped on ice,

or simply tripped mid-
flight,
a pheasant stumbles—

then we hear the shot.
All this beside
that stretch of land

in which a farmhand's
fencing.
We see before we hear

the thud.
He's straining wire
as if he's tuning strings

of a long guitar.
And then we come
across the body—a fluster

in the mud,
a final flare
before the fire falters.

Paul Muldoon (1951–)

When Paul Muldoon wrote a poem to mark the birth of his daughter, he imagined her delivered into a world that is as close as any to the landscape of his own poetry, a country filled with particulars whose very names verge on poetry. "The Birth" conveys the new life it celebrates into what Muldoon calls "the inestimable / realm of apple-blossoms and chanterelles and damsons and eel-spears / and foxes and the general hubbub / of inkies and jennets and Kickapoos with their lemniscs / or peekaboo-quiffs of Russian sable / and tallow-unctuous vernix, into the realm of the widgeon— / the 'whew' or 'yellow-poll,' not the 'zuizin.'"[1]

Like Muldoon's work in general, this is poetry that derives from the sounds of the words, and from the subtle interplay of origins those sounds suggest. The sober Old English roots of *apple* and *blossoms* tether Muldoon's flight into the general hubbub of derivations that move the poem from the Spanish plains where horsemen bred jennets, to the Midwestern plains roamed by the Kickapoos, to the Russian steppe with its winds softened by quiffs of sable. And then, recalling the fundamental business of the poem, Muldoon mixes elements of Anglo-Saxon and Latin derivation to transform that peekaboo-quiff into the fatty sheath covering the newborn, that tallow-unctuous wrap or stole of vernix.

Along the way, the poem's alphabetical ordering of its images emphasizes that Muldoon is himself as likely to have gleaned the words from a foray into the wilds of the *Oxford English Dictionary* as from the world to which its entries refer. At the same time, though, this catalogue of things is like a post-Poundian ABC of the natural world that highlights Muldoon's attention to the material stuff of nature and human culture.

That nervous pleaching of the bookish and the practical is characteristic of Muldoon. In an early poem, he traced his own origin, and the lexical genealogy of his poetic style, back to his parents in "The Mixed Marriage":

My father was a servant-boy.
When he left school at eight or nine
He took up billhook and loy
To win the ground he would never own.

My mother was the school-mistress,
The world of Castor and Pollux.
There were twins in her own class.
She could never tell which was which.[2]

Muldoon was born in 1951 in County Armagh in Northern Ireland. His father, not quite a servant boy, was a day laborer and market farmer, his mother a teacher at a local school. Profiting from its hybrid vigor, Muldoon's poetic language draws as readily from one parent's world as from the other's, taking as much energy from the utilitarian directness of *billhook* and *loy,* a pruning knife and a spade, as from the high classical music of names like Castor and Pollux. This early poem is already conscious of the sonorous effect of clanging the two registers against each other: "She had read one volume of Proust, / He knew the cure for farcy. / I flitted between a hold in the hedge / And a room in the Latin Quarter."[3] Proust, farcy; a hedgerow in County Armagh played against the Parisian labyrinths of the Latin Quarter. Muldoon's version of his childhood concentrates on the space separating his parents' worlds, and finds in between a field on which to play out the struggle Seamus Heaney identifies as the "tension to which all artists are susceptible, just as the children of temperamentally opposed parents are susceptible."

> The child in this case is the poet, and the parents are called Art and Life. Both Art and Life have had a hand in the formation of any poet, and both are to be loved, honoured and obeyed. Yet both are often perceived to be in conflict and that conflict is constantly and sympathetically suffered by the poet.[4]

Like Heaney, who found that "Two buckets are easier carried than one" and so "grew up between,"[5] Muldoon habitually portrays himself as an inhabitant of the gaps between opposing worlds, between art and life, or between Proust and the cure for farcy. In the divided sectarian landscape of Northern Ireland, though, that liminal temper can put the poet in the difficult position of having no place at all, as in "The Boundary Commission" where the poet, facing a boundary like the one that divides Northern Ireland from the Republic, is left to "wonder which side, if any, he should be on."[6]

As a counter to that border homelessness, Muldoon's second commercially published volume, *Mules,* had wondered whether those things in between, like the offspring of a mixed marriage, couldn't "have the best of both worlds."[7] In subsequent poetry, he has been making imaginative mixtures in which that might be possible, even true. His poems have moved from musing on cross-breeds like mules and the children of mixed marriages to a kind of poetic husbandry, grafting language and stories from contrasting cultures onto the stock of his own Ulster upbringing. "The Birth" is a small recent example.

Earlier, "Immram," the long poem in *Why Brownlee Left*—the volume that followed *Mules*—played a turn on the barnyard sense of *mule* by imagining the poet's father employed as the sort of mule hired to do the practical work of smuggling: "This is how it was. My father had been a mule. / He had flown down to Rio / Time and time again."[8] This version of the mule, the smuggler rather than the hybrid, is an apt emblem for another side of Muldoon's work. It's an image that allows him to smuggle his own hallucinatory mix of cultural references into the baggage of the Immram, a genre of medieval Irish poetry that describes a voyage or journey. At the same time, the poem captures a possibility fading away in the distances of family history—a possibility that lived, briefly, in his father's aborted plan to emigrate.

The fleeting, half-remembered quality of hallucination and gesture, though, is only one facet of Muldoon's poetic style. While he reaches for essences that are already nearly lost—like his mother confronting the twin faces in her class, Muldoon, when he imagines kneeling at the grave of his father and mother, can "barely tell one from the other"[9]—his poems hold out the hope that the past those memories contain can still be somehow preserved, inscribed on the present. A poem might provide a way to resuscitate those disembodied voices of one's own past, and of the shared past of literary and popular culture.

Like his later collections, the poems in *Annals of Chile* collect fragments of disappearing memory, sifting them together so that the personal and the popular both become, in an odd sense, literary and open to reading. In "Incantata," an elegy for the artist Mary Farl Powers, Muldoon finds in Powers's artistic medium, intaglio printing, a metaphor for this kind of poetic activity. Powers, the poet, and the reader blur into the *you* of the poem, reflecting the way the sources of memory and the various acts of remembering become almost indistinguishable as time passes. Finally, we can hardly tell one from the other. Each remembering, like each reading of a poem, is analogous to a fresh inking of the intaglio plate, and each produces what printers call a new state. "Incantata" denies the reality of a fate that can keep these things linear and discrete, but the denial opens up a gap between loss and recovery, in which the story of loss becomes its own kind of recovery, in which the poem itself has, to borrow the phrase from "Mules," the best of both worlds.

Notes

1. "The Birth," *The Annals of Chile* (New York: Farrar Straus Giroux, 1994), p. 31.
2. "Mixed Marriage," *Mules* (London: Faber and Faber, 1977), p. 42.
3. Ibid.
4. Seamus Heaney, *The Government of the Tongue* (London: Faber and Faber, 1988), p. xii.
5. Seamus Heaney, "Terminus," *The Haw Lantern* (London: Faber and Faber, 1987), p. 5.
6. "The Boundary Commission," *Why Brownlee Left* (London: Faber and Faber, 1980), p. 15.
7. "Mules," *Mules*, p. 52.
8. "Immram," *Selected Poems* (New York: Noonday Press/Farrar Straus Giroux, 1993), p. 66.
9. "Milkweed and Monarch," *The Annals of Chile*, p. 10.

Wind and Tree

In the way that the most of the wind
Happens where there are trees,

Most of the world is centred
About ourselves.

Often where the wind has gathered
The trees together and together,

One tree will take
Another in her arms and hold.

Their branches that are grinding
Madly together and together,

It is no real fire.
They are breaking each other.

Often I think I should be like
The single tree, going nowhere,

Since my own arm could not and would not
Break the other. Yet by my broken bones

I tell new weather.

The Mixed Marriage

My father was a servant-boy.
When he left school at eight or nine
He took up billhook and loy
To win the ground he would never own.

My mother was the school-mistress,
The world of Castor and Pollux.
There were twins in her own class.
She could never tell which was which.

She had read one volume of Proust,
He knew the cure for farcy.

I flitted between a hold in the hedge
And a room in the Latin Quarter.

When she had cleared the supper-table
She opened *The Acts of the Apostles,*
Aesop's Fables, Gulliver's Travels.
Then my mother went on upstairs

And my father further dimmed the light
To get back to hunting with ferrets
Or the factions of the faction-fights,
The Ribbon Boys, the Caravats.

The Boundary Commission

You remember that village where the border ran
Down the middle of the street,
With the butcher and baker in different states?
Today he remarked how a shower of rain

Had stopped so cleanly across Golightly's lane
It might have been a wall of glass
That had toppled over. He stood there, for ages,
To wonder which side, if any, he should be on.

Why Brownlee Left

Why Brownlee left, and where he went,
Is a mystery even now.
For if a man should have been content
It was him; two acres of barley,
One of potatoes, four bullocks,
A milker, a slated farmhouse.
He was last seen going out to plough
On a March morning, bright and early.

By noon Brownlee was famous;
They had found all abandoned, with
The last rig unbroken, his pair of black
Horses, like man and wife,
Shifting their weight from foot to
Foot, and gazing into the future.

Gathering Mushrooms

The rain comes flapping through the yard
like a tablecloth that she hand-embroidered.
My mother has left it on the line.
It is sodden with rain.
The mushroom shed is windowless, wide,
its high-stacked wooden trays
hosed down with formaldehyde.
And my father has opened the Gates of Troy
to that first load of horse manure.
Barley straw. Gypsum. Dried blood. Ammonia.
Wagon after wagon
blusters in, a self-renewing gold-black dragon
we push to the back of the mind.
We have taken our pitchforks to the wind.

All brought back to me that September evening
fifteen years on. The pair of us
tripping through Barnett's fair demesne
like girls in long dresses
after a hail-storm.
We might have been thinking of the fire-bomb
that sent Malone House sky-high
and its priceless collection of linen
sky-high.
We might have wept with Elizabeth McCrum.
We were thinking only of psilocybin.
You sang of the maid you met on the dewy grass—
And she stooped so low gave me to know
it was mushrooms she was gathering O.

He'll be wearing that same old donkey-jacket
and the sawn-off waders.
He carries a knife, two punnets, a bucket.
He reaches far into his own shadow.
We'll have taken him unawares
and stand behind him, slightly to one side.
He is one of those ancient warriors
before the rising tide.
He'll glance back from under his peaked cap
without breaking rhythm:
his coaxing a mushroom—a flat or a cup—
the nick against his right thumb;
the bucket then, the punnet to left or right,
and so on and so forth till kingdom come.

We followed the overgrown tow-path by the Lagan.
The sunset would deepen through cinnamon
to aubergine,
the wood-pigeon's concerto for oboe and strings,
allegro, blowing your mind.
And you were suddenly out of my ken, hurtling
towards the ever-receding ground,
into the maw
of a shimmering green-gold dragon.
You discovered yourself in some outbuilding
with your long-lost companion, me,
though my head had grown into the head of a horse
that shook its dirty-fair mane
and spoke this verse:

Come back to us. However cold and raw, your feet
were always meant
to negotiate terms with bare cement.
Beyond this concrete wall is a wall of concrete
and barbed wire. Your only hope
is to come back. If sing you must, let your song
tell of treading your own dung,
let straw and dung give a spring to your step.
If we never live to see the day we leap
into our true domain,
lie down with us now and wrap

yourself in the soiled grey blanket of Irish rain
that will, one day, bleach itself white.
Lie down with us and wait.

Quoof

How often have I carried our family word
for the hot water bottle
to a strange bed,
as my father would juggle a red-hot half-brick
in an old sock
to his childhood settle.
I have taken it into so many lovely heads
or laid it between us like a sword.

A hotel room in New York City
with a girl who spoke hardly any English,
my hand on her breast
like the smoldering one-off spoor of the yeti
or some other shy beast
that has yet to enter the language.

The Mist-Net

Though he checked the mist-net
every day for a month

he caught only two tiny birds;
one Pernod-sip,

one tremulous crème-de-menthe;
their tiny sobs

were his mother's dying words:
You mustn't. You mustn't.

Meeting the British

We met the British in the dead of winter.
The sky was lavender

and the snow lavender-blue.
I could hear, far below,

the sound of two streams coming together
(both were frozen over)

and, no less strange,
myself calling out in French

across that forest-
clearing. Neither General Jeffrey Amherst

nor Colonel Henry Bouquet
could stomach our willow-tobacco.

As for the unusual
scent when the Colonel shook out his hand-

kerchief: *C'est la lavande,
une fleur mauve comme le ciel.*

They gave us six fishhooks
and two blankets embroidered with smallpox.

from 7, Middagh Street

Wystan

Quinquereme of Nineveh from distant Ophir;
a blizzard off the Newfoundland coast
had, as we slept, metamorphosed

the *Champlain*'s decks
to a wedding cake,
on whose uppermost tier stood Christopher

and I like a diminutive bride and groom.
A heavy-skirted Liberty would lunge
with her ice-cream
at two small, anxious

boys, and Erika so grimly wave
from the quarantine-launch
as might as truly have been my wife
as, later that day, Barcelona was Franco's.

*

There was a time when I thought it mattered
what happened in Madrid

or Seville
and, in a sense, I haven't changed
my mind; the forces of Good and Evil
were indeed ranged

against each other, though not unambiguously.
I went there on the off-chance
they'd let me try
my hand at driving an ambulance;

there turned out to be some bureau-
cratic hitch.
When I set out for the front on a black burro
it promptly threw me in the ditch.

I lay there for a year, disillusioned, dirty,
until a firing-party

of Chinese soldiers
came by, leading dishevelled ponies.
They arranged a few sedimentary boulders
over the body of a Japanese

spy they'd shot
but weren't inclined to bury,
so that one of his feet stuck out.
When a brindled pariah

began to gnaw
on it, I recognized the markings of the pup

whose abscessed paw
my father had lanced on our limestone doorstep.

*

Those crucial years he tended
the British wounded

in Egypt, Gallipoli
and France, I learned to play

Isolde to my mother's Tristan.
Are they now tempted to rechristen

their youngest son
who turned his back on Albion

a Quisling?
Would their *chaise-longue*

philosophers have me somehow inflate
myself and float

above their factories and pylons
like a flat-footed barrage-balloon?

*

For though I would gladly return to Eden
as that ambulance-driver
or air-raid warden
I will never again ford the river
to parley with the mugwumps
and fob them off with monocles and mumps;
I will not go back as *Auden*.

*

And were Yeats living at this hour
it should be in some ruined tower

not malachited Ballylee
where he paid out to those below

one gilt-edged scroll from his pencil
as though he were part-Rapunzel

and partly Delphic oracle.
As for his crass, rhetorical

posturing, "Did that play of mine
send out certain men (*certain* men?)

the English shot . . . ?"
the answer is "Certainly not."

If Yeats had saved his pencil-lead
would certain men have stayed in bed?

For history's a twisted root
with art its small, translucent fruit

and never the other way round.
The roots by which we were once bound

are severed here, in any case,
and we are all now dispossessed;

prince, poet, construction worker,
salesman, soda fountain jerker—

all equally isolated.
Each loads flour, sugar and salted

beef into a covered wagon
and strikes out for his Oregon,

each straining for the ghostly axe
of a huge, blond-haired lumberjack.

*

"If you want me look for me under your boot-soles";
when I visited him in a New Hampshire hospital
where he had almost gone for a Burton
with peritonitis
Louis propped himself up on an ottoman
and read aloud the ode to Whitman
from *Poeta en Nueva York*.
The impossible Eleanor Clark
had smuggled in a pail of oysters and clams
and a fifth column
of Armagnac.

Carson McCullers extemporized a blues harmonica
on urinous pipkins and pannikins
that would have flummoxed Benjamin Franklin.
I left them, so, to the reign
of the ear of corn
and the journey-work of the grass-leaf
and found my way next morning to Bread Loaf
and the diamond-shaped clearing in the forest
where I learned to play softball with Robert Frost.

*

For I have leapt with Kierkegaard
out of the realm of Brunel and Arkwright

with its mills, canals and railway-bridges
into this great void
where Chester and I exchanged love-pledges
and vowed

our marriage-vows. As he lay asleep
last night the bronze of his exposed left leg
made me want nothing so much as to weep.
I thought of the terrier, of plague,

of Aschenbach at the Lido.
Here was my historical
Mr W. H., my "onlie begetter" and fair lady;
for nothing this wide universe I call . . .

Milkweed and Monarch

As he knelt by the grave of his mother and father
the taste of dill, or tarragon—
he could barely tell one from the other—

filled his mouth. It seemed as if he might smother.
Why should he be stricken
with grief, not for his mother and father,

but a woman slinking from the fur of a sea-otter
in Portland, Maine, or, yes, Portland, Oregon—
he could barely tell one from the other—

and why should he now savour
the tang of her, her little pickled gherkin,
as he knelt by the grave of his mother and father?

*

He looked about. He remembered her palaver
on how both earth and sky would darken—
"You could barely tell one from the other"—

while the Monarch butterflies passed over
in their milkweed-hunger: "A wing-beat, some reckon,
may trigger off the mother and father

of all storms, striking your Irish Cliffs of Moher
with the force of a hurricane."
Then: "Milkweed and Monarch 'invented' each other."

*

He looked about. Cow's-parsley in a samovar.
He'd mistaken his mother's name, "Regan," for "Anger":
as he knelt by the grave of his mother and father
he could barely tell one from the other.

Incantata   *In memory of Mary Farl Powers*

I thought of you tonight, *a leanbh*, lying there in your long barrow
colder and dumber than a fish by Francisco de Herrera,
as I X-Actoed from a spud the Inca
glyph for a mouth: thought of that first time I saw your pink
spotted torso, distant-near as a nautilus,
when you undid your portfolio, yes indeedy,
and held the print of what looked like a cankered potato
at arm's length—your arms being longer, it seemed, than Lugh's.

Even Lugh of the Long (sometimes the Silver) Arm
would have wanted some distance between himself and the army-worms
that so clouded the sky over St Cloud you'd have to seal
the doors and windows and steel
yourself against their nightmarish *déjeuner sur l'herbe:*
try as you might to run a foil
across their tracks, it was to no avail;
the army-worms shinnied down the stove-pipe on an army-worm rope.

I can hardly believe that, when we met, my idea of "R and R"
was to get smashed, almost every night, on sickly-sweet Demarara
rum and Coke: as well as leaving you a grass widow
(remember how Krapp looks up "viduity"?),
after eight or ten or twelve of those dark rums
it might be eight or ten or twelve o'clock before I'd land
back home in Landseer Street, deaf and blind
to the fact that not only was I all at sea, but in the doldrums.

Again and again you'd hold forth on your own version of Thomism,
your own *Summa*
Theologiae that in everything there is an order,
that the things of the world sing out in a great oratorio:
it was Thomism, though, tempered by *La Nausée,*
by His Nibs Sam Bethicket,
and by that Dublin thing, that an artist must walk down Baggott
Street wearing a hair-shirt under the shirt of Nessus.

"D'éirigh me ar maidin," I sang, *"a tharraingt chun aoinigh mhóir"*:*
our first night, you just had to let slip that your secret amour
for a friend of mine was such
that you'd ended up lying with him in a ditch
under a bit of whin, or gorse, or furze,
somewhere on the border of Leitrim, perhaps, or Roscommon:
"gamine," I wanted to say, "kimono";
even then it was clear I'd never be at the centre of your universe.

Nor should I have been, since you were there already, your own *Ding*
an sich, no less likely to take wing
than the Christ you drew for a Christmas card as a pupa
in swaddling clothes: and how resolutely you would pooh-pooh
the idea I shared with Vladimir and Estragon,

with whom I'd been having a couple of jars,
that this image of the Christ-child swaddled and laid in the manger
could be traced directly to those army-worm dragoons.

I thought of the night Vladimir was explaining to all and sundry
the difference between *geantrai* and *suantrai*
and you remarked on how you used to have a crush
on Burt Lancaster as Elmer Gantry, and Vladimir went to brush
the ash off his sleeve with a legerdemain
that meant only one thing—"Why does he put up with this crap?"—
and you weighed in with "To live in a dustbin, eating scrap,
seemed to Nagg and Nell a most eminent domain."

How little you were exercised by those tiresome literary intrigues,
how you urged me to have no more truck
than the Thane of Calder
with a fourth estate that professes itself to be *"égalitaire"*
but wants only blood on the sand: yet, irony of ironies,
you were the one who, in the end,
got yourself up as a *retiarius* and, armed with net and trident,
marched from Mount Street to the Merrion Square arena.

In the end, you were the one who went forth to beard the lion,
you who took the DART line
every day from Jane's flat in Dun Laoghaire, or Dalkey,
dreaming your dream that the subterranean Dodder and Tolka
might again be heard above the *hoi polloi*
for whom Irish "art" means a High Cross at Carndonagh or Corofin
and *The Book of Kells:* not until the lion cried craven
would the poor Tolka and the poor Dodder again sing out for joy.

I saw you again tonight, in your jump-suit, thin as a rake,
your hand moving in such a deliberate arc
as you ground a lithographic stone
that your hand and the stone blurred to one
and your face blurred into the face of your mother, Betty Wahl,
who took your failing, ink-stained hand
in her failing, ink-stained hand
and together you ground down that stone by sheer force of will.

I remember your pooh-poohing, as we sat there on the *Enterprise,*
my theory that if your name is Powers

you grow into it or, at least,
are less inclined to tremble before the likes of this bomb-blast
further up the track: I myself was shaking like a leaf
as we wondered whether the I.R.A. or the Red
Hand Commandos or even the Red
Brigades had brought us to a standstill worthy of Hamm and Clov.

Hamm and Clov; Nagg and Nell; Watt and Knott;
the fact is that we'd been at a standstill long before the night
things came to a head,
long before we'd sat for half the day in the sweltering heat
somewhere just south of Killnasaggart
and I let slip a name—her name—off my tongue
and you turned away (I see it now) the better to deliver the sting
in your own tail, to let slip your own little secret.

I thought of you again tonight, thin as a rake, as you bent
over the copper plate of "Emblements,"
its tidal wave of army-worms into which you all but disappeared:
I wanted to catch something of its spirit
and yours, to body out your disembodied *vox
clamantis in deserto,* to let this all-too-cumbersome device
of a potato-mouth in a potato-face
speak out, unencumbered, from its long, low, mould-filled box.

I wanted it to speak to what seems always true of the truly great,
that you had a winningly inaccurate
sense of your own worth, that you would second-guess
yourself too readily by far, that you would rally to any cause
before your own, mine even,
though you detected in me a tendency to put
on too much artificiality, both as man and poet,
which is why you called me "Polyester" or "Polyurethane."

That last time in Dublin, I copied with a quill dipped in oak-gall
onto a sheet of vellum, or maybe a human caul,
a poem for *The Great Book of Ireland:* as I watched the low
swoop over the lawn today of a swallow
I thought of your animated talk of Camille Pissarro
and André Derain's *The Turning Road, L'Estaque:*
when I saw in that swallow's nest a face in a mud-pack
from that muddy road I was filled again with a profound sorrow.

You must have known already, as we moved from the "Hurly Burly"
to McDaid's or Riley's,
that something was amiss: I think you even mentioned a homeopath
as you showed off the great new acid-bath
in the Graphic Studio, and again undid your portfolio
to lay out your latest works; I try to imagine the strain
you must have been under, pretending to be as right as rain
while hearing the bells of a church from some long-flooded valley.

From the Quabbin reservoir, maybe, where the banks and bakeries
of a dozen little submerged Pompeii reliquaries
still do a roaring trade: as clearly as I saw your death-mask
in that swallow's nest, you must have heard the music
rise from the muddy ground between
your breasts as a nocturne, maybe, by John Field;
to think that you thought yourself so invulnerable, so inviolate,
that a little cancer could be beaten.

You must have known, as we walked through the ankle-deep clabber
with Katherine and Jean and the long-winded Quintus Calaber,
that cancer had already made such a breach
that you would almost surely perish:
you must have thought, as we walked through the woods
along the edge of the Quabbin,
that rather than let some doctor cut you open
you'd rely on infusions of hardock, hemlock, all the idle weeds.

I thought again of how art may be made, as it was by André Derain,
of nothing more than a turn
in the road where a swallow dips into the mire
or plucks a strand of bloody wool from a strand of barbed wire
in the aftermath of Chickamauga or Culloden
and builds from pain, from misery, from a deep-seated hurt,
a monument to the human heart
that shines like a golden dome among roofs rain-glazed and leaden.

I wanted the mouth in this potato-cut
to be heard far beyond the leaden, rain-glazed roofs of Quito,
to be heard all the way from the southern hemisphere
to Clontarf or Clondalkin, to wherever your sweet-severe
spirit might still find a toe-hold
in this world: it struck me then how you would be aghast

at the thought of my thinking you were some kind of ghost
who might still roam the earth in search of an earthly delight.

You'd be aghast at the idea of your spirit hanging over this vale
of tears like a jump-suited jump-jet whose vapour-trail
unravels a sky: for there's nothing, you'd say, nothing over
and above the sky itself, nothing but cloud-cover
reflected in a thousand lakes; it seems that Minne-
sota itself means "sky-tinted water," that the sky is a great slab
of granite or iron ore that might at any moment slip
back into the worked-out sky-quarry, into the worked-out sky-mines.

To use the word "might" is to betray you once too often, to betray
your notion that nothing's random, nothing arbitrary:
the gelignite weeps, the hands fly by on the alarm clock,
the *"Enterprise"* goes clackety-clack
as they all must; even the car hijacked that morning in the Cross,
that was preordained, its owner spread on the bonnet
before being gagged and bound or bound
and gagged, that was fixed like the stars in the Southern Cross.

The fact that you were determined to cut yourself off in your prime
because it was *pre*-determined has my eyes abrim:
I crouch with Belacqua
and Lucky and Pozzo in the Acacacac-
ademy of Anthropopopometry, trying to make sense of the *"quaquaqua"*
of that potato-mouth; that mouth as prim
and proper as it's full of self-opprobrium,
with its *"quaquaqua,"* with its "Quoiquoiquoiquoiquoiquoiquoiq."

That's all that's left of the voice of Enrico Caruso
from all that's left of an opera-house somewhere in Matto Grosso,
all that's left of the hogweed and horehound and cuckoo-pint,
of the eighteen soldiers dead at Warrenpoint,
of the Black Church clique and the Graphic Studio claque,
of the many moons of glasses on a tray,
of the brewery-carts drawn by moon-booted drays,
of those jump-suits worn under your bottle-green worsted cloak.

Of the great big dishes of chicken lo mein and beef chow mein,
of what's mine is yours and what's yours mine,
of the oxlips and cowslips

on the banks of the Liffey at Leixlip
where the salmon breaks through the either/or neither/nor nether
reaches despite the temple-veil
of itself being rent and the penny left out overnight on the rail
is a sheet of copper when the mail-train has passed over.

Of the bride carried over the threshold, hey, only to alight
on the limestone slab of another threshold,
of the swarm, the cast,
the colt, the spew of bees hanging like a bottle of Lucozade
from a branch the groom must sever,
of Emily Post's ruling, in *Etiquette*,
on how best to deal with the butler being in cahoots
with the cook when they're both in cahoots with the chauffeur.

Of that poplar-flanked stretch of road between Leiden
and The Hague, of the road between Rathmullen and Ramelton,
where we looked so long and hard
for some trace of Spinoza or Amelia Earhart,
both of them going down with their engines on fire:
of the stretch of road somewhere near Urney
where Orpheus was again overwhelmed by that urge to turn
back and lost not only Eurydice but his steel-strung lyre.

Of the sparrows and finches in their bell of suet,
of the bitter-sweet
bottle of Calvados we felt obliged to open
somewhere near Falaise, so as to toast our new-found *copains*,
of the priest of the parish
who came enquiring about our "status," of the hedge-clippers
I somehow had to hand, of him running like the clappers
up Landseer Street, of my subsequent self-reproach.

Of the remnants of Airey Neave, of the remnants of Mountbatten,
of the famous *andouilles*, of the famous *boudins*
noirs et blancs, of the barrel-vault
of the Cathedral at Rouen, of the flashlight, fat and roll of felt
on each of their sledges, of the music
of Joseph Beuys's pack of huskies, of that baldy little bugger
mushing them all the way from Berncastel through Bacarrat
to Belfast, his head stuck with honey and gold-leaf like a mosque.

Of Benjamin Britten's *Lachrymae,* with its gut-wrenching viola,
of Vivaldi's *Four Seasons,* of Frankie Valli's,
of Braque's great painting *The Shower of Rain,*
of the fizzy, lemon or sherbet-green *Rana*
temporaria plonked down in Trinity like a little Naugahyde pouffe,
of eighteen soldiers dead in Oriel,
of the weakness for a little fol-de-rol-de-rolly
suggested by the gap between the front teeth of the Wife of Bath.

Of *A Sunday Afternoon on the Island of La Grande Jatte,* of Seurat's
piling of tesserae upon tesserae
to give us a monkey arching its back
and the smoke arching out from a smoke-stack,
of Sunday afternoons in the Botanic Gardens, going with the flow
of the burghers of Sandy Row and Donegal
Pass and Andersonstown and Rathcoole,
of the army Landrover flaunt-flouncing by with its heavy furbelow.

Of Marlborough Park, of Notting Hill, of the Fitzroy Avenue
immortalized by Van "His real name's Ivan"
Morrison, "and him the dead spit
of Padraic Fiacc," of John Hewitt, the famous expat,
in whose memory they offer every year six of their best milch cows,
of the Bard of Ballymacarrett,
of every ungodly poet in his or her godly garret,
of Medhbh and Michael and Frank and Ciaran and "wee" John Qughes.

Of the Belfast school, so called, of the school of hard knocks,
of your fervent eschewal of stockings and socks
as you set out to hunt down your foes
as implacably as the *tóraidheacht* through the Fews
of Redmond O'Hanlon, of how that "d" and that "c" aspirate
in *tóraidheacht* make it sound like a last gasp in an oxygen-tent,
of your refusal to open a vent
but to breathe in spirit of salt, the mordant salt-spirit.

Of how mordantly hydrochloric acid must have scored and scarred,
of the claim that boiled skirrets
can cure the spitting of blood, of that dank
flat somewhere off Morehampton Road, of the unbelievable stink
of valerian or feverfew simmering over a low heat,

of your sitting there, pale and gaunt,
with that great prescriber of boiled skirrets, Dr John Arbuthnot,
your face in a bowl of feverfew, a towel over your head.

Of the great roll of paper like a bolt of cloth
running out again and again like a road at the edge of a cliff,
of how you called a Red Admiral a Red
Admirable, of how you were never in the red
on either the first or the last
of the month, of your habit of loosing the drawstring of your purse
and finding one scrunched-up, obstreperous
note and smoothing it out and holding it up, pristine and pellucid.

Of how you spent your whole life with your back to the wall,
of your generosity when all the while
you yourself lived from hand
to mouth, of Joseph Beuys's pack of hounds
crying out from their felt and fat "Atone, atone, atone,"
of Watt remembering the *"Krak! Krek! Krik!"*
of those three frogs' karaoke
like the still, sad *basso continuo* of the great quotidian.

Of a ground bass of sadness, yes, but also a sennet of hautboys
as the fat and felt hounds of Beuys O'Beuys
bayed at the moon over a caravan
in Dunmore East, I'm pretty sure it was, or Dungarvan:
of my guest appearance in your self-portrait not as a hidalgo
from a long line
of hidalgos but a hound-dog, a *leanbh,*
a dog that skulks in the background, a dog that skulks and stalks.

Of that self-portrait, of the self-portraits by Rembrandt van Rijn,
of all that's revelation, all that's rune,
of all that's composed, all composed of odds and ends,
of that daft urge to make amends
when it's far too late, too late even to make sense of the clutter
of false trails and reversed horseshoe tracks
and the aniseed we took it in turn to drag
across each other's scents, when only a fish is dumber and colder.

Of your avoidance of canned goods, in the main,
on account of the exceeeeeeeeeeeeeeeeedingly high risk of ptomaine,
of corned beef in particular being full of crap,

of your delight, so, in eating a banana as ceremoniously as Krapp
but flinging the skin over your shoulder like a thrush
flinging off a shell from which it's only just managed to disinter
a snail, like a stone-faced, twelfth-century
FitzKrapp eating his banana by the mellow yellow light of a rush.

Of the "Yes, let's go" spoken by Monsieur Tarragon,
of the early-ripening jardonelle, the tumorous jardon, the jargon
of jays, the jars
of tomato relish and the jars
of Victoria plums, absolutely *de rigueur* for a passable plum baba,
of the drawers full of balls of twine and butcher's string,
of Dire Straits playing "The Sultans of Swing,"
of the horse's hock suddenly erupting in those boils and buboes.

Of the Greek figurine of a pig, of the pig on a terracotta frieze,
of the sow dropping dead from some mysterious virus,
of your predilection for gammon
served with a sauce of coriander or cumin,
of the slippery elm, of the hornbeam or witch-, or even
    wych-,
hazel that's good for stopping a haemor-
rhage in mid-flow, of the merest of mere
hints of elderberry curing everything from sciatica to a stitch.

Of the decree *condemnator,* the decree *absolvitor,* the decree *nisi,*
of *Aosdána,* of *an chraobh cnuais,*
of the fields of buckwheat
taken over by garget, inkberry, scoke—all names for pokeweed—
of *Mother Courage,* of *Arturo Ui,*
of those Sunday mornings spent picking at sesame
noodles and all sorts and conditions of dim sum,
of tea and ham sandwiches in the Nesbitt Arms hotel in Ardara.

Of the day your father came to call, of your leaving your sick-room
in what can only have been a state of delirium,
of how you simply wouldn't relent
from your vision of a blind
watch-maker, of your fatal belief that fate
governs everything from the honey-rust of your father's terrier's
eyebrows to the horse that rusts and rears
in the furrow, of the furrows from which we can no more deviate

than they can from themselves, no more than the map of Europe
can be redrawn, than that Hermes might make a harp from his *harpe*,
than that we must live in a vale
of tears on the banks of the Lagan or the Foyle,
than that what we have is a done deal,
than that the Irish Hermes,
Lugh, might have leafed through his vast herbarium
for the leaf that had it within it, Mary, to anoint and anneal,

than that Lugh of the Long Arm might have found in the midst of *lus*
na leac or *lus na treatha* or *Frannc-lus,*
in the midst of eyebright, or speedwell, or tansy, an antidote,
than that this *Incantata*
might have you look up from your plate of copper or zinc
on which you've etched the row upon row
of army-worms, than that you might reach out, arrah,
and take in your ink-stained hands my own hands stained with ink.

The Train

I've been trying, my darling, to explain
to myself how it is that some freight train
loaded with ballast so a track may rest
easier in its bed should be what's roused

us both from ours, tonight as every night,
despite its being miles off and despite
our custom of putting to the very
back of the mind all that's customary

and then, since it takes forever to pass
with its car after car of coal and gas
and salt and wheat and rails and railway ties,

how it seems determined to give the lie
to the notion, my darling,
that we, not it, might be the constant thing.

Hard Drive

With my back to the wall
and a foot in the door
and my shoulder to the wheel
I would drive through Seskinore.

With an ear to the ground
and my neck on the block
I would tend to my wound
In Belleek and Bellanaleck.

With a toe in the water
and a nose for trouble
and an eye to the future
I would drive through Derryfubble

and Dunnamanagh and Ballynascreen,
keeping that wound green.

The Loaf

When I put my finger to the hole they've cut for a dimmer switch
in a wall of plaster stiffened with horsehair
it seems I've scratched a two-hundred-year-old itch

with a pink and a pink and a pinkie-pick.

When I put my ear to the hole I'm suddenly aware
of spades and shovels turning up the gain
all the way from Raritan to the Delaware

with a clink and a clink and a clinky-click.

When I put my nose to the hole I smell the floodplain
of the canal after a hurricane
and the spots of green grass where thousands of Irish have lain

with a stink and a stink and a stinky-stick.

When I put my eye to the hole I see one holding horse dung to the rain
in the hope, indeed, indeed,
of washing out a few whole ears of grain

with a wink and a wink and a winkie-wick.

And when I do at last succeed
in putting my mouth to the horsehair-fringed niche
I can taste the small loaf of bread he baked from that whole seed

with a link and a link and a linky-lick.

Tithonus

Not the day-old cheep of a smoke detector on the blink
in what used to be the root cellar,
or the hush-hush of all those drowsy syrups
against their stoppers

in the apothecary chest
at the far end of your grandmother's attic,
nor the "my sweet, my sweet"
of ice branch frigging ice branch,

nor the jinkle-jink
of your great-grandfather, the bank teller
who kept six shots of medicinal (he called it "therap-
utraquist") whiskey like six stacks of coppers

stacked against him by the best
and brightest of the American Numismatic
Society from the other side of 155th Street,
nor the in-the-silence-after-the-horse-avalanche

spur-spink
heard by your great-great-grandfather, the Rebel yeller
who happened to lose a stirrup
and come a cropper

at the very start of the Confederate offensive in the west,
nor even the phatic

whittering of your great-great-grandmother ("such a good *seat*")
whose name was, of all things, Blanche,

nor again the day-old cheep of a smoke detector on the blink
in what used to be the root cellar
but what turns out to be the two-thousand-year-old chirrup
of a grasshopper.

It Is What It Is

It is what it is, the popping underfoot of the Bubble Wrap
in which Asher's new toy came,
popping like bladder wrack on the foreshore
of a country toward which I've been rowing
for fifty years, my peeping from behind a tamarind
at the peeping ox and ass, the flyer for a pantomime,
the inlaid cigarette box, the shamrock-painted jug,
the New Testament bound in red leather
lying open, Lordie, on her lap
while I mull over the rules of this imperspicuous game
that seems to be missing one piece, if not more.
Her voice at the gridiron coming and going
as if snatched by a sea wind.
My mother. Shipping out for good. For good this time.
The game. The plaything spread on the rug.
The fifty years I've spent trying to put it together.

Harry Clifton (1952–)

Harry Clifton was born in Dublin in 1952. He remained there to attend University College, where he received an M.A. in Philosophy in 1975. Since then his link to home has been stretched. When Clifton wrote to Derek Mahon with a "word about the text" of his 1992 volume *The Desert Route*, a selection of poems written between 1973 and 1988, he explained that the collection has its "beginning and ending in Ireland, with intervening periods of residence in Africa and Asia, and tries to organize fifteen years of travel and experience into an approximate arc . . . There is always, too, the umbilicus back to Ireland."[1]

This early segment of Clifton's approximate arc carried him through two years of teaching in Africa and a period during which he administered aid programs for Indo-Chinese refugees in Thailand. The atmospheres of Africa and the East that derive from these experiences are ambient in the poems of *The Desert Route*. The interplay of the traveler's exoticism and the present "umbilicus back to Ireland" works within the framework of steady yet casual meter and rhyme to give the poems what Mahon calls a "journalistic facility," and an easy authority that is reminiscent of Auden or Fenton.[2]

"The Death of Thomas Merton" is an early example of Clifton's ability to find the lie in expectations of both the exotic and the familiar, "so your mind records it, a sin of omission / In a mystic journal."[3] Evoking the interaction of contradictory traditions and positions that Clifton's poems thrive on, "Merton" anchors its worldly reportage inside the brilliantly recreated consciousness of the Catholic monk and student of Zen, taking Merton's death by electrocution in a bath in Bangkok as an ironic circuit by which the poem can shuttle its energy between the life of the world and the life of the mind. Clifton's particular achievement in this poem lies in the deftness with which he anchors this biographical closure in its historical moment. He manages to retain the tense relationship of biography to history in the poem's easy unbalancing act between corruption and wisdom, or Merton's own roles of priest and "holy fool."

However exotic or familiar the setting, Clifton would continue to demonstrate his dexterous ability to make all places *the* place and no place. Like his Asian and African poems, Clifton's echo of Hart Crane in "Euclid Avenue," for example, projects a voice at once compellingly familiar with its one current place and congenitally alien from all. The same alienation is audible in "Eccles Street, Bloomsday 1982," in which the memory of Joyce and the record he made of their city gives the inhabitants of Dublin a momentary sense of their own reality. But, as Clifton puts it in another poem, it might be that after the years of travel, "Where we live no longer matters / If it ever did. . . ."[4]

NOTES

1. Quoted in Derek Mahon's Foreword to *The Desert Route* (Loughcrew, Ireland: Gallery Press, 1992), p. 9.

2. Ibid.

3. "The Death of Thomas Merton," *The Desert Route*, p. 40.

4. "Where We Live," *Night Train through the Brenner* (Loughcrew, Ireland: Gallery Books, 1994), p. 25.

The Walls of Carthage

Augustine, ended the priest,
Put it all too well.
Here am I, a priest
In my late forties, still

In the desert, still
Relativity's fool.
Wherever it is the will
Of *lycée*, college, school,

As here, God to conclude
From premisses, I am sent
For lectures, *journées d'études.*
Oases of discontent,

Paris, Maynooth, Louvain,
Define my forty-year desert,
My home from home, terrain
Of groundless visions, assert

The same topography
As he, Augustine, mapped.
Godless in Carthage city,
A dialectician, trapped

In a waste of comparisons,
His speech is my speech, speech
Of failure, of a man
Old enough now to preach

Of a God he may never know
Under the sun—a mirage.
So, with Augustine I tell you,
Alexandria, Carthage,

We, in inferior reason,
Travel until we fall,
To compare, in a desert season,
The beauty of their walls.

The Desert Route

Exempted from living, abandoned
To some infinite fascination he has
With a gentle goat by a wall,
Here where the trade routes start

The idiot sits, clad in the cast-offs
Of a town full of tailors,
Unembarrassed
By any such thing as self.

Around him in chaos, preparations
For the desert . . . camels genuflecting
To necessity, loaded with iron bedsteads,
Struggling to rise; and donkeys

With lank, hopeless penises,
Jesuit eyes,
Marking time.
                    In time they all set out,
Like free beings, across a desert

He will never go through again, relieved
Of space and time
To be lost in. Doesn't even notice
How everything still moves outwards

To the same end . . . the camel trains,
The slow asphalting-gangs
On the superhighway, laying down
Lines of purpose, almost merging

At times, almost parallel,
Except at the border, where a soldier
With three stripes, wishing himself elsewhere
Is waving the landrovers on . . .

Monsoon Girl

In the airconditioned drone
Of a room we rent by the hour,
You go to the telephone,
Lovely and naked, to put through a call
For drinks, or hire a car
To take us home.

Your nudity dapples the walls
With shadows, and splashes the mirrors
Like a vision, in the blue light
That bathes you, a pleasure-girl
On a lost planet, sincere
But only at night.

Outside, it will rain
For weeks, months on end. . . .
We'll come here again
As we did before, where Chinese women,
Blank and inscrutable, attend
Nightly to our linen.

We'll come again
In drunkenness, for the child's play
Of lovemaking, or to part the rain
Like curtains of jet beads,
And dream the rainy months away
On pampered beds

Where forgetfulness lies down
With executive power
After hours, in a tangle of legs
And juices, a world turned upside down,
And I feed on the lotus-flower
Of your delicate sex.

At three, we'll be driven back
Through depths of Bangkok
Already tomorrow. There will be roads
Closed, and a dope squad
Flashing its query through windowglass,
Letting us pass. . . .

There will be lights
In Chinatown, sampans on the river—
The poor starting early. Elsewhere the night
Will separate us, having seeded within you
Miscarriage of justice forever,
And the rain will continue.

Death of Thomas Merton

Losing altitude, you can see below you the flames
Of the Tet Offensive, giving the lie to your visions
Of Eastern mystics, like uncensored newsreel
In which the slaves of history are spreading the blame—
And so your mind records it, a sin of omission
In a mystic journal. Meanwhile the wheels
Descend for Bangkok, with one of the Catholic great,
In late October, Nineteen Sixty Eight.

A clean declaration. One a.m. and you're through
The bulletproof glass of security, like a conscience
Filtered through judgement, leaving behind
Temptations you were dead to, years ago—
Hippies frisked for heroin, women and incense
For the American soldiers. Only the life of the mind
You hide on your person—all the rest you can shed
Like a stale narcotic. Shortly, you'll be dead.

So wake before daylight, breakfast alone,
Remembering what you came for. Below you a river
Seeps out of Buddhist heartlands, not in meditation
But in commerce, irrigating zones
Of military fleshpots, where the barges deliver
Rice and Thai girls, and a drifting vegetation
Drags at the chains of destroyers, moored in Bangkok—
And you wait to be chauffeured, at nine o'clock,

To the other side of the city. . . .
                              Spiritual masters
Shrunken to skin and bone, await you in silence
On a neutral ground of Buddhas, golden and hollow,

Smiling from inner space, beyond disaster
To an old complacency. Starving for non-violence
In saffron robes, their shavenheaded followers
Beg on the streets. From an airconditioned car
You can see them in passing, as cut off as you are—

Cut off from each other, disconnected by history
In Paris and Calcutta, linked alone by the airspace
Of a temporal pilgrimage. Diplomatic immunity,
This is your saving grace—to restore mystery
To a common weal, and resurrect from disgrace
The nonpolitical, kneeling in the unity
Of a moment's prayer, with the Dalai Lama and wife—
For the flash-photographers of *Time* and *Life*.

Judas has other betrayals. At your last supper
In a Hungarian restaurant, among friends in Bangkok,
It's left to the Chinese waiter to overprice you—
So unworldly. You can switch from corruption
Suddenly into wisdom, through an electric shock
Turning your hair white, resolving your crisis
Into anticlimax. But it leaves you dead,
With a powerline shortcircuited through your head. . . .

A small embarrassment, for the United States—
Your motherhouse at Gethsemani awaits
Its anti-hero. A gaggle of monks are released
To New Haven for the day, to identify and separate
Among the Vietnam dead, the maimed in crates
From an Air Force plane, this body of a priest
And holy fool—from beyond the international
Dateline, and the jungle war with the irrational.

The Distaff Side

Elopement and civil wedding . . . the sham squire
Looks back on it all, remembering Guadeloupe
Where they lived on nothing, cooked and sang for the troops—
Himself and this runaway daughter. God knows why

They ever came back, to dampen the fires
Of passion in Ireland, to put down roots and die.

Because *she* wanted to. Because it made sense.
Because, as she keeps repeating, nothing intense
Goes on forever. . . . Restless, he hears from bed
The brokenhearted weeping of a daughter
And wishes he was somewhere else instead
Like back in the army, ladling stew before slaughter

From an old field-kitchen, safe in the middle of war—
But no such luck. The pillowtalk of a spouse
So down to earth she makes even sex a chore
Admonishes, chides, "The day you become breadwinner
I'll pacify children . . ." sends him out through the house
As nude as a ghost. Already, tomorrow's dinner

Bleeds on the flagstones, waiting to be skinned
From a day of boyish hunting. . . .

How did the years
Imprison him here, in an Irish house and grounds,
With a redhaired wife, who sees him when she can—
Divorced from history, stalking Wicklow deer,
A jealous minder of children, a kept man?

"Tomorrow I'll take you fishing . . ." he quiets his daughter
While out on the Eastern Marches, wholesale slaughter
Drains the silos. . . . Nobody knows him, his rages
Are all domestic, tantrums at bad little girls
Upsetting the basket of eels he gathered for ages
And starting their passionate journeys back to the world.

Euclid Avenue

after Hart Crane

The blazing stanchions and the corporate lights—
Manhattan over the bridge, from Brooklyn Heights—
Were energies like yours, without a home,
That would not be condensed inside a poem

But endlessly dispersed, and went to work
For time and money, hovering over the masses
Like terrible angels. . . . Now, I stand in New York
And watch those energies sweat themselves out, like gases

Through a subway grille, to keep the derelicts warm
In a new depression. Or, at station bookstalls,
Calm at the eye of the electric storm
I drink your words, like prohibition alcohol

Capital hides from itself. On soundless trains
Through Middle America, citizens fishing in creeks
That rise and flow nowhere, disappear again
In a private wilderness you were born to seek

And lose yourself in. But none of them will thank you—
They, nor the desolate children that they raised
On a thousand streets called Euclid Avenue
For travelling inwards, damning with faint praise

The forces that they freed, to blast through gravity
Into a loveless, extraterrestrial space
Like night bus stations, galaxies of strays—
The sons and daughters of the human race.

Eccles Street, Bloomsday 1982

Onesided, stripped of its ghosts,
The half that was left of Eccles Street
Stood empty, on that day of days
My own unconscious feet
Would carry me through
To a blind date, or a rendezvous.

Invisible pressure, invisible heat
Laid down the blue coordinates
Of an Hellenic city
From Phoenix Park to the Merrion Gates,
Where disconnected, at one remove
From wisdom, or eternal love,

A million citizens worked, ate meals,
Or dreamt a moment of Joyce,
And felt themselves wholly real,
The equals of fate, the masters of choice,
As I did too, on Eccles Street,
Before ever you and I could meet

In the larger scheme. . . . Coincidence
Ruled invisibly, the casual date
Upstaged by Greek infinities
Moving among us like common sense,
Imprisoning, setting me free
To dream and circumambulate

In a myth too young to be formed.
I would build it myself, from the ruined door
Of Bella Cohen's bawdyhouse,
From other basements, other whores
Unbuttoning their blouses
Forever, while traffic swarmed

And the lights outside turned green and red
On shifting planes of reality—
And you, eternal student, read
Of Joyce in the National Library,
Or stood in the crowd, my love unseen,
At the unveiling in Stephen's Green.

An hour went by, on Eccles Street—
Two drunks, at ease in the Mater portals,
Swigged, and sang Republican songs.
I watched a line of taxis wait
And saw where real grass had sprung
Through mythic pavements, already immortal,

Green as life, and unresearched.
I had come, only that morning,
From Ringsend docks, and Sandymount Church,
Along the arc of odyssey,
With my invisible yearning
To break the circle, set myself free,

As you had yours, until one day
In the prefigured city,
Where every step is a step of fate
And recognition comes only later,
We would meet, you and I,
Weigh anchor at last, and go away.

Firefly

It was zigzagging along
In the dusk, when I snatched it

Out of its path of flight
Like the hand of God

Delaying it, temporarily,
Between the why and the wherefore

Of my cupped palms
That glowed, like a votive lamp

Pulsating yellow, so I knew
It was alive in there

In the attitude of prayer
I carried ahead of me

On the latening road—a principle,
A mustardseed of light

That belonged in the dance of atoms
Around me, energies

The dark released
And I, too, had a hand in.

Where We Live

Where we live no longer matters
If it ever did, the difference
Between North and East, South and West,
Belfast Central, or Budapest,
Currency changed, like innocence,
For the life that was going to be ours.

Let us admit it. There are powers
No border can contain.
They sit with us, the uninvited guests,
Wherever our table is laid,
Accepting a second coffee,
Awaiting the end of the story.

They were in ourselves
From the beginning. Dark and placeless,
Tropic suns, or the greys of Ulster
Meant nothing to them. Your skies, my skies,
Everywhere in between
Was a place they could work unseen.

Here, they can rest a while
In our latest exile. Groundless,
Taking root anywhere,
Living on thin Italian air,
Our house is their house,
With the bats and the swallows,

Angels and demons, ghosting
The warm red sandstone
Of borrowed quarters. Leave us alone!
Wherever life is an open question
They have beaten us to it
Already, come into their own.

They are the lightnings
That transfigure us, our troubles—
Homeless, the ancient weather
That travels inside us
And breaks out, here or there,
The days we despair of each other.

In Hoc Signo

The straws in the wind—
Who feeds on them? Nobody here
Is poor enough,

Thank God. The starving cats
And mongrels have the rubbish bin
And the poor in spirit

Seek solace in the bar.
The door of the church is always locked
Since the chalice was stolen,

But the heraldic animals
Stabled for winter
Are safe as in Ark or Manger.

Christmas approaches.
Blue Adriatic mists
Creep inland, up our valley—

The winds from Greece
Reversing themselves, occluding us
At the desired height

Of contemplation.
Plato and the Gospels,
She and I—what more do we need

Than our two bodies, our two minds,
To link each other
And the world we left behind?

Sometimes, out of the blue,
A telephone rings, rings off—
The outer world trying to get through,

The buzz and static
Of interconnected voices—
Europe, America . . .

Then nothing. Silence.
A horsebell in the mists,
Time dripping from the eaves,

The IN HOC SIGNO of the bar,
The closed church—
And a cripple, playing Patience

Under dirty yellow streetlights,
Greeting us in the English
He learned as a prisoner of war.

Taking the Waters

There are taps that flow, all day and all night,
From the depths of Europe,
Inexhaustible, taken for granted,

Slaking our casual thirsts
At a railway station
Heading south, or here in the Abruzzo

Bursting cold from an iron standpipe
While our blind mouths
Suck at essentials, straight from the water table.

Our health is too good, we are not pilgrims,
And the nineteenth century
Led to disaster. Aix, and Baden Baden—

Where are they now, those ladies with the vapours
Sipping at glasses of hydrogen sulphide
Every morning, while the pumphouse piano played

And Russian radicals steamed and stewed
For hours in their sulphur tubs
Plugged in to the cathodes of Revolution?

Real cures, for imaginary ailments—
Diocletian's, or Vespasian's.
History passes, only the waters remain,

Bubbling up, through their carbon sheets,
To the other side of catastrophe
Where we drink, at a forgotten source,

Through the old crust of Europe
Centuries deep, restored by a local merchant
Of poultry and greens, inscribing his name in Latin.

The Canto of Ulysses

As the eye reads, from left to right,
Ulysses' canto, what comes next,
The day, already spread like a text
On the ceiling above me, asks to be read.
Anxiety, or increasing light,
Whatever wakes me, fills my head
With the oceanic billows
Of a slept-in marriage bed.

The shutters go up, like thunder,
On the street below. If the soul fed
On coffee, aromatic bread,
Niceties raised to the power of art,
We would long ago have knuckled under
To perfection, in the green heart
Of Italy, settled here,
And gone to sleep in the years.

But what was it Dante said
About ordinary life? My mind wanders
Like Ulysses, through the early sounds,
A motor starting, taps turned on,
Unravelling Penelope's skein,
Unsatisfied, for the millionth time,
With merely keeping my feet on the ground—
As if I could ever go home!

Money, like a terrible shadow,
Unsuccess, and middle age,
Darken my vision of the page
I scan from memory, where it says
Women will all be widows

To the quest, neglected fathers,
Ageing, live out lonely days,
And coastlines merge with each other.

Sound of a passing train at dawn
Through Umbrian fields, of wheat and vines,
Through cloisters and bird sanctuaries,
Feeding on overhead powerlines,
Obsesses me, like the need to be gone,
Vitality, or cowardice,
The sail of Ulysses, west of the sun,
Dwindling in ptolemaic skies.

What did you say to me last night?
"Where you go, I go." Sleep on that
While I watch you, curled,
Uxorious, my one satisfaction
At the heart of the known world,
Stippled with mediterranean light,
Its yellow streaks already latent
With afternoon heat, and stupefaction.

Any day now, we hand back the key
To habit, peace, stability,
The seasonal round, festivities
Of wine and cherry. Think of the fuss
Of what to take, and leave behind—
Shade for the soul, our miniature trees
Of olive, oak, and southern pine—
Before the seas close over us.

The Black Book

About the terrible politics of this island
Let us educate ourselves anew. Hand it to me,
The black book you were reading, with the names,
The negotiations, the graves dug up

In the lonely places, bogs and border marches,
And the executioners, doing time
In the open prison of their own kitchens,
Reminiscing, over hot strong cups of tea.

The names, of course, are changed, and the places
Falsified. Where X met Y
One ancient day, to seal the fate of Z,
Is a grey zone of compromise now,

Or call it a housing estate. I grew up next door
To murder. You combed your hair
With soldiers in the mirror, closing in.
Let us not argue then, on the lesser points,

But hand me the little black book, with the names, the places,
Like a lost undersea continent
Rising forever, to rediscover itself
In our own eyes, and call itself Ireland.

Gerald Dawe (1952–)

Gerald Dawe was born in Belfast in 1952. He left Northern Ireland in 1974 and lived in Galway until 1992, when he moved to Dublin. Where he might feel at home is more difficult to say. Dawe left Belfast because of the way the sectarian tensions, at a peak in the late 1960s and early 1970s, were affecting the shape of lives in the city. But unlike Michael Longley Dawe has never been able to identify fully with the life he created for himself in the West of Ireland. "Maybe the vagrant Huguenot blood in my veins and the mixtures of Irish and Scottish also there disqualify me from ever having a clear sense of home," he writes. If his displacement entailed "no great movements across hemispheres or continents, just a subtle seachange through those complicated and sometimes deadly chambers that divide one part of this island from another," that is not to say it is of less significance than that of the thousands of Irish émigrés. The idea of home has become for Dawe "both smaller and greater; less centred on the one particular place and more open to elsewhere without losing sight, at the same time, of what actually makes this place or that *a home*."[1]

Not surprisingly, given this uncentered appreciation of home, Dawe's most intricate views of Ireland have been those from far away. His own "childhood 'British' way of life," for example, drew into clearer focus during his travels in Australia. That former British colony "had a feel of sturdy expectations and civic-spiritedness that bears close resemblance to the '50s in which I grew up in Belfast and the seaside resorts I went to every year on the north-east coast."[2] In "The Likelihood of Snow / The Danger of Fire," written at Canberra in the Australian Capital Territory, Dawe reflects on the various sorts of distance that separate him from the community of Northern Ireland and asks himself "why it could be so easy to forget about home / and all the mumbo-jumbo about one's *people*."[3] It *could* be easy, but apparently isn't. Dawe's thoughts, among Australia's "emblazoned butterflies" and "imperious cockatoos," flutter continually back to Northern Ireland and its people. But if, from this distance, Dawe's sense of isolation remains acute, the distance nonetheless gives him the perspective to see isolation itself as the characteristic effect of a Northern Irish sensibility. His people, Dawe concludes, are ultimately unknowable because they keep to themselves, "or, like me in another hemisphere, / they disappear in dreams."[4]

The dreams in his poems are ultimately the ones Dawe shares with others who have, literally or symbolically, left home. "When I left the North," he says in the preface to a volume published in 1995, " . . . I took with me a battery of images which would eventually surface in my own poetry."[5] Dawe's recent poems still hold on to these images like the outdated maps remembered by "Refugees": "Old Europe— / the rough edges, borders; the spaces, countries."[6] In "The *de facto* Territory" Dawe makes it clear that these old maps bear an uneasy relation to his present landscape.

"In Memory of James Joyce" expresses a similar regret over the fading of a distinctly literary past. The poem recalls a Bloomsday Dawe spent in Galway, where instead of tracing the steps of Leopold Bloom as Dubliners do "schoolgirls in greys and blacks / sped past with U2 badges on racing-bikes." The city's apparent indifference to the day leads Dawe to question the value of Joyce's work:

> The pity is, would it have been any
>
> different if they had known about
> your woman, Nora, or how you both managed
> moving from flat to flat
> and put their country on the map
>
> of a mostly indifferent universe?

The pity built into Dawe's question implies a negative answer, but if Joyce offers little to the ordinary citizens of Galway in this poem, he still warrants the special respect of fellow artists. Dawe ends the poem paying those respects. "I tip my hat as you pass by," he writes, "a preoccupied man in shabby gutties."

Along with his poetry, Dawe, who teaches at Trinity College, Dublin, is acclaimed for his insightful, if contentious, literary criticism. He is, as Seán Dunne writes, "one of those rare critics no society can afford to be without, one who keeps the lines of communication open and whose aims are essentially earthed in political decency and in a belief in the shaping power of the imagination."[7]

NOTES

1. "Going Places," *False Faces: Poetry, Politics and Place* (Belfast: Lagan Press, 1994), p. 13.
2. "Thinking of Oz," *False Faces*, p. 96.

3. "The Likelihood of Snow / The Danger of Fire," *Sunday School* (Loughcrew, Ireland: Gallery Press, 1991), p. 28.

4. Ibid, pp. 28–29.

5. *Against Piety: Essays in Irish Poetry* (Belfast: Lagan Press, 1995), p. 14.

6. "Refugees," *Heart of Hearts* (Loughcrew, Ireland: Gallery Press, 1995), p. 33.

7. Seán Dunne's assessment of Dawe, drawn from a review in the *Irish Times*, is quoted on the jacket of *Against Piety*.

Secrets

I was coming-of-age in a sparse
attic overlooking the sluggish tide.

Down the last flight of stairs
a grandfather clock struck

its restless metronome to those
who went about their business

with a minimum of fuss. My
puritan fathers, for instance,

stumbled from separate beds
and found their place

under the staunch gaze
of monumental heroes, frozen

stiff in the act of sacrifice;
they had always been

tightlipped about God-
knows-what secrets.

The Desert Campaign

On a day-trip to Donaghadee
I am free and easy,
scanning eyes over the bay
like a real sea-captain.

There certainly are women
in floral printed skirts
and, settling through news-
papers, grandmothers with

bright blue rinses chat
about making do and watch

stretch-marked daughters
carry on the way they used to,

as the various husbands,
unaccustomed to the sun,
unbutton shirt-fronts or stand
giddily at the water's edge.

I am dive-bombing
beneath the promenade wall,
leaving in my wake
a ruined city and on

my bended knees
discover an oasis
where sultry hussies drive
shaggy beasts to drink.

The Lundys Letter*

You staged the ultimate *coup de grâce*
for the Union's son turned republican.
I can see you shivering in the cold
of an East Belfast morning, outside
school, the bikes upended, the quad
blown by a dusty wind, and rows of
windows, some cellophaned, gaze
back at the encroaching estate.

Even your voice was different, haughty
we thought, the grand dismissive way
you demonstrated learning, or in *Tartuffe*
worked a subtle authority over our
ragged rebelliousness that we
should sit through such performances
of high art in a secondary school!

A generation growing but no hard-hats
for us or the miserable one-step up

a slippery ladder to civil service.
I don't know where you went; we got
lost in London or tried our wings
on an amalgam of desperate love
and politics at the new university.

And then the next time it was a warm
summer's day at Woolworth's when
the ground shook and a tailor's dummy
crashed through sheets of glass,
and there was hardly time to ask
how you were keeping as shoe-boxes flew
all over the place and the bomb
finished its work on down High Street.

Walking to the Dole, the clang in my ears
of sirens and trampling feet,
it was another lock of years
before I saw you in a pub by chance,
barely the same, chose not to recognise—
I only bear witness now to what was,
and hear your prefect's voice of derision
shout to a smoking third-form class.

Outside Queens

The trees were probably elm
but for what we knew oak would do,
sitting on the low wall a few
years before it all happened,
the great redbrick façade behind
its sweep of contemplative lawn.

We read what we could get
our hands on and walked the town
regurgitating it till that day
I remember your choleric outburst
in the library, *"Yeats*

never drank from the well of the People!,"
the hush as the rest of us shifted
in those awkward moulded seats.

Gangling in the sun later, a busy
afternoon, the road full of students,
it sounded as if a war-cry
had burst from your tautened lips
against The Books, bloody dreams,
the interrogated silence outside Queens.

Carlyle in Ireland

Carlyle holds his head.
The coach bumps towards Galway.
In the fields the dead
glisten and slowly wave.

The desolation he can
handle. In Eyre Square
pigs tethered to the Lord's
railings, shrouded leaves.

"I can taste the Atlantic
far better than take in
the gabble of people
shawled in such resentment.

These letters must
tell the truth of my
anger at their disorderly
rage.
            Or did I dream it?"

A face like sea-foam
all skull and bone,
mouthing for pity's sake
in the middle of a field

choked with weed.
"Oh for men, pickmen,
spadesmen, and masters
to guide them!"

The Likelihood of Snow/
The Danger of Fire

Around five, in the next garden, a rooster
starts up his rusty banter and the first flight,
coast to coast, soars through an endless sky.
We are hatching in the bedroom downstairs
our special dreams, maybe of home—who knows?—
heads together, facing, I suppose, the sun,
which has left you to this evening's viewing,
with a good fire down and the curtains drawn
on shining streets and the likelihood of snow.
Sprinklers will soon play across the impeccable lawns
and the puppetry of emblazoned butterflies begin
with air-conditioning, humming like a ship's engines,
while the two imperious cockatoos
take to the surrounding suburban trees.

I've been asking myself, head crooked in arms,
why it could be so easy to forget about home
and all the mumbo-jumbo about one's *people*.
Mine, if such they are, look for all the world
like great Deniers, the staunch, unflappable self-
deceit of always seeming to be in the right
and the fear of being found out that they are not.
I have watched since childhood their marches and parades,
with banners aloft, swords and bibles displayed,
and I have passed the banks of clipped hedges, the front rooms
with oval mirrors and cabinets full of photographs—
the husband in the Army, son in the Boys' Brigade,
a fallen brother, the Royal Wedding—
and never known my *people* since they kept

to themselves in desperate innocence,
or persist behind transparent walls to explode in hate,
or, like me in another hemisphere,
they disappear in dreams:
as stewards on ocean-going liners,
managers of building societies,
multi-national executives,
further up or down the scale of things,
the accents mellow to a faint American twang
or a touch of the Anglo,
we to whom no surface is deep enough
grin and bear the nonchalant enquiry,
"Where do you come from?"
and know that the only real news here today
is the danger of fire.

Canberra

A Story

What caught my eye
was the white enamel of the bath
installed by the black lake
for cattle to drink, in safety.
We lived there for a time
and I remember being told
about this pike
that was supposed to have
scoured the lake bottom for years
till one day a visiting boy
eagerly fished him up
to the incredulous daylight
and inside they discovered
barbed-wire, a rat's bones.
I think of it laid out
on the formica table-top,
a hellish, aggrieved mouth,
and the stench simply everywhere.

The *de facto* Territory   *for Dennis O'Driscoll*

The truth is, with all this going
back and forth, I end up imagining
the midlands as the Urals or the Steppes;
really I am passing through
the wheatfields of somewhere else.

Backpackers discuss itineraries
and their impressions of France;
behind the ruins of a Big House
brand new bungalows appear.
I'm lost in the morning's paper—

but did they make Tipperary
or chance the *Express* to Belfast?

The Third Secret

The seas on either side of us
are slowly meeting, so they say.

I think we are quite simply
returning to constituent parts,

whether long in the tooth
or weak in the heart.

Crete Summer

Amongst these, my fellow humans,
are the silver-bespectacled Dutch,
overweight Germans, and bright Danes.
We speak in smiles and nods,

read the same pulp fiction, drink *bier*
or bottles of water and look aghast

at tree-wasps, armies of ants;
the need to "Please not flush papers away."

Clothes, towels, and swimsuits dry
on ornamental hedges and amazing bushes.
For three weeks we are tinkers
with nothing left to lose.

The humdrum of language is
pierced suddenly with Greek laughter
and an English mother's voice
gives her daughter what-for.

Last night the grey sirocco
descended on island and bay; an owl
eclipsed our whitewashed courtyard.
Today only a tiny greenfly lands

on my pale thigh. I lie, silently
with those who have, for the time being,
little on their minds—veterans
idling under an inescapable sun.

In Memory of James Joyce

Just thought I'd drop you a line
given the fact that I happened to be walking
the same streets as you once did.
It was, of course, raining,

and down by Nuns' Island the houses faded
to a faint pointillist light.
At the derelict mill up-for-sale,
schoolgirls in greys and blacks

sped past with U2 badges on racing-bikes.
They'll keep going till they are far
from Rahoon, Wellpark and Castlelawn.
The pity is, would it have been any

different if they had known about
your woman, Nora, or how you both managed
moving from flat to flat
and put their country on the map

of a mostly indifferent universe?
Heading into town, the Curragh Line
is like the road in *The Great Gatsby*
except the billboard here is the dump.

Every house is an El Dorado
while an ancient tower teeters on the brink.
So much for the past. We must make
our own choices and live with them—

immaculate blinds and ornamental brasses—
as the Corrib seeps into glinting lakes.
What would you think of the new estates
hugging either shore, or the Telecom mast

picking up our fervent calls across the water
to a son that's gone, or a daughter?
I tip my hat as you pass by,
a preoccupied man in shabby gutties.

    Bloomsday, Galway 1987

The Night's Takings

for Cathal McCabe

The whores had disappeared by the time
we got there and the barman smiled,
totting up the night's takings.
So here we were, two Northern lads perched
on high stools in the middle of Europe,

the last snow black on the cobblestones,
a way down marble stairs to the seen-
it-all-before janitor, the ballroom kitted
out for ex-party types, the local mafia,
as we looked along the longest street—

the shoplights dimmed, the watchful mannequins,
the clackety-clack of the military,
the wary taxi, the metallic sky,
and the inevitable echo
that is neither here nor there.

Text Messages

Sloe gin. Single malt. The occasional grappa.
Wine from Lorenzo, wine from the valley. Marsala.

Open all the doors. Open all the windows, the sun's caught
up with us in our mountainy retreat.

The arrow garden defies the landslides, the wind
and the rain. Your home is built on solid ground.

The poignancy of driftwood, the cloud formation.
Snow on the mountaintops and, on the lake, drifting swans.

And then, before you know it, the windows shuttered,
the rain spills down through the brilliant sunshine.

All the shadows are angles you half imagine
in the actual rise and fall of this home from home.

Amidst the farmhouses and vine groves,
the dark valley, you knock the light off.

At the airport you go your separate ways.
Who will turn back a second time to wave?

An Evening in the Country   *for Olwen*

Their children run free in the adjoining field
where an abandoned car sits in a heap.
I am cutting back dead branches from a tree.

A tractor edges along our common boundary.
That would be Tuam over there, but I still can't tell
for certain the direction I am facing.

A Child of Prague floats in its red
alabaster cloak; creamery lorries arrive at dawn,
and there is a man who sits by the grave

of his young wife beseeching her to come home.
The hedges bristle with cobwebs and dew,
bramble swings out from a collapsed wall.

I hack my way through, clearing the garden.
The children's voices rise and fall;
we lift up our heads for a second and listen.

A magpie cackles, its dusty tail up in arms
with this rook circling overhead. Does one know
the other by wingspan, the gimp of its beak?

Beneath me, lost for words, you play.
It's coming on evening in the country,
swallows showing off in the lucid light.

Nuala Ní Dhomhnaill (1952–)

When Máire Mhac an tSaoi asked herself whether writing poetry in Irish is nothing more than a "benign anachronism," her argument to the contrary found its strongest evidence in the work of Nuala Ní Dhomhnaill. "No poet could be more rooted in her medium than Nuala," Mhac an tSaoi wrote in 1995,

> no poet's work demonstrates more clearly than hers that particular access to an ancient, but intensely living and relevant, world, which is the unique property of the Irish language; yet no poet writing in Ireland today has a greater following among fellow-poets writing in English than she. The primeval universality of her themes breaks through the magic thicket of her rich and complex language, an ominous folk-force that invades the consciousness and takes over, at once liberating and appalling.[1]

Ní Dhomhnaill's popularity among English-language poets in Ireland probably accounts in some degree for the strength of her influence outside Ireland and for the acute attention translators have given her poems. As Mhac an tSaoi points out, "she translates splendidly,"[2] in part, one assumes, because the vigor of her Irish verse has encouraged translation by some of Ireland's most talented contemporary poets—Seamus Heaney, Michael Longley, Derek Mahon, John Montague, and Medbh McGuckian, to name only a sonorous few. In Paul Muldoon, Ní Dhomhnaill has found the most sympathetic translator imaginable. The match of the two poets' voices is so striking that Muldoon's translation of Ní Dhomhnaill's Irish in *The Astrakhan Cloak* is generally spoken of in critical circles as a collaboration. Muldoon's earlier translation of her "Ceist na Teangan" as "The Language Issue" catches something of both the risk and the expanded possibility Ní Dhomhnaill courts when she edges her Irish poems out into the world to find their English correlatives. Though Ní Dhomhnaill's poems have for the most part landed in very congenial laps, and come with a snug rightness into English, Mhac an tSaoi is probably onto something when she says they could not have been conceived in English, "any more than you could create an original Henry Moore in papier mâché."[3]

Early in Ní Dhomhnaill's life Irish became her language of strength and of private thoughts. Like Medbh McGuckian, she identifies herself with a particular place of strength, what bullfighters call the *querencia*. In her case this space is the Gaeltacht region of County Kerry. Ní Dhomhnaill finds in her family's moving from England to Kerry the beginning of her sense of affiliation, of being inside a particular culture:

> When I arrived in Kerry after living in my own world in a big garden on Sutton Manor Coalfield, there were other little girls my age that I could play with—the first time ever—and also the landscape and the language, and I fell madly in love with it. My parents, who were both doctors, formed a little Irish enclave on a Lancashire coal mine, but we were always outsiders. In Kerry I was related to everybody, so there was a real sense of belonging. I still find that when I come back from Kerry I can write poems more easily.[4]

Despite this talk of ease, Ní Dhomhnaill's poems have the atmosphere of conversations that don't come out easily at all, but build and build until the pressure forcibly extrudes a poem. As a schoolgirl she kept her diary in Irish to cloak her thoughts in an extra layer of privacy. Something in the privacy of the worlds her poems depict suggests that Irish may still have the same protective function. In "Aois na Cloiche," translated by Derek Mahon as "The Stone Age," Ní Dhomhnaill describes a love affair in terms, at once mythic and intimate, that echo her use of Irish. As the poem builds to its climax, the poet's stony resistance to communication eventually effects, by its own properties, its own release, "growing until it erupted like a volcano."[5] The implication is that her radiant poems burst to the surface of consciousness in much the same way.

Nuala Ní Dhomhnaill was born in 1952, grew up in the Gaeltacht in Counties Kerry and Tipperary, and attended University College, Cork.

NOTES

1. Maire Mhac an tSaoi, "Writing in Modern Irish—A Benign Anachronism?" *The Southern Review*, vol. 31, no. 3 (Summer 1995), p. 425.

2. Ibid.

3. Ibid., p. 426.

4. Medbh McGuckian and Nuala Ní Dhomhnaill, "Comhrá, with a Foreword and Afterword by Laura O'Connor," *The Southern Review*, vol. 31, no. 3 (Summer 1995), pp. 587–588.

5. "The Stone Age," *Pharaoh's Daughter* (Loughcrew, Ireland: Gallery Press, 1990), p. 69.

Abduction

The fairy woman walked
into my poem.
She closed no door
She asked no by-your-leave.
Knowing my place
I did not tell her go.
I played the woman-of-no-welcomes trick
and said:

"What's your hurry, here's your hat.
Pull up to the fire,
eat and drink what you get—
but if I were in your house
as you are in my house
I'd go home straight away
but anyway, stay."

She stayed. Got up and pottered
round the house. Dressed the beds
washed the ware. Put the dirty clothes
in the washing-machine.
When my husband came home for his tea
he didn't know what he had wasn't me.

For I am in the fairy field
in lasting darkness
and frozen with the cold there
dressed only in white mist.
And if he wants me back
there is a solution—
get the sock of a plough
smear it with butter
and redden it with fire.

And then let him go to the bed
where lies the succubus
and press her with red iron.
"Push it into her face,
burn and brand her,
and as she fades before your eyes

I'll materialise
and as she fades before your eyes
I'll materialise."

[Translated by Michael Hartnett]

Young Man's Song

My two hands
on your breast
your two birds' nests
your flock bed
your skin flows—
as white as snow
as bright as lime
as fine as a bunch of flax.

I stretch my shoulder
when I feel
your tongue in my cheek
your mouth beneath my teeth.
A trench is opened up
by the sock of my plough.
When I reach the furrow's end
I buck.

I am the púca
who comes in the night—
nest robber
world-plougher:
I destroy the surrounding reeds,
I reclaim your bogland.

[Translated by Michael Hartnett]

The Shannon Estuary Welcoming the Fish

The leap of the salmon
in darkness,
naked blade
shield of silver.
I am welcoming, full of nets,
inveigling
slippery with seaweed,
quiet eddies
and eel-tails.

This fish
is nothing but meat
with very few bones
and very few entrails;
twenty pounds of muscle tauted,
aimed
at its nest in the mossy place.

And I will sing a lullaby
to my lover
wave on wave,
stave upon half-stave,
my phosphorescence as bed-linen under him,
my favourite, whom I, from afar have chosen.

[Translated by Nuala Ní Dhomhnaill]

As for the Quince

There came this bright young thing
with a Black & Decker
and cut down my quince tree.
I stood with my mouth hanging open
while one by one
she trimmed off the branches.

When my husband got home that evening
and saw what had happened
he lost the rag,
as you might imagine.
"Why didn't you stop her?
What would she think
if I took the Black & Decker
round to her place
and cut down a quince-tree
belonging to her?
What would she make of that?"

Her ladyship came back next morning
while I was at breakfast.
She enquired about his reaction.
I told her straight
that he was wondering how she'd feel
if he took a Black & Decker
round to her house
and cut down a quince-tree of hers,
et cetera et cetera.

"O," says she, "that's very interesting."
There was a stress on the "very."
She lingered over the "ing."
She was remarkably calm and collected.

These are the times that are in it, so,
all a bit topsy-turvy.
The bottom falling out of my belly
as if I had got a kick up the arse
or a punch in the kidneys.
A fainting-fit coming over me
that took the legs from under me
and left me so zonked
I could barely lift a finger
till Wednesday.

As for the quince, it was safe and sound
and still somehow holding its ground.

[Translated by Paul Muldoon]

The Stone Age

That was the year the rain
fell out of the skies
not in buckets or in torrents
but in showers of stone.

The snow lay like a toxic powder
on flower-gardens and lawns,
unmelting and immovable
as quartz.

There was no call for statues
in the public squares,
no call for garden gnomes;
the people were there already, frozen stiff.

The sun rose each morning, a great Fomorian eye,
and aimed its radiation at every bush
or bit of grass that tried to grow
or even dared to sneeze.

Imagine a stone getting up each morning,
shaking its rocky shoulders
and moving its stony tongue,
trying to speak; well, that was me.

No use to light fires and fight the frost.
An immense crystal grew from the supersaturated
solution of our self-regard,
growing until it erupted like a volcano.

Whatever we lacked then, it wasn't heat.
Looking back on it now, that year
seems to have stretched the length and breadth
of countless aeons.

[Translated by Derek Mahon]

The Smell of Blood

I wake up, and my hands are sticky
With the smell of blood.
And though there's not a smudge nor blot
In eyeshot, nor any soul
That I know missing (I've counted them, each one,
And they're all present and correct),
Still, it seems my hands are sticky
With the smell of blood.

I swear my hands are sticky
With the smell of blood.
I've rummaged underneath the mattress,
In cubbyholes, behind doors,
For fear the body of a rotting king or courtier—
Polonius behind the arras—
Might lurk behind this smell of blood
That's sticking to my hands.

Hell's freezing over with sour water
And icy cataracts pour from the tap.
My hands are hacked, the skin is all volcanic
Cracks from this eternal pumice-stone,
And I don't know how many bars of *Sunlight* soap
Have shrunk into exhausted slivers
Since I'm stuck forever with this stink of blood
That's on my hands.

[Translated by Ciaran Carson]

Why Bridgid, or Bríd, Never Married

Why Bridgid, or Bríd, never married
though every stick of her furniture,
her trousseau, her ware, her share of knick-knacks,
were packed and ready the day before

is because
>   at nine on the wedding morning
her father and two of the children were got
hanging stone-dead from the branch of a tree,
tied up in new ropes, the wind and the daylight shot

clean through them all, with the tracks of the bullets
plain to be seen, and though the killer's still on the run
that put a stop to their gallop, and that is why
in the heel of the reel Bridgid, or Bríd, never married.

[Translated by Peter Fallon]

Aubade

It's all the same to morning what it dawns on—
On the bickering of jackdaws in leafy trees;
On that dandy from the wetlands, the green mallard's
Stylish glissando among reeds; on the moorhen
Whose white petticoat flickers around the boghole;
On the oystercatcher on tiptoe at low tide.

It's all the same to the sun what it rises on—
On the windows in houses in Georgian squares;
On bees swarming to blitz suburban gardens;
On young couples yawning in unison before
They do it again; on dew like sweat or tears
On lilies and roses; on your bare shoulders.

But it isn't all the same to us that night-time
Runs out; that we must make do with today's
Happenings, and stoop and somehow glue together
The silly little shards of our lives, so that
Our children can drink water from broken bowls,
Not from cupped hands. It isn't the same at all.

[Translated by Michael Longley]

The Language Issue

I place my hope on the water
in this little boat
of the language, the way a body might put
an infant

in a basket of intertwined
iris leaves,
its underside proofed
with bitumen and pitch,

then set the whole thing down amidst
the sedge
and bulrushes by the edge
of a river

only to have it borne hither and thither,
not knowing where it might end up;
in the lap, perhaps,
of some Pharaoh's daughter.

[Translated by Paul Muldoon]

The Crack in the Stairs

There's a crack in the flight of stairs
at my very core
that I simply can't get round or traverse.
For days on end, I can do little more

than rummage and root
through the gloom
of the cellar, or try out
the dusty furniture I trundle from room

to lower room: there's a rose withered
in its pot; a china dog slumped
on the mantel; an oleograph of the Sacred Heart
and, before it, a paraffin lamp

that's long since snuffed it. The drapes
have been shredded by moths, as well
as the nightly phantom-troop
who leave a familiar, all-pervasive smell.

The piano is under lock and key
and the lock is hard
with rust, while I myself cannot break free
of what's eating away at my heart.

Other days, though, I'm so full of vrouw-vroom
I'll take the flight
of stairs with a single bound, into some upper room
where I'm blinded, blinded by the light.

[Translated by Paul Muldoon]

Cathleen

You can't take her out for a night on the town
without her either showing you up or badly letting you down:
just because she made the Twenties roar
with her Black and Tan Bottom—O Terpsichore—
and her hair in a permanent wave;
just because she was a lily grave
in nineteen sixteen; just because she once was spotted
quite naked in Cannought, of beauties most beautied,
or tramping the roads of Moonstare, brightest of the bright;
just because she was poor, without blemish or blight,
high-stepping it by the ocean with her famous swan's prow
and a fresh fall of snow on her broadest of broad brows—

because of all that she never stops bending your ear
about the good old days of yore
when she crept through the country in her dewy high heels
of a Sunday morning, say, on the road to Youghal
or that level stretch between Cork and Douglas.
There was your man Power's ridiculous
suggestion when he was the ship's captain, not to speak

of the Erne running red with abundance and mountain-peaks
laid low. She who is now a widowed old woman
was a modest maiden, meek and mild, but with enough gumption
at least to keep to her own
side of the ghostly demarcation, the eternal buffer-zone.

For you'd think to listen to her she'd never heard
that discretion is the better part, that our names are writ
in water, that the greenest stick will wizen:
even if every slubberdegullion once had a dream-vision
in which she appeared as his own true lover,
those days are just as truly over.
And I bet Old Gummy Granny
has taken none of this on board because of her uncanny
knack of hearing only what confirms
her own sense of herself, her honey-nubile form
and the red rose, proud rose or canker
tucked behind her ear, in the head-band of her blinkers.

[Translated by Paul Muldoon]

Persephone Suffering from SAD

Now don't go ringing the cops,
Mum, and don't be losing the bap:
I admit I was out of line
and over the top
when I hitched a ride
with that sexy guy
in his wow of a BMW.
But he was such a super chat-up
I couldn't give him the push.

He booked us a foreign holiday
no travel agent runs—
his car so jet-propelled with revs
the engine soared on wings.
He said he would buy me velvet gowns

and satin underthings,
and his credit's fine. He leaves
me space, though I'd have to say
there's not much light in the place.

He's signing me the title deeds
to all his stately homes.
He's for putting my name in lights
as a star on the silver screen.
He has me flooded with rings
and pearls, but the menu's pretty thin—
I've just been served a pomegranate:
it's crimson, dripping with seeds—

a veritable *Céad Míle Fáilte* of drops of blood.

[Translated by Medbh McGuckian]

Ten Ways of Looking at a Magpie

Magpie, your black and white
has put to flight
every bird smaller than yourself.

The hawthorn has caught you at
your work among the stonechats,
breaking up their meeting.

Beneath them you flew,
over and under and through,
till you left them not even a nestling.

In the meadow's edge
the linnet kept its eggs,
but you drove her from the bushes

as you have driven since
the pair of goldfinch
that had settled in the fuchsias.

Nor is the tiny goldcrest
safe in its nest
from you rudely pilfering the hedge;

and you come the heavy
with the yellowhammer
on its day out in Kerry.

But worse than all of them
the blackbird and his hen
you put out of action in my back garden.

And it's your infernal din
that really does my head in,
you bullyboy without pardon,

your crowning glory of abuse,
whether bailiff or terrorist,
foulmouthed, two-faced magpie.

[Translated by Medbh McGuckian]

You Are

Whoever you are, you are
The real thing, the witness
Who might lend an ear
To a woman with a story
Barely escaped with her life
From the place of battle.

Spring, the sweet spring, was not sweet for us
Nor winter neither.
We never stepped aboard a ship together
Bound for America to seek
Our fortune, we never
Shared those hot foreign lands.

We did not fly over the high hills
Riding the fine black stallion,
Or lie under the hazel branches

As the night froze about us,
No more than we lit bonfires of celebration
Or blew the horn on the mountainside.

Between us welled the ocean
Waves of grief. Between us
The mountains were forbidding
And the roads long, with no turning.

[Translated by Eiléan Ní Chuilleanáin]

The Prodigal Muse

As I said to his godship,
to quote my little horrors,
in the *Bunscoil* lingo,
"You can bugger off, dickhead!

"It's all a cod—
I'm practically at death's door,
not a penny to my name,
sacrificed as a penance
on your damn altar,
and what the hell
have I got to show for it?"

Whereupon he ups
and lands me with you.
You saunter back in
as cool and dandy
as if you'd not been
on your travels
since the Lord-knows-when.

You sit yourself down
in your old favourite armchair
pulled up to the fire.
I come out in
an all-over body-rash,

my erect nipples
in for a nuzzling
by the stomach of the chimney
stack, or the cubby-hole
under the stairs.

[Translated by Medbh McGuckian]

A Recovered Memory of Water

Sometimes when the mermaid's daughter
is in the bathroom
cleaning her teeth with a thick brush
and baking soda
she has the sense the room is filling
with water.

It starts at her feet and ankles
and slides further and further up
over her thighs and hips and waist.
In no time
it's up to her oxters.
She bends down into it to pick up
handtowels and washcloths and all such things
as are sodden with it.
They all look like seaweed—
like those long strands of kelp that used to be called
"mermaid-hair" or "foxtail."
Just as suddenly the water recedes
and in no time
the room's completely dry again.

A terrible sense of stress
is part and parcel of these emotions.
At the end of the day she has nothing else
to compare it to.
She doesn't have the vocabulary for any of it.
At her weekly therapy session

she has more than enough to be going on with
just to describe this strange phenomenon
and to express it properly
to the psychiatrist.

She doesn't have the terminology
or any of the points of reference
or any word at all that would give the slightest suggestion
as to what water might be.
"A transparent liquid," she says, doing as best she can.
"Right," says the therapist, "keep going."
He coaxes and cajoles her towards word-making.
She has another run at it.
"A thin flow," she calls it,
casting about gingerly in the midst of words.
"A shiny film. Dripping stuff. Something wet."

[Translated by Paul Muldoon]

Matthew Sweeney (1952–)

During the first decade of his career, from the appearance of his first commercially published volume, *A Dream of Maps,* in 1981, to the publication of *Cacti* in 1992, Matthew Sweeney was busy, as Ian Sansom puts it, "squeezing the Heaney out of himself." Sweeney's poems, that is, were moving in the direction of ever greater simplicity; or perhaps it would better capture his minimalist tendency to say that his poetry was becoming less and less complex, "forcing his language to its absolute minimum."[1]

Sweeney clearly began his career with values other than simplicity in mind. His early poems, those in *A Dream of Maps* and *A Round House,* can approach the limit of verbal excess, as in "The Servant," a poem lumbered with ivory hands, silver tureens and mauve velvet curtains.[2] Despite the exuberance of that early language, however, there is something in the precision and crispness of the images it describes that accords with the lucidity of poems in Sweeney's later volumes. By the time *Blue Shoes* was published in 1989, Sweeney had pared his language to fit the narrative minimalism shared by the early and late poems alike. His subjects can still be grave—"Where Fishermen Can't Swim" or "Dredging the Lake"—but the poems almost always tighten themselves around a few vivid images, their drama downplayed by Sweeney's concise and colloquial diction. At their most successful these poems recall Beckett, not least because their inventive yet strikingly simple narratives resemble poetry in translation, or poetry caught, like Beckett's, between two languages.

In "The Lighthouse Keeper's Son," for example, Sweeney's casual acceptance of the repetitive mechanics of ordinary human lives (captured in the colloquialism of "umpteenth time") takes on the tinge of something like existential anger in the poem's last line, in which the lighthouse beam searches the sea "for nothing."[3] This may be an optimistic image, the lighthouse not searching for anything because there's fortunate scarcity on these shores of ships in trouble. At the same time, the ambiguity of the phrasing picks up the purposelessness in that possibility, sending back a glint of nihilism into the vast terrain of the wobbling land, the pockmarked moon, the seven stars of the Plough. The lighthouse keeper's duties—like the boy's search for an excuse and, perhaps, our search for meaning in the poem, or in life—looks to be "for nothing": to no end. And the poem, reaching that end, ends without an ending; there is no final stop to its one sentence.

Throughout a career built on poems like this, Sweeney has remained, in the words of *Observer* reviewer Peter Porter, "a great deceiver": "Wearing his *faux-naïf* narrator's smile he tells you relaxed stories in gently persuasive verse. Suddenly you are plunged into fear or strangeness, yet Sweeney seems not to have changed his pace or raised his voice."[4] It shouldn't be surprising—given Porter's description of Sweeney as the sort of avuncular teller of tales to children whose portrayal of strange worlds and possibilities always skirts the boundary between delight and terror—that Sweeney has published children's fiction, as well as two collections of verse for children. Reading this work, one has the feeling that Sweeney has still not changed his pace or raised his voice. But imagining these poems directed toward an audience of children makes his recognizable themes more than usually unsettling when they surface in *The Flying Spring Onion*, the collection of children's verse Sweeney published in 1992.

In the last ten years, Sweeney has been content to let a little Heaney back into his work. Recent poems like "Guardian of the Women's Loo in Waterloo" retain his characteristic humor and inventiveness, while adding layers of linguistic and rhythmic complexity. In "Sweeney" he puts his own stamp on the medieval Irish myth of a mad king transformed into a bird that Heaney himself translated as "Sweeney Astray." In a version of the story that fits perfectly alongside his other poems, Sweeney imagines the king as a suburban husband who at first dismisses as psychosomatic the feathers pushing through his pores, but is forced to leave his house for an oak branch in the back yard after he pecks his wife while trying to kiss her one morning.

Matthew Sweeney was born in Donegal in 1952. He studied in Germany at the University of Freiburg. He has lived in London, Berlin, and Timisoara.

NOTES

1. Ian Sansom, review of *Cacti*, *Times Literary Supplement*, 6 November 1992, p. 26.

2. "The Servant," *A Round House* (London: Allison & Busby, 1983), p. 55.

3. "The Lighthouse Keeper's Son," *Blue Shoes* (London: Secker & Warburg, 1989), p. 10.

4. Peter Porter, review of *Blue Shoes*, *The Observer*, 23 April 1989, p. 44.

A Round House

Will somebody build me a round house
low on a headland. With thick walls
& shrunken windows, a view on all sides.
And an acre of sandy grass.

I will move there, like the birds in winter.
Unloading a trunk & domestic trophies,
then quickly a bucket of whitewash
while the dry wind lasts.

Fields away, the weather-station
will probe the sky.
Ships will cross in the distance
with goods for the city.

I will have rabbit-snares,
a boat for cod. And a high
fence for summer, its day-trippers.
I will invest in a gun.

The Servant

I am summoned: a double handclap
from my mother's ivory hands
and I fill the silver tureen
with pumpkin soup the colour of oranges.
I enter on feet of air.
Her smile subsides like a wave on sand
pointing me towards the curtain
of mauve velvet where I must stand.

Wine is shared. A toast to mother
updates a grace before meals
then the ladle becomes a wand
and oohs climb from warmed stomachs.
My timing is pre-set—

I conjure the plates away
to return, hidden by conversation,
with shark fillets in lime & butter.

I picture the absent fins & teeth
& a red dye in the sea.
Remove the bones, wheel in a trolley
on which a boar, freed from the spit,
sits in a juniper sauce.
Another wine now, old & crimson
then marble potatoes, celeriac matchsticks
& olive lentils puréed in butter.

I bring dessert, despite protests—
its exact identity mother's secret
though I smell figs & honey
in a foam the lightness of clouds.
Dispatched to the kitchen to grind coffee
I glance at the night through glass—
a slide where the stars are dandruff,
the moon a fingernail-clipping.

Captain Marsh

Captain Marsh has gone to work
in a locked room on the second floor.
He is not pleased by steps approaching.

We are close enough. Listen, he types
with two fingers and barks at mistakes
as if at insolent cabin-boys.

All winter he is marooned here
by his own orders. An electric fire
and a whiskey-bottle are his comforts.

He has not spoken to us in months
though sometimes notes escape the room
requesting steak or lamb curry.

Nights when we can't sleep, we hear
the clacking of his machine far up
disturbing the pigeons on the rooftop.

What is his great vocation? When
will he reveal this late crop,
this surge that has replaced the sea?

We ask, we make crude guesses, laugh.
Sometimes we wait outside the room
as he walks the boards as if in pain.

Preparation for Survival

for Philip Casey

Somewhere a man is swathed in furs
and is growing a beard of ice.
A survivor from an expedition
to set a flag at the absolute north
he chose to stay there
and learned to withstand cold.

He flies an aerial from the flagpole
and each month a plane leaves Greenland:
meat and coffee parachute down.
A temporary pleasure. The trade-
winds practise with pollen
above the submarines far south.

Audience at the war theatre,
fire will briefly light his sky
then a finite crackle on the radio.
Expert now in the disciplines of snow
he is learning to spear moose
or to fish through portholes in the ice.

Simultaneous Stories

There was the story of a power station
sinking into the very bog that fed it,
an inch or so a year, and still it burned
all the turf around it, so the hi-fis,
shavers, and vibrators could drone on
as near as upstairs, as far as the city.

And at the same time there was a hill
two of us climbed, earning our sleep,
to the wide, uncanny blue of the ocean
where a glimpse of Scotland bobbed.
Coming down, we found a ruined pram
from the 1950s, and spooked a hare
to skedaddle on up the promontory.

Relics

The cleaver, hung on the scullery wall
these twenty years, gleamed once,
suffered the rasp of the backyard stone
to joint with ease the lambs he bought
on those monthly trips to Carn fair.
The basin that once caught lamb's blood
for black pudding, holds clothes-pegs
in the back bedroom where he slept
and on whose walls a holster hung
through my childhood, empty of its gun.
The backyard dancehall that he built
is a giant junkroom, with old papers
and coats, beds, prams, cans of paint.
The big house with poky rooms is flaking.
The mangle in the washhouse rolls
as it did for him, though the clothes
are machine-washed and spun dry.

The garden is a hedged-in field
where windfalls hide in the long grass.
The turkey stuffing alone survives
from his kitchen ways. The turfhouse walls
are rusted and patched with zinc,
and contain the hulk of the generator
by which, in advance of the government,
he brought electricity to the house.

The Lighthouse Keeper's Son

got arrested
as he wobbled home
on a lightless bicycle
after a late drink,
and he asked the cop
if the pockmarked moon
wasn't light enough
not to mention the Plough's
seven stars,
and his dad's beam
igniting the road
twice a minute,
then searching the sea
the umpteenth time
for nothing

Where Fishermen Can't Swim

Back there where fishermen can't swim,
where the ice-age coast of Donegal
leaves rocks among the waves,
a lobster-boat cast off, whose engine
croaked before the rocks were by.

The youngest in the crew leapt out
onto a rock to push the boat away,
then laughed when he couldn't jump back.
But exactly when did he realise
that the boat would float no nearer;
that all those pulls on the engine cord
would yield no shudders; that no rope
or lifebelt existed to be thrown;
that those flares were lost in cloud;
that the radio would bring a copter
an hour later? He had forty minutes—
to cling while the waves attacked,
to feel the rock gradually submerge.
And they had forty minutes of watching,
shouting into the radio, till he cried
out, sank from view, and stayed there.

Pink Milk

When the goats ate the red carnations
and the next morning's milk was pink,
the abbot loved it, demanded more

but the monks loved their flower-garden
and turned to cochineal, to crushed ants,
to paprika, all stirred in milk

to no avail—the perfume was gone
and the abbot grumpy, so carnations
were sacrificed to rampant goats

whose beards jiggled as they chewed,
who looked up at the watching monks
while the abbot watched from a window

and in the kitchen, a leg of pork
thawed on a hook from the ceiling,
and blood dripped into a milk-jug.

Donegal, Arizona

for Dermot Seymour

He put Donegal in the oven,
cooked it awhile, and got Arizona.
And he siphoned all that rain
and the troublesome Atlantic
into waterholes in the desert
and the Colorado River.
A few tons of gelignite
moved the hills together
to make the Grand Canyon,
and he stretched all the toads
to make Gila monsters,
and bought a few steamboats,
and buried gold in the hills.
The Indians were difficult
but he advertised abroad,
then the Mexican ambassador
signed the Treaty of Guadalupe
all over again, and Derry
stared at Sligo over a void.

The Wobble

Halfway across the ravine,
watched by more than a thousand
and a further million on TV,
he wobbled and almost fell.
Maybe the gasp held him up,
righted the wheel of his unicycle,
gave his legs a surge
that powered him across.
As the crowd hauled him off
and carried him aloft,
he thought of the wobble,
how it had tried to send him

down onto the steer-bones
at the ravine's bottom,
his cry echoing out over
the cries of the thousand,
till it suddenly cut off—
and he asked those carrying him
to return him to the ravine,
to his rope, still strung there,
and he took the unicycle,
turned the pedals and sent it
back where it had come from,
alone this time, the crowd quiet,
until halfway across, it fell
with a clatter and a cloud of dust.

An End

I want to end up on Inishtrahull,
in the small graveyard there
on the high side of the island,
carried there on a helicopter sling
with twenty speedboats following.
And I want my favourite Thai chef
flown there, a day before,
and brought to the local fishermen
so he can serve a chilli feast
before we head off up the hill.
A bar, too, it goes without saying,
free to all, the beer icy,
the whiskey Irish, and loud
through speakers high on poles
the gruff voice of Tom Waits
causing the gulls to congregate.
Get Tom himself there if you can.
And in the box with me I want
a hipflask filled with Black Bush,

a pen and a blank notebook,
all the vitamins in one bottle,
my addressbook and ten pound coins.
Also, a Mandarin primer.
I want no flowers, only cacti
and my headstone must be glass.

The Bat

In through the open French window
flew the bat, past my head
as I stood peeing into the river
that flowed beneath the house
which the bat quickly explored, round
the barn-sized living-room,
up the cracked stairs, two flights
to the attic where the kids slept
but they wouldn't tonight, not while
the bat stayed. So we opened
the skylight, despite the wasp's nest
on the drainpipe, and I stood
with a glass of the local red wine,
calling to the bat, like Dracula,
Lovely creature of the night,
come to me, I am your friend,
while it looped the length of the room,
with the kids on the stairs, laughing,
but not coming in. And it stayed
past midnight, till Joan
cupped it in her hands
and carried it downstairs
to the same French window,
where I stood, calling after it,
Lovely creature of the night,
come back, I miss you,
come to me, I am your friend.

The Volcano

When they phoned to tell us
the volcano was finally erupting,
we threw a few things in a bag—
your best sari, my Armani suit—
grabbed the monkey and ran.
For a minute the car wouldn't start,
then we were off, rattling
down that mountain road, the stench
of sulphur in the air, you
whitefaced and silent at the wheel.
When you took a corner too quickly
and the car nearly turned over
the monkey started screeching,
so I crooned that country song
it loved, turning to look behind me
to see if lava was following
but all I saw was
a herd of donkeys, galloping,
and the sky filled with crows,
as if the mountain was emptying
of all its creatures, and all,
including us, would get away.
And as you slowed down
I put my hand on yours and squeezed,
thinking of the lava
entering our house
and swarming over the chairs,
turning them into sculptures
that one day we'd come back and see.

Guardian of the Women's Loo in Waterloo

Centimes, francs—I've a drawer full of them.
I'm not supposed to take them but I do.
At least they pay, these French women.
They don't stand there, smirking, saying
I'm broke, I'm going to wet myself,
or worse, vaulting over the metal bar
to run and lock themselves in a cubicle.
As if I'd leave my seat to stop them!

The things that go on behind me, sometimes—
sex, drugs-dealing, even a murder, once.
It's not my job to police the joint.
That's Angela's territory, when she's here.
More often than not she's doing the rounds,
but I like it when I get to talk to her,
hear her gossip, who's bonking who
in the disused waiting room on platform 12.

Sometimes she calls me back to show me
what's been left behind—knickers,
puke, a used condom (I let no men in!)
a lipstick-smeared photo of Brad Pitt.
Once there was the name Steve in blood
all over the back of the door, but the saddest,
the one that stayed with me, was a dead baby
propped up in the corner, wearing a bow.

I tell you, I want out from time to time.
The Eurostar's just across the platform,
I could go to Paris and not come back,
lose myself in Montmartre, an artist's flat
overlooking steps, but who'd take over, who'd be
guardian of the women's loo in Waterloo,
with all the tact, let live, let go by, that's needed?
20p entrance? That's half of it. The skill's in the rest.

Animals

A narrative is all right so long as the narrator sticks to words as simple as dog, horse, sunset.

                                        Ezra Pound

Admit it, you wanted to shoot that dog
who stood barking on the edge of town,
right from the start of sunset, until
the clock in the square struck twelve
and the hotel's horse started to whinny,

sending you out from your musty bed
to the window that you flung open,
before sticking your head out and shouting
in bad French, "Fuck off, animals,
some of us are trying to sleep here!"

At that, the dog barked louder, faster,
and the horse galloped round the field,
and a rooster, fooled by the noise,
began crowing, and two cats fought
openly, on an adjacent wall.

Closing the window was all you could do,
that and turning on the shower until
the animals were lost in the hiss,
and you slept there on the bathroom floor
till light brought the squawking of gulls.

Sweeney

Even when I said my head was shrinking
he didn't believe me. Change doctors, I thought,
but why bother? We're all hypochondriacs,
and those feathers pushing through my pores
were psychosomatic. My wife was the same
till I pecked her, trying to kiss her, one morning,

scratching her feet with my claws, cawing
good morning till she left the bed with a scream.

I moved out then, onto a branch of the oak
behind the house. That way I could see her
as she opened the car, on her way to work.
Being a crow didn't stop me fancying her,
especially when she wore that short black number
I'd bought her in Berlin. I don't know if she
noticed me. I never saw her look up.
I did see boxes of my books going out.

The nest was a problem. My wife had cursed me
for being useless at DIY, and it was no better now.
I wasn't a natural flier, either, so I sat
in that tree, soaking, shivering, all day.
Every time I saw someone carrying a bottle of wine
I cawed. A takeaway curry was worse.
And the day I saw my wife come home
with a man, I flew finally into our wall.

The UFO

A UFO landed in Ireland in '54,
in Donegal, in my back garden.
At the controls was my grandfather,
and not wanting his craft to be seen,
he had a house built around it,
or he added bricks to the turfhouse
till his spaceship had a coat
and no earthly visitor could guess
that alien splendour was there.
I was two when it landed
but I can just about remember.
I can hear the noise it made—
a humming that scared me,
as if it might take off again,

scattering bricks everywhere,
taking my grandfather away,
but he walked into the house
and switched the lights on—
no need for paraffin and matches,
just a bulb hanging there
like our own small moon,
and this was repeated in every room,
and a copper kettle boiled
away from the fire,
and my grandfather took me
out to the turfhouse
to see the thing being fed,
but I closed my eyes
stuck my fingers in my ears,
and cried.

Exiled

They'd blindfolded me, thrown me in a plane
(I knew it was a plane when it lifted off),
flown me somewhere for more than an hour,
then dumped me out and powered away.

I was lying on the ground with hands tied.
I had no idea where I was, or why.
I wondered what my wife would think,
or if I'd ever see her pretty face again.

I struggled to my feet and started walking—
small steps, though. I could be on a cliff.
And gradually I heard the bleating of goats,
then smelt them, felt them brush past me,

as hands undid the blindfold, the rope,
and a young man was standing there, smiling,
speaking a language I didn't recognise.
I thanked him, as he waved me to follow.

Frog-Taming

Any fool can learn to catch a frog—
the trick is to do it blindfolded,
lying there, in the wet grass,
listening for the hop and the croak.

And the real trick is to keep it alive,
not strangle it, or squeeze it dead—
that way you can take it home
and tame it, make it your pet.

But early on, keep the cat locked up.
Soon she'll get used to her odd sibling—
meanwhile put a bit of time into
picking a suitable name for a frog.

And research a frog's ideal diet,
also the best sleeping arrangement—
water somewhere nearby, of course,
and plenty of air, plenty of air.

Be sure to play the frog the right music
so it can learn hopping tricks—
ones it can reproduce on the cleared table
when you have dinner guests around,

while you find your blindfold and put it on,
holding your hands out and grasping
the air the frog has just vacated—
making it clear you're deliberately missing.

Thomas McCarthy (1954–)

Thomas McCarthy was born in 1954 at Cappoquin in County Waterford. He attended University College, Cork, and has been a librarian with the Cork city libraries since 1974. He sees the library as an ideal setting in which to foster the poetic interests planted by his family history. "Both a family background in politics and a deep interest in history," he writes, "have given me tremendous motivation to continue writing. I feel that I have been handed my themes from the beginning of my career, and all I need to do is work out the implications of those themes in my work. My vocation as a public librarian is an ideal one for a writer; I have constant access to archive materials and books."[1]

History and politics, though, are mediated in McCarthy's poetry by his reverence for individual experience. "I have *The Irish Times* for the morning / you were born," he writes in one poem. "You are already / part of the archive of my love for you."[2] McCarthy's archival explorations are undertaken as forays into a life as lived. As a result, his early interest in history and politics most frequently surfaces in his poems in the form of poetic riffs on intimate scenes from the lives of historical figures. The number and variety of personalities represented—from Edouard Vuillard and Vladimir Nabokov to Charles Stuart Parnell and Éamon de Valera—reflect McCarthy's wide reading of literary, cultural, and political history. These biographical poems display a marvelous ability to connect historical situations to the lives they condition. McCarthy's selection of well-known subjects stands in tension with his concentration on the private moments that, more than public occasions, articulate for him the human truth of the history to which each personality has contributed. At times the gravity of history can seem to diminish under the weight of personal material entering the poem from the poet's life as well as the subject's. The poet's private engagement with Picasso's work, for example, nearly obscures the particular situation of Guérnica and the Spanish

Civil War in "Picasso's 'Composition au Papillon,'" giving the artist a heroic posture—"Leonardo reincarnate" or "Cuchulain of canvas"—that transcends history.[3]

But while the density of historical event is dispersed, the broadening of association strengthens the poem, linking the civil war in Spain to the Irish tradition through Cuchulain, and, by extension, to the undeclared civil war still under way in the North when "Picasso's Composition" was written. The poem's conclusion translates both the biographical *Bildungsroman* and the variously implied civil wars into a playfully contrived rhetoric of culture and nationalism: "Truth is / we are all born to an artless, provincial stench. / If we are lucky, Picasso, we die French."[4]

In "Hugh MacDiarmid," a poem that reflects on the idiosyncratic gifts of Scotland's strongest twentieth-century poet, McCarthy appears more eager to situate his subject's life within the troubled history of his nation: "Scotland's past was a parcel of ill-luck, / with you, its covering letter, gone astray. / History can't close on the Sabbath Day, / nor poetry."[5] But again the intimate details of personality drive the poem's apprehension of history. The poetic voice signals the shift to private concerns by substituting MacDiarmid's given name, Christopher Grieve, for the pseudonym that gives the poem its title.

McCarthy's many poems on the life of Éamon de Valera are similarly situated to look forward to the public life from early moments of private crisis. "Sometime within that structure of / loneliness," he writes of the future Irish prime minister's early period of doubt in "De Valera's Youth," "he found words. Decades / after, small girls would bring flowers."[6]

De Valera's political future is forecast here by honorific bouquets, but, for McCarthy himself, an interest in flowers tempers the political commitments of his writing life. "I have a keen interest in gardening and in visiting old gardens," he says. "If I were fifteen years younger, I would study rose-breeding and growing. My real heroes are not writers but great rose-breeders such as Kordes, Mailland, and Sam MacCready."[7] One of McCarthy's earliest poems shows the figure of the heroic gardener already in place. "Breaking Garden," playing on the military concept of breaking camp, watches an older couple, one a soldier, the other a gardener, deal with change in terms of the occupations by which their lives have been defined. The gardener's ongoing attention to beauty in the face of adversity is an apt figure for McCarthy's work as a poet.

NOTES

1. "Thomas McCarthy," *Contemporary Authors*, vol. 133, p. 265.

2. "Cleaning White Shoes, II: The Month of June," *Seven Winters in Paris* (London: Anvil Press, 1989), p. 33.

3. "Picasso's 'Composition Au Papillon,'" *Seven Winters in Paris*, p. 58.

4. Ibid.

5. "Hugh MacDiarmid," *Seven Winters in Paris*, p. 59.

6. "De Valera's Youth," *The Sorrow Garden* (London: Anvil Press, 1981), p. 19. This poem is not included here, but a companion piece, "De Valera's Childhood," is.

7. "Thomas McCarthy," *Contemporary Authors*, vol. 133, p. 265.

Daedalus, the Maker   *for Seán Lucy*

Dactylos was silent and impersonal;
hidden behind false names, he achieved
a powerful *persona*. There was only
his work; a chipping of rock into form
and the rhythmic riveting of bronze,
diminishing his need for company.

Learning to keep silent is a difficult
task. To place Art anonymously at
the Earth's altar, then to scurry away
like a wounded animal, is the most cruel
test-piece. A proud maker, I have waited at
the temple doors for praise and argument.

Often I have abandoned an emerging form
to argue with priests and poets—
only to learn the wisdom of Dactylos:
that words make the strangest labyrinth,
with circular passages and minotaurs
lurking in the most innocent lines.

I will banish argument to work again
with bronze. Words, I have found, are
captured, not made: opinion alone is
a kind of retreat. I shall become like
Dactylos, a quiet maker; moving between
poet and priest, keeping my pride secret.

Breaking Garden

He's reluctant to move; old campaigner
Familiar with siege. He had spent hours
On violent streets during the 'thirties,
Refusing to move despite batons and gas:
But this is the year of forced migration;
Letters, books are stuffed in bags like grain,

Pictures and paperweights, crumbling squadrons
Of files await the retreating campaign.

Patricia's more resigned. Quiet in acquiescence:
She moves quickly between rows of growth,
Deciding which plants must stay. I watched her
For days. With two sheepdogs for lieutenants
She tested the tallest stems; made a note
Of the tough ones, those likely to endure.

Her Blindness

In her blindness
the house became
a tapestry of touch.

The jagged end of a dresser
became a signpost
to the back-door,

bread crumbs crunching
under her feet told
her when to sweep
the kitchen floor;

the powdery touch
of dry leaves in
the flower-trough
said that geraniums
needed water.

I remember her beside
the huge December fire,
holding a heavy mug,
changing its position
on her lap; filling

the dark space
between her fingers
with the light
of bright memory.

The Poet of the Mountains

Every Sunday she prepared the brown oak table
For breakfast and listened to new writers
On the wooden wireless, while she ladled
Fresh milk from the yellow stone pitchers
By the wall. The English words that broke
Across her small kitchen were seldom spoken

When she was young. Then, it was all Irish:
Those brown words had curled about her childhood
Like collies home from a long cattle-crush
Or an alphabet of trees in the Abbey wood
Where she picked bluebells with her uncle
And caught words off the air as they fell.

She had spent all her days in the company
Of women. They had churned milk in the dairy
With her, taken weak lambs across the hills,
Or spoken in black shawls as far as chapel:
All their days were taken up in a great swell
Of work. They had to wash, sew, milk and kneel.

But at night, I imagine, she would lie awake
And listen to the mountains for her own sake.
She would listen to the linen wind at night
As it flapped the wet clothes. She would steal
Into the children's room to dream and write;
To be a whole person, a picker of bluebells.

De Valera's Childhood

The roots of the grandeur of the world plunge into a childhood

Gaston Bachelard

I

Something from his sad youth
I've been following through;
to be found, perhaps, at his
childhood Limerick village,

in the small streets, the grey
school buildings where his
copying-desk and dutiful hand-
writings are preserved. There

even his absences were seen
as duty-filled: work that gives
a clue toward understanding—
cold dutiful hours spent

before school delivering milk
to neighbours, soaking gallons
of folklore and folk-solitude
from the morning world of work.

II

Lloyd George was wary of his
fox-like comings and goings:

"all that is truly dark
and furtive and violent in

the Irish mind" was what
he thought. He should have

known that such an animal
existed only in colonial

thought. Our home fox wanted
to hunt in its own word-wood.

III

Once, in a blindness lit by memory,
De Valera recalled the penniless days
after College, herding another man's
wild cattle. A long funeral

snaked its way through the roads
below the hillside where he stood.
"Shall I end like that?" he thought,
"end all purpose within its source,

like a flower gone full cycle in
its seed, like a fox turning over
to give death with birth." Like that
old fox he spent the final years,

staring at roads from the brushwood
of memory, retracing his steps
down wound-roads to childhood
where a broken soul could be restored.

In Memory of My Father

Sometimes I return to where he belonged,
to his most real world of felled trees
and timber bridges;
                          and I find, where
time has had time to play,
his first dimly-lit woodlanders' hut
covered by time's macramé
of loosened ropes and beams.

Next winter when growth stiffens
I shall uncover the black derrick-beams
of his circular saw and, perhaps, the
smashed axle of an old steam truck

and (if I am really lucky) the smell
of woodsmoke from across the river
and tea brewing by the river and
him hiding his paints and sketching-pad
before calling his labourers to rest.

A Meeting with Parnell

That day's event began with a lady's parasol
tripping across the grey Victorian sands
of Dublin and two polite female calls
for help. The passing bather lent a hand.

With an athletic zest he pursued her shade,
catching it beautifully near the pebble wall
while her child and its day-nurse delayed
as their mistress practised her protocol.

"You *are* a kind man," she said, when she saw
that he was a handsome one. "Please sit here
and take a little shade. Nobody will know:
I'm a Castle person, so you need have no fear."

"I must warn you, Madam, about who I am,"
the dark man announced, "I'm the awful Parnell."
Then she feigned boredom with political games;
Things like State Affairs, she said, *make one ill.*

The sun blazed at the edge of the Century
where they spoke, and the sea came in
to wash their flirting feet. He held her baby
in his scandalous hands and it seemed

to enjoy his cheerfulness. All that afternoon
its small joy stretched across the Dublin sand,
as if it knew what foes were sharing the sun;
as if it felt a new life seeping from the land.

The Provincial Writer's Diary

On cold nights in November he read late
and worried about the gift of fiction;
he was enveloped in a shell of lethargy.
Everything was let go—
even his diary lay idle for a whole month
while he chased provincial loneliness
from the corners of his mother's house.

Everything became consumed by the Personal:
furious theatre work killed some time,
strolling with his bachelor friends, fishing,
or the steady cumulative ritual of walking
beyond the city to stretch its grey limits.

But nowhere could he find (within those limits
of thought) the zeal that would consume life.

He lived far from the heroic. On Monday
mornings he would stalk the grey ghettos
of the North side and low-lying tenements
for absentee school-children. He would be taken aback
by the oppressive stench and filth of their lives.
One morning he thought, as if explaining all misery,
that such homes were the nests of the Military.

Mr Nabokov's Memory

For my first poem there are specific images
herded like schoolchildren into a neat row.
There is an ear and human finger hanging
from the linden tree in the Park north of
Maria Square and, between there and Morskaya
Street, other images of defeat. Such
as a black article in a Fascist newspaper
blowing along the footpath, or an old soldier
throwing insults at lovers out walking.
Even the *schveitsar* in our hallway
sharpens pencils for my father's meeting
as if sharpening the guillotine of the future.
There is only Tamara, who arrives with the poem
as something good; her wayward hair tied back
with a bow of black silk. Her neck,
in the long light of summer, is covered
with soft down like the bloom on almonds.
When winter comes I'll miss school to listen
to her minor, uvular poems, her jokes,
her snorting laughter in St Petersburg museums.
I have all this; this luxury of love; until
she says: "a flaw has appeared in us,
it's the strain of winters in St Petersburg"—
and like a heroine from a second-rate

matinée in Nevski Street she steps into the womb
of the Metro to become a part of me forever.

So many things must happen at once in this,
this single chrysalis of memory, this poem.
While my son weeps by my side at a border
checkpoint, a caterpillar ascends
the stalk of a campanula, a butterfly comes to rest
on the leaf of a tree with an unforgettable
name; an old man sighs in an orchard
in the Crimea, an even older housekeeper
loses her mind and the keys to our kitchen.
A young servant is sharpening the blade
of the future, while my father leaps
into the path of an assassin's bullet
at a brief August lecture in Berlin.
All these things must happen at once
before the rainstorm clears, leaving one
drop of water pinned down by its own weight.
When it falls from the linden leaf I shall
run to my mother, forever waiting forever
waiting, with maternal Russian tears,
to listen to her son's one and only poem.

The Non-Aligned Storyteller

Soon there would be no reason to remember Parkers in that place. Because the
present prevails . . .   Patrick White: *The Tree of Man*

Everything that happened here, that could be trapped
By light, lies abandoned in my shop:
Who would bother to look, now that my lease
Is up? I have photographic plates
Of weddings as old as any villager's memory;
A perfect plate of the first Model T in town,
A file of annual Blackwater floods, action shots
From the Carnival held for the Abbey chapel—

All of them useless. I gave my only child
A box of unclaimed, unknown Communion
Prints, perfectly justified and guillotined;
So perfect, in fact, that the subjects couldn't pay.
The first thing I photographed in this town
Was fire, a subject dangerous and ephemeral
Brought on by politics. The new Party
Had made its first great leap. That time,
The poor in celebration burned tar in barrels.
Fire made a kaleidoscope of wet streets.

I loved to stroll about in windy rain to watch
Streets training themselves to be abandoned.
By then the young had begun to disappear,
Leaving a melancholia like a dark pothole
That only the rains could fill. In the long
Afternoons of Sundays there would be a flood
Of black shawls and a brief sleet of children
As well as a drought of able-bodied men—
Factories overseas had claimed them, or a combination
Of TB and the ever-promising vagrant sea.
The villagers never trusted me, so for years
I photographed only what they could trust and see:
Corpus Christi processions, sycamore trees, local
Football teams or scullers bolting down the river.
But politics was the most awkward field. I hung
Around to collect images at the centre of its
World; dragging old men from the stifling alcoves
Of meetings. I didn't know what I was meant to see

Because I was called in at the end of events
With camera and tripod. My wife arranged
The lights above their heads. She created
An aura of strength around their tired faces,
A sort of grey metallic, a solder of wisdom.
Their chairman I remember best. He wore
A gold watch-chain to every meeting;
He had a voice as revered as a Miraculous Medal—
That gold chain sparkled in my best photographs,
Though I tried to dampen it in the negative.

His secretary owned innumerable fields.
I photographed him in one perfect moment
During a 1960 snowstorm; a starched
Figure caught against a herd of yearlings.
My wife remembers them too, under our lights,
As they held resolutely to tenancies and laws.
"If only they had strength," she used to say, when
They were building anew, shedding bloody days.

Picasso's "Composition au Papillon"

When I contemplate your magic gifts tonight,
alone, the back-boiler creaking, the frosty moonlight,
I am reminded that you were Leonardo
reincarnate, the Cuchulain of canvas.
Paint never buckled under such pressure—
Guernica, vulgar goats, the portraits of Olga;
even something as brittle as "Composition au Papillon"
has the finished look to make gods finite.

In Paris, at fifty-one, you could play God
with cloth, string, a thumb-tack, oil. Truth is
we are all born to an artless, provincial stench.
If we are lucky, Picasso, we die French.

Hugh MacDiarmid

Here on the Celtic fringe ice is very thin;
if you speak a word of English I'll fall in,
into the *muckle toon* of florid talk,
the quagmire of manners, the velvet catwalk
of bourgeois courtesy. Let us kiss each other
on the arse for luck, and not stir
again until I've praised as best I can

your own gift, and your genius, Scotland.
How you suffered at the hands of others,
dear Chris! The air was very thin
between cabins, the kirk too full of nerves
to challenge those who came to burn and sin.
Dr Grieve, remember the good luck
of having a postman for a father
and a post-office full of Victorian books
to cheer you while you waited there.
Scotland's past was a parcel of ill-luck,
with you, its covering letter, gone astray.
History can't close on the Sabbath Day,
nor poetry. They festered in the volumes
that you took away. Poor man's child, say
"I'm sorry. I know too much for my age.
My bourgeois teachers are in a rage."

The sentimental masters would have you praise
our unique Celticness, the infinite
boredom of the picturesque, braes
at break of day. I can hear you say
"What about the slums, the insomniac
nature of poverty and disease?"
You had a continent elsewhere
to write about: Stalin's land
that you and they could barely understand.

As Benedict of Clusa used to say
to the troublesome Bishops of Aquitaine
"I have two houses full of books,
I meditate upon them every day."

How much of Scotland fell apart
when you broke down, how many mere tits' eggs
that would have pleased the pious kirk?
More natural achievements took their place:
a winter mezereum, differential calculus,
that dragged you into a wider arc
to stare amazed at the mere *material*.
There, on the material fringe, the ice

was very thin. You swallowed more
than Scotland whole when you jumped in.

November

The sun has burned the toast of the morning
yet again. Outside our window, late mist
is blown upriver. A thrush begins to sing;
it spits through the flaky Saturday haze.

In the yard there isn't much left of autumn.
Frayed Virginia leaves in the corner
are the summer's disquieting shrapnel—
one year on, an Arts Council grant winds down.

Life that is fragmentary and difficult
has had space to run with outstretched arms;
the blame and lack of love you might have felt
is deeper now. Our child bawls like an alarm

as he has done every night for two years.
Has he found me wanting? I would not wish him
the father I had; hopeless father
who couldn't shield us from the bitching parish

of his own misery. The house was claustrophobic
but only with his own troubles.
It takes so long for a father to learn love,
to ditch the hero for the outstretched hand.

We survive self-knowledge like the memory
of war or a car crash. Not only ourselves
are victims but those who teach us to love.
Each year vanities fall away like leaves

to expose more of our basic structure,
all lopped branches and cankered scars.
Here is memory, here is the recent humus
of trouble. The new gutter sheds tears.

Each gust of wind traps more retreating leaves,
keeps them cornered, makes a damp imprint
of whatever wound. The full year grieves
like a bomb-victim in a basement

and poems come like ballads of the IRA,
under pressure but not admitting love;
primed to defend the hot selected areas.
There, time stands still, more naked and unkind

as years pass overhead. In the shopping mall
of parenthood we are lost. There are fractious walks
in the park, tired shoulders in a wood
or seaside strolls where once was horny talk

before love-making. These, the recurring images
of you, seashells, stones on a sunlit beach,
dolphins, these come to me at the edge
of autumn. They are out of reach

too often now. Pressure of the domestic,
ritual duties of the house. We yearn for more:
domesticity is only interim music.
Love feeds at the edge beyond the seashore

from where it springs. Leaves brush against
the breakfast window. You are asleep once more
after a night of lustful happiness
stolen from the kids. Let's get a divorce

from them and hide in the foliage. Toast
is burning for you through the breakfast news.
The purple dregs of wine in a glass—
Californian, and ripe as figs

against a November wall—have not lost
their sexual taste. The night was seed-filled
and hot as any night in adolescence.
The deep tannin of love still holds.

Only poetry itself is ever autumnal,
wanting to drag in and to store too much.
Better to lose as much again, overturn creels
of possible images. One cannot store touch

or the sensuous moment. The year hangs
now from the cliff of autumn. Winter fills
us already with its compositions, its strange
cleansing light. Rain has washed window-sills

and left them gasping. The haze has lifted.
I breakfast on the good words between
us now. Winter arrives with its gifted
techniques. Leaf fragments adhere to glass, seem

like marmalade pieces left on a plate
or sweet-papers blown across a beach.
I move to the grill to turn up the heat
for more toast. Sunlight is within reach

if only I could touch the lintel of November.
Familiar smells, the grill-pan warms.
November, your birthday. Love breathes upon fear
the way a kiss moistens an exposed arm.

Patrick Street

Today, the passionate light of a city in the South,
                                        red light
of October and its various shades. Sunlight
                                in a passing car
like a stunned moth on a theatre poster:
                        the heartbeat
of what has happened here and what's to come.

Louis MacNeice in America

Your *Autumn Journal* is still in my hand
as I leave Grennan's Vassar. A cinnamon roll
crumbles when I find your imaginary islands,
Marlborough and Achill. The train edges

apologetically across the marshalling-yard
of the Hudson. Coffee stains your stanzas.

It is your voice more than any other
that I hear on my Amtrak journeys.
In Plattsburg, New York State,
a teenager flirts with a tired conductor:
Sir, do you think I'm a slut? I'm psychosexual!
The narrator in you would make a poem of this,
for you were the poet of the damaged.

Beside me a priest fears for the Berlin wall,
a professor fears for the life of the Pope,
an illegal immigrant fears for Ireland.
How you would have connected all
these things, as you connected friends
with their fulfilled and unfulfilled hopes.

While there's life and cigarettes there's hope.
Sanguine heart, you described hope without faith;
blessed particulars without God or Lenin;
life highly glossed like lipstick on a cup
                    or the rim of a glass.
How quickly you understood there was less sin
in America than in any other place.

The Cappoquin Cricket XI

Memory is a *plein air* studio,
contemporaneous, ourselves looking on:
like this Edwardian afternoon in Cappoquin.
It is a resolute moment above our town,
a game of cricket ended. Eleven men
kneel down awhile before letting go.

Young men, no doubt, from the best families
                    of my native town,
the top eleven of the freehold name-plates.

Each one is at ease with the photographer
twelve years before the Free State
made such self-assurance legitimate:

Frahers, Oldens and Whites, Collenders
and Walshes, a young Kenny from the square,
Laceys born to be factory managers,
Barrons and Currans, Bolgers and Sargents.
Boarding-schools and monsignor uncles
will uplift the more banal trades.

Here we find the past at its most naked,
men fully dressed in cricket whites, prosperous,
not an Ireland to be imagined or made
whole in national speeches, but the thing itself:
social power and its immortal oneness
as well-connected as a Diocesan priest.

One player with flowing black curls
and perfect smiling teeth, he'll inherit
an import business and a river boat.
A youth with eyes and mouth that never smile
will make his fortune as a Sweepstake agent.
None of them, as far as I can tell,
will lose in love; none will marry a local.

Connections will be made from other towns.
Middle-class in a poor, congested land,
their destinies seem relentless, destined.
A nation awake, soviets and flying columns,
to the very end nothing disturbs the pattern.
Bourgeois chances were theirs to take

on afternoons never as tendentious
as my own bitter speculation is.
Words are things I hurl from Twig Bog Lane.
They stick for a moment to such perfect ease:
a simple photograph, the white comfort
of sport. Only, my childhood is a jealous critic
and burns the plate at their bended knees.

Dennis O'Driscoll (1954–)

Dennis O'Driscoll has been called a poet of the everyday, but his poetry finds its greatest intensity in the meeting of the ordinary with the marvelous and terrible anomalies that occasionally disrupt its reassuring boredom. In his first collection, *Kist,* the small quotidian events the poems describe are continually transformed into versions of destruction and death. "C'mon Everybody," for example, begins with what looks like a simple critique of conformity in a technological age: "every morning / everybody in the world / begins the day with radio." But this short poem then speeds toward the worst-case conclusion to its scenario: "nobody looks outside where clouds / are gathering in a mushroom shape / forecasting bad weather."[1]

The raw encounters with death and disease in *Kist* give way to more artistically shaped models of tragedy in O'Driscoll's later work. Always, though, his poems teeter in the fragile instant in which tragedy is indeed impending, the moment that holds "the terminal diseases still dormant in our cells."[2] Like the protagonist of "G-Plan Angst" (later renamed "Middle-Class Blues") what these poems fear most "are the stories that begin: / *He had everything. . . . Then one day.*"[3]

O'Driscoll found his poetic métier in *The Bottom Line,* the volume he published in 1994. The author biography on the book's flap declares that O'Driscoll has "worked in offices since he was sixteen," a fact that may explain why the poems in this collection so convincingly portray the office as the landscape of catastrophe in a minor key. The threats in this sequence of fifty lyrics are subdued: the secretary who might reciprocate a married businessman's interest, time wasted on work that can't be billed. But they feel ominous in the confined space of the office cubicle. Death in *The Bottom Line* is dressed in tasteful business attire, but eventually "his / cellular telephone will toll for you."[4] *The Bottom Line* closes with a kind of year-end statement about the spread of business throughout the lives of everyone it touches: "In the end of the day, for my successors too, / what will cost sleep are market forces, vagaries / of share price, p/e ratio, the bottom line."[5] A similar business model informs O'Driscoll's views on what he might call the manufacturing of Irish poetry. "Like any small indigenous industry, Irish Poetry Inc. looks abroad for growth," he wrote the year after *The Bottom Line* appeared. "Poets born into this country, with its limited local resources and its marginal domestic market, try to export their produce to America, and spend a good deal of time marketing it there. Becoming a poet in Ireland is a matter not so much of apprenticeship as audition. Successful poets need to be seen and heard; and (as is claimed of beauty pageants) 'personality' counts for a great deal if you are to win the star prizes: transatlantic trips, prominence at literary conferences, triumphal entry into the canon of Irish studies."[6]

In his more recent work O'Driscoll has continued to catalog the dissatisfactions of the ordinary working life and to voice the fear that even that disappointing life won't last long enough to suffice. News in an O'Driscoll poem is mostly bad. Travel is business travel, made up of treks at dawn through familiar terminals in unfamiliar cities. Against this backdrop of despair, however, O'Driscoll is uniquely adept at registering small tremors of fulfillment, like those expressed in "Home," and the pleasures, like birdsong heard at the edge of the parking lot, that may be found on the margins of the workday.

Dennis O'Driscoll was born in 1954 in Thurles in County Tipperary. He spent nearly a half century working in the civil service. In addition to poetry, he has published a wide range of commentary on contemporary Irish literature.

NOTES

1. "C'mon Everybody," *Kist* (Mountrath, Portlaoise, Ireland: Dolmen Press, 1982), p. 28. This poem is not included in this anthology.

2. "Here and Now," *Hidden Extras* (Dublin, Daedalus, 1987), p. 13.

3. "G-Plan Angst," *Hidden Extras*, p. 12. Renamed "Middle-Class Blues" in *New and Selected Poems* (London: Anvil Press Poetry, 2004).

4. "(32)," *The Bottom Line* (Dublin: Dedalus Press, 1994), p. 22.

5. "(50)," *The Bottom Line*, p. 31.

6. "Troubled Thoughts: Poetry Politics in Contemporary Ireland," *The Southern Review*, vol. 31, no. 3 (Summer 1995), p. 639.

Porlock

this is the best poem I have never written
it is composed of all the stunning lines I thought up
but lacked the time or place or paper to jot down

this is a poem of distractions, interruptions, clamouring telephones
this is a poem that reveals how incompatible with verse my life is
this is a home for mentally lapsed poems

this is the lost property office of poetry
this is my poem without a hero, conceived but never born
this is a prisoner of consciousness, a victim of intelligence leaks

this is the poem that cannot learn itself by heart
this is the poem that has not found its individual voice
this is the poem that has forgotten its own name

this is my most unmemorable creation
these are my most disposable lines
this is the poem that dispenses with words

Breviary

STORM

a vein of lightning slits the sky
discharges a haemorrhage of rain

IDOLATRY

the strawberry is a sacred heart
a tooth here is a foot in heaven

HOSPITAL

between pre-natal and mortuary
the research unit

MANNA

> a yolk of moon
> its shell speckled with stars

ARS POETICA

> butchers put price tags on meat
> or neatly trim the fat around its edge

ARS EDITORIA

> each body of work is tested by the surgeon
> for the regularity of its beat:
> he scans it thoroughly for jarring rhythms, stress
> rejects superfluous appendices and checks the x-ray's proofs
>
> his failures are remaindered, their circulation stopped

NIGHT WATCH

> to get to sleep
> he started to count sheep
> but they too were
> being led to the slaughter

EVERGREEN

> God perches at the apex
> of his star-decorated tree
>
> a Christmas fairy
> that can withhold or grant our wish
>
> waving wand or stick
> conducting the music of the spheres

HERITAGE

> what looks like chalk dust
> floats down from the blackboard sky
>
> knee-deep in its white detritus
> children climb out from the rubble

where killed friends and teachers lie
and try to build a snowman

THE FATHER

after William Carlos Williams

so much depends
upon the familiar sound
of his red car

coming at night
around the final bend
toward home

scattering white chickens
and shattering glazed puddles
of rain

Middle-Class Blues

He has everything.
A beautiful young wife.
A comfortable home.
A secure job.
A velvet three-piece suite.
A metallic-silver car.
A mahogany cocktail cabinet.
A rugby trophy.
A remote-controlled music centre.
A set of golf clubs under the hallstand.
A fair-haired daughter learning to walk.

What he is afraid of most
and what keeps him tossing some nights
on the electric underblanket,
listening to the antique clock
clicking with disapproval from the landing,
are the stories that begin:

He had everything.
A beautiful young wife.
A comfortable home.
A secure job.
Then one day.

Normally Speaking

To assume everything has meaning.
To return at evening
feeling you have earned a rest
and put your feet up
before a glowing TV set and fire.
To have your favourite shows.
To be married to a local
whom your parents absolutely adore.
To be satisfied with what you have,
the neighbours, the current hemline,
the dual immersion, the government doing its best.
To keep to an average size
and buy clothes off the rack.
To bear the kind of face
that can be made-up to prettiness.
To head contentedly for work
knowing how bored you'd be at home.
To book holidays to where bodies blend,
tanned like sandgrains.
To be given to little excesses:
Christmas hangovers, spike high heels,
chocolate eclair binges, lightened hair.
To postpone children until the house extension
can be afforded and the car paid off.
To see the world through double glazing
and find nothing wrong.
To expect to go on living like this
and to look straight forward. No regrets.

To get up each day neither in wonder nor in fear,
meeting people on the bus you recognise
and who accept you, without question, for what you are.

Man Going to the Office

(a painting by Fernando Botero)

They all rush to the windows as he leaves.

Wife, child, sister-in-law and servant wave,
though they might also be dismissing him, pushing him away,
wiping him out of their lives with imaginary dusters,
holding palms out for their share of his alms.
Now that his business-suited back is turned, they can relax:
mother pours another coffee, crocheted with cream,
and flicks through glossy magazines, winnowing crumbs of toast;
the open window ideal for sunbathing or keeping track of neighbours;
the afternoon free for an unmolested nap, when sister gardens
and the infant's pudgy mouth is hushed with jelly beans.

As he bustles back through the front door at night, muttering,
he will find an immaculate cloth set, a hot meal ready.
After hanging up his bowler crown, dabbing his regal moustache,
he will sit, enthroned, at the head of the rectangular table
permitting the poodle, a foppish courtier, to lick his feet,
throwing it rinds of meat and bread.
And the ladies-in-waiting will pamper him,
bridling their impatience or stifling scorn,
careful not to exasperate him like clients
or provoke, like inefficient secretaries, a fit of spleen.

3 AM

I'll give him a minute longer
before I break the news.
Another minute of innocence and rest.

He is in the thicket of dreams
he will still be struggling with
as he stirs himself to take my call
wondering who in Christ's name
this could be.
           One more minute, then,
to let him sleep through what
he's just about to wake to.

from The Bottom Line

[6]

A life of small disappointments, hardly meriting
asperity or rage, an e-mail cc-ed
to the wrong address, an engagement
missed, a client presentation failing
to persuade: nothing you can't sweat off
at gym or squash. But, in the dark filling
of the night, doubts gather with the rain
which, spreading as predicted from the west,
now leaves its mark on fuscous window panes;
and you wait for apprehensions to dissolve
in the first glimmer of curtain light.

[9]

How did I get this far, become
this worldly-wise, letting off steam
to suppliers, sure of my own ground?
What did my dribbling, toddling stage
prepare me for? What was picked up
from rag books, sticks of coloured chalk,
cute bears, during those gap-toothed years?
So embarrassing the idiocies of my past,
seen from the vantage of tooled-leather
and buffed teak, hands-on management
techniques, line logistics, voice mail.

[18]

Women who matter in our lives
—secretaries, wives, one taking on
the other's features in the dark—
adapt their habits to our needs,
shrewd about what should be packed
for the tour of brand distributors,
which calls to allow, how to treat
our moods, our swears: we like our
secretaries efficient, young, breaths
of fresh air, able to laugh off risqué
jokes, remain tight-lipped as wives.

[48]

You could do it in your sleep, the dawn
trek through another empty terminal,
vinyl undergoing a mechanical shine,
gift shops shut—cigars, frilled silk
behind steel grilles—bales of early
papers bursting to blurt out their news . . .
Fanning stale air with your boarding pass,
if you look up from your business-class recliner
during the safety drill, it will be only
to eyeball the stewardess; you itch
to switch your laptop on, rejig the unit price.

[50]

Sensor lights tested, alarm code set,
I burrow into the high-tog, duckdown duvet;
the number-crunching radio-clock squanders
digital minutes like there was no tomorrow.
Who will remember my achievements when
age censors me from headed notepaper?
Sometimes, if I try to pray, it is with
dead colleagues that I find myself communing . . .
At the end of the day, for my successors too,
what will cost sleep are market forces, vagaries
of share price, p/e ratio, the bottom line.

Talking Shop

What does it profit a man to own the poky
grocery shop he sleeps above, unlocking at eight,
not stopping until some staggeringly late hour?

Even before opening, he has driven his van
to the market, replenished supplies of bananas,
apples—nothing too exotic for local demand.

Seven days, he takes his place behind formica,
the delights of his mother's age preserved
in shelves of jelly, custard, sago pudding.

Peaches on his waterlogged display outside
will still be smarting from the previous day's
rain as though steeped in their own juice,

cabbage-leaves prismatic with drops.
A propped radio brings up-to-the-minute news
or, in slack periods, he reviews things

at first-hand, standing sentry in the doorway,
watching nobody come or go from the plain-
faced cottages opposite: once they unleashed

mid-morning shoppers; now wives work,
supermarkets supply all but a few spontaneous
needs: shoelaces, low-fat milk, shampoo.

Finally, having wound the shutter down again,
the life he leads is his business exclusively.
Perpetual light shines on the tiny cash box.

You will see for yourself, through the slats,
the rows of cans like tin hats, suits of armour,
maybe hoarded as a foretaste of impending war.

Home

when all is said and done
what counts is having someone
you can phone at five to ask

for the immersion heater
to be switched to "bath"
and the pizza taken from the deepfreeze

Tomorrow

I

Tomorrow I will start to be happy.
The morning will light up like a celebratory cigar.
Sunbeams sprawling on the lawn will set
dew sparkling like a cut-glass tumbler of champagne.
Today will end the worst phase of my life.

I will put my shapeless days behind me,
fencing off the past, as a golden rind
of sand parts slipshod sea from solid land.
It is tomorrow I want to look back on, not today.
Tomorrow I start to be happy; today is almost yesterday.

II

Australia, how wise you are to get the day
over and done with first, out of the way.
You have eaten the fruit of knowledge, while
we are dithering about which main course to choose.
How liberated you must feel, how free from doubt:

the rise and fall of stocks, today's closing prices
are revealed to you before our speculating has begun.
Australia, you can gather in your accident statistics
like a harvest while our roads still have hours to kill.
When we are in the dark, you have sagely seen the light.

III

Cagily, presumptuously, I dare to write 2018.
A date without character or tone. 2018.
A year without interest rates or mean daily temperature.
Its hit songs have yet to be written, its new-year
babies yet to be induced, its truces to be signed.

Much too far off for prophecy, though one hazards
a tentative guess—a so-so year most likely,
vague in retrospect, fizzling out with the usual
end-of-season sales; everything slashed:
your last chance to salvage something of its style.

To a Love Poet

I

Fortysomething did you say? Or more?
By now, no one could care less either way.
When you swoop into a room, no heads turn,
no cheeks burn, no knowing glances are exchanged,

no eye contact is made. You are no longer
a meaningful contender in the passion stakes.
But a love poet must somehow make love,
if only to language, fondling its contours,

dressing it in slinky tropes, caressing
its letters with the tongue, glimpsing it darkly
as though through a crackling black stocking
or diaphanous blouse, arousing its interest,

varying the rhythm, playing speech against
stanza like leather against skin, stroking words
wistfully, chatting them up, curling fingers
around the long flowing tresses of sentences.

II

Never again, though, will a living Muse
choose you from the crowd in some romantic city—
Paris, Prague—singling you out, her pouting lips
a fountain where you resuscitate your art.

Not with you in view will she hold court to her mirror,
matching this halter-neck with that skirt, changing her mind,
testing other options, hovering between a cashmere
and velvet combination or plain t-shirt and jeans,

watching the clock, listening for the intercom or phone.
Not for your eyes her foam bath, hot wax, hook-snapped lace,
her face creams, moisturisers, streaks and highlights.
Not for your ears the excited shriek of her zip.

Look to the dictionary as a sex manual.
Tease beauty's features into words that will assuage
the pain, converting you—in this hour of need—
to someone slim and lithe and young and eligible for love again.

Tulipomania

And who on earth would blame them,
those Dutch merchants prepared
to give up everything they owned
for the pearl of great price
that is a tulip bulb?

What house wallowing in canal mud,
like a rigged-out ship marooned
in harbour, could hold its own,
however secure its moorings,
against the ground-breaking tulip egg
that incubates in spring, sprouting shoots
of incandescent plumage: tangerine feathers
rippled with pink, streaked with aquamarine?

And who, with his priorities in place,
would hesitate to exchange
his very home for the tulip that leaves
no blood-red trail of perfume
but proceeds to make its bed
in the tactile gloss of satin sheets?

What crinoline gown, what silk
chemise, slithering to the boards
of a lead-windowed bedroom,
could compare with this stranger
bearing arcane knowledge from
a stream-splashed crag in Tien Shan
or the snow-melts of Tashkent?

Who wouldn't want to fade out
in a blaze of glory? Who wouldn't
sacrifice himself on an altar
of urn-shaped tulips, a pyre
of flaming crimsons, smoky maroons?

Who wouldn't be the better
for the lesson of those petals,
dropping off like share values,
precious metal rates,
leaving time to meditate on fortune,
speculate on loss?

The Clericals

How slowly, in those pre-flexi days, the cautious hands
of standard-issue civil service clocks moved, leaving you
impatient to change into flowered polyester frocks,
cheesecloth skirts, bellbottoms, platform shoes,
finding the sequinned night still young at 2 AM,
held in its velvet embrace under the gaze
of a ballroom's crystal moon, a disco's excitable lights.

Marys, Madges, Kathleens, it seems an age
since you guarded public hatches or sat in cream
and mildew-green gloss-painted offices, updating
records, typing carbon-copy letters on demand
for bosses, serving them leaf tea, checking the tot-ups
for payment warrants on slim adding-machine rolls,
date-stamping in-tray correspondence, numbering files.

The years have not been at all kind to you.
Your lives have not withstood the test of time:
not a spare cardigan draped on a chair-back,
not a card-index, not a hard-copy file remains
from the glory days of 1970-whatever when
your generation held the monopoly on being young:
twenty-firsts, all-night parties in a friend's friend's flat . . .

Your youth was snatched from your manicured grasp,
lasting no longer than the push-button hall lights in red-brick
houses where you returned by taxi in a pay-day's early hours,
barely allowed time to step inside and locate your bedsit key
before the darkness resumed: you unlocked the warped
plywood door in the eerie silence of a sleeping corridor,
set the fluorescent alarm clock on the prowl for morning,

undressed, flopped on the foam mattress, dreamt.

While Stocks Last

As long as a blackbird
still mounts the podium
of the aspen tree, making
an impassioned plea for song.

As long as blue tits, painted
like endangered tribesmen,
survive in their rain-forest
of soaking larch.

As long as the trilling lasts
above the office car park

and hands tingle to inscribe
in the margins of buff files,

"The skywriting of a bird
is more permanent than ink"
or "The robin's eagle eye
questions these projections."

Vigil

Life is too short to sleep through.
Stay up late, wait until the sea of traffic ebbs,
until noise has drained from the world
like blood from the cheeks of the full moon.
Everyone else around you has succumbed:
they lie like tranquillised pets on a vet's table;
they languish on hospital trolleys and friends' couches,
on iron beds in hostels for the homeless,
under feather duvets at tourist B&Bs.
The radio, devoid of listeners to confide in,
turns repetitious. You are your own voice-over.
You are alone in the bone-weary tower
of your bleary-eyed, blinking lighthouse,
watching the spillage of tide on the shingle inlet.
You are the single-minded one who hears
time shaking from the clock's fingertips
like drops, who watches its hands
chop years into diced seconds,
who knows that when the church bell
tolls at 2 or 3 it tolls unmistakably for you.
You are the sole hand on deck when
temperatures plummet and the hull
of an iceberg is jostling for prominence.
Your confidential number is the life-line
where the sedated long-distance voices
of despair hold out muzzily for an answer.
You are the emergency services' driver
ready to dive into action at the first

warning signs of birth or death.
You spot the crack in night's façade
even before the red-eyed businessman
on look-out from his transatlantic seat.
You are the only reliable witness to when
the light is separated from the darkness,
who has learned to see the dark in its true
colours, who has not squandered your life.

Diversions

Lean on the green recycle bin
        in the yard where roses run amok,
scent intensified by last night's rain.

Lift your eyes to the sunlit hills: hedge-
        perforated fields are first-day issues
tweezered askew in your childhood album.

Rest on the laurels of your elbows.
        Consent to mind and body going
their ways amicably, a trial separation.

*

Even the distant glimpse of a dozen
        hormone-puffed cattle can sometimes
be enough to raise your spirits from their rut.

Or an uncouth stream—only slightly
        the worse for farm waste—topped up
from some unfathomable source.

You ache to touch the hem of its current
        as you drive by, reach out like a willow leaf,
contrive a way, in passing, to partake.

Mary O'Malley (1954–)

Mary O'Malley was born in Connamara in 1954 and didn't publish her first volume of poetry until 1990. Since then she has quickly written another five collections and established a superlative reputation as a poet engaged in what Eavan Boland calls a "negotiation between inheritance and instinct."[1]

The give and take Boland has in mind is evident in the way O'Malley has reworked classical myths involving women. She has, for example, revisited the Persephone myth on a number of occasions, in "Ceres in Caherlistrane," "Persephone Astray," and "The Wineapple." In each of these O'Malley uses the story —of a maiden's abduction and her mother's grief—to reflect on the relationships mothers have with their daughters, or that daughters have with the world they find when they leave home. Two of these poems take the form of a mother addressing a daughter who is about to leave, giving the myth an eerily modern twist.

O'Malley makes a similar turn on another myth in "PMT—The Movie," a poem that imagines the dismemberment of Actaeon by Diana's nymphs as a particularly violent result of a contemporary complaint. (PMT is the British acronym for the malady known in the United States as PMS.) "Actaeon had been gorgeous," O'Malley writes, "but day twenty-six / was not auspicious among the maidens." The poem is—as much as a rewriting of the Greek original—a response to the way Irish poets in the patriarchal tradition have used material of this kind. O'Malley's imaginative reworking of the Actaeon material might be set alongside, for instance, Michael Hartnett's version, which uses contemporary language and minimalist form to turn the original story into a short imagist lyric focused on the suffering of the man: "Four hounds went south, / one had your liver in his mouth. / Poor Actaeon."

But while the grand themes of myth are frequent subjects for O'Malley's poetry, she is equally adept at adjusting the way poets see the everyday material of Irish life. Her depictions of the diminutive Irish currach, a small boat made of hide or canvas stretched over a sparse wooden frame, offer a case in point. Often the currach figures only as an incidental atmospheric detail, as in O'Malley's "The Wound," which begins with a "legend" that "tells of three men / in a currach, fishing." But the currach has also given poets an emblem for poetry's passage between different worlds. Máirtín Ó Direáin uses the currach in "Homage to John Millington Synge" as a shuttle between life on the Aran Islands when Synge went there at the turn of the twentieth century and the legendary past of mythic figures like Deirdre and Naoise, whose tragic love Synge portrayed in one of his plays. In a similar way, when Michael Longley describes his own visit to the Aran island of Inisheer in "Letter to Derek Mahon," he imagines that the currach which ferries the two poets from the Irish-speaking island to their waiting boat is crossing a "bilingual" sea. But one of the vessel's most striking appearances comes in another O'Malley poem, "Canvas Currach II," which envisions the currach as a strangely sleek woman in a slinky black dress that clings to her ribs.

> The black canvas drawn like a dress
> over the ribs is skin this time.
> Not even a treacherous shift
> separates her from the waves.

As the poem continues O'Malley uses the metaphor as a way of understanding the risky intimacy fishermen adopt by necessity with the sea. The boat gives them access to the sea's treasures—as ordinary as fish or as miraculous as gold coins and ambergris—but the dance they do with the thinly dressed vessel also puts them in dangerous proximity to death:

> She shoulders up the lumps of water
> between her and sanctuary
> as good as the oarsmen she has drawn;
> they are her luck, and the red-tipped oars
>
> dip like fingers into a sea of bones.

Reworking the usually masculine imagery of seamanship, O'Malley manages both to open up the poetic tradition of maritime poetry to women as well as men, and to connect the subject matter she has appropriated with the flashing epiphanies of poetry itself.

After living for some time in Portugal, O'Malley has now settled in her native County Galway.

NOTE

1. Eavan Boland, "Introduction," *Three Irish Poets, an Anthology: Paula Meehan, Mary O'Malley, Eavan Boland* (Manchester: Carcanet, 2003), p. xiv.

Credo

There is a risk
that every consideration of silk,
each velvet hush between lovers
is stolen from other women.

That consenting acts of love
are only enjoyed
over the staked thighs
of the unsaved women of El Salvador,

that I have no right
to claim kinship with war women,
their ripe bellies slit like melons
while I guard

the contentment of my children,
agonise over which small
or great talent to nurture,
which to let die.

But while I am yet free
to observe the rights of womanhood
I will relish and preserve
the sigh, the sway, the night caress

yes, and the dignity of my children.
I will anoint my wrists with scent,
fold fine sheets, hoard
sheer stockings and grow a red rose.

I will hold them all for you
in an inviolate place,
the hallowed nook beside my heart
that no man knows.

Every step I dance
each glance of love and glistening note
from a golden saxophone
is an act of faith for I believe

in the resurrection of the damned.
I believe your day

is an arrow loosed,
it is burning along a silver bow

to meet you rising to your power
like a crocus in the snow.

The Shape of Saying (ix)

They call it Received English
as if it was a gift you got
by dint of primogeniture.
Maybe it was. Old gold words
toned like concert violins,
tuned to talk to God.

After the French and Latin wars
I relished the poppies of Donne
though I thought this graceful foreign tongue
was only meant for men—
all right for the likes of Coleridge
but it gave me unpleasant dreams.

They say we cannot speak it
and they are right.

It was hard and slippery as pebbles,
full of cornered consonants
and pinched vowels, all said
from the front of the mouth—
no softness, no sorrow,
no sweet lullabies—
until we took it by the neck and shook it.

We sheared it, carded it, fleeced it
and finally wove it
into something of our own,
fit for curses and blessings
for sweet talk and spite,

and the sound of hearts rending,
the sound of hearts tearing.

The Wound

Nothing changes. The legend tells of three men
in a currach, fishing.
A big sea rose up and threatened to engulf them.

They cast lots to see who was wanted—a young man.
As the swell hung over him
he grabbed a knife and pitched in desperation,

cold steel against the wave.
The sea withdrew and all were saved.
One man heard a cry of pain and prayed.

At nightfall a woman on a white horse
enquired and found the house.
"My mistress is sick and only you can save her,"

she said and gave him guarantees.
They took the road under the sea
to a palace where a beautiful woman lay.

His knife was buried in her right breast.
"This is the knife you cast into my flesh.
You must pull it out with a single stroke,

or I will die by midnight." He did
and the wound became a rose. She offered
the treasures of her green underworld,

a pagan kiss. The same old story. She begged:
"This scar will ache forever if you go."
Then a choir of lost men whispered,

"Stay here and she will have your soul,"
so he blessed himself, refused and went above
to the simple solid world he understood.

Canvas Currach II

The black canvas drawn like a dress
over the ribs is skin this time.
Not even a treacherous shift
separates her from the waves.

The people on this coast know the sea
holds or gives up whom she will
and yields occasional miracles—coral,
gold coins, ambergris.

She shoulders up the lumps of water
between her and sanctuary
as good as the oarsmen she has drawn;
they are her luck, and the red-tipped oars

dip like fingers into a sea of bones.
She makes shore. Now all depends
on what they call this sleek stranger—
jetsam or treasure.

Ceres in Caherlistrane   *for Colum McCann*

Somewhere near forty-second street,
a girl, copper-haired, sings for a hawk-eyed man.
He tastes, in the lark's pillar of sound
honey and turf-fires. A tinker's curse rings out:

This is the voice of Ireland, of what we were.
He approves. Her hair gleams. There is a vow.
Later, she skips into the grafitti-sprayed subway.
At the edge of hearing, a laugh, a man's death cry,

a woman's love call are carried out of the tunnel's
round mouth caught in the snatch of a tune.
She has no idea these underriver walls
are shored up with Irish bones, black men's bodies.

She thinks all the buskers in New York are down
here tonight like cats. She hears them—a keen,
a skein of blues. They speed her passage. She hums,
picking up the echoes in her river-run.

In Galway, her stooked hair ripens that Summer.
At Hallowe'en there are wineapples. A seed caught
in her teeth will keep the cleft between this world
and the next open, the all souls' chorus a filter

for certain songs that rise from a cold source.
Brandy and honey notes replace spring water—
the gift price to sing an octave deeper
than sweet, tuned to a buried watercourse.

Pegeen Mike's Farewell to the Playboy

The strand is white, the tide is out,
the last ferry has pulled away from the pier.
Below a line of council houses
a red scarf lies on the sand,
a wound fading at the edges.
This is where the knife stabbed the island
again and again and again.

A breeze plays softly with skin.
A young bull roars out of memory, cut.
A timber-ended tourniquet
clips the absence off neatly.
The wind stirs the silk, fingers
the scarf, picks it up. It struts
across the limestone catwalk.

You were looking for one red image—
just a streak to relieve the grey.
You thought there were only the haws,
poison berries, a swish of fuchsia. Here, love,
adventure is not playacting. The dark man
takes his place by right.
When night falls, blades flash.

The Boning Hall

the wreck and not the story of the wreck
the thing itself and not the myth

Adrienne Rich

No one goes diving into coffin ships* but if they did
with the desire for pearls quelled they'd see wonders:
limbs streaming by, the rush of blood, oxygen, water,
bubbling with the slipstream. Then the flesh stripped
to the bones, flensed and the master saying "measure twice,
cut once, the same for a steel boat as a set of pipes."

Bone pipes. A phosphorescent shape, not fish,
not seal-woman but essence, slips
through the eye of a needle, of a storm
past the fabulous galleons, the gold coin,
down to where the black water is
and the little open-mouthed bone-harp sings
not of the names for things you cannot say
but the long round call of the thing itself.

The Ballad of Caitlin and Sean*   *i.m. Michael Hartnett*

His hands explored her rounded hills,
the mounds and underground passages.
He was here to discover on this journey
a country he could love like no other. Never
like this before, even with India. He mapped her,
would have planted her but this was Connaught.

For a while she was his border country
the boats, the guns, his brush with wildness.
She was his destiny, he said, so Irish with her temper
such a woman, with her hysterics and demands
for repeal. He loved and understood her
as he never had his home counties. She said,

"That's what they all say," but loved his hands,
his faith in maps, the shine and glint
of astrolabe and compass. She whispered,
"My love you will betray me like all your kind
but be for a time my safe house."
Because his bedtime stories brought rest

from the poison and sweetness of her own language
she relished English, the bladed consonants of his love.
The vowels that bubbled out of his mouth
like glass beads, so perfectly oval, are the real reason
why after all these years
she teaches his bastards their shamed lineage.

Persephone Astray

I've always kept a unicorn
and I never sing out of tune

Sandy Denny

At solstice I slide deep into it, up for it this once,
choice, chance, downfall, the inevitable winter vortex.
In a stone tower near the shops, the cards.
The reader is motherly. She lays them out.
In the centre, malevolent goat's head
red body packed tight, grin like toothy fruit
a helix of sprung life from eyes to sex
the king of hell pirouettes like a TV presenter.

Lifting him, she revealed a card of sun or stars.
He proffers wrinkled fruit. Something stirs in me.
My eyes rake the deck for swords.
It's time to go dealing. My hands burn across the cards.
I make three cuts. I will meet him halfway
be what he made me, queen of the dead.
"It's time to get rid of him. He blocks the light."
The reader's eyes are Chagall blue.

I'll be his mirror, the foxed surface spread like skin
or painted on, watery, stagnant, the sky silvered
with lake light, the bog sucking me in
but don't make me leave him
in the shade of his own terrible mother.
I'll tumble-the-wildcat if that's what it takes
but this time I want him with me, my six months' dark side
when I surface into the pale wash of March.

"He renegued before and got you by trickery.
Now you want to bring him home and have fun.
The cold wind will wither your skin.
Do you think your mother bargained for nothing?
It can be done. A breath let out, the graded sink
the space between the hips turning to ballast.
The body rests in lotus on the bottom. Then panic, flight
upwards propelled by the lungs straining.

Pearl fishers know the best training
and sponge divers. Ask them. Teach the mind
to overcome instinct." Live in the intellect's light
accurate and harsh as middle-age lines?
Alright. I'll go down with the gloomy bastard again
and come up on my own but I want to smuggle in
great cataracts of Spanish sun. Stella, he called me. Stella.
Now his red star will go out but the crops will ripen.

PMT—The Movie

It arrives a day early for once, bloody but unbowed,
living proof that God's a man. Taken by surprise again
Diana wonders whether Actaeon might have been
better left to his gazing, after all those breasts were full
and with the water splashing, the way the sun slanted
in the groves would make Sam Goldwyn hire
the lighting technician.

                                This happened every month
and you'd think, she said to her nymphs,
a goddess would know if the rage that whirled through her

like a ninja and attacked whoever crossed her path
was cyclical and came from the swollen place between
her hips. Tell that to your CAT scan, she told the gynaecologist.
I feel it comes from the red hot centre of my brain
and I'm listening to my instincts.

              The nymphs agreed,
had the same problem and now they were synchronized—
Actaeon had been gorgeous but day twenty-six
was not auspicious among the maidens.
Now he was just pitiful and made scary noises.
Maybe those evening primroses could have saved him,
such a pretty flower. Pity Zeus hadn't said what they were for.

The Wineapple

Daughter you are moving out and it is time
for this story about Demeter and Persephone.
You'll remember most of it from when
you were small: the working mother,
a strange lustre on the leaves the child gathers,
the ground opening, the man.
He shaded his eyes from the light, not the deed—
nowadays there is nothing that cannot be told.

You are moving out into the half-way house
and this is the story of half a year, childhood robbed.
It is the mother's point of view,
and we may differ on details as night from day
as daughters and their mothers do,
except in this: flower was your first full word.
You snatched one from the maelstrom of bougainvillea
at our neighbour's gate, an offering in magenta.

Some things are fated or let us say so with hindsight
because otherwise madness lies crouched in every night.
It is never as simple as it seems, this point of view.
There are daughters emerging from the ground
and mothers entering. But back to the story, the sound
of war between a woman and the king of hell. Demeter knew

from her own begetting that the gods' weaponry was crude
and would pay any ransom. A sullen bargain was made.

The gods fight dirty. So do mothers—they claw
time back line by line. The legend is told well. It sketches
over the uglier close ups. The story is hard enough
but not uncommon. He offered marriage and girls are tough.
So Zeus said. We know the cut earth bleeds as heavily now as when
the poem was written down and before that again
when the girl paused too long—it is said she ignored warnings—
by a stream and the new fruit died on the stem.

Remember the seeds in her teeth, how she had to stay
six months of every year with her kidnapper—you won't.
But on this cusp look carefully at the two houses of your life.
Choose neither. Wine. Apple. There's enough mapped out.
Separate juice from pulp. Rent a temporary room in the sun
and try to figure out what keeps so many stars from falling.
No, hardly hope. Will it add anything to say this is neither lament
nor epithalamium? All I can give you in spite of invocation

and the calling back of hard words piercing the silence
like sub-atomic particles is a splash of holy water, good perfume.
Touching, the invisible worlds physicists believe in despite new facts
that turn their temples inside out. This is the oldest story of all.
Open-ended. Home, the point of departure and return.
Among the jumble of skirts and jumpers waiting to be packed,
the gold shoes we chose together, for the heels and thongs
are impatient to be off. These are the bookends of your song.

Bowbend

Pink rain, a flock of waders turn in the sun
and there is nothing but the space between
dimensions, a luminous choreography
of the birds absence; a trick that
no matter how often we see it calls back
the ghosts of faith or wonder, to disappear again

perfectly rehearsed, like a shoal of mackerel
making their iridescent bellies dark.

Aillbrack Georgics

Plant something where the sun reaches,
shield the seedlings from the wind,
and grown, they will shelter you
and mark the edge of the storm.

If your nature is the salt ridge,
reap the wind, on the spring tide,
harness the white island horses
and plough the rocks under a full moon.

Calypso

The moon juts her high rump over the town,
the tide rises with intent to clarify and drown.

In a dream, a boat moves over the grass.
I know her, twenty-eight foot and a mast.

The Lister engine drums like a snipe. She cuts
towards me. Two swift strokes,

Matisse blue, part the water in a V.
All I want, after the fire's hard craquelure,

is this shape, the square root of love reduced
to longing, a soft vowel held by two hard

consonants. The dreamworld insists
it is dangerous to burn away more than this.

The debris of my years is plaited into her rough tide.
I steer for the point, with its shield of stormcloud.

I will try to find, on this journey, someone
who has the recipe for honeycombs.

I leave my home—there are no companions—
and step aboard my father's boat with this instruction:

forget the stars. The cleated angle where the sky
meets to form a roof is all you can rely on now.

Two flicks of the oars and she responds, light as a wishbone,
the gods' capricious gift for this art of being alone.

Paula Meehan (1955–)

Skirting a line between the mythic and the mundane, Paula Meehan has fashioned a distinctive poetic style from a brand of magical realism in which the real is the motive force of the magic. Her mystical world is not the conventional landscape of legendary Ireland, but a deeply personal terrain in which the imagination charges ordinary occurrences—a glimpse of her father at morning, a grandmother's talk over tea, a walk along a river in winter—with transcendental significance.

A native of Dublin and a lifelong denizen of its inner-city districts, Meehan wields a poetic vocabulary that comes, as Eavan Boland has said, from "a lexicon of iron, water, and quick-witted reflection."[1] She manufactures poems like "'Would you jump in my grave as quick?'" out of the raw material of remembered expressions, their poetry a kind of patina that appears when their colloquial philosophies are annealed in the forge of modern urban life.

Other poems work a similar transformation on the world Meehan sees around her. In "My Father Perceived as a Vision of St Francis" she first perceives her father's presence in the rattling soundtrack of an ordinary day—"I heard / him rake the ash from the grate, / plug in the kettle, hum a snatch of tune"—before witnessing his saintly metamorphosis, an effect created by the happenstance synchronicity of a few ordinary elements. The sun, the breadcrumbs, the birds, the father's accidental posture: what turns the scattered details into poetry, and the moment into a housing-estate epiphany, is a triumph of the imagination that occurs when a chance thought flickers through the mind stitching them all together.

Meehan's ability to spark these small moments to life comes in part from the subtle way she works with poetic form. When she sends rhymes rippling across the ordinary language of her poetry, for instance, their enchanting resonances never buck against the rhythm and pitch of everyday speech. In "The Pattern"—

a poem that seems to stumble upon her mother's legacy to her—Meehan recaptures the vitality of a dwindling memory partly by dismantling the formal pattern she at first sets for herself, a quatrain that rhymes abba in the poem's opening stanzas. As long-held ideas about her mother give way to the mother's own story, the quatrain form evaporates. It later returns—as if Meehan is reasserting her own control—only to be overwhelmed again by the story. Remembering her mother, it seems, Meehan is losing track of her own pattern. But she does so in a way that recognizes her mother's deeply rooted influence on her life's work. By the end of the poem, the snatch of speech it seems created to remember becomes a joke about its own form: "'One of these days,'" her mother says, "'I must / teach you to follow a pattern.'"

While her touch is delicate, Meehan is not afraid to take on the most substantial themes. Undercurrents of tragedy course through her poems. In some, such as "The Man who was Marked by Winter," death is "the secret current underneath" ordinary experience. Other poems probe the moment of infinite possibility just at the cusp of tragedy, trying to imagine alternative stories, but often colliding with the stony reality of inevitability, as in "Take a breath. Hold it. Let it go." The bereaved mother in "Child Burial" also imagines turning back time, not simply to bring her son back to life, but to alter the course that carried him first into life and then into death. "I would spin / time back," the mother says, "take you in again // within my womb." In the end the poem's regression back through time gives a literal reality to the wound of his loss: "you would spill from me into the earth / drop by bright red drop."

If death lurks like a chilling undertow beneath Meehan's poetry, sex is a kind of magic she can use to conjure either menace or humor. Desire is linked to death in "Child Burial" and "'Would you jump in my grave as quick?'" But it is *art* and desire that get all mixed up in the winking sexiness of "Fruit," in which a museum-goer, "Alone in the room / with the statue of Venus . . . couldn't resist / Cupping her breast." And sex itself becomes an art in Meehan's mock-biblical hymn to the sexual pleasures offered by "The Tantric Master." That poem is also a good emblem of the way her own art works. Meehan admits preferring the delights the master specializes in—the real stuff of sensory experience—to any talk about their meaning, and it is the pattern of experience, rather than any decoding of that pattern, that her poems constantly strive to recreate.

NOTE

1. Eavan Boland, "Introduction," *Three Irish Poets, an Anthology: Paula Meehan, Mary O'Malley, Eavan Boland* (Manchester: Carcanet, 2003), p. xi.

from Mysteries of the Home

Well

I know this path by magic not by sight.
Behind me on the hillside the cottage light
is like a star that's gone astray. The moon
is waning fast, each blade of grass a rune
inscribed by hoarfrost. This path's well worn.
I lug a bucket by bramble and blossoming blackthorn.
I know this path by magic not by sight.
Next morning when I come home quite unkempt
I cannot tell what happened at the well.
You spurn my explanation of a sex spell
cast by the spirit who guards the source
that boils deep in the belly of the earth,
even when I show you what lies strewn
in my bucket—a golden waning moon,
seven silver stars, our own porch light,
your face at the window staring into the dark.

The Pattern

Little has come down to me of hers,
a sewing machine, a wedding band,
a clutch of photos, the sting of her hand
across my face in one of our wars

when we had grown bitter and apart.
Some say that's the fate of the eldest daughter.
I wish now she'd lasted till after
I'd grown up. We might have made a new start

as women without tags like *mother, wife,*
sister, daughter, taken our chances from there.
At forty-two she headed for god knows where.
I've never gone back to visit her grave.

First she'd scrub the floor with Sunlight soap,
an armreach at a time. When her knees grew sore
she'd break for a cup of tea, then start again
at the door with lavender polish. The smell
would percolate back through the flat to us,
her brood banished to the bedroom.

As she buffed the wax to a high shine
did she catch her own face coming clear?
Did she net a glimmer of her true self?
Did her mirror tell what mine tells me?

I have her shrug and go on
knowing history has brought her to her knees.

She'd call us in and let us skate around
in our socks. We'd grow solemn as plants
in an intricate orbit about her.

*

She's bending over crimson cloth,
the younger kids are long in bed.
Late summer, cold enough for a fire,
she works by fading light
to remake an old dress for me.
It's first day back at school tomorrow.

*

"Pure lambswool. Plenty of wear in it yet.
You know I wore this when I went out with your Da.
I was supposed to be down in a friend's house,
your Granda caught us at the corner.
He dragged me in by the hair—it was long as yours then—
in front of the whole street.
He called your Da every name under the sun,
cornerboy, lout; I needn't tell you
what he called me. He shoved my whole head
under the kitchen tap, took a scrubbing brush
and carbolic soap and in ice-cold water he scrubbed
every spick of lipstick and mascara off my face.

Christ but he was a right tyrant, your Granda.
It'll be over my dead body anyone harms a hair of your head."

*

She must have stayed up half the night
to finish the dress. I found it airing at the fire,
three new copybooks on the table and a bright
bronze nib, St. Christopher strung on a silver wire,

as if I were embarking on a perilous journey
to uncharted realms. I wore that dress
with little grace. To me it spelt poverty,
the stigma of the second hand. I grew enough to pass

it on by Christmas to the next in line. I was sizing
up the world beyond our flat patch by patch
daily after school, and fitting each surprising
city street to city square to diamond. I'd watch

the Liffey for hours pulsing to the sea
and the coming and going of ships,
certain that one day it would carry me
to Zanzibar, Bombay, the Land of the Ethiops.

*

There's a photo of her taken in the Phoenix Park
alone on a bench surrounded by roses
as if she had been born to formal gardens.
She stares out as if unaware
that any human hand held the camera, wrapped
entirely in her own shadow, the world beyond her
already a dream, already lost. She's
eight months pregnant. Her last child.

*

Her steel needles sparked and clacked,
the only other sound a settling coal
or her sporadic mutter
at a hard part in the pattern.
She favored sensible shades:
Moss Green, Mustard, Beige.

I dreamt a robe of a color
so pure it became a word.

Sometimes I'd have to kneel
an hour before her by the fire,
a skein around my outstretched hands,
while she rolled wool into balls.
If I swam like a kite too high
amongst the shadows on the ceiling
or flew like a fish in the pools
of pulsing light, she'd reel me firmly
home, she'd land me at her knees.

Tongues of flame in her dark eyes,
she'd say, "One of these days I must
teach you to follow a pattern."

Child Burial

Your coffin looked unreal,
fancy as a wedding cake.

I chose your grave clothes with care,
your favourite stripey shirt,

your blue cotton trousers.
They smelt of woodsmoke, of October,

your own smell there too.
I chose a gansy of handspun wool,

warm and fleecy for you. It is
so cold down in the dark.

No light can reach you and teach you
the paths of wild birds,

the names of the flowers,
the fishes, the creatures.

Ignorant you must remain
of the sun and its work,

my lamb, my calf, my eaglet,
my cub, my kid, my nestling,

my suckling, my colt. I would spin
time back, take you again

within my womb, your amniotic lair,
and further spin you back

through nine waxing months
to the split seeding moment

you chose to be made flesh,
word within me.

I'd cancel the love feast
the hot night of your making.

I would travel alone
to a quiet mossy place,

you would spill from me into the earth
drop by bright red drop.

The Man who was Marked by Winter

He was heading for Bridal Veil Falls,
an upward slog on a dusty path.
Mid May and hot as a mill-

stone grinding his shoulders, his back.
Each breath was a drowning.
And who's to say if it was a mirage

the other side of the creek's brown
water. He saw it, that's enough,
in the deep shade of a rocky overhang—

the spoor of winter, a tracery of ice. If
we'd reached him, we'd have warned him of the depth,
the secret current underneath.

He must have been half crazy with the heat.
He stripped off. Waded in.
His feet were cut from under him. He was swept

downriver in meltwater from the mountain.
She clutched him to her breast, that beast of winter.
One look from her agate eyes and he abandoned

hope. He was pliant. She pulled him under.
If she had him once, she had him thrice.
She shook his heart and mind asunder.

And he would willingly have gone back to her palace
or her lair, whichever; whatever she was,
he would have lived forever in her realms of ice.

She must have grown tired of his human ways.
We found him tossed like a scrap on the bank,
hours or years or seconds later. His eyes

stared straight at the sun. His past is a blank
snowfield where no one will step. She made her mark
below his heart, a five-fingered gash—*Bondsman*.

Fruit

Alone in the room
with the statue of Venus
I couldn't resist
cupping her breast.

It was cool
and heavy in my hand
like an apple.

My Father Perceived as a Vision of St Francis   *for Brendan Kennelly*

It was the piebald horse in next door's garden
frightened me out of a dream
with her dawn whinny. I was back
in the boxroom of the house,
my brother's room now,
full of ties and sweaters and secrets.
Bottles chinked on the doorstep,
the first bus pulled up to the stop.
The rest of the house slept

except for my father. I heard
him rake the ash from the grate,
plug in the kettle, hum a snatch of a tune.
Then he unlocked the back door
and stepped out into the garden.

Autumn was nearly done, the first frost
whitened the slates of the estate.
He was older than I had reckoned,
his hair completely silver,
and for the first time I saw the stoop
of his shoulder, saw that
his leg was stiff. What's he at?
So early and still stars in the west?

They came then: birds
of every size, shape, colour; they came
from the hedges and shrubs,
from eaves and garden sheds,
from the industrial estate, outlying fields,
from Dubber Cross they came
and the ditches of the North Road.

The garden was a pandemonium
when my father threw up his hands
and tossed the crumbs to the air. The sun

cleared O'Reilly's chimney
and he was suddenly radiant,

a perfect vision of St Francis,
made whole, made young again,
in a Finglas garden.

"Would you jump into my grave as quick?"

Would you jump into my grave as quick?
my granny would ask when one of us took
her chair by the fire. You, woman,
done up to the nines, red lips a come on,
your breath reeking of drink
and your black eye on my man tonight
in a Dublin bar, think
first of the steep drop, the six dark feet.

Dharmakaya

for Thom McGinty

When you step out into death
with a deep breath,
the last you'll ever take
in this shape,

remember the first step on the street—
the footfall and the shadow
of its fall—into silence. Breathe
slow-

ly out before the foot finds solid earth again,
before the city rain
has washed all trace
of your step away.

Remember a time in the woods, a path
you walked so gently

no twig snapped
no bird startled.

Between breath and no breath
your hands cupped your own death,
a gift, a bowl of grace
you brought home to us—

become a still pool
in the anarchic flow, the street's
unceasing carnival
of haunted and redeemed.

That Night There Was a Full Moon, Little Cloud

Granny's up late and she's hemming her shroud.
The run and fell of it, the seemingly
seamless kilter of the over halter
that she'll slap or dash, again biting in
with what's left of her teeth. After the tea
she'll read my leaves and though the voice falters
the vision's crystal. She knows my black sin

my deep delved delight in the self same
sin. I exult in it. A lump of coal
on a white linen tablecloth—*my soul:
a picture of it,* my granny says. My name

should be harlot or scarlet. I am doomed.
She sees. She tells me I am beautiful.
That I'll never have children, but a song
for every child I might have had and none
got easy but writ in the blood of men
who've displeased me. She swears it's true. No room
of my own till the grave. The moon's strong pull
will claim me as daughter. No blame. No wrong.

Take a breath. Hold it. Let it go.

The garden again. Finglas.
My younger sister on the coalshed roof playing circus.

Early June—elderblossom, sweet pea.
The morning carries the smell of the sea.

I'm above in the boxroom looking down at her
through the window. Eldest daughter

packing what will fit in a rucksack,
what of seventeen years I can hoist on my back.

I don't know where I'm going. She steps out
on the narrow breeze block fence. If I shout

I'll startle her. She'll fall.
I swallow back a warning, the call

of her name become a lump in my throat,
something stuck there all these years, a growth

I've tried to bawl out, dance out, weep.
The inarticulate foolish gestures of grief.

She falls anyway. I could not save her.
Then or now. My younger sister

stepping out, her tongue between her teeth,
a rapt concentration that stills the world beneath her feet.

I hold my breath. A sequinned leotard,
her velvet slippers, a cast-off battered

umbrella for balance. The spotlight blinds her,
the crowd is hushed, the tiger

paces his cage, the ringmaster
idly flicks at a fly with his whip. She falters.

I hold my breath. She finds her centre.
Then or now, I could not save her.

The Bog of Moods

The first time I cross the Bog of Moods
I misread the map.
The Bog of Moons I thought it was
and watched as your white cap

lifted by a sudden squall
was cast before me into the canal
a full moon itself on the jet black water
shattering the perfect mirror

of the starry heavens. Seeds
of light prolific as common duckweed,
fen sedge, pollution-intolerant arrowhead.
Bistort. Bulrush. Bog Bean. Bur-reed.

The low down belly rooted naming
of these wet toed, turf sucking
mockers at our hamfisted, clubfooted clumsy
taking of each other. Glory be to whimsy

and misreading that have us cross the Bog
of Moots or Moos. For yes, they're there—
the slow moan of them squelching through the fog
of their own breaths, swinging full udders,

dainty hoofs picking through bladderwort
and crowfoot. Hells bells! And helleborine!
The harder you look, the more you will have seen;
and I say forgive me for the tense and curt

way I've been all day. The world
has shrunk to the proportion of the narrowboat.
I was a termagant curled
in the prickly armour of my pre-menstrual overcoat

barking at the moon, the mood,
the moot, the moos, until the moment when we stood
hand in hand under the stars and you showed me the rare
and lovely Grass of Parnassus, far

from its usual habitat. And something loosened
and came right, as if the land
herself was settling down, plumping out her skirts,
prepared to take her ease, and done with birth.

The Tantric Master

For I shall consider his beautiful navel firstly
—an altar!—whereat I've often offered flowers,
the yellow buttercup especially, a monstrance I can elevate
to the memory of his mother who surely taught him to pet.
And honeysuckle and meadowsweet and the wild dog rose:
one for its scent, one for its sound, and one for the tone of his skin
that is all petal to me.
                    For I shall consider
secondly each individuated pore of his entire body
and consider each at length having nothing better
to do with my time, and each being a universe unto itself.
This I call rapture.
                    And thirdly, to make no bones
about it, being the crux, the hardest part of the matter,
I shall consider his noble and magical wand. He do good
business throughout the night with it. He enchant,
and spellbind and wind me round his little finger;
or, on a moony night in April, even his little toe.

Which brings me to his nails: he keepeth that trim and smooth
the better to pleasure me. So subtle his touch I can feel
the very whorls of his fingerprints and could reconstruct from memory
his mark on my breast. Each ridge the high mountain,
each trough the deep canyon, unfathomable;
but I, having buckets of time, do fathom, do fathom.

For I shall consider the mesmeric draw of his nipples,
like standing stone circles on the broad plain of his chest,
megalithic power spots when I lay my hot cheek
on the cool of his belly and sight through the meadows
and the distant forests the trajectory of sun and other stars.

His mouth, I won't go into, being all cliché in the face of it,
except to say the dip of his lip is most suited to suction and friction,
and other words ending in tion, tion, tion, which come to think of it
when I'm in the grip of it, is exactly how I make sweet moan.
                              For I shall consider
him whizzbang dynamo and hellbent on improving my spiritual status.
You can keep your third eyes and your orbs sanctimonious
the opening of which my Master believes *is* the point.
He says I'm a natural and ultimate enlightenment a mere question of time.
But in patient devotion I'll admit to deficiency. The theory of being
not a patch on just being is. Yap I distrust! Show me.
Don't tell me the way. The right place for talk of this ilk
is not during, not after, and foretalk will get you nowhere at all.
The best that I hope for in our daily instructions
is the lull between breaths, spent and near pacified.

from Suburb

Desire Path

For days before the kids were gathering stuff—
pallets and cast-off furniture, the innards of sheds,
the guts of Barna huts. Local factories on red alert
for raiding parties under cover of dark.

I watched them lug and drag fair-got and knocked-off
gear across the park, to the gap in the hedge,
to their deep ditched hoarding spot where they kept
it dry and guarded against the rival gang's attack.

They reminded me of bees, making to the flower
or worker ants. Their comings and goings wore

the grass away until there was only bare earth
on their preferred track—a desire path

inscribed on the sward. I reckon seen from above
it must look umbilical to some object of exotic love.

A Woman's Right to Silence

When the silence of the grave
steals over me as it does
like a mantle that comforts each day

I fancy it could save
me, the way the fuzz
on a sweet peach, say

the one you gave
me in bed not an hour ago nuzz-
ling up and making even the grey

of this spring morning easier to bear
can save me; or those first
ash leaves that as I decide

which skirt to wear
start their slow deliberate burst-
ing from the bonny black bead,

allow me claim silence as a rare
and fine sister, not in the least a curst
state, but ecstatic, free, untried.

Death of a Field

The field itself is lost the morning it becomes a site
When the Notice goes up: Fingal County Council—44 houses

The memory of the field is lost with the loss of its herbs

Though the woodpigeons in the willow
The finches in what's left of the hawthorn hedge
And the wagtail in the elder
Sing on their hungry summer song

The magpies sound like flying castanets

And the memory of the field disappears with its flora:
Who can know the yearning of yarrow
Or the plight of the scarlet pimpernel
Whose true colour is orange?

And the end of the field is the end of the hidey holes
Where first smokes, first tokes, first gropes
Were had to the scentless mayweed

The end of the field as we know it is the start of the estate
The site to be planted with houses each two- or three-bedroom
Nest of sorrow and chemical, cargo of joy

The end of dandelion is the start of Flash
The end of dock is the start of Pledge
The end of teazel is the start of Ariel
The end of primrose is the start of Brillo
The end of thistle is the start of Bounce
The end of sloe is the start of Oxyaction
The end of herb robert is the start of Brasso
The end of eyebright is the start of Persil

Who amongst us is able to number the end of grasses
To number the losses of each seeding head?

                              I'll walk out once
Barefoot under the moon to know the field
Through the soles of my feet to hear
The myriad leaf lives green and singing
The million million cycles of being in wing

That—before the field become solely map memory
In some archive on some architect's screen
I might possess it or it possess me
Through its night dew, its moon-white caul
Its slick and shine and its profligacy
In every wingbeat in every beat of time

Cathal Ó Searcaigh (1956–)

Cathal Ó Searcaigh writes in Irish, often about rural Ireland, but just as frequently about a broader world in which he sees his own rural life reflected and sometimes contrasted. Ó Searcaigh lives on a farm in County Donegal where the material stock of nature and rural life is close at hand. But he is less a nature poet than a poet of human nature. Even his poems on natural subjects display his distinguishing concentration on human sexuality and its correlatives in sensuous, sometimes roughly sensual, landscapes. Looking at "the lifeless villages in the foothills," in "A Runaway Cow," Ó Searcaigh perceives the landscape with an eye trained by Beat poetry to see "little white bungalows, attractive / as dandruff in the hairy armpit of the Glen."[1] (The English word *dandruff* stands out in the Irish text like a stray flake of the stuff it names.) In a similar way, Ó Searcaigh can still sense in the urban environment of Dublin or London the substance of agrarian life, so that the poem included here as "Puddle (High Street Kensington, 6 P.M.)" turns his glimpse of that West London shopping district into a small urban georgic.

Ó Searcaigh studied at the Institute of Higher Education in Limerick, where he focused on modern languages—French and Russian, as well as Irish. His eye for those poem-shaped things in the landscape of human culture is especially discerning of the way language and poetry have shaped each other. His own poetic project has been to find, in the shape of his poetry, a way of restoring vigor to the Irish language, his mother tongue. In "Caoineadh," included here in Seamus Heaney's translation "Lament," Ó Searcaigh hears the death rattle of that language, but nonetheless holds out hope that her anger might come "howling wild out of her grief." It almost goes without saying that it is in Ó Searcaigh's poetry and that of fellow poets writing in Irish that the language still manages, as he puts it in that poem, to "bare the teeth of her love."[2]

Cathal Ó Searcaigh was born in County Donegal in 1956. He worked as a television news presenter in Dublin, and has been writer-in-residence at the University of Ulster and Queen's University, Belfast. He lives near Mount Errigal, the highest point in County Donegal, and spends part of each year in Kathmandu.

NOTES

1. "A Runaway Cow," trans. Patrick Crotty, *Modern Irish Poetry: An Anthology*, ed. Patrick Crotty (Belfast: Blackstaff, 1995), p. 409.

2. "Lament," trans. Seamus Heaney, *By the Hearth in Mín a' Leá*, ed. Frank Sewell (Todmorden, UK: Arc Publications, 2005), p. 25

The Well   *For Máire Mhac an tSaoi*

"It'll set you up for life,"
said old Bríd, fire in her eyes,
handing me a bowl of well-water,
the cleanest in all Gleann an Átha
from a well kept by her people's
people, a family heirloom
tucked away in a secluded spot
with a ditch like a moat around it
and a flagstone for a lid.

When I was coming into my own
back in the early sixties here,
there wasn't a house around
without some sort of well;
everyone was all chuffed then
about how clean and healthy
theirs was kept and wouldn't let
a speck of dust cloud its silver
lining; and if a hint of red-rust
was found, they bailed it out
right away using a tin bucket;
then to keep their well sweet,
freshened it regularly with kiln-lime.

From our family well sprang
bright clearwater full of life.
With tins and crocks, they dipped into it
day after day and any time their throats
were parched by summer's heat,
it slaked and soothed them in fields
and bogs—a true pick-me-up
that set them hop, skip and jumping
for joy, cleansing them all their lives.

For a long time now, running water
snakes towards us from distant hills
and in every kitchen, both sides
of the glen, water spits from a tap,
drab lacklustre water that leaves

a bad taste in the mouth while
among my people the real thing
is forgotten about. Bríd once said,
"it's hard to find a well these days,"
as she filled up another bowl.
"They're hidden in bulrushes and grass,
choked by weeds and green scum
but for all the neglect, they've lost
not a drop of their true essence.
Find your own well, my lad,
for the arid times to come.
They dry up who steer clear of sources."

[Translated by Frank Sewell]

On Such a Day

for Lillis Ó Laoire

I remember one Sunday long ago. An eternal Summer Sunday. I went
on a journey in a blue car. A journey towards the Light.

Time and weather were no more; clock and calendar. I was driving in
eternity. I was God wandering.

It was hot. In the depths of heaven I plunged the sponge of my imagina-
tion and when I squeezed it afterwards poetry flowed from it. Poetry
that wet and cooled me.

The grass was warbling and singing on the trees. The birds were green-
ing in the fields. The clouds were bleating in the pastures. Not one sheep
was in the sky.

I chanced upon a stream that was dying of thirst. I began to cry and it
recovered quickly. I picked up a small hill that was walking by the way-
side. It said it was doing a course in mountain-rescue. I remember it left
its cap behind in the car.

But the wind I met at the top of the Glen said she was going that way
later and would return the cap to him. The poor wind! I came upon her
suddenly. She was sunning herself at the top of the Glen. She was na-
ked. But the instant she saw me, she drew the air shyly around her and
spoke gently.

They were all as kind as she. The stones invited me into their company and when they quietened talkatively about me I understood the meaning of silence. I listened to a small flower playing a sonata on her petal-piano, music that pleased my nose. The lake drew my picture.

And the day, host of the Light, I'll remember forever. He was so well-mannered and polite doing his duty; attending to and anticipating my needs. He didn't close the doors nor pull the blinds till I informed him I was going home. He worked overtime just for my benefit.

And night came home with me, her sleek and slender body rustling about me; the black skies of her dress twinkling all around me. She enthralled me with the sound of her voice.

I remember that Sunday long long ago. And though time has destroyed it.

I believe in miracles still.

[Translated by Gabriel Fitzmaurice]

When I Was Three   *For Anraí Mac Giolla Chomhaill*

"That's muck! Filthy muck, you little scamp,"
my father was so severe in speech
while I was messing happily
in my mud-trench by the road.
"Out with you from that muck
before you freeze to death!"

But I continued shuffling, having fun,
all the time screaming with delight:
"Muck! Muck! It's my own muck!"
But the word was nothing in my innocence
until I felt the squelch of wellies
and, through the dripping wet of clothes,
the shivering knowledge of water.

Ah! Muck of destiny, you drenched my bones!

[Translated by Thomas McCarthy]

Sweeney's Eyes

I'm drawing near the top of Bealtaine,
black-hearted as the night, climbing
sloping brows of land and mind,
pushed back by the bitter wind.

She was my treasure, my Gort a' Choirce.*
I brought her from wildness to cultivation
but her natural bent is returning;
there's yellow-eyed weeds in the field I love.

I see Venus above Dún Lúiche,
winking her eye, coming on and coming on;
and suspended over the black dress of sky,
the moon like a breast Mucais has cupped.

Through light and dark, Bealtaine flames,
I squeeze sideways in one mad rush.
Lights in the glen shiver before me:
under the lids of those hills: Sweeney's eyes.

[Translated by Frank Sewell]

Puddle (High Street Kensington, 6 P.M.)

There are times when I taste
in the churning city street
a bowl of buttermilk
in a poem's shape.

[Translated by Donald McNamara and Wes Davis]

A Runaway Cow   *for Liam Ó Muirthile*

I'd say he'd had too much
of the desolation that trickles down
through the glens and the hillocks
steadily as a hearse;
of the lifeless villages in the foothills
as bare of young folk as of soil;
of the old codgers, the hummock-blasters
who turned the peat into good red earth
and who deafened him pink year after year
with their talk of the grand sods of the old days;

of the little white bungalows, attractive
as dandruff in the hairy armpit of the Glen;
of the young people trapped in their destinies
like caged animals out of touch with their instinct;
of the Three Sorrows of Storytelling
in the pity of unemployment, of low morale,
and of the remoteness and narrow-mindedness
of both sides of the Glen;
of the fine young things down in Rory's
who woke the man in him
but wouldn't give a curse for his attentions;

of clan boundaries, of old tribal ditches,
of pissing his frustration against the solid walls
race and religion built round him.
He'd had too much of being stuck in the Glen
and with a leap like a runaway cow's one spring morning
he *cleared* the walls and *hightailed* away.

[Translated by Patrick Crotty]

Buachaill Bán*

To be in love with a man:
that's a tale I haven't the words for yet,
to tell it, to say it out
in a way that won't come back on me.

How I would like
to loosen the tongue of this silence
that chokes me;
that smothers me every day.

Sometimes when I'm here in the back kitchen,
the ghosts of the house become childish,
and do kids' stuff, shouting "Mammy, Mammy . . ."
The table looks at me pityingly,
his smooth face greasy with dirt.
The pots and pans start
babbling and splashing in the sink.
The floor looks like shit . . .
his trousers hanging off him
as he skirs round heedlessly.
And the kettle, the kettle doesn't just deafen me,
it goes right through me
when it rasps out
its cold, sad,
light-metal music.

Then, in the dead of night,
he brings me his love
and gets his fill, until daybreak, of the joys of my youth.
He wraps himself up in my breast, presses into my warmth,
seeks the manly comfort
that exudes from my skin;
and in this calm,
he shrinks in stature
as I tackle him
in the sport of bed and hands;
as I spread out miraculously
in an ocean of enticement

drawing this ship
with its cargo of hope
into a harbour of content . . .

Now, I am the shore, the safe haven,
the anchor bed
that gives shelter and protection—
the port in which even I lose myself
in the depths of an abyss
and I don't know why.

[Translated by Frank Sewell]

After the Epiphany

Worse for wear the alms
bowls lie abandoned
behind the church.

Ravaged by woodworms,
all they collect now
are silver coins of snow.

[Translated by Donald McNamara and Wes Davis]

A Fresh Dimension

Like silence you come from the morning mist,
musk of bog-myrtle on your heather cloak,
your limbs—bright streams lapping joyfully
around me, limbs
that welcome me with skylarks.

You see me truly
in the majestic lakes of your eyes—
Loch an Ghainimh on the right, Loch Altán on the left,
both plainly visible, full of sky,
the complexion of summer on their cheeks.

And you loosen to the mountain air
your girdle of the hazy heat of May;
you loosen it, my love,
that I may wholly see
the beloved boundaries of your body

from Log Dhroim na Gréine to Alt na hUillinne,
from the Malaidh Rua to Mín na hUchta,
below and above, body most beautiful,
every hollow and curve, every sunspot,
every love-spot I'd forgotten

since last I was with you.
I see them again, love, the resplendence
I'd forgotten in the misery of the city.
Oh! don't let me stray again:
Shelter me here between the bright causeway of your legs,
add a fresh dimension to my poem.

[Translated by Gabriel Fitzmaurice]

The Ruined House in Mín na Craoibhe

What's left of the old place,
its bare-bones frame,
draws music out of the wind.

With the door and windows gone the way
of the roof's safe-haven of slates,

every last hole in the wall's a penny-
whistle that whistles its own wild tune.

From gable to gable the house
abandons itself
to a storm-tossed melody.

That's my kind of music:
A lilting the like of which
you'll never hear in a semi-detached

where a family whiles its time away—
however windy the day.

[Translated by Donald McNamara and Wes Davis]

To Jack Kerouac

The only people for me are the mad ones, the ones who are mad to live, mad to talk,
mad to be saved, desirous of everything at the same time, the ones who never yawn
or say a commonplace thing but burn, burn like fabulous yellow roman
candles . . .   On the Road

Thumbing through your work tonight the aroma of memories came
from every page.

My youth rewoke and I felt rising in me the dreamy beat that imitated
you at the start of the '70s.

1973. I was hooked on you. Day after day I got shots of inspiration from
your life which lit my mind and stretched my imagination.

I didn't see Mín a'Leagha or Fána Bhuí then, but the plains of Nebraska
and the grassy lands of Iowa

And when the blues came it wasn't the Bealtaine Road that beckoned but
a highway stretching across America.

"Hey man you gotta stay high," I'd say to my friend as we freaked
through California's Cill Ulta into Frisco's Falcarragh.

Your book lies shut on my breast, your heart beating under the skin
cover in the muscle of every word.

Oh man I feel them again, those highs on youth's Himalayas from coast
to coast we roamed together, free, wild, reckless:

A hitchhiking odyssey from New York to Frisco and down to Mexico
City.

A mad beat to our lives. Crazed. Hurtling down highways in speeding
cars, skidding over the verge of sanity on the wings of Benzedrine

We crossed frontiers and we scaled dreams.

Celebrations at every turn of life's highway, binges and brotherhood
from Brooklyn to Berkeley; booze, bop and Buddhism; Asian verse;
telegrams from a Sierra eternity; marijuana and mysticism in Mexico;
frenzied visions in Bixby Canyon

Orpheus emerged from every orifice.

O I remember it all Jack, the talk and the quest.

You were the wild-eyed poet walking free, searching for harmony,
searching for heaven.

And although it is said there's no shortcut to the Gods you opened one
up now and then, harnessing your mind's Niagara with dope and divin-
ity

And in those rapturous moments you generated the light you saw eter-
nity by

And that guided you, I hope, the day of your death, home to Whitman,
Proust and Rimbaud.

My road is before me "a road that ah zigzags all over creation. Yeah
man! Ain't nowhere else it can go. Right!"

And someday, on the road of failing sight and knotted limbs

Or a less distant day, perhaps

Death will face me at fate's crossroads

My gentle companion across the frontier

And then, goddamit Jack, we'll both be hiking across eternity.

[Translated by Sara Berkeley]

Lament

in memory of my mother

I cried on my mother's breast, cried sore
The day Mollie died, our old pet ewe
Trapped on a rockface up at Beithí.
It was sultry heat, we'd been looking for her,
Sweating and panting, driving sheep back

From the cliff-edge when we saw her attacked
On a ledge far down. Crows and more crows
Were eating at her. We heard the cries
But couldn't get near. She was ripped to death
As we suffered her terrible, wild, last breath
And my child's heart broke. I couldn't be calmed
No matter how much she'd tighten her arms
And gather me close. I just cried on
Till she hushed me at last with a piggyback
And the promise of treats of potato-cake.

To-day it's my language that's in its throes,
The poets' passion, my mothers' fathers'
Mothers' language, abandoned and trapped
On a fatal ledge that we won't attempt.
She's in agony, I can hear her heave
And gasp and struggle as they arrive,
The beaked and ravenous scavengers
Who are never far. Oh if only anger
Came howling wild out of her grief,
If only she'd bare the teeth of her love
And rout the pack. But she's giving in,
She's quivering badly, my mother's gone
And promises now won't ease the pain.

[Translated by Seamus Heaney]

The Clay Pipes

You won't be the one to turn away when death
rolls in towards you like the ocean.

You will hold to your steadfast gaze,
as it comes tiding in, all plash and glitter
from the rim of eternity.
You will keep your head.
You will come to your senses again as it
foams over the ridged beaches of your brain
and you will take it all in

and know it completely:
you will be a child again, out on the strand
at Magheraroarty, your body
abandoned altogether
to the lift of the Atlantic.
But before you went the whole way then away
into nothingness, you would touch the bottom.
And this will be what happens to you here:
you'll go through a black hole of initiation,
then reach the land of the living;
but the seal of the brine will be on you forever
and you'll have depth as a person:
you'll walk from danger of death into the truth.

Here is the best image I can find:
you are like the forest people of Columbia
I read about in the library,
a tribe who smoke clay pipes, coloured pipes
that used to have to be made from this one thing:
basketfuls of clay
scooped out in fatal danger
in enemy country, in a scaresome place
full of traps and guards and poisoned arrows.
According to this article, they believe
that the only fully perfect pipes
are ones made out of the clay
collected under such extreme circumstances.

[Translated by Seamus Heaney]

Kathmandu

For Dermot Somers

Kathmandu is here to change you
not for you to change it

    O Kathmandu   dark stranger   wild Sadhu of the mountain
I met you last night in a rowdy nightclub
      now you stroll into my poem
you sit down at this poor altar of the word

with your mountain dusk
　　that falls like a feather
with your alarm-horns that send my mind
　　racing in a rickshaw of imagination
with your rucksacks that are bursting with dreams
　　with your shops greedily eyeing
　　my purse
with your dogs that keep your nights up　　barking endlessly
　　with your dreams that fly like swallows
　　in the skies of your eyes
with your lovely boys' sunny laughter as they walk
　　arm in arm
　　together
with the busy lethargy of your streets
　　with your fluent smiles
　　that whisper secrets to me
with the birth-pangs of your virginal maidens
　　with the sighs
　　you raise like a mountain
with your laughter that opens to me like a glen
　　with your cow pouring the pure milk of its gaze
　　into my saucepan eyes
　　this morning
with your traffic coughing up its smoky lungs
　　with the solemnity
　　and hilarity of your bargaining
with the spicy aroma of your imagination
　　with the dazzling colours
　　of your dark
with your Hippies whose withered flowers lie in Freak Street
　　with your mystical treks
　　loudly proclaimed
　　in hopeful Thamel
with your wide-eyed Stupa in Swayambhu who looks
　　right at me with a child's innocence
with your young waiter in the Pumpernical who lays the sun's
　　syrupy pancake on my plate at breakfast
with your streets of bright Sari's swaying like lilies
　　in a breeze of business

with your streets where Bhúpi Sherchen walked
    in desire for words
    for desire
with the inky dark you give me so I can write
    about the night
    smothering my soul
with the water-jets of your skin—the Bishnumati and the Bagmati—
    swollen with dirt and sewers
and which give you weak turns in the midday heat
    and wild dreams
    in the dead of night
with the riches of your bookshops that dumbfound me
    with the cicadas you have singing
    in my weary limbs
    when I sleep
with your beautiful boys whose lovely cheeks
    are wind-and-moon coloured
their hair the colour of your mountain's darkest berries
    with your bright boys in the Tantric Bookshop
    who petted me gently and modestly
    with the green breeze of their eyes
with your temples that open up to me like rhododendrons

O Kathmandu   dark stranger   wild Sadhu of the mountain
    you who sway between Yak and Yeti
    as I do between Yin and Yang
take me   body and bones
    dress me in the precious stones
    of your music
let your passionate poinsiattas redden my cheeks
    lift me up to the mountains of your thoughts
that are gathered together like a herd of sheep one afternoon
    thoughtfully chewing things over
you who are accustomed to loss
    pour blessings on me
don't leave me here like a love-letter dumped at the side of the road.

[Translated by Frank Sewell]

The Pink Lily

Everything was bathed in its own nature.

—*Seán Ó Ríordáin*

I'm walking round the table, all agitated.
Standing for a moment opposite the window.
Staring at the pine trees in the holly-garden
shaking their heads and swaying their arms
in the wind—a perfumed veil sloping off
the shoulders of Soipeacháin. I take a mouthful
of tea. Put on a cassette. A clarinet concerto
of Mozart's. Music full of joy and vigour.
I brush the floor. Do the dishes. Flick
through my Dinneen. Throw old half-written
pages into the fire and search the whole time
through memory, mind and imagination
for words flowing fast with feeling.
Holy and precise words to enliven my poem
for all eternity with quiddity and clarity.
Words to bring it out into the light.
Motionless, the huge pink lily stares
wide-eyed at me from her clay vase.

I put on my coat and hurry out. Turn
left at Tobar na Coracha. Head on up
Bealach na Míne out to the hanging slopes
of Loch an Ghainimh to the very top of Malacha.
Finding neither peace nor release from this
word-weariness, I head back home. The lily
is where she was: stayed-put and placid, prim
and petalled, pretty-facing me, greeting me
with patience and loving looks, never blinking
or turning away her glad-eye as handsome
and bright as the glinting eye of a bridge.

The force I feel to express myself in words,
the lily has long since mastered. She needs no more
art than nature itself to declare her genius.

Enough for her to be who and what she is,
to stay put and placid in her clay vase,
expressing herself clearly and confidently
from stalk to scent, in her shape and silence.
If I step too close to her, she tenses,
trembles. She is all feeling, watching, sensing,
celebrating life in the scarlet of her soul.
Has this flower overpowered me? No.
Though I'd be happy with that incarnation
in another life, all I want now is
to be as human as the lily is *lilium*,
as much myself as that lily in the pink.

[Translated by Frank Sewell]

Sic Transit

Somewhere or other
we've lost our way
between the Battle of Kinsale
and the Chinese takeaway.

The threads of our story
have broken loose
between Four Green Fields
and Fruit of the Loom.

Our Irish is rotting
with the plaque of English
though we dip our tongues
*in tobar an dúchais.**

Our stomachs stick out
over our arses,
with nothing to keep us
but shreds of seanchas

and crummy jokes
that tumble and fall
between the Bistro
and the Golden Grill.

Oh, we're weaving our futures from our past,
McGee-ing our homespun wraps,
Levi-ing our kacks with King Billy's flax—
oh, we're weaving our futures from our past.

We're half-prehistoric
and half-intertextual,
half-postmodern
and half-bisexual.

One day you find us,
a people on the prowl,
herding dinosaurs,
with Finn McCool;

next day we're feeling up
Katie McWeir
or beating the pants
off Queenie at poker.

Some nights, we joy-ride,
quick as a shot,
subarooing Letterkenny
in a hot-wired chariot

nicked under the nose
of the Hound of Ulster . . .

Oh, we're weaving our futures from our past,
McGee-ing our homespun wraps,
Levi-ing our kacks with King Billy's flax—
oh, we're weaving our futures from our past.

We're thatch-roofed
and bungalow mod-conned;
we're Marilyn Monroed
and Poor Old Womaned;

we're salmon-shortaged
and microwaifish;
we're Old Wives' Taled
and satellite-dished;

we're traditional welled,
and CD walkmaned;
we're cross-bordered
and station wagoned;

we're horsepowered
and Vauxhall Cavaliered;
we're local gossiped
and search engineered;

we're barmbracked
and pina colada'd,
we're cheesecaked,
and tossed salad;

we're set-danced
and hokey pokeyed;
we're sean nós-ed*
and karaoke'd.

Oh, we're weaving our futures from our past,
McGee-ing our homespun wraps,
Levi-ing our kacks with King Billy's flax—
oh, we're weaving our futures from our past.

[Translated by Frank Sewell]

Peter Sirr (1960–)

Peter Sirr's poems are filled with the convolutions and complexities that are likely to arise in a native language frequently submerged in alien idioms, and they read like the kind of travel letters that must be written when, as he puts it in "Destinations," "there is not only / nothing to say, there is nowhere to send it."[1]

Sirr was born in Waterford in 1960 and spent a number of years living abroad. After studying at Trinity College, Dublin, he lived for a time in Holland and in Italy. Now settled in Dublin, Sirr has trouble looking at Europe as simply the storehouse of "the canonical past we try to catch up on." His travel and efforts at "engagement with what is currently happening" have tended to disrupt a unified view of western tradition. Language encountered in all its undomesticated variety, he finds, is too complicated to support a linear, apostolic literary succession. "To acknowledge the Babel-like, explosive nature of what we call Europe is, maybe, to begin to understand what it might mean to us."[2]

The idea that the *meaning* of Europe, for an Irish poet, might lie somewhere near its linguistic variety proposes the analogy between travel and writing that is at the center of much of Sirr's cosmopolitan poetry. Poems like "Destinations" use the common link of linguistic discovery to connect the fascinations—and the boredom—of travel to the act of writing. The prerequisites of the two activities overlap in Sirr's catalogue of "Some Necessary Equipment" in a sequence called "Death of a Travel Writer"; travel and writing, by his account, call jointly for "Sensible clothes; a robust character; / paper, pens; agility; lack of money; / a compass; a troubled childhood."[3]

In "Rough Guide to July 18" the poet imagines he sees the insufficiency of his own achievement in the disappointing gap between the description in the travel guide and the reality it describes. The poem opens with an image that unfolds like a cinematic postcard, replete with ubiquitous swarming Vespas and a beach boy who "congratulates his deckchairs, slapping them on the back."[4] But, growing increasingly uneasy with the almost arbitrary derivation of these images from the actuality of experience, the poem later reconsiders its own earlier line—"Antonio . . . *congratulates* his deckchairs?"—and finally concludes that this kind of "sudden, breeze-like notion" is, though not "accurate nor, particularly, appropriate," what both travel and poetry come to in the end. It is a conclusion Sirr accepts with equanimity, calling his linguistic discovery a "celebration, though what of / you couldn't say and, for that, wouldn't want to."[5]

What Sirr presents in the poem's sudden and breeze-like imagery here is the sort of openness to discovery that, while it might sacrifice accuracy, is capable, equally, of causing a poem or triggering the traveler's departure for the next seaside town. This logic holding travel close to writing, though, is often complicated in Sirr's mind by unpredictable gusts of desire. Love, in "A Journal," is a "huge place, unmappable, / going everywhere at once."[6] And Sirr's travel writer, accomplished to some degree in both his vocations, finally dies "Of loneliness and lack of sex," having "discovered the lost empire. / Having discovered her."[7] Ultimately, as in "Of the thousand ways to touch you . . .," even the lover's touch becomes a kind of travel, and follows the outline of desire like a tram route chosen at random out of Baedeker.[8]

Peter Sirr served as director of the Irish Writers' Centre in Dublin and editor for *Graph.* Now editor of *Poetry Ireland Review,* he writes a lively blog on contemporary poetry called "The Cat Flap."

NOTES

1. "Destinations," *Ways of Falling* (Loughcrew, Ireland: Gallery Press, 1991), p. 30.

2. "Looking for Poetry in Europe," *Colby Quarterly,* vol. 28, no. 4 (December 1992), pp. 218–219.

3. "Some Necessary Equipment," *Ways of Falling,* p. 76.

4. "Rough Guide to July 18," *The Ledger of Fruitful Exchange* (Loughcrew, Ireland: Gallery Books, 1995) p. 22.

5. Ibid., p. 23.

6. "A Journal," *The Ledger of Fruitful Exchange,* p. 60.

7. "Death of a Travel Writer," *Ways of Falling.*

8. "Of the thousand ways to touch you . . .," *Ways of Falling,* p. 48.

Translations

The strange fruits for which we have no name
Are ripening in the nearest thing to heat;
Hazy flocks flap close relations of the wing
And make the noise our language knows

As the rapid machine-gunfire of crickets
Hugely amplified, vivid concerti
For bin-lid and orchestra, the break for coffee
At a convention of electric drills.

Hard to believe our million
Variants of light have never fallen here
Or were not so quickly transformed
By what they fell on none was recognised;

To behold the lovely sketches published
Immediately our mapmaker returned
And know in our hearts his hatchings lie
Since everything here depends

On our having no way of expressing it,
On the wind blowing from a fifth direction
Over the fabulous inland mountains
Where clouds of yeti drift

And the shepherds are continuing students
Of the idea of height;
On night arriving in a chaos of equivalents
As dreamed of couples make furry love

On the plains, and nearby, in cartoon
Houses, thickets aflame with claws,
The little family groups sit down
To half the words for food.

Journeying Inland

We're learning a new language
To guide us through the strange
Territories of each other.
Limbs invent their own shy grammar
And eyes command the basic tenses
Yet how small our transactions are!
Our words still are known resorts
Whose camouflage we gladly accept.

Straying, we falter and betray
Our tourists' fear of the unexpected—
In our minute by minute Berlitz
There are many structures that elude us.
We stall above watermelons, wallets of snakeskin,
And calculate the moment when
Our tongues will drop the glossy news
Which our lithe fingers now compose.

While the light fades we sit on terraces
Facing brochure beaches, and I imagine
The journey inland where only our own
Skills can protect us, remote
Mountain villages of our adventures
Together, the blinding cottages
Flowing in the liquid heat,
The slurred salutations of the villagers

Which we'll never
Exactly interpret. We sit a long time
Here, listening to crickets
Spray the undergrowth with lead;
Watching, on our colliding shores,
A man in silhouette
Hold a shell to his ear like a transistor
And strain to hear the airwaves pour.

Destinations

1

Something outside is ablaze with surprise.
The sun comes through
with a hungry clarity, taking its own.
The desk, and everything on it
rise to the light, as if they were dawning
on some quick mind, that holds them now
in wonder: lost things, beginnings, after all this time
discovered. Nothing here is mine. My own hands
lighten, as in a joy of recognition,
freed at last from the silent room, from their dark life.
The next one has already begun. . . .

2

Friends in their far rooms, the dead
in their endless homes,
streets that wander in the blood, addresses
still familiar, and those
hardly remembered, lives
held, relinquished . . .

3

Neither loved nor known, barely imagined:
a somehow friendly silence,
a place blank but hospitable, a body yearned for
but neutral: letter after letter comes, is scanned,
discarded, touch after touch arrives and is dissolved.

4

A landscape intent or convalescent:
everything there
is foretaste, echo, a tremor of entrance,
a still warm absence. It is the childhood of gods
or their ancient boredom. Here I come
in the small hours to explore, my hands empty,
my mind sucked dry: there is not only

nothing to say, there is nowhere to send it.
Yet here also I stay, invented by the air
and growing into it, each day
a little more securely: the first of my kind
amazed by my life, that lingers, and is spacious.

"Of the thousand ways to touch you . . ."

Of the thousand ways to touch you
I select this one
the finger running gently
from toe to thigh and back again
its route fixed, like a tram
snug beneath its wires
                    above
my finger now, bolt after bolt of blue fire
rocking the air. . . .

from Death of a Travel Writer

Some Necessary Equipment

Sensible clothes; a robust character;
paper, pens; agility; lack of money;
a compass; a troubled childhood;
mosquito nets; anger; tinned pears;
ointments; a strong stomach;
a weak heart; a small typewriter;
credit cards; memories; good boots;
impressive gifts; words; a folding stool;
weapons; a curious sexuality;
binoculars; acne; a motionless adolescence;
whiskey; cigarettes; an inadequate body;
magazines; books; telephone numbers;
faith; cruelty; Van Houten's cocoa;
gas burners; matches.

Cures*

For jaundice a stunned bat worn around the waist
until it dies for epilepsy glowworms in a cloth
loosely tied, laid on the stomach
for deafness a lion's ear for melancholy an ostrich
for desire a sparrowhawk, camphor, *calandria*

For drunkenness a little bitch half-drowned
its head rubbed against the veins
for dimness of the eyes a salve of apple leaves
for dropsy the spindle tree for migraine
aloe, myrrh, poppy oil and flour

For barrenness hazelnuts, convolvulus, water pepper
for baldness bear's grease, ashes of wheaten straw
for the heart storksbill, nutmeg, for the devil mulled copper
for vexation compress of aspen for catarrh tansy
for worms cherry seeds for fever tormentil, honey

Rowans plums sapphire emerald in wine
topaz in a ring to show poison for fleas dried earth
for hatred a doe for silence the sea for pride
alabaster, oak, leopard, the wrecked sun
creeping to its hut, the night hugging and hoarding

its secret alphabets . . .

from Pages Ripped from July

Rough Guide to July 18

At this moment in the town's history
(long, bloody
in 1554 seven thousand slaughtered
heads down on the Bitter Stone)

a boy walks out of the house of his parents
towards the field where his girl waits;

the mini-market is closing on Via Roma
(Hier spricht man Deutsch);* fish

relax on platters, Vespas swarm in the piazza
and down on the beach
Antonio furls his blue umbrellas,
congratulates his deckchairs, slapping them on the back

till the sand flies; from lidos, from belvederes
Freddie Mercury John Lennon Lucio Battisti
("I giardini di marzo si vestono di nuovi colori");*
a camper wobbles towards its site, behind it

the Morettis (corso Venezia, Milano, nine hours
on the autostrada) grit their teeth, curse;
someone has left *Bild* on a table, scandalizing
the breeze; Bepì takes his postcards in

(tan breasts the waves caress, the sun going down
on the tiniest of G-strings) and surprising mullet
swim head to tail towards death
out by the eastern promontory, caught

by the nets of the *trabucco* (peculiar
to this coast, a gift of the Phoenicians—
beams, winches, lines, platform,
a live mullet as bait) but

(floundering, distressed) not after all
enough: it's not how much surprises but how little
not what's there at all but the absences,
the willful omissions; not the thousands dead

but those alive, untouched, the shoals
unbaited, not even imagined, the vegetation ignored,
the majestic forest within easy reach, cool,
probably fragrant, the burning fields, the endless palms

unlooked for, the bright flowers, those especially, purple,
with spiky leaves   the entire
tradition of observation, of the heart
open, exulting at what lies before it.

Disprized. Disprized. But then (a recovery?)
the diary opens again its generous arms,
the page forgives the (winged, giddy)
far from encyclopaedic eye

and, besides, Antonio *congratulates* his deckchairs?
This after all is what it comes to,
is really about, let us admit it, neither
accurate nor, particularly, appropriate

but a sudden, breeze-like notion, even
a kind of celebration, though what of
you couldn't say and, for that, wouldn't want to
(it goes on, past the end, fish after fish

swimming in: the cicada-click of heat,
the puddle-calm sea, shutters of the new palazzi,
July day in southern Italy
too heavy to haul, the platform anyway too small.

from A Journal

Love pines for its own country
the seasons arrive
with a punctual, private ache
and everyone agrees
that something has changed: the heart
shifted on its twig, the hands flown
the black river of the telephone
frozen over. A sudden, faltered prayer
Thin ice of absence, hold for us
Black winter of our love, see us home

*

Here are words without a landscape
Here's a shape without trees or weather

Walk here and you'll walk uncovered
Talk here and there's just *I want you*

to keep repeating like a half-wit
in a starved language. Think of it

as the ur-cry from which
a thousand cognates will emerge, each

lovelier than its neighbour: unshakeably
the difficult words take root, brilliantly

flower in the waiting mouths

*

How could I not celebrate it?
Days on a single hair
a month on your laughter:

how the dolphin plunges
for sheer joy into the light
how the green lakes turn to rapids

how some gentle creature
lingers all day in the corner
of your mouth
                    Love

wait for me
where the first crystals shatter
and the darkness grows unsure

let us still be there
when summer comes
and the white nights forgive the winter

let the god who comes between us
tumble from his chair
into an everlasting stupor

*

This huge place, unmappable,
going everywhere at once, borders
like eels, skies a blue confusion

The watched fire blazes and the blood
shifts again that branched out here

a faint rhythm growing stronger
startling into harvest her long hair
her body I must ache to gather

*

How will they live again
these streets that have led
to one place only, these dark statues
with their outstretched arms

We prowl our secret cities
for the afternoons where no one lingers
but us: the squares are all deserted
the traffic stilled

and in the bar the glasses are polished
over and over, each one lifted to the lamp
and rubbed so fiercely
our bodies thin to its gleam

Our secret cities burn to glass
as we return to the only room
though later they'll have their time
rising with the light to transform

my tongue in you to ferocious stone
our fingers to the streets below
Now my whisper turns to roar
and with an old politeness

the room makes itself clear
a cupboard we had never seen before
clothes that must be ours
slumped in strangeness on the floor

Habitat

I searched a long time but things had shifted.
Now I come from Lighting with a small lamp
to where a woman stands brushing her hair
as if privately, in a bedroom mirror.

The place vanishes around her
and couples tranced in kitchens finger shiny wood
and disappear, as I am about to, floating off
on a linen basket, a laundry chest, a whole rack of rugs.

I'm moving towards the centre, over the chimney breasts,
the fiery domes: my shadow sprawls in garden childhoods,
my lamp brushes the sky, in my arms
a woman brushing her hair
as if privately, in a bedroom mirror.
We wake in a place we have no name for,
the pillows that light our heads
filled with the moon's feathers, the downy stars.

And still we wander from room to room
in a daze of purchase, amazed by desire,
fingering galaxies, opening drawers,
touching the darkness
as if it might be ours, as if we could choose,
as if the store, the stars, our lives
were waiting for us,
the lights still burning, the place still open.

Going Back

The routes don't remember us,
the language doesn't pine for our mouths

but a solid city still roots in the bone
and not a brick is missed, not a scent, not a shimmer,

nothing's lost, the map's already drawn,
hidden, forgotten and again stumbled on

of the zoo, the avenues, the window
from where I gaze across at the laundry,

shepherding my wash through its endless cycle,
the students still smoking on the library steps,

the bookshop still in the square,
these yards of water in which two cyclists

wobble and disappear, this sandwich,
this cup of coffee, this return

to an old life that hasn't happened yet,
that still happens, still wakes to itself

surprised, still walks out for the first time
without a map, without a clue,

towards the market . . .

From the Sunken Kingdom

The lost continent moves towards us.
Atlantis, Atlantis
we have searched so long.
Mountains dissolve, a great lake opens, the sky
is a blue astonishment. The voice says
Go to it, settle on it, push
the heavy doors. Dust greets us, cobwebs, spectral linen.
Nonetheless we enter, nonetheless lie down.
The ropes are loosed, the drift begins, the mountains
are dark above us. A long journey, the land
aching beneath us. Are we moving still?
We look up at the lost stars, try to count them, try
to rope them in. Beyond them, the far peoples
stirring faintly, waiting for us to return
with leaves, promises. *The world is safe again, open
the doors.* They stand there, listening,
their hands heavy with keys
as many and as ancient as our own.

Settling

Now that the last box lies flattened against a wall
and everything hangs as if forever
we can learn to live here and not mind

that something keeps on moving,
something stays far away from us,

that sometimes we lie back
and nothing holds us, that concentratedly
a spider will cross the floor or absently
dust shift in its sleep, a draught wake a door knob;
that the house will have its quiet

in which nothing, and no one happens,
that all night it will pace, rearrange the furniture,
shake the photos from the albums, and enjoy
at last the sound of its own breath
gusting through the dark.

Office Hours

The workers disappear into their buildings,
the work itself falls through the air,
sinks into corners, remembers itself.
A notebook wakes up in a drawer;
in a forgotten diary, under mounds of clutter,
the umpteenth PAYE week of the year*

is drawing to a close
as early lunch floats up from the restaurant
and rain pummels the fire escape.
Today's rain, last year's rain . . .
the door opens
and someone lumbers in

drenched in eighteenth-century rain,
the rain of the great squares, Luke Gardiner's rain,
the Earl of Drogheda's rain;*
stands there shaking the rain from his cloak,
wanting his lunch,
then crosses the chessboard flagstones

and approaches us, a large, fretful
impatient gust.
But we're impatient too

and walk through him as through our own
scurrying selves that come towards us
with their stacks of paper and unmissable deadlines

and maybe one of them will stumble,
lift his head, stall
long enough to stare out a window
and sing our lost labours
in rooms for the never completed,
for the ongoing review, the unfinished application,

the meeting still searching for a conclusion.
The delicate letter weighs up its options,
the fax we have been waiting for
is coming through, the fax machine itself
is on the way
and though the diary's run out

and the taxes are paid
our working lives continue
in their own time, the cables are laid, the calls
are put through to our desks again,
our hands fallen into the air
nonetheless persist . . .

*

This is where they came:
addressograph, adding machine,
adhesive tape dispenser, even the ashtray.

Smoke fills the office and no one
bats an eyelid, they're busy
with ballpoint pens, box-files and bulldog clips,

their thoughts are fixed on the slow clock,
the clack of coat hangers
and consequential loss, the costs

of carbon paper and calendars.
A clerk is searching in a drawer
from which in time will emerge

a double-hole punch and a dry-ink marker
while someone with a big desk
is speaking importantly into a dictaphone

and there's more to duty than drawing pins;
an invoice rots in a folder, unsuspected,
ungoverned, unforeseen, the list finder's

missing and the marginal lever
appears to be broken.
Someone reaches for paper clips,

someone is patiently removing staples
from a statement: here, at last,
is the single-hole punch,

a forest of treasury tags. All
here is shortfall, a feast of stolen
vetro-mobiles files

and ghosts of effort disbelieving,
leaning against the Xerox
staring at a bundle

of discarded safety statements:
the trailing cables, the blocked
access/egress routes,

the broken chair
no one has yet rendered secure
pending disposal or repair,

here is the uneliminated spillage,
the unreported life, here
are sandwiches, flasks, a language

pressed against a window staring out
rubbing the steamed glass of the words
to see what else is there

The Leavetaking of the Ceremonious Traveller

"Congedo del viaggiatore ceremonioso" by Giorgio Caproni

Friends, I think it best
that I should now begin
taking down my suitcase.
Even if I don't know exactly
the time of arrival, nor what stations
come before mine, certain signs
inform me, reaching my ears
from the places hereabout,
that I shall have to leave you soon.

Kindly excuse me
the slight disturbance I cause.
I have been happy among you
since we left, and am much
in your debt, believe me,
for your excellent company.

I would love to spend more time
conversing with you. But that's the way.
Where I'm supposed to catch the connection
I have no idea. I feel however
that I shall often recall you,
transplanted to my new seat,
while already my eye sees from the window,
beyond the damp smoke of the large cloud
approaching us, the red disk of my station.

I take my leave of you
without being able to conceal
a slight frustration.
It was so pleasant to talk
amongst ourselves, sitting opposite
each other, to mingle faces (smoking,
exchanging cigarettes)
and all our tale-telling
(the easy way we can tell others)
even to be able to confess

things which, even if pressed
(mistakenly) we'd never dare reveal.

(Pardon me. It's a heavy case
even if there's not much in it.
I wonder indeed why I bothered
bringing it, and what possible use
it will be to me. But all the same
I have to carry it, if only from habit.
Excuse me please. There we are.
Now that it's in the corridor
I feel freer. Please excuse me.)

I was saying how nice it was
to be together, chatting away.
We've had such disputes,
it's only natural,
and nearly come to blows—
what could be more normal?—
more than once, only courtesy
restraining us. However that may be
I want to thank you all again,
and from the bottom of my heart,
for your marvellous company.

I take my leave of you, doctor,
and of your eloquent doctrine.
Farewell, slender little girl, your face
so gently coloured, that whiff
of playground and meadow . . .
Goodbye, soldier
(O sailor! On earth
as in heaven and at sea).
Farewell peace and war
and to you, Father,
who asked me (in all jest)
if I had it in me to believe
in the *true* God.

Farewell to knowledge
and farewell to love.
Farewell too to religion.

It seems I've arrived.
Now that I can hear the brake
more vigorously applied
I leave you finally, dear friends.
Farewell. Of one thing I'm certain,
that I have reached a calm
desperation, undismayed.

I'm getting off. Enjoy the rest of your journey.

Vona Groarke (1964–)

The characters in Vona Groarke's poetry seem always to be thinking about houses. The speaker in "Patronage" remembers that she "was born in the ballroom of Maria Edgeworth's house" and has never returned there; a house, she says, "is one place trapped in another." "Around the Houses" makes a joke out of the colloquial phrase that—made into a plural—gives the poem its title, musing on "the ratio of internal / to external air around the vernacular // houses of Irishtown."[1] The scenes that unfold in various kinds of public "houses" turn into family dramas in poems like "The Courthouse" and "Trousseau," the latter set in a railway "station-house." In "The Big House" a stack of hay bales is mistaken for a ruined estate of the kind the title names, just the sort of house Maria Edgeworth's family occupied in the Ireland of the eighteenth century.

It is in "Open House," a poem that starts in the gap between the real estate agent's description and the reality of an anonymous suburban housing development, that Groarke finally makes the motivation for her interest in houses explicit. Looking at a strange house allows her to try on other lives, letting her imagination expand into the shape of the house, its neighborhood, the relationships that living there would entail. The rhetoric of real estate marketing refers to every house as a "home," but Groarke writes about houses as a way to think about homes—what it means to leave home or try to make a new one someplace else.

Groarke's interest in place and displacement also shows up as an interest in language. In "A Tree Called the Balm of Gilead" she wonders how a North American tree has come "to rest on waste ground beside / my home."[2] But her curiosity enters the poem as a kind of wonder at the way the one tree, a Balsam Poplar, can lead to names as different as "Tacamahac" and "Balm of Gilead." Her most recent collection, *Juniper Street,* hears the coming together of place and language in a landscape's "local accent."

Groarke has herself heard several different local accents. She was born in the Irish Midlands in 1964 and has lived abroad while teaching at Wake Forest University, Villanova University, and the University of Manchester.

NOTES

1. "Around the Houses," *Other People's Houses* (Oldcastle, Co. Meath: Gallery Press, 1999).
2. "A Tree Called the Balm of Gilead," *Shale* (Oldcastle, Co. Meath: Gallery Press, 1994).

A Tree Called the Balm of Gilead

What is it that is done
and undone in a name?
How is it that the Tacamahac
from North America has come
to rest on waste ground beside
my home, to be named in my book
of trees the *Balm of Gilead*?

Patronage

Arriving from Bath, they were a strange ménage—
a family thrown together by four marriages,
and having nowhere else to go. Four daughters
older than their new mother, and single still:
their chances harried by a father's debts.

He tinkered with prospects and arrangements of trees,
laid out a town to bear his family name,
devised a railway to cut across the bog,
and so made an impression, and settled down
to oversee a world of prudence, tact, reserve,

and writing books. One daughter worked
at a table made of wood from the estate.
While her sisters stitched bright patterns
in a lace-work plot of pleasantries and chat,
she took a clutch of unstrung characters

and muddy syllables, and set them in a landscape
of her own. In which her father recognised a flaw
and had her slightly shift the view from where
she stood, to take in the symmetry of poplar trees
that secured them from the wilderness beyond

but could not distinguish them, after all,
from a future placed elsewhere;

a time beyond him when their house
becomes a final home for the old,
its rooms converted by nuns to maternity wards.

I was born in the ballroom of Maria Edgeworth's house.
I have tried to imagine the line that takes you
from muslin and moonlight to my mother's screams
and then to me, her last, her unstrung child.
But a room will always cover more than it reveals.

A house is one place trapped in another.
With the windows shut and the doors locked up,
it passed for a place no one would choose to leave.
And when they found their way to a separate life,
something of what they could not leave remained.

I have never returned to Maria Edgeworth's house,
but I've passed behind it on the Longford train
and seen them sitting out in the garden.
I've noticed how they turn towards us as we pass,
how their faces are lost in the shadow of the house.

Trousseau

I do not wear white as a general rule,
but that day in Finse, between trains,
I could have found a use
for even the veil and wedding-dress
I hadn't bothered with the day before.

While he was gone to check the times
I went through our holiday bags,
tossed our clothes onto the platform,
and picked out what was white, or almost white;
underwear mostly; socks; my slip; his torn T-shirt.

With these he helped me plot a line
laying each one down to touch another
so that they spanned from the tracks
to the unpacked snow
behind the station-house.

When our train pulled out again
we were bickering over the window seat
from which we could just about make out
a broken trail of underwear
subsiding in the snow.

Not even the final blaze of ice
seen from the westbound Oslo train
was as lavish, as immediate as this:
our wedding gift to a world
that wanted nothing, held nothing of us.

Open House

At first glance every house looks much the same
as the others adjoining and sharing the name
of Sycamore Court (though there's barely a tree
to be seen and there's certainly no royalty).
Instead we have seventy-six ideal homes
laid out with the stature of so many tombs
in seven straight lines that all run parallel
concluding in debris that doesn't bode well
for the "intimate setting" or "rural surrounds"
suggestive to buyers of huge estate grounds.
At least when I viewed the plans for Number 6
I saw something more than just mortar and bricks:
I saw myself, permanent, rooted at last,
with all the aplomb of the propertied class;
I saw myself sacrosanct, safe and secure
inside the enclosure of my own front door,
my neighbour and I quite distinct from each other
blissfully unconcerned with all the bother
of civil exchanges and how-do-you-do's
that are the first step, as everyone knows,
to cars in your drive and complaints about noise,
to cameras and telescopes trained on your house,
to asides about guests who have clearly slept over,
suggestions about how to deal with your lover,
and comments about how your clothes really sit

so neatly now that you've been getting fit.
Moreover I'd swear that I've recently seen
my neighbour from two up at my Wheelie Bin
looking like somebody looking for clues
to my personal hygiene or liking for booze.
Which he'll probably share with the woman who's out
adjusting her garden from morning to night.
Or the man who accepted his wife's nomination
as Chair of the Residents' Association
which, needless to say, is an onerous duty
that needs dedication, and so he must duly
jot down all the numbers of visiting cars
and bring the lists weekly on up to the guards
to ascertain if that jeep parked at my fence
might harbour a convict of evil intent.
Or if my new boyfriend whom he called a *pup*
when he got the two fingers should be locked up.
This neighbourly interface is all forestalled
by the containing gesture of four straight walls
that keeps me safely in and them safely out
save for a rousing, occasional shout
that I won't really mind if it won't really last,
that I'll probably eavesdrop with my drinking glass
pressed up to the wall and my casual ear,
only listening to what they don't mind if I hear.
It's only breeze blocks, plaster, paint, insulation
that maintain this illusion of neat isolation,
but how can we really be quite so distinct
when the smell of my own bin advances the stink
of next door's, and the same weeds, regardless of source
will choke all our flowers with impartial force?
And it's not just a network of pipes that connects us
with life's deeper purpose: we're joined in a nexus
that overrides each individual claim
to freedom, uniting in one lofty aim
all for one, one for all (unless it applies
to my ride-on mower, my new set of pliers).
And, in theory, I'm perfectly keen to subscribe
to the notion of residents being a tribe
with certain shared interests and some common ground.
But must the subscription be two hundred pounds?

All of which keeps me up, calculating and mean,
imagining bedrooms which I've never seen
with layouts that probably look just like mine
with too little space, too much country pine.
But even allowing for different tastes
as to where the master bed ought to be placed
along with the lockers and pink wicker chair,
I still can imagine that my bed will share
a similar setting, against the same wall
as the bed of the stranger I should one day call
to ask if he has been receiving my post
though doubtless he'll tell me to go and get . . . lost.
Now here we are, just as close as two ticks
who've been separated by one course of bricks
and the fact that my feet both point to the west
while his are in line with his ultimate rest.
Other than that, I could almost reach over
to tussle his hair or to pull back the cover.
But the distance between us may never be breached
and my sleeping partner may never be reached
unless, by an accident or design flaw,
the wall that divides us should crumble and fall,
or else be rolled back by the great hand of fate
as happened to Lazarus, or the guests on *Blind Date*.
So that we might meet for the very first time
unsurprised by the question of *Your place or mine?*

Folderol

I have been walking by the harbour
where I see it's recently sprayed
that *Fred loves Freda,* and *Freda cops Fred.*
Which reminds me of you, and the twenty-four

words for "nonsense" I wrote on your thighs and back
(the night you came home from her house with some cock-
and-bull story of missed connections and loose ends)
with passion-fruit lipstick and mascara pens.

Including, for the record: blather, drivel, trash,
prattle, palaver, waffle, balderdash, gibberish, shit.
Thinking I had made a point of sorts, but not
so sure when I woke up to find my own flesh

covered with your smudged disgrace
while you, of course, had vanished without a trace.

The Big House

I took it for another ancient ruin
with gaping windows and the roof all in.
But as we drove up underneath its bulk
I saw that what was darkening our truck
was not the shadow of a burnt-out pile
but a stack of tightly-packed hay-bales
built up like bricks, its façade high
and monumental, latticed to the sky.

Around the Houses

"Oh no," she said, "you're wrong. Underwood
never came here. And if someone did

write about the ratio of internal
to external air around the vernacular

houses of Irishtown, Ballinadrum,
I'm sure it could not have been him.

For everyone knows he turned off in Clogher
and never made it this far."

The Courthouse

One day a month, it becomes a kind of fortress
besieged by lads with haircuts and new ties
shifting between their cigarettes and briefs—
men of letters sprawled on granite walls
wherein a flurry of vowels and balding wigs
is thick around the pillars and closed doors.
On other days, the silence is upheld:
no one breathes a word; new light is thrown,
unnoticed; a damp patch slurs;
the windows, in their cases, rattle on.

The Couch

A gap-minder on the Gortmore road
when the cattle are on the move,
I am flap and holler, borrowed bluff,
and none of it will last long enough
to see a ruck of them scatter,
the brown of them take any hold.

Wait on a while, say thirty years,
for one to stray through the gate
of my sitting room, to come to a standstill
by the hedge of the window sill, to squat
and haunch, to lie low as a brown heat
splayed for refuge in the gap of four a.m.

To Smithereens

You'll need a tiller's hand to steer this through
the backward drift that brings you to, as always,
one fine day. August 1979. A sunlit Spiddal beach.

Children ruffle the shoreline. Their nets are full
of a marvellous haul of foam and iridescent sand
and water that laughs at them as it wriggles free.

They hardly care: they are busy spilling buckets
of gold all over the afternoon. But further back,
something spreads over the beach like scarlet dye

on the white-hot voice of the radio. The mams
and aunts pinned onto Foxford rugs put down
their scandalous magazines and vast, plaid flasks

as a swell from over the rocks showers them
with words like *rowboat, fishing, smithereens.*
You hear it too, the news that falls in slanted beats

like metal shavings sprayed from a single,
incandescent point to dispel themselves
as the future tense of what they fall upon.

Let's say you are lifted clear of the high-tide line
into another order of silence. Exchange the year.
The cinema's almost empty. She has taken you

to *Gandhi* at the Ritz. You are only a modernist
western wall away from the Shannon and the slipknot
of darkness the river ties and unties in the scenes.

Her breath is caught up in it: she's nodding off.
Her head falls back on the crimson plush and then
her carriage bears her on and on, shunting towards

the very point where all the journeys terminate
with the slump and flutter of an outboard engine
reddening the water with its freight. It's here

that every single thing casts off, or is brightly cast,
into a flyblown, speckled plural that scatters tracks
in the heat and dust of the locked projection room.

The railway bridge one up from ours shakes out
each of its iron rails in readiness, and she is woken
by words that spill over the confluence of the Ganges

and the Shannon at our backs. "To smithereens?"
she says. "I'm pretty sure it's Indian. It means
to open (like an Albertine); to flower."

The Local Accent

This river is pronounced by granite drag.
It is a matter of inflection, of knowing what
to emphasize, and what to let drift away,
just as a slipping aspen leaf makes barely a flicker,
one gaffe in the conversation between the current
and the flow; a stifled yawn, a darkness reimbursed;

while, underneath, the thing that falls through shadow
is full of its own occasion. Weighty and dull,
it longs for water, the lacquer and slip of it,
the way it won't allow for brightness on its back,
but flips around to where its fall is a wet-wool,
sodden thing about to break at any moment, and undo.

Something is coming loose like aspen leaves, or froth.
Or maunder, letting itself down like rain into a river
immersed in getting on with what it separates:
the sulk of damp soil; the stiff articulation of the shore,
the giddy vowels sprayed over the drag and ebb
of voices leaking through the rain over the town.

Everything arrives at a standstill under the bridge.
The town grips the river and all the words for elsewhere
or for being there have had their edges worn off
and their meanings powdered to a consonantal darkness
where they dissolve, like happenings, into traffic
and asphalt, or otherwise, in the river and its silt.

This river is pitched so far from the sea
it announces itself in elision, as though everything
unsaid could still bed down in depth and unison,
underwriting words for going on and every other way

in and out of this one place. Excepting the blood-red
trickle of sky, and what it overrides, what slips beneath.

Archaeology

Call it proof, then, this thing that will survive
like an axehead or the map of a town
where no one ever lived. A story told
as if through frosted glass, all taken up with plot
and happenstance, with the singular moment
of when such-and-such occurred. As if.

Let's look at the detail. Take that woman
stubbing out a cigarette over there. She could be
distressed or paranoid or bored. She says nothing:
she's no help at all. There is only the butt in the ashtray,
the used-up time, the way her coat is slumped
and how she doesn't wear it when she leaves.

Take Jane. She said, "I lost my key, but anyway
I hadn't locked the door." Jane knows a thing or two
about moving this along. More than the key,
more than any lock. More than the fragments
of a glazed milk jug can tell about why she threw it
at his upright head, and why he didn't duck.

The stain on the carpet could be spilled milk
or leaking pipe. Patches underneath a wooden seat
might look like prints, but whose—the pregnant woman's
or the nervous man's? And what of all this anyway,
whose evidence grows paler by the hour? What if
only *cigarette* survives, or *leaking pipe*? Or even Jane?

Who then will read a single word or two
and take from this that once there was
a language and a page, a person writing
and re-writing this for days? A hand,
a desk, some form of light, a life inferred
from one of these details. Or maybe all.

Let's skew it with a spray of last night's dreams:
rain that tasted of copper; houses made of silverfoil;
a piglet in a babygro, for fun. And then, at last,
to tie the whole thing up, a woman on an unknown road,
waving a cloth so red it bleeds out on her hand,
the empty road, an inscrutable sky.

Why I Am Not A Nature Poet

has to do with Max and Nemo
scarcely out of a plastic bag three weeks ago
and into our new fishbowl
when Nemo started swelling up,
spiking pineapple fins and lying sideways
like a drunk in a gutter
lipping some foul-mouthed shanty to the moon.
"Dropsy," Ed in the Pet Centre said, who,
three weeks ago, swore they could live fifteen years.
"Put him in the freezer. Kill him quick.
Don't leave him in the bowl to rot
or the other one will eat him and die too."
I buy drops instead that cost
what three new goldfish would.
Eve makes a *Get Well Nemo* card
and talks to him when she passes,
calling him "little guy" and "goldilocks,"
playing "Für Nemo" on her keyboard.
I don't know. Max, I think, fine-tunes
his hunger and has a bloodless, sly look
to him now. He knows I'm on to him.
I tap the glass, shoo him away
whenever I see him closing in
on Nemo's wide-eyed slump
but I can't stand sentinel all night.
I'm in the kitchen when I hear the shout,
"Come up, see what's going on."
I take the stairs two at a time,

ordering the right words in my head:
Choice . . . Fault . . . Nature . . . Destiny.
Eve's face is level with the fish
and behind the bowl so it's magnified,
amazed, like an open moon.
"Max is nudging Nemo," she says.
"He's helping him turn round."

Juniper Street

We go to sleep by artificial moonlight.
The floodlit stadium times itself out at midnight
and a thicker weave of darkness plies the room.

We sleep under the eaves, where nights of late
have eddied in the wind's plump, elevated arch.
We wake to only dawn's blindsided gaze.

Just last week, the icicle tree at our door
was in full bloom. The breeze made a show of it.
We picked one bud with the longest stem

to set in the freezer where it has since drooped,
given itself up to the kitchen's heated breath.
Now March is opening and closing, like a valve.

Snow-melt in the gutters keeps new time,
ice slurs on the lean-to, the Swiss Alps
of the swimming pool drape over our own roof line

and the ticking flagpole sees out the month with us.
This morning, the trash was dappled on the lawn
where squirrels are sifting with Victorian aplomb,

tails aloft like pinkies off a cup. Chrome riplets from
next door's chimes, like first notes of some oriole
or wren, slip over the path, are pounced on by a hawk

in the ginkgo preening himself to call upon a light
just come into its own. Then the laburnum school bus
swerves into view, and the children's on-the-run

goodbyes settle on the porch with my unplanted kiss.
I am queen of the morning: nothing to do but to fiddle
words or quote the gilt-edge of our neighbour's forsythia

gaining on our own trim laurel shrub. Or tell you now
that even in January, with our snow-boots lined up
in the hall, I slipped your leather glove onto my hand

and felt the heat of you as something on the turn
that would carry us over the tip of all that darkness
and land us on the stoop of this whole new world.

Enda Wyley (1966–)

Enda Wyley was born in Dublin in 1966. She grew up in Dalkey, a seaside suburb that still had the air of a fishing village when she was a child in the 1970s. Perched on a rocky promontory southeast of Dublin's center, the little town mixed nineteenth-century architecture and dramatic coastline in a setting guaranteed to stimulate a young poet's imagination. In that environment it is not surprising that Wyley began to write at an early age. Her first poems were published when she was still in high school, and after receiving a teaching degree at Carysfort College, she decided to focus on poetry full time at the University of Lancaster, where she received an M.A. in creative writing.

The collection Wyley put together at Lancaster set the tone for the early part of her career. *Eating Baby Jesus*, published in 1994, opened with a series of poems about the failure of love. Most of these, like "Love Goes Home," take the form of lyrics uttered by a woman who has lost her lover either to another with more authority in the relationship—a wife, a former flame—or to an alternative to love, like an attractive stranger or the comfort of friendship reached for in preference to the anxiety of romance.

Her next collection, *Socrates in the Garden*, worked a similar vein of material, but in poems like "Five Definitions of a Butterfly" Wyley was beginning to reframe private and public experience by returning the poem's attention again and again to its subject, trying to catch it from every angle, setting a pattern for poems that could return in a similar way to the things we've loved and lost, each time redefining both the love and the loss.

In her latest volume, *Poems for Breakfast* (2004), Wyley balances unhappy love and illicit love with a wry winking humor, in a sense combining the strains that had once found separate expression in poems as different as "Love Goes Home" and "Eating Baby Jesus." In "Mint Gatherers" what seems a typical subject for an

Irish poem—the recollection of a mundane rural task like gathering mint—becomes an occasion for something completely different. Wyley's poem, rather than following the mint gatherer on his chore, stays at home with two lovers who take advantage of the time alone. "Diary of a Fat Man" undertakes an even more playful revision of the sort of love poems that might have appeared in one of Wyley's earlier volumes. The abandoned lover in this poem, when his weight drives his former partner away, turns hardship into opportunity, giving a literal shape to his love of food.

That Wyley is the author of one of the two unlikely poems in this collection that reflect on the cures of Hildegard of Bingen says something about her imaginative range, her poetic influences, and her private life. Hildegard was a medieval anchorite and composer whose migraine-induced visions inspired a plethora of vocal compositions and guided her description of remedies for ailments ranging from constipation (try psyllium) to epilepsy (eat a biscuit made of flour, mole blood, and the feet and beaks of certain waterfowl). Peter Sirr's "Cures" takes these remedies as material for a poetic catalog, while Wyley's "Women on a Train, Poets in a Room" lists "Hildegard of Bingen's cures" among the stories poets tell. The two writers' shared interest in the subject recalls the kind of mystical transmission Hildegard's memory might well provoke, but it occurs in close quarters. The volume in which Wyley's poem appears is dedicated to Sirr, to whom she is also married.

Love Goes Home

for Gitte

Love, in this early hour of our final day,
parting seems easy to you
as the pressing into my hand
of a list of things you have left me to do
when you're gone away.

    I will try to emulate you;
    try to dust our past clean
    like dirt webs swiftly wiped
    from your thread-leafed spider plant
    or the dark-covered books you give me,
    too heavy, you say, to pack—
    will try when your name
    falls through my door
    on your still incoming mail
    to newly address, then forward on
    all my thoughts of you.

But love, in the early hours of our last day,
do not ask me to call goodbye
or wave at your bobbing back-window head;
I know the taxi that takes you away
will fume a bleak image in the morning sky—

you nestling somewhere else
into a waiting bed, finding the home you left
for a while, in her warm stirring pulse.

The House

You built this house in me;
when you left, I felt the rafters' peak
grow and pinch below my appendix mark,
while from two chimneys further up
panic smoked along my heart pipes.

What can I do with you gone?
I let hours twist me on down halls
that stretch my skin inside out;
in other rooms half-built by you,
intruders squat on tasteless chairs.
—Don't fool yourself, he won't be back.

You will, you will.
I want to be a mammoth place
with wind rushing
your homecoming in—
and all my doors springing wide.

The Waitress Has Transformed

The waitress has transformed.
Her flat hair curls,

her pale lips redden.
She has seen your face

and transformed.
As I hide my face in your chest

I am jealous
that you continue to order more—

endives, guacamole, fettucine—
until in the sea of food I sink

to watch you place
a gherkin in her mouth.

Eating Baby Jesus

On a Monday mitch, for something to do,
Gummo crunched Alpen with Eucharist—
a ten year old's breakfast

of roughage and baby Jesus
creamed in a stolen chalice.

No stain glass here,
no well kept shrine—
a graffitied church
in a housing estate.
On the priest's home top,

housekeeper screeching
in Gummo's head
like last night's lifted cars,
he is a young roof protester—
a prisoner raining down

piss on the prison yard.
He can climb the school railing later—
tall, iron tree with rust spikes
and there, lodged in its roots
on the playground side,

a brick.
He wants to send concrete ripples
far across the window sea
of classroom heads bobbing on calm.
A child's face splinters within

and crayon blood figures out
sudden red on a sum copy page.
For this I could dangle Gummo,
roping him upside down
like the kittens they gut live

on this wasteland's torture branch;
but I know he is fast away,
his hair damp as council walls,
his pulse racing a ghetto beat
he will run, through row upon row

of boxed grey—
hope always dim for him
as headlights in winter smog

from the coal-burning tombs of babies
named after soap stars

and a visiting Pope.

Love Bruise

Afterwards she found it by accident,
shaped like a huge cougar prowling below
the jungle basin of her pelvic bone—
a tawny bruise that rode
her outer thigh's skin folds.

> *—I banged into a table edge,*
> *a car door bit into my side,*
> *where a knee-high daughter pinched*
> *greedy for my attention, I bruised.*

Days later it is fading—
becomes only a flash of pebble,
now purple, thumb-print size
under the waterfall roll
of dirt and suds from her morning shower.

> *—I grazed myself on the trellis nails,*
> *rusty diamonds on the garden wall,*
> *was hit by snowballs pelted at me*
> *one school-closed January day.*

She tells herself all these things,
over and over—even in her sleep.
They are easier than the truth:
the pain of your pull within her—
then away from her when you go.

Talking to the Bees   *for Maighréad Leonard*

The city far away, in this place
silence falls with the Angelus bells
and *císte cróin* baked the night before
is today rough-round, a solid cake crucifix-marked,
uncut, not to be topped with loganberry red
she preserved in the heat of mid-July
till this woman of the kitchen is ready
to raise her head from prayer
and we are all given the nod to eat.

But once in this place, the city far away
when the baking of bread was her mother's domain,
she ran free of the house, down the slope
where neighbours' farm-sheds seemed to bark
so full of tied-down dogs
that the old mountain ash ahead
became her bright rowan guard
to jump to if one of them unleashed.

And always the river rush
under the road-way loudly
or sometimes throbbing, approaching
like an imminent rare car
turning the road to school.
Then, what secrets could she have known—
her child's belly spread over the moss wall,
her tiny fingers threading the Dubhglas River's flow?
Did she stare so long that she felt
the whole world move before her
or see in the dark water stones
things that might come to her?

Her husband going out to tell the bees
—*Tá sé faoi chré*, our son is dead,*
the old magic and sadness waxed
in honey-caves for the bread
she carries in her satchel
on the two mile path to class—
not knowing these things yet,
her little face bright as a rosehip berry,

her morning thought a young river trout
leaping, escaping the set night-lines.

Five Definitions of a Butterfly

(after the end of the IRA ceasefire, Feb. 9, 1996)

I

Sometimes your name
can mean a cluster of weeds—
wild flowers lance-shaped, a bright orange glow
in the run-down tangle of our minds.

II

I know long ago it was thought, that witches
became you—stealing away on your wings,
eggs and cheese, milk or cream,
the farmer's eyes buttered with sleep.

III

Then again, when you choose to,
you can become slang—
a young woman showily dressed,
making a quiet room giddy, capricious.

IV

Or I have seen you as a salt-water fish—
butterfly titled, silvery flat in your tropical swamps,
your enormous mouth popping
the first and last vowel of your realm. Africa.

V

But that night, you were a red admiral
flapping so frantic against the fluorescent light,
that your craziness magnified in our glass net,
made us free you out into the night air.

How could we have known you would be
the very last light we would see
before electricity in our mountain home failed
or that panic would beat—a bat trapped indoors,

its ultrasonic cries echoing
our black fear,
while we are left fumbling, hopeless
in deep corners of the impossible dark.

The Soul Kisses Goodbye

I am the soul
who leaves your body
but at the door comes back
to kiss you once
then, lonely, comes back
again and again,
my grief, jagged petals falling
on the floor of your mouth
that was always mine.

Again and again, I turn
to trawl the water caves
of your mind
where your lovers
have often drowned
trying, one last time, to catch
all those thoughts
you so assuredly pouched
in your eyes now fallen
to a desperate close.

Twice, three times
I become,
where the devil of pain
tries to dig its claws,
an angel at rest
on shoulders—
a definite breeze

cooling down the heat
of your people's loss.

They lift their heads
from the side of your bed
gone suddenly cold
and feel me kissing
your body goodbye,
over and over—
you who harboured me
so well in life
with love.*

Mint Gatherers

While you are off gathering mint,
we stain our fingers
with a fresher smell
in the long, narrow room—
its tiny window making
four perfect purple squares
out of the far away mountain—
that room with the yellow blanketed bed
that holds us wrapped in heat and love
over the kitchen, below the Alpine spider,
our own spindly guard and his soft cylindrical web
in the angle of the latticed door.
The house is ours for that brief time

while you are off gathering mint
in your neighbour's field high on the hill.
You raise your hand in the afternoon heat,
rub water across your cheek, can lick already
the green coolness on the roof of your mouth—
while we back there, taste each other.
There are no words. The lizards lie still
in the cool of the old barn. The lime tree shades
the balcony where we rise at last to stand,
now waiting for you to come back,

certain you'll hang from hooks
in the old kitchen ceiling
a bunch of fresh mint leaves to dry,
just below where we had lain.

Emperor

While others might relax after love,
he is up and about in his boxer shorts,
watering flowers on the balcony—
not caring that it's overlooked
by a hundred city windows opposite.

Back inside, he pads barefoot
their apartment's wooden floors,
blasts Wagner's *Ride of the Valkyries*,
sucks dates, climbs up on a fold-out chair
to check on the highest shelf

Commodus's exact background
in his encyclopaedia,
before the wood beneath his feet
flips back, his toes are caught red sore
and he shouts his pain to the waking walls.

Then he is that ancient emperor—
everybody, everything against him
and hearing the mob's gleeful roars
in the theatre where his anger rules,
he feeds her to the lions.

Women on a Train, Poets in a Room

After reading Louis MacNeice

Inside, the locked heart
and the lost key.
Outside, the light winking

on the waste of sea.
I clutch the red book
of hard-won rhymes
and am warmed by its beat
that is easily the rhythm
of this late afternoon
over railway tracks sea-ward—
and know I am not alone.
The women wear rings—
which men are theirs?—
their heads bent reading too.
The girl with her pony-tail bobbing,
has her back to mine,
the plant leaves
on her knees rising,
while beyond the misted window
the rocks growl
like sea men coming for us—
but we speed on, each locked
in our own different hearts,
not giving the key away.

Outside, the light winks on a waste of sea
and I step from the station
into my real home
where poets tell their stories—
the Bog of Moods, a woman
jumping to her death from Putney Bridge,
Hildegard of Bingen's cures . . .
We write in a winter place of late-night milk and toast,
the cracked floor paint sticking to our bare feet like snow,
the old woman next door making ghost sounds
into the early hours—her Glenn Miller playing,
her doors eerily opened and shut—but then
our bedroom shakes us awake with morning
and the secrets of the sumac tree.
We step from the station into a familiar place,
feel it is our home—
find that the light in the room is a poem.

Diary of a Fat Man

I am so fat now
that the woman I love
will not lie down with me—
so I make her shape in the mountains
of potatoes I boil and mash,
feel her breasts in the dough I knead and prick,
her bread nipples rising erect at 200 degrees Celsius,
hear her noises gurgling with the bubbling
of tomato, ginger, cinnamon,
her kisses extra sweetness oozing.

Skin, heaped spoons of crème fraîche,
eyes, sharp kiwi green.
arms, the curve of bananas, melons, fresh bread rolls,
mouth, a dazzling lemon split apart—
I am so fat now
she is all of this to me and more.
I make my bed in the sitting room,
unable to climb the stairs.
I sleep with my heavy boots on,
unable to pull them off.
Sometimes she passes by my door—
the dart of a thin shadow,
her breasts suddenly shrivelled
as an avocado's outer layer,
her skin rough like uncooked rice,
her eyes two empty plates pleading,
I look at you
and can never eat again.

Her voice has the rancid stench
of food left over for weeks.
She is becoming nothing—
ice-cream melted on a hot kitchen floor,
boiled water evaporating in a room.
But I make her again—my woman.
Her love among the carrots, onions,

broccoli, steak and garlic
is so heated in my thick, tasty stew
that I do not notice
her open the front door
then leave the house for good—
the smell of food
a jaded world forever clinging
to her hair, her skin and clothes.
Not hearing, I scoop, scoop,
scoop from my pot
into the biggest
bowl I can find.

Sara Berkeley (1967–)

The landscape of Sara Berkeley's poetry is not one most readers would recognize as essentially Irish, but her rich poems of memory and loss are given a resonant tension by the stretched ties to her native country. Berkeley was born in Dublin in 1967 and lived there until 1989, when she graduated from Trinity College. After years of travel that included a period studying with Robert Hass at the University of California at Berkeley, she now lives in a rural area north of San Francisco. For all the time and distance, she says in a recent poem that she is still "always leaving Ireland."[1]

Berkeley's poetic voice is that of an Emily Dickinson suddenly at large in the social world. She has a sharp eye for details of the natural landscape, but the rumble beneath her poetic language is most often the noise made by the tectonic plates of personality as they shift beneath the surface terrain of relationships. While she has said that she doesn't struggle with issues of nationality,[2] Berkeley does use her foreignness—in Northern California, say, or New South Wales—as a poetic stand-in for deeper, more ubiquitous kinds of alienation. Estrangement from places and people is such a characteristic feature in her poems that it sometimes becomes difficult to tell which is the more alien presence, the poet or the foreign place in which she finds herself. In "Fault" the two blur together, the poet's lurking strength seemingly revealed in the distinctively feminine power of a personified California geography. "The fault sniggers beneath the highway" and "cracks her knuckles publicly," but like the poet keeps herself aloof. The fault's secret is its potential energy, which will one day "burst her corset of rock" because, again like the poet, "she was not meant / for the brittle rib-cage of the bay." "Valley," which was originally published as a companion piece to "Fault," plunges into the midst of this environment, so that "Wherever you look / she answers back" with the hard jewel "eyes" of the landscape.[3] The personification throughout the poem embodies Berkeley's eco-romanticism in the bony particulars of an environment that articulates its relationship to human life through human technology.

Other poems deal precisely with the risk that technology might foreclose this sort of immersion. "Convalescent" distinguishes the poet's affective involvement with the environment from the disengagement of those who turn away from nature, "shedding muddy boots and things, / slamming their private doors / on rooms with sofas and TVs."[4] Berkeley's sensitivity to the way the ordinary amenities of domestic life can separate us from nature may be one result of growing up in a household without television. She herself has credited its absence with provoking her interest in writing.

During the long gap between the publication of *Facts About Water* in 1994 and her latest volume, *Strawberry Thief*, in 2005, Berkeley, who had already published a collection of short stories, wrote a novel, *Shadowing Hannah*. Her subsequent poems, perhaps drawing on that experience as a fiction writer, have inclined more toward narrative. Like many of Berkeley's earlier poems, "Patagonia" and "Hawkesbury River, NSW" are focused on moments at which the course of a life changes. But in these more considered later works those moments have been transformed into imaginative travelogues, as if the poet, no longer content to describe the passing scenery, has finally taken control of the itinerary.

NOTES

1. "Alstroemeria," *Strawberry Thief* (Oldcastle, Loughcrew, Co. Meath, Ireland: Gallery Press), p. 40.

2. See Ann Owens Weeks, *Unveiling Treasures: The Attic Guide to the Published Works of Irish Women Literary Writers: Drama, Fiction, Poetry* (Dublin: Attic Press, 1993), p. 34.

3. "Fault" and "Valley" appeared as "Valley Poem I" and "Valley Poem II" in *Wildish Things: An Anthology of New Irish Women's Writing*, ed. Ailbhe Smyth (Dublin: Attic Press, 1989). The titles used here are taken from Berkeley's *Facts About Water, New and Selected Poems* (Dublin: New Island Books/Canada: Thistledown Press/Newcastle-upon-Tyne, UK: Bloodaxe Books, 1994).

4. "Convalescent," *Home Movie Nights* (Dublin: Raven Arts Press, 1989).

Out In the Storm

This storm explodes while it is still dark,
I have no light to watch my flight
From here on up—riding, riding my storm.
She blows the sky aside for me to pass
And from her back the ground looks
Faraway. Rainswept. Black.
A coiled coastline writhes in a swirl of sea,
Lightning spills yellow road across the fields.
She swoops. Riding storms is fun.
She bucks and rears like real horses.
Who is old in her timeless gale?
She blows a tunnel through the years.
Winded words from the doubling trees
As she gallops past. Riding storms is easy!
Gliding on a tide of rain—
Oaks are not afraid of rain.
Time to bring her home, my storm
But reining her is hard.
And long after she has bolted to another sky
Below me waits the road, yellow in the silence
And the oaks that are never afraid.
Driving storms is fun until they crash.

Launderette

The harbour town is washed with dirty greens,
I hum an old lullaby until it hurts
and the dim lines of poplar trees
breathe in time to the breaking
and the healing of the sea.
I find the slatted comfort of the wooden seats,
sit facing the machines,
watching them digest their wet, cotton meals,
and through the tumbling heat

his shirts grasp feebly at the glass door,
dancing for me, pleading with me,
so I concentrate
until the helpless linen tells how heavily his life lies,
how he wakes late to feel the dark come down,
obliterate the comfort of old things, childhood things,
long put away, dust-mantled;
and I try to fold something more
into the warm damp of clean clothes—
something he will come upon,
intent in that unguarded moment
leaning back to catch the second sleeve,
something blue-green,
or all the colours of a child's wish.

Home-Movie Nights

Ratcheted, in stills,
how thin and brown the smooth-limbed
brothers, throwing off their casts of sand
(Bury me! I am a dead man!)
framed in loose rolls of celluloid,
and I, smaller even than the buried ones
up there on our sitting-room wall.
I was once caught under a giant wave,
they brought me out alive
(they did not save my life,
for I was saved on celluloid)
but through the wave I saw them dive for me,
all my life they brought me, pearl-like, from the waves,
and now, well used to handling the names
of men long gone from me and unfamiliar grown,
and opening the letters home,
I do most of my
wringing of hands
alone.

Emily Dickinson

From anything that touches her she may recoil,
go no further
but retreat upon it all and reap
words that are born and unfurl under careful hands,
words that come from her trance
in a silent monotone.

Then the Alice-like fall
swings from dull thud to thud of her hitting earth.
In her long descent, did she howl?
I worry about that sound
and watch how her own nouns
jostle her now she is down,
her thoughts are an empty train, doors open,
and no-one getting in.

At times she has nodded drily at the abyss,
it is not sunny at this time so there are no shadows,
but maybe down there genius lightly spirals,
words landing squarely, perfect fits;
I edge warily, all blows glancing,
until my mind connects with a bright shock.
Somewhere, a train pulls off.

Convalescent

There's smoke in the air although it's Spring,
people are shedding muddy boots and things,
slamming their private doors
on rooms with sofas and TVs,
I fall into the wind,
it rights me, mildly,
and I walk like a convalescent
down a tree-lined path,
wood-soothed, thinking of bough

and bark and all that will come
of the nutshell,
the circles in the circles
that the lathe handles lovingly
with its gaze,
the hacked limb a lumberman heals
with his dab of bright paint.
Somewhere friends are waiting,
lies in their hands,
hands by their sides.

The Courage Gatherer

With the sun too close
a loose wind catches me off guard,
dreams flock to my skirts
and cling there like a litter
I'd steal sleep to feed.
Asked exactly how I feel
I answer from the fields and summer lanes
where I have come
gathering courage.
A wing shadow strobes the lane
from time to time the future sinks
with the black doubt of people leaving me—
but hope comes out in her lovely shimmer,
her hair behind, untied,
fresh on the morning, never fully woken,
never still,
I follow with my arms full
of the songs she leaves,
all of the same brave tune.

Fall

(U.C. Berkeley 1989)

We sit over Indian bones
and over the silent, sitting up, buried ones.
Bob Hass laughs about Dickinson
and tells us it is
okay to be slow,
and confusion
is all part of what is meant to be.

I finger the silence
that follows a poem's end.
It is the sound
of having been there, the hard despair
that follows pain getting words
and after rain you can hear the drops
staying in the trees.

Sometimes the day tumbles early
but coming up from the Mining Circle
the grass yearns down to the figure of a girl
in bronze, green as rain, and such bewilderment
is part of what is meant to be.

Fault

I was not built for
the dull rumble of the valley air,
the great steel birds
that fly with a dark grey
whine, grazing the sky.
They fly low in the blue face of it,
they spell out its naked state,
the clouds are at bay.
The fault sniggers beneath the highway,

she cracks her knuckles publicly
but keeps apart her joy,
narrow and deep; some day
she will send a flame
from the scorched well of the earth
and burn off the teeming human layer,
she will burst her corset of rock
and take the air,
she was not meant
for the brittle rib-cage of the bay.

Valley

Wherever you look
she answers back.
You know her by the jewels
set shallow and close
for eyes that narrow
and are never shrewd.
You know her by the good bones,
the many thoughts that fall on gold,
her friends are few
or they hide; her smile is broad
while out of the bullets of fast cars
she invents a war,
under their hail of horns
only such surface gestures can be made,
the nod, the solemn wave.
When there is cause to celebrate
her laughter is canned,
a cast of hawks falls on her parade.
I know her for a young girl,
virginal, pure,
you skin your knuckles
trying to knock some love from her.

Undertow

I was not gently led
into that inner room.
From where I lay, it always
seemed another room away,
and feeling the wall for a door
I felt the cries of all those girls before
being drawn, drowned,
promised and offered and led
to the very core, and whether willing
or in dread, all
swooping low and following
the flow and irresistible tide
knowing the undertow
was where they always died,
abandoning
every distinguishing sign,
mole, tilt and curl,
number and name,
until they were all
the same and it fell
cold as a cave in the room,
they stood holding the spent flame,
wanting to put it down,
bury it now it was done
and move with the ease of girls
who know themselves,
into a different room.

Once their sound
turned down, my hands
began to burn
from holding memory's hand.
I laid them flat on the cool sheet
and turned my other cheek,
lying easy in a white bed, wondering
when I would be given up
for dead.

Dogwood and Iris

Above the valley fog, below the snow,
we're looking for gold,
and here's the sun, proving
by the cut of shadows and the play of leaves
that there is more to now than what we see.

In fact, since April is the time for iris,
purple-frilled and curiously low to the ground,
we have struck it rich; the old
dogwood by the covered bridge
shines out among the river's things,
and there it is: the gold of poppies in the weeds.

On our return
the fire glows, the milk is warm,
the radio announces sunset at 7:24.
You want to see those poppies in a jar,
but I tell you in late afternoon
they fold up tight against the coming dark.

The irises have hunkered down.
I watch the sun lose power
and hold for comfort to the thought
that every day is borrowed time, and to the memory
of the dogwood blossom nobody can see,
and the gold we didn't mine.

First Faun

Late Winter, the deer come down
for food; hungry for love,
they stalk the traffic on perfect legs,
doe-eyed, nowhere near
appropriately scared.

I slow my Villager on Knight's Hill,
a buck taps his white cane

off the centre divide;
I cannot hear you over all the noise
in both our lives.

You once said to let Nature
take her course, and I know
that water finds its own level,
but this—I grip the steering wheel
with both hands, the buck reaches

high ground, I breathe a sigh,
then a next breath, and a next,
into the absence,
into the rising tide,
and rather than wait

for sadness to cover my eyes
from behind, I drive on
toward the village of the world
where enough food, a warm bed,
put me in with the lucky few.

All day the deer play
catch-me-if-you-can on the Miracle Mile;
Spring rain shakes out the trees,
and I can almost touch the veils
that ripple down between our lives.

Coming home, old sun
lays her gold leaf on every stone,
unpins her hair into the wind;
any morning now, the first faun
folded quietly by the road like a stillbirth.

Patagonia

I drive by the reservoir, the hills
smudge into an early dark,
frog song springs out of the loaded air
and the rain begins,

long skinny filaments on my windowpane.
What surprises me now
is how I can forget the course is changed:
I think we are still heading
for the Cape of Good Hope, banderole aloft,
on our mettle, tacking into the game.
Instead, we ride anchor off Fire Land,
Patagonia, with its dry squall lines,
its sheep, Magellan's desperate straits,
its Indians in their overshoes—this is the place
all Winter breaks out.

Hawkesbury River, NSW

I was a schooner,
I was a rigged cutter with sixteen oars,
fire on a bed of earth in my hold.

I liked to be on the river without purpose,
the swell from the mailboat washed at my hopes;
I ran my oars idly through the mangrove swamps.
At Milson Island the kids from town
fished from the jetty with silver spools,
white prawns for bait,
and all news carried equal weight.

On the Bauer Point foreshore I berthed in the dawn,
the river revealed at its own pace
its purpose; beyond the mouth,
the trades laughed in the face
of the great winds that govern hurricane and calm
and fanned into motion my knot of flame.

I was moved by the tide beyond fear,
left my old ways by the shore and struck out
with a good tailwind, plain sailing
for the Solomons and their bold promises—
whale teeth, coconuts, and pearls.

Venus Awake

after Delvaux's 'Venus Asleep' (1944)

Everyone's in a spell but I'm not caught.
Make the hammers yield your deep summer music
across the creek, I in my kitchen, listening
and listening; I have never listened before.

It could have been anything,
dulcimer, cithara, musical stones,
but the past decided that it was piano I owned,
the yellowing ivories that brought you to my home.

I was unprepared,
tired, almost beyond forgiving.
In my high-ceilinged room
you brought everything into tune;
now the notes fall where they should fall,
a weightless and effortless flow.

I know how late it is
to dream of little death and desire.
Up on my wall
Venus and the skeleton and the dressmaker's girl
inhabit the moonlight of Delvaux's unreal
tableau. You can come to my door
any pale silver night,
you can enter there without call.

Glaces, Sorbets

Paris was grey this morning
out our tiny bathroom window.

One more book and we'll need new shelves,
the whole apartment knows it.

How many Fridays? Hundreds and
hundreds of Fridays, but never before

these particular leaves on the silk trees, such a
newborn green; this young sunshine, this wind.

I do not know how long we'll be married.
They say love hangs on for dear life

hands at the throat
until you cut it down.

Conor O'Callaghan (1968–)

Conor O'Callaghan's poetry often flirts with our inclination to misread and misrepresent the past, turning our histories, both public and private, into fictions. Even the present, in an O'Callaghan poem, is subject to misreading. "I am," he writes in "Ships," "given to mistaking / the rumble of cranes around dawn / for dry shapeless thunder at sea."[1] Mistaking x for y in this and other poems serves as a metaphor for the way poets make metaphors, but also for the way the mind tends to distort lived experience in memory, in order to make sense of it or make it fit with the images we have of ourselves.

O'Callaghan likes to call attention to the role these fictions play in individual lives. In "The Middle Ground" he writes about the way growing older makes a fiction of the past by putting our present lives into a conflict with our past preferences. But O'Callaghan is himself more fascinated than disturbed by the way age alters the assumptions that define a person's relationship to the larger culture—from a youthful disdain for tennis shirts to the sense that any woman over thirty is, as he puts it, a granny—making it impossible to say whether it is the past or the present that might reveal the truth about ourselves.

That the truth lies somewhere in between, in the contradiction itself, may account for O'Callaghan's apparent pleasure in cultivating all sorts of momentary confusion. He has written, for instance, three different poems called "The Swimming Pool." There are two poems called "Seatown" in the book of the same name. There is also one called "Slip," which is easily mistaken for "Ships." Another poem, "The Oral Tradition," interprets its title phrase in sexual rather than the literary terms we might expect on diving into a poem of that name.

The particular mistake described in "Ships"—which invites us to revise our image of seaside Ireland, replacing distant thunder with the rumble of gantries that do the heavy lifting of maritime trade—lays emphasis on the way the Irish poetic tradition may itself have fostered the misrepresentation of reality by encouraging writers to dwell on romantic images that, as the playwright Brian Friel once put it, no longer match the landscape of fact. In a poem not included here, "The Modern Pastoral Elegy," O'Callaghan vents his frustration with the conservative nature of that poetic tradition through some gentle ribbing of his versifying elders, but more often he simply wrestles with the conventions themselves, as in "East," a poem that expresses his preference for the unromantic dreariness of modern Ireland's Eastern seaboard over the more exotic West.

The landscape of O'Callaghan's poetry is anything but romantic Ireland. What most distinguishes his work is his knack for turning the unpoetic elements of contemporary popular culture into poetry that doesn't sacrifice grace and intelligence in the acquisition of topicality. The internal resonance and formal grace of poems like "East" and "September" make them sound at times like the cosmopolitan Louis MacNeice, but their subject matter owes more to Patrick Kavanagh, who in the 1950s recommended that Irish poets try the dog track now and then as an antidote to Yeats's emphasis on peasants and hard riding country gentlemen. O'Callaghan does exactly that in "East," which imagines "a dreary eastern town that isn't vaguely romantic, / where moon and stars are lost in the lights of the greyhound track." He also manages to make poetry out of Pitch & Putt, a shortened version of golf that is popular in parts of Ireland. The game becomes a kind of metaphor for the ennui of the unemployed when it appears in poems in *Seatown*, but its bigger job is to change the rules of writing Irish poetry.

O'Callaghan was born in Newry in 1968 and grew up in Dundalk. He has published three books of poetry—*The History of Rain*, *Seatown*, and *Fiction*—and has written extensively on cricket and soccer. He has taught at Villanova University and Wake Forest University and now lives in Manchester with his wife, the poet Vona Groarke, and their two children.

NOTE

1. "Ships," *Seatown* (Oldcastle, Co. Meath: Gallery Press, 1990).

September

It must be a cliché to think, however brief,
that light on a wall and our voices
out in the open are the pieces
we shall look upon in retrospect as a life.

There is a danger of circumstance smothering
even the smallest talk. If a breeze
shakes another colour from the trees
we say a word like *withering*

without the slightest hint of irony.
After a season of fruitful conversation
and reflective pauses in the garden
we say we know what it means to be lonely.

Today the first moment of autumn tolls
like a refrain from the nineteen thirties.
The voices of friends and courtesies
are interrupted by thunder and the radio crackles.

We shall remember it as the impending doom
and use this afternoon as an example of decay
when there is nothing left for us to say
and September has outstayed its welcome.

Today our clothes will be spoiled by rain.
We shall drag from the lawn the chairs and table
that all summer made us comfortable.
Though all of that remains to be seen.

The Last Cage House in Drogheda*

Made bi Nicholas Bathe in the ieare of our lord 1570 bi hiv Mor carpenter

Maybe a final order from the sheriff was sent
after the neighbours complained it was an eyesore
and, because the oak had been stolen from Mellifont,

claimed that some god had settled an old score
when the floorboards smelt and the beams were rotten.
But who lived there, and where they went, is forgotten.

All that survives is an unpeopled picture
with the first owner's inscription. It traps
in pencil on a page of mist the architecture
of a crumbling age and someone's understandable hopes
that the place where so many people once lived
would, despite the weather, be somehow saved.

Maybe the heir in a family of settlers
left instructions for the lot to be pulled down
after he returned to a different cold in Chester.
Or a pail that caught two centuries of rain
was thrown away, and with it a clatter
of tenants stepped out to freedom and squalor.

The only certainty is that one morning in Drogheda
in 1825 an amateur draughtsman turned up early,
and for half a day passers-by stopped and saw
the corner of Shop St. and Laurence St. differently.
Then tea-chests filled with earthenware and spoons
were stacked onto the cobbles in the late afternoon.

And someone alone upstairs probably recognised
history being listened to from a particular angle
for the last time, while boys whistling outside
could see no meaning in the single
martin rising from the thatch, or yellow bars
on the floor and worktop that were just wiped bare.

Say someone who had shared one room with her husband
and with her husband's friend and his nephew;
who wondered if anything that had been left behind
could be used again, and thought how the years flew;
who, with the final call, put a spray of harebells
in a jam jar on the ledge, to be gathered in the rubble.

Mengele's House

It was considered
the finest in its street
on the outskirts of Buenos Aires.
Splashing and screams were heard
during the long July heat
in adjacent gardens.

Nobody has lived there
since the last family fled.
Now and then a researcher comes,
or a would-be buyer
armed with rosary beads
noses around the bedrooms.

Since all the glass
was kicked from a window
by legless students,
the lambency of trees
is free to come and go
in the gutted kitchen.

Out the back are piles
of twigs and compost,
a seventies lawnmower
and aquamarine tiles,
exactly as they were left
by the last owner,

who talked about himself a lot,
chatting across the fence,
but never had the neighbours
past his gate,
and never even once
darkened their doors.

In the neighbourhood
he's remembered still.
He was the old misery
who had strange kids,
a swimming pool,
and a history.

The History of Rain

for Johnny McCabe 1903–1993

These are the fields where rain has marched
from time to time. This is the year that
is measured in consistent downpours, until it spills
on the foreground of a basin covered, the tone of dull enamel.

In the half rush to shelter, these unripe blackberries
and woodbine drifts at the level crossing distract a generation
that knows the probability of sitting through August, the blight

of reticence raising a month past an average fall.
Or that later sees the lost patch momentarily bleached
as if by an hour of recorded sun and the history of light.

In the photograph of 1940, my granduncle and his mother.
Late that tall summer they fold their sleeves and step
into the front yard to watch a swarm of veined clouds pass.

As if the full world might still end here,
away from the horizon of more populated storms.

Forgetting that soon they will run back to the house
and the wireless babbling, and listen to the gentle clapping
on slate and galvanised roofs where the sky begins,
suddenly uncertain at the border of an even longer decade.

Pigeons

Busty never asked me why I came around.
Twice a week we cycled to the farthest hill
to shake his pigeons from a *Marietta* box, knowing
they'd be back before us in half-light on the wall.

He was with my father, on short-term hire.
I invented messages to go and watch sheet metal
being splintered to gold. The others laughed
behind his back because he hardly spoke at all.

Then the welders were let go, and he was gone.
On the first evening of the holidays

I found his yard in tatters, the loft on its side,
the wire spattered with feathers, white and grey.

I kept trying the bell, and listening to it ring
in the hall until night built behind the town.
There was no answer. My mother told me
to sit in the front room and calm down.

He spoke its name each time he threw a pigeon
in the air and saw it broke from the initial stutter.
I felt a small heart in my palm for days after,
and my father's taunt: "I told you he wasn't all there."

The story goes . . . he packed his bags
and sat out all night; he was heard at dawn,
shouting and shouting; the whole of Dundalk
woke to clouds flyblown with homing pigeons.

The Mild Night

I have taken an armchair into the garden
to enjoy the quietness at the end of May.
This is the way the mild night begins.

I have turned off the only lamp in the kitchen,
blown out the candles and put them away.
I have taken an armchair into the garden.

The lights in the trees can barely be seen
as evening comes and the land falls away.
This is the way the mild night begins.

The road past the house is lit with whitethorn
and grey poplars shine just long enough to say
I have taken an armchair into the garden.

The light on the grass, the blackening sun,
the sunflowers, the sky, the open wind all say
This is the way the mild night begins.

I have forgotten all I have said of pain
to enjoy the quietness at the end of May.
I have taken an armchair into the garden.
This is the way the mild night begins.

Silver Birch

Here, in time, the words for trees will
be darkness's other names (lime, ash, evergreen)
and will alter what happens. Today I read
the pages where a generation falls still.

In my book the plain of Birkenau
opens into the surrounding fields
of silver birch that once sealed
it within its name . . . *from the German* . . .

The branches of the past rumble in the wind.
Some parents tell their children to go on
listening to the trees before they are gone,
that each leaf is a minute turning to the ground.

I read of the gypsy encampment near their home
and the day in October when it is lit with war.
I read of those who pass through there
for years to come, remembering their freedom.

The day is gone. My longest memory of trees
is the one in which I walk across a road
to where silver birch leaves are darkened on one side.
The shadows from a story will survive like this.

Seatown

Sanctuary of sorts for the herons all day yesterday
waiting for the estuary to drain and this evening
for two lights queuing like crystal at the top of the bay.

Last straw for the panel beaters only just closed down
and the dole office next to the barracks and the gold
of beer spilled on the pavements of Saturday afternoon.

Home from home for the likes of us and foreign boats
and groups with oilskins and unheard-of currencies
in search of common ground and teenage prostitutes.

Reclaimed ward of bins left out a week and dogs in heat
and the fragrance of salt and sewage that bleeds
into our garden from the neap-tide of an August night.

Poor man's Latin Quarter of stevedores and an early house
and three huge silos swamped by the small hours
and the buzz of joyriders quite close on the bypass.

Time of life to settle for making a fist of love
and glimpsing new dawns and being caught again
and waking in waves with all the sheets kicked off.

Point of no return for the cattle feed on the wharves
and the old shoreline and the windmill without sails
and time that keeps for no one, least of all ourselves.

May its name be said for as long as it could matter.
Or, failing that, for as long as it takes the pilot
to negotiate the eight kilometres from this to open water.

Pitch & Putt

Its is the realm of men
and boys joined in boredom,
the way of life that sees
one day on a par
with the next and school breaks
dragged out too long.

Theirs is the hour killed slowly,
the turn for home
in diminishing threes and twos,

the provisional etiquette
of shared tees,
conceded defeat.

Theirs the loose end,
the nationality of ships
in the absence
of shop to talk,
the freedom to be hopeless
and still come back.

Theirs the blather
of the last twoball
accepting flukes
for what they are,
the greenkeeper collecting flags
and shadows in their wake.

Ships

I am given to mistaking
the rumble of cranes around dawn
for dry shapeless thunder at sea,
to going weeks on end without sleep.

~

Her father tended the pile light
like an allotment of lettuce,
too wordless in times and levels
to care, too fogbound to notice.

~

I've come around to thinking ships
are the only visible bridge
between the earth's darkened centre
and its sunlit peripheries.

~

Just once, I called her bluff between
the grain stores and two waves of heat.
Days after, on a rush-hour train,
her salt was still on my fingers.

~

Lately I find I can lie here
listing their grey ports in my head—
Hull and Bergen and Bilbao
and Riga—without drifting off.

~

I have taken it all on board:
her distance and her brother's death
and her big wedding to a prick
of a stevedore from abroad.

~

Behind the chimney smoke at eight
and the park and pitch & putt flags
and the bypass, a coal freighter's
constellation edges away.

~

Just once, let me be her husband,
climbing in behind her after
a twelve-hour shift, stirring her with
sweet nothings in a foreign tongue.

East

I know it's not playing Gaelic, it's simply not good enough,
to dismiss as someone else's all that elemental Atlantic guff.
And to suggest everything's foreign beyond the proverbial pale
would amount to a classic case of hitting the head on the nail.

But give me a dreary eastern town that isn't vaguely romantic,
where moon and stars are lost in the lights of the greyhound track
and cheering comes to nothing and a flurry of misplaced bets
blanketing the stands at dawn is about as spiritual as it gets.

Where back-to-back estates are peppered with satellite discs
and the sign of the *Sunrise Takeaway* doesn't flick on until six
and billows from the brewery leave a February night for dead
and the thought of smoking seaweed doesn't enter your head.

And while it's taken for granted everyone has relatives in Chicago
who share their grandmother's maiden name and seasonal lumbago,
it's probably worth remembering, at the risk of committing heresy,
as many families in Seatown have people in Blackpool and Jersey.

My own grandmother's uncle ran a Liverpool snooker hall
that cleaned up between the wars and went, of course, to the wall.
I must have a clatter of relatives there or thereabouts still
who have yet to trace their roots and with any luck never will.

I know there's a dubious aunt on my father's side in Blackburn,
a colony on my mother's in Bury called something like Bird or Horn.
I have a cousin a merchant seaman based in darkest St Ives,
another who came on in the seventies for Man. Utd. reserves.

If you're talking about inheritance, let me put it this way:
there's a house with umpteen bedrooms and a view of Dundalk Bay
that if I play it smoothly could be prefaced by the pronoun "my"
when the old man decides to retire to that big after hours in the sky.

If it comes down to allegiance or a straight choice between
a trickle of shingly beaches that are slightly less than clean
and the rugged western coastline draped in visionary mystique,
give me the likes of Bray or Bettystown any day of the week.

If it's just a question of water and some half-baked notion
that the Irish mind is shaped by the passionate swell of the ocean,
I align myself to a dribble of sea that's unspectacular, or flat.
Anything else would be unthinkable. It's as simple as that.

The Count

There's this pal of a pal who earned his stripes
snipping surplus nipples from made-for-TV flicks.
As little as six or seven frames apiece,
they curled in a box at his feet like locks of hair
or like shavings planed from a strip of maple.

Me? I like to think I get my kicks elsewhere.
Still, his nickname lingers on the tip of my tongue
whenever I lose all hope of something worth seeing
and hit the standby through a late double bill,
or whenever I cut my teeth on a sweet red apple.

The Middle Ground

We wear this weather the tennis shirts
we once thought a scream. We compromise
when it comes to cuisine and the arts.
We find birth moving. We vote for peace.
We praise long stretches and hire a strimmer.
We call our doctor by his Christian name.
We flick through catalogues in bed. In summer,
we intend to watch less telly, join a gym.

We save up our statutory days of leave
like pesetas in a jar. We place our trust
in the laws of averages and nature. We love
our tots in ways our parents were against.
We do jobs around the house, and see to it
the sitter doesn't walk home on her own,
and phone out for a pizza on Friday night,
and blow every other New Year on the sun.

Our sisters aren't grannies when they're thirty.
Our daughters don't stand in nite-club queues
using language, smoking, looking tarty,
in their teens and gangs and platform shoes.

We don't blare car horns at all hours,
or leave beer cans and cigarette butts
on the pavement. We don't piss in doors.
We don't blame others, or fuck like rabbits.

We wake instead to Sunday's civic order,
still together, to heaven in a garden centre,
an agnostic grace, a roast, and getting older,
milder, lying out the back on plastic furniture.
When the golden hour throws in '80s hits
we hated then, we know the words, we reminisce.
We don't mind if the ground that separates
the high-rises and the horsey set is ours, this.

Heartland

    It's still going,
        the post-tea siesta
in the towns, and much later than planned,
    when I say my so longs
        and get away
into that antiquated heartland
    full of huckster shops
    and halls and the warmth
with which midsummer flatters itself.
    I make shapes,
        corkscrewing north
and fiddling now and then with the sunroof.

    After nine, ten,
        it's still good and bright.
So I pull over in Durrow
    for a pee, a cone,
    give the legs a bit
of a stretch and come around somehow
    to bluffing a bum
    with a plastered hand

about the Land Leagues and the famine
   in a hotel ballroom
      where a two-piece band
is programming its drum machine.

   Outside, on the green,
      as if from a shipwreck,
five Spaniards in a hired Toyota
   have settled on
      hitting West Cork
before the day's done. I run the motor,
   flick on the lights.
   What darkness follows
is just the Irish underwater darkness
   of horse chestnuts,
      handball alleys
and burger joints with hanging baskets.

   The horizon
      all the way up
goes into one of its purple patches.
   On the roadside grazing
      there are even sheep
marked with aquamarine, and midges,
   with fields of rape
      streaming towards
the dimmers. I pass out and am passed
   by nothing. A tape
      of bluegrass standards
meanders through both sides twice at least.

   The shortened night
      on the long finger,
between Monasterevin and Kildare,
   for a minute,
      or slightly more,
it starts to feel as if its shutter
   won't fall again,
      not properly,
or ever, and I am diving upwards

through seas of corn
   or maybe barley
and any second now will break the surface.

Fiction

None of this is true.
We're still all
we crack ourselves
out to be.

Our hereafters
have not been laid
in a plot
with my loose ends.

You're not miles away.
The slow numbers
were never
swayed alone to.

I don't blame you,
smiling in the mirror
at a face
you've just made up.

from Loose Change

I "THE PEACOCK"

We've perfected the disappearing trick.
I'm thinking especially of that old lie
called sentiment and sentiment's rhetoric
that we, together or alone, no longer buy.
Remember reading Carver's "Feathers" to me,
the one about the meal, the peacock dancing?

When you were done I offered you a penny.
You shut your eyes and said exactly nothing.

II "THE HERON"

Dead master. Old posturing taxidermist.
Forgive me when I can't help but hear
my granddad and his like being dismissed.
Or call it, if you prefer, a bookish night too far,
contemplating sonnet after well-made sonnet,
when I think "Stuff that . . . *Ignorant men!*
They knew what they knew and acted on it,
as opposed to some folks I could mention."

V "THE BULL"

I once hitched a lift in a pick-up
from a senator with a thing for voodoo,
and I once got legless in a china shop
with Lee Harvey Oswald's widow,
and I once left my mark on the divan
of twins who grew up in Daytona,
and I once got through to Bob Dylan
but omitted to push Button A.

X "THE SALMON"

St Brigid's night, and we lie in separate beds.
All about us the flood-level raises the stakes
above regret's loose change and our heads.
I know, even as I go through whatever it takes
and fuss over the blister on my thumb again,
you're swimming away from me in darkness
where Castletown crosses into the Creggan
and silver water is given to breaking its banks.

XX "THE HORSE"

A spin in the roles we've saddled on each other:
the upholder of vision to see the abstract through
and the pleb with a bag of chips on his shoulder.

The last straw is an *assiette Anglaise.* I ask you,
"How would the horseman know to pass by
if not by whoa-ing his nag to a standstill?"
We tour the landmarks of Roquebrune, badly,
stopping off only for Camels and petrol.

L "THE WOODCOCK"

There are five sides to every story, I'm told.
So let me raise a glass and toast this much,
one last time. Let love come in from the cold,
even if love finds you in someone else's crush
or someone else in yours that's grown too long.
Let us greet the leaf, the blossom and the bole.
Let us praise, together, the harbingers of spring
in your step and your girlish way on the mobile.

C "THE STAG"

Nineteen hundred and ninety-nine.
I test it between my teeth
when it drops again from the phone.
Take it from me, my sweet,
a high hill is a lonely place.
If only I had the exchange rate
I could begin to pay the price
of screwing my way out of a rut.

Signing Off

It's just about time to round things up.
Thanks again. That was the sound
of white noise being blown
on a patter that's all for now.

Until next time. After this,
you're on your own. It looks like snow.
Here's a little something to take us
all the way to silence. Wrap up well.

Justin Quinn (1968–)

The author of three books of criticism, Justin Quinn, who was born in Dublin in 1968 and published his first volume of poetry in 1995, is already one of the most distinct voices in the rising generation of literary critics. It is a generation charged, as he sees it, with finding an alternative to both the ideologically driven criticism that dominated the academy in the last quarter century and the earlier style of aesthetic analysis that focused on literary texts in isolation. Exhausted by both ways of looking at the world, Quinn says, younger critics "are writing books which span this divide and renew our sense of the particularly literary aspects of poems, while also attending to political contexts and the ways in which poetry matters to lives."[1]

Quinn's own criticism—largely concerned with twentieth-century Irish and American poetry—is a case in point. And his take on a poet like Wallace Stevens, whose poetry resembles some of his own in its inwardness and opulence, says a lot about the way he practices both criticism and poetry. (Quinn, for his part, says that while studying Stevens for his doctoral dissertation he "consciously tried not to write like him.")[2] He argues that for Stevens "the space of nature, far from allowing him to escape societal concerns, was the greatest occasion for his engagement with them." Looking at nature is a way of thinking about perception. "And thus," Quinn writes, "to think in general about how ideologies change lives he observes a bouquet and its surroundings, the premise being that ideology, if it is to take purchase on reality, must transform the space of immediate human perception."[3]

It is not surprising, in this light, that one of the Czech poets Quinn most admires, Petr Borkovec—Quinn translated a volume of Borkovec's poetry and dedicated a section of his *Fuselage* to him—writes about landscapes as a way of transcending what Quinn calls the "poetry of witness" that might be expected from a Czech writer pressed by the changes his country has undergone in the last decades. Quinn himself is just as likely to write about a vacuum cleaner or an espresso machine, but the effect is similar. Looking at a Hoover is for him a way of thinking about how we live now, but in particular terms. His sharp-eyed views of urban spaces work the same way. "The buildings stand for this," he writes in a sequence titled "Prague Elegies": "Some years ago / a revolution swept through them, the junta / folded away with its acres of red bunting."[4]

That is not to say that Quinn is not interested in considering historical change in the abstract. In the book-length *Fuselage* he creates a kind of thought experiment on the nature of subjective experience in an age of globalization. Quinn himself doesn't seem troubled by the phenomenon—he once said he likes having a McDonald's in Prague, where he now lives. But *Fuselage* reads like the transcript of an uneasy dream about cultural transformation. Its untitled sections slip between moments of exultation and flights of paranoia. In the background is a version of the fear, which Quinn downplayed in one essay as a political bugbear, that "small cultures will dissolve in the currents of globalization." Or to give it the form specific to his adopted city: that the EU as "the emergent superstate will swallow us whole and leave us like zombies watching Euronews on a loop."[5] The poem—as if its atmosphere were distilled of two parts Benjamin, one part *Blade Runner*—unfolds in a hypermodern world where "Junkies veer and drift / through the concourse of the Metro," their heads full of Benjamin's messianic time. But its focus is on ordinary people who aren't sure what to make of the spinning scene around them.

Quinn's early poetry reveled in linguistic difficulty, making use of a recondite vocabulary wherever the opportunity arose. And *Fuselage* is a formal *tour de force*. But his recent work has a lighter touch. Poems like "Coffle," "Borscht," and "Solstice" produce their effects with delicate rhymes and tender attention to the things and people they consider. There are no spotlights on their subjects, but rather, as Quinn puts it in "Coffle," a "Slow fade to / their works and days."

Quinn studied literature and philosophy at Trinity College, Dublin, where he received a Ph.D. He moved to Prague in 1992 and has remained there to teach at Charles University.

NOTES

1. Quinn, *Gathered Beneath the Storm: Wallace Stevens, Nature and Community* (Dublin: UCD Press), pp. 1–2.

2. Oxford Poetry Archive: http://www.oxfordpoetry.co.uk/texts.php?int=ix2_justinquinn

3. *Gathered Beneath the Storm*, p. 2.

4. Section XX from "Prague Elegies," *Waves and Trees* (Oldcastle, Co. Meath: Gallery Press, 2006).

5. Quinn, "Letter from Czechia," *Yale Review* 93.1 (Jan. 2005), p. 47.

The 'O'o'a'a' Bird

Once there was a time
    I sang in trees,
And forest reached right to the rim
    Of everything that was.

The pristine world spun free
    Of fences then
Without the empty clarity
    Of plaza, field or plan.

My song had origins
    Of bole and sky,
As much as come-ons to the hens,
    Whom I loved, and they me.

(But listen to your music:
    Blasting sennets
From drills at road-works, or asthmatic
    Engines under bonnets,

An electronic chirrup
    When your travel-pass
Is good for one more day, the blip
    You need to know you'll last.)

You couldn't stand our freedom.
    You laid your laws
That silenced us, in this your time
    Of consonants, fences, chainsaws.

Instructions

Hold the lamp-flex hard,
    Its cool fluent plastic against your palm.
Nothing will seem to happen. Then think: inside, onward,
    Coursing to the strange-branched metal plant
        Electrons race until they come
    To the end, and explode constantly in pure event.

Then know this: when you meet
A friend you haven't seen for years
(They'd been away and just got back) by chance on the street,
It's just the same. Moments before perhaps
You were gently slipping unawares
To where nothing ever happens, and years elapse

Without your ever seeing
The city's streets and crowds and trees.
(And anyway, in good times cities are self-effacing.)
But something comes to light and elbows through
To re-existence, generosities
Zoom into shot from nowhere—and wake you.

Or more hugely, more naturally,
Meet the woman that you love.
That's like sitting up at night, and *late* drifts into *early*.
The hours pass, and then for a moment your head drops down
In doubt. Whisper: *What do I believe?*
And raise it to see, with utter shock, the sun.

from Days of the New Republic

XI Attics

The clouds go and the ash trees stand
Like nervous-systems in the sky,
Fleshless. Alive in every bend
And tilt to weather, this is psyche,
Breath beneath the breathing wind.

The stolid roofs look on, their attics
Lungs that hold their breath for decades—
Old furniture suspended in a matrix
Of fifty-year old air, old blankets,
Coinage from the old republics,

Boardgames, clothes, and tax-receipts,
The bedposts of the bed your grandparents
Slept together on, its sheets.

Year in, year out these wait like plants
That never grow, a sky of slates,

In this their garden, this the place
To where each life of objects used
Is drawn and eventually migrates
Forever. Her pictures gather dust,
Your room cleared out for space.

XVII Ur-Aisling

Once when the world had not yet happened,
I was dozing in a forest clearing,
When I heard somebody's footfalls and
Sat up to see a woman staring
Straight at me. Beauty. She proclaimed:

"Make me a nation as you will."
She paused and thought. "Make of its past
What you can." Her face was pale
And red hair blazed about it. Her breast
Moved with a power which I now felt as well.

So I thought "Fine!" and did the lot.
First I laid mythologies
Like slabs across the open land,
Then infrastructure and nostalgias
Unto completion. The hour was late.

She came again, now changed with time,
Which shocked me, but still beautiful.
"You have usurped my power and name—
Your work misjudged, these people pitiful."
I shrugged. "So usurp it back again."

XX Geography

Start with the nothing-could-be-simpler
Line where skies depend on seas,
Endless talks on talks, palabra
Of reflections and replies
To what winds howl and rainstorms jabber.

Then move in toward the bay, forever
Just about to close its grasp
Around a lake, the green drugged river
Seeping out like mountain soup
Into the largesse of saltwater.

It's all around you now, its growth,
Its thru-ways, hoardings, open shops,
Its people crowding every width
Of pavement, cranes above the rooftops,
Mayoral, watching life beneath.

And then the suburbs. You're there somewhere
On some road, ridiculously named,
Living at a certain number,
Waking up from rooms you dreamt
To where you gradually remember.

Apartment

You're drawn up to a tree's height in the air.
You leave the lift, unbolt the bolted door
And slam it shut behind you, home once more.
Relief. Unzip. Undress. Run the shower,

Unopened mail left waiting on the shelf.
Water scalds your body, steaming open
Your every pore, limbs slide around the soap in-
Side the tub. Step out and dry yourself.

Looking out the window, you see the forest,
Its black bar, the still-light sky and left
Of this another block, another lift,
Another hundred lives that felt the frost

In the fifteen minutes from the Metro home,
And lean back with a drink into the chair.
You watch one woman and then become aware
She's stopped her rhythmic strokes, put down her comb

And sees you. One instant and you have exchanged
It all. And nothing, when you twist the blinds
And turn back to your book that maybe binds
Huge things together, has everything arranged

From nations to the Derridean trace,
Voluted columns after columns of prose
That put things in perspective, balance praise
With scorn to hold the pantheon's roof in place.

It suddenly shivers like the trompe l'oeil
It maybe is beside the recent vision
Of a woman home from work, her earned seclusion,
So like you that you wonder if some play

Of light threw your reflection back into
Your drowsy eyes or you back into hers.
The moment of mirage and truth occurs
In the apartment buildings' interview,

A different kind of world from what you read,
A different kind of life from what you had
For years in that old house beneath the Hrad.
You find yourself inside this block of concrete

That's setting fast, like everybody else
Halfway to being bar-graphs, stacked in boxes
Across the south-town's *locus*
Un*amœnus* and dog-shit-covered green-belts.

And look at these, what's more, these ringing blocks
Laid down upon the whiteness of the page.
They try to draw you into their stiff cage.
(Whose wires are far too wide. Which no key locks.)

"Yes, and . . . ?" Well, life, as Joseph Cornell knew,
Is always an affair of different boxes.
Take these ones. Be my guest. What this place lacks is
Chaos. Impulse. Colour. Over to you.

from Six Household Appliances

1 HOOVER

It picks up mainly pieces of us,
Small flakes of skin, odd hairs, an eyelash,
Then paperclips and grains of food
Gone hard where they fell three weeks past.

Every so often it's fit to burst
And there's this touching scene: the bag,
Split sometimes down the middle, is lifted
From the plastic vacuum chamber
And you can see it all conjoined
In wadded bliss at last: us there
With everything we sidelined, edged
Off tables, worktops, chairs and shelves
While forging our lives on ahead.

Dumped in the bin. The bag replaced.
And I'm off roaming round the flat
Again with this huge hungry wheeze,
This loud dog on a leash, resolved
To clean up, get our lives in order.

3 MOCHA EXPRESS

Despite its tight corset
It stands full-bodied on the searing hob
With one black arm akimbo. Of course it
Seethes the whole while long, since that's its job,

But otherwise stands firm.
The little Java surging to its crown
Does not erupt beyond its form
And make a Pompeii of the flat and town;

I have to say I'm grateful.
As well as for the thimblefuls of tar
That take god knows how many cratefuls
Of coffee bean to make, and months to mature.

The grounds sit in their chamber
While underneath the water churns in turmoil
   Until the pressure and the temper-
Ature get to it and a gathering thermal

   Lifts it into flight.
It showers up through the perforated floor
   And infiltrates the cell outright.
The least and last ground is cleansed of all flavour.

   Then filtered by the moke
It bubbles up the home straight—huff and puff.
   See how the aperture gives a choke
And gushes forth the pure, the dark brown stuff.

   Which is all very well
Until you clean the tiny cauldrons out
   And prize apart the clam-tight shell
Inside of which the grounds adhese like grout:

   It's such a mess to wash.
The attitudes in which they came to grief—
   Sucked clean of essence by the whoosh
Of my need for refreshment and relief—

   Those terror-stricken forms
Crumble like shale as the water takes its toll.
   Across the sink they sweep enormous
Estuaries . . . then vanish down the plughole.

Poem

after Ladislav Skála*

I am a rock
Perched on the fifth floor
Of this apartment block

Which was exploded
About eight years ago;
That is, a breath, a cloud.

from Fuselage

Observe the sky: it changes
and remains the same. Cope
of cloud manoeuvres, flow
and fusillades of rain.
You fall up through it

endlessly, you never
come upon its edge.
Its flame is various,
is light and luxury
one moment, then sheers off

and leaves the streets and houses
closed and utterly bereft,
their people sunk back down.
Junkies veer and drift
through the concourse of the Metro.

Lodged inside their skulls
are jewels of *Jetʒʒeit*. Expanse
of joy and mainly power,
"vital, consecrating, celestial,
all things dissolve into

the waves and surges of
an ocean of light." The world
is spinning fuselage
& swerves & bends & swoops
in answer to our will

though we don't see or know
each other, what spirit
each is of. We flame forth
beautifully, apart;
shimmer, slide and flow.*

***

I wake early into
the already azure day.
The leaves, still sleeved in dew,

adjust themselves and sway
like tiny tremor-gaugings.
The black rampaging gangs
that flooded to-&-fro
throughout the night in dreams
(in time to passing trams)
linger briefly, then go.

Receding southwards, deep
into the continent,
a goods train threads one steep
green river valley bend
after another. Thunder
slow-fades to faint trundle.
The fields of yellow rape
stretch both ways from the river
to the interior;
they ripple and stand ripe.

Gaze folded into gaze,
flesh into flesh, like forests
risen in a maze.
The earth is widely forced
by myriad points of view.
So many—wakeful, new—
that flock and scintillate,
each with its glint of self,
plying its trade, its sylph
of silver concentrate.

The moving crowds are caught
by different tracts and cameras.
They wander into shot
and join the swelling arras
for a few moments when
they are the people, then
drift out of their bit parts
back into open day.
I spread my arms and pray.
I love how each day starts.

The roots of this tree stretch
to the entrails of the world

for its deep water; they fetch
it up into the curled
leaf waiting at the height
inside the sky's blue heat,
and for the heavy fruit—
stone folded in sweet flesh.
Eyes that see afresh,
in joy, have this dark root.

Set deep within the eye—
desire: its shuttles and warps
furiously multiply.
The overlapping orbs
load tales into the earth
of death and monstrous birth,
of pristine female beauty
relaxed and unconcerned
that all the world is burned
by some god for her body.

For mine. I stand in clay
and slowly I am covered
by my love's glint and play,
who once moved through the covert,
oblivious and free,
joy of a body, fear
of nothing, and first light
gathering everywhere,
before a sudden flare
of day-star. Then my flight.

*for Petr Borkovec**

from Prague Elegies

XX

A flagstone of old ice pulls and then lets go.
The river sweeps it turning through the country
unlocked with thousands more and rapidly shunted
away as all the rivers start to flow.

The buildings stand for this. Some years ago
a revolution swept through them, the junta
folded away with its acres of red bunting.
Another change rippled across the tableau

and rearranged those sleeping in the ground
with tiny landslides of record and surmise.
I walk to work and back through the city's maze,

the sun comes out and millions of ghosts turn round,
suddenly able to breathe if I can translate
the words: I was in Prague. I was flooded with light.

Pool

I dive into this rippling box of blue
and swim. Cliffs rise up on two sides of it
into the immense air and straying breezes.
The hurdling muscles thoughtlessly knit
the head back down and through, back down and through.

Hands wipe the water back, both sides at once,
the movement mirroring across the spine,
which clenches and then whips its length back out;
it ramifies the body's old design
out to the walls in small successive fronts.

Give or take a hundred people here
whose different wavelengths splash into my own:
the surface scintillates, self-cancelling.
A haze from off it is the single zone
of cool amidst the marvellous heat this year.

Their limbs are twisted in so many shapes,
pale corrugations hanging in the depths
that almost slip to anonymity.
Old skin goes floating by in stippled crêpes
and young flesh is mere shimmer; it escapes

the eye and then comes back; it has no mark
of child or knife. Miles off, across the plains,
the corn swells in its sheath beneath the sun,
so modified that bugs crawl in its grains
and doze off into everlasting dark.

Such black interiors, such tiny spans
are gathered up in sheaves; the grain is poured
into the gleaming silos and stands there,
the summer's pure gold surplus, traded, stored;
its bread soft clouds and sun held in your hands.

A flock of starlings spirals, streams and sports
itself in utter pleasure through the air
like swarms of fluent print about whatever
comes back in answer to its force, its flair,
its rapid glints through beryl, black and quartz;

like sentences that traffic to and fro
year after year between a man and woman
in antiphons of amour and attack,
a kind of covert, marriage acumen
through which comes almost everything they know.

These are the fat, the roseate
characters of all childhood memories—
tendresses, rebukes, the long days brought to book;
they drift back into distant centuries,
become a folk song whistled with regret

along a bosky lane as evening comes,
the flowers and florets pouring out themselves
to make a massive fragrance that resounds
with bug-chorales and bird-calls through the shelves
of lindens, beech-trees, ash and large viburnums.

The girls go by in bathing suits of blue
and yellow, sky and sun, half pales of green,
half pales of red, like flecks or fillips of
the season, ideas wandering through a scene,
the gestures and the laughter just on cue

and for that they are all of beauty, as though
that were to be in time, borne on a wave
running beneath the years, into the winter's
declivities and pleats that are a grave
for multitudes of leaves beneath the snow,

then twisting into this bright festival:
they scud its foaming peak, they hook and saunter,
their wake embellished hectically with drafts
of wide desire. Offstage there is some thunder,
then minutes later the whole sky has gone still.

*

A giant cloak of forests and of heaths
extends across the land mass from the ocean
to the interior, marked here and there
by clearings fretted with the complex motion
of ploughs and oxen, of small heroic feats

as tribes migrate and marry into others,
their languages spread further or erased
without a spoor that leads back to their lives.
Some might have glimpsed it just too late, amazed,
their children put to death before their mothers.

Their naïve labours were in vain, the breeze
dispersed these tribes like smoke throughout the air.
And what of it? Their blood is gone by spring
and foliage uncurls from everywhere,
a wall of trees behind a wall of trees.

This is a negative: take all the Levant,
the trade and culture creased in green oases
strewn widely through the undulating sands
and out of this comes Christendom's first traces,
the stories of how bread is newly leavened,

relayed across the Mediterranean—
its diamond facets and its glistening foam,
its lucent deeps that seagulls drift above
and heroes stray across in search of home—
in moving ripples from a Galilean.

Julian, baulked, could only but admire
the vast Hercynian expanse; it threw
him into gloom—the silence and the dark,
the endless solitude. He said he knew
of nothing like it in the Roman Empire.

But dazzled by their own rights and their worth,
their Caesar's sway and martial mastery,
the Roman citizens forgot outlying countries
left to their independence, and gradually
confounded their grand Empire with the earth.

Vague populations flitting in the shadows,
exchanging places, offering resistance,
dispersing in the trees which knit behind them;
their muddy languages, their strange subsistence
with no harvest, no livestock in the meadows:

this forest folded his gaze in its main
and lost it there forever in among
so many other sallies and tourbillions.
It's almost gone now, levelled for a song
that's to be heard in cities of the plain,

song of sporadic sirens and autobahns;
of streetcars ringing, trundling at full tilt
along the river that broke its banks last year
and rose and rose—the swirling mud and silt,
contagion rife throughout low-lying lands—

then sank again into its marble walls
to its habitual glittering through the country;
of children crying out in fright and play
about the pool, the splashes and the sundry
echoes off the cliffs, the counter-calls

around this theatre fringed with swaying ash.
The rocks rise from the ground into the air,
loom greatly there, the wild flowers on their ledges
so many, so many sprouting everywhere
for all the world like some great wave's panache.

Coffle

On small, hard shelves,
serried and stacked,
autonomous selves
(a moving tract

of loves and salts)
rise from the grey
fluorescent vaults
of the subway

and then break through
to the city's haze.
Slow fade to
their works and days.

Borscht

All that occurred
through their long days
spent in the earth,
in summer's blaze,

is here, the taste
of esculent roots
generously laced
with cream and croutes,

dug from a steppe
where last night's ice
drew in some schlepp
and closed its vice.

Solstice

Deep in the ground
the massive turn
of spring comes round.
The sun will burn

the earth for days
and days, a toy
within its gaze—
like luck, or joy,

or like Aeneas
coming home
to what we see as
ancient Rome.

David Wheatley (1970–)

Born in Dublin in 1970, David Wheatley is the author of four collections of poetry and more than two dozen scholarly articles. Also a prolific journalist, he has surveyed the changing landscape of contemporary literature for *The Times Literary Supplement*, *The Guardian*, and *The London Review of Books*, among others. He is co-founder, with Justin Quinn, of the journal *Metre*, and editor of the collected poems of James Clarence Mangan, as well as two literary anthologies—one dedicated to children's verse, the other collecting poetry from County Wicklow, where Wheatley was Writer in Residence.

As busy as Wheatley's resumé shows him to be—in one of his "Sonnets to James Clarence Mangan" he admits that he can't manage to "refuse / demands for instant copy from the press. . . . alas / the only work I'm paid for is . . . reviews"—he writes poetry that sinks into experience as if time were standing still. In "A Skimming Stone, Lough Bray" his spellbound attention to the formal elements of the simple act of skipping a stone leads to a poetic form that seems to recreate the action's elements:

> Watch the stone brush
> the water beneath it
> and never fall below,
> dip for an instant,
> rise again
> and glide like so, like so.[1]

Wheatley's poems sift through washes of sensory input in the way the listener in "AM Radio" tunes through the "chaos of voices" that spark across the late-night airwaves. Even noise eventually gets parsed into sense, as when the static in that poem resolves into "the sound of the world's / axis turning / as I finger the dial."[2]

But for Wheatley making sense of chaos doesn't mean reducing it to one fixed meaning. In "AM Radio" the silence between stations blurs into the silence of night itself, and even the poem's title swings between two meanings—radio on the AM band and radio in the A.M. hours.

When Wheatley quotes Christopher Ricks in an essay on Northern Irish poets —Ricks says the poets of Heaney's generation are distinguished by "an intense self-reflexive concern with the art of poetry itself in poems; and . . . a thrilled perturbation at philosophical problems of perception and imagination"—he comes close to pinpointing a description of his own poetry.[3] For Wheatley this concern with the art of poetry takes shape partly in self-reflexive *themes*. "The race is on," he writes in one sonnet, "Your poems gather speed, / realising time is running out." Another asks, "what's / a poem if not a message in a bottle?"

But he is equally concerned with the relationship between perception and poetic *form*. Often that means writing in traditional forms that give an orderly structure to perception and imagination. It can also mean experimenting with those forms, as he does in "Sonnet," a poem that satisfies the lyrical and narrative desires we bring to sonnets, even as it overturns the conventions of the form itself. Its fourteen lines—the number itself making the poem's strongest claim to be seen as a sonnet—are made up of two-word phrases that have the ring of colloquial currency: "stretch pants cashback pound shop store card." Although the duple combinations echo the iambs of the conventional sonnet, the lines Wheatley makes from them stop two beats short of a sonnet's pentameter. And they make sense without syntax. Whether read left to right or up and down it feels as if a lyrical story is trying to emerge from the apparently random combination of words. Whatever the rank of words might mean, its formal arrangement invites us to think about the way poems themselves manage to manufacture sense.

Wheatley was educated at Trinity College, Dublin, where he received a doctorate. He now teaches at the University of Hull.

NOTES

1. "A Skimming Stone, Lough Bray," *Thirst* (Oldcastle, Co. Meath: Gallery Books, 1997).

2. "AM Radio," *Thirst*.

3. Christopher Ricks, "Andrew Marvell: 'Its Own Resemblance,'" in *The Force of Poetry* (Oxford: Clarendon Press, 1984), pp. 34–35. Quoted in Wheatley, "'That Blank Mouth': Secrecy, Shibboleths, and Silence in Northern Irish Poetry," *Journal of Modern Literature*, Volume 25, Number 1, Fall 2001, p. 3.

A Skimming Stone, Lough Bray

for Justin Quinn

Skim a stone
across the lake surface,
marrying water and air:
turn this brick
of earth, while it flies,
from stone to living fire.

From stone to living
fire ablaze
on the lake's faceted skin—
tideless, the plaything
of wind and rain,
as now of this skimmed stone.

Watch the stone brush
the water beneath it
and never fall below,
dip for an instant,
rise again
and glide like so, like so.

Hear it echo back
each new contact,
brushing against the surface,
like a whip cracked
from shore to shore
of this walled-in, echoing place.

Skim a stone
across the lake surface,
never suspect it may fall—
as long as there's water
left to walk on,
air for its echo to fill.

AM Radio

The static
is the sound of the world's
axis turning
as I finger the dial,

a chaos of voices
gasping for breath,
the short wave snoring
its dreams in white noise.

After-hours radio.
There is nothing to stay
awake for and nothing
to make me drift off.

Punctual, various
headlines leap time zones,
pips mark the hours
like morse ultimata;

one phone-in show host
keeps punting the dull
sludge of insomniac
chatter *ad nauseam.*

Sleep is beyond me:
each shake of my head—
half defiance,
half resignation—

stays creased in the pillow
I roll on. This smooth plastic
box devours sleep,
spits dreams out

and builds invisibly,
wide and high
as the room's four walls,
its babel in air.

And at odd moments,
unlooked-for, silence
descends between stations. . .
And it is as much

as my ear can do
to tell the radio's
tiny silence
from that of the night.

A Garden In September

Inch by inch the oblong slab of sunlight
wins over the lawn;

we shift the wooden bench hourly
to stay in the shade

and watch the cardinal purple of tangling hebe
and wide-open clematis embroider

the far wall, where ants scramble
and leaves cover snails

spared the attentions of midday.
I have only to spill a glass of water

for the sun to lap it up at my feet.
But summer is ending,

and for more than the worm
the blackbird twitches impatiently

before swallowing. The tarmac
that baked so long in the heat has burst

to reveal a clump of underground mushrooms
already dead and beginning to stink,

and tomorrow something will be
not quite the same as we found it today

but still cause for neither regret nor alarm:
the chalked hopscotch grid in the lane

beginning to fade, the cat on the wall
picking its way more cautiously

through the scattered mosaic of jagged glass.

Autumn, the Nightwalk, the City, the River

How early the autumn seemed to have come that year,
the drizzles like moods, the tightness in the air.
Walking was different: nervous, brisker now
under the streetlights' tangerine conic glow;
needing gloves and scarves. I had both,
and a raincoat pulled up tight around my mouth.
Direction never mattered on those streets.
Once I walked all night and called it quits
somewhere miles from home, then caught the first
bus back. What mattered was being lost.
Anywhere would do: I remember suburbs
plush with hatchbacks parked on tidy kerbs,
privets, cherry blossoms, *nouveaux riches'*
houses named for saints, complete with cable dishes;
and then the streets where every window was
an iron grid across its pane of glass,
the garden weeds in cracks, a noise ahead—
a bird, a cat—enough to make me cross the road.
Any light was harsh: all-night Spars
and the lit façades of Georgian squares
I'd hurry past; headlights glared like search-
beams in their hurtling, quizzical approach.
But landmarks were always a magnet. I'd be out
for hours—in sight of open fields—and spot
a pub or spire I knew, then find myself
being led by it, with inarticulate relief,
back in. Home was defeat but consolation too,
reassurance there was nowhere else to go.
The clubs all shut, town was deserted all over:
the only living thing would be the river;
and one night following it, I got a sense
of how, if anything did, it left the dead-ends

of the place behind, moving like a dream
as past barracks, churches, courts, the lot, it swam,
the lights reflected on its surface so many jack-
o'-lanterns promising no going back,
for it at least if not for me. I followed it
all the way to the quay-end and then sat
as long as I thought it would take to reach the last buoy
and from there, already forgetting dry land, open sea.

from Sonnets to James Clarence Mangan

I

Fishamble Street, the Civic Offices
turning the sky a bureaucratic grey
above a vacant lot's rent-free decay:
craters, glass, graffiti, vomit, faeces.
One last buttressed Georgian house holds out
precariously against the wreckers' ball
or simply lacks the energy to fall
and rise again as one more concrete blot.
Ghost harmonics of the first *Messiah*
echo round the Handel Hotel and mix
with bells long redeveloped out of use
at Saints Michael and John's, a ghostly choir
rising and falling until the daydream breaks . . .
Silence. Of you, Mangan, not a trace.

6

If poetry wells up from some true source
Pierian spring water's all we need,
Pope innocently thought—who never tried
The Phoenix, Mulligan's, The Bleeding Horse.
What welled up there, an evening's work done,
were beer and whiskey streams to ease your drought,
overflowing, when your purse allowed,
to raging floodtides of oblivion.

Which lasts longer, poetry or drink?
Posterity's a cheque no barman yet's
agreed to change, and fame a low-class brothel.
And yet what better place than down the sink
for words, like streams, to find the sea, and what's
a poem if not a message in a bottle?

10

An east wind unleashed in Siberia,
your land where "nothing blooms," whips in from
the sea and quickly makes itself at home
outside my window in suburbia.
Spain, Prague, Russia . . . Stuck here all your days,
you conjured dream and nightmare worlds in rhyme,
but never pictured anything as grim
as row on awful row of semi-d's.
If only you like me had known the leafy
suburbs pastured on our mortgages
you could have forgone all your Shangri-las
to pioneer Siberia-sur-Liffey
in a brave new world of double glazing, hedges,
hose pipes, patios and second cars!

11

A folio creaks open, coughs a decade
of stored-up dust into your prying face.
Wrinkled, foxed, strong evidence of fleas . . .
the book itself is scarcely less decayed.
The race is on. Your poems gather speed,
realising time is running out.
And not for you alone: leaking rot,
the barren harvests run to barren seed.
But at your College desk your books retain
their unavailing charm, a Provost's bust
still pledges learning's universal salve.
That can no more save the land from ruin
than spare you that incalculable waste.
That spectacle. Your country left to starve.

13

The yawning earth absorbs another guest.
A knot of mourners plumed in heavy crêpe
thins to a single hooded, female shape.
Then no one. Corpse to bone to soil to dust,
dust to dust, then even that much gone.
I skulk among Glasnevin's plaster Christs,
the well-kept gravel paths and nettle wastes,
the rows of plots in search of . . . here's the one.
IHS: *In hoc signo,* "I have
suffered?" They blend like the rain and sodden earth
as the sun drowns. A few late rays hang on
to probe the fading script. *In memory of* . . .
No farce of flesh and blood but, given birth
to into death, MANGAN graved in stone.

14

Let the city sleep on undisturbed,
new hotels and apartment blocks replace
the Dublin that we brick by brick erase;
let your city die without a word
of pity, indignation, grief or blame,
the vampire crime lords fatten on its flesh
and planners zone the corpse for laundered cash,
but let your heedless cry remain the same:
"The only city that I called my own
sank with me into everlasting shade.
I was born the year that Emmet swung
and died my fever death in '49:
my words are a matchstick falling through the void
and scorch the centuries to come with song."

Jaywalking

A busker plays the guitar left-handed;
my hands, carrying
a plastic bag and a paper,

have been reversed in the glass façade
my double advances from
to greet me crossing the road.

However I follow it,
his clumsy rush
to the kerb leaves me scarcely

time to keep up or remember:
is it on the left
or the right that cars drive here?

If there was a clock, alive
to the danger, the second hand
would have gone into alarmed reverse.

Now I'm surrounded,
stuck on the white line
in what feels like the last scene from

Invasion of the Body Snatchers,
eye to eye
with my passing reflection.

I rewind to your terse goodbye
of the previous night
("Watch yourself out there")—

like mirror writing
read in a mirror,
travestied into meaning at last.

Poem

The roof has fallen but the house still stands.
Birds drop to our table from the open sky.
I cup and drink the rain from shivering hands.

Nothing could be simpler than my wants:
to go on living here not bothered why
the roof has fallen though the house still stands.

Some would assail the builders with complaints
(our bed was waterlogged last night). Not I,
cupping and drinking the rain from shivering hands.

You call it folly, I call it romance,
to weather each new test and still get by.
So what if the roof has fallen? The house still stands

and we still thrive in the muck and damp like plants,
nourished by the forces we defy.
I cup and drink the rain from shivering hands

and lie in the dark. The sea breeze roars and rants.
Drive us out? I'd like to see it try.
The roof has fallen but the house still stands.
I cup and drink the rain from shivering hands.

Stan

Stan: the bouquets in the window
spell his name. He is turning
the corner, out of view,

as I press for the traffic to stop,
four black cars slinking
behind him. The hearse pulls up.

Stan, though he has an appointment, has time.
I signal discreetly, *wouldn't you rather . . .*
sure of what feels like a rule of thumb

until the driver uncurls his fist
and extends a finger politely
demanding *you go first.*

Sonnet

stretch pants	cashback	pound shop	store card
hubcaps	tailfin	souped-up	Escort
breakbeat	ringtone	dole day	cheques cashed
loan shark	small change	rat boys	bag snatched
tin can	tomcat	backstreet	dosshouse
TV	late lunch	warmed-up	Chinese
black dog	tongue stud	real nails	fake tan
red light	road rage	brain-dead	Leeds fan
handbrake	wheelspin	pub crawl	big screen
spiked drink	lift home	knocked up	sixteen
knocked up	knocked out	well gone	all gone
all day	all week	stay home	what's on
chat shows	pig out	hard stuff	hard case
hard luck	fuck life	fuck off	now please

Gable End

Tá Tír na nÓg ar chúl an tí . . .

—Seán Ó Ríordáin*

Their day never to come, they have gone to the wall.
Like holy beggars they seem to have lost all will.
Their love affair with the future has made them ill,

the people who speak neither English nor Irish
and stand the ground only they could cherish
by the gable end of the last house of the parish,

shouldering their burden not to be borne,
the people who are neither native nor foreign.
Somewhere among these streets my mother was born

and now I too return to prod at the past,
content if I can be the unnoticed guest
and drop dead letters to myself in the post,

delivered and thrown away at the gable end
as I must have been, to end up lost and found
sharing my postcode with the rain and wind.

I paint myself into the tightest corner
and, though I could not be a slower learner,
mouth the slogans on each flag and banner

that I might join the gable end people
at last, surrendering to their appeal
and saying a prayer beneath their dreary steeple,

though they believe in neither Church nor God
but only the straw on which they make their bed,
outcast on the world. Yet they seem glad.

And we too are glad, making ourselves at home
among the averted gaze, the grating hymn,
the shout in the backstreet, the sanctified harm,

the shopping centre and the tourist trail:
security discreet; all of it real,
only our appetite for it still on trial,

and the signs in which we saw it all foretold—
*Quis Separabit,** *What We Have We Hold*—
urgently redundant, self-fulfilled

like us and fading as we lose all will,
our day come and gone, the pair of us still
with nowhere to shelter but this gable wall.

Sinéad Morrissey (1972–)

The far-flung landscapes of Sinéad Morrissey's poetry—in just her first three volumes she strays from Northern Ireland through Japan, China, Germany, and Australia—attest to her nomadic spirit and the flexibility of her poetic vision. But you don't have to dig far beneath the surface of her poems to see that Morrissey's native soil is poetry itself. Whatever her subject, Morrissey seems to be thinking simultaneously of the reality she's depicting and the art that perceives that reality through language.

"The Juggler," for example, is a kind of sideshow *ars poetica* in which the performer's anachronistic skill is tantamount to poetry. The supple craft the juggler troubles himself to master serves no practical purpose and it requires a lifetime's practice to hone its techniques to a point of effortless performance—the "game," as Morrissey puts it, "whittled // To art."[1] His achievement is in the momentary control his art demonstrates over a world that—by physical gravity and metaphysical chance—seems otherwise conditioned toward the failure of human endeavors.

There is also something of the artist in the haphazard tourist in "China" who catches on her digital camera a face she hadn't known was there, as if to say it's in trying to capture what you think you see, or think you know, that you come to discover what you had in fact been missing in your happenstance perception of the world. This is the way a poem discovers what language already knows. In Morrissey's poetry even choosing a place to live may acquire a similar poetic valence. In "The Fort-Maker," for example, a Fitzcarraldo figure who for no good reason turns the building of his house into an epic three-year struggle finds that doing something so difficult and meaningless for the love of the task turns the world around him into a work of art, visible "In a stilled frame, everywhere he looked."[2]

Morrissey was born in Portadown, Northern Ireland, in 1972, and grew up in Belfast during the Troubles. Her development as a poet occurred at an extraordinary rate and she wasn't yet ten years old when she wrote her first poem. Early on, Morrissey was captivated by the rhythmic effects of poems with insistent beats—she singles out works like Stevenson's "From a Railway Carriage" and Poe's "The Raven"—and she was then thrilled to discover that writing poetry came easy to her. At fourteen, Morrissey told an interviewer, she "fell under the dangerous spell of Sylvia Plath, like so many teenage girls with literary aspirations."[3] But if her interest in Plath was conventional, her talent was extraordinary, and four years later Morrissey won the Patrick Kavanagh award, making her, at 18, the youngest recipient of that prize. She went on to study at Trinity College, where she became a member of Michael Longley's creative writing group. Over the years Plath has been supplanted by Les Murray, the Australian poet she now points to as the strongest influence on her own work.

Morrissey's Belfast background is evident in a poem like "Tourism," which reflects on the question the city faces as it enters the 21st century: whether to revise or cash in on the war-torn image of itself—the kind of image Morrissey had drawn in earlier poems like "Double Vision" (not included here) and "English Lesson."

But the city's troubled past is more often transmuted in her work into a kind of faith in the humanitarian efficacy of poetry. "The Gobi from Air," a poem that remembers the journey W. H. Auden and Christopher Isherwood made to China in 1938, is about the way a single striking image can kindle an antagonism toward injustice, or catch a human element otherwise lost in the headline snapshots of history. Her recent long poem "The State of the Prisons" is similar in the way it imagines images sticking in the mind as emblems of injustice. The section included here captures the transformation of eighteenth-century prison reformer John Howard, focusing on the period during which, as the poem puts it, he "metamorphosed into an enthusiast."[4] The process—driven by images and the rhythms of his personal history—looks a lot like the making of a poet.

Notes

1. "The Juggler," *There Was Fire in Vancouver* (Manchester: Carcanet, 1996).
2. "The Fort-Maker," *There Was Fire in Vancouver*.
3. "Sinead Morrissey—Interview with Declan Meade," *The Stinging Fly*, vol. 1, 14.
4. "The State of the Prisons," *The State of the Prisons* (Manchester: Carcanet, 2005).

The Juggler

He must have practised for hours
Between the bins and the mattresses
Of a rented back yard
To dance the seven painted skittles
Off his fingers like that.
He has the game whittled

To art. God knows what
Anachronism he took up before,
Using medieval skills to stop
Time: he puts the clock back
Nine hundred years
With this side-show for a quack

Or diversion for a king.
Still, or because of the drain
Of things modern, we ring
Him with faces. He knows
How we anticipate failure
And that what he owes

His audience is a defiance
Of breakdown. We watch as his magic
Creates the radiance
Of a spinning blue arc, brought
Slowly to standstill. Natural begrudgers,
We are nevertheless caught

By the weightlessness, the controlled
Mechanics of air

With all the improbables cajoled
Into truth, we are not as far out
From faith as we were.

There Was Fire in Vancouver

There was fire in Vancouver,
And we leaned out into the night to watch it
Set light to the East End.
It had taken stand on Commercial Avenue.

We marvelled at the darkness of the city,
All neon dulled by the superior flame,
And wondered would it bestow its dance
On the Ginseng Teahouse in Chinatown, on Jericho Pier.

There were no sirens, hoses, buckets even,
Scattering streets and "Fire!" "Fire!"
We seemed the only ones conscious of the bright crusade
And we watched with Moses standing in our heads.

English Lesson

Today I taught the Germans about Northern Ireland.
High on their interest, I paraded as a gunman
On the Falls Road. Death holds the attention—
BANG! blew them off their seats and I got away scot free.

"A fiddler in a death-camp"—
Beyond the lot of it.

The only honesty is silence.

The Fort-Maker

It was too late for invasion
By the time he'd set his hungry eye on the hill
Above the town, and thought of the view.
War was not the reason

For the three years' haulage—
It was sheer love.

And because his need
Was a beginning and an end to all things,
His house became a circle of windows—
Catching ruins and birds
And the blank faces of the sea
In a stilled frame, everywhere he looked.

Restoration

1. ACHILL, 1985

Once I saw a washed up dolphin
That stank the length of Achill Sound,
Lying on the edge of Ireland.
The Easter wind ripping it clear
Of all its history,
And the one gull watching it,
Abandoned by the tide.
I remember how its body,
Opened in the sun,
Caught me,
And I remember how the sea
Looked wide and emptied of love.

2. JUIST, 1991

The North Sea booms tonight
And there are no lights the length
Of the fifteen mile beach,
And no stars

The sea is revealing itself
By its own light light revealing
Essences of light:
Meeresleuchten, lights of the sea

One touch and the water explodes
In phosphorescence
No one knows if it lives
It is as though God said

Let there be light in this world
Of nothing let it come from
Nothing let it speak nothing
Let it go everywhere

Tourism

Like the relief of markets,
their saffron-coloured cloths and carpets,
purification where two rivers cross, or the widening line of light
entering Newgrange on the winter solstice—

a manufactured prophesy of spring—
the Spanish and the Dutch are landing in airports
and filing out of ships. Our day has come.

They bring us deliverance, restitution,
as we straighten our ties, strengthen our lattés,
polish our teeth. We take them to those streets
they want to see most, at first,

as though it's all over and safe behind bus glass
like a staked African wasp. Unabashedly, this is our splintered city,
and this, the corrugated line between doorstep and headstone.

Next, fearing summary,
we buy them a pint with a Bushmills chaser
and then on to the festering gap in the shipyard
the Titanic made when it sank.

Our talent for holes that are bigger
than the things themselves
resurfaces at Stormont, our weak-kneed parliament,

which, unlike Rome, we gained in a day
and then lost, spectacularly, several days later

in a shower of badly played cards. Another instance, we say,
of our off-beat, headstrong, suicidal charm.

So come, keep coming here.
We'll recklessly set chairs in the streets and pray for the sun.
Diffuse the gene pool, confuse the local kings,

infect us with your radical ideas; be carried here
on a sea breeze from the European superstate
we long to join; bring us new symbols,
a new national flag, a xylophone. Stay.

Street Theatre

They started with sweetness and light,
their faces white as *Mikado* lovers,
their eyes elliptical.
Their ache (a seagull)

was abated (a swan).
Shame was brief—
it came as a bat
hung up in the chest's wall.

It flapped twice in panic,
then slept.
Boredom was a rock that rolled between them.
They ate their dinner off it.

Finally they dealt each other
a deck of disappointments,
snatched them up, flashing,
and swallowed them as swords.

There wasn't an ending proper.
They simply stood back to back
in a frozen unnecessary duel
and waited for coins.

Between Here and There

No one seems sure of the reason why aprons
are tied to the necks of stone babies in temples.
The priest says "honour."
The guide to Kyoto City mentions "cold
on their journey away from us to the heaven for children."
I look at them squatting in Buddha-reflection,
wrapped up to the throat in teddy bears and trains.

*

There's a graveyard for miscarriages under Ikeda Mountain
as stark as a bone field. No flowers, tangerines, sake or aprons
but a basin of stone bodies in two parts: square body, round head.
Like oriental soldiers contained by a wall, they would go walking—
spill over with all of the energy for life that fell out of them too soon.
Except that even in stone some bodies have opened—
loose balls in the basin where heads have rolled.

*

Inside the biggest wooden building in the world
sits Japan's greatest Buddha. One hand raised as a stop sign to evil.
The other is flat, flat with comfort and promise, flat enough
for all of us to nuzzle his thumb. His lily flower opened.
His crossing was a falling into light.
Fall with me, he says, *and you'll be raised to the heights
of the roof of the biggest wooden building in the world.*

*

When Nagasawa visits the house of the dead
he leaves at the door his camera and tripod
his champion karaoke voice his miracle foot massage
his classroom dynamics his rockhard atheism
and slips onto the tatami of the prayer room
as the man who can chant any you-name-it soul
between here and Ogaki to paradise.

To Encourage the Study of Kanji

I've been inside these letters it seems for years, I've drawn them
on paper, palms, steamed mirrors and the side of my face
in my sleep, I've waded in sliced lines and crossed boxes.

They stay, stars in the new-moon sky,
as dead as the names of untraceable constellations.
Intricate, aloof, lonely, abstracted,

some other mind made them and still since then
they've shrunk to a hint at a fairytale. Say I thread beads.
Say I remember a sky of walking pictures.

Forty Lengths

Before goggles, the pool was a catch of beleaguered heads
being raced against each other by omnipotence.

But now that I, too, have been strapped back and capped
like a pre-war flying enthusiast—

shoulders to the rear, the aerodynamic necessity
of not having hair—I see

how solidly we occur under water.
Now all the world's a blur, except for down here

in this makeshift polar enclosure
where I follow one white-limbed swimmer after another

to the wall. We do not resemble fishes, so much as frogs
or the diving waterboatman with his fringed hind legs.

And I find myself back—to the womb,
most obviously, but even better than that—to the film

I played in my head as a child
to make myself sleep: me up in the sky

like Lucy, not needing to breathe, or be tired, or be told, or be older—
wishboning through the stratosphere.

from China

7

I find I have made a ghost
of you—I'm sorry—as I
aimed my camera foolishly
at the passing coloratura
of mountains and fields,
and snapped them anyway,
knowing I'd never get them back
the way they were being given,
at that precise instant, and caught them,
yes alright, adequately enough, but somehow
also caught your watchful face
filling the window without
its source. Confucius refuses
to speak about spirits. *Till you know*
about the living, how are you
to know about the dead? he pronounces
to the ever-curious Tzu-lu.
And I wonder, if I can make ghosts
of the living with my dinky, digital
machine, is it possible I can also
make the dead visible? And I set my camera
more deliberately now on the vast, peopleless
expanse, then check its screen
to see if I've got anything
in its wide-eyed little net.
I don't know what I expected—
one or two of the million Yangtze
drowned, perhaps, still draining their ears
by banging the sides of their heads, or looking after
the vanishing tumult of the train
for directions home?

The Gobi from Air

1

Auden's face in age
looked like this place.

The same wind-chiselled flair.
The same doubt as to where

decorousness
really ought to begin and end.

Ten thousand barrels of sand
overturned

on the streets of Beijing in a year.
Some days they fear

that the earth
is raining.

2

His addiction to war
delivered him here—

a three-month-old letter
wherever he went.

His trains all avoided the front.
The Japanese shielded their eyes

from the sun, and kept on killing.
He toured warehouses, brothels, remembering,

out of everything,
damp fungus frothing

on the fingertips
of the mill girls in Shanghai.

Polar

after Brecht

My darling, lest you vanish back
To the vast frontier you fled from
Once its darkness
Failed to break—
Baying for bathwater, bedlinen, *me*—
Without a further word,
Allow these gifts:

Six pairs of pearl-stitch knitted socks,
An Aran with a fingered ridge, a scarf
To trap a boulder in.
For even though you're lean
And craven, I'd rather have you
Round and down and rollable.
I want to hap you up

So that you stagger off, surrounded
By my warmth, on your journey
North. I want to wrap
Your delectable backside
(Which I chew on so immoderately
When I'm out of my right mind)
In all the wool of Scotland.

Forgive me this redress. Forgive
The need to staunch my loneliness
On your enormous absence.
Even the furniture sags without you.
I invent a war to send you
Off to, but it's only a war
With nature. They say it's winter

When you're up there
Nine months of the year
(The solstice dragging its feet
With the weight of the planet);
That the sky is merely on fire

With its own futility; and the snow geese—
Inconsequential company.

Zero

for Joseph

Whatever else it was he stole from the East—
indigo, gold, a brace of abused and temporary women,
frankincense, the inevitable spice or two,
or the fruit that shed itself with such feral sweetness
on the tongue it begged re-naming—
Alexander also stowed nothing—
that double nick in the Babylonian plaque which,
of everything, was the easiest to store
(the women were a nightmare)
precisely because it lived nowhere
and therefore everywhere: in two spare horseshoes
angled together, in the kiss of a thumb and forefinger,
in the sigh at the bottom of a poured-out water jar,
in the memory of some noon-white city square
wherever luck ran out, or faith, or anger—
                                        but
when Alexander delivered zero to the Greeks
they turned and saw (or thought they saw)
a wellhead blacken in front of them—
an incredulous, bricked-in "O"—
unravelling into inkiness like a sleeve, the kind
you might toss a stone into and never hear the splash,
though you stand and wait, your ear awash in silence,
for an hour—and over it the bric-a-brac of kitchens appeared
suspended in the sunshine—knives, lemons, sieves, pots, bowls—
a funnel of dailyness, which the wellhead then swallowed
like a child, and, sensing where it could lead,
this number/no-number that would eat the world,
the Greeks turned back to Alexander in the advancing shade
and smiled: for there were still angles, there were still
three old angels skipping over heaven carrying harps and signs.

from The State of the Prisons

2

God sent an earthquake when I was twenty-nine
And lured my soul to suffering like moths to the flame.
November 1755. As my first wife was lain
In an oak box in Whitechapel, 20,000 attested dead
Flared across the pages of the *Gentleman's Magazine*.
The death toll left me breathless, but decided.

Resolved for Portugal, I dismissed my servants,
Sorted my affairs, and was heading for the wreckage on the Lisbon Packet
On the 14th day in January, when the French attacked.
We were captured as prisoners of war, whipped,
And forced on our knees to swear a blood-felt testament
To dungeon existence. Later we were shipped

To Carhaix, then finally released. I came home.
Washed. Grew well. In time became Sheriff of Bedford.
The villagers and tenants prospered.
My French adventure faded from view. And then the County Trials,
Irregular as women, rolled round again to Cardington,
And everything changed. At the first sitting of the Assizes

The prisoners entered, pulling on long chains.
A muscle jerked in my thumb. The judge was eminent,
Bored, ecclesiastical, inured to the stench of sweat and excrement
That flowered where they stood. I was reeling back to a stone hole
And darkness interminable, as the felons' crimes
Were pronounced against them in a nasaloid drone.

When it was over, I barked six questions at the Crown officials.
Why are they not clean? Why so thin?
Why ill? Why are felons and debtors, women and men,
Chained and tried together? Why, when chosen for release,
Do debtors stay listed on the turnkey's roll call?
What fees remain to pay? Justice sat asleep

In a rolled wig. I metamorphosed into an enthusiast.
And so it was my journey started to every prison in Europe,

Shuttling between nations like an evangelist. Or *a Cook*
Of the Unfortunate (as Burke put it). I, too, was on a voyage of discovery.
I, too, would make maps. A continent of misery, unchartered, vast,
Opened before my eyes. I vowed to regulate the colony.

Through the Square Window

In my dream the dead have arrived
to wash the windows of my house.
There are no blinds to shut them out with.

The clouds above the Lough are stacked
like the clouds are stacked above Delft.
They have the glutted look of clouds over water.

The heads of the dead are huge. I wonder
if it's my son they're after, his
effortless breath, his ribbon of years—

but he sleeps on unregarded in his cot,
inured, it would seem, quite naturally
to the sluicing and battering and pairing back of glass

that delivers this shining exterior . . .
One blue boy holds a rag in his teeth
between panes like a conjuror.

And then, as suddenly as they came, they go.
And there is a horizon
from which only the clouds stare in,

the massed canopies of Hazelbank,
the severed tip of Strangford Peninsula,
and a density in the room I find it difficult to breathe in

until I wake, flat on my back with a cork
in my mouth, stopper-bottled, in fact,
like a herbalist's cure for dropsy.

NOTES TO POEMS

PERMISSIONS ACKNOWLEDGMENTS

INDEX OF TITLES

Notes to Poems

Padraic Colum (1881–1972)

19 Pan is the Greek god of flocks and herds. Wotan is the Germanic form of Odin, the supreme deity of Norse mythology. Dana, sometimes Danu, is the Celtic mother goddess referred to in the term *Tuatha Dé Dannan*, or people of the goddess Dana.

21 "Shall I Go Bound and You Go Free?" and "She Moved Through the Fair" are restorations of Irish traditional songs of which one or two lines were in existence; they were written for traditional music collected by Herbert Hughes and published with these words in one of his collections" (author's note).

23 Khayr ad-Din (d. 1546), known as Barbarossa or "redbeard," was a pirate who became commander of the Ottoman navy. Abu ʻabd Allah Muhammad XI (d. 1527), called Boabdil in Spanish, reigned as sultan of Granada from 1482 to 1492. The Serbian prince Lazar Hrebeljanovic was defeated by forces of the Ottoman Empire at the Battle of Kosovo in 1389. Charlemagne (d. 815), King of the Franks, was in 800 crowned emperor of the Holy Roman Empire by Pope Leo III. Arthur, the legendary king of Britain, is the hero of medieval legend cycles and later romances. "Gaelic Finn" refers to Finn MacCumhaill, the hero of the Fenian or Ossianic cycle of Irish tales and ballads.

25 Latin, "hail and farewell." The phrase has a long tradition of use in poetry, from Catullus to Swinburne to Billy Collins. Colum's poem is a translation from Catullus.

26 A co-founder of the Irish-nationalist organization Sinn Féin, Arthur Griffith (1871–1922) in 1921 helped negotiate the treaty that established the Irish Free State. He served as the president of Ireland's revolutionary parliament, the Dáil Éireann, from 1919 until his death in 1922.

Targe is a poetic term for a light shield or buckler.

27 Roger Casement (1864–1916), Irish nationalist and British diplomat, was executed for his role in planning the Easter Rising of 1916.

A word of Gaelic origin, *ochone* is an expression of sorrow or regret.

Blee, an archaic and poetic term meaning color or hue.

Austin Clarke (1896–1974)

31 Author's note: "This is merely a glimpse of *Buile Suibhne,* a middle-Irish romance of a king who, cursed by a saint, wandered in madness through the woods. The story, published by the Irish Texts Society for the first time in 1913, has escaped attention. George Moore regarded it as one of the great stories of the world, and its natural colour inspired him in his second to last story, the Norman-Irish romance, *Ulick and Soracha.*"

The name Kieran or Ciarán is associated with several early Irish saints, including a contemporary of St Patrick.

Mannanaun MacLir is a sea god who also appears in Clarke's play *The Plot Succeeds* (1950).

Glenveigh (more often spelled Glenveagh), or "Glen of the Birches," is an area on the shore of Lough Veagh in County Donegal.

32 Author's note: "The women bound to the rafters. The Furies appeared in this manner to the doomed."

33 Achill Island, most of the land mass of which is peat bog, lies off the west coast of County Mayo.

A dolmen is a megalithic stone tomb. In its most common construction the tomb is made up of upright stone pillars on which rests a flat stone slab.

34 Author's note: Midna is "a magician who played slumber-music on a reed outside the camps of the Fianna."

The Culdees formed an early monastic order in Ireland and Scotland that long lay outside canonical control. Their reputation as caretakers of the sick and injured would have attracted the ravaged Suibhne.

The Greek goddess Mnemosyne, the mother of the Muses, personifies memory.

The setting of the poem is the area just east of Phoenix Park in Dublin. Manor Street, where Clarke was born, or "got," angles down toward the River Liffey from the northwest, running into Blackhall Place near what is now Ellis Quay. The Hospital and Free School of King Charles II, known as the Blue Coat School, occupied buildings on Blackhall Place beginning in 1783. Kingsbridge Station has been called Heuston Station since 1966. The Guinness brewery and storehouse are nearby off Market Street.

35 Dr Steevens' Hospital on Steevens Lane, the first public hospital in Dublin, was founded by Grizell Steevens (1653–1747) in 1717, drawing on an estate willed to her by her late brother, the physician Richard Steevens (1653–1710), with the intention of establishing a hospital upon her death. The building was completed in 1733 and Dr Steevens' Hospital served patients, in particular Dublin's poor, for more than two hundred years. Clarke's editor Hugh Maxton notes: "The Steevens family were Cromwellians, and perhaps for this reason Madam Steevens (as she was known) was reputed to have the facial features of a pig. This is said to have been the result of a beggarwoman's curse on her mother. Clarke appears to merge mother and daughter." *Selected Poems of Austin Clarke*, ed. Hugh Maxton (Dublin: Lilliput Press, 1991), p. 246.

St Patrick's Hospital, the psychiatric facility where Maurice Devane is treated, was established by a bequest from Jonathan Swift. The Hospital occupies buildings on Steevens Lane. Clarke was himself treated there in 1919.

40 A drosky is an open, four-wheeled carriage much used in Russia.

41 A fearsome creature from a traditional Dublin ballad in which a Twangman stabs to death a commercial traveler who steals the heart of his "mot" (girlfriend).

In the Old Testament story (Genesis 38) Onan spills his seed on the ground. The name has thus become a figure for masturbation.

42 Author's note: "*The Romance of Mis* was edited by Brían Ó Cuív. This ancient story seems to anticipate the curative methods of Freud. I am indebted to Professor David Greene for his translation. I have ventured to add a few stanzas about dream analysis." Clarke's note explains further that Mis "is pronounced Mish. Ruis is Ruish." In the version of the story Ó Cuív published in *Celtica* in 1954, Mis is driven mad by the death of her father in the Battle of Ventry and afterward lives in the forest, killing and eating animals and humans. After many years (seven score in one version, three hundred in another) the new King of Munster offers a reward to anyone who can bring her safely to him. All who attempt the task are killed until the king's harper, Dubh Ruis, ventures into the forest and lures her with his harp. Soothing her with music Dubh Ruis seduces Mis in the hope that sexual intercourse may bring her back to her senses. Dubh Ruis slowly civilizes Mis, teaching her to cook her food, rather than devouring animals raw, and to clean and clothe herself. Eventually he takes her

back to his home and marries her. See Brían Ó Cuív, "The Romance of Mis," *Celtica*, vol. 2, part 2 (1954), pp. 325–333; Ó Cuív's English summary is quoted by Maxton in *Selected Poems of Austin Clarke*, p. 274.

43 Clarke glosses *geilt* as "a mad person."

A cantred is a district made of villages.

The Paps of Dana and Mount Brandon are in County Kerry.

A farl is a flat, usually triangular, bread or cake common in Ulster.

44 Clarke glosses *suantree* as "a soothing song."

47 A Sidhe-mound is a hillock of earth associated in Irish legend with a race of fairies.

C. DAY LEWIS (1899–1963)

55 "Laois: Pronounced Leash. Ballintubbert House was the poet's birthplace" (note to *Collected Poems*).

60 Markievicz: pronounced Markievitch (Author note.)

62 Sidhe: pronounced she. People of the faery mound (found in Irish mythology and W. B. Yeats) [Author note.]

LOUIS MACNEICE (1907–1963)

101 Maud Gonne MacBride (1866–1953), Irish actress and Republican activist with whom W. B. Yeats was infatuated.

102 Orange bands: paraders representing Protestant Unionist groups.

Kathleen ni Houlihan: A figure for Ireland.

103 Arthur Griffith: founder of Sinn Féin; Joseph Connolly: Irish nationalist interned after the Easter Rising in 1916; Michael Collins: Irish nationalist assassinated during the Civil War in 1922 as a result of his role in the Anglo-Irish Treaty negotiations; Ourselves alone: a translation of "Sinn Féin."

106 Tir nan Og: In Irish mythology the land of immortal youth.

SAMUEL BECKETT (1906–1989)

117 Chapelizod: the name of this village on the River Liffey west of Dublin derives from Chapel of Isolde. It is the legendary burial place of that medieval princess.

Nepenthe is the remedy for grief that Helen gives to Menelaus and Telemachus in Book IV of the *Odyssey*. In Book X Hermes gives the herb Moly to Odysseus to immunize him against Circe's magic.

JOHN HEWITT (1907–1987)

126 Grace Darling, the daughter of a lighthouse keeper stationed on one of the Farne Islands off Northumberland, was celebrated for assisting her father in the daring rescue of victims of the wreck of the SS *Forfarshire* in 1838. Grace O'Malley (c. 1530–1603), known as Granuaile, a corruption of the Gaelic Gráinne, was a Mayo-born pirate who took part in rebellions throughout the 1580s.

128 yowes: Ulster dialect for ewes

129 Hewitt's paternal grandparents were born in Kilmore parish, Co. Armagh.

MÁIRTIN Ó DIREÁIN (1910–1988)

137 The poem "is based on the life of one of the hereditary landlords of Aran. In Ó Direáin's book of prose sketches, *Feamainn Bhealtain (May Seaweed)*, he mentions how the landlord's cattle were driven over a cliff at the time of the Land League and how the islanders had to pay compensation" ("Introduction," *Selected Poems / Tacar Danta*, selected and translated by Tomás Mac Síomóin, Douglas Sealy (Co. Kildare, Ireland: Goldsmith Press, 1984), p. xv. This information puts the incidents of the poem in the early 1880s. The Land League was founded in 1879 by Charles Stewart Parnell and Michael Davitt to resist the mistreatment and eviction of tenant farmers.

138 Frieze, in this sense, is a coarse woolen cloth.

141 Cill na Manach; Church of the Monks.

John Millington Synge (1871–1909), Irish writer associated with the Aran Islands and chiefly known for his plays, including *The Playboy of the Western World*.

142 Deirdre and Naoise are the ill-fated lovers whose legendary elopement is the subject of Synge's play *Deirdre of the Sorrows*. A currach is a small boat of leather stretched over a wooden frame. "Ceann Gainimh (Sandy Headland) is at the north eastern corner of Inishmaan. Coill Chuain (The Wood of Cuan) is one of the places in the West of Scotland where Deirdre and Naoise lived during their exile" (*Selected Poems / Tacar Danta*), p. 129n. Inishmaan is the middle island in the Aran chain.

Pegeen Mike, the heroine of *The Playboy of the Western World*, is loosely affianced to Shawn Keogh (Shawneen) before falling in love with Christy Mahon, the playboy.

143 "The embalmed head of Blessed Oliver Plunkett (1621–81), Archbishop of Armagh, who was hanged, drawn and quartered at Tyburn, is enshrined in St Peter's Church, Drogheda" (*Selected Poems / Tacar Danta*, p. 133n.)

144 George Berkeley (1685–1753) was appointed Bishop of Cloyne in 1734. In this poem Ó Direáin is referring to Samuel Johnson's famous refutation of Bishop Berkeley, described as follows in James Boswell, *The Life of Samuel Johnson* (New York: Alfred A. Knopf, 1992), pp. 295–296: "After we came out of the church, we stood talking for some time together of Bishop Berkeley's ingenious sophistry to prove the nonexistence of matter, and that every thing in the universe is merely ideal. I observed, that though we are satisfied his doctrine is not true, it is impossible to refute it. I never shall forget the alacrity with which Johnson answered, striking his foot with mighty force against a large stone, till he rebounded from it—'I refute it *thus.*'"

145 Sruthán is on Inis Mor, the largest of the Aran Islands.

PADRAIC FIACC (1924–)

162 Norman Dugdale: poet associated with the Belfast group.

163 Ards: a peninsula on the coast of County Down in Northern Ireland.

165 François Mauriac (1885–1970), French novelist and poet who won the Nobel Prize for literature in 1952.

166 Leitrim, Longford, and Cavan are contiguous counties in north-central Ireland.

167 Irish-born labor organizer Michael J. Quill (1905–1966) helped found the Transport Workers Union of America.

168 *Terribilita* is a term used to describe an artist's ability to inspire awe through the representation of intense emotion, often in the depiction of facial features.

169 Patrick Rooney was killed in August 1969 when machine-gun fire from a British army unit struck the Falls Road apartment building in which the boy was sleeping. The soldiers were attempting to quiet a clash between the Catholic residents of the Falls neighborhood and Protestant loyalists who had staged what the Catholics saw as an invasion. Five other Catholics were killed in the incident.

170 Fenian is term a that originally named the heroes led by Fionn MacCumhaill in the so-called Fenian cycle of Irish epic. The term was applied to nationalists from the nineteenth century on. "Get" is British and Irish slang for bastard.

PEARSE HUTCHINSON (1927–)

175 Nansen passports: international identification cards proposed by the Red Cross and issued by the League of Nations as passports for stateless refugees beginning in 1922.

The passport was named for Fridtjof Nansen, the League's High Commissioner for Refugees, who was awarded the Nobel Prize later in 1922. A number of Russian artists—Marc Chagall, Anna Pavlova, Igor Stravinsky, and Sergey Rachmaninov, among them—used Nansen passports to reach the West after the Russian Civil War.

176 *Fleadh Cheoil* is Irish for "festival of music." The term often refers to the annual national festival put on by *Comhaltas Ceoltóirí Éireann*, the Society of the Musicians of Ireland.

177 "*An Nollaig sa tSamhradh:* Christmas in Summer. From a love-song by Seán Ó Neachtain (1655–1728), Roscommon-born poet and novelist" (author's note)."

178 Gaeltacht: region of western Ireland in which Irish is the vernacular language.

"The Gaelic means, in verse 2: The Gaelic is less than the water in that glass; in verse 3: I speak with strangers. I believe it's right to be speaking with strangers. (Strangers, here, has the sense of outlanders, foreigners, runners-in.) In verse 4: Ah, son: don't be breaking a boat. This last was said to my friend Liam Barry in Carraroe" (author's note).

180 "The first country is Transylvania; I read a book about it twenty years ago and, to my shame, I've forgotten both the title and author. The second country is Ireland, my authority is Dinneen. The third country is Guatemala, which I read about in Luís Cardoza y Aragón's 'Guatemala: en las líneas de su mano' (Fondo de Cultura Económica, Mexico)" (author's note).

Achnasheen is a remote village northwest of Inverness in the Scottish Highlands. Talisker is a single-malt Scotch whisky praised by Robert Louis Stevenson in "The Scotsman's Return from Abroad": "The king o' drinks, as I conceive it, Talisker, Islay or Glenlivit."

182 "The black sticks of the devil: from one of the *dis*approving Gaelic names for the pipes: maidí dubha an diabhail. Barcelona: the Catalan poet Salvador Espriu has a line, 'tornar a les coses el seu nom' (to give things back their name), and walking one day in Barcelona I realized it might mean, quite simply, to put the street-names in Catalan, not Castilian, the language of the conqueror. Belfast: the name is an Anglicization of the original Gaelic, Béal Feirste" (author's note).

183 The hybrid phrase accepts that "the little lad's a mistake," or perhaps, although Irish adjectives normally follow the nouns they modify, "the lad's a little mistake."

184 "She fell asleep in the sun: I owe this expression to the poet and scholar Dáithí Ó hÓgáin, who found it for me in the archives of Roinn Bhéaloideas Éireann (the Department of Irish Folklore), University College, Dublin. For that I am grateful to him, as I am to Áine McEvoy (the woman from Kerry) who gave me that incompa-

rable phrase 'leanbh ón ngréin,' and to my friend from Tiernahilla (County Limerick), the poet Pádraig de Vál, for the line 'garsúinín beag mishtake'" (author's note).

185 The model of miners working the Barnsley Main Seam is in York Minster cathedral. The features of the cathedral that Hutchinson focuses on include a 14th-century effigy of Prince William (1103–1120) and the Five Sisters Window in the North Transept. A massive grisaille work comprising over 100,000 separate pieces of glass, the window was completed in 1250 and is now dedicated to the women who died in the 20th century's two world wars.

Honiton, Devon, was the scene of so-called bread and butter riots in 1766. In one incident lace workers forcibly seized grain held by local farmers. See E. P. Thompson, *The Making of the English Working Class* (London: Penguin, 1991), p. 69. Merthyr Tydfil, in south Wales, was an important center of iron production in the late eighteenth and early nineteenth centuries. In 1831 miners and iron workers there staged an armed uprising against the town's industrialists, leading to clashes with the local bailiffs and the 93rd Highland Regiment, which was sent to quell the unrest.

186 Brú na Bóinne, an area defined by a bend in the Boyne river north of Dublin, is the site of a complex of Neolithic chamber tombs.

"In the last verse, line 2. 'Where the Air is Clear' means Mexico City. It's the title of the English translation of the novel by Carlos Fuentes which first made him famous, namely 'La region más transparente del aire'—literally, the most transparent region of the air. In other words, Mexico City. I can't think of any translation more brilliantly found, so different, so much more crisp and lyrical, yet entirely faithful" (author's note).

187 "This poem is for Paddy Joe Hill, because on that memorable day in 1991, when the Birmingham Six came out of court vindicated, one of the first things he said to the world was: 'It's English justice, not British—we can't blame the Scots or the Welsh'" (author's note).

RICHARD MURPHY (1927–)

193 Grace O'Malley (c. 1530–1603), known as Granuaile, a corruption of the Gaelic Gráinne, was a Mayo-born pirate who took part in rebellions throughout the 1580s.

194 On 28 October 1927 a powerful storm struck the area of Cleggan Bay off County Galway, capsizing fishing boats and killing some forty-five fishermen.

195 The poem is set in the west of Ireland where the River Corrib flows into Galway Bay.

196 Ailsa Craig is a manufacturer of marine engines.

198 Éamon de Valera (1882–1975), Irish Republican who served as the President of Ire-

land's revolutionary parliament and, after introducing a new constitution in 1937, as Prime Minister of the Republic of Ireland.

ANTHONY CRONIN (1928–)

221 Second Officer aboard the R.M.S. *Titanic*.

224 Ship of the Leyland Line that some believe was within sight of the *Titanic* at the time of the disaster.

225 Shady financier who as a member of Parliament proposed criminal proceedings against the White Star Line.

THOMAS KINSELLA (1928–)

250 The *Táin Bó Cúailnge* is the legendary tale of Queen Medb's cattle raid on the neighboring province of Ulster. Kinsella translated parts of the epic in 1969 and here describes his retracing of the routes taken by its heroes.

JOHN MONTAGUE (1929–)

265 In Irish mythology the Fomóiri were a hostile older race of sea-roving gods who clashed with the Tuatha Dé Danan upon the younger race's arrival in Ireland.

The Clogher Valley (from *Clogh-oir,* golden stone, or simply stony place) in County Tyrone provided the landscape for the stories and novels of William Carleton (1794–1869).

266 "We have the Irish again" (author's note). *Tír Eoghain* is the original Irish spelling of Tyrone.

Irish chieftain Hugh O'Niall (more often, O'Neill) (d. 1616) was born in Tyrone, where he was fostered by the O'Hagan clan. His army was defeated by the English at the Battle of Kinsale in 1601.

270 Irish writer Brendan Behan (1923–1964) lived on Herbert Street in Dublin when Montague arrived there the late 1950s.

Molly Malone is the heroine of "Cockles and Mussels," a ballad popular in Ireland from the 19th century on. She works as a fishmonger, wheeling her barrow through the streets and calling out to customers until a fever kills her, whereupon her ghost takes over the job.

JAMES SIMMONS (1933–2001)

278 Derived from *a chuisle, mo chroí,* "pulse of my heart," the phrase is used as a term of endearment.

286 A village outside Derry, Northern Ireland, Claudy was the scene of an IRA bombing that killed nine in July 1972.

DESMOND O'GRADY (1935–)

303 Hugh O'Neill died in exile at Rome in 1616, some fifteen years after his defeat at the Battle of Kinsale.

BRENDAN KENNELLY (1936–)

311 Ireland's Grand Canal connects the city of Dublin to the midlands by linking the River Liffey to the River Shannon.

316 "Clean," "A Holy War," and "There Will Be Dreams" reflect the philosophy behind Oliver Cromwell's campaign against Catholic Ireland in 1649 and 1650.

318 The comic strip *Count Curly Wee,* which appeared in the *Liverpool Echo* beginning in the 1940s, has been reprinted in the *Irish Independent* for several decades. Its two-panel strips with verse captions recount the adventures of the debonair Count Curly Wee, an unusually well-dressed pig, and his friend Gussie Goose.

319 "Service," "Halcyon Days," "A Second's Eternity," "Lough Derg," and "The True Thing" speak from the perspective of a fictionalized Judas Iscariot.

321 A small lake-isle on Lough Derg, Station Island, is a pilgrimage site where penitents undergo a three-day ritual known as St Patrick's Purgatory.

322 Daniel O'Connell (1775–1847) was an Irish nationalist who agitated for Catholic Emancipation. Molly Malone is the heroine of "Cockles and Mussels," a ballad popular in Ireland from the 19th century on. She works as a fishmonger, wheeling her barrow through the streets and calling out to customers until a fever kills her, whereupon her ghost takes over the job.

SEAMUS HEANEY (1939–)

334 The term "croppy" was applied to Irish rebels at the end of the 18th century in reference to their short-cropped hair, thought to have been adopted in imitation of French revolutionaries for whom short hair was a signal of anti-aristocratic sentiment.

It was at Vinegar Hill near Enniscorthy, Co. Wexford, that Irish rebels suffered a decisive defeat by the British in June 1798.

T. P. Flanagan (1929–): watercolor painter born in Northern Ireland.

354 Hughie O'Donoghue: English painter, born 1959.

Michael Longley (1939–)

362 Cromlech: a megalithic tomb, dolmen.

364 The Shankill and Falls Road neighborhoods are, respectively, Protestant and Catholic enclaves bordering each other in west Belfast.

Currach: a small boat made of skins stretched over a wooden frame.

369 Duncher: Belfast dialect term for the flat cap or bunnet known in the United States as a "newsboy."

371 Hoy is the second largest of the Orkney Islands, Stromness a village north of Hoy across Hoy Sound, on the larger island known as "The Mainland."

374 John Lavery and William Orpen, both Irish-born, both served the British as official war painters during the First World War.

Seamus Deane (1940–)

388 Art Mac Cumhaigh was born in Creggan, Co. Armagh, in 1738.

Eamon Grennan (1941–)

409 "The robin is an American robin, which belongs to the thrush family (*turdus migratorius*)" (author's note).

Michael Hartnett (1944–1999)

415 Irish for "I love you."

422 Hartnett's refrain, "*mánla, séimh, dubhfholtach, álainn, caoin,*" uses the Irish words for a series of attributes: gentle, slender, black-haired, lovely, smooth.

Evan Boland (1944–)

482 *Mise Eire* is Irish for "I am Ireland." Boland's title echoes that of a poem by Padraic Pearse, who was executed for his role in the Easter Rising of 1916.

Bernard O'Donoghue (1945–)

531 *Lepus Timidus Hibernicus* is the scientific name of the Irish hare.

538 *Ter conatus* is Latin for "thrice attempted." O'Donoghue's title refers to a phrase repeated twice in Virgil's *Aenead*, at 2.792–94 and 6.700–702:

ter conatus ibi collo dare bracchia circum
ter frustra comprensa manus effugit imago,
par levibus ventis volucrique simillima somno.

"Three times he tried to throw his arms around her/his neck; three times the form, embraced in vain, fled from his hand, just like light winds, and very similar to a winged dream."

In Book II Aeneas is attempting to embrace the ghost of his dead wife, Creusa, in the midst of burning Troy. In Book VI he is in the underworld attempting to embrace the ghost of his dead father, Anchises.

FRANK ORMSBY (1947–)

552 Stephen Donoghue (1884–1945), Lancashire-born Catholic jockey who won ten consecutive championship titles between 1914 and 1923. Sir John Lavery's portrait of Donoghue is held in a private collection, but a sketch for that work is in the Ulster Museum.

Felicia Dorothea Browne Hemans, 1793–1835.

554 Nicolas-Philippe Ledru (1731–1807), known as Cotte-Comus, a magician and mountebank noted for theatrical performances that included fortune telling, mirror tricks and sleight of hand.

CIARAN CARSON (1948–)

560 The RIC, Royal Irish Constabulary, was Ireland's national police force between 1870 and 1922, when the partition of the island divided its duties between the Garda Síochána in the Irish Free State (later the Republic of Ireland) and the RUC or Royal Ulster Constabulary in Northern Ireland. *Peeler,* in the following line, is British slang for a police officer. The term derives from the name of the Home Secretary, Sir Robert Peel, who in 1829 established the London Metropolitan Police Force, an institution that was soon replicated throughout the United Kingdom.

561 *Tip* is a British noun for a dump, or place where trash is deposited.

The hugely popular *Irish Melodies* of Dublin-born poet Thomas Moore (1779–1852) appeared in ten volumes beginning in 1807.

At the Battle of Clontarf, fought on Good Friday in 1014, the High King of Ireland Brian Boru defeated the rebellious King of Leinster and an army of Viking mercenaries. Boru himself was killed in the battle; according to one account he was assassinated by a retreating Viking while praying in his tent.

The riddle is a version of the one asked of Oedipus in Sophocles' *Oedipus the King*.

563 The Belfast streets Carson mentions are named for battles and figures of the Crimean War.

Durex is a brand of condom sold in the United Kindom.

565 *The Angelus:* a print of the often-reproduced 1857/59 painting by the Frenchman Jean-François Millet (1814–1875), which depicts two peasants pausing in their work in a potato field to mark the Angelus, a devotional rite observed in the morning, noon, and evening, at times traditionally signaled by the ringing of a church bell.

566 Hatchet Field lies on Black Mountain north of Belfast.

567 The White Ensign, a flag bearing a red cross on a white field with a Union Jack in the canton, or upper left corner, was flown by Nelson at the Battle of Trafalgar. It is the only ensign now in use by the Royal Navy.

569 The term *aisling* applies to both a fantasy or dream vision and a poem incorporating that vision. The *aisling* traditionally includes the appearance of a supernatural woman, often representing Ireland.

Tom Paulin (1949–)

577 "Letter to R. S. Crossman" appeared in W. H. Auden and Louis MacNeice's *Letters from Iceland* (1937), a collection of poetry and prose that sprang from a trip the two men made to the island in the summer of 1936. Paulin may remember the letter "sadly" because Labour politician and writer Richard Crossman (1907–1974) served after the Second World War on the Anglo-American Palestine commission that recommended further Jewish immigration into Palestine, a move that runs counter to Paulin's position on Israel.

Doochary is a hamlet and Bloody Foreland (Cnoc Fola) a headland, both in the Rosses area of County Donegal.

578 Maud Gonne MacBride (1866–1953), Irish actress and Republican activist with whom W. B. Yeats was infatuated.

579 Basil Stanlake Brooke, Viscount Brookeborough (1888–1973), who served as prime minister of Northern Ireland from 1943 to 1963, was known for his aggressively Unionist and pro-Protestant policies and remarks.

Desertmartin, in County Londonderry, Northern Ireland, is a village with just under three hundred inhabitants.

Squaddy is slang for an ordinary soldier.

582 The kosangas takes its name from a brand of liquefied petroleum marketed in Ireland.

Boreen, from the Irish bótharín, is a small road.

583 A rath is an earthen ring fort.

584 Thrawn is a Scots term meaning twisted, also applied to a deviant or irritable person.

MICHAEL DAVITT (1950–2005)

592 The railway line between Cork and Skibbereen, a center for the manufacturing of linen and woolen cloth in County Cork, became an important trade route in the late 19th century. Youghal is a seaside town east of Cork.

593 CIE: Córas Iompair Éireann was founded by the Transportation Act of 1944 to manage public transportation by road and rail. Originally a private company, it was nationalized in 1950.

597 *Regulum Mundi*, Latin, "prince of the world."

598 The IRA announced its first Christmas ceasefire in 1974 but the tradition lapsed after a year and 1990 marked the first Christmas ceasefire in 15 years. In mid-October 1994 Loyalist paramilitary groups in Northern Ireland signed on to the ceasefire the IRA had announced several weeks earlier. The British government began talks with the IRA that December. This ceasefire broke down two years later.

PAUL MULDOON (1951–)

645 Irish for "I got up in the morning . . . to go to the big fair."

GERALD DAWE (1952–)

679 "Lieut. Col. Lundy was Military Governor during the Siege of Derry in 1689. He departed the city and to the besieged population he became a symbol of betrayal. Those considered to follow in his footsteps are known as Lundy's" (author's note).

MARY O'MALLEY (1954–)

766 *Coffin ship* is the term sometimes applied to the crowded, often poorly provisioned ships on which Irish emigrants fled the potato famines at the middle of the nineteenth century.

"Caitlin Ní hUallacháin and John Bull" (author's note); O'Malley is referring to the female symbol of Ireland and the male symbol of England.

CATHAL Ó SEARCAIGH (1956–)

795 Gort a' Choirce, literally "field of oats," is the Gaeltacht townland in County Donegal where Ó Searcaigh was born.

797 *Buachaill Bán* is Irish for "fair-haired boy."

807 Irish for "well of heritage."

809 *Sean nós* is Irish for "traditional," as in traditional music. O Searcaigh's phrase "we're *sean nós*-ed" is a punning non-traditional way, using English and Irish elements, to say "we're traditional."

PETER SIRR (1960–)

816 Author's note: "From the *Physica* and the *Causae et Curae* of Hildegard of Bingen, quoted in *Hildegard of Bingen* by Sabina Flanagan, Routledge, 1989, pp 80–105."

817 Idiomatic German expression meaning "German spoken here."

The line, meaning "March gardens are dressed in new colors," is from the song "I Giardini Di Marzo" by Italian singer-songwriter Lucio Battisti (1943–1998)

823 PAYE, an acronym for Pay As You Earn, is the payroll deduction system of the Irish Revenue Commission.

Luke Gardiner (1745–1798), a banker, and Henry Moore (d. 1714), the third Earl of Drogheda, owned and developed property in Dublin during the 18th century. Moore, in particular, left his stamp on the street names of the city: Henry Street, Earl Street, Drogheda Street (now O' Connell Street), even Of (now Off) Street.

ENDA WYLEY (1966–)

850 "*Tá sé faoi chré:* he's under the earth" (author's note).

853 "An t-anam a phóg an corp—the soul that kissed the body—an old Irish story where the soul, having left the dead body, cannot resist turning back to kiss it farewell repeatedly, having been protected by it in life" (author's note).

CONOR O'CALLAGHAN (1968–)

874 "*Cage house:* Tudor style timber framed house" (author's note).

JUSTIN QUINN (1968–)

898 "In Czech the word 'skála' means rock" (author's note).

899 "This is indebted to Reginald Shepherd's poem 'Locale' from his collection *Wrong*. The passage quoted is from Ralph Waldo Emerson's 'The Over-Soul.' *Jetzzeit* was glossed by Walter Benjamin as a 'time of now shot through with chips of Messianic time'" (author's note). [The quotation from Emerson is approximate. *Jetzzeit* is more commonly spelled *Jetztzeit*.—ed.]

901 Petr Borkovec: a young Czech poet whose work Quinn has translated.

DAVID WHEATLEY (1970–)

919 The epigraph "Tá Tír na nÓg ar chúl an tí," drawn from Seán Ó Ríordáin, is Irish for *Tír na nÓg—the mythical land of youth—is at the back of the house.*

920 Latin for "Who will separate us."

PERMISSIONS ACKNOWLEDGMENTS

SAMUEL BECKETT

"Whoroscope," "Enueg I" and "Something there" from *Collected Poems in English and French*, copyright © 1977 by Samuel Beckett. "Tailpiece" from *Watt*, copyright © 1953 by the Estate of Samuel Beckett. Used by permission of Grove/Atlantic, Inc.

"Whoroscope," "Enueg I," "Something There," and "Tailpiece" from *Collected Poems 1930–1978*. Reprinted by permission of Faber and Faber Ltd.

SARA BERKELEY

"Dogwood and Iris," "First Faun," "Patagonia," "Hawkesbury River, NSW," and "Venus Awake" from *Strawberry Thief* (2005). By kind permission of the author and The Gallery Press, Loughcrew, Oldcastle, County Meath, Ireland. "Fall," "Fault," "Valley," and "Undertow" from *Facts about Water* (1994) by kind permission of the author c/o The Gallery Press, Loughcrew, Oldcastle, County Meath, Ireland.

"Glaces, Sorbets," "Out In the Storm," "Launderette," "Home-Movie Nights," "Emily Dickinson," "Convalescent," and "The Courage Gatherer" reprinted by permission of the author.

EAVAN BOLAND

"In Coming Days" and "An Elegy for my Mother in Which She Scarcely Appears" from *Domestic Violence*. Copyright © 2007 by Eavan Boland. "Athene's Song," "The Poets," "New Territory," "Yeats in Civil War," "The War Horse," "The Famine Road," "Suburban Woman," "Making Up," "Mise Eire," "The Achill Woman," "Outside History," "That the Science of Cartography is Limited," "The Pomegranate," "Story," "The

Mother Tongue," "Irish Poetry," and "Quarantine" from *New Collected Poems*. Copyright © 2005, 2001, 1998, 1994, 1990, 1987, 1980, 1975, 1967, 1962 by Eavan Boland. Used by permission of W. W. Norton & Company, Inc., and Carcanet Press Limited.

CIARAN CARSON

"The Exiles' Club" and "Patchwork" from *The Irish for No;* "Home" and "The Forgotten City" from *Breaking News;* "Soot," "The New Estate," "Dresden," "Belfast Confetti," "Campaign," "Bloody Hand," "The Ballad of HMS *Belfast,*" "The Rising of the Moon," "Spraying the Potatoes," and "Catmint Tea" from *Selected Poems;* "Zugzwang" from *For All We Know*, as published in *Ciaran Carson: Collected Poems*. Reproduced by permission of Wake Forest University Press.

   "The Exiles' Club," "Patchwork," "Home," "The Forgotten City," "Soot," "The New Estate," "Dresden," "Belfast Confetti," "Campaign," "Bloody Hand," "The Ballad of the HMS *Belfast,*" "The Rising of the Moon," "Spraying the Potatoes," "Catmint Tea," and "Zugzwang" [II] from *Collected Poems* (2008). By kind permission of the author and The Gallery Press, Loughcrew, Oldcastle, County Meath, Ireland.

AUSTIN CLARKE

All poems from *Austin Clarke: Collected Poems,* edited by R. Dardis Clarke with an introduction by Christopher Ricks (Carcanet Press and The Bridge Press, 2008). Reprinted by permission of R. Dardis Clarke, 17 Oscar Square, Dublin 8, Ireland.

HARRY CLIFTON

"The Black Book" from *Secular Eden: Paris Notebooks 1994–2004* (2007). Reproduced by permission of Wake Forest University Press.

   "The Walls of Carthage," "The Desert Route," "Monsoon Girl," "Death of Thomas Merton," "The Distaff Side," "Euclid Avenue" and "Eccles Street, Bloomsday 1982" from *The Desert Route* (1992); "Firefly," "Where We Live," *"In Hoc Signo, "* "Taking the Waters," and "The Canto of Ulysses" from *Night Train Through the Brenner* (1994). By kind permission of the author and The Gallery Press, Loughcrew, Oldcastle, County Meath, Ireland.

PADRAIC COLUM

All poems from *The Collected Poems of Padraic Colum* (Devin Adair, 1953). Reprinted by permission of Clíona Máire O'Sullivan.

ANTHONY CRONIN

All poems from *Collected Poems* (2004). Reprinted by permission of the author and New Island Books.

MICHAEL DAVITT

"In Howth," "Clay Memories," and "The Terrorist" translated by Philip Casey; "Joe" translated by Jason Sommer; "For Bobby Sands on the Eve of his Death" translated by Michael O'Loughlin; "To Pound, from God" translated by Paul Muldoon from *Rogha Dánta/Selected Poems* (Raven Arts Press, 1987). Reprinted by kind permission of Moira Sweeney, Philip Casey, Jason Sommer, Michael O'Loughlin, and Paul Muldoon.

"The Mirror," "August," and "Third Draft of a Dream" translated by Paul Muldoon; "O My Two Palestinians" translated by Philip Casey from *Bligeard Sráide* (Coiscéim, 1983). Reprinted by kind permission of Moira Sweeney, Coiscéim, Paul Muldoon, and Philip Casey.

"Ceasefire" and "So Long" translated by Louis de Paor; "The Call" translated by Paul Muldoon from *Scuais* (Cló Iar-Chonnachta, 1998). Reprinted by kind permission of Moira Sweeney, Cló Iar-Chonnachta, Louis de Paor, and Paul Muldoon.

GERALD DAWE

"Secrets," "The Desert Campaign," "The Lundys Letter," "Outside Queens," and "Carlyle in Ireland" from *The Lundys Letter* (1985); "The Likelihood of Snow/The Danger of Fire" and "A Story" from *Sunday School* (1991); "The *de facto* Territory," "The Third Secret," and "Crete Summer" from *Heart of Hearts* (1995); "In Memory of James Joyce" and "The Night's Takings" from *The Morning Train* (1999); "Text Messages" and "An Evening in the Country" from *Lake Geneva* (2003). By kind permission of the author and The Gallery Press, Loughcrew, Oldcastle, County Meath, Ireland.

C. DAY LEWIS

All poems from *The Complete Poems of C Day Lewis* published by Sinclair-Stevenson (1992), Copyright © 1992 in this edition The Estate of C Day Lewis. Reprinted by permission of the Random House Group Ltd.

SEAMUS DEANE

"Power Cut," "Derry," "Roots," "Gradual Wars," "Osip Mandelstam," "History Lessons," "Guerillas," "Exile's Return," "Breaking Wood," "Tongues," "Homer Nods," "The Churchyard at Creggan," and "Reading *Paradise Lost* in Protestant Ulster 1984" from *Selected Poems* (1998). By kind permission of the author and The Gallery Press, Loughcrew, Oldcastle, County Meath, Ireland.

"Shelter" and "The Broken Border" Copyright © Seamus Deane, 1977. Reproduced by permission of Sheil Land Associates Ltd.

PAUL DURCAN

"Self-Portrait as an Irish Jew" from *Greetings to Our Friends in Brazil* (1995); "Lady with Portable Electric Fence" and "The Second Coming" from *Cries of an Irish Caveman* (2001) by Paul Durcan, published by Harvill. Reprinted by permission of The Random House Group Ltd.

"They Say the Butterfly is the Hardest Stroke," "The Kilfenora Teaboy," "In Memory: The Miami Showband—Massacred 31 July 1975," "The Haulier's Wife Meets Jesus on the Road Near Moone," "Flower Girl, Dublin," "My Belovèd Compares Herself to a Pint of Stout," and "A Snail in My Prime" from *A Snail in My Prime* (Harvill Secker, 1995). Copyright © Paul Durcan. Reproduced by permission of the author c/o Rogers, Coleridge & White Ltd., 20 Powis Mews, London W11 1JN.

JOHN ENNIS

"Bright Days," "Circa July 27," "The Croppy Boy," "Villanelle," "A Drink of Spring," excerpt from "The Burren Days," "Questions for W. C. Williams," "Deep Ploughing," "Sinking Wells," "Devotees Gathering Round Jim Morrison's Grave," excerpt from "Letter to Connla," and excerpt from "Telling the Bees" from *Selected Poems* (1996). Reprinted by permission of Dedalus Press.

"Old Style Country Funeral" from *Goldcrest Falling* (2006). Reprinted by permission of the author and Scop Productions.

PETER FALLON

"The Lost Field," "Fostering," "My Care," "Caesarean," "Country Music," "The Old Masters," "Windfalls," "Birches," and "Storm at Sea" from *News of the World: Selected and New Poems* (1998); "I.176–203 (I could, if I'd not seen you back away . . .)," "II.401–413 (The farmer's chores come round . . .)," and "IV.116–148 (Indeed, if I were not already near the limit . . .)" from *The Georgics of Virgil* (2003); "Fair Game" and "The Company of Horses" from *The Company of Horses* (2007); excerpt from "Gravities: West" from *Eye to Eye* (1992). By kind permission of the author and The Gallery Press, Loughcrew, Oldcastle, County Meath, Ireland.

PADRAIC FIACC

All poems from *Ruined Pages: Selected Poems* (Blackstaff, 1994). Reprinted by permission of the author, Gerald Dawe, and Aodán Mac Póilin.

EAMON GRENNAN

"Women Going," "These Northern Fields at Dusk," and "Shed" from *So It Goes* (1995); "A Gentle Art," "In the National Gallery, London," "Wing Road," "Men Roofing," "Breaking Points," "Kitchen Vision," "The Cave Painters," and "Sea Dog" from *Selected and New Poems* (2000); "To Grasp the Nettle," "Killing the Bees," and "Detail" from *Still Life With Waterfall* (2001); "End of Winter" and "Raeburn's Skater" from *Wildly for Days* (1983). By permission of Graywolf Press and by kind permission of the author and The Gallery Press, Loughcrew, Oldcastle, County Meath, Ireland.

VONA GROARKE

"The Couch," "The Local Accent," "Archaeology," "Juniper Street," "To Smithereens," and "Why I Am Not a Nature Poet" from *Juniper Street* (2006). Reproduced by permission of Wake Forest University Press and by kind permission of the author and The Gallery Press, Loughcrew, Oldcastle, County Meath, Ireland.

"A Tree Called the Balm of Gilead," "Patronage," and "Trousseau" from *Shale* (1994); "Open House," "Folderol," "The Big House," "Around the Houses," and "The Courthouse" from *Other People's Houses* (1999). By kind permission of the author and The Gallery Press, Loughcrew, Oldcastle, County Meath, Ireland.

MICHAEL HARTNETT

"A Small Farm," "Sickroom," "Poor Actaeon," "For My Grandmother, Bridgit Halpin," "Bread," sections 1,2,9 from "Anatomy of a Cliché," sonnet 9 from "Thirteen Sonnets," sections 1,2,3,5,8 from "Notes on My Contemporaries," "Pigkilling," "Death of an Irishwoman," and sections 1,5,7 from "A Farewell to English" from *Collected Poems* (2001). By kind permission of the Estate of Michael Hartnett and The Gallery Press, Loughcrew, Oldcastle, County Meath, Ireland.

SEAMUS HEANEY

"The Early Purges," "Digging," "Death of a Naturalist," "Follower," "Personal Helicon," "Requiem for Croppies," "Bogland," "Anahorish," "The Grauballe Man," "Punishment," "Hercules and Antaeus," "Sonnet II from Glanmore Sonnets," "The Otter," "Sloe Gin," "Widgeon," "Sections VII and XII from Station Island," "Wolfe Tone," "Sections iii, viii, xii, xxii, and xlviii from Squarings," "Weighing In," and "The Gravel Walks" from *Opened Ground: Selected Poems, 1966–1996*. Copyright © 1998 by Seamus Heaney. "The Loose Box" from *Electric Light*. Copyright © 2001 by Seamus Heaney. "The Blackbird of Glanmore" and "The Turnip-Snedder" from *District and Circle*. Copyright © 2006 by Seamus Heaney. Reprinted by permission of Farrar, Straus and Giroux, LLC and Faber and Faber Ltd.

JOHN HEWITT

"Because I Paced my Thought," "Gloss, On the Difficulties of Translation," "Mary Hagan, Islandmagee, 1919," "O Country People," "Once Alien Here," and "The Glens" from *The Selected Poems of John Hewitt*, edited by Michael Longley and Frank Ormsby (2007); "Ars Poetica," "Bogside, Derry, 1971," "Freehold: III Townland of Peace," and "The Last Summer, for Roberta (1975)" from *The Collected Poems of John Hewitt*, edited by Frank Ormsby (1991). Reproduced by permission of Blackstaff Press on behalf of the Estate of John Hewitt.

PEARSE HUTCHINSON

All poems from *Collected Poems* (2002). By kind permission of the author and The Gallery Press, Loughcrew, Oldcastle, County Meath, Ireland.

PATRICK KAVANAGH

All poems from *Collected Poems*, edited by Antoinette Quinn (Allen Lane, 2004). Reprinted by kind permission of the Trustees of the Estate of the late Katherine B. Kavanagh, through the Jonathan Williams Literary Agency.

BRENDAN KENNELLY

"Halcyon Days," "A Second's Eternity," and "Lough Derg" from *The Book of Judas* (1991); "Home," "Old Irish," and "Still to be done" from *Glimpses* (2003); "James Joyce's Death-mask," "The Hill of Fire," "The Celtic Twilight," "Good Souls, to Survive," "The Limerick Train," "At the Party," "Union," "The Singing Girl Is Easy in Her Skill," "Clean," "A Holy War," "There Will Be Dreams," "The Big Words," "Service," and "The True Thing" from *Familiar Strangers: New and Selected Poems 1960–2004* (2004). Reprinted by permission of Bloodaxe Books.

THOMAS KINSELLA

All poems from *Collected Poems 1956–2001* (2001). Reprinted by permission of Carcanet Press Limited.

MICHAEL LONGLEY

"Epithalamion," "Persephone," "Badger," "Letter to Derek Mahon," "Wounds," "Wreaths," "Second Sight," "Remembering Carrigskeewaun," "An Amish Rug," "Ceasefire," and "The White Garden" from *Selected Poems* (1998); "The Horses," "An Elegy," "The Branch," and "The Rabbit" from *The Weather in Japan* (2000); "Pipistrelle," "The

Painters," "Leaves," and "Edward Thomas's Poem" from *Snow Water* (2004); "Laertes" from *Collected Poems* (2006). All published by Wake Forest University Press and Jonathan Cape. Reproduced by permission of Wake Forest University Press and The Random House Group Ltd.

LOUIS MACNEICE

All poems from *Collected Poems of Louis MacNeice* (Faber and Faber, 1966). Reprinted by permission of David Higham Associates Ltd.

DEREK MAHON

"Glengormley," "In Carrowdore Churchyard," "A Disused Shed in Co. Wexford," "Courtyards in Delft," "A Garage in Co. Cork," "The Globe in Carolina," "Ovid in Tomis," "Antarctica," "The Hudson Letter, I, VIII, X," and "The Yellow Book, XIX (On the Automation of Irish Lights)" from *Collected Poems* (1999); "The Cloud Ceiling" and "New Wave" from *Harbour Lights* (2005). By kind permission of the author and The Gallery Press, Loughcrew, Oldcastle, County Meath, Ireland.

THOMAS MCCARTHY

All poems from *Mr Dineen's Careful Parade: New and Selected Poems* (1999). Reprinted by permission of Anvil Press Poetry Ltd.

MEDBH MCGUCKIAN

"Red Armchair" from *Marconi's Cottage* (1991); "Querencia," "The Blue She Brings with Her," "The Dream-Language of Fergus," "No Streets, No Numbers," "Marconi's Cottage," and "Captain Lavender" from *Selected Poems* (1997); "Shoulder-Length, Caged-Parrot Earrings" and "Self-Portrait in the Act of Painting a Self-Portrait" from *Shelmalier* (1998); "The Good Wife Taught her Daughter" and "The Currach Requires No Harbours" from *The Currach Requires No Harbours* (2006). Reproduced by permission of Wake Forest University Press.

"Red Armchair" from *Marconi's Cottage* (1991); "Smoke," "The 'Singer,'" "The Heiress," "Querencia," "The Blue She Brings with Her," "The Dream-Language of Fergus," "No Streets, No Numbers," "Marconi's Cottage," and "Captain Lavender" from *Selected Poems* (1997); "Shoulder-Length, Caged-Parrot Earrings" and "Self-Portrait in the Act of Painting a Self-Portrait" from *Shelmalier* (1998); "The Worship of the Plough" from *The Face of the Earth* (2002); "The Good Wife Taught her Daughter" and "The Currach Requires No Harbours" from *The Currach Requires No Harbours* (2006). By kind permission of the author and The Gallery Press, Loughcrew, Oldcastle, County Meath, Ireland.

PAULA MEEHAN

"Dharmakaya," "That Night There Was a Full Moon, Little Cloud," "Take a breath. Hold it. Let it go." "The Bog of Moods," "The Tantric Master," "Suburb: Desire Path," and "A Woman's Right to Silence" from *Dharmakaya* (2002). Reprinted by permission of Wake Forest University Press and Carcanet Press Limited.

"Death of a Field" from *Painting Rain* (2009). Reprinted by permission of Carcanet Press Limited.

"Mysteries of the Home: Well," "The Pattern," "Child Burial," "The Man who was Marked by Winter," and "Fruit" from *The Man Who Was Marked by Winter* (1991); "My Father Perceived as a Vision of St Francis" and "'Would you jump into my grave as quick?'" from *Pillow Talk* (1994). By kind permission of the author and The Gallery Press, Loughcrew, Oldcastle, County Meath, Ireland.

JOHN MONTAGUE

"The Water Carrier," "A Drink of Milk," "Old Mythologies," "Forge," "To Cease," "The Country Fiddler," "Like dolmens round my childhood . . . ," "A Lost Tradition," "A Grafted Tongue," "Sweeney," "Killing the Pig," "Herbert Street Revisited," and "Guide" from *Collected Poems* (1995); "The Family Piano" from *Smashing the Piano* (1999); "White Water" from *Drunken Sailor* (2004). Reprinted by permission of Wake Forest University Press and by kind permission of the author and The Gallery Press, Loughcrew, Oldcastle, County Meath, Ireland.

SINEAD MORRISSEY

"The Juggler," "There Was Fire in Vancouver," "English Lesson," "The Fort-Maker," and "Restoration" from *There Was Fire in Vancouver* (1996); "Tourism," "Street Theatre," "Between Here and There," and "To Encourage the Study of Kanji" from *Between Here and There* (2001); "Forty Lengths," "China: 7 'I find I have made a ghost . . . ,'" "The Gobi from Air," "Polar," "Zero" and "The State of the Prisons: 2 'God sent an earthquake . . .'" from *The State of the Prisons* (2005); "Through the Square Window" from *Through the Square Window* (2009). Reprinted by permission of Carcanet Press Limited.

PAUL MULDOON

"Tithonius" and "It Is What It Is" from *Horse Latitudes*. Copyright © 2006 by Paul Muldoon. "Hard Drive" and "The Loaf" from *Moy Sand and Gravel*. Copyright © 2002 by Paul Muldoon. "Wind and Tree," "The Mixed Marriage," "The Boundary Commission," "Why Brownlee Left," "Gathering Mushrooms," "Quoof," "The Mist-Net," "Meeting the British," "7, Middagh Street: Wystan," "Milkweed and Monarch," "Incantata," and "The Train" from *Poems, 1968–1998*. Copyright © 2001 by Paul Muldoon. Reprinted by permission of Farrar, Straus and Giroux, LLC.

"Tithonius" and "It Is What It Is" from *Horse Latitudes;* "Hard Drive" and "The Loaf" from *Moy Sand and Gravel;* "The Train" from *Hay* by Paul Muldoon; "Milkweed and Monarch" and "Incantata" from *The Annals of Chile;* "The Mist-Net," "Meeting the British," and "7, Middagh Street: *Wystan*" from *Meeting the British;* "Wind and Tree," "The Mixed Marriage," "The Boundary Commission," "Why Brownlee Left," "Gathering Mushrooms," and "Quoof" from *Selected Poems.* Reprinted by permission of Faber and Faber Ltd.

RICHARD MURPHY

All poems from *Collected Poems* (2000). Reprinted by permission of Wake Forest University Press and by kind permission of the author and The Gallery Press, Loughcrew, Oldcastle, County Meath, Ireland.

EILÉAN NÍ CHUILLEANÁIN

"The Absent Girl," sections 1,6,7 from "Site of Ambush," "The Second Voyage," "Old Roads," "Letter to Pearse Hutchinson," "Séamus Murphy, Died October 2nd 1975," "Wash," "Pygmalion's Image," "The Pig-boy," "St Mary Magdalene Preaching at Marseilles," "The Architectural Metaphor," "Woman Shoeing a Horse," "Studying the Language," "Anchoress," "Agnes Bernelle, 1923–1999," "Borders," and "Gloss/Clós/Glas" from *Selected Poems* (2008); "Ferryboat" from *The Second Voyage* (1986); "The Liturgy" and "Chrissie" from *The Magdalene Sermon* (1989). By kind permission of the author and The Gallery Press, Loughcrew, Oldcastle, County Meath, Ireland. All poems except sections 1, 6, 7 from "Site of Ambush" reprinted by permission of Wake Forest University Press.

NUALA NÍ DHOMHNAILL

"The Stone Age" translated by Derek Mahon; "The Smell of Blood" translated by Ciaran Carson; "Why Bridgid, or Bríd, Never Married" translated by Peter Fallon; "Aubade" translated by Michael Longley; "The Language Issue" and "As for the Quince" translated by Paul Muldoon from *Pharoah's Daughter* (1990); "The Crack in the Stairs" and "Cathleen" translated by Paul Muldoon from *The Astrakhan Cloak* (1992); "Persephone Suffering from SAD," "Ten Ways of Looking at a Magpie" and "The Prodigal Muse" translated by Medbh McGuckian; "You Are" translated by Eiléan Ní Chuilleanáin from *The Water Horse* (1999); "A Recovered Memory of Water" translated by Paul Muldoon from *The Fifty Minute Mermaid* (2007). By kind permission of the author and The Gallery Press, Loughcrew, Oldcastle, County Meath, Ireland.

"Abduction" and "Young Man's Song" translated by Michael Hartnett; "The Shannon Estuary Welcoming the Fish" translated by Nuala Ní Dhomhnaill from *Selected Poems: Rogha Dánta* (Raven AAs Press, 1991). Reprinted by kind permission of the author.

CONOR O'CALLAGHAN

"The Count," "The Middle Ground," "Heartland," "Fiction," excerpts from "Loose Change," and "Signing Off" from *Fiction* (2005). Reproduced by permission of Wake Forest University Press and by kind permission of the author and The Gallery Press, Loughcrew, Oldcastle, County Meath, Ireland.

"September," "The Last Cage House in Drogheda," "Mengele's House," "The History of Rain," "Pigeons," "The Mild Night," and "Silver Birch" from *The History of Rain* (1993); "Seatown," "Pitch & Putt," "Ships," and "East" from *Seatown* (1999). By kind permission of the author and The Gallery Press, Loughcrew, Oldcastle, County Meath, Ireland.

MÁIRTÍN Ó DIREÁIN

All poems from *Selected Poems/Tacar Danta* (Goldsmith Press, 1984). Reprinted by kind permission of Tomás Mac Síomóin and Douglas Sealy.

BERNARD O'DONOGHUE

"Poaching Rights" from *Poaching Rights* (1987). By kind permission of the author and The Gallery Press, Loughcrew, Oldcastle, County Meath, Ireland.

"Pied Piper" and "*Ter Conatus*" from *Here Nor There* (1999); "The Day I Outlived My Father," "A Candle for Dolly Duggan," "Artistic Block," "Usefulness," and "The Potato-Gatherers" from *Outliving* (2003). Published by Chatto & Windus. Reprinted by permission of The Random House Group Ltd.

"*Lepidus Timidus Hibernicus*," "Enterprise Culture," "Con Cornie," "The Humours of Shrone," "Madonnas," "Lastworda Betst," and "A Noted Judge of Horses" from *The Weakness* (Chatto & Windus, 1991); "The Iron Age Boat at Caumatruish," "Nel Mezzo del Cammin," and "Staples" from *Gunpowder* (Chatto & Windus, 1995). Reprinted by kind permission of the author.

DENNIS O'DRISCOLL

"Diversions" from *Reality Check* (2008). Copyright © 2008 by Dennis O'Driscoll. Reprinted by permission of Copper Canyon Press, www.coppercanyonpress.org, and Anvil Press Poetry Ltd.

"Breviary" from *Hidden Extras* (1987); "Porlock," "Middle-Class Blues," "Normally Speaking," "*Man Going to the Office*," "3 AM," "The Bottom Line: 6, 9, 18, 48, 50," "Talking Shop," "Home," "Tomorrow," "To a Love Poet," "Tulipomania," "The Clericals," "While Stocks Last," and "Vigil" from *New and Selected Poems* (2004). Reprinted by permission of Anvil Press Poetry Ltd.

DESMOND O'GRADY

"The Poet in Old Age Fishing at Evening," "Professor Kelleher and the Charles River," "Reading the Unpublished Manuscripts of Louis MacNeice at Kinsale Harbour," and "Purpose" from *The Headgear of the Tribe* (1978); "THE Celtic Sura: *The Poet and his Dog*" from *A Limerick Rake: Versions from the Irish* (1978); "Paraphernalia: Origins" from *His Skaldcrane's Nest* (1979). By kind permission of the author and The Gallery Press, Loughcrew, Oldcastle, County Meath, Ireland.

"Celts in Europe," "Ovid from Exile," "Hugh O'Neill in Rome," and "The Poet's Request" from *The Wandering Celt* (2001); "The Old Head of Kinsale Says" from *On My Way* (2006). Reprinted by permission of Dedalus Press.

"Self-Portrait of Reilly as a Young Man" from *Reilly* (Phoenix Press, 1961). By kind permission of the author.

"Kinsale" from *Tipperary* (1991). Reprinted by permission of Salmon Poetry.

MARY O'MALLEY

"Credo," "The Shape of Saying (ix)," "The Wound," "Canvas Currach II," "Ceres in Caherlistrane," "Pegeen Mike's Farewell to the Playboy," "The Boning Hall," "The Ballad of Caitlin and Sean," "Persephone Astray," "PMT—The Movie," "The Wineapple," and "Bowbend" from *The Boning Hall: New and Selected Poems* (2002); "Aillbrack Georgics" and "Calypso" from *A Perfect V* (2006). Reprinted by permission of Carcanet Press Limited.

SEÁN Ó RÍORDÁIN

"Second Nature" translated by Ciaran Carson from *First Language* (1993). By kind permission of Wake Forest University Press, the author and The Gallery Press, Loughcrew, Oldcastle, County Meath, Ireland.

"Death" and "The Moths" translated by Thomas Kinsella from *New Oxford Book of Irish Verse*, edited by Thomas Kinsella (1986). Reprinted by permission of Oxford University Press.

"Tulyar" translated by Criostoir O'Flynn from *Irish Humorous Poetry* (1999); "My Mother's Burial," "Mount Melleray," "Claustrophobia," and "Fever" translated by Patrick Crotty from *Modern Irish Poetry: An Anthology*, edited by Patrick Crotty (Blackstaff Press, 1995). Reprinted by kind permission of Cló Iar-Chonnachta and Patrick Crotty.

CATHAL Ó SEARCAIGH

"The Pink Lily" translated by Frank Sewell from *By the Hearth in Mín a' Leá* (Arc Publications, 2005). Reprinted by permission of Arc Publications and Frank Sewell.

"Sic Transit" translated by Frank Sewell from *On the Side of Light*, edited by James

Doan and Frank Sewell (Arlen House, 2002). Reprinted by kind permission of the author and Frank Sewell.

"To Jack Kerouac" translated by Sara Berkeley from *The Bright Wave: Poetry in Irish Now/An Tonn Gheal* (Raven Arts Press, 1986). Reprinted by kind permission of the author and Sara Berkeley.

"On Such a Day" and "A Fresh Dimension" translated by Gabriel Fitzmaurice; "When I Was Three" translated by Thomas McCarthy; "The Clay Pipes" and "Lament" translated by Seamus Heaney from *Homecoming: Selected Poems,* edited by Gabriel Fitzmaurice (1993); "The Well," "Sweeney's Eyes," "Buachaill Bán," and "Kathmandu" translated by Frank Sewell from *Out in the Open,* edited and translated by Frank Sewell (1997); "Puddle," "After the Epiphany," and "The Ruined House in Mín na Craoibhe" translated by Donald McNamara and Wes Davis. Reprinted by kind permission of Cló Iar-Chonnachta and Donald McNamara.

"A Runaway Cow" translated by Patrick Crotty. Reprinted by kind permission of Cló Iar-Chonnachta and Patrick Crotty.

FRANK ORMSBY

"Travelling," "A Northern Spring: 1: *The Clearing;* 3: *Cleo, Oklahoma;* 4: *The Lesson of the War;* 6: *I Died in a Country Lane;* 8: *I Stepped on a Small Landmine;* 13: *Apples, Normandy, 1944;* 14: *They Buried Me in an Orchard;* 15: *The Night I Lost World War II;* 18: *On Devenish Island;* 35: *Some of Us Stayed Forever,*" and "The War Photographers" from *A Northern Spring* (1986); "Sheepman" and "My Friend Havelock Ellis" from *A Store of Candles* (1986); "The Gap on my Shelf," "The Gatecrasher," "The Graveyard School," excerpt from *The Memoirs,* and "You: The Movie" from *The Ghost Train* (1995). By kind permission of the author and The Gallery Press, Loughcrew, Oldcastle, County Meath, Ireland.

"On Devenish Island" from *Ripe for Company* (Ulsterman Publications, 1971); "A Small Town in Ireland" from *Being Walked by a Dog* (Ulsterman Publications, 1978). Reprinted by kind permission of the author.

TOM PAULIN

"Chagall in Ireland" and "Not Musical" from *Wind Dog.* Copyright © 1999 by Tom Paulin. "August 39" from *The Invasion Handbook.* Copyright © 2002 by Tom Paulin. Reprinted by permission of Faber and Faber, Inc., and affiliate Farrar, Straus and Giroux, LLC.

"States," "Thinking of Iceland," "In the Lost Province," "Desertmartin," and "Presbyterian Study" from *Selected Poems, 1972–1990;* "Painting with Sawdust" from *Walking a Line.* Reprinted by permission of Faber and Faber Ltd.

JUSTIN QUINN

"The 'O'o'a'a' Bird," "Instructions," and "Days of the New Republic: XI Attics, XVII Ur-Aisling, XX Geography" from *The 'O'o'a'a' Bird* (1996); "Apartment," "Six Household Appliances: Hoover, Mocha Express," and "Poem" from *Privacy* (1999). Reprinted by permission of Carcanet Press Limited.

Fuselage: "Observe the sky . . . "and "I wake early . . ." from *Fuselage* (2002); "Prague Elegies: XX," "Pool," "Coffle," "Borscht," and "Solstice" from *Waves and Trees* (2006). By kind permission of the author and The Gallery Press, Loughcrew, Oldcastle, County Meath, Ireland.

JAMES SIMMONS

"The Not Yet Ancient Mariner," "Macushla, Machree," "Lot's Wife," "A Muse," "In the Wilderness," "Outward Bound," "Stephano Remembers," "Drowning Puppies," "Epigrams," "On Circe's Island," "Claudy," and "Exploration in the Arts" from *Poems, 1956–1986* (1986); "The Publican" from *Selected James Simmons* (Blackstaff Press, 1978). By kind permission of the Estate of James Simmons and The Gallery Press, Loughcrew, Oldcastle, County Meath, Ireland.

"Intruder on Station Island" from *Mainstream* (1995); "Night Song from a Previous Life" from *The Company of Children* (1999). Reprinted by permission of Salmon Poetry.

PETER SIRR

"Translations" and "Journeying Inland" from *Marginal Zones* (1984); "Destinations," "'Of the thousand ways to touch you . . . ,'" and "Death of a Travel Writer: Some Necessary Equipment" from *Ways of Falling* (1991); "Cures," "Pages Ripped from July: Rough Guide to July 18," and excerpt from "A Journal" from *The Ledger of Fruitful Exchange* (1995); "Habitat," "Going Back," and "From the Sunken Kingdom" from *Bring Everything* (2000); "Settling," "Office Hours," and "The Leavetaking of the Ceremonious Traveller" from *Nonetheless* (2004). By kind permission of the author and The Gallery Press, Loughcrew, Oldcastle, County Meath, Ireland.

MATTHEW SWEENEY

"The Lighthouse Keeper's Son" from *Blue Shoes* (Secker and Warburg, 1989); "A Round House" and "The Servant" from *A Round House* (Raven Arts, 1983). Reprinted by kind permission of the author.

"Captain Marsh," "Preparation for Survival," "Simultaneous Stories," "Relics," "Where Fishermen Can't Swim," "Pink Milk," "Donegal, Arizona," "The Wobble," "An End," "The Bat," "The Volcano," "Guardian of the Women's Loo in Waterloo," "Animals," and "Sweeney" from *Selected Poems* (2002); "The UFO," "Exiled," and "Frog-Taming" from *Sanctuary* (2004). All published by Jonathan Cape. Reprinted by permission of The Random House Group Ltd.

DAVID WHEATLEY

"A Skimming Stone, Lough Bray," "AM Radio," "A Garden In September," and "Autumn, the Nightwalk, the City, the River" from *Thirst* (1997); "Sonnets to James Clarence Mangan (#s 1, 6, 10, 11, 13, 14)," "Jaywalking," and "Poem" from *Misery Hill* (2000); "Stan," "Sonnet," and "Gable End" from *Mocker* (2006). By kind permission of the author and The Gallery Press, Loughcrew, Oldcastle, County Meath, Ireland.

ENDA WYLEY

"Love Goes Home," "The House," "The Waitress Has Transformed," and "Eating Baby Jesus" from *Eating Baby Jesus* (1993); "Love Bruise," "Talking to the Bees," "Five Definitions of a Butterfly," and "The Soul Kisses Goodbye" from *Socrates in the Garden* (1998); "Mint Gatherers," "Emperor," "Women on a Train, Poets in a Room," and "Diary of a Fat Man" from *Poems for Breakfast* (2004). Reprinted by permission of Dedalus Press.

Index of Titles